FORGIVEN

FORGIVEN

*The Rise and Fall of Jim Bakker
and the PTL Ministry*

CHARLES E. SHEPARD

ATLANTIC MONTHLY PRESS *New York*

Printed in the United States of America
Second edition

Library of Congress Cataloging-in-Publication Data
Shepard, Charles E.
    Forgiven : the rise and fall of Jim Bakker and the PTL
ministry /
    Charles E. Shepard.
    Includes index.
    1. Bakker, Jim. 1940–   . 2. PTL (Organization). 3.
Evangelists—United States—Biography. I. Title.
BV3785.B3S48   1989   269'.2'092—dc20   89-34053
ISBN 0-87113-398-9 (pb)

The Atlantic Monthly Press
19 Union Square West
New York, NY 10003

First printing

To Jody, with all my love

"Jim, God does not bless falsehood, and the Bible says He resists the proud. . . . Unless you face reality and ask God's forgiveness, He is going to bring you down. God is speaking to you through things that are happening. I pray that you will get His message."

—Pat Robertson's closing words in a private letter to Jim Bakker, September 15, 1977, ten years before Bakker's fall

CONTENTS

INTRODUCTION

In the year of his disgrace, Jim Bakker secured the celebrity status he had coveted for so long. At the beginning of 1987, he had a position of prominence in the charismatic-Christian world. His ministry claimed six hundred thousand supporters and reported revenues of more than $120 million in a year. Within three months, Bakker had become a recognized celebrity in tens of millions of American households. He and his wife, Tammy Faye, seemed to be everywhere: in the headlines, on the cover of national magazines, on the TV news shows, in Johnny Carson's late-night monologues.

To many in his new secular audience, Bakker was a cartoon character, the latest hypocrite to sully the revival tent with greed and adultery. To a handful of his longtime supporters in the church, Bakker was a man unfairly condemned, a prophet proclaiming a gospel of love and prosperity who had sacrificed his personal happiness to build a first-class resort for Christians. In between were many who had once worked at Bakker's side. At PTL they had been blinded by Bakker's propaganda, by the relentless pace of the work he demanded, and by their eagerness to please their boss and their Lord. Forced out of that insular world, they came to recognize that Bakker could accommodate no reality besides his own. Now they were able to see how he had manipulated his audience and staff for his own ends. They realized that Jim Bakker should never return to PTL. Yet many believed that once, in his early years in television ministry, Jim Bakker had been anointed of God.

After a lifetime before the camera, after all the headlines, Jim Bakker remained a mystery, even to those once closest to him. Was he a man of God corrupted by power, fame, and money? Was he a sincere, driven preacher exploited by those around him? Was he a con man from the start? Why did so many believe in him so ardently, for so long?

The truth is discernible in the fine details of Bakker's life story—in Muskegon, where he was born and raised; in Minneapolis, where he attended Bible school; in Portsmouth, Virginia, where he started his career as a TV evangelist working for Pat Robertson; in

Orange County, California, where he began a second TV ministry; and in Charlotte, North Carolina, where he took over a local religious TV show and built it into a corporation with assets of nearly $180 million.

The story of Jim Bakker and the PTL ministry is also a tale of social, religious, cultural, and technological change. Bakker was one of the pioneers of mass TV ministry, a field so crowded twenty-five years after his first TV broadcast that even established figures such as Jerry Falwell and Oral Roberts had to struggle to sustain revenues, their difficulties compounded by the PTL scandal. Bakker and PTL prospered, in part, because of instantaneous satellite transmission and cable television. Together, these innovations opened an inexpensive path into America's living rooms and began a quiet revolution that continues to transform broadcasting.

In exaggerated form, Bakker's rise from working class to wealth mirrors the passage of Pentecostal Christians into mainstream society. Once relegated to what Bakker called the "wrong side of the tracks," Pentecostals began to share the plenty of America in the decades after World War II. To many, Jim Bakker and his rich man's life-style and ostentatious ministry symbolized how far those once known as "holy rollers" had climbed up the social ladder. His booming PTL ministry also represented vindication of sorts for the Pentecostal church; its belief in the supernatural manifestations of the Holy Spirit in modern times had inspired the charismatic renewal that swept through mainline Christian denominations in the sixties and seventies and created a bigger, more enthusiastic, and more affluent audience for Bakker.

Jim Bakker's story is a chilling reminder of the fragility of the safeguards against fraud in religious broadcasting. The stakes are enormous: TV evangelists raise hundreds of millions of dollars each year over the public airwaves, virtually all of it exempt from federal and state income taxes. It is an odd marriage, God and television, and too often its progeny mimic the worst secular hucksters, their slick salesmanship and rationalized deceit cloaked by the disarming glow of godliness. The changing political landscape of the seventies and eighties compounded the hazard. With evangelicals wielding more political power and Ronald Reagan ushering in an era of deregulation, the government had been increasingly unwilling to challenge the excesses of some TV evangelists. As a result, Bakker could get caught misleading his viewers but escape without punishment. The IRS could find further cause to question PTL but be obliged under federal law to step gingerly and quietly, offering no public hint of the outrages it had discovered years before. And industry and church groups, protective of their own, did little to make up for the government's inaction.

Perhaps most troubling in the Bakker-PTL story is its demonstration of the awesome power of television. Though he had other talents—creativity, determination, and a knack for marketing—Jim Bakker succeeded in large part because he could perform on-screen. Without that talent, Bakker would likely have accomplished little in the church. He lacked the gifts for being a teacher and counselor that make a good pastor, and his performances off-camera had little of the magnetism of an entertainer like Jimmy Swaggart.

Pentecostals and charismatics voted Bakker into prominence with their TV dials and dollars. In doing so they mimicked secular America. More and more, our society's heroes are instant celebrities from the broadcast world—actors and actresses who populate prime-time fantasies, singers with the hottest music video, athletes with the most home runs or the quickest moves to the basket on the TV game of the week. Our political leaders are those who perform best before bright lights and Minicams. Substance and offstage character mean less and less. Should we be surprised when those who seek a hero in the church do the same?

As an investigative reporter for the *Charlotte Observer,* I spent three years, 1984–87, writing about mismanagement, deceit, and abuse of trust in the PTL ministry. My final series of articles began with the story that prompted Jim Bakker's resignation on March 19, 1987: his 1980 sexual encounter with a woman named Jessica Hahn and the $265,000 payoff four years later to keep his indiscretion a secret. That story, and the series of exclusives that followed in the weeks afterward, made my reporting an integral part of the story of Jim Bakker and his PTL ministry. Thus, out of necessity, I play two roles in this book: one as historian, the other, in the final years of this narrative, as occasional participant.

I haven't been content to rewrite the now-familiar news stories of the past. Without jobs, bosses, or a ministry to protect, scores of Bakker's relatives, friends, and former colleagues agreed to give freely of their memories and opinions. Like me, they were eager to replace stereotypes and sensationalism with a balanced portrait of Jim Bakker, his PTL TV ministry, and, by extension, the business of TV evangelism. This book has been strengthened immeasurably by my access to thousands of pages of confidential, previously unpublished documents—internal memos, private correspondence, and detailed reports by PTL's outside lawyers, auditors, and other professional counselors. Memories fade and people shade the truth, but, barring forgery, the printed word never changes its story.

My interest in this subject began in 1978 in the newsroom of the *Charlotte Observer,* where I watched my colleague and friend Allen Cowan pursue the truth about PTL and wrestle with Bakker's early efforts at disinformation. I am indebted to Jeannie Falknor for believing in me, the story, and our newspaper's duty to pursue it. Ken Friedlein was her able successor.

The list of colleagues who have given counsel and support, both for my reporting and for this book, is long. I was fortunate to work with fellow investigative reporter John Wildman on my first major PTL story; he taught me a boundless appreciation for public record, and his reporting on John Wesley Fletcher and David Taggart has shed further light on two of Jim Bakker's most intriguing associates. I am also indebted to reporters Frye Gaillard, Tex O'Neill, Gary Wright, Elizabeth Leland, and Jim Morrill; book-page editor Dannye Romine; editor Foster Davis; and librarian Sara Klemmer and her colleagues. Many others at 600 South Tryon have provided their support and encouragement. *Observer* editor Rich Oppel and publisher Rolfe Neill have extended editorial wisdom and generous moral and material support. Mark Ethridge III, then managing editor, encouraged me to take a leave of absence and write this book, never imagining how long it would take. Hank Durkin, Beth Hartness, Bill Fleming, and Bob De Piante have provided much good-natured help with computers. Dottie De Piante's TV transcripts have been invaluable. I owe special thanks to my chief "landlord," Mark Wilfley, and his colleagues in the *Observer*'s circulation division for their generous aid and genuine interest.

This book would not have been possible without the hard work, sharp mind, and good cheer of research assistant Sallie Locke. I thank Barbara Booth, Angela Williams, Robin Boggs, Cecilia Hamilton, and Cheryl Finn for their help.

I am indebted to the hundreds of family members, friends, and former associates of Jim Bakker's who have extended their trust. I have identified many of them by name in the text and footnotes; only a few have asked to remain anonymous. Ellen Baker (with one "k," as she will tell you with a laugh), PTL's video librarian, has been a tremendous help. The new leaders of PTL have also been of great assistance. They include Harry Hargrave and his colleagues during Jerry Falwell's tenure, PTL trustees David Clark and Red Benton, and numerous employees of PTL and its successor, Heritage Ministries.

I am especially grateful to those who, in 1987, helped unveil the truth of the Jessica Hahn payoff and other misdeeds under the Bakker-Dortch administration. A few remain unnamed at their request. Others have agreed, at my urging, to emerge from the shadows. I owe particular thanks to Al Cress, Jim Cobble, Roger Flessing, Jerry Ogg, Jr., and John Stewart.

My agent, Rafe Sagalyn, has set a high standard for this book from its inception in May 1987; his editorial advice has made this a much better book. Ann Godoff, my editor at Atlantic Monthly Press, has provided thoughtful and enthusiastic leadership for a newcomer to the world of book publishing. I am terribly grateful to her and her hard-working and cheerful assistant, Nancy Lewin.

I owe my deepest thanks to my family: to my parents, Chuck Shepard and Jo Shepard, who have set a standard of excellence from the start; to my four-year-old son, Ben, who one day will understand who this Jim Bakker fellow is that his dad is writing about; to his young brother, Sam; and most of all to my wife and fellow reporter, Jody Jaffe, to whom this book is dedicated, for her support, editorial counsel, and willingness to abide another evening at the office and just one more conversation about Jim and Tammy.

CHAPTER ONE

MUSKEGON

"To do the best possible in everything I do"

Nourished by America's faraway wars and far-flung highways, Muskegon, Michigan, prospered during Jim Bakker's childhood. Cargo ships streamed into Muskegon's harbor on their way up and down the new St. Lawrence Seaway. Continental Motors churned out tank and airplane engines for the military. Trains lurched through town carrying coke and scrap metal destined for the Campbell, Wyant, and Cannon foundry in Muskegon Heights. Plant #1 dominated the center of Muskegon Heights, a smaller inland city whose terrain belied its lofty name. Inside the foundry, molten iron hardened into engine blocks for tractor-trailer rigs.

Today, the boom is a faded memory. The foundry was boarded up in 1982, leaving a solemn reminder of economic reality in America's rust belt. Four blocks north, beneath a canopy of oaks, Sanford Street has surrendered its claim to upward mobility. Two motorcycles roost on the front porch of the three-story house Jim Bakker once called home.

A mile further north, across the line into Muskegon, Terrace Street has also shed its middle-class veneer. There, next to the lot that once contained a gas station, is the building where Jim Bakker says God first called him to preach. The Central Assembly of God now fills fancier, more spacious quarters on the edge of town. The old sanctuary is spare, reflecting the simple tastes and humble means of the Reverend Robert Rieben and his working-class congregation thirty-six years ago. Brown brick adorns the facade, but the side walls are a humbler cinder block, testimony to a disdain for aesthetics that Jim Bakker would later revile.

Near Muskegon's once-thriving harbor, preservationists have rescued the Victorian mansions built by Muskegon's captains of industry. The most famous is the Webster Avenue home of the city's patron, Charles Hackley. His three-story Queen Anne house is an ornate reminder of Muskegon's late-eighteenth-century heyday, when forty-seven sawmills spat out the lumber that rebuilt fire-ravaged Chicago. When Hackley finished his home, it contained eleven fireplaces, sixteen stained-glass windows, lavish carved wood fixtures, and an octagonal Gothic turret.

Three doors down is the Loescher house, a simpler three-story home named after the owner of a local tannery who lived there in the early twentieth century. The house had become worn by 1955, the year fifteen-year-old Jimmy Bakker convinced his parents to buy it. With three of four children out of the nest, the Bakkers hardly needed the extra room. Four years later, Jimmy was gone as well, to Bible school in Minneapolis. He would seldom return to Muskegon as an adult.

Bakker preserved an idiosyncratic version of his past in the climate-controlled world he built in the Carolinas, stuffing and mounting it to validate his ministry. On his television show, he talked often about his childhood, speaking with seemingly remarkable candor. Recast for dramatic effect and psychic relief, Bakker's bygone days offered him the hopes and hurts to validate the path he chose as a man, a minister, and a corporate executive.

Grandfather Joe Bakker was a foot soldier in the Pentecostal movement that swept through America at the beginning of the twentieth century. He evangelized with the same determination his grandson would later show. He doled out Bible tracts on street corners, inside the county jail, from his bicycle. But his was not a gentle spirit. Joe Bakker was righteous and implacable. He told strangers puffing on cigarettes that they were destined for hell. During one of his regular Sunday afternoon visits to the jail, an offended prisoner gave Bakker a black eye.

Joe Bakker inspired similar distaste in those who knew him best.

In the early twenties, he organized the small prayer meetings that eventually became the Central Assembly of God. But the church did not revere this founding father. His eccentric testimonies ran too long. The youngsters were scared of him. He feuded with church leaders. Eventually, he began attending services at a black church in town.

When he died, in his ninetieth year, some of Joe Bakker's siblings acknowledged to his grandchildren that they thought Joe was a bad seed. His proselytizing seemed incongruous. He had dedicated his life to rescuing the unsaved. His family even doubted his own suitability for God's celestial kingdom.

Joe Bakker also harvested bitterness at home. He and his wife, Alice, a gentle German-born woman of Jewish blood who limped from an old case of polio, raised nine boys and girls to adulthood. Joe insisted that his children quit school after the eighth grade and go to work full-time; he was suspicious of the worldly influence of school, and he needed money to support his family and help with the grueling work on his celery farm in the mucklands outside Muskegon.

As adults, two of Joe's daughters were unable to conceive children; there was talk in the family that the hard labor in the fields was to blame. John Bakker, Joe's eldest son, died four years after his father, still cursing the old man. In his late teens, John had applied for admission to a Bible school. The school accepted him, but Joe intercepted its letter; later, John found out that he had missed his chance at further schooling. John Bakker had a fiery temper like Joe's, and he stopped talking to his father. Months before his death in 1967, Joe Bakker refused his son's final request for forgiveness. Father and son would never see each other again.

Years later, one of the family's pastors, Bernard Ridings, mused that it was a wonder there had never been a murder in the Bakker family. As a grown man, Andy Bakker, another of Joe's sons, had knocked his father down and jumped violently on the prone man. Inside their grandfather's home, two of Joe's grandchildren watched, noses mashed against the screen door. Another son pulled Joe and Andy apart, yelling, "Andy, you don't have to kill him!"

Alice Bakker, Joe's first wife, died in 1949 at age sixty-eight, the victim of diabetes. Joe Bakker met his equal in his second marriage.

3

Kathrina Magdelina Ralph was a retired missionary in the Assemblies of God. Six years older than Joe Bakker, she was hardly the compliant wife Alice had been. Married in June 1951, they butted heads for five years. Privately, Joe's family relished the patriarch's predicament.

In the harsh winter days of 1956, as Kathrina neared death from malignant tumors on her face and in her stomach, seventy-seven-year-old Joe Bakker took to his downstairs workshop. When one of the grandchildren dropped by, Kathrina asked why Joe was making such a racket with his saw and hammer.

Grandson George Bakker, then thirteen, was evasive. He knew the answer to the question, but he could hardly tell the dying woman that her husband was piecing together a pine box lined with a straw-stuffed feed sack so he could save money on her coffin. George alerted his father, John, and Joe's kids discussed their dilemma with the family undertaker. After Kathrina died in March, the funeral home cautioned Joe Bakker that state law banned burial in homemade coffins. It might have been a lie, but it helped avoid another Joe Bakker outrage.

The empty casket sat in Joe Bakker's workroom for years, a macabre counterpoint to the religious tracts stacked high inside his house. After he had grown and married, George Bakker would bring his young ones by to peer through the window at the box, a monument to the unlovable patriarch of the Bakker clan.

Jim Bakker's father, Raleigh Bakker, escaped much of the bitterness and primal fury that infected his older brother John. While John turned his back on the church and tended bar, drank, cussed, and smoked cigarettes, Raleigh accepted the strictures of his father's Pentecostal faith. John was brusque; Raleigh, who bore a certain resemblance to Clark Gable, was known for his courtly manner and for a flirtatiousness that earned him a reputation as a ladies' man.

But Joe Bakker's mark was indelible. Raleigh Bakker could be stubborn, harsh, and hotheaded. When he made up his mind, there was no changing it. Men in the Bakker clan clung to their opinions with a steadfastness they benignly attributed to their Dutch blood. Growing up, listening to his father, his uncle Raleigh, and his other relatives debating the Jews' control over the US financial system or the inequities of government subsidies for farmers, it seemed to George Bakker that the fewer facts these men had to back up their claims, the more passionately they stuck to their positions. Years later, that same closed-minded conviction would color Jim Bakker's televised tirades against his accusers—be they government agencies, the local newspaper, or Jimmy Swaggart.

Raleigh's beliefs bordered at times on the eccentric. He insisted that he had seen two angels during a trip to Florida. He said that he had met the ghost of his beloved sister-in-law in his home in Muskegon. He discouraged his children from drinking milk or eating fresh bread, and he blamed his oldest son Bob's lung and kidney disease on the rosin Bob used when he bowled.

Raleigh was a proud man comfortable boasting about his initiative and frugality. "I don't care to brag, but I was good at everything I did because I set my mind to it. I don't believe in fooling around," he recalled. He seemed to thrive on his children's successes and bruise at their missteps. Months after Jim Bakker's disgrace in 1987, Raleigh Bakker declared that his humiliated youngest son was the most popular person in the country. Best known, perhaps, but hardly most popular. Speaking that same day about his daughter-in-law Tammy, Raleigh Bakker sounded more like an irritated husband. "Who wants a wife sitting there in her boudoir making her face up for a couple hours each morning, getting up early so that Jim can't see her without her makeup? That would be a trial for me if that woman spent that kind of time in front of the mirror."

Raleigh's wife, Furnia, lacked her husband's charm. She was inclined to be self-centered, nervous, fretful, and dependent on her mother and husband. Like her son Jim, she was quick to withdraw in social settings, but she could be outspoken when she had something on her mind. Relatives and friends considered her a cold woman, a sharp contrast to her nurturing mother, Armilda Irwin, and gentle older sister, Maude.

Furn was a dutiful housewife, faithful to the Dutch tradition of cleanliness and tightly wedded to her domestic routine. She kept the rich woodwork in her Webster Avenue home shining with lemon oil. But she seemed indifferent to the emotional needs of her four children. She complained to Bob, her firstborn, about how she had suffered during his birth. Later, when Bob had his own first child, the forty-one-year-old Furn let him know that she did not care to be, or be called, a grandmother. When Furn's teenage son Norm had his leg amputated, she stayed away from the hospital because hospitals made her nervous. Her sister Maude tended the boy instead.

Raleigh Bakker and Furnia Lynette Irwin were teenagers when they met in church in 1923. They married three years later. The bride, a stenographer for an insurance company, had just turned twenty. The groom marked his twentieth birthday ten days later.

Within a year, they conceived their first child. Robert Raleigh Bakker was born on Valentine's Day, 1928. Five years later, Furn gave birth to a second boy, Norman Joseph Bakker. At birth, the doctors noticed a small spot on the infant's right leg. Within days, it had spread, turning the leg purple from thigh to shin. Doctors in Ann Arbor diagnosed the growth as a hemangioma, a benign mass of small blood vessels. A surgeon trimmed the tumor, and the doctors at the University of Michigan hospital tried to shrink the remaining vessels with x-rays. The treatment stunted Norman's leg, weakened his right side, and rendered him sterile. When Norman was nineteen months old, Raleigh and Furn had their one and only daughter, Donna Jean. Their fourth and final child was born on January 2, 1940, five weeks premature, at Muskegon's Mercy Hospital. Furn, then thirty-three, had wanted a girl, a playmate for Donna. She was disappointed, and she cried that day in her hospital bed. The nurse comforted her with assurances that the new boy was cute.

The Bakkers named their newborn son James Orsen Bakker. They chose a middle name made famous fourteen months before when Orson Welles had stunned his radio audience with a reading of H. G. Wells's *The War of the Worlds.*

From the beginning, show business was in Jim Bakker's blood.

During the year of his marriage, Raleigh Bakker took a job at Sealed Power Corporation's piston-ring plant in Muskegon Heights. He was guaranteed forty cents an hour, more if he worked hard, and Bakker did. He was never sick and rarely took a vacation. For the next seventeen years, he monitored a machine that trimmed, bored, and smoothed cast-iron pistons to tolerances of a ten-thousandth of an inch so they would run smoothly inside car and truck engines. During the Depression, Bakker kept his job as the number of wage earners in Muskegon County dropped from eighteen thousand to six thousand. During World War II, Raleigh Bakker moved up a notch, taking a job making special tools and repairing plant machinery. He nearly made tool-room foreman, but a company consolidation cost him the job. "If I had had more education," he said later, "I would have been probably vice president or president of the company." Instead, when he retired in 1969 after forty-three years, Raleigh Bakker had never earned more than fourteen thousand dollars a year.

The newborn Jim Bakker came home to a cramped two-bedroom house in a blue-collar neighborhood. A single vent in the middle of the house furnished heat, and hot water came off a wood-fired stove. Sister Donna slept on the living-room sofa, and the three Bakker boys shared a bedroom. Bob—a few weeks short of his twelfth birthday when the baby arrived—slept on the upper bunk bed. The bottom was Norman's. When Jim was big enough, he joined Norman on the single mattress. The younger brothers slept together until 1947, when Jim was seven and Norman thirteen. That year, Bob married and moved out.

Furn Bakker's parents, Armilda and Emmett Irwin, lived next door, and their home became a refuge for young Jim. Armilda Irwin, sixty-six at Jim's birth and a seamstress by profession, encouraged the boy. As an adult, Bakker would have his fondest memories of his grandmother. She talked to him for hours. She fed him ice cream and pie. She bathed him in the unconditional love and nurturance that a child seeks from his parents, feeding an appetite in Jim that would never be satisfied.

As Bakker later put it, Grandma Irwin "believed" in him. That was something he rarely, if ever, said about his own parents.

> The one friend I could always count on was Grandma Irwin. The sun always seemed to shine at her house, even though it might be raining outside. She had given me the small New Testament that I read at night, and her open love had reached inside my heart. . . .
>
> She was the one person in my life against whom I can never remember feeling even a twinge of resentment. There was something about the way she lived and loved that made you feel special.

It was to his maternal grandmother that Bakker dedicated his first major building project at PTL. The shrine symbolized more than the generosity and love of a single individual. People like Grandma Irwin—Bakker fondly called them "Grandma Grunts"—formed the core of Jim Bakker's army of believers. These gray-haired women had an abiding faith in Jesus Christ and a mother's trust of and protectiveness toward the evangelist with a boyish face and childlike character. In them, Bakker found an army of surrogates for the departed Armilda Irwin.

Armilda—Mildy to her friends—was the undisputed boss at home. Her husband Emmett had never found a conventional career. He did some farming, some carpentry, a bit of everything. By 1940, the year of Jim's birth, a directory of Muskegon residents listed Emmett Irwin's occupation as "huckster." Emmett was willing to peddle whatever turned a buck: apples, Christmas trees, tomatoes, mops, blankets, even books about the Titanic. His face was familiar in Muskegon's black neighborhoods, where he found a market for the fish he and his young companions reeled out of the lakes that surround Muskegon. Emmett, who died when Jim was sixteen, was known to some as Kingfish, perhaps in recognition of both his love of fishing and his similarity to the manipulative character on radio's "Amos and Andy Show."

If young Jim drew his zeal from Joe Bakker and his faith from Armilda Irwin, his instinctive talent as a salesman flowed from Emmett. His grandfather liked to sell and was brash enough to sell iceboxes to Eskimos. Once, when he wanted to peddle a rowboat sitting in his yard, he slapped paint on one side of the boat—the side facing the street—and stuck a for-sale sign out front.

Emmett was a blusterer who relished bending the rules of convention so dear to his wife. Some days he attended church with his pajamas poking out below the cuffs of his pants, a rumpled contrast to his neatly dressed wife. Inside the church, he sometimes dozed behind a songbook or yanked out his dentures and polished them with spit. He had no particular sense of humor, but the youngsters in church found him comical.

A month before Jim's second birthday, the Japanese bombed Pearl Harbor. The war transformed Muskegon County. At war's end, 36,000 people held industrial jobs in the area, up from 14,000 before the war. At Continental Motors, the payroll soared from 700 to nearly 5,000 workers. Recruiters had to scour the South for workers to fill the city's factories. The forties saw the county's population climb thirty percent to over 121,000.

At home, Raleigh and Furn Bakker fought their own battle with the rebellious Bob. At age thirteen, he jumped a train headed to California, carrying a jar of peanut butter and a loaf of bread. He got frostbite in Colorado and was sent home. Later, he stole his father's car and drove to Texas. The police arrested him there, and Raleigh flew south to pick up his car and his boy.

In March 1944, a month after his sixteenth birthday, Bob dropped out of tenth grade. He wanted to play football, but his parents said no. The Bakkers' refusal was considered sensible parental discipline in the Pentecostal community. The church thought the football crowd too worldly, too cozy with forces of sin like pool halls and beer joints. If he wanted to see a ball game, Bob had to sneak in.

Six days after he turned seventeen—just months before the end of World War II—Bob enlisted in the navy. He was back in eight months. He had suffered what the woman he later married considered a nervous breakdown; some family members prefer to dismiss it as shrewd acting. Back home, he saw a psychiatrist at government expense.

To support himself, Bob worked in a shoe store, using his considerable talents as a salesman. Handsome and charming, he had more drive and practicality and fewer insecurities than his youngest brother. He eventually became the top salesman in a chain of thirty-five shoe stores to the delight of his father. Bob married in February 1947, after a whirlwind courtship that began with a chance meeting in a roller-skating rink. He had turned nineteen the day before. Jim, seven, served as ring bearer.

Bob wanted to be a minister in the Assemblies of God. He enrolled in North Central Bible Institute in Minneapolis. Later, he transferred to Central Bible Institute in Springfield, Missouri, the home city of the Assemblies of God.

By Bob's wedding day, Raleigh and Furn Bakker had settled into a more spacious Dutch colonial home on Muskegon Heights' Sanford Street. The three-story house was a short walk from Raleigh's job and an undisputed step up the social ladder. The Bakkers'

neighbors included a local superintendent of schools, factory owners, a doctor, a Continental Motors plant manager, and the coach
of the high school's football and basketball teams.

In Jim Bakker's memory, the house became a cause for shame;
his recasting of Sanford Street exemplified his profound capacity to
remake reality. Out of conscious design or impulsive emotion,
Bakker replaced the truth with images more likely to elicit sympathy, favor, or money.

Bakker described the house bleakly in his ghostwritten 1976
autobiography.

> My father's name is Raleigh Bakker. He worked as a machinist
> in a piston-ring plant and made a decent living. But I thought
> we lived in poverty. . . .
>
> I was even embarrassed about my family's house. A cement
> block structure . . . the house had been painted with what
> Daddy thought would be buff-colored paint. It turned out to
> be orange!
>
> That house stood out on the block, looking like an oversized
> Florida citrus. Whenever someone drove me home from
> school, I'd ask to be dropped off several blocks away so they
> wouldn't see the house.

The home was hardly so pitiful. What Bakker called cement blocks
were decorative stones, textured and beveled. The house had a
porch across the front and a gabled roof. At the second story, the
stone facing gave way to painted wood shingles. Neighbors and kin
remember the house painted dark tan, its trim a dark green.

Some family friends envied the place. Norm's fiancée, Dorothy,
lived in an aging farmhouse. To her, the Bakkers' home was beautiful. It had handsome varnished woodwork and fireplaces upstairs
and down. Donna had her own bedroom. Eventually, Raleigh fixed
up a bedroom for Jim in the attic so he would no longer have to
share quarters with Norm.

Bakker's best friend on Sanford Street was his neighbor Sonny
Singer. Sonny's parents sold auto parts and unclaimed freight, and
the boys shared a keen entrepreneurial spirit. They mowed lawns
and raked yards to raise a buck. Both creative, they soon discovered
they could make bigger money in sales than in lawn care. Grown-
ups, they realized, loved to buy from kids. The boys bought water-

melons, cantaloupes, and flowers at Smitty's gas station, loaded the produce on Sonny's red wagon, and sold it door-to-door. With the help of other children in the neighborhood, they collected newspapers to recycle. Once, they filled the back half of the church bus Raleigh drove with newspapers. That effort made fifteen dollars for each of them, big money in an era when a movie cost sixteen cents and popcorn five.

The boys made the big time after Sonny's dad shut down his stores and stored the unsold inventory—cleaning pads and pots and pans—in the Singers' basement. One weekend, while Sonny's parents were away, Sonny and Jim loaded the wagon and traveled from house to house. Cleaning pads cost ten cents, a teakettle went for six bucks. They emptied the basement, earning $263 in the process. Sonny's father, amused at their enterprise, let the boys keep sixty-three dollars.

Jim and Sonny were both small for their age. Jim seemed to stop growing between his fifth and eighth years, and his parents wondered if he would be a midget. His parents remember his weight hovering at twenty-eight pounds; others remember thirty-eight. He turned his weight into a chant, calling out "eight pounds, eight pounds, eight pounds" as he bounced down the stairs. Jim displayed no embarrassment at his height then, but as an adult five foot seven inches tall, Bakker would surround himself with men of short stature.

Living on Sanford Street, Jim's horizons reached no farther than the shops downtown. He told Sonny that he wanted to be a shoe salesman when he grew up, just like his brothers. By the time he turned thirteen, he was helping Norm at the shoe store.

To Singer and the other kids on the street, the neighborhood seemed a wonderful place to grow up. Jim and Sonny roamed all over. They bicycled to the cemetery on the edge of town. They scouted the swamp at the end of Peck Street, a wonderland of frogs and turtles and snakes. Those who knew young Bakker remember him being content in this little universe.

In Bakker's version of his youth, he was dogged by fear and convinced of his inferiority. He was, without dispute, a poor student. According to his autobiography, he was ashamed not only of his house, but "it seemed like anything I had was inferior to what other kids had. Year after year, I wore the same tattered blue baseball jacket with prominent white stitching, until the stitching unraveled completely." Later, his parents said they would not have allowed their boy to wear such a shabby coat.

If Jim was afraid of his shadow, he showed few signs of it to his buddies who gathered in the alley behind his house. With his cousin George, Jim would pour a line of gasoline down the alley, strike a match, and watch flames dance along the path. The children would also tie bricks to the end of a chalk line, stretch the string tight across the alley, set the bricks on garbage cans, and wait for cars to hit the line. As one playmate remembered, "We were always raising hell." Once the kids pulled American flags off the soldiers' graves at Saint Mary's Cemetery. The mother of one of Jim's co-conspirators made her son go back and replace them.

Short and uncoordinated, young Bakker never cared for sports like his friend Sonny and his own siblings did. Brother Bob was a skilled bowler and a solid softball player. Donna, a quiet tomboy, was a demon with the football. Despite his bad leg, even Norm played ball.

Of all Raleigh and Furn Bakker's kids, Norm seemed to have the most reason to feel sorry for himself. He wore a built-up shoe to compensate for his short leg. By age sixteen, one leg was a full foot shorter than the other. That year, surgeons amputated Norm's right leg above the knee and fitted him with an artificial leg. Jim was not quite ten years old.

In fall 1953, with Norm newly married and thirteen-year-old Jim starting eighth grade, the Bakkers moved back across the tracks to Muskegon and Jim Bakker's third childhood home. Raleigh thought the house on Sanford too expensive to heat. The new home on McLaughlin Street had a good roof, fussy Dutch former owners, and a Michigan cellar for storing fruit and vegetables that appealed to the practical Raleigh.

Jim had already discovered television at his friends' homes. His favorite show, and the nation's, was "I Love Lucy." One night, Raleigh Bakker announced to the family that he was buying a television set—despite the jeremiads emanating from the church. Raleigh's father had condemned the appliance as "hellevision." Furn was nearly in tears at her husband's decision. "I never thought you'd weaken," she told him.

Young Jim was also transfixed by his new tape recorder. He

needed one for speech class, he told his father, and Raleigh picked out the best he could find, a reel-to-reel with a clear tone and a price tag of more than a hundred dollars. Jim carried the recorder back and forth from junior high so he could practice at home.

With the new machine, Jim Bakker taught himself how to read and court an audience, skills that would propel his career as a TV evangelist. If he liked what he heard on the reel-to-reel, he left it on the tape. If he didn't, he taped over it. He watched himself speak in front of the mirror to polish his bearing. If he liked the fellow on the glass in front of him, he knew the people would like him too.

Jim disliked the new neighborhood on McLaughlin Street, which was more modest than Sanford Street. In 1955, the fifteen-year-old noticed an advertisement for a old mansion downtown on Webster Avenue. The Bakkers toured the house. Inside they found eleven-foot ceilings, sprawling bedrooms, and rich wood paneling and trim, including quarter-sawed oak wainscoting beneath the dining room's coffered ceiling and an ornate mahogany and mirrored mantelpiece over the downstairs fireplace. Webster Avenue had once been the poshest of neighborhoods, a king's row. The street had been paved with brick and overlooked the city's harbor on Muskegon Lake. But in 1955, the neighborhood was in decline. The Red Cross and a day-care center had moved in on the same block, and blacks—an ominous presence to many in the older Bakkers' world though not to Raleigh Bakker—lived on the next block.

Jim persuaded his parents to buy the house, much as he would persuade his father, a devoted Ford man, to buy a used Cadillac. In June 1955, the summer before Jim started high school, the Bakkers bought the fraying house for $12,500. It was a deal frugal Raleigh Bakker could appreciate: the house had room for boarders on the second floor, and he could also rent out space over the separate three-car garage. Within a few months, Jim's sister, Donna, a clerk at Woolworth's, married a telephone installer. Jim was the only child left at home.

Years later, Raleigh Bakker blamed his youngest son's fancy taste on Aunt Martha, Grandma Irwin's sister. Jim thought that his great-aunt, the wife of an Ohio blanket salesman, was the wealthiest woman in the world. She made a show of her money. Her home in Lima, Ohio, was spacious and strewn with statues and mementos. When she arrived by train for a visit, she brought what seemed like suitcase after suitcase for her jewelry, mink coat, and new outfits for each occasion. "That's where he got his ideas, because he never got it from us," Raleigh Bakker said disdainfully. "I don't think he knows that she lived on borrowed money all her life."

Jim also glimpsed the good life when his mother's two brothers visited. They came in their campers, or a yacht, or a huge, wood-paneled Chrysler town car. Each had marshaled the Irwin entrepreneurial flair with a success that had escaped their father. One sold coffee to restaurants in Lansing, the other caskets to the bereaved in Chicago. "Don't put your bones in any old basket," went Uncle Bill's pitch, "lay them neatly in an Acme casket."

If Aunt Martha was the future to young Jim, the Central Assembly of God epitomized the past. Family and church were indistinguishable in his world. His grandmother taught Sunday school, his dad was the consummate usher. The church was his principal social center, a place to meet girls and show off the outsiders he dated.

Services at Central Assembly consumed Wednesday nights and most of Sunday. The dos and don'ts of Pentecostal life touched virtually every corner of life during the rest of the week. No smoking, no dancing, no drinking, no pool playing, no movies, no consorting with the world of sin.

> As a child I was taught the big eye. In fact, in our Sunday school department we had this eye about six feet wide, and it said, "This eye is watching you, you, you." So we sang a little song that said, "Be careful little eyes what you see; be careful little feet where you go; because looking down from up above is your Father." And we had this image that God had this big club, and if we step out of boundaries, He was going to bash us.

Bakker's generation of Pentecostal youth was torn between these traditional prohibitions and the allure of American popular culture and mainstream values. With television, the entertainment industry and advertising agencies could establish a beachhead in even the holiest of homes. High school, even college, was within the reach of Joe Bakker's grandchildren; with this opportunity came further exposure to the way the other half lived. The forties brought economic revival. Now, more Pentecostals could afford the fruits of affluence—big cars, fancy clothes and jewelry, and money for leisure activities.

As they got older, Jim and his cousin and friend George Bakker cringed at the church's lack of sophistication: the parishioner who bellowed "Amen" at the most inappropriate times; the traveling evangelist who named names during the McCarthy era, including those of improbable communists like Lucille Ball and Bob Hope; the used barracks that Pastor Rieben used to house his church camp north of Muskegon.

Rieben rolled up his sleeves and got the job done without caring how it looked. He believed in living with as little as possible. He turned down pay raises over his family's objections. He painted church classrooms purple because he got the paint free.

Dedicated to evangelizing, Rieben sent recruiters in church buses to enlist youngsters from government projects and the hardscrabble countryside. Sunday-school enrollment swelled from just 83 in 1948 to 550 in the mid-fifties. Many of the newcomers were down and out: the father a drunk, his wife struggling to raise a half-dozen kids in a home with a dirt floor. They were the sort of folks drawn to the Pentecostal movement in its infancy. But Central Assembly was beyond that now, and even Rieben's children were embarrassed at the ragged recruits. The stalwarts in Rieben's congregation might live simply, but they were proud of their steady jobs and clapboard homes and dreams of more.

Jim stayed in the church, trying to bend the rules without breaking them. He went to school dances but avoided the dance floor; instead, he took pictures or spun records as a deejay. He went to movies. He tried smoking. He dated girls who wore makeup but asked them to abstain from cosmetics when they joined him at church.

If he had been crippled by shyness and timidity—and his friends and family don't remember young Jimmy that way—that persona had been shed by his teenage years. Jim cultivated an image of distinction and self-assurance. As a teenager, he later told his employees at PTL, he believed that God cared most about the way he dressed and wore his hair. He slicked his hair into a seamless ducktail, not the more common crew cut. Friends at church made jokes about Crisco in his hair. Jim put his wardrobe together with the same care—the worst thing you could do, a friend from church remembered, was step on Jim's white bucks.

Jim shopped carefully for trendsetting outfits. He taught his friend and cousin George, two years younger, to be a classy dresser and helped him secure a charge account at the men's shop when George was only fifteen. Often, people really don't get to know you, he told George, so the only impression they get is how you look.

George was impressed by his cousin. Afternoons and weekends, Jim sold shoes downtown. George watched from the back room and decided that his cousin was a superb salesman. He spoke well, and he had a boyish charm that appealed to the maternal instincts of the women customers. Jim had a handle on the world. He had ideas, he knew where he was headed, he knew how to act around girls. When he had a date, he made sure he found a girl to date George.

Others saw this same self-confidence and keen sense of direction in young Jim. One was Bill Harrison, a thirty-year-old graduate of the University of Michigan who was teaching journalism, photography, and English at Muskegon High School, a massive three-story structure housing twenty-two hundred students. Harrison, a dark-haired man who resembled Jim's father, was no guardian of convention. He let his students be what they wanted to be and didn't insist on bending them his way. He let his students see him as a human being, and he seemed to treat them like adults. "You were always very soft, always very kind," Jim told Harrison on a 1986 PTL broadcast.

Harrison nurtured his students' creativity. He encouraged them to be daring, to shoot for the moon if they wanted to get off the ground. It was that advice that Bakker continued to follow at PTL.

In young Bakker, Harrison found a boy eager to learn, easy to teach, drawn to center stage, and brimming with ideas. Jim had so many ideas, in fact, that he needed someone he respected to curb his enthusiasm, Harrison thought. Coupled with his creative spark, Jim had tremendous energy, a knack for selling himself, and a willingness to try what others said couldn't be done.

With Harrison's help, Jim learned photography and journalism and joined the camera club and newspaper, both advised by Harrison. Jim sold advertising for the paper and was given the title of ad manager. He also took photos, and soon he and his camera were a familiar presence on campus.

It was at the newspaper that Bakker found his first grand audience.

The school paper, the *Campus Keyhole,* was perpetually broke. To pay its bills, it published an edition on auto safety to win a lucrative competition sponsored by Kemper Insurance. With the prize money, it balanced its budget. In the fall of 1956, as he started his second year at Muskegon High, Jim introduced a new way to raise money: produce a variety show in the school's eleven-hundred-seat auditorium using amateur and volunteer professional talent. He produced the fund-raiser for the next three years—and took a big step toward a career raising money onstage.

The TV variety show, a staple on America's networks since the war's end, was big news that year. One Sunday night during the summer of 1956, NBC premiered a variety show hosted by Steve Allen of the "Tonight Show," which competed with Ed Sullivan's successful CBS vaudeville show. That season, both men battled for viewers, using appearances by a teenage singing sensation named Elvis Presley to capture ratings. By season's end, Allen had pulled NBC neck and neck with CBS on Sunday nights.

Show business fascinated Jim. He loved theater. He acted in school plays, helped with the technical work behind the massive high-school stage, and appeared in a Christian film produced by a Muskegon gospel film company. Several friends were certain that Jim would end up working in theater in New York. His 1957 high-school variety show was set in Manhattan. The set mimicked its skyline, and the show's slogan was There's no business like show business.

Jim's star attraction that first year was Marlene Way, a twenty-year-old Elvis Presley impersonator from Muskegon. That fall, Way had appeared twice in one week on Steve Allen's programs, making her an instant celebrity back home and at the high school, her alma mater. She agreed to perform in the *Keyhole*'s variety show, and her appearance pushed the show's net profit to four hundred dollars, four times more than Bakker had hoped.

Jim and Way became instant friends. Jim seemed to feel comfortable around the bubbly five-foot soldier's wife from a working-class home. Jim was lots of fun once Way got beyond his surface reticence. She thought he was a born organizer, she loved his fresh sense of humor, and she considered him an exemplar of purity. She was not troubled—in fact, she hardly noticed—the four years' difference in their ages.

Way thought that Jim was searching for his place in two contrary worlds, one where teenagers dressed properly and never missed church, another where youngsters wore black and danced to Elvis, the personification of defiance. In a visit to Way's home, Jim confided that he had spent some time the evening before with some youngsters in show business, the sort he wasn't used to being with, the sort the church disapproved of. These friends didn't share his family's standards, but they really weren't bad, he told her. Jim said he couldn't enjoy himself because he didn't know which way he should go. He summed up his dilemma with a rhyme that stuck in Way's memory. "Should I be good or should I be a hood?"

Eventually, Jim agreed to fill in as Way's manager. He helped Way haul her makeup and props to performances. He ran tapes of Elvis's music while she lip synced. On one trip to a local nursing home, Jim rescued Way from disaster with his intuitive feel for his audience. Way couldn't get a response from the elderly audience. Two songs fell flat. Offstage, Jim whispered a suggestion: "Jailhouse Rock." He flipped on the record, jumped onstage, and began dancing the bop while Way lip synced. The ladies started to smile; they came alive. One approached Way afterwards. "This has been the most fun I've had in a long time. Please come again."

Jim's grades won no applause, and he failed to graduate in June 1958 after his senior year at Muskegon High, a fact noticeably absent from accounts of his youth. But his repeated senior year became a time of triumph. Harrison named him editor of the *Keyhole.* He ran the campaign for a candidate for student-council vice president, and she won. He served as technical director of the senior play and acted in the school drama club's December production of *Gentlemen Prefer Blondes.* A week later, on December 12, 1958, he executed his third and most ambitious variety show.

The *Keyhole* promoted the extravaganza without restraint in its issue of December 1, 1958, devoting space on five of its eight pages to articles and pictures about the show. The newspaper he edited provided Bakker with his own cheering section, much as PTL's in-house newspaper would years later.

> "This year's Variety Show is filled with fun, excitement, and terrific entertainment from the opening curtain to the finale. The members of the cast have gone all out to make this the best show yet," quoted Jim Bakker, producer-director of the *Keyhole* Variety Show.

The show would be Jim's last, the newspaper said. "Jim Bakker is graduating, and it seems no one else wants to take over his sleepless nights and hectic days." Bakker had spent months in preparation, the paper said, and had lined up thirty acts and a cast of more than three hundred. Bakker had even tried to move the show from the high school's hardwood stage to a larger theater in Muskegon. School officials said no.

Bakker scheduled a black rock 'n' roll group from Muskegon High, a Marilyn Monroe impersonator, the school's sixty-piece orchestra, and a kick line. The *Keyhole* stories also promised a "hilarious number" by Miss X, described only as a secret member of the cast, and music from "Michelo Zenone, concert pianist of Detroit."

The night's drawing card was Miss Michigan, a blonde named Patience Pierce. Jim had lined up the state's beauty-pageant winner with calls to the governor's office and assurances that the beauty queen would have a chauffeured car and dressing room. Even as a teenager, Jim had a knack for talking people into things. He persuaded local companies to donate food and door prizes to help boost attendance. He borrowed hearses to chauffeur his celebrity guests.

Bakker showed less finesse at working with the people under him, a pattern that would dog him throughout his TV ministry. His great expectations and attention to detail alienated some schoolmates. He showed little patience when he wanted a job done, and his brusque manner left younger students cold. Years later, Bakker recalled telling Harrison, "I wish the staff would just do what I would tell them to do. Ours is not to wonder why, ours is but to do or die." Harrison had gently corrected him. "Everyone has a right to know why," he told Jim. It was one bit of wisdom Jim Bakker wasn't ready to learn.

19

To host his final show, Jim chose a short, effervescent female student and a twenty-two-year-old local actor, Steve Zarnas, who also played the mysterious Miss X. Zarnas remembered Bakker as a promoter with infectious enthusiasm, willing to try the outrageous. But Bakker tolerated no loss of control. He dismissed a suggestion from Zarnas to change one of the actor's routines, and Zarnas noticed, with irritation, that Jim seemed to take credit for the cast's ideas.

The *Keyhole*'s next issue proclaimed the show a "huge success" and carried a picture of the cast taking its bows, with Jim at center stage. He closed out the night with a triumphant party at his home on Webster Avenue that stretched into the early hours of the morning.

Jim's so-called concert pianist from Detroit, "Michelo Zenone," was a teenager named Louis Michael Zenone. Jim had befriended Louis at Camp Faholo (the name a contraction of faith, hope, and love), an Assemblies of God camp in central Michigan where Jim and friends from church went each summer. The two became devoted friends. Louis visited the Bakkers in Muskegon, and Jim stayed with the Zenone family at their home on Detroit's east side.

Zenone was a talented performer. He acted, played piano, and played the organ for his Assembly of God in Hamtramck. As an adult, Zenone became a successful professional entertainer, working as a musician, actor, conductor, and composer under the name Louis St. Louis. He served as music director for the first production of *Grease* and composed a popular song added to the musical's movie version. Years later, Zenone said that *Grease* was the story of the lives the other kids, free from the strict rules of the Pentecostal church, led while he was growing up in the fifties.

Zenone considered his boyhood friend a showman in the style of Mike Todd. Jim had a rich imagination and an entrepreneurial touch. In his pensive moments, Jim would appear to be busy thinking up another plan, another way to do something—a pattern that continued through his adult years. Like several of Bakker's friends in Muskegon, Zenone expected Jim to go into show business, perhaps as a producer.

Two days before he graduated from high school, Bakker told his readers in the *Keyhole* that theater was his favorite interest. Jim talked about his ambitions with Zenone's mother, Ana. "I would like to be a star in show business. But it's just for a few chosen ones. I have a different way," Ana Zenone recalled hearing him say. Ana Zenone doesn't remember asking—or Jim Bakker ever saying— what that different way was.

Jim surprised many friends and relatives when he announced that he wanted to attend Bible school in Minneapolis. George Bakker thought that his cousin shared his own eagerness to put the church behind him.

Jim could have chosen to stay in Muskegon and work, like his father, brother, uncle, and sister-in-law, at the Sealed Power Corporation. He might have sold shoes for a living, as he had done at night and on weekends. But his senior-year girlfriend, Sally Wickerink, remembers that Bakker was eager to escape his provincial hometown, where social life revolved around McDonald's and taking a spin to the Ovals, a popular lakeside spot. Bakker had talked of photojournalism, but he seemed to have grown out of the role of silent witness with his variety-show successes.

Attending North Central put Jim onto the path that his eldest brother, Bob, had walked with seeming promise nearly ten years earlier. In Bible school in Springfield, Missouri, however, Bob Bakker had fallen in with men who espoused doctrine that the Assemblies of God considered false. He dropped out of school, a bitter disappointment to his parents, who considered their firstborn the smartest of their four children and the offspring with the greatest promise as a preacher.

In 1954, Bob had decided to start all over in Houston, with his wife Joan, brother Norm, and Norm's bride Dorothy. The brothers got jobs in a traveling carnival, Bob as a barker, Norm as the poor fellow who lies on a bed of nails. Norm soon returned to Muskegon, Bob to Springfield. Bob Bakker and his wife separated in 1955, a few weeks before Raleigh and Furn bought their new home on Webster Avenue. After eight years, Joan Bakker was weary of her husband's temper and mental instability.

Bob returned to Muskegon. In 1956, Jim's seventeenth year, Bob Bakker's fall was complete. He married a nineteen-year-old girl he had met selling magazines, forfeiting any chance of working as a minister in his parents' church. He could no longer take the strain of running a shoe store. He took a job at Sealed Power as a machinist, much like his father. By 1963, he was earning $125 a week. His ex-wife drew $55 a month in welfare to support their two children.

Bob Bakker remained an outcast from the Assemblies. The church in Muskegon knew of his involvement in a church that sanctioned dancing and drinking wine and considered the Bible as just one, not the only, source of God's word. There was talk, too, of free love in this heretical church. When Bob joined his parents at services one day and helped Raleigh take up the collection, the church brethren asked him to stop, a defensible decision considering his apostasy. Jim Bakker told the story many times as an evangelist, his words brimming with resentment at what he considered the church's lack of forgiveness.

With Bob Bakker's fall, the mantle of ministry fell on Jim, the only boy left at home. Young Jim knew he was a second and distant choice.

> My brother, Bob, was the one that was called. My brother Bob graduated from Bible college and could sing and speak and had tremendous ability. Very charismatic . . . I was the runt of the litter. Bob was the tallest one, good-looking, dynamic. People liked him. And the Devil just destroyed his life.

Bakker was living out the dreams of his much-maligned paternal grandfather as well.

> Grandpa Bakker was a very dominant, hard man—a Hollander of the first sense. But he loved the Lord and he had this call of God . . . he had this something inside of him that he had to tell the whole world about Jesus Christ. . . .
>
> So, it's like, you know, I don't have any choice. You know, it's like a mantle somehow has come down . . . this whole thing, now, has kind of slid on down, and I have to do it.

Bakker told another story of his commitment to Christ while he was a traveling evangelist and during his early years in TV ministry. Bakker spun a wrenching tale of true-life redemption to explain his decision to choose the ministry. His "testimony" lent authority to his ministry and appeal to his altar calls. But like so much of the history Bakker created, it was partly illusion.

As Bakker told the story in his autobiography, he had slipped out of a Sunday-night church service and gone cruising in his father's '52 Cadillac with a girl from church. They talked and listened to rock 'n' roll music. Turning back into the driveway at Central Assembly, Jim hit three-year-old Jimmy Summerfield. The boy recovered, and Jim, chastened by the experience, surrendered his life to God. For the rest of his senior year, he wrote, Jesus "became the only thing in my life. I knew I couldn't control my own destiny anymore . . . my future was entirely in the hands of God."

After the accident, Bakker's autobiography said, young Jim quit working as a disc jockey for school clubs and read the Bible intently. One passage, Acts 10:42, drew his eye repeatedly: "And he commanded us to preach." Over the next few months, the book says, he felt that God was calling him into the ministry. Then a secretary at his church who boarded at his home suggested that he consider North Central Bible College, her alma mater. By summer, Jim made up his mind to go to Minneapolis.

Bakker did run over the Summerfield boy. But the accident happened not in late 1958, Jim's final year of high school, but two years earlier, on December 16, 1956, about the time Marlene Way performed in the first of Jim's three variety shows. Bakker's friends and relatives describe the accident as a trying moment for sixteen-year-old Jim, who feared at first that he had killed the toddler. But they do not remember the dramatic conversion described by Bakker.

Sunday-night services at Central Assembly had just ended, and young Summerfield was rolling down a snowbank near the street as Jim pulled into the parking lot in the dark. Jim's cousin George was in the front seat of the car, not a girl. As the car rolled over Jimmy, the tire left an imprint across the little boy's chest. As Jimmy was rushed to the hospital, Jim pounded his hands against the side of the church in anguish.

Young Jimmy's collarbone was crushed, his lung ruptured. Jim Bakker visited the hospital that night with his father. Raleigh Bakker appealed to Summerfield's father to take a moment to speak to Jim. "Jim's going to lose his mind if you don't talk to him." Charles Summerfield, an assembly-line worker at an office-furniture plant and one of Raleigh Bakker's fellow ushers, assured Jim that he was not to blame. The police later reached the same conclusion. Inside

Hackley Hospital, doctors reinflated Jimmy Summerfield's lung, and his breathing returned to normal a few hours before sunrise. The next morning, Jim learned that Jimmy would survive. Before he went home, young Summerfield had a new stuffed animal, a gift from Jim Bakker.

Jim showed little interest in organized religion at school. He rarely talked about his faith. He ignored a solicitation to join the active Youth For Christ club at Muskegon High. By his final months in high school, though, Jim showed more interest in religion, at least in public displays of faith.

In March 1959, Bakker read from the Scriptures at Muskegon High School's Easter service, another performance his paper promoted on its front page. In its Easter edition, Jim ended his column:

> Almost everyone knows the Easter story of Christ's crucifixion and how He arose on the third day, but do we realize the real meaning of His death or do we drown the real meaning in a maze of new clothes and Easter gaieties? In this Easter season let us concern ourselves with the real meaning of Easter. Attend the church of your choice, not only this Easter Sunday but every Sunday.

Jim's girlfriend, Sally Wickerink, a Methodist with her own thoughts of going into the ministry, heard Bakker preach at Central Assembly. She found him charismatic, his preaching full of drama.

Bakker's yearbook entry indicated no ambition to enter the ministry. Some classmates expressed their plans "to do everything to the honor and glory of God," to become a missionary or "to please the Lord in everything I do." Bakker's entry was more egocentric, a prophetic slogan for a man who would be consumed by his own mission. At age nineteen, Jim Bakker's ambition was "to do the best possible in everything I do."

CHAPTER TWO

BIBLE SCHOOL

"The cutest girl I had ever seen"

As if to compensate for his earlier lack of fervor, Jim Bakker fell in at North Central with the Holy Joes, students who made a grand show of spirituality. With monastic dedication, he prayed for hours in a basement room, kneeling on pillows that cushioned the concrete floor, surrounded by walls of whitewashed Minnesota stone. Some mornings he would return to his room at daybreak and sleep through his classes. Later, Bakker recalled with pride how students laughed when he declared he would win the world for Jesus. In his telling, the gesture illustrated his spiritual calling. Inside North Central Bible College, Bakker's asceticism and bold declarations smacked of faddism and self-promotion.

With a population of almost five hundred thousand, Minneapolis was ten times the size of Muskegon. North Central was an obscure presence in the city. It had 360 students, fewer than Bakker had graduated with at Muskegon High. It was unaccredited, though it had begun offering a four-year program and college degree. The students kidded about their one-building campus, a stately five-story Victorian brick structure that had once been a hospital and now held classrooms, offices, and carefully segregated boys' and girls' dorms. Most of its students came from blue-collar homes. North Central's morning schedule of classes left room for afternoon and evening jobs to pay the costs of school.

Bakker was hungry for the stage, and he soon found it twelve blocks away inside the Minneapolis Evangelistic Auditorium, an old theater on the seedy end of Nicollet Avenue. MEA was run by a husband-and-wife team of Assemblies of God ministers, Russell and Fern Olson. A friend had told Jim to go hear Fern, a onetime traveling evangelist, preach.

Fern Olson was a rousing preacher, a pulpiteer of tremendous power. If Russell Olson looked like central casting's idea of a friendly police sergeant, she might have doubled for actress Shelley Winters. She was warmhearted, outgoing, and flamboyant, with a taste for loud, wide-brimmed hats and flowing, Kate Smith style gowns that softened her substantial girth. She sang in a no-nonsense, belt-out-the-words style.

During his Holy Joe phase, Bakker crossed the salt-and-pepper marble floor of MEA's lobby and received for the first time the baptism of the Holy Spirit, a distinctive rite of passage for a Pentecostal. Russell Olson was holding the service that day, which Bakker later described.

> Without even thinking, I walked toward the center of the room with several others. . . . "Lord," I said in desperation, "I give up."
> The moment I spoke those words, the Lord baptized me with the Holy Spirit, and immediately I began speaking in a language that I hadn't learned. For what seemed like hours I was lost with God. When I drifted back to earth, the world was practically empty of people, and I was singing.
> "I've been with Jesus, and I'm so happy," I sang, "and I can feel it in my soul."

By late October, Bakker was on the MEA program himself for a week of nighttime teen rallies. At the Olsons' auditorium, he found the launching pad for a career that blended theater and the church. The program was titled "Rock for Teens." It had the singular flavor of a Jim Bakker production. The featured talent that night—as it had been ten months earlier for Jim's last high-school variety show—was Jim's church-camp friend from Detroit, Louis Zenone. For the variety show, he had been Michelo Zenone, concert pianist. Now, Bakker promoted Zenone as the young man who had starred as Hypo in the Christian film *Teenage Rock*. Zenone played the piano and organ. Joyce Gore—the church secretary from

Central Assembly, where she had also sung as a soloist—performed. She was cast as a nightclub singer turned sacred recording artist. In fact, she had never been a nightclub singer.

Bakker came wrapped in a similar born-again package. The program billed the earnest-looking young man with the Bible in his left hand as a teen who had gone "from rock 'n' roll disc jockey to rock of ages." As a high-school student, Bakker had played a bit part in "Teenage Rock" himself, posing as an unsaved student who spins records for his classmates. Young Bakker spoke a single line in the film, "Let's get our girls and get out of here." The film—shown during the fall 1959 rallies at MEA—offered celluloid proof of Bakker's salvation. The world of make-believe was redefining reality in Jim Bakker's world, as it would many times in the future.

Bakker was deft at introducing speakers. You could tell he liked crowds. He was a glib, enthusiastic talker onstage even though he could turn shy in person. Star struck, he also enjoyed the access to traveling celebrities. When a big-name evangelist —a W. V. Grant, a Gordon Lindsay—finished speaking, Bakker often asked his roommate Bob Cilke to walk up to the stage with him to meet the celebrity. Cilke customarily demurred; Jim usually went ahead. Jim seemed eager to hitch himself to a star, to become someone special overnight.

MEA existed on the fringes of the official North Central community. Russell Olson had grown up in town, pastored a church there, hosted a local radio show, and taught the science of preaching at North Central. But services in the auditorium had more pizzazz than traditional Pentecostal worship, and the Olsons had not affiliated the auditorium with the Assemblies of God. North Central preferred its students from Assemblies homes to attend churches in the denomination.

MEA had little traditional church structure, and Jim rose to the position of youth director quickly, the way he preferred. The Olsons nurtured the youngsters around them, and the two older ministers were welcome friends for a newcomer.

The Olsons served as models for Bakker as he carved out an identity for himself behind the pulpit. Fern Olson was his "spiritual mother." A simple, childlike trust in God was a cornerstone of the Olsons' ministry, and eventually it became central to Bakker's. Russell Olson had displayed that sunny faith when he opened the auditorium in 1953. "I've got a big God, and I know He'll help me," he told the audience.

The Olsons also embraced divine healing, a cornerstone of Pentecostal theology and soon an integral part of Jim Bakker's ministry. The Assemblies of God and other full-gospel denominations hold that modern-day believers, like Christ's disciples at the time of Pentecost, can be filled with the Holy Spirit. Under that divine influence, they can talk in unknown tongues or heal the spiritually or physically ill. It was with such displays of healing powers that evangelists like Oral Roberts and Kathryn Kuhlman gained notoriety in Bakker's youth. Some faith healers, however, made claims that aroused suspicion within the ordinarily sympathetic Assemblies of God. One MEA speaker claimed that he could see through his glass eye.

Early in his first year at North Central, Jim had had a falling-out with his first roommate. He begged Cilke and Cilke's roommate, Tom Byrtus, to let him take the empty bed in their room, and they agreed. Cilke and Byrtus came from Michigan too, and their room, one of the biggest in the school, had a sink, a rarity at North Central.

Cilke, Jim's closer friend, had grown up in Petoskey, Michigan, his dad a sales manager for an auto-parts firm, his mom a bookkeeper. Cilke was a good listener, sensitive to others and an intuitive judge of character. He was direct and open. Cilke sensed a certain reserve in his new roommate. He felt that Jim had an inner world he would never share. And he sensed that Jim wanted to replace something missing within through his pursuit of the extravagant, the unusual, the supernatural. Jim always seemed to thirst for a new high—a quality that others would see in him throughout his years at PTL.

To pay his bills, Bakker bussed tables at The Tea Room, the restaurant on the fourth floor of the Young-Quinlan Company store six blocks up Nicollet from MEA. Designed to resemble a Florentine palazzo, the store offered its monied clientele the "finest fashions in America" from its corner location on a section of Nicollet that some considered the Fifth Avenue of the Upper Midwest. The ladies at the restaurant flaunted their furs. Even Jim's boss in the Tea Room was classy, with her "long cigarette, the furs, big diamonds, big car, and Estée Lauder perfumes." Young-Quinlan's was Jim's back door into the world of the wealthy, and he seemed to enjoy what he found.

By his second year, Jim was active in theater and journalism at North Central, much as he had been at Muskegon High. He played a part in the annual missions play, along with Cilke and the son of the Assemblies of God's district superintendent in North Dakota, an enthusiastic, athletic kid named Sam Johnson who, twenty-five years later, would join Bakker's staff at PTL. Bakker took his role seriously, and his gift for theater impressed his classmates. He was picked to edit the monthly school paper, the *Northern Light.* He took charge, showed lots of energy, and displayed an eagerness to find new ways of doing things. In an editorial, he declared, "I believe if we band together, we can touch the world with the Gospel of the Lord Jesus Christ."

Bakker showed little discipline in his studies. He stumbled in the classroom as he had in Muskegon. He had the ability to get B's and, with hard work, might have earned some A's. But he settled instead for C's, if he completed his coursework at all, and some at the college wondered if the young man had what it took to complete what he started. But Bakker, full of energy, was intent on pursuing his own dreams—and determined that others wouldn't stand in his way. Then, and with growing intensity in the years to follow, Bakker displayed disdain for those in authority, for those whose rules of right and wrong restrained his single-minded pursuit of his own ends.

> I don't know why, in my denomination we always wore a certain type of glasses. And they all carried themselves in a certain way, and they were untouchable. And they were an image more of discipline, the principal image again. They had that image of authority, that they were always right. And they were the one. And I've never been able to obtain that.

If Raleigh and Furn Bakker had once represented harsh judgment and austerity, they were joined now by Bakker's professors at North Central. Eventually, the casting would change—to Pat Robertson, the federal government, the *Charlotte Observer,* and finally to evangelists Jimmy Swaggart and Jerry Falwell.

Jim talked with his friends about becoming a traveling evangelist. In those days, North Central students had two leading models, Oral Roberts, from Tulsa, Oklahoma, and C. M. Ward, who hosted the Assemblies of God's national radio show. The ministry of Billy Graham, one of America's most prominent evangelists, was headquartered in Minneapolis, but Graham was a Baptist and an unlikely mentor for a young Pentecostal.

TV evangelism was in its infancy in the late fifties. On a trip home for Christmas, Bakker told his former girlfriend, Sally Wickerink, that he was interested in a TV ministry. "I want to do something different," she remembers him saying. "I want a female partner. Nobody's done that."

In November 1960, forty-two-year-old Oral Roberts arrived in Minneapolis for a week-long crusade sponsored in part by MEA. Roberts was one of the few evangelists who had added television to his work in the long-established soul-winning medium of radio. That year, 330 radio stations and 140 TV stations carried Roberts's sermons each week. Roberts employed 350 people and claimed an annual budget of $3 million.

Abundant Life, as the crusade was called, was vintage Roberts. He sat in an elevated chair, looking down at those who stepped forward to be healed. He clasped each believer's head forcefully. His muscles tightened, his hands twisted, and he invoked the Holy Spirit's curative powers. "Father, heal these crossed eyes, pull them straight!" he intoned over one boy, carried forward in his father's arms. "Oh, brother, they sure look good! Look at them!" In six days, Roberts raised $15,838 and laid hands on more than three thousand people.

By this time, Bakker had met the young woman who would become his lifelong partner, a minuscule first-year Bible-school student named Tammy LaValley. He had noticed her in a hallway.

> My neck almost broke as I turned to watch her walk away. She was absolutely the cutest girl I had ever seen. She was wearing white socks, gym shoes, and a stiff purple crinoline skirt. . . . Even without makeup, she was a little doll.

Tammy came from International Falls, Minnesota, an outpost along the Canadian border. She had grown up poor, the oldest of eight children living in a home that lacked an indoor bathroom. Only later did Bakker discover, as he put it, that Tammy lived in a hillbilly's house and wasn't a spoiled little rich kid. Her parents had divorced when she was still an infant. She had been raised by her mother and stepfather, a paper-mill worker. She had followed a fiancé to Bible school, but had severed the engagement soon after she arrived.

The Bakker-LaValley courtship was swift and passionate. Tammy later described their romance.

> He weighed 130 pounds and I 73. We looked great together. We went to church on our first date. After church, on the way back to school, Jim very suddenly stopped walking and said, "Tammy, I can't see you any more . . . because I have fallen in love with you. My mother and dad want me to finish school." . . .
>
> We continued walking. Again he stopped dead in his tracks and said like a general giving an order, "Tammy, kiss me!" He said it with such force that I never questioned if I should or shouldn't. I had never given a boy a kiss on a first date, but that wasn't going to stop me now. I reached over and kissed him, and WOW! I, too, was in love.
>
> When we got back to school, he asked me to go out the next night. So I did. On the second date he asked me to go steady. He asked me to go out the third night. I did, and he asked me to marry him. "Yes, Jim. Yes!" I said. I had no doubts. . . . I felt it in the Spirit that it was of the Lord.

The two saw each other almost daily. They ice-skated, they worshipped together. Their friends thought they looked cute with each other. Bakker took Tammy to meet his parents in Muskegon. They spent much of the trip under a blanket in the backseat of his sister Donna's car, making out. Bakker wasn't shy about sex. Once, slipping his underwear off before an evening out with Tammy, Bakker explained to a friend that it helped him get more aroused when he brushed up against his date.

As the romance with Tammy blossomed, it began to hurt their studies. Jim began to consider doing the "honorable" thing. "Tammy and I were deeply in love. She was the only girl for me. I believed God had brought us together and we were destined to be married."

North Central stood in the way of that destiny. Students had to have permission to date. Ballroom dancing was frowned upon because it brought young bodies in contact. Public display of affection, or PDA, was forbidden between men and women. Even an arm around a girl drew a talking-to from the dean, and Jim was admonished several times. Marriage, a potential distraction from studies, also broke the rules. Students were not allowed to marry during the school year. If they did, they had to sit out a term before returning.

Raleigh Bakker sternly objected to the marriage. You've gone to Bible college to learn to preach or be a missionary, he told his youngest son. You don't need to be in a hurry. The elder Bakkers didn't object to Tammy; they thought she was an attractive little thing, a bit nervous perhaps. She still looked like a girl. She didn't wear high heels or garish makeup. Applying the scriptural injunction to be modest, North Central strictly prohibited lipstick and mascara.

During her stay in Muskegon, Tammy tried on the wedding gown that Jim's sister Donna had worn five years earlier.

> I had no sooner put the gown on when Jim's dad walked in. He just gave us a real hard look, turned around, and slammed the door. We all just sighed. This was my first suspicion that there might be trouble.

At the end of the trip, Jim and Tammy climbed into Norm and Dorothy's car for a lift to the train station in Chicago. Norm's car broke down on the way, and the four jumped on a train but had to leave the wedding gown behind in the car. The auto was towed back to Muskegon. There Raleigh Bakker took—and kept—the wedding gown.

Raleigh Bakker drafted a letter to press his point. You two haven't known each other long enough to marry, wrote the elder Bakker, who had himself married at nineteen. There's enough risk marrying someone you've known for years. As he remembered it later, he also wrote to Jim that he loved Tammy dearly, "But I'm thinking of your welfare."

On April Fools' Day, 1961, as Raleigh Bakker mailed his warning letter, Jim and Tammy were married. Jim was twenty-one,

Tammy had just turned nineteen. There had been little preparation for the ceremony, which was scheduled around one of Jim's youth services at the auditorium. Russell Olson officiated in MEA's Garden of Prayer, a dimly lit chapel in the basement, carpeted in green and decorated to resemble old Jerusalem. Instead of Donna's wedding gown, Tammy wore a mint-green dress borrowed from Jim's boss at the Tea Room. Jim's sister—whose husband attended North Central—served as matron of honor. Bob Cilke was best man.

Jim stuck with his job at the Tea Room, Tammy worked as a sales clerk at Woolworth's, and the two did youth work at night for the Olsons. Living in a third-floor walk-up, Jim and Tammy were now free to indulge their libidos. Inside the Tea Room one day, Jim confided to a co-worker that he had seen a doctor because he felt so weak; the doctor concluded that he had tired himself out making love to Tammy so often.

Tammy described those days in her autobiography:

> Jim was so in love all he wanted to do was stay home and play house. . . . Jim had almost given up church totally and didn't want to go to church. . . . One day Sister Fern called Jim and said, "Jim Bakker, if you don't get back to church and do what God wants you to, your wife is going to be the minister." . . .
> It scared Jim, so he started going back to church.

The newlyweds never returned to North Central as students. In his year and a half in college, Bakker had gotten no formal theological training. If he took the introductory course in religious doctrine, he did not complete it. Later, when his ministry spread to national television, the shallowness of his preaching did not surprise his former professors.

In the place of Bible college, Bakker wrote later, he and Tammy got "a rich Bible school" from Russell and Fern Olson and the speakers at MEA. Bakker sought Fern Olson's lessons in the evangelist's trade.

> "What's the key to success as an evangelist?" I asked her one Sunday morning after the [Sunday-school] class lesson had ended.

Without a moment's hesitation, she said, "Results." I nodded my head recognizing the truth of what she said.

"If you want to be a successful evangelist and have churches call you," she continued, "you must get results. It's nice to have a theory, but only results will demonstrate the value of the theory."

Passing up a chance to run a concession stand with his brother Norm at a Chicago yacht club, Jim decided to hitch his star to a missionary with big plans.

In his autobiography, Bakker identified the man as Dr. Samuel Coldstone. Coldstone had come to Minneapolis in search of money—a familiar routine within the Assemblies of God, whose missionaries raise money to support themselves overseas. Saving the unchurched was heart and soul of the evangelical tradition in which Bakker had been immersed for all of his twenty-one years. The calling of missionary offered respect and a passport to the world beyond. Coldstone's project had the flavor of celebrity: as Bakker remembered it, the missionary planned to evangelize along the Amazon River in a yacht once owned by Errol Flynn.

The Bakkers began soliciting contributions at churches in Minnesota and Michigan and, at the invitation of a pastor visiting the MEA, in Burlington, North Carolina. There, the Bakkers learned that Coldstone was a fraud. The newlyweds decided to stay in the South and travel from church to church as evangelists.

The one-week revivals may have appealed to Bakker the performer, but the life-style did not. Bakker felt smothered staying at preachers' homes. One church put up Jim and Tammy in its evangelist's apartment, a ragtag walk-up with a collapsing bed and no toilet or bath. In some churches, the sanctuaries were so dirty that the Bakkers cleaned up before preaching.

In photographs from that era, Jim looks poised and in control. Tammy is still the woman-child, the turn of her hands or the catch in her smile hinting at unease before the camera. The pictures are black and white, exaggerating the spare sanctuaries in which the Bakkers preached and the detached, even stern, faces that looked out upon them. Jim and Tammy Bakker's energy must have been a welcome relief to these leaden souls.

The Bakkers became familiar faces in Assemblies of God

churches between Maryland and the Carolinas. They circulated their schedule for admirers. Larger churches began to call with invitations. That meant more money, enough to buy a travel trailer. Bakker was busy enough to miss his uncle's fiftieth wedding anniversary and the 1963 funeral of his beloved Grandma Irwin. She would have wanted him to go on with his revival, he recalled later, and he didn't want to see her corpse in a coffin.

The Bakkers' revivals offered something for the entire congregation. The couple fashioned hand puppets from bubble-bath containers; there was a piglet named Susie Moppet with a sassy tongue like Tammy's. The kids loved the puppets. The Bakkers salted their routines with simple lessons about God and Christian values. Jim and Tammy promised the young ones their choice of souvenirs from a treasure chest of small toys and cheap games from the five-and-dime. The goodies helped ensure good audiences, a common measure of an evangelist's success.

Jim Bakker had polished his soul-saving tale of redemption for the grown-ups: here I am, the one-time rock 'n' roll disc jockey, the driver who nearly crushed the life out of a toddler, saved by the Lord, look what Christ can do for you. The story of Jimmy Summerfield was the climax of Jim's crusade. It got results—a stream of men, women, and children rising from their seats, walking to the altar, and committing themselves to the Lord.

Young Bakker began to recognize the influence his personal misfortune gave him over audiences, and he and Tammy developed an appeal based on their own troubles that would prove successful time and time again at PTL.

One day, as he and Tammy drove along a Virginia highway, their twenty-eight-foot trailer slipped its hitch and slammed into a telephone pole. During services the next day, Tammy broke into sobs. Jim told the church about the trailer's demise. "Lord, I don't know what you have in mind, but I give up. I surrender to your will." With that, Bakker knelt at the altar and wept. Then, as Bakker remembered it, "unbelievable revival broke out. Young people came forward and gave their hearts to the Lord, older folks got their hearts of stone softened by the Holy Spirit, and healings were reported by the score. . . . Our trailer had not been wrecked in vain."

Traveling evangelists were a fixture in the Pentecostal world.

Churches looked to their pastor to teach and counsel. The minister willing to abide that gritty work and numbing routine was often not the sort to render stirring performances in the pulpit. Itinerant evangelists—polished, enthusiastic, flamboyant—could revive a congregation's passion for God. It was for that purpose that Norfolk, Virginia, pastor Gordon Churchill scheduled the Bakkers to preach a two-week revival in October 1964, a few months after Jim Bakker had been ordained as a minister in the Assemblies of God.

Churchill and his wife produced a crude half-hour kids' show each Saturday night on WYAH, a struggling Christian TV station in Portsmouth, Virginia. Churchill suggested that the Bakkers take over the show for a few weeks, and the Bakkers agreed. Jim and Tammy's puppets were more polished than the Churchills' flannel cutout figures. Their performances made an impression on the station's owner, and a year later the Bakkers agreed to join the station and its parent, the Christian Broadcasting Network. Jim was twenty-five, Tammy twenty-three. In September 1965, WYAH— short for Yahweh, the Hebrew God—broadcast the Bakkers' first TV program. It was called "Come on Over."

CHAPTER THREE

PAT ROBERTSON'S CBN

"We're on the verge of bankruptcy"

Jim and Tammy had a way with kids; at 4'10", Tammy even looked like one. The Bakkers worked their TV show without a script, and "Come on Over" was delightfully unpredictable. The crew enjoyed the thrill of flying by the seats of their pants as much as the kids in the audience did. Jim might burst out laughing at a cameraman's off-camera joke and chase the crew member around the studio, brandishing his microphone. One day, Jim and Tammy took over the camera, switching places with the cameramen. One of the men posed as Jim. The other took over Tammy's puppet.

The Bakkers hosted the kids' show from a mock front porch inside WYAH's Portsmouth studio. Jim played the straight man, and Tammy worked the puppets. The Bakkers had a full cast of inanimate supporting actors: Zippy the talking mailbox, a puppet named Charlie the Happy Christian, and Danny, who sat on Jim's lap just as Charlie McCarthy had sat on Edgar Bergen's. Among the most prominent characters were blunt-talking Susie Moppet and an alligator named Allie—a figure reminiscent of Ollie, the scatterbrained dragon, on the "Kukla, Fran and Ollie" TV show. Early on, the Bakkers borrowed ideas freely from their counterparts in the secular entertainment world.

The Bakkers had little money to spend on the show; in 1964, Christian television was hardly a path to riches. The TV station had been defunct when Pat Robertson, a born-again Christian and the son of one of Virginia's US senators, had purchased it four years earlier. WYAH broadcast on UHF Channel 27, a signal few televisions in the Tidewater area could even pick up. When the Bakkers arrived, the station was still searching for an audience.

What they lacked in their production budget, the Bakkers made up with their new ideas and their energy. They drew young fans to the studio in scores. Kids waited as long as four weeks for tickets. Up to five thousand letters a week poured into Zippy the Mailbox.

Television was turning Jim and Tammy into celebrities. Bakker, so eager to be in the company of the famous, knew how to foster and exploit the mystique. The Bakkers made promotional visits to local malls. They rode a float in Norfolk's annual Oyster Bowl Parade. Eventually, the children's show was renamed the "Jim and Tammy Show." CBN dedicated one of its two studios to the program, and the set inside Studio B grew more elaborate. It eventually stood every bit as sturdy as a real house, with a gabled roof and stairs inside so scenes could be shot from the upper windows.

Though Jim gave the program its low-key religious flavor, people at the station thought that Tammy was the creative spark behind the show and the more solid person off-camera. She was sweet and sincere and comfortable around people. She wore wigs but used makeup with restraint. She could express the emotions Jim bottled up. When the Bakkers got together with friends, Tammy was the life of the party. Jim might sit in silence watching television.

As Bakker told it later, he had agreed to work for Pat Robertson in exchange for a promise from the Yale law school graduate and former seminary student that Bakker could inaugurate a late-night Christian talk show modeled after Johnny Carson's program on NBC. The weeknight program premiered on November 28, 1966, with Bakker hosting. The program was named the "700 Club," a moniker borrowed from an earlier CBN effort to raise ten dollars from seven hundred supporters. (Robertson remembered the "700 Club" not as Bakker's idea but as an outgrowth of the earlier telethon. Years later, Robertson said he would have turned down any suggestion that CBN pattern a program after Carson's.) The Bakkers' children's show had helped awaken the TV audience to the possibilities of Christian broadcasting and had given Christian television a foothold in the mass market. With the "700 Club," Bakker began shaping an entire generation of religious programming.

Unable to afford big-name guests from out of town, Bakker interviewed local pastors and intercepted celebrities and ministers passing through. Often, Tammy sang or played piano, organ, or accordion, as she had on the road. Viewers called in their testimonies, and volunteer phone counselors passed along the most remarkable stories for Bakker to use on the air.

The "700 Club" became a showcase for Jim's growing talent before the camera. If Pat Robertson, aristocrat and Ivy Leaguer, spoke to the educated and sophisticated, Bakker, the Bible-college dropout, spoke to the common man. He was tailor-made for CBN's audience of traditional Pentecostals, the same working-class folks Bakker had grown up among and preached to on the road. He weeded big words out of his public vocabulary to heighten his appeal to the masses. Whereas Robertson could come off as arrogant or detached, Bakker seemed warm. Bakker lived by his heart, not his head, and he had a gift for making his TV audience feel what he felt—or seemed to be feeling. Once touched, they responded. Some offered their tales of healing and saved souls; others offered their money to promote the novel cause of Christian television.

The results could be breathtaking. Early in his tenure at CBN, Bakker rescued a telethon that had fallen $40,000 short of its $120,000 goal. Robertson included the story in his 1972 autobiography.

> "Our entire purpose has been to serve the Lord Jesus Christ through radio and television," [Bakker] said emotionally, his voice almost breaking. "But we've fallen short. We need $10,000 a month to stay on the air, and we're far short of that. Frankly, we're on the verge of bankruptcy and just don't have enough money to pay our bills." His voice broke and he began to cry.

Off-camera, a producer asked Robertson to intervene. Robertson—typically not one for such talk of doom and gloom—told the producer to hold steady, telling him,

"God is about to do something great."

And he was. Immediately the phones in the studio started ringing until all ten lines were jammed. . . . People called in weeping. . . . By 2:30 A.M. we had raised $105,000, and we finally signed off the air.

The telethon resumed the next day and continued all week. It was, Robertson wrote, as if Pentecost had come all over again.

The tactic was one Bakker would use repeatedly over the next twenty years: declare a crisis, dramatize it, often to the point of outright distortion, and wait for the viewers to respond. Yes, CBN did have a problem. But had the $40,000 gap truly put CBN "on the verge of bankruptcy"?

Bakker's colleagues at CBN—and later at PTL—noticed Bakker bending the truth occasionally. Rarely did anyone challenge him. Exaggeration, a common marketing ploy in the secular world, was a pardonable sin in the business of saving souls and financing ministries. If an evangelist could exaggerate the number of people he had saved at services, then Bakker could bend the truth about CBN's finances. The ends justified the means.

Despite his histrionics and hyperbole, many of Bakker's CBN colleagues considered his commitment to God's cause genuine. Bakker disdained scripts and preproduction planning on his "700 Club" broadcasts; he complained that too much structure diminished the presence of God. Bakker seemed to have a keen sensitivity to what was known as the move of the Holy Spirit. With that tangible divine presence, the sick were healed, believers spoke in unknown tongues, and the unchurched—in the studio and at home watching television—found Jesus.

Robertson later recalled one particular night at CBN.

The holiness of God came into the new studio in such an awesome way that Jim Bakker, who was on the air, suddenly said, "We are on holy ground here in the studio, and we'll have to take off our shoes."

I looked around, and everyone in the studio was taking off his shoes. Jim was right. The glory of the Lord was filling the room, and I, too, took off my shoes. Jim handed me the microphone. "I'm going to pray," he said, and stepped over to one side and began to praise the Lord. . . .

> The anointing of the Holy Spirit was so intense in the room that one of the cameramen put his arm up over the camera and began to weep uncontrollably until there was a pool of water, a puddle, under his feet. We stayed on the air until 2:30 A.M. praising God and answering the phone as people called in and told of wonderful miracles that had happened as they were watching.

Bakker became gifted at the word-of-knowledge healing style popularized by faith healer Kathryn Kuhlman of Pittsburgh. CBN carried Kuhlman's TV program; Bakker had attended her miracle services and interviewed her on the "700 Club." Like Kuhlman, Bakker didn't claim to possess healing power. He was merely a messenger, identifying those in the studio audience or at home watching television whom God was healing of arthritis or cancer or curvature of the spine. Occasionally, viewers called or visited WYAH and said, yes, I'm the one Jim talked about, and, yes, I've been healed. The testimonies sharpened the staff's sense of purpose, and they deepened the viewers' devotion to God and to Jim Bakker.

In the supernatural universe of healing and the Holy Spirit, there is no scientific test to distinguish true anointing from talented acting or psychotic self-deception. By its very nature, the full-gospel church, with its doctrine of latter-day gifts of the Holy Spirit, sanctions highly subjective relationships with God. In doing so, it leaves its faithful vulnerable to manipulation by leaders who claim that God has set their course. To its critics, the movement turns Christianity on its head, breeding enthusiasm, not enlightenment, promoting religion based on "experience, emotion, phenomena, and feelings," not on the Word of God as recorded in Scripture.

For many of Bakker's true believers, particularly those who knew Bakker in his early years in television, even the evangelist's 1987 fall from grace would not alter their conviction that Bakker was a man touched by God. God has few untainted vessels at his disposal. He must content himself with what is available, they thought, and Jim brought many in his audience to Him. Bakker got results; who he was underneath the mask and how he was able to seduce his audience were questions set aside for another day.

* * *

At the start, Jim and Tammy Bakker were industrious employees, working long hours alongside CBN's dedicated, overworked staff at the TV station and its sister radio station, WXRI. Creative and driven, Jim Bakker had ambitious plans for CBN. When he served a stint as program director, he created a half-dozen new shows. He developed elaborate sets to lend authority to the broadcasts. He pushed for color, and WYAH broadcast in color before the local ABC affiliate.

But members of CBN's staff began to feel resentful as the Bakkers capitalized on their fame. The couple formed a business called Jim and Tammy Interprises. They cut an album of songs and stories with an outside producer. As the children in the audience left the studio each day, the Bakkers and their secretary hawked Jim and Tammy merchandise—a book of sing-along songs, a coloring book full of their fantasy characters, a $2.95 Susie Moppet doll. Some colleagues wondered why the Bakkers were raising money for themselves, not CBN.

The Bakkers found several different ways to supplement their income. They bought houses, spruced them up with paint and wallpaper and resold them. Tammy sold costume jewelry at work and at parties in her home. Friends say that her business did very well.

The Bakkers seemed to have an uncanny knack for arousing their admirers' generosity. Women walked up and handed Tammy diamond rings. Fans offered money, clothes, even cars. Cash and gifts for individual evangelists—"love offerings," some called them—were an accepted part of evangelical culture. Pat Robertson and his family lived rent-free in a supporter's four-bedroom southern mansion in the country with columns out front and huge magnolia trees all around.

Status symbols and "nice things" were important to the Bakkers, especially to Jim. Jim and Tammy were willing to eat beans and struggle until payday to pay for Jim's sharp clothes, their Cadillac, Tammy's mink, the fur rug and the white baby grand piano in the living room. Colleagues watched the Bakkers' spending grow more flamboyant. The couple showed little regard for the consequences to CBN's public image or internal morale. When Bakker bought a black Cadillac, Pat Robertson suggested to Bakker that the car looked like it belonged to the Mafia, not a minister. Bakker replaced it.

In spring 1969, the Bakkers bought a $35,000 waterfront home in Sterling Point, a pricey neighborhood across the Elizabeth River from Portsmouth popular with the area's affluent Jews. Some CBN employees grumbled. They had no food in their icebox and were scraping together donations to pay a co-worker's medical bills, and here Jim and Tammy were buying a home in one of the area's nicest neighborhoods. In the world of Christian ministry, the private life of an employee—particularly a minister with a high profile on television—was never truly private. Bakker would never reconcile himself to this reality.

During his third year at CBN, Bakker suffered a nervous break-down. He blamed the collapse, as he preferred to call it, on long hours and constant pressure, including complaints from viewers about the guests he featured on the "700 Club." One day, Bakker went home sick. The next morning, "my nerves were jangled and I felt as though I was losing all the restraints that held my life together. I couldn't even bear to talk with anyone. I wanted only to be away from people." Bakker couldn't sleep; he said that a shower felt like an assault by hundreds of tiny needles.

> Problems loomed completely out of proportion to their actual size. It seemed as if whatever little control I had over myself might snap any minute, and I'd be floating in an emotional stream unable to return.

Bakker's doctor gave him medicine for dizziness. His nerves failed. The physician prescribed tranquilizers, but they agitated him. Finally, the doctor ordered him home for a month and pre-scribed a special diet of cream and milk—apparently to remedy the ulcers gnawing at Bakker's stomach. Bakker feared that he was losing his mind.

To believe Jim, the path to good health was short and easy. He realized that he had abused his body with too little rest and too many meals on the run. He took time to fish. He mowed his lawn. And, he wrote later, he surrendered his problems to God. Soon he was ready to return to work.

After eight years of marriage, Tammy was eager to have a baby. A year before, a CBN viewer had offered Jim and Tammy the chance to adopt their unwed daughter's child. Tammy was excited. Jim, worried that they had no time for children in their schedule, refused. Instead, he telephoned his brother Norm, who, rendered sterile by the childhood x-ray therapy, adopted the baby instead.

It was hard to imagine the Bakkers as parents because they seemed so much like children themselves. But some friends at CBN thought a child might put a check on the prima donnas. Jim and Tammy's doctor suggested that a child might help pull Jim out of his emotional breakdown. Tammy gave birth to a daughter in March 1970. She had her father's dark hair and heavy eyelids. The looks were Dad's but the names were unmistakably Mom's: Tammy Sue. Susie Moppet had come to life.

Parenthood was a shock to the Bakkers and to their marriage. Tammy hallucinated from what she thought was a too-heavy dose of painkillers administered during labor. She withdrew into a shell for months. She wouldn't let Jim touch her. "She didn't want a physical relationship," Jim told an interviewer later. "This is bound to offend any man." Jim talked of divorce.

After nearly a year, Tammy began to regain her composure—in time for the Bakkers' final crisis at CBN.

Pat Robertson, who had served in the Marine Corps before law school, was a tough boss. He seemed to enjoy drafting policy manuals and insisted that rules be followed. Robertson once adopted a weight policy, warning staff members that they would be fired if they didn't meet insurance-company standards for height and weight. He offered an incentive: employees would get five dollars for each pound they lost. To save his job, one member of the TV crew lost sixty pounds, using speed and diuretics to do it. Robertson failed to make good on the promised reward.

Bakker chafed at the walls CBN built around him. In his early years, Bakker repeatedly threatened to quit. After Bakker refused to work a Saturday-night shift on WXRI, Robertson told him to pay a hundred-dollar fine or resign. Bakker walked out. That night, as Bakker told it, he and Tammy watched and wept as their colleagues at CBN hosted the children's show that had been theirs. By week's end, Jim was back in Robertson's office. Each man admitted that he wanted to make amends. Jim said he didn't have the money for the fine; Robertson paid it from his own pocket.

In fall 1971, Robertson hired a twenty-eight-year-old producer-director named Jerry Horstmann, a recently born-again Christian. Horstmann had more than ten years of experience in secular television, most of it in nearby Norfolk. From the outside, Horstmann had considered WYAH, Channel 27, a joke. The programming was amateurish, the signal was weak, and he thought that the healing and casting out of devils was fakery.

Horstmann did admire the Bakkers' kids' show, even though he considered the hosts phonies. Why, he wondered, did Tammy always cry at the same point when she sang "The Blood Will Never Lose Its Power" on the "700 Club"? He was determined to expose the Bakkers.

With Horstmann's arrival, the Bakkers entered the period that Tammy Bakker later described as "three years of torture." Horstmann directed Bakker several times a week—by then Robertson had taken over the "700 Club" twice a week—and heard much that deepened his suspicion. The Bakkers often talked of their sacrifice, but what Horstmann knew of their life suggested otherwise. Jim no longer worked with the intensity of most of CBN's staff. He showed little consideration for his crew's schedule, routinely pushing the "700 Club" past midnight, even to one or two in the morning if he sensed a soul ready for saving or the Holy Spirit ready to descend. Bakker could sleep in the next morning, but his crew was expected back at 9 A.M.

The children's show was WYAH's strongest in-house program, and by 1972 CBN had begun syndicating it to stations in Charlotte, Canada, and out West. CBN, growing with the acquisition of other TV and radio stations as well, saw the potential for a national audience. Bakker regarded his contribution with a self-importance that unsettled director John Gilman. Gilman remembers Bakker telling him that CBN was built on Jim and Tammy. No, Gilman answered, Jim and Tammy were built on CBN. Without Pat's vision and leadership, there would be no Christian Broadcasting Network, he told Bakker.

A few months after Horstmann's arrival, Robertson promoted him to production manager. He commissioned Horstmann to take a detailed look at CBN's spending on television, which was running in or near the red.

Robertson thought that the children's show was costing CBN

$100,000. Horstmann learned that the price tag was $187,000, nearly one of every five dollars CBN spent. Horstmann looked at the Bakkers' pay. Together, the couple earned about three hundred dollars a week, slightly more than Robertson. That, Horstmann thought, seemed reasonable. So did a housing allowance of about two hundred dollars a month.

Horstmann was troubled most by the Bakkers' perks. A clothing allowance. A weekly appointment to have Tammy's hair done. A secretary who baby-sat for Tammy Sue, looked after dogs Beefy and Tweety, and fetched medicine, roses, and the first mink stole Bakker ever gave his wife. Horstmann decided the perks had to go.

Bakker was defiant. He telephoned Robertson from Horstmann's office; Robertson stood up for Horstmann. Afterwards, Bakker sulked, and Horstmann deepened their rift with overt hostility and pettiness. He threatened to take away part of Studio B—a move that would save CBN the staff time spent striking sets in the other studio—if Bakker didn't stop playing star and start applying himself.

Robertson had been patient with his temperamental charges. A pragmatic man, Robertson had given Bakker little of the authority he wanted. He recognized that Jim was best suited to be a lieutenant, not the general; on-air talent, not behind-the-scenes management.

Horstmann complained to Robertson that Bakker was undercutting him and trying to win the staff's loyalty. Bakker had bad-mouthed a management decision to discourage staff members from ministering to one another on company time. Bakker complained that his bosses were professionalizing CBN, taking the ministry, the Holy Spirit out of the organization.

As Horstmann remembered it, Robertson's first answer was to suggest that they pray for the Bakkers. The impatient Horstmann couldn't fathom that attitude. Robertson, a Baptist before embracing full-gospel theology, was not as highly emotional as the Bakkers. But soon he began to grow impatient as well. When Bakker threw a fit, Robertson began telling him it was time to grow up.

Robertson was eager for CBN to reach beyond its traditional Pentecostal audience. They were programming to the spirit, he told his staff, but they needed shows that minister to body and soul as well. At PTL, Bakker's ministry would take a similar turn. But for now, Bakker was uneasy with Robertson's plans.

On election night 1972, as Richard Nixon buried George McGovern in an electoral landslide, Bakker filled in for Robertson on the "700 Club" while Robertson broke in with vote counts from the polls. The interruptions annoyed Bakker. The public could get the returns from a secular station, he thought. To Bakker, it seemed that Pat was being insensitive to the workings of God.

In his autobiography, Bakker said little about the animosity festering in both camps by November 1972. He claimed that outwardly, things couldn't have been better, but that he and Tammy had felt unsettled for months. And, "the eighth day of November 1972 arrived, and as I dressed for work, the Lord spoke to me, 'I want you to resign your job at CBN today.' "

In fact, Bakker had been eager for a sign from God to depart. He and Tammy had put their house in Sterling Point on the market. If it sold, they thought, then God would be sending them a message to leave. Finally Bakker gave up waiting. The house sold, but not until after Bakker's decision to quit.

God's purpose, Bakker said in years to follow, was to multiply ministries, not to divide them. God gave him that message as he left a good-bye party at CBN. "God could not have comforted my troubled heart more perfectly," he wrote. "His words reassured me that He was in charge."

CHAPTER FOUR

FROM CALIFORNIA TO CHARLOTTE

"This is the hour of God's visitation for Charlotte"

Amid the social turmoil and antiwar protests of Richard Nixon's first term as president, a quiet awakening of religious fervor set the stage for Jim and Tammy Bakker's ascent. Members of mainstream denominations—from Catholics to Presbyterians to Baptists—began embracing the Pentecostal tradition. These neo-Pentecostals or charismatics, as they would later be called, were dissatisfied with the detached style of worship and distant relationship with God they found in their home churches. In the charismatic experience, the newcomers found a God who seemed more real in their daily lives. Buoyed by their discovery, many turned enthusiastically to evangelism, hoping to share the good news of their new Christian faith with family, friends, and strangers.

By 1972, the charismatic renewal had blossomed in Charlotte, North Carolina, as it had in Tidewater Virginia. Each Friday morning, 150 men met for breakfast, song, and shared prayer at a restaurant downtown. One of these men was Bill Flint, thirty-eight, a regional sales supervisor for a food manufacturer who had been transferred to Charlotte from Portsmouth four years earlier. In the

Tidewater region, with its population of nearly six hundred thousand, Flint had seen the power of Christian television and radio. He told his friends in Charlotte, "I want you all to agree we're going to bring Christian television and radio to this city."

One night in early 1972, Pat Robertson and his wife, Dede, spoke to the local chapter of the Full Gospel Business Men's Fellowship. Afterwards, the chapter's director asked the Flints to take the Robertsons out to eat. Under the A-frame ceiling of a pancake house, Robertson listened as Flint described his hope to bring Christian television to the 250,000 residents of Charlotte and surrounding Mecklenburg County. "Well, brother, keep praying," Robertson told Flint, "because God can do anything."

Flint soon spotted an opening. An independent UHF TV station in town, WRET, was struggling through its second year of broadcasting old movies, cartoons, syndicated programs, and reruns. The station was owned by Ted Turner, a thirty-two-year-old Atlanta business whiz with a passion for yacht racing. On a Saturday morning in February 1972, Turner begged his audience to send cash to keep WRET out of bankruptcy. He pledged to repay the money once Channel 36 got on its feet.

Flint dispatched a letter to Robertson. The letter arrived the same day that CBN's efforts to begin syndication on a Christian TV station in Indianapolis fell through. That April—seven months before the Bakkers' sudden departure from CBN—Charlotte became CBN's first affiliate as WRET inaugurated twenty hours of CBN programming, including the "700 Club" and the Bakkers' children's show (a local paper mistakenly called it "The Jim and Tabbie Show"). Two months later, Bakker spent a week in Charlotte, producing the "700 Club" live and hosting a telethon over the weekend. CBN's resident fund-raising whiz hoped to collect $22,000. He was enthusiastic about the early response. "After being here only a few days, there is no doubt about it. This is the hour of God's visitation for Charlotte."

Soon CBN opened an office in Charlotte for volunteers to field calls for prayer and crisis counseling. Martha Wheeler, a CBN volunteer whose husband served as WRET's general manager, was hired to run the office. Over the next six months, 17,500 calls were logged in. The success of the secular WRET as a vehicle for syndicating CBN's weekday Christian programming established a model that Robertson's ministry would soon replicate in more than 150 other cities.

Jim and Tammy Bakker returned that fall for another broadcast. They spoke at a charismatic Presbyterian church in Charlotte during their stopover. During the service, Jim fretted openly about the hundreds of dollars in repairs his Cadillac needed. A Charlotte couple in the audience was touched by his plight. "They didn't have any money. He needed help. . . . He wept during the service. That wrenched my heart," the woman recalled. After the service, the woman and her husband, whose company manufactured and distributed cosmetics, approached Bakker and offered him new clothes and a car. Squiring him about in their custom-built Lincoln, they purchased what Bakker described as an entire wardrobe of clothes—shirts, shoes, coats, socks, and pants. The husband suggested the car be a Chevrolet or Ford, but Bakker told him he'd like a car like the Lincoln. "My husband told him he didn't think he was ready for that." Bakker never got the car, simple or fancy, and the generous couple came away offended at Bakker's attitude.

Bakker wasn't finished using the couple, though. In his autobiography, Bakker retold the story—without identifying his benefactors and without mentioning the couple's offer of a car, his suggestion of a luxury auto, or the pitiable story that prompted the couple's gesture. Instead, he gave the credit to an anecdote he had told about divine intervention during an earlier speaking engagement in Atlanta. "That praise story brought blessing after blessing to all who heard it, including me!"

Six weeks after their trip to Charlotte, the Bakkers resigned from CBN. Martha Wheeler from Charlotte was staying at the Bakkers' home temporarily while she helped with a WYAH telethon. One night, the three sat around the Bakkers' kitchen table and talked about Jim and Tammy's future.

The Bakkers decided to go back on the road to raise money for religious TV stations. With help from Martha Wheeler and her husband, Sandy, and a check from Bill Flint, the Bakkers set up a nonprofit corporation for their new work called Trinity Broadcasting Systems. In February 1973, it obtained its incorporation papers. By then, Jim and Tammy, who had sold their Portsmouth home at a $15,000 profit, were hosting telethons at stations in South Carolina, Indiana, and Arizona.

In Tucson, Jim saw his brother Bob for the last time before his death on February 21, 1973, a week after his forty-fifth birthday. Bob Bakker had been sick for a year with Wegener's granulomatosis, a rare disease that afflicts the lungs and kidneys. He lost sixty pounds, bleeding from the rectum and vomiting in the back room of the shoe store where he filled in as a salesman. Bob chose not to fight the fatal illness. Bob had never been one for social convention, shopping for his clothes at the Salvation Army and taking his sixteen-year-old daughter to a nudist camp. He had lived an intense life and seemed ready to escape it. Days before his death, his first cousin and friend, Marge Bakker Klages, gave Bob the book *Jonathan Livingston Seagull.* The story of the bird seemed to give the deathly ill Bakker a metaphor for his solitary flight through life.

From Arizona, the Bakkers drove their camper to Pasadena to visit Marge Klages, the firstborn daughter of John Bakker. There, Jim Bakker met Paul Crouch, who had served as assistant pastor at the Bakker family's church in Muskegon after Bakker had left for Bible college. Crouch was now general manager at Channel 30, a TV station owned by a Glendale church. Crouch knew the Bakkers' talents and CBN's reputation for polished programming in the largely amateurish field of full-gospel television. Channel 30 carried the "700 Club" and the Bakkers' children's show, whose reruns were still broadcast by CBN.

By mid-March, Crouch had left Channel 30. The station had been looking for a way to get its signal into San Bernardino, and Crouch had discovered an available UHF transmitter. Soon he and Bakker were planning a new Christian TV station—and a new program for Bakker.

Over breakfast in Costa Mesa, California, Bakker spelled out his plans to Alex Valderrama, a talented young member of Crouch's staff. "We can set this world on fire," Jim stated confidently. The Lord had given him the ability to raise money, and Paul had the contacts and business know-how they needed to start a station in Los Angeles, one of the nation's top TV markets. Valderrama, a Roman Catholic turned Pentecostal from Whittier, California, was excited at the chance to create a new kind of programming. Christian television had a lot of competition; to thrive, they would have to do a lot more than just turn on the cameras.

Bakker recruited a second member of his creative team from the Phoenix station where he had hosted a telethon a few weeks earlier. "I want you to know that you're good," Bakker told Roger Flessing as he ran audio at KPAZ one afternoon. "You ought to be preaching the Gospel instead of hawking junk."

The Phoenix station, Channel 21, was struggling. It was the city's only UHF station, and few TV sets received its signal. With no ratings to speak of, the station couldn't attract advertisers. To make money, KPAZ auctioned merchandise from local businesses over the air—the "junk" Bakker had referred to—and in return gave the businesses an equivalent sum in advertising.

In those early days of Christian broadcasting, everybody pitched in. One of only fifteen employees at KPAZ, Flessing ran camera, audio, and switching equipment for "The Gap," an evening show clumsily modeled after the "700 Club." It was, Flessing joked later, the only religious talk show that lived up to its name. Flessing also worked as on-air talent. He was sports director. He supplied the voice of the slow-witted puppet Buford T. Small Person on the "Bozo the Clown" show and doubled as Bozo's promoter, Gordon Fleet, Man on the Street.

Like Bakker, Flessing had grown up in the Assemblies of God. But his childhood world in postwar Sacramento had been more sophisticated and socially established than Bakker's wedge of working-class Muskegon. Flessing was born eight years after Bakker, his dad an elementary-school principal, his mother a secretary to a state legislator and local pastor. Like Bakker, Flessing considered himself shy; the sandy-haired boy had conquered his unease with wry humor and a hearty laugh. Like Bakker, he gravitated to the stage, putting on satirical routines for high-school assemblies and Youth for Christ rallies that borrowed material from Bob Newhart, Bill Cosby, and the Smothers Brothers.

Flessing was ambitious and successful. He earned A's during his final two years of high school, played golf, and presided over the student body in his final year. His ambition was to be president of the United States; he lived in a world where such dreams seemed within reach for a Pentecostal boy.

Flessing's father had taught his oldest son to ask questions. Flessing often turned that scrutiny on the figures of authority in his life. When he replaced his political ambitions with plans to become a minister, Flessing was soon at war with the powers that be at the Assemblies of God Bible college in Santa Cruz. Movies were prohibited, so he went to movies. He poked fun at the college and denomination in his comic routines. It seemed to Flessing that the college was pursuing a course that hadn't worked for twenty years. It wasn't teaching its students how to think. Eventually he dropped out, and in 1972, he accepted the job at KPAZ.

Bakker and Flessing were both dreamers. Flessing was impressed by Bakker's plan to turn an abandoned air-force base into a TV complex, using the hangars as studios. Bakker liked Flessing's ideas for documentaries and a children's show, and he called Flessing "the most creative person I'd ever seen." Bakker asked Flessing to co-host his new talk show. Flessing said no. He didn't want to be the talent, but he told Bakker he was ready to be his director.

On April 24, 1973, the new California ministry secured office space in Santa Ana under Bakker's Trinity Broadcasting Systems, Inc. A month later, Bakker and Crouch began broadcasting. They called their new TV show "Praise the Lord."

Unable to afford a full staff, Bakker invited viewers to come to the studio and learn to run a camera. As a result, the directors— Flessing, Dale Hill, Bakker's friend and colleague from CBN, and Sam Orender, who had worked with Hill at a Greenville, South Carolina, Christian station—taught as they directed the live show. This is pan, this is tilt. Put your hand on the grip, now crank it all the way. See the throttle. Now roll that back and forth to work the zoom. Pretend you're framing a still photograph, but be ready at any time for that picture to go on the air.

Trinity supplemented its nighttime talk show with reruns of the Bakkers' children's show. A friend on the staff in Portsmouth copied the old programs and sent them to California on the sly. Bakker believed that he had the right to the shows. Eventually, Robertson wrote to demand that the rebroadcasts stop, and Bakker began producing his own children's show in California.

Soon after Robertson discovered the pirating, he gave orders to bulk-erase CBN's tapes of the Bakkers' children's show. For months, CBN had aired reruns, keeping the Bakkers' name before the public. Now, Robertson was fed up.

Much as Bakker had run afoul of his colleagues in Virginia, so his alliance with Crouch quickly disintegrated. The staff noticed lots of meetings behind closed doors. The walls were thin, and shouts of "This is my ministry" became a familiar refrain. Tensions were most noticeable between Tammy Bakker and Crouch's wife, Jan, women so similar in appearance and manner that many thought they were sisters. Both were flashy and expressive, vivid counterpoints to their more restrained husbands.

A year after his sour departure from CBN, Jim Bakker found himself in crisis again. The Bakkers complained to friendly staff members that Crouch was curbing their authority and that his friends dominated the board of directors. If he hadn't recognized it in Virginia, Bakker now realized that he needed to be supreme commander to thrive. With Crouch controlling the money, he could never have unlimited power.

Crouch was a cautious manager. He preferred to save money— the finances of the new ministry were always precarious—and Jim wanted to do more and do it better. Bakker wanted a postage machine to make it easier to reach Trinity's supporters, or "partners," by mail. Crouch said they couldn't afford it.

The two men disagreed about the path Trinity should take. Jim was eager to produce a nationally syndicated show, and his allies on the production staff wanted to create new kinds of Christian programming. Crouch wanted to acquire a network of TV stations as CBN had begun to do.

The Bakkers also felt threatened by Crouch's pastor, Syvelle Phillips of Santa Ana's First Assembly of God. Phillips's church had supplied much of the money behind Trinity, and the forty-four-year-old minister was anxious to see the fledgling TV ministry run in a decent, businesslike way, under the leadership of respected men in the community. Years later, without naming Phillips, Tammy Bakker complained about the pastor, whose church she had attended sporadically.

> The pastor from Paul's church began to come around talking to Paul about Jim. He would say, "Jim is far too emotional for California. He shouldn't be praying for the sick, or talking about the baptism of the Holy Spirit on the air." . . .

> [During a telethon] Paul's pastor got on the air, and in front
> of that entire television audience denounced Jim.
> "I do not, nor does the board agree with the things that are
> going on. We don't like the way PTL is being conducted and
> we are going to do our best to change it and make it the way
> it ought to be."

Phillips didn't remember making any such statement on the air.
Nor, years later, did he recall raising the issue of Jim's emotionality.
But he did believe the gifts of the Holy Spirit were more suitably
displayed in church, not on a mass medium like television.

One day, Bakker ordered more than $1 million of equipment.
Phillips and others were terrified at the prospect of owing that
much money, and they told Bakker he couldn't do it. Bakker had
a much better grasp of television's power than the men behind the
California ministry, Phillips later said. Bakker understood what the
others didn't—that he could indeed raise the money to pay for
the equipment.

Watching the battle lines being drawn, Valderrama wondered if
the southern Californians were intimidated by Bakker, an outsider
from the East who could win over the LA market. Though Bakker
had never lived in the Southwest, his syndicated CBN shows had
made him a minor celebrity in the area. Crouch, an awkward-
looking man without Bakker's charm in front of the TV camera,
was not well known to viewers. Jim and Tammy had a remarkable
effect on their audience. Viewers answered their appeals for money
and testimonies in dramatic numbers.

As Bakker and Crouch grew apart, the staff in Santa Ana began
taking sides, as they had at CBN before Bakker's departure. One
night, Bakker prepared to fight an on-air coup by Crouch, suggesting to Valderrama that he experience technical problems if Crouch
tried anything. Valderrama watched that night poised to kill the
audio and fade to black. Nothing happened—that night.

In spring 1973, after a year of broadcasting, Ted Turner ordered
CBN off his Charlotte station. Pat Robertson had added commercials and secular programming to CBN's Atlanta station. Turner
was trying to make a go in Atlanta with his Channel 17, and Robert-

son was now competing for syndicated family shows in the Georgia market. Turner felt that the arrangement at WRET—which gave CBN access to the airwaves and to donations from the Charlotte market—was effectively helping Robertson compete in Atlanta. Publicly, the WRET general manager, Sandy Wheeler, said only that the parting resulted from "irreconcilable differences between managements." Wheeler, the husband of CBN volunteer Martha Wheeler, told the press that the station would soon air other religious programs.

As Bakker prepared his new show in California, a handful of volunteers hammered together a simple set inside the studio at WRET. When they finished, Bill Flint anointed the set—a host's desk between two banks of phones and blue shag carpet on the floor—with olive oil, a simple gesture mirroring the Charlotteans' earnest commitment to spreading the Gospel.

The volunteers expected Bakker to play a central role in the new program replacing CBN in Charlotte. On May 16, 1973, a Charlotte newspaper even reported "Trinity Broadcasting System, a new Charlotte-based religious network headed by Reverend Jim Bakker, formerly with CBN, [had] resumed 'praise and prayer' programs."

But days before the inaugural broadcast, Bakker called Martha and Sandy Wheeler to say he was not coming. As one former PTL employee recalled, Pat Robertson had telephoned Bakker and asked, out of personal loyalty, that Bakker not work with the Charlotte ministry for the time being. Robertson apparently still hoped to return to WRET. And Bakker, facing the choice between Charlotte and southern California, preferred the promise of the enormous West Coast market and his developing partnership with Crouch.

In Virginia, Robertson and his staff were deeply suspicious of the Charlotte operation. As the CBN theory went, Bakker had started CBN's Charlotte affiliate to create the audience, mailing list, and other groundwork for Bakker's new ministry in Charlotte. When Bakker left CBN, they allege, he used a CBN mailing list to write an angry letter to CBN supporters in Charlotte. And, they say, he then used Sandy Wheeler's influence to force CBN off of WRET. "It was very painful, because I really felt a great love and affection for Bakker," Robertson told the author of the authorized biography published during his presidential campaign. "The people in Charlotte had been so gracious to us. I was sorry that they might get hurt and exploited and used." In fact, the CBN conspiracy theory seems more a measure of residual bitterness between Robertson's staff and Bakker than accurate history. Bakker's autobiography bent the truth as well. It ignored Bakker's planned participation in the Charlotte broadcast altogether.

Tim Kelton, a local Foursquare Gospel pastor and radio-show host, was recruited by the Wheelers at the eleventh hour. Instead of being Bakker's guest, Kelton was told he was needed as host. He was assured that the Bakkers would come soon, and he was told to make nothing of their absence. They're coming, he told viewers, and he and his co-hosts did what they could to sustain the impression that WRET's program was part of Bakker's ministry. Eventually, Bakker began sending tapes of his California show, which ran intermittently in Charlotte. The two ministries shared a single board but functioned largely as separate entities.

That summer, Sandy Wheeler summoned a dozen volunteers to a conference room at WRET. He stunned them with the news from California: Jim Bakker had sent orders to stop opening the mail. He wanted them to send it all to Santa Ana, where his staff would open it, collect any offerings, and pay for WRET's airtime. He also wanted them to stop producing the local program altogether and to air only his tapes from California.

Proud of what they had accomplished, the volunteers agreed on a firm no. They were angry. Who did Jim Bakker think he was? They were carrying the ball, and he wanted to shut them down. A vision of local Christian television had inspired them, not a longing for television imported from distant Los Angeles. They agreed to approach Bakker carefully so that he wouldn't interpret their response as mutiny. Some suspected that Bakker, insecure and seemingly naive, was being manipulated by his allies in California. They agreed to urge Jim to come to Charlotte, if only for a weekend.

Sandy Wheeler and a volunteer named Larry Hall flew to Los Angeles to negotiate a truce. The two men met with Crouch, Bakker, and an attorney. Over the phone, Bakker had portrayed Crouch as the villain in the matter: he's the one in charge, I don't really want to do this. That day, Bakker melted into the shadows as the conversation went from simmer to boil.

The Californians explained that they didn't trust the North Carolinians and the way they handled donations. The visitors from Charlotte thought that Crouch looked down on the East Coast show as a mere satellite operation run by a bunch of dumb country folks.

Wheeler and Hall objected, telling Crouch he couldn't take control of what wasn't his. The Charlotte men offered the only acceptable option: splitting the two operations and creating two separate corporations and boards. Crouch began to bluster. Hall remembers him saying he would shut them down. The conversation grew loud and hostile. Years later, Hall described the exchange as the most un-Christian thing he had ever heard. Finally, the Californians agreed. The Crouch-Bakker enterprise would take the name Trinity Broadcasting Network, and Charlotte would remain Trinity Broadcasting Systems. Bakker elected to stay with Crouch.

A few months later, Bakker telephoned Charlotte. He was hysterical. He and Tammy were being thrown out, their ministry was being taken from them.

As Bakker explained it in his autobiography, the issue of who controlled the California ministry crystallized over the role of Melodyland Christian Center, a thriving charismatic church in Anaheim across from the entrance to Disneyland. Trinity had been borrowing cameras from Melodyland, hauling them between Anaheim and its studio in Santa Ana each weekend. That fall, the board of directors was asked to place the entire ministry under Melodyland's control in the interests of financial stability and to improve Trinity's chances of getting an FCC license. Bakker was against the merger, feeling that he had promised his viewers that the station would be theirs. He feared that becoming associated with a single church or denomination could alienate some viewers and make it harder to raise money.

In his book, Bakker said that the board voted, five to one, to affiliate with Melodyland. The directors then asked Bakker, the sole dissenter, to step down. That day, the Bakkers sobbed in their office. They had been told to clean out their desks and leave immediately, with no severance pay.

As Syvelle Phillips, Crouch's pastor, remembered, Bakker left shortly after Trinity's directors blocked Bakker's effort to install himself as president over Crouch. No one had told Bakker to leave,

Phillips said; Bakker had simply concluded that he would not be the dominant figure at Trinity.

Crouch has refused to discuss the details of what happened between the two men. He has said that Bakker's book is inaccurate at a number of points, but declined to "reopen old wounds." In a 1983 history of Trinity, however, Crouch described Bakker's last-ditch effort to secure control of the California ministry.

> Jim and I, who had worked together beautifully in the early formative days of the ministry, began to grow farther apart in the concept and goals of the ministry. As a result of the confusion and dissension which followed, God began to lift His blessing and we began to suffer serious financial needs. . . .
>
> Jim and I both lost our spiritual direction for a time. One day in my office, Jim Bakker finally suggested that I leave the ministry. He offered to secure some financing to pay back the gift of $20,000 that Jan and I had made to get the station started. . . . But God would not release me nor could I find peace in any thought of leaving the ministry He had called me to.
>
> There followed a chapter in our lives so dark and filled with such despair that I do not even like to think about it or recall it in any way. I do not fully understand why it is that those whom we love the most seem to hurt us the worst.

Bakker wanted to appeal his case on the air, to tell his viewers that he had been wronged. He was still determined to succeed in California. He and the staff loyalists who followed him out of Trinity's door began holding prayer meetings at Jim and Tammy's home. They managed to secure a mailing list—Bakker felt that he had a right to the information—and his fellow exiles put out a mailing. Supporters gave the Bakkers and their aides free meals, food, and department-store gift certificates, generosity Bakker regarded as the handiwork of God. The outcasts bought secondhand black-and-white monitors, stored a camera in Bakker's garage, and found a building in Orange County. Inside, he and his staff chalked out a studio layout. The proposed lease included an option to purchase.

Bakker's new ministry was called Dove Broadcasting Corporation. In its first financial statement, the ministry reported donations of $6,336.83 between November 23 and December 31, 1973. On

January 4, 1974, Bakker approved Dove's articles of incorporation, with Orange County listed as its principal place of business.

Within a few days, Jim and Tammy Bakker left LA for Charlotte, where they had agreed to help with a telethon for the Charlotte ministry. The California loyalists waited for Jim's return and the start of his new ministry in southern California.

With its dominant influence over American life, television seemed a natural ally in the charismatics' crusade to spread their gospel to every corner of the country. But, as the idealists in Charlotte had discovered, Christian television wasn't immune to human frailties or the corrosive influence of money and power. Vast sums of cash had to be raised from the public, a daunting task that too often called for questionable means to achieve a spiritual end. To the intense pressure of producing daily television was added the responsibility of managing donors' gifts. In this fledgling industry, there were no long-established corporations or vigilant government agencies to assure professional, moral, and psychological suitability for the job. This was the frontier, and anybody could stake their claim. Too often, money was misspent because of greed, internal politics, and inept management.

By January 1974, Bakker had demonstrated his shortcomings for the role he so badly wanted to play—top man in a TV ministry. He was temperamental, opportunistic, and unable to function within an organization unless he had total control. But Bakker had a proven name in this emerging world. He was a celebrity, a creative TV genius, and an unrivaled money-raiser with an apparent commitment to spreading the Word. If anyone could turn Charlotte's new TV show into an evangelistic success, it was Jim Bakker.

The stage at Charlotte's Ovens Auditorium was bare on Sunday afternoon, January 13, 1974. A pair of spotlights fell on a stand-up microphone, and Jim and Tammy Bakker slipped out between the curtains and into the glow. The crowd of more than twenty-four hundred rose and cheered. In the audience, Tim Kelton, Bakker's substitute in the host's chair, was stunned as he listened to the Bakkers gloss over their absence. They cried about how hard things had been out West. They snuggled up to the crowd. Kelton felt the young TV ministry slip into Jim and Tammy's hands.

Kelton arrived at WRET the next day an hour before airtime for his customary prayers with his co-host and telephone counselors. When Bakker arrived that morning, he didn't say hello. He took his place at the host's desk and opened a Bible. Kelton greeted him. Bakker looked up and smiled, said nothing, and turned back to his Bible.

At eleven o'clock, the director signaled that the show was on the air. Bakker turned to Kelton and greeted his co-host and the audience with an enthusiastic smile and a bubbly hello. He seemed to be another man. To the viewers, it looked as if the two men had been talking all morning over coffee at Shoney's. Kelton had discovered what others at PTL would realize in the years to come: Jim Bakker, like a gifted actor, could assume many different faces, shedding one for another as if he were changing channels on a television set.

Later that week, Bakker chatted with Kelton in the corridor outside the studio. It was their first conversation of any substance. Bakker wanted a new car, and he told Kelton that he was willing to accept a reasonable price for the old Cadillac he wanted to sell. Kelton wasn't interested. He knew Charlotte—he had graduated from high school there—and he knew the mores of the small Foursquare Gospel church he pastored. He drove a three-year-old Oldsmobile Cutlass. "Jim, I've been in the ministry now a few years, and it is my opinion as a young minister that every pastor who drives a Cadillac gets flak. I don't need any flak."

Bakker made no apologies. "You're going to have to pray and get over that mentality," he told Kelton. If you drive a worn-out car, Bakker believed, you get worn-out offerings.

Buoyed by his welcome in Charlotte, Bakker telephoned his loyalists in California. Come out here for six months, he proposed, and we'll help these people build a studio. Once the studio is open, we'll come back. The Californians began arriving within days, and the paid staff doubled to about twelve. Within a few weeks Bakker had decided to stay permanently.

Four days before the Bakkers' first appearance at Ovens Auditorium, the Wheelers had leased an empty furniture store for the Charlotte ministry. As Bakker settled in, work began on a studio inside, and soon Bakker announced plans to finish in time for a June telethon—the first of Bakker's many ambitious construction schedules at the Charlotte ministry. The staff put in split shifts at the new studio, bracketing the daily two-hour taping at WRET. Inside, they constructed a small chapel and two studios, as CBN had in Portsmouth.

Though Bakker offered the Charlotte ministry a chance to become another CBN, some questioned whether the insecure, moody, and unpredictable arrival was the right man for Charlotte. One critic was board member Bob McAlister, a charismatic minister in Charlotte. Another man, Jim Moss, owner of a local janitorial firm, an active Trinity supporter, and an occasional co-host before Bakker's arrival, considered Bakker immature and paranoid. But Bakker's commitment to saving souls impressed Moss, and he soon changed his mind.

Bakker didn't hold the reins of power when he first arrived. Martha Wheeler, then forty years old, managed Trinity from an office in the ministry's new home. She was the sort of woman with whom Bakker rarely felt at ease. The daughter of a career editor at the Associated Press, Wheeler was college educated, self-assured, accustomed to getting work done, and willing, sometimes to a fault, to speak her mind. Physically, she stood a few inches taller than Bakker. With her style and physical presence, many in the ministry—even those fond of her—found her overbearing.

Sandy Wheeler, her husband, was quieter. He had a sense of humor and sharp business sense. He had earned his credentials in educational television; he had served as the first station manager for WETA in Washington, D.C., and had run KTWU in Topeka before taking the job at WRET in Charlotte. A "new Christian," Wheeler committed himself enthusiastically to the fledgling Charlotte ministry. Seven months after Bakker's appearance at Ovens Auditorium, Wheeler quit his job at WRET to serve as president and general manager of the Charlotte ministry. A brief newspaper story announcing the move made no mention of the Bakkers. Some people close to Bakker sensed that the evangelist was uncomfortable with Sandy Wheeler's expanding role.

As he had with Crouch in California, Bakker began to chafe at the Wheelers' authority. If Bakker wanted something, it had to come through the Wheelers—they handled the money. The Wheelers began to curb Jim, to say no. If Jim wanted something, he wanted it then. He never made enough money, he never had a big enough car. Nothing seemed good enough. The Wheelers saw the ministry getting out of hand. Bakker might raise donations for a piano, but by the time the piano arrived, the money had often been spent on something else, and donations for the next project would have to pay for the piano. Growing revenues papered over the risk: in January 1975, the ministry was earning $144,000 a month.

One winter day, Martha Wheeler slipped on a patch of ice and shattered her left ankle. For four months she wore a full leg cast. She moved about first in a wheelchair, then with a walker. As she recuperated, the Bakkers sold their new home, which was next door to the Wheelers, and purchased a $60,000 house in another neighborhood. The move was symbolic: within weeks, Bakker had decided he could no longer tolerate the Wheelers.

As was so often the case in Bakker's life, there was a sharp discrepancy between his public history and others' accounts of the same events. In his autobiography, Bakker described a gloomy financial picture—one, in fact, that he would institutionalize during his tenure at PTL. As always, the fault lay with others.

> I was not actually involved in [Trinity's] business affairs. I didn't sign checks. . . . Others decided where and when the money should be spent. . . .
>
> Throughout 1974, in spite of the ministry's great progress, I began to feel uneasy. There seemed to be a tremendous drag on the Holy Spirit within the work . . . something was holding back more progress and results.
>
> People who sold us goods and services constantly called to complain that their bills were not being paid. I began to ask the bookkeeper some questions for which she didn't seem to have any answers. I asked the [Wheelers], who were serving as business managers, and they didn't seem to have any answers either.
>
> Tammy had already become worried sick over these problems and I decided it wasn't worth it to continue; I would resign.

But Jim Moss, then serving as vice president, told Bakker to wait, that God was working something out. Then God spoke to Bakker.

> "I'm not going to require you to quit this time," the Lord said. "This is the ministry I have established for you." . . .

> Together with the bookkeepers, we began to look through the records. "It looks like this ministry is bankrupt," Moss said. . . .
>
> The image of Trinity Broadcasting had become tarnished as a result of the debts. The ministry needed a change of image— from the one of not paying bills to one of doing everything properly in the sight of God and man.

To other insiders, the showdown seemed a straightforward struggle for control, not a Bakker defense of fiscal responsibility. Bakker complained to board members that he couldn't work with Martha and Sandy. Sandy wasn't a minister and they weren't spiritual, he would say; it made no sense to have them in charge. Bakker gave the board an ultimatum: us or them.

Sandy Wheeler argued his case in turn, telling the board that he believed God wanted them at Trinity. He cautioned the other board members—Moss, Flint, Hall, and A. T. Lawing, the owner of a service-station-equipment business—that "This is a mistake that you'll live to regret. You never let the talent run the business."

The board sided with Bakker; he seemed indispensable. Now he held the titles of president and chairman of the board. Martha Wheeler, livid, stumped out with her walker. Years later, witnesses still remembered the sound of her protests. This bitter moment marked the beginning of a tradition at PTL: the Wheelers became the first of many one-time Bakker intimates abruptly ushered from their jobs in the ministry.

The Wheelers felt betrayed; Martha Wheeler sued. Her court papers complained that she had been "wrongfully and unjustifiably terminated" from her $1,300-a-month job at an improperly convened board meeting. In its written response, Trinity denied any wrongdoing. A quiet out-of-court settlement followed. Trinity was still small and obscure; the local newspaper carried no word of the coup or the lawsuit. Years later, the Wheelers refused to discuss their departure. For the family, one friend said, it that would be like digging up a corpse.

CHAPTER FIVE

A VILLAGE FOR PTL

"I'm going to build my vision"

Soon after the departure of Martha and Sandy Wheeler, Charlotte began to notice the evangelist with the choir-boy looks and the burgeoning audience and budget.

As they had in Portsmouth, the crowds swelled inside the studio where Bakker taped his TV program. Eager to broaden the telecast's appeal, the ministry replaced the name Praise the Lord with the less explicitly religious name PTL Club. Bakker began to fashion a plan to expand his ministry's building on Charlotte's Independence Boulevard. He wanted to do it cheaply. No Taj Mahal, he said, just adequate facilities to broadcast the Gospel. "I was determined not to sink hundreds of thousands of dollars into elaborate and expensive-to-maintain buildings."

Soon Bakker did an about-face, one of many during his tenure at Trinity, which was known increasingly as PTL. He showed little restraint in his on-air declarations. Eager to please his audience—an enthusiastic viewer was a generous donor—Bakker told America what he thought it wanted to hear. Often, that meant bending the truth. If he sensed his donors, known as "partners," were uncomfortable with his fancy car, paid for by the ministry, he would persuade the board to drop the auto allowance and raise his pay accordingly. Then he would declare on the air that PTL no longer paid for his car. In Bakker's hands, half-baked plans were transformed into projects supposedly just weeks from completion. A decision to get rid of a car that he or Tammy disliked became a grand gesture of sacrifice.

One of Bakker's advisors had found a three-story Georgian mansion on a twenty-five-acre site in suburban Charlotte. Bakker gushed when he saw it. "I've loved this kind of property ever since I was a kid." The house had been on the market for years, and the owners were willing to sell for $200,000 in cash and a letter showing that the owners had donated $150,000 to PTL. This added enticement cost only the US Treasury—not Bakker's ministry.

The mansion could be converted to offices, but it had no space suitable for TV studios. Bakker soon announced plans to build a fifty-four-thousand-square-foot studio called the International Counseling and Broadcast Center. What had once seemed a sensible step—adding space for the ministry's growing staff and studio audience—had taken on a life of its own. With little forethought, a young TV ministry operating out of a $1,870-a-month rented furniture store found itself waist deep in a $3-million building program. Bakker was doing precisely what he had said he would not do.

Bakker was a master of packaging, and his partners hardly seemed to notice the turnabout. As Bakker told it, God had directed him to create a tourist attraction for the Christian faithful, a miniature version of Colonial Williamsburg. Bakker called it Heritage Village, the very name Muskegon preservationists had chosen two years earlier for the Bakker family's neighborhood on Webster Avenue. Bakker explained that he had picked the name because he associated the Williamsburg design, like Christianity, with the American heritage. He broke ground for the new studio on October 30, 1975.

By late 1975, Bakker had been the subject of profiles in the *Charlotte Observer,* the city's predominant newspaper, and its sister afternoon newspaper, the *Charlotte News.* The *Observer*'s religion writer, Mary Bishop, recognized the support that would soon propel PTL to national attention.

From Augusta to Anaheim, those who find solace in Bakker's "PTL Club" show are showering it with an estimated $350,000 a month and praise for helping them get miraculous healings from suicide wishes, impending blindness, and fearsome knots in their flesh.

With gifts of cash, diamonds, and furs, Bakker appears to be pumping the three-year-old television ministry into an empire, one that vows to build a multimillion-dollar Vatican of mystical fundamentalism in Charlotte where the multitudes can come for Bible teaching and to see the show.

The reporter interviewed a coal-miner's wife from Earlington, Kentucky. Her simple words spoke volumes about the trust that Bakker's partners placed in the evangelist. "I have so much faith in Jim Bakker," she told the reporter. "All I know is that the Lord is using him in a powerful way."

The Christianity that Bakker espoused, Bishop wrote, "is a happy, down-home gospel laced with a lot of laughing and smiling, upbeat musical numbers, promises of an abundant life, and reassurances that 'God loves you.'" The reporter watched from inside the newly purchased mansion as Bakker—not a hair out of place, dressed immaculately in a blue suit with red stitching—supervised delivery of Williamsburg-reproduction furniture.

In those early days in Charlotte, Bakker looked like middle America. His sideburns flared to a stop in a line with the Howdy Doody grin that had made him self-conscious as a teenager. A mod haircut swept across his forehead and over his sizable ears. His ties were loud, his sports jackets vivid plaid with broad lapels. He was a TV star, but he still looked approachable.

Ever mindful of his image, Bakker dressed up his past with care. The profile in the *Charlotte News* described him as a graduate of North Central Bible College, not a dropout. The story suggested that Bakker had moved to Charlotte because he was wasting his time between two headquarters. It said nothing about his acrimonious departure from California or his earlier decision to sever his half-hearted ties with the original Charlotte ministry. Bakker revealed his salary—$22,100—to the *Observer* but refused to say how much he received as his housing allowance. Newspapers, he explained, "make too much of the money thing."

As Bakker supervised construction at Heritage Village, his staff busily signed up TV stations, creating a syndication network much like Pat Robertson's at CBN. They targeted grass-roots America first, buying cheap airtime in cities like Dothan, Alabama; Canton, Ohio; Chattanooga, Tennessee; and Paducah, Kentucky. Bakker's videotapes were shipped, or "bicycled," from station to station. By the close of 1975, PTL had forty-six affiliates carrying its program. Bakker's target was to broadcast his show in every TV market in America.

It was an ideal time to build a nationwide TV ministry. The charismatic renewal had created a mass audience, enthusiasts eager to find a home for their new faith; Bakker drew support from these people as well as from the broader evangelical community. *Newsweek* ran a cover story proclaiming born-again Christianity "the most significant—and overlooked—religious phenomenon of the seventies." A few weeks after the magazine article, Baptist Sunday-school teacher Jimmy Carter was elected president.

Religious services broadcast from local churches still dominated religious programming in America, but these "Sunday ghetto" programs had little allure to a mass audience. CBN represented PTL's only serious competition, and CBN was more interested in the nation's largest markets. There was space on the airwaves for PTL: ABC affiliates all over the country had little to draw viewers during the morning, and many jumped eagerly at PTL's proposal to buy two hours of airtime each weekday morning.

As PTL's network of affiliates grew, so did the task of raising money in each market. In the early years, Bakker would only rarely solicit contributions on his daily show. Instead, he and his staff would produce semiannual telethons at each affiliated station to pay for airtime. From Binghamton, New York, to Greenwood, Mississippi, to Jackson, Tennessee, the telethons brought live religious television—and Bakker himself—to the evangelist's growing national constituency.

By May 1977, PTL had begun laying another path to America's living rooms, assembling plans for an around-the-clock menu of Christian programming to beam to local cable systems by satellite. Once complete, the satellite network would represent a great leap forward for Bakker's program. Instead of waiting days or weeks for videotapes to arrive, local TV stations would be able to pick up PTL's satellite feed and broadcast the program live. Like PTL, the technology was young but promising; satellite dishes were still rare at TV stations, and the cabling of America was in its infancy.

* * *

Watching Bakker piece together his new ministry, some of his former colleagues at CBN concluded that Bakker wanted to match Robertson step for step. A month before PTL's board had voted to move ahead with its satellite network, CBN had dedicated its satellite earth station, the first owned and operated by a Christian ministry, and had begun beaming programming to American cable systems. Six weeks before PTL announced its purchase of the Park Road mansion, Pat Robertson decided to buy 142 acres in Virginia Beach as the home for his broadcast facility, offices, and university.

Once PTL reached 170 broadcast stations, it declared itself the nation's fourth-largest TV network behind CBS, NBC, and ABC. The distinction gave Bakker something close to the superlative he longed for, but the "accomplishment" was questionable. Once it had signed the top 120 markets, PTL's search for affiliates was hardly worth the expense, considering the tiny audiences it yielded. And, though it might have fewer affiliated stations, CBN still had a larger audience.

Bakker recruited old friends from his days in Virginia and California to join his staff. Henry Harrison, who had been Bakker's Ed McMahon at CBN, agreed to leave Virginia and take the other seat at the host's desk. Harrison was a gentle, roly-poly man raised by a sharecropper from the tobacco fields of eastern North Carolina. A forty-seven-year-old radio announcer, Harrison received the baptism of the Holy Spirit from Pat Robertson in 1964 and went to work at CBN three years later. There, he befriended Bakker, renting a room from Jim and Tammy and naming Jim best man at his second marriage. Robertson officiated at the ceremony.

Bakker, scarred by his departure from CBN and ouster from California, liked Harrison for his willingness to surrender the limelight. "You know when to keep quiet, and I don't feel threatened by you," Bakker told him. "There have been times when I felt that the person sitting in the co-host chair had aspirations of filling mine."

Bakker hired Phil and Ruth Egert, two more friends from his days at CBN. Phil, retired from the military, became staff photographer; Ruth became Jim's secretary. Bakker called Roger Flessing, who had been freelancing in Santa Ana since the falling-out with Paul Crouch, to be a director. Flessing and his wife, Kathy, felt that the Lord wanted them to make the move. Flessing thought he might be able to reach beyond the limits of the talk-show format at PTL. He loved to take a blank TV screen and bring it to life, just as a painter would fill a canvas. If PTL could exploit the creative potential of television, Flessing was fond of saying, it could "make the Gospel unavoidable."

That spring, Flessing and Alex Valderrama outlined their plans for new programming. They envisioned documentaries about what was happening at Heritage Village, how to raise your family, and the work of evangelists like Kathryn Kuhlman. The two men wanted to broaden PTL's scope, attract more viewers, convert more people, and possibly leave PTL's mark on secular TV. It was the sort of idealistic vision Bakker claimed to embrace wholeheartedly. "We've got to come up with new methods to reach people," he would say.

During Bakker's final year in Virginia, Pat Robertson had produced a ghostwritten autobiography, *Shout It from the Housetops.* At age thirty-five, Bakker was ready to publish his life's story. In the early months of 1976, writer Robert Paul Lamb interviewed Bakker in his car, his office, over dinner. But with just twelve weeks to write the book, Lamb had no time for serious research. He had to content himself with chats with a few members of Bakker's tight-lipped family and conversations with a few staff members.

Lamb chose to focus on Bakker's boyhood insecurities. By page four of *Move That Mountain,* Lamb had sketched a youngster hounded by fear, ashamed of his family's house, and crippled by feelings of inferiority. The emotions were raw and startling and gave the book the ring of truth. For years, journalists would regurgitate the book's account of Bakker's past as authentic. In fact, it was marred by factual errors, large and small.

There was a short leash on Bakker's seeming self-awareness. The book gave Bakker's childhood demons little credit for influencing his adult life. That role was reserved for the inner voice that Bakker identified as God, a supportive, generous figure who represented the polar opposite of the cold, judgmental, and tight-fisted parental figures who towered over Bakker's youth.

July 4, 1976, the nation's bicentennial, marked a day of triumph for Jim Bakker. PTL released his autobiography. Heritage Village was ready for its grand dedication; its new TV studio was finished and so were several smaller buildings, flower gardens, and walkways. The grounds were storybook-handsome, with white picket fences and spacious lawns, and the staff wore colonial costumes. Among Bakker's guests were two men who represented the darkest moments of his career: Pat Robertson, in a sober business suit, and Paul Crouch, glistening in a white suit and white shoes. Bakker awarded Robertson a plaque of honor.

The new TV set was PTL's finest ever. Telephone counselors sat sixty strong to Bakker's right, their visibility a measure of the central role prayer phones played on Bakker's program, much as they had at CBN. Volunteers jotted notes on prayer forms whether the caller needed healing for hemorrhoids or female problems or any of some forty other ailments. The forms were passed to Bakker, and he picked some out to receive extra public prayer.

When Bakker appealed for calls, the phones jumped to life. Usually the phones sounded sequentially, moving up the bank of counselors. Sometimes, in what the faithful considered the work of the Holy Spirit, the ringing jumped forward or backward to a counselor ideally suited to minister to the caller. An alcoholic might end up talking to a staff member who had once had a drinking problem.

The callers were hurting people with no one to turn to. PTL could help. The mass ministry offered a friendly voice to those who sought no more and an introduction to Christ to those who sought an answer. One counselor later commented that unless you had taken the calls, you could hardly imagine the depth of human need.

The work gave a sense of purpose to volunteers and staff; telephone counseling was one of the idealistic sides of an industry that, because of its reliance on the costly medium of television, had to devote tremendous energy to raising cash. Counselors tracked the success stories—"praise reports," they were called—and the most dramatic were retold on the air and spread through the ministry by memo and word of mouth. Like the testimonies from guests who appeared on Bakker's show, the phoned-in praise reports testified eloquently to the healing power of a sympathetic voice and to the PTL partners' abiding faith in God's power over their daily lives.

Osgood, Indiana: The doctor said I had stones in my gallbladder. He said the next time I had to be put in the hospital I'd have to have surgery. I knew I didn't have to be cut on so I called PTL. The lady who talked and prayed with me was so wonderful and encouraging. God healed me completely.

Shippensburg, Pennsylvania: I have been sending prayer requests for my son who has been on drugs and drinking. He has accepted the Lord and was baptized this month. Truly a miracle!

Collinsville, Illinois: I wrote you when I was thinking about ending my life. A pastor was sent to me that started a Christian school just one block from my home. They made me understand even with both legs missing there is something for me to do for the Lord. I am studying the Bible and getting my life back together now.

Bakker's staff saw other indications that its work for TV evangelism was worthwhile. Local ministers across the country—especially preachers in the Assemblies of God and other Pentecostal denominations—reported a marked surge in the numbers of new worshippers at their churches Sunday mornings. And the clergy told Bakker's staff that their longtime church members had become more enthusiastic in their faith.

With Heritage Village complete, PTL had burst from obscurity into the evangelistic big time. Bakker proclaimed its success as testimony to God's blessing. "The hand of God is on it, and that makes all the difference in the world." Between April 1975 and March 1976, PTL took in nearly $5.5 million, up from $817,454 the year before. Its net worth had soared from $129,000 to more than $2 million. Everybody likes a winner, and Bakker shone with the aura of success. "Remember," he wrote to his partners, "with God, NOTHING IS IMPOSSIBLE."

In the early years, a spirit of mission, teamwork, and community infused PTL. Staff members pitched in to help throughout the ministry. They and the growing corps of PTL volunteers showed a selflessness that flowed from their dedication to Jesus, the paradigm of sacrifice, and from their conviction that God had blessed PTL for its soul-winning work.

The ministry was small enough for everyone to know one another, and once a month the staff and relatives gathered for family night. Together, they guffawed at embarrassing outtakes and parodies pieced together by the crew. Into a tape of Tammy singing "Jesus Keeps Taking Me Higher," Flessing and Sam Orender spliced pictures of the studio audience dozing off and a shot of a hand, supposedly Tammy's, ludicrously laden with jewelry and motioning insistently for more audio inside the studio. Back then Bakker could appreciate good humor, and he was less consumed with monopolizing center stage. "There are no big shots at PTL," he wrote in a 1976 article in PTL's *Action* magazine. "This is a team effort, and everybody connected with the ministry knows it." His picture was a reliable fixture on the cover of PTL publications, but the work of individual staff members was generously applauded inside the magazine.

The protective shell around Bakker thickened steadily. Despite the ministry's dedication to human love and caring, Bakker seemed most comfortable with inanimate objects. He could charm an audience through the neutral lens of a camera or from the safe distance of a studio stage, but in person he kept his distance from all but his closest circle of associates. Where once they could approach Bakker directly, rank-and-file staff members now found Ruth Egert guarding access to Bakker. In the later years, new staff members and volunteers would be instructed not to speak to Mr. Bakker unless he spoke first. He rarely did.

As PTL settled into Heritage Village, two more shells formed around the reclusive Bakker. On the village's twenty-five acres, Bakker had created a miniature world where his version of reality reigned. As he supervised construction on the site, Bakker found and embraced the role of master builder, an obsession that would eventually erode his dedication to ministering on television.

Bakker's rewards were considerable. Consumed with designing, supervising construction, and decorating, Bakker was spared many of the gritty management tasks for which he had little patience. Should something go wrong, Bakker could explain that he had been too busy to read that memo or spot this financial crisis or correct that breakdown in ministry operations. The role of master builder furnished Bakker a broader scope for his restless urge to create. The new buildings he erected—which also brought more dollars and more donors—became sweet affirmation of Bakker's claim to his throne.

But Heritage Village drove a wedge between Bakker and the woman who had been his constant companion for fifteen years. Later, Tammy described her resentment of Jim's long hours at Heritage Village.

> I felt Jim should care as much about me as he did about that building project. I just had to fight for any time I got with Jim. One morning he didn't come home until three o'clock in the morning. . . . I thought Jim didn't care, that I was a second spot to him. I just could take no more.

Tammy had been pregnant when Jim decided to move his ministry to Heritage Village. In 1975, a week before Christmas, Tammy gave birth by Cesarean section to her second child, a boy named Jamie Charles. She had hated the pregnancy. She had gotten sick, felt unattractive, and missed the attention she got at PTL, which was a salve for her deep-seated insecurities. During her pregnancy, she confided to a friend in a moment of frustration that she sometimes hoped she would lose the baby.

Bakker had not helped matters with his decision to go on with the show—his TV program—while the doctor delivered Jamie Charles. Tammy had given him permission to go, but she had wanted him to stay, to play protector as he had been willing to do in years past—and as Tammy's natural father had failed to do in International Falls.

Off the air, Tammy Bakker showed little enthusiasm for being a mother. She seemed to love babies, but other priorities readily interfered, and she relied heavily on family and co-workers to watch her children. Tammy sustained herself with relentless motion, usually in the direction of local malls. She needed to buy something every day, to indulge her "shopping demon" even if just with a trinket from K-mart. Buying seemed to make her feel whole, just as building sustained her husband.

Bakker's subsidized life-style and expensive taste began to raise eyebrows at PTL. PTL's cleaning lady cleaned Bakker's home, and the ministry picked up the tab for lunches and dinners that stretched the definition of business. Tammy didn't like the new carpet in a PTL-owned home where the Bakkers lived briefly. She ordered it ripped out and replaced.

One night, an elderly woman volunteering at PTL announced that she would not be returning. "I had a dream last night," she explained, "and I believe it was a message from God. I saw a table laid out beautifully with food. Someone walked on the table, scattering the food. Yet some continued to eat, to consume all that was put before them." She had asked God to explain the dream. He had said, "Children have played at my table and defiled my food. People who are starving will eat this food. People who are knowledgeable will not." The volunteer did not know the identity of the defiler. But she knew she would no longer sit at the table.

The Bakkers seemed to move into a new home every six months. They had bought their first in March 1974, their second in December of the same year in Charlotte's Woodbridge subdivision. While they still owned the second home, they evidently lived in two others, including one owned by PTL. By spring 1976, the Bakkers were adding a new master bedroom, garage, and sun deck to the Woodbridge home. The addition included a gas grill, gas-fire log, two toilets, three sinks, and a Jacuzzi whirlpool set in an open enclosure off the master bedroom and walled in on three sides by mirrors. All in all, by an internal ministry account, the work cost $73,153, exceeding the $60,000 the Bakkers had paid for the house and land.

The Bakkers had a knack for window dressing and a drive to make things look right—just right. "My home is my hobby," Bakker told an interviewer while on his way home to help Tammy wallpaper the kitchen. The Bakkers' stamp was unmistakable: a surfeit of chairs, the baby grand, glitzy accessories, and walls covered with pictures. It was as if they had to mark everything, to leave the notice This Is a Jim and Tammy Creation.

In November 1976, two months after the final building permit was issued for the Woodbridge renovations, the Bakkers donated the property to PTL. Bakker packaged the gift as evidence of his commitment to the ministry and his disdain for material possessions. As several of Bakker's vice presidents remembered, Bakker gave PTL a debt, not an asset. PTL's prime contractor had done much of the work at Bakker's home. PTL was stuck with the bill for the improvements and with the $50,000-plus mortgage Bakker had used to buy the house. The Bakkers continued to live in the house, with PTL paying for yard work, a maid earning four hundred dollars a month, and utility bills averaging more than five hundred dollars a month.

The Bakkers' personal interests were becoming indistinguishable from PTL's. Five days after Bakker signed his Woodbridge home over to PTL, he ordered his staff to buy him a year-old Corvette sports car for $8,450.

Jim Moss, the board member whom Bakker had named executive vice president, told Bakker the purchase was wasteful and immature. PTL needed that money to pay ministry bills, he said. Bakker was annoyed and told Moss that it was none of his business. A few days later, Bakker decided to get rid of the car. Tammy didn't like the two-seater either; it had no room for the kids.

Driven by a sense of unlimited potential, by early 1977 Bakker and his staff had set their sights on acquiring as many as seven TV stations, the legal limit. For a time, PTL pursued KPAZ in Phoenix, Roger Flessing's old station, but they emerged with little to show but a ten-thousand-dollar legal bill. Paul Crouch acquired the station instead.

Bakker had more luck with an independent TV station in northeastern Ohio. WJAN in Canton had been among the first stations to broadcast the "PTL Club." The program had an unusual prime-time slot at nine in the evening, and the strong response made Canton a cherished market. Worried that another evangelist might buy the station, Bakker agreed to purchase WJAN for $2.5 million. Later, some of Bakker's deputies concluded the station's market value had in fact been less than $1.5 million.

In theory, the TV station, along with the planned cable network and Heritage Village, was bait to bring Bakker's audience closer to Christ. Winning souls, Bakker wrote at the close of 1976, was the most important part of PTL. The world, he said, was PTL's God-given missions field.

In 1977, PTL began to make good on its stated commitment to worldwide missionary work. Overseas evangelism was a cornerstone of the Assemblies of God—twenty years earlier Bakker's denomination had named its soul-recruiting strategy the Global

Conquest. Missions were also a proven stimulus to charitable donations. In early 1977, PTL picked a host for a Spanish version of Bakker's show. PTL produced "Club PTL" and helped pay for airtime in Central and South America. By October, the Spanish program was carried in thirteen countries at a cost over ten months of more than $112,000.

On June 13, 1977, Bakker invited his talk-show guest, Assemblies of God minister Paul Yonggi Cho of Seoul, Korea, to become PTL's surrogate in Asia. Seoul had been one of the Assemblies of God's fastest-growing evangelistic centers, and Cho's church was considered one of the world's largest.

Cho was stunned. He answered Bakker's suggestion with a polite, "Praise God. Amen." Bakker continued, "We can do the same thing just as we are doing in Latin America. And I will tell you if Dr. Cho can help us to get the time, we will produce it. . . . And we will raise the dollars to buy the time." Cho agreed to make arrangements when he returned to Asia. The next month, Roger Flessing left for Korea to begin drawing up plans.

For more than a year—even before the July 1976 dedication of Heritage Village—Bakker had talked of creating a country retreat that would include a rustic worship center, homes for retired ministers, and buildings for Bible and soul-winning seminars. He also wanted Heritage Village to grow, but the city of Charlotte had rewritten its zoning rules after Bakker began building on the Park Road site. The change, prompted by complaints from PTL's neighbors, limited PTL's growth at Heritage Village.

Bakker's plans for his country retreat grew bolder. During spring 1977, he talked of spending $50 or $100 million to create a Christian retirement center and university. In May, the newspapers carried talk of a July 4 groundbreaking and plans for a campground, twelve-story hotel, and a liberal-arts university. Within four years, PTL expected an enrollment of twelve thousand students, four thousand more than attended the Charlotte campus of the University of North Carolina. At its May 13, 1977, meeting, Bakker's board agreed to seek property for the development, tentatively named the Positive Total Living Center. In PTL's July magazine for partners, Bakker described the university as the second step towards world evangelism after the satellite network.

But PTL's search for property in the rolling countryside south of

Charlotte and along the border with South Carolina moved slowly. And PTL was running short of money. Bakker's ignorance of corporate finance and his compulsion to forge ahead—he proudly proclaimed that PTL was the world's fastest-growing ministry—had begun to take their toll.

Within days of Bakker's on-air offer to Cho, PTL announced that it was postponing the groundbreaking for the Total Living Center. Later that summer, Bakker announced that PTL's debts had put a halt, at least temporarily, to the expansion plans. Privately, PTL staff members told a reporter to take Bakker's grand plans with a grain of salt, that his ideas often didn't jibe with fiscal reality. "Jim Bakker is not a financial person. He's not a nine-to-five, dollars-and-cents person," one staff member told a reporter.

This statement could have been made in any year of Bakker's tenure at PTL, up through his departure in 1987. But only in Bakker's early years were his aides willing to be so candid about their boss in such a public setting. For now, it was OK to say that the emperor wore no clothes.

With the Total Living Center on the shelf, the fledgling missions outreach became Bakker's leading inducement to donors. PTL devoted the cover of the August 1977 *Action* magazine and its first two stories to PTL's international missions work. "God is now breaking through foreign barriers for PTL in every major continent," the magazine declared. No mention was made that month of the Total Living Center. Publicly, Bakker pledged that buildings would take a backseat to PTL's missions work.

> And I am going to make you a promise today. . . . With God's help anything that we build, including the School of Evangelism, unless God sends us money from other sources, foundations, businessmen coming together, I will not ask the people to build that type of building or any expansion in that particular area. . . .
>
> I believe every penny that comes in over and above the actual minimum cost to keep us on the air and the budget needs to go to world evangelism and world missions.

Bakker bathed the missions outreach in passionate hyperbole. The PTL's Korean outreach is "the beginning of one of the greatest revivals man has ever known," he told his PTL audience. Bakker vowed he was committed to international broadcasts. "I would rather die than selfishly say we are going to have it in the United States and we are not going to give this message . . . every place there is a television set." Bakker also declared that PTL's goal was to give ninety percent of its income to missions.

By autumn, Bakker's staff was discussing a Brazilian version of the "PTL Club" with the Reverend Robert McAlister. McAlister, the respected Charlotte minister who had cautioned against Bakker's return in 1974, was now a missionary in Brazil. During his appearance on the "PTL Club" show of October 20, 1977, Bakker offered to outfit a studio in Brazil "just like we are going to send to Korea." The two men agreed on the air.

Five weeks later, Bakker was swept up with enthusiasm for Elias Malki, a missionary working in Lebanon who hoped to establish a one-hundred-thousand-watt AM transmitter on Cyprus and beam the charismatic message through Israel and the Arab world. Bakker acknowledged that he was stretching his ministry's resources. "I have got more projects than Carters have little liver pills, as my grandma used to say. But this is one project that I just feel has got to be."

Bakker routinely behaved as if PTL's fiscal barrel was bottomless; he called it faith in God. Trust, and He will provide. Faith defies reason; it is "something you can hope for but can't see."

> Talk negatively and you will have a negative life. . . . As soon as we speak in faith, God starts the wheels turning in our life. We move ahead victoriously. . . . Don't lose your vision. Don't camp at your problem. When you are negative, your life is going to be like a mudhole. You stay stuck in it . . . hitch up to faith in God who is bigger than any problem. And never be afraid to fail. . . . Follow the dream and vision God has given you.

"God told me so"—an accepted notion in the personal faith of the Pentecostals—cloaked Bakker's psychic demons and failings as a manager. His impulsiveness, thirst for control, and chronic disregard for economic and legal realities became signs of devotion to God. "God didn't call me to manage a business, He called me to win souls!" Bakker wrote to his donors. "We never know what we're going to do until we do it," Bakker said. "The mood changes according to the flow and direction of the Holy Spirit."

But Bakker could not afford to be totally cavalier with money; after all, he needed suppliers to survive, and he liked to boast that he had directed his staff to make sure PTL's finance operation was "so clean it squeaks." With that charge from Bakker, a Californian named Bill Perkins arrived in spring 1977 to take over PTL's finance and accounting department. Perkins had given up a better-paying job as a financial analyst for Sandia National Laboratories in Livermore to lend a hand to a ministry in need. A layman in the Assemblies of God and the treasurer of his home church, Perkins was a spiritual man with a fervent commitment to evangelism, a prophet's insight, and an unerring sense of propriety. For Perkins, a righteous end could never justify shady means.

Even before taking the $450-a-week job, Perkins cautioned Bakker by letter that he needed a complete audit by a widely recognized CPA firm. "The acceptance of your ministry by millions of people is so crucial that you cannot afford even the slightest suggestion that financial or procedural irregularities resulted in an investigation by some governmental agency."

Once he arrived, Perkins sought to mend relations with the creditors bruised by the financial ups and downs of the young ministry. He instructed the staff to adopt an austere budget. Perkins challenged standard operating procedure at PTL in other ways. He cautioned against loans to employees, a practice he feared might jeopardize PTL's vital tax-exempt status. He tried to improve documentation of business expenses. "Signing a PTL American Express charge ticket, in and of itself, is not sufficient to qualify for a legitimate business expense," he told the staff by memo. He even prodded Bakker gently, through his secretary, to make sure that his expense records met IRS requirements. He attached a batch of inadequate receipts to his memo:

> Jim Bakker pointed out, when on a business trip he is often under the press of business, such that he is likely to neglect these details—most of us have this problem but not nearly to the degree he would.
> It will take perseverance and patience on your part . . . don't hesitate to pin Jim down. He truly wants to maintain a good

account and his efforts will go far towards encouraging others
to do likewise.

Inside and outside PTL, Bakker encountered increasing questions
about his conspicuous spending. Evangelists, like politicians, are
natural targets for public and press skepticism; nothing stirs mass
righteousness like the whiff of hypocrisy from the morally correct.
Bakker's style made matters worse. He polarized those around him;
either people loved him or they couldn't stand him. Each side
unleashed its rhetoric in letters to the local newspapers. Bakker's
admirers called him a "messenger of God" and his program inspirational. A critical Baptist minister said that PTL played on viewers'
emotions and exploited scriptural ignorance. Others condemned
the luxuries at Heritage Village as alien to the principles of Christ.

Bakker defended the ministry, saying that it was dedicated to
helping troubled churches. Bakker disclosed that PTL had given
$15,000 to rebuild a black church damaged by fire; it had turned
over a box of diamond rings, silver bars, and furs to a drug-rehabili-
tation group and given one thousand dollars to a ministry aiding
Appalachian children. Bakker told his critics that the ministry used
new Cadillacs because people donated them; they were building a
swimming pool with a whirlpool bath under the new studio because
the staff worked long hours and needed to relax and exercise.

The questions nagged at board member Larry Hall, who had
returned from a PTL telethon in Montgomery, Alabama, with a
sobering lesson in PTL's duty to spend its money wisely. A woman
had emerged from the studio audience with one hundred dollars
to give Hall for PTL. She told him that her son was a housebound
invalid and that she could rarely attend church. For her, and for
many of PTL's older and handicapped viewers, Bakker's two-hour
program brought church inside her home. The woman asked Hall
to come by the next morning and pray with her. Hall found her in
a shack, its walls paper-thin. Her son was about eighteen years old,
crippled and most likely retarded. If anyone needed that one hundred dollars, it was the woman and her son.

Back in Charlotte, Hall learned that Bakker had decided, on his
own, to use handmade brick, shipped from Pennsylvania, for the
new studio, which was being built to resemble the Bruton Parish
Church in Williamsburg, its steeple disguising a broadcast antenna.

The brick cost PTL more than double what it would have paid for a less-showy local product. Hall was also unhappy with Bakker's decision to turn the board-authorized staff swimming pool into an opulent Grecian spa with mirrored walls and a floor covered with quarry tile. Classical columns were erected, and saunas were installed in the men's and women's dressing rooms, with a whirlpool in between. Rowing machines and other athletic equipment lined the balconies around the pool.

By September 1977, PTL felt besieged, a Pentecostal outcast in a city of haughty mainline churches and unfriendly secular reporters. A local radio station carried a continuing satire starring Brother Bill Taker and his Pass the Loot Club. Homosexuals complained about PTL programs that featured Anita Bryant, who was then fighting to repeal a Dade County, Florida, ordinance banning discrimination against homosexuals. PTL's neighbors around Heritage Village resisted PTL's plan for a building to service its new satellite dish. An unfavorable zoning decision prompted a PTL spokesman to state, "We are being treated like second-class citizens in this country."

County tax officials contested PTL's claims that it owed no property taxes. The Better Business Bureau decided that PTL was submitting too little fund-raising information to join its list of approved charities. The state of North Carolina asked PTL to stop raising money until it filed a financial statement and obtained a license. PTL refused and sued, complaining of unconstitutional meddling in church affairs. Eventually, Bakker prevailed in court, but the publicity cemented the impression that the ministry had something to hide.

Like a defiant teenager, Bakker took criticism badly, even as he invited it. He slipped reflexively into the role of victim, one who must forge ahead with his divine mission at great personal cost. In his hands, the world became the great condemner, as stern and fast in its judgments, perhaps, as his father had been. It was good against evil, God against Satan.

"Now, today, I face the biggest test this ministry has ever gone through," he wrote to his supporters in August 1977.

> I have been attacked from every side. My honor has been in question. Some people have looked at me as though I were a

common crook. I have been called everything in the press but a child of God. All of this has hurt so deeply, sometimes I felt I could not go on.

Though he condemned the press before his congregation, Bakker and his deputies tried to mend PTL's image. PTL declared that its finances were an open book. As Perkins had recommended, PTL hired an outside accounting firm in May 1977. Two months later, PTL released a financial statement. Bakker took the extraordinary step of ordering an audit of his personal finances for distribution, hoping to show that he was not personally benefitting from the ministry.

> I believe our partners and our people and our friends deserve to know the truth. I believe they deserve to know everything that goes on. And so I try to be as transparent as glass. . . .
> I will actually be publishing exact figures of my own salary. And I feel—you know, I hate to go throwing all that kind of stuff around because to some people it is going to make me look like I am a pauper. To other people, it is going to make me look like, boy, I am rich.

The Haskins and Sells audit of the Bakkers' personal assets and liabilities showed the couple's net worth was less than $24,000. PTL chose to keep to itself a detailed schedule of the Bakkers' assets that showed that the Bakkers owned jewelry worth $8,500—more than one-third of their net worth.

Bakker compared his salary to that of successful secular talk-show hosts, a stance he would often take over the next ten years. "Our little organization is valued at $3.8 million," Bakker said. "If I'm big show biz, how come I'm not making $3 million like Johnny Carson or Mike Douglas? Why am I not taking home this much money?" His job, Bakker explained, was akin to hosting the "Tonight Show" and presiding over the NBC network. The analogy sounded convincing, particularly when no mention was made of the considerable difference in size between the huge network and PTL, with its payroll of three hundred.

Though Bakker portrayed himself as a victim of religious persecution, other TV evangelists took issue with his conduct. Within his own industry, Bakker was acquiring a questionable reputation. Fortunately for Bakker, almost all of the complaints of other religious broadcasters would remain private until the upheaval of 1987.

Pat Robertson was perturbed by the reports he was getting from Charlotte. Robertson's staff had pressured PTL to focus its efforts on markets where CBN didn't broadcast; if CBN and PTL were vying for the same stations, the argument went, then local stations were likely to take advantage of the competition to raise rates. But CBN's early syndication had concentrated on the largest American markets and Bakker was eager to get into the bigger cities as well. Soon the two ministries found themselves in competition, and Robertson heard from his staff that PTL was playing dirty. In addition, Bakker had skillfully left the impression that PTL owned the distinction of building the first Christian satellite dish, though PTL was a year behind CBN in the move into that broadcasting technology.

Disgusted, Robertson wrote to Bakker on September 15, 1977. His letter was scalding and prophetic, informed by Robertson's seven years with Bakker.

As you requested when you telephoned, I insured that none of our people were making any overtures whatsoever which would conflict with the airing of the "PTL Club" on Channel 36 [WRET] in Charlotte, and we have not in any way moved to cause any inconvenience to you in your plans.

You can imagine my shock when I learned today from an officer of Channel 18 [in Charlotte] that members of the "PTL Club" have approached [a station official] with a specific request to purchase the time that the "700 Club" has been buying on their station.

This was reminiscent of an incident a year or two ago when we specifically refused to accept your affiliate in Savannah, Georgia, because we did not feel it was ethical, and within weeks our kindness was repaid by your attempt to take away our Orlando affiliate and your entry into the Hartford market which played a part in ruining a transfer of license which we had been working on at great expense for some months. Now this new evidence of duplicity, coupled with recent purchases either in competition with us, or on the same station as we are on, make me question seriously your financial wisdom, your ethics, and your truthfulness.

I might add that the outrageous claims about your satellite project "to be on the air by the end of April," "the first ever to broadcast twenty-four hours a day,"—when you knew an

April date was impossible and you also knew that CBN had already done what you were claiming—were patently false and misleading. You know that a satellite project can cost up to $6 million and that the only market for yours now is a tiny part of the US cable industry, because your project is in direct competition with CBN which already is covering the market, yet you continue to make untrue claims about it to the public. This is a totally uncalled for waste of the money of God's people merely for the purpose of gratifying your personal ego and unbelievable competitive spirit.

Jim, God does not bless falsehood, and the Bible says He resists the proud. This competitive spirit and financial wastefulness has brought about many of the troubles you are now in. Unless you face reality and ask God's forgiveness, He is going to bring you down. God is speaking to you through things that are happening. I pray that you will get His message.

The letter must have been a blow to Bakker. Earlier that year, in a letter thanking CBN for its ten-thousand-dollar donation to PTL, Bakker had gushed to Robertson, "I appreciate this gesture of love more than you will ever know. I trust that someday I will be able to do something to show my love and respect that I hold in my heart for you." Nearly a year after Robertson's damning letter, Bakker told an interviewer that he had never fought with his old boss. "We've never had any words with each other. When I left, he told me I always had a job there, and there's been times lately when I've been tempted to take him up on that."

Shortly after Robertson's letter arrived, Texas evangelist James Robison declined an invitation to appear on the "PTL Club." He publicly expressed his reservations about Bakker's ministry. "I get the impression from watching the 'PTL Club' that he implies if you all support PTL, you'll prosper. I don't agree with that philosophy. Rather than get people right with God, it seems they're trying to get them more involved with the ministry of PTL."

Bakker had embraced the philosophy of seed-faith giving espoused by Oral Roberts: give to God and you shall receive back many times over, for God wants his people to prosper and rewards their generosity. Seed-faith was one manifestation of the prosperity gospel, the emerging leitmotif of many of America's charismatic-Pentecostal TV preachers. The doctrine put God's stamp of approval on the growing affluence and new-money showiness of both evangelical America and its TV preachers. It also helped to perpetu-ate the TV ministries, which prospered on the harvest of their donors' seeds of faith.

In November 1977, Bakker received a confidential three-page letter from a perturbed Gene Scott, who now controlled KHOF, the Glendale, California, religious TV station that Crouch had left in 1973. A year earlier, as the Charlotte press and local ministers had questioned PTL's commitment to the needy, PTL had listed a gift of $318,000 to Scott's Faith Center Church as an example of its generous support of other ministries. Bakker, eager to make the right impression, had bent the truth once again. As Scott told it, the "gift" merely fulfilled an agreement Bakker had made to secure airtime in the Los Angeles market he so coveted; instead of paying for airtime directly, PTL was to return a percentage of the money it raised from KHOF viewers. Bakker had refused to acknowledge his misstatement publicly, and Scott complained.

> The only difference that I have ever felt between us involves a simple telling of the truth, which I thought was a conviction we equally shared. . . .
> I really wish you no harm, Brother Bakker, and believe you when you preach that the Christian community needs to come together.
> Someone must take the first step to activate the witness of Christian love, so this letter is an honest attempt to heal the breach between us. . . . I believe that we should do more than talk about Christian love. . . .
> I believe that truth without love is a harsh caricature of Christlikeness, and love without truth brings no glory to God.

Scarred by his experiences in Virginia and California, Bakker was determined to ensure that he would never again have to struggle with an unsympathetic board of directors. Bakker demanded total allegiance; if you weren't totally with him, you were against him. Dale Hill, a trusted friend and colleague from CBN and Trinity, took a seat. So did Flessing and Moss. Bakker's board thus included three of his closest allies—and subordinates.

In August 1977, Bakker tried to force out board member Larry Hall, who worked for IBM but had been volunteering at PTL since its inception in 1973. Bakker had tried to recruit Hall to the staff job of telethon coordinator, and Hall was eager to say yes to Bakker's offer. He was dazzled by Bakker's ability to raise money, his instinctive sense of what worked on television, and the moxie that let him execute it spontaneously. He had watched Bakker announce in one telethon that God had assured that PTL would raise the money it needed to pay WRET. Bakker told everyone on the set to pray silently. God, he said, will make up the difference. Conventional wisdom held that dead airtime was fatal to a telethon. Instead, pledges came in by the armload. Hall's wife, Carolyn, warned him that if he accepted Bakker's offer, he would become Bakker's servant, just as Moss had. Reluctantly, Hall told Bakker no. "You've missed God's will in your life," Bakker told him.

On the board, Hall had acquired a reputation as a hothead. At the board's May 1977 meeting, he pressed the directors to hire the Big Eight accounting firm of Haskins and Sells, a move Bakker privately resisted. Hall resented that the PTL president seemed to want a raise at every meeting. That May, the board unanimously boosted Bakker's salary to seven hundred dollars a week plus a housing allowance. When Moss asked Hall to cosign a PTL check to pay the Bakkers' moving expenses, Hall balked. No matter how nice the house, the Bakkers were never satisfied, he thought. He knew that PTL employees had packed and moved PTL's first family. Tammy hadn't had to lift a finger. "I'll get A. T. to sign" Moss told Hall, alluding to board member A. T. Lawing. "Fine," Hall rejoined. "Put it on A. T.'s conscience."

A year had passed since Hall had recognized the sobering implications in the juxtaposition of the squalor in the Alabama shack and the lavishness of Bakker's Heritage Village. Now Hall questioned Bakker's plans for the Total Living Center. When Hall had visited Bakker in California in 1973, Bakker had said that he wanted to build a place for Christians to go for fun like Walt Disney's Disneyland, just up the highway in Anaheim. Now, years later, Hall saw Bakker actually pursuing that idiosyncratic vision. "You're building your dream, not God's dream," he told Bakker. If the Bible was unfailingly true, as Bakker ostensibly believed, then he should work to feed the hungry, clothe the naked, and propagate the Bible, Hall said. If Jesus was to return soon, then PTL should be out building people, not buildings. Pay the TV stations' bills first, Hall said, and use the money that remains to expand PTL's broadcast outreach. Bakker was unmoved. "I am going to build my vision."

Bakker was livid when he discovered Hall working on a telethon for a Florence, South Carolina, TV ministry in summer 1977. It was the same sort of work Hall regularly did for PTL in telethons on the road—and the same work Bakker had done for ministries all over the country since his days at CBN. But Bakker didn't like the Florence evangelist.

During the board's August 1977 meeting, Bakker voiced his complaints. Hall was there, along with Bakker, Moss, Hill, Flessing, and Lawing. Bakker raised a second issue, challenging Hall's right to work for a religious broadcasting company interested in opening a TV station in Florida. Bakker declared the dual service a conflict of interest. Hall offered to resign from the Florida board, but Bakker asked Hall instead to resign from PTL. "At this point," minutes of the meeting read, "Hall apologized and said he repented of his association with Channel 52," the Florida company.

Moss suggested a compromise: let Larry resign from Florida or from PTL. Bakker made a motion giving Hall seven days to make a choice. "One way or the other," the minutes concluded, "Hall must decide."

Thirteen days later, nearly a week after the deadline, Hall wrote Bakker a two-page letter.

> For the past seven days, I have been praying, fasting, and seeking God about the direction for our future. To be very honest, I feel that I have found the mind of the Lord on what we are to do.
>
> For the past five years, I have felt that God had me involved with PTL. . . . We have never sought personal gain from the ministry and everything has been done as unto God. . . . God has reconfirmed to me that I am to continue with PTL because He put me on the Board of Directors. . . .
>
> God directed us to help get this [Florida] station on the air in the same manner that He spoke concerning our commitment to PTL. Roger Flessing has consulted PTL's FCC attorney. . . . [He says] there is no legal, moral, or ethical conflict of interest and that my involvement would in no way jeopardize PTL's satellite license. . . .
>
> The very essence of PTL has always been giving and this is what we were doing. . . . I cannot regret the intent of my heart.

The letter did no good. Bakker wanted Hall out, and Hall's late response had given him an excuse. At its January 5, 1978, meeting, the board removed Hall. Minutes of the meeting made no reference to Hall's August letter to Bakker.

For months after he sent that letter, Hall had tried to reach Bakker. When a letter from PTL arrived accepting his resignation—which he had in fact never tendered—his wife, Carolyn, was livid. She called Moss. "You tell Jim," she told Moss, "if he doesn't meet with me Monday I will be in the *Observer*'s office and I will answer all questions they ask truthfully." The Halls' phone was busy that weekend with calls setting up the meeting with Bakker. He could not afford a scandal.

Monday afternoon, Larry and Carolyn Hall walked into Bakker's office at Heritage Village. Bakker had Moss and Flessing at his side. He seemed petrified. Bakker had never been one for confrontation, preferring to leave the dirty work to others, to avoid the consequences of his decisions.

At the start, Carolyn Hall tried to put her onetime friend—the man who had presided over the funeral of her infant son two years before—at ease. She told him that she had had no intention of going to the paper, that she only wanted a meeting with him. She spoke about how they had been friends with Bakker before he was anybody, how they had done nothing wrong, how even if they had, Bakker hadn't given them a chance to make up for it.

Larry Hall added his voice. "You may not know this. I'm the best friend you ever had. I didn't rip you off, I didn't make money off you. And you hated me for it. I go off and help another ministry, and what do you do, you get upset about it."

Bakker broke into tears. "People either hate my guts or they try to use me because I'm Jim Bakker. I need friends, I need you as a friend," he told them. He asked Carolyn to go talk to Tammy. Once, the two women had been very close. Carolyn Hall found Tammy inside a PTL home next to Heritage Village. She reassured Tammy, telling her not to worry, that they were all still friends.

Two weeks later, the Halls spotted the Bakkers at a Charlotte mall. As they watched, Jim turned around and walked in the other direction. "Let it go," Carolyn Hall told her husband. "You have done your part."

CHAPTER SIX

HERITAGE USA

"The ox is in the ditch"

On a Friday morning in November 1977, Bakker and his top deputies gathered in a conference room at a beachfront resort on Kiawah Island, near Charleston, South Carolina. They had come to talk about PTL's future. "Our goal is to bring the Gospel of Jesus Christ to every living person on earth. Don't lose sight of the goal," Bakker said. They must work together, he said, and not lose PTL's overall goal by setting their sights on individual parts of the ministry—be it the Total Living Center, the satellite, or television. They must not let financial considerations override his vision. "Follow the Holy Spirit," he said, "don't organize it out."

Three months earlier, Bakker had promised his TV audience that he would not build the Total Living Center without outside financing. Instead, he pledged to spend PTL's extra revenues on evangelism. Bakker had a new commitment for his executives at Kiawah, who had come to the beach to piece together PTL's first budget. He told them that from now on, he would not buy property or start a major construction project without having the money in hand. His staff had seen the strain that Heritage Village had put on PTL's operating budget. As Bakker and his aides trimmed their wish lists from $54 million to $32 million, they made no provision to pay for the Total Living Center, a project whose price Bakker put at $100 million.

Within weeks, Bakker informed his staff and board that he had approved a contract to buy twelve hundred acres of land, most of it just over the state border into South Carolina. "I believe that God really wants us to have this property. He has spoken to me. This is really important," Bakker told Flessing.

In two years, history had repeated itself. Once again, Bakker had turned 180 degrees and moved ahead with a large building project totally at odds with his promises to his partners. Bakker was fond of saying that life at PTL felt like a roller-coaster ride; without question, the ministry moved swiftly, plunging from highs to lows without warning. The metaphor was appropriate in another way. PTL, though always changing, always stayed the same, like the roller coaster that takes the same path, over and over. As the years passed, patterns appeared behind the facade of changing names of Bakker's projects, staff and Satanic enemies. Where some grow wise with age and experience, Bakker ossified, a self-centered man-child sheltered by success and self-deception.

The story was sad, inspiring, and sobering. Sad because a man with such talent and drive could not put his demons to rest, instead taking an enormous toll in money and human capital. Inspiring because many of the men and women at his side and in his army worked with such devotion to a higher cause, trying to make amends for the transgressions of their leader and his often self-serving consorts. And sobering because so many people had been deaf for so long to the truth, many of them duped by the convincing "reality" of the TV image that has such a hold on modern America.

As packaged by Bakker, the Total Living Center was to serve as a breeding ground for evangelism, supposedly PTL's paramount cause. Bakker's program was now broadcast at all hours of the day all across the country, and PTL struggled to get volunteers to answer its prayer phones during off-hours. The Total Living Center would offer training in counseling and the Bible to partners, who could then serve as "a mighty army" of counselors from their campsites, each of which would have its own phone jack. Students at Heritage University would be able to do the same from their dorm rooms, and year-round residents would volunteer from their homes and apartments. This "training and service to Christ . . . is the main reason we are building the Total Living Center," Bakker told his partners.

Really this whole thing was born out of the need to reach out on these phone systems. We just couldn't get enough counselors. There's no way, physically, to get enough counselors even in here to do the job when the thing goes wild and they're all ringing off the hook.

On his thirty-eighth birthday, January 2, 1978, Bakker broke ground for what he proclaimed "the greatest project ever in the history of Christianity." Three days later, PTL's board unseated the absent Larry Hall, who had opposed the project, and ratified the decision Bakker had already made for them, agreeing to buy the acreage for the Total Living Center and to hire a general contractor.

Bakker was already making plans for the major university he said that God had directed him to build. Like new buildings, missions programs, and financial crises, universities were a potent lure for donations in the religious broadcasting industry. "It is a very appealing thing for people to want to support," Bakker said privately. By late March, PTL had scheduled a September opening with a projected enrollment of at least three hundred graduate students. Within five years, Bakker expected to have an accredited four-year university. He called Heritage University "the most important project in PTL's history."

When Tammy Bakker learned her husband was going ahead with the Total Living Center, she cried silently. Oh no, she thought, we need a break, not another building program. The task consumed her husband. He woke at dawn to sketch his latest idea. He spent afternoons on the site of the Total Living Center, which he soon began calling Heritage USA. There, he was busy deciding where to lay roads, which trees to save, where to build.

Heavy construction began in March 1978. Soon, something seemed to be going up on every corner of the site. Everything was a priority, a contractor working for PTL joked privately. Bakker had scheduled the dedication ceremony for July 4, ignoring gentle suggestions from his staff that he move more cautiously. With such a tight schedule, saving time, not money, was uppermost in Bakker's mind. Water lines that should have cost $4 a foot to install cost $6.75. To compound matters, Bakker kept changing his plans. He wanted to make sure everything looked just right. Dirt moved here one day had to go back there the next.

With no financing—Bakker was still trying to secure a $50 million loan—PTL had to absorb the escalating building costs in its operating budget. Making payroll became a struggle. The missions staff repeatedly submitted check requests in their effort to secure the money that PTL had promised to a program for feeding children in India. Moss had trouble negotiating for better airtime in the United States and overseas.

As money grew tight that spring, Flessing and Orender built a sense of anticipation in PTL's TV audience with a series of comic spots starring Flessing as an announcer earnestly promoting Heritage USA's July opening, and Orender, unseen behind the wheel of his persistent green VW, as a partner too impatient to wait until summer. Flessing used gentle humor to prod Bakker, hoping the message might sink in after the laughs wore off. He saw that Bakker didn't respond well to direct confrontation. Flessing's goofy video routines promoting Heritage USA—he shot a sequence in the dark after staging the fall and destruction of a chandelier being installed in one building—subtly parodied the enthusiastic pitches Bakker delivered during on-camera visits to construction sites at Heritage USA. Over lunch one day in 1978, as Bakker and his lieutenants struggled with the consequences of Bakker's massive building plan, Flessing joked to his colleagues that he had found a verse of Scripture with insight for PTL, and he needed to share it. "What sort of man before he goes out to build a house does not stop and count the cost?" he asked. Then he looked at Bakker and declared "I think we've found the man." One executive laughed so hard he fell out of his chair. Bakker—the man who had not counted the cost—threw his napkin, spoon, and fork at Flessing.

Publicly, Bakker clung to expressions of confidence. As PTL tried to come up with $1 million for its general contractor and $200,000 for its payroll in May 1978, he told an interviewer,

> People talk like there's a lack somehow in God, like there's somehow a shortage. And if we build something for a Christian retreat center, that we wouldn't have the money to send to India [to feed the hungry] or we wouldn't have money to do this or we couldn't have the money to do that. There is no shortage in God, believe me.

Bakker touted his plans to spend profits from Heritage USA on world evangelism. "We're gonna be able to do more, not less, because this whole thing is set up to be self-supporting, all the way through." Supposedly, all the millions PTL was spending on new buildings and roads was really creating money for the charitable work of the Lord. It was an appealing notion to PTL's donors, and one that PTL continued to brag about for years, even as many operations at Heritage USA lost money and survived on subsidies from the TV audience.

It was not until the eve of the scheduled opening of Heritage USA that Bakker was ready to acknowledge the crisis he had created.

On June 19, Bakker met with his vice presidents. "You may not like some of the things I'm going to say today," he warned them. "But God has shown me what to do. . . . If you don't agree with these moves, you have the option of resigning. . . . I feel a new anointing and a new desire to win souls. And I think it's because I'm making these positive changes." Bakker detailed a battery of cost-cutting measures and new responsibilities for his staff, for both executives and the rank and file.

Two days later, for the first time ever, PTL staged a wholesale layoff of staff members. Sixty people, nearly one of every ten on the staff of 690, were dispatched. Privately, Bakker told his board that he planned to let another forty go in two weeks. He expected to cut $5 million from PTL's budget.

The layoffs were a wrenching blow for an organization supposedly dedicated to love and caring and for Bakker, so eager to safeguard PTL's image. PTL's new personnel director was let go four months after moving his wife and three children from Chicago. Bakker's PR man—reportedly blamed by Bakker for a *People* magazine picture showing Bakker's ample belly hanging out during a trip to the bowling alley—was fired a few weeks before his child's birth.

Staff members complained that Bakker had cut out time for devotionals—the sort of cost-cutting measure Bakker had condemned as a CBN employee. "They turned the place into a sweatshop," one said. Workers said they had repeatedly been asked to work overtime without pay, in violation of federal law. One told a reporter that Bakker had threatened to lay off workers earlier that month, on Father's Day weekend, because he thought too few employees had turned out for volunteer cleanup duty at Heritage USA. Bakker said later that he might have voiced such a threat, but he had only been joking.

As the sixty were laid off, Bakker circulated a tough memo to his staff, spelling out principles he himself would repeatedly break in the years to come.

> It is a hard thing to let people go, but God has spoken to my heart that we must not be slothful in business. God told me that He would remove His blessing from this ministry if we continue to pay people whose spirit is not right, whose work is not up to par, and for duplicated positions, overhiring in some areas, and financial pressures in the ministry.
>
> We must bring the PTL budget into a position where we can live within the income. . . . We are looking at attitude—those who are willing to work, those who say they are missionaries working here for the glory of God and truly will act like it, giving that extra effort . . .
>
> We have the Heritage USA to open in just a few days. Our workdays have dropped down to eight people on some Saturdays. . . . I understand there are reasons that people cannot come every Saturday. However, I believe when the "ox is in the ditch," extra effort is needed on all parts. . . .
>
> To coin a phrase, "Ask not what your ministry can do for you, but what you can do for your ministry."

That summer, Bakker was forever making what one executive remembered as his "little blue hen" speech, a variant of the fable about the little red hen whose animal friends wouldn't share the drudgery of making bread from scratch and who therefore got none of the finished food. The little blue hen—blue was Bakker's favorite color—was forever asking his staff for the impossible. We need this brick wall built by day's end. The wall most likely got built, the staff exhausted itself doing it, and the little blue hen decided he really wanted a fence built of wood or stone. When he couldn't get the absolute devotion he wanted for his next task, the little blue hen pouted aloud that he would have to do the job himself.

The layoffs had lifted the lid off PTL, baring the consequences of Bakker's mismanagement. On June 25, an article on the *Observer*'s front page opened with a quote from an unnamed PTL employee, "PTL's problems are not financial. They're manage-ment." Nearly everyone believed the obvious: that Heritage USA was the biggest culprit. Bakker defended the complex. He had no regrets, he said. "People respond to these projects. People need a goal, an incentive."

A day before PTL announced the staff layoffs, Bakker's board voted to raise his weekly salary from seven hundred dollars to a thousand dollars, retroactive one month. Board member James "Johnny" Johnson, a retired Marine Corps officer who had served as assistant secretary of the navy under President Nixon, declared that Bakker would earn $500,000 in most organizations for the load he carried. "Walter Cronkite makes $750,000 a year, and he gives out bad news." Moss suggested that Bakker get a raise; Flessing seconded the proposal.

The $52,000 salary may have been reasonable, but Bakker rec-ognized that news of his raise during this time of austerity could compound his image problems. Immediately after the vote, Bakker recommended—and the board agreed—that PTL stop releasing financial information to the press. Eleven months had passed since Bakker had told his TV audience that he wanted to be as transpar-ent as glass.

In public, Bakker tried to sustain the image of openness. He told an interviewer that his board had decided to cut back the release of information. He neglected to mention his key role in the board's decision.

> It's been a policy of the board of directors and people like
> Johnny Johnson who just believe you don't gain anything by
> having a lot of indiscriminate things in the press . . . that's part
> of the philosophy of the advisors that have been advising me
> on what to do about the press and the media.

On June 27, two days after the *Observer* story raised questions about Bakker's management, Bakker announced on the air that he and Tammy had decided to give "every penny we have, our entire life's savings" to PTL. "And we have cut out everything at PTL possible. . . . We are cutting out anything that we consider fat, that is not necessary in the ministry." Bakker did not say how much he had in savings. As Perkins remembered it later, Bakker's gift totaled between two and three thousand dollars.

Bakker trumpeted the donation in a July letter to his partners, turning his gesture into another fund-raising device. "Tammy and I have given our largest gift ever to PTL. . . . I have done all I know to do." He said nothing about his raise. As much as he bristled at suggestions that ministers should not drive luxury cars or live in fancy houses, Bakker recognized the sway those standards held over his Christian audience. He knew he couldn't afford to appear to ask what his ministry could do for him. He publicly distanced himself from the world of wealth and materialism, even as he willingly embraced it in private.

> The richer you get the more miserable you become. Timothy 6:6 says "But godliness with contentment is great gain." I'd rather be poor and have the Lord than rich without Him. The reason it's harder for the rich to get into the kingdom of God is because of their heart attitude. They are usually so selfish in their hearts, they have no room for Jesus. With God you don't need anything else. . . .
>
> I believe the trumpet is going to sound soon. When it does, only what has been done for God will count. . . . [God's] waiting for you. All this other that you're holding on to in this world is just carnival junk. It's plastic and just junk. . . . Sin is like that when it's finished. You can buy the finest materials and even then it will eventually rust out. The things you accumulate you can't take with you when you die. It will all rot, burn, and decay.

Even as he poured millions of PTL dollars into Heritage USA, Bakker proclaimed his unbridled commitment to missionary work. "I love missions so much," he told his studio audience after his June 16 broadcast. "It brings me to tears sometimes to see their dedication. I've lived so comfortably here in the United States. We all have. . . . It's only right that we support those who go among disease and need in other places to share the Gospel."

For weeks after Korean pastor Paul Yonggi Cho's June 1977 appearance on Bakker's program, the Asian mission had taken center stage on the PTL broadcast. PTL had raised $277,000. By fall 1977, Bakker portrayed the project as all but complete. "We are getting ready to ship the cameras. We are going to have a special packet of cameras for Korea," he said in October 1977. In fact, no cameras had been bought. Bakker claimed that broadcasts would start within days. They didn't. On May 9, 1978, when a guest surprised Bakker on the air by asking, "You are on in Seoul, aren't you?" Bakker stammered back, "We are just—we are building the studios there." In fact, PTL was not building a studio.

Behind the scenes, PTL had encountered several problems in trying to make good on Bakker's impulsive promise. PTL had promised TV equipment for the Korean show, but Korean customs duties threatened to double PTL's cost. And Cho's church had encountered objections from the Presbyterian church in Korea, which cut off, at least temporarily, Cho's access to airtime. According to PTL's March 1978 magazine, however, all barriers had been overcome. The magazine reported that after meetings in Korea, the red tape hampering delivery of PTL TV equipment for Cho's new studio had disappeared. "And permission was granted. This month, equipment is being purchased and sent to Korea to set up the new studio."

As the anniversary of Bakker's offer to Cho approached, Cho and his staff grew frustrated and embarrassed. On June 8, 1978, Cho's assistant wrote to Bob Manzano, who ran PTL's missions department. The assistant complained that overseas visitors kept asking to see the studio PTL claimed to have built. "They all think it is 'up and going.' " Eight days later, the assistant wrote to Bakker that Cho was disturbed by the slow progress. "I think this is mainly due to the fact that in his worldwide travels everyone is always telling him how wonderful it is that he *now* has TV studios in operation and all paid for and provided by PTL. . . . I think you can understand his situation."

Behind the scenes, PTL was also balking at fulfilling its promises to Bob McAlister, the missionary who was to begin his own version of the "PTL Club" in Brazil. PTL had agreed to give McAlister $50,000 a month in May, June, and July of 1978. With Heritage USA draining PTL's cash, Manzano could get no more than ten thousand dollars in May—even as Bakker was telling his donors about the Brazilian programs PTL was supposedly sponsoring.

McAlister was just as frustrated as Cho. On a June day that Bakker professed his love of missions to his studio audience, missions director Manzano telephoned McAlister, at Bakker's direction, to say that he must call his Brazilian program by the name PTL, not the name McAlister had planned to use. McAlister was furious. He had just laid off his orchestra because PTL had failed to make good on its promises.

Three days later, McAlister wrote to Manzano.

> Having not heard any more from you concerning the promise of money for our [air]time charges for the first three months, we emptied the existing accounts and paid the bill on the 15th.
>
> Now, after three days of real soul-searching, we feel that it would be unwise for us to rely on the promises of PTL for the future of this work. If you have been unable (or unwilling) to take care of such a relatively small commitment as $150,000 in three monthly gifts, how can we gear a program that requires us to spend over a million dollars. . . .
>
> I don't think it is necessary for me to comment on the recent decision of PTL to strive for "uniformity" in their overseas efforts. Historically, this kind of empire complex is not new and these kinds of decisions are usually made by people who are completely ignorant of the realities of world conditions.

In a second, confidential letter to Manzano, McAlister complained, as California's Gene Scott had the year before, about PTL's handling of money designated by donors for specific projects.

> I think the use of money that has been designated is a very real symptom of an illness that can only cause great pain to the heart of the One who is the truth. Your assurance that $52,000 had been received and was in the bank for Brazil was an encouragement to us to go full steam ahead. For it to be used for anything other than missions—even temporarily—is a clear violation of conscience, and that puts a cloud over everything that has been said about PTL's desire to be involved in effective missions. . . .
>
> I have come to believe that the most dangerous aspect of television ministry is the pure mathematics of the thing. The outreach is so great; the possibilities so vast; the influence (and power) so tremendous, that a person who does not have a very clear vision of what he is called for can easily be chewed up in the great maw of some "ministry" that is far less than the Gospel. . . .

> Opportunity can be a trap. One must return to his origins
> and find out Who called him, and for what purpose.

In early July 1978, Manzano briefed Bakker and other top executives on PTL's overseas programs. Bakker was visibly upset that PTL promises had not been kept. He pounded the table. "I'd rather go to jail for not paying my bills than renege on my missions commitments," one vice president recalled Bakker's saying.

Bakker said it as if he meant it. At that moment, he probably did. But PTL had grown too big and complex for Bakker's simple answers and plastic reality. Manzano couldn't get the money to fulfill the commitments because PTL didn't have it because Bakker had committed so much cash to building Heritage USA. When it came right down to it, Bakker was unwilling to sacrifice his personal agenda so that PTL could make good, in a timely fashion, on its corporate promises and Bakker's public declarations. But the declarations served their purpose: Bakker could claim, as he later did to investigators from the Federal Communications Commission, that he had told his staff to do the right thing.

Nine months after the retreat on Kiawah Island, Bakker's once cooperative executive staff had become frustrated and suspicious of one another. In mid-August, the contractor at Heritage USA walked off the site. He vowed not to return until PTL had paid more than $500,000 in delinquent invoices. But PTL's problem was not simply cash flow. Bakker's vice presidents wanted more dialogue with Bakker, a clearer chain of command, and well-defined division of authority. Bakker often delegated responsibility without power. He second-guessed his managers and shuffled responsibility constantly, assigning more power to those whose stock was up at the time regardless of their suitability for the job. The consequences of Bakker's leadership were evident to bankers from North Carolina National Bank in Charlotte. In early August, a bank vice president explained to Bakker his reluctance to grant PTL a loan.

> . . . we . . . do not find conventional wisdom in your approach
> to expand your facilities without adequate financing or financial planning. We usually view such expansion as fiscally dan-

gerous. . . . Our exposure to your organization has led us to conclude that it is suffering from inadequate professional management in most areas except those directly related to television production. And, because of this, we have concern over the organization's long term viability.

By early August, Bakker seemed to recognize that he was no longer capable of running PTL. He named an executive committee—Moss, Manzano, Flessing, and finance director Herb Moore—to act on his behalf. "This ministry has grown to such a tremendous degree that I am no longer able to follow through on all the many details to keep PTL running smoothly." Soon, the executive committee agreed that PTL needed a more businesslike image.

Shortly thereafter, Bakker decided that he, not Manzano, would represent PTL at a mid-September world conference of charismatics in Singapore as part of an extended trip around the world. He would be joined by Flessing, then his favored executive, a cameraman, and Phil and Ruth Egert. His purpose, he told an interviewer before leaving, was to get firsthand exposure to people in need. "Mine is a mass ministry. But it's just so wrong to get to the point where all you see is masses, where you just talk in numbers. I want to go into the ghettoes. . . . I'm going to visit those people [who write to PTL] in their homes and talk to them and pray with them and listen."

As Bakker flew from Los Angeles to Honolulu on his way to Singapore, a telegram arrived from Cho's church in Seoul. The Koreans were still waiting for PTL to pay them the $5,369 that they had spent to participate in the televised April dedication of PTL's satellite dish. They had heard nothing from PTL in months, and embarrassing requests to visit their nonexistent studio continued. "I am sorry but we feel you owe us some kind of explanation," the telegram read.

A PTL secretary forwarded the message to Bakker's deputies. "From the sound of this," she wrote, "it could be a potentially embarrassing situation for Jim when he arrives in Seoul and thought perhaps you would want to handle this right away." The bill was quickly paid, but the timing was not lost on Cho.

En route to Singapore, Bakker telephoned Manzano at home. His missions chief was entertaining Jim Moss and his wife and another PTL couple. Bakker ordered Manzano to fly to Singapore immediately. He hated confrontations, and he wanted Manzano to protect him from the hostility he expected to encounter at the conference. Moss picked up the telephone. He chastised Bakker for not taking Manzano from the start, as Moss had recommended.

Bakker asked Manzano what it would take to placate Bob McAlister, the missionary in Brazil whom Bakker expected to see at the conference. Manzano suggested paying $50,000, a third of PTL's pledge, and Bakker agreed. He told Manzano to have the financial office draw up a postdated check, and to bring the check with him.

The next morning, Manzano learned that McAlister wasn't coming to Singapore. He telephoned McAlister, who told him that he didn't want PTL's money or to be associated with PTL. PTL's finance director told Manzano that PTL didn't have $50,000 to give McAlister anyway.

Manzano arrived in Singapore on the final day of the conference. His trip had cost PTL more than five thousand dollars. In Bakker's suite, Manzano told Bakker that McAlister had turned down the money. "I would have taken it," Bakker replied. At that moment, Manzano later told FCC investigators, he thought to himself, That is the difference between you and Bob McAlister.

Soon, Bakker left for Seoul and a meeting with Cho. En route, he asked Flessing to draw up plans for the Korean studio. Flessing obliged, sketching them on a napkin. On Bakker's orders, Flessing telephoned Charlotte and ordered the staff to begin crating equipment for shipment overseas.

The eleventh-hour effort came too late. Face to face in a Seoul hotel room, Cho politely told Bakker that his own church would provide all the equipment for broadcasts in Korea. Instead, PTL should devote its attention and money to creating a PTL program in Japan. Bakker tried to change Cho's mind; with his reputation at stake, cost was no longer a concern.

> I said, "Dr. Cho, please, let me send equipment." I said, and I had already called before I reached Korea, and I . . . had worked with Roger Flessing on how we could get this thing moving and get the equipment to Korea. I said, "We will send our cameras from our remote truck. We will send our lighting from our amphitheater. . . . We will send our audio systems which we already had in our trucks." . . .

The equipment was already being packaged on our loading dock in Charlotte, NC, at my request through Roger Flessing to our staff.

Cho stood his ground, saying that he had to save face.

Weeks later, an Assemblies of God missionary wrote to Bakker that Cho no longer harbored any animosity toward him but that Cho believed he needed up to two years to restore the confidence of his church members and his credibility with the American donors whose money had not been used as promised. Cho passed along word through an intermediary that PTL should "count the cost"—the same scriptural allusion Flessing had joked of—before making any commitments to broadcasts in Japan. He also cautioned PTL not to give its Japanese show great publicity before the Charlotte ministry had the resources to support it.

The mishandling of the Korean program still dogged Bakker. In a speech in Chicago, Cho spoke critically of PTL. Relying on Bakker's word, his church had spent hundreds of thousands of dollars but had received none of the money it had been promised. Bakker asked his go-between, missionary Maynard Ketcham, to write to Cho. Ketcham declined in a memo to Bakker.

> I have had a continued check in the Spirit which I believe comes from the Lord. It appears to me that if I write to Brother Cho . . . I will only worsen the situation. . . . This is a situation that time, and time alone, will heal. Rightly or wrongly, Brother Cho has been deeply hurt.

Just as PTL's attempts to fund missions in Korea and Brazil had accomplished little, Bakker's ambitious plans to teach toddlers, graduate students, and everyone in between at Heritage USA fared poorly in execution. Things had begun badly in early 1978, when Bakker hired one man and Manzano another for the same job as dean of the PTL university. The project was a classic example of a grandiose Bakker plan played for its maximum public-relations value but crippled by bumbling management and acute financial difficulties.

The school had become more than even Bakker had apparently intended. Manzano had encouraged Bakker to create a university with a full-fledged liberal-arts college, not merely the schools of communications and evangelism Bakker had originally planned. Bakker seemed to like the grander scale. He had heard that Oral Roberts University in Tulsa had thousands of students on its waiting list, and Bakker, with his fondness for superlatives, wanted a school as big—or bigger.

By June 1978, PTL had laid off Bakker's original choice for dean, Donald Barnhouse, Jr., a communications professor at Drexel University in Philadelphia and the son of a Presbyterian minister who had been a pioneer in Christian radio. In a somber letter, Barnhouse later cautioned Bakker about those he saw around the PTL president.

> I will still pray for you and for the work and the people of PTL, but in a different mood. I still think that you could be a David, a man after God's own heart; but I believe strongly that something is wrong and that you need a Nathan. I will pray that you will be stripped of flatterers and favor-seekers, and surrounded by men of Godly strength who will dare to tell you what is right if you are momentarily blinded, as we all are at times.

Eleven months later, Bill Perkins would invoke the same biblical parallel. Nathan the prophet had exposed David's sin with Bathsheba; David, recognizing what he had done, had fallen to his knees and repented.

F. Brooks Sanders, the man whom Manzano had hired away from his job as director of educational technology at a community college in Binghamton, New York, inherited the dean's job from Barnhouse. By early summer, he had lost his faith in Manzano, his boss, who was giving him little real authority and, he thought, freely reinterpreting Bakker's instructions. Manzano was insisting on history, physics, and mathematics—incongruent offerings, Sanders thought, for a school of evangelism. Manzano had prohibited Sanders from telling instructors hired by Barnhouse that they were not needed. Sanders complained in a five-page, single-spaced memo to Roger Flessing, who shared his distrust of Manzano.

> This is unkind, un-Christian, unwise, and uncalled for. These people should have been notified as quickly as possible. . . . We are going to have a number of professors, along with their friends and acquaintances, who are going to be alienated from

the PTL Club Ministry, and my understanding of the financial situation at this moment is that we can afford very little alienation.

Manzano seemed willing to bend the truth for his own ends, Sanders wrote. He had heard Manzano trying to close a real-estate sale for PTL over the telephone. Applying pressure to the owner, Manzano warned that Bakker would call off negotiations if the deal wasn't consummated before Bakker's return from a trip out of town.

> While this may have been Jim's attitude, I got the distinct feeling from Bob's asking the Lord's forgiveness when he got off the phone for stretching the truth that Jim had not specifically communicated anything like this to him. I find it hard to believe that the Lord's work is done in anything but the Lord's ways, and that means a strict adherence to the truth.

Sanders had also seen Manzano mislead Bakker into believing that all was progressing well at the school.

> This practice has been referred to under various terms. Some call it bending the truth, some call it situational ethics, and Machiavelli referred to this practice as the necessary tool in the pursuit of power politics.

Sanders was not the first to raise questions about Manzano. Three years younger than Bakker, Manzano had run an independent charismatic church outside Charlottesville in the early seventies. He appeared on Bakker's show in fall 1976, and Bakker hired him in March 1977 to edit PTL's *Action* magazine. His job description grew quickly to include public relations, missions, and the university. Manzano was a sweet-and-sour man—gracious, witty, erudite, perceptive, pompous, arrogant, and flamboyant in equal measure. He was hardly an angel. At home, he drank and he smoked. Some of his colleagues didn't trust him to tell the truth.

One day, Flessing learned that Manzano's PTL bio sheet might contain some exaggerated claims. As he remembered, he walked into Manzano's office at Heritage Village and set the document on Manzano's desk. "Bob, this isn't true," he told Manzano. "We can't have this out if it's not true." Flessing told Bakker about the exchange. Bakker did nothing. Years later, Manzano denied making any false claims or even being confronted by Flessing. Manzano said a PTL bio sheet giving him credit for a degree from CCNY (he had attended but had not graduated from the school) and a doctorate from UCLA (he had never attended the university) was a fabrication someone at PTL had prepared after his departure from the Charlotte ministry. Manzano had in fact earned his doctorate in philosophy from Union University of Los Angeles, a correspondence school from which Johnny Johnson, a PTL board member and a friend of Manzano's, also claimed a doctorate. Manzano had sought the degree, he said later, to acquire the credentials to organize the university Bakker wanted. He had worked hard, he said, and had gotten all A's.

At PTL, Manzano allowed himself to be misrepresented as what Bakker called "our token rich boy." A 1976 *Observer* article described Manzano as the grandson of a successful New York developer. "The results of that success are apparent in the Persian rugs, Tiffany lamps and hand-carved antiques that abound in Manzano's home." In fact, Manzano was raised first in a New York City housing project on the Lower East Side, then in Jamaica, Queens, the oldest of three sons of an RCA recording engineer. His parents had emigrated from their native Puerto Rico. Both his grandfathers were working class, and neither ever lived on the mainland. Years later, asked about the false account of a rich grandfather, Manzano insisted he had never made the claim. He had inherited money from relatives, he said. Pressed further, Manzano said he used the term "relatives" loosely; those who had remembered him in their will were not blood relatives, he acknowledged.

Heritage University and PTL's new grade school opened in September 1978. Each had about three hundred students. PTL's money problems had halted construction of the university's pyramid-shaped home at Heritage USA. Classes met everywhere, in tents, at a leased supper club, and at Heritage Village. The university students bunked down in the chalets built to house paying guests.

That fall, an accreditation team visited Heritage University. Its report was discouraging, if predictable, and hardly described the model school Bakker had bragged about to his audience that summer. The team concluded that their visit was premature—Heritage University was not ready to be licensed.

Bakker's seige mentality deepened during the summer of 1978. After a broadcast in early August, Bakker told his studio audience that reporters were telephoning staff members at midnight and threatening them with bodily harm if they refused to criticize PTL. In fact, *Observer* reporters had been telephoning staff members while researching a story about PTL's failure to pay overtime; they had not threatened anyone or called so late at night. Reporter Frye Gaillard, in the "PTL Club" audience that day, confronted Bakker afterwards.

"How can you say things like that? Do you know that you're lying, or can't you tell the difference?" Gaillard asked. The lanky thirty-one-year-old towered over Bakker.

"My information is that you're doing exactly what I said," Bakker replied.

Gaillard indignantly jabbed his finger at Bakker as the two walked towards Bakker's office. "I want you to look me in the face and say you believe that I would call someone on your staff at midnight and threaten them."

Bakker, who had seemed to enjoy his talks with Gaillard, backed off. "Well, maybe you didn't do that. People were telling me they were frightened," Bakker said. "Sometimes I just get so caught up in what feels true."

Years later, this moment remained vivid in Gaillard's memory. To Bakker, the truth was not what was true but what Bakker thought ought to be.

Two months earlier, Bakker had granted Gaillard a ninety-minute interview, one of the most far-ranging he would ever give at PTL. Adept at reading an audience, Bakker showed a thoughtfulness that impressed Gaillard, one of the *Observer*'s most talented writers and commentators.

> You know we all like to think we're totally committed to God. Totally. We'd like to be perfect. I have just as many faults as anybody, and I have areas in my life, I'm sure, that I'll never

win total victory over, and I don't think God will ever allow me to. . . .

I think I want everybody to love me; I think everybody does that. I don't like to have critics.

Bakker presented himself as a man of the people, an executive in close touch with what was happening in his ministry.

I guess I've been one of the Indians so long that it's hard for me to be a chief. I just don't like the "big I, little you" business at all. I just don't like it. So I feel as Christians the Bible makes us equal. I believe in leadership and headship but I don't believe in people having lordship over one another. . . .

Once he had preached fire-and-brimstone sermons. Now he thought preaching love was more effective than holding a club over the heads of the faithful in case they stepped out of bounds. Love was PTL's biggest theme now, he said.

I think a lot of people thought they were alone; a lot of Christian people felt they were the only ones in their community . . . and the program has done a lot to bring these people together. . . .

The God that I know, that I see in the pages of the Bible, and the God that I have learned to know personally is a compassionate, loving Savior who cares for people.

Bakker defended his use of television to promote religion. "I believe we have a better product than soap, than automobiles. We have eternal life. I believe in what I'm preaching. I believe in it a million percent. I believe in it with every fiber of my being, and why shouldn't I use the most effective means of communication today?"

Television is a very intimate medium, one he thought "should be shared as a friend. I look at the cameras as a friend, the people there as a friend. . . . It's a one-to-one medium." With his TV show, Bakker hoped to offer the viewer an illustrated sermon, presented by the people themselves. With PTL, viewers felt that they had a program—and a church—truly concerned about their individual problems. The stories PTL talked about on the air, he said, were about simple, everyday problems and how God can help solve them.

> You know a lot of people think we preach utopia, that every-
> thing is going to be right if you accept Christ. That's not true.
> I don't preach that. I talk about problems. I cry when I'm
> on-camera. If I am at a point where something is going wrong,
> and there's a real emotion of tears, I'll cry or I will laugh.

Gaillard asked Bakker what happened when God spoke to him, if his voice was audible or if he spoke to Bakker's heart. Bakker replied that the voice was an inner one. When God spoke to him, he said,

> I make a decision in that area, no one will ever change me.
> Now if I make a decision, and I'm not sure it's God, anybody
> could come and persuade me if facts were right. But I won't
> look at facts if God told me to do something. . . .
> That's the reason Heritage Village is here and the new
> Heritage USA is being built . . . without any financing at all.
> It's impossible to do what's being done . . . but I was able to
> hold on to the fact that I knew this was what God had told me
> to do. And so we did it. And every day we've made it. . . .
> I know who Jim Bakker is, and Jim Bakker's not God. I want
> to tell you, Jim Bakker's not a holy man. The only good thing
> that can come through Jim Bakker is if it comes from God
> through him, ministering the Word of God. That's the only
> good. I would say, if it's good, it's God, if it's bad, it's Jim
> Bakker. . . .
> I dislike flaunting prayer as a spiritual badge. . . . I try my
> best to communicate with God throughout my day, constantly.
> I take Him into everything I do, decisions I make, everywhere
> I go, and it's no superspiritual thing. It's just simply talking to
> God, even on a simple matter of when you're driving down the
> road, you're praying, you're talking, you're sharing.

In his lengthy profile in the *Observer,* Gaillard introduced another side of the man ridiculed by so many outside PTL. Those who know Bakker well, he wrote, "throw out adjectives such as humble, com-mitted, kind, or loving. . . . He does, in fact, demonstrate a grasp of the human, and humane, dimensions of Christianity. . . . Bakker displays an easygoing attentiveness to people—turning a boyish, grinning shyness into an asset that makes others feel special.''

As Bakker crisscrossed Asia, Africa, and Europe in September and October 1978, PTL's image at home wilted even further. The *Observer* published a story challenging Bakker's claims that financial institutions didn't lend to religious groups. Eight days later, the *Charlotte News* reported that Bakker had purchased a $25,000 houseboat that summer, days after announcing that he had donated his savings to PTL. The new forty-three-foot Drifter houseboat, which actually cost $30,000, had two bedrooms, a kitchen, bathroom, built-in television, and gas barbecue grill. The purchase was the first celebrated example of what would become a pattern for the Bakkers: an extravagant purchase made as PTL limped through a financial crisis. Inevitably the press found out about the purchase and Bakker defended himself indignantly. For a man with such superb timing on the air, it was a curiously self-destructive display. It was as if a part of Bakker wanted to rid itself by public humiliation of the Jim Bakker who thirsted for homes, cars, and boats, who couldn't tolerate in his private life the frugality that each crisis imposed on his ministry.

When the houseboat story broke, PTL executive Bill Perkins learned that the newspapers were checking into the possibility that the ministry had furnished Bakker's six-thousand-dollar down payment. The suggestion troubled Perkins, who now served as vice president of international administrative operations. Not only had Bakker made a big show of giving his life's savings to the ministry a few weeks before, but he had called on PTL's partners to boost their giving as well. Perkins took his concerns to Herb Moore, PTL's finance manager.

Moore told him to ignore the newspapers, that PTL wouldn't have anything to worry about if it didn't talk to the press. Perkins took a contrary position: if the ministry handled everything properly, it wouldn't have to worry about leaks. The six thousand dollars was merely a loan, Moore told Perkins. It was perfectly legal as long as Bakker repaid the money within a year.

Perkins disagreed. Bakker was a board member and corporate officer of a tax-exempt corporation, the sort of figure the IRS prohibited from receiving anything beyond reasonable compensation for his work. Perkins suggested that the board would have been willing to give Bakker a six-thousand-dollar bonus. Perhaps, Moore said, but "there wasn't any way he could have gotten board approval in one day, and Jim wanted the boat that day." At PTL, when Jim wanted something, he got it. If someone said no, he didn't last long.

Later, Perkins related the conversation in a memo to Bakker. His account exemplified the willingness of some of Bakker's aides to sanction questionable conduct in the interests of appeasing their boss.

> The most disturbing statement Herb made during our discussion was when he said he didn't feel it was wrong to bend ethics a little if it was necessary. He said "none of us would even have a job at PTL if it wasn't for Jim Bakker." I acknowledged that he was correct on that score, but we can protect Jim Bakker and spare the ministry devastating embarrassment if we just take the time to do things right. . . . Someone is going to have to say "No!" or at least "Wait!" when it is for your own good.

When Bakker finally explained the houseboat purchase to his TV audience, he supplied a version different from Moore's. "Nobody bothered to ask me that I had sold my manuscript, and I am going to pay for my boat that I bought. And I did buy a boat. . . . I wouldn't steal a penny from this ministry."

Bakker amended that story in later years. In secret testimony, Bakker said that he had instructed Moore to set aside his raise and accrue the rest on the books until PTL's cash flow improved. When he decided to buy the boat, Moore informed him that he had accrued the six thousand dollars necessary for down payment. Later, after a 1986 newspaper article pointed out the conflicting explanations, Bakker told his viewers that royalties had financed his monthly payments, but the accrued salary had supplied his down payment.

Bakker's explanations were a vivid illustration of Bakker's willingness to deceive. Mathematically, Bakker could not have accrued enough money to pay the six-thousand-dollar down payment. The board had voted Bakker's three-hundred-dollar weekly raise on June 20, effective retroactively to May 15. On July 14, Bakker directed Moore by memo to pay him only six hundred dollars of his weekly one-thousand-dollar pay. Bakker bought the houseboat less than three weeks later. If Moore had set aside four hundred dollars a week, Bakker would have needed fifteen weeks to raise six thousand dollars in gross salary. Under PTL policy, Moore was required to withhold taxes. So Bakker would have needed even more time to build up the six thousand dollars.

Though he clung to the accrued-salary story by avoiding specific dates, dollars, and numbers, Bakker knew better. In a July 1979 phone call, Perkins explained the mathematical impossibilities to Bakker. Bakker blamed the transaction on Moore, saying that his finance chief had told him to handle it that way instead of borrowing the money. Of course Bakker did not share this more candid explanation with his audience.

In the days before Bakker's return from his world trip, Moore and Perkins faced off again, this time about a newspaper story alleging that PTL had failed to make its $35,000-a-month payments into its employees' retirement fund. Moore acknowledged privately that the story was accurate but refused to admit it publicly— even though PTL still owed three monthly payments.

On a Friday afternoon four days before Bakker's return, Moore fired Perkins, ostensibly because he had asked PTL's accountant about the six-thousand-dollar houseboat payment.

Perkins took his case to Bakker, beginning a campaign for the truth that would cost him his place at PTL. Perkins was Bakker's worst nightmare: informed enough to see through half-truths, wise enough to know there was a better way, and willing to sacrifice his paycheck on the altar of righteousness. Three days after he was fired, Perkins completed a seven-page, single-spaced memo to Bakker telling him that it should be his decision, not Moore's, to fire him.

Perkins raised broader questions as well. He was troubled by PTL's growing reliance on secular commercial ventures to finance the ministry. "If God doesn't supply sufficient funds for a new venture, maybe its His way of saying 'I don't want you to get involved in that venture, at least not now.' " He recommended that Bakker concentrate on TV ministry, the work God had called him to do. "If we tackle too many diversified projects, aren't we likely to become mediocre or ineffective in all of them?" God might be telling PTL to stop, he said, much as the Deity had halted Abraham's sacrifice of his son Isaac.

Before his return from Europe, Bakker asked executive vice president Moss to terminate Manzano. Moss refused to fire his friend, thinking that Bakker was making Manzano his scapegoat for PTL's unfulfilled missions promises. Bakker, unable to accept responsibility for his own shortcomings, had to pin the blame on someone else, Manzano later told federal investigators. Moss thought that Manzano had done as much as Bakker would allow him to do. The job of firing Manzano was left to Flessing.

Bakker tried to appease Perkins with the offer of a job as treasurer of a semi-autonomous world-missions division, but he gave Perkins no chance to air his concerns. Later, Perkins tried to meet with Bakker privately, waiting for nine hours without success. Finally, he delivered another letter.

> Some of our people . . . have been mistreated in a manner which would never be tolerated in a reputable secular organization. . . . Jim, you appoint people to an elevated position with great fanfare, and that is fine. But when you become disenchanted with them, they are summarily removed by someone else without so much as an explanation or opportunity to discuss their deficiencies with you and rebut any unfavorable comments about their performance. . . .
>
> Employees [who have been fired] stood in front of me and with tears streaming down their faces said "Why, Mr. Perkins? Why?" I had to turn my face because I had no answer and couldn't get one. Jim, it's wrong, it's wrong, and I cannot turn my head any longer!

Perkins had experienced this sort of treatment himself. He had been moved abruptly from one vice-president's post to another, and Bakker had not talked to him about it for two days—and then only discussed it when Jim's sister, Donna Puckett, arranged a twenty-minute conversation between the two men.

Perkins chided PTL's finance staff for its treatment of creditors. They "have been lied to, avoided, ignored, and treated in anything but a Christian manner . . . [and] have good cause for mocking God." Accounting was in such disarray, Perkins wrote, that "many people have begun to wonder if the chaos is deliberate to cover something. . . . My dismissal for asking *only superficial* questions, which revealed lies and inconsistent statements, has given me sincere doubts."

Perkins said he could not, in good conscience, allow his integrity and reputation to be tarnished by association with a less-than-upstanding organization. "There is a black and white—a right and a wrong—manner of doing business." Perkins demanded the resignation of Herb Moore, and he asked for an apology to his wife and daughters. "I await your direct, *personal* response."

The letter insulted Bakker. It was just the kind of condemnation Bakker couldn't tolerate, no matter how accurate it was. Perkins got no answer to his letter.

Bakker emerged from his world trip with a renewed passion for missions. Once again, he was ready to declare them PTL's top priority. He promised to send more money to a program for the hungry in India, and his staff drafted a plan to put ten percent of each day's receipts into a separate missions account.

Bakker hardly sounded like the man who had spent millions on Heritage USA. "We cannot continue to evangelize as we have," he told his studio audience on October 11. "It isn't fair to put all our money into the US where there's so much access to the Gospel. We need to put the emphasis overseas, reaching the world."

The next day, PTL's staff packed the studio at Heritage Village to hear Bakker's report on his trip. He was irritated at all that had happened in his absence.

> We have so lowered the level of Christianity that the Body of Christ has become gray and muddy. To bring revival we must fall on our face and ask God to examine our hearts and motives. Because if we don't, we are going to pay for our bickerings, slanderings, and backbiting.
>
> We are keeping back revival because we won't bury our feelings. Don't point your finger at another but at yourself. . . .
>
> Get your eyes off me, and off those around you, and get your eyes on Jesus. . . .
>
> I saw those missionaries [in India], old and young alike, staying up all night to make bread for those hungry children and they receive no pay. They do our work. At least we can

give flour, milk, and provide equipment for their hospital. The least we can do is build orphanages and schools. But no, we have to fight over who is the greatest in the Kingdom of God. . . .

If it wasn't for the souls of men, for what I know this thing can do, I would have quit a long time ago. Because I am tired of the battle of PTL. I'm tired of this living hell I've been through this year.

A harangue from Bakker was not enough to correct the missteps undermining the ministry. PTL soon failed to meet a payroll on time, and Bakker said that without money from his partners "I don't know how this ministry can avoid beginning a sell-off of equipment and property and a close down. There is no way." Bakker acknowledged that some blamed his obsession with Heritage USA for PTL's money crisis. That was a smoke screen for the Devil, he insisted; PTL's real problem was rapid growth. PTL hadn't sent the envelopes that partners needed to mail their monthly pledges, and that, he said, had cost PTL $20 or $30 million.

Bakker was back in the papers soon with another public relations gaffe: he and his family were moving into a $200,000 donated house in Foxcroft, one of Charlotte's priciest neighborhoods. Bakker could sense the toll that the increasingly aggressive local newspaper coverage was taking on his credibility. He believed that the Knight-Ridder newspaper chain, which owned the *Charlotte Observer* and the *Charlotte News,* wanted to destroy religion—a notion that his friend and fellow evangelist Rex Humbard had pressed on Bakker after Humbard's troubles with a Knight-Ridder newspaper in Ohio. Bakker, so quick to play the martyr, pressed his case in a November interview.

It's the sowing of the seed of the questioning all the time. . . . Truth is not damaging. I love the truth. But half of the truth is damaging. . . .

We have nothing to hide, and that's one of the things I resent from the media. . . . You're always looking for some dark secret, a skeleton in the closet. . . .

How would you feel to have many people overlooking your shoulder day after day after day just waiting for you to make a mistake? Waiting for you to fail, like an artist painting a painting . . . [with] somebody behind you looking to see if you're making the wrong stroke. . . .

I figure if I stay honest, and sincere, and continue to do the work that God called me to do, that time will prove I am an honest man, and I'm doing an honest job, and PTL is right. Because I will survive. And I will stay steady. And I will survive through it. And that's what I've got going for me.

Bakker said he was ready to walk away from his job and the public exposure that came with it.

It's pretty hard for a president of a ministry to resign, especially when he's a public spokesman for the ministry. But I would. I would give it all up today if I had my own personal desires.

It's bigger than I am. The budgets are so horrendous that they're not enjoyable to live with in any way, shape, or form. I challenge anyone who'd have to come up with between $1 and $2 million a week to stay alive to want to live with that kind of budget. . . .

I no longer have privacy. . . . I would like to have a family life. I would like to have, but because I love God and love people, and love their lost souls enough, I have devoted my life to reaching them.

Of course Bakker did not resign. But within days he had lost several of his most talented lieutenants. Flessing was the first to go; his was a gentle departure. He told the press that he wanted to reassess his personal priorities, but that he still held a "deep love and appreciation" for Bakker and PTL's staff. Privately, he was frustrated that missions were not getting the priority Bakker had promised so grandly weeks before. Back home, faced with the realities of Heritage USA, Bakker decided that building a new road and repairing the tennis courts were more important than finding $50,000 for a TV show in Japan.

One day during his final weeks, Flessing sat in the executive dining room inside the mansion at Heritage Village as Bakker delivered another inspirational speech to his executives. The veterans had heard it before, particularly the pledge not to start a building project without money in the bank. The weariness showed. Valderrama toyed with a model airplane, another longtime executive drew on the table cloth, and Jim Moss dozed on the sofa.

Within days of Flessing's resignation, Valderrama, vice president of production, announced that he too was leaving. Then PTL's vice president for television quit. Bakker left the door open for all three to return.

For Perkins, there was no warm good-bye. With no answer from Bakker to his last letter, Perkins mailed a resignation to PTL's board in December. He attached his earlier memos to Bakker.

> Off-camera in our day-to-day management operations we have become somewhat less than honorable. . . . Unilateral decisions, with far-reaching legal as well as moral consequences, have been made and implemented without your knowledge and consent, and in some cases, apparently even without the knowledge and consent of the President or his Executive Committee. . . .
>
> The business community will measure our Christianity and see our Christ through our manner of doing business with them. They will never understand a faith that is adequate to build for the Glory of God, but inadequate to pay them *what* we promised *when* we promised.

Three days later, PTL's board gathered for the first time in six months. In attendance were Bakker, Moss, Johnny Johnson, A. T. Lawing, a Charlotte surgeon named Forbes Barton, and several staff members. During the meeting, the board approved amendments to PTL's bylaws. The new bylaws spelled out very specific terms of Bakker's tenure. James O. Bakker was elected president of PTL for life, with power to appoint his successor. He could be removed, the bylaws read, only if found mentally incompetent or convicted of a criminal felony or of immoral conduct.

CHAPTER SEVEN

THE FCC
INVESTIGATION

"If I said it on the air, I believed it"

On January 9, 1979, as Bakker approached his fifth anniversary in Charlotte, he met with *Charlotte Observer* reporters Allen Cowan and Frye Gaillard. The reporters had pieced together an article on PTL's overseas TV programs that would forever change the course of Bakker's ministry. The reporters had learned that PTL had raised hundreds of thousands of dollars for those missions efforts—in Korea and Brazil, chiefly—but had used the money to pay bills at home. In the Blue Room of the Heritage Village mansion, Bakker defended himself.

> Every penny that has been raised will go if it hasn't already gone. When I make a commitment, I don't put a time span on what I do. . . .
>
> You're trying to prove a dark conspiracy. . . . I've got other facts that will [prove] this stuff wrong, and if you want to rush into print you'll just destroy more credibility. The people of the United States don't really believe the *Charlotte Observer* loves PTL.

The reporters pressed Bakker to explain his claim that PTL had 20 million viewers. Bob Manzano, who had concocted the numbers, had acknowledged to the reporters that the claim was a "total fabrication." And, he said, he had told Bakker so the year before. Bakker did not take kindly to being caught. "All right, you guys really got me. You found an error. We made a mistake in judgment. [My public relations man] will correct that mistake. What more can we do, beg your forgiveness?"

Nine days later, the *Observer* published its story across the top of the front page. "The PTL Television Network has diverted hundreds of thousands of dollars contributed for specific overseas missions programs, using the money to finance other projects and pay its bills at home," the article began. The article was firm, but balanced. Bakker was quoted. Bill Perkins and Roger Flessing, sources for the story along with Manzano, were given a chance in print to say that they still believed in Bakker and were convinced that he intended to honor his commitments overseas, eventually.

Flessing recalled Bakker's table-banging declaration the summer before that he wanted his missions commitments fulfilled. "But nothing changed," Flessing told the newspaper. "That's Bakker's problem. He thinks that saying it makes it true."

Externally sincere in his on-air declarations, Bakker had trouble keeping his passion alive off the set; he had a short attention span. "His concerns would change. That is the nature of his personality. At times, he would be interested in missions. At other times, he could care less," Manzano later told federal investigators. The plodding job of building TV programs in faraway countries—shows hosted by someone else and played to a distant audience—offered little food for Bakker's craving for change, excitement, and self-glorification.

It would be a source of frustration to Bakker's staff for years to come. Bakker would unveil his projects with great enthusiasm and flourish. But soon he would be on to the next project, often creating impediments—financial and otherwise—to the completion of his earlier dreams.

One PTL vice president likened Bakker to a dragon. While his staff tried to make Bakker's ideas work, he would spin around and propose something new for another part of the ministry. As the dragon turned, his tail would knock down all that his staff had built in trying to execute his earlier ideas. Then Bakker would look back and see the wreckage and ask, Why can't we get things right?

Bakker attributed his steady stream of new projects to the urgency of accomplishing all that PTL could in the final days before the Second Coming of Christ. Bakker's new ideas served a more practical purpose—they gave PTL's partners further reason to give to Bakker's ministry. Imperceptibly, more and more of the substance of Bakker's ministry became a means to perpetuate the institution. Instead of listening to God, some PTL employees thought, Bakker was focusing his energies on finding ways to raise money.

The three executives quoted in the *Observer*'s front-page story had been unable to change Bakker. The men had agreed to talk on the record, they said, because they were unwilling to tolerate a pattern of deception and misinformation plaguing the ministry.

The *Observer* story forced Bakker to account for his failure to follow through with his on-air promises and for his misleading words. In his five years in Charlotte, Jim Bakker had cemented his internal control over the PTL ministry. Many of those who objected to his misdeeds had left. Now, for the first time, he would be held accountable to a higher force with the power to punish him—the federal government.

A few days before the *Observer*'s story appeared, a letter arrived in Bakker's office from former vice president Bill Perkins. Perkins wanted Bakker to know why he had given an interview to the newspaper.

> I am convinced now that had we cooperated with the newspapers they would have been far more sympathetic about mistakes and errors in judgment. However, when they became convinced that some executives were trying to cover their wrongs and then you attacked them for printing what facts they did have (and there were no lies printed), they felt no obligation to show any special sympathy. In fact, they became suspicious.

Perkins challenged Bakker to read the newspaper's story with an open mind.

> There are two questions you must ask yourself about their article when you read it: is it true and are the inaccuracies, if any, due to your refusal to provide them with the correct

information? If it is true, are you angry because the truth in their article is embarrassing?

On January 18, the day the story appeared, Bakker condemned the article as untrue on his daily program. "All of our missionary commitments for 1978, all committed funds that you have sent to me, have been paid except the Asian fund . . . contrary to any rumors or innuendos." Bakker made no mention of PTL's unmet promise to McAlister of more than $100,000. In a broadcast later that month, Bakker dismissed the story as hearsay, gossip, lies, and half-truths. "There's nothing worse than a half-truth and a truth together because it's still a lie."

The morning of the *Observer*'s story, Bakker gave a $56,000 check to Elias Malki, the Lebanese missionary Bakker had promoted on his program in late 1977. PTL had collected that sum for Malki's proposed transmitter in Cyprus. But PTL had held the money after Manzano had discovered that the project—aimed at introducing Christian radio broadcasts to the Middle East—would cost millions. Manzano had also uncovered troubling information about Malki's personal style, program quality, and Arabic skills. To compound matters, Malki had worked as a courier for CBN. "One cannot be in two ships at the same time," Manzano had written to Malki.

Malki had buttonholed Bakker in Singapore, however, and Bakker had promised he would give Malki every cent PTL had received for Cyprus. In October 1978, Bakker asked Malki to appear on the "PTL Club" sometime that fall. A few days before Malki's arrival in January 1979—as the *Observer* story was being prepared—Bakker ordered a check drawn for Malki.

Bakker did so over his staff's objections: finance director Moore and executive vice president Moss thought the transmitter would never be built. They argued that giving the money to Malki violated PTL's duty to its donors to see that their money was wisely spent. But Bakker wanted to save face, to make good on his word no matter what. As Moss remembered, "Mr. Bakker was real concerned . . . the article had appeared, and he is saying, 'I want it all paid, I want it all paid.' "

For years afterwards, Bakker's staff dogged Malki for an accounting of the money and progress on the Cyprus project. Three years later, Malki informed Bakker's staff that he was still negotiating for property in Cyprus. By 1989 the proposal for a Cyprus transmitter had been dropped altogether.

Like Bill Perkins, university dean Brooks Sanders found Bakker's style of leadership insidious. When Bakker stood and declared "the Lord told me," others were powerless to object. The invocation of God's name could cover all sorts of excesses. Sanders saw Bakker playing with his employees' lives as if they were toy dolls, and he found Bakker's demeanor in sharp contrast to the kind, gracious manner of many on Sanders' staff at PTL.

As the university opened in fall 1978, Bakker finally grasped the cost of his ambitious proposals. By early winter, he had decided to change the school to an unaccredited internship program. Sanders was given only five employees to run the whole school. He felt fresh out of miracles and soon accepted an offer of six months' severance pay. PTL announced that it would offer one-year internships. Within a few years, PTL would drop those as well, reducing the school to an apprenticeship program. The building that donors had underwritten as a home for PTL's university would instead house PTL's headquarters, including Bakker's office.

In February 1979, Bakker faced what he most feared: a mutiny on the board. Several directors were unhappy with Bakker's leadership. The board had told Bakker gently in late 1978 to hire a general manager; he had too much to do at PTL to run everything, they said. In the early weeks of 1979, Bakker's critics on the board considered replacing him as PTL's top operating executive, leaving him with the duties of TV host. As Moss remembered it, he halted the coup, refusing to convene a board meeting until Bakker—then in Florida—was present to hear the directors.

Once Moss had been one of Bakker's most valued associates. Moss, forty-seven, complemented Bakker nicely. He had roots and connections in the Carolinas, he was tall, good-looking, and athletic, and he possessed the seamless charm of a master salesman. While Bakker offended the community, Moss worked to appease it. He was not, however, without his critics. Some found him vain, many considered him too political, and others questioned his veracity.

By summer 1978, Bakker had removed Moss as executive producer of the "PTL Club," a position he had given Moss four years before. Early in the new year, Bakker asked Moss to take the job back. Moss refused. He no longer wanted to work that closely with Bakker, preferring instead to work with the stations carrying PTL's program.

> I told him if he wanted me out of the ministry all he would have to do was ask me as a friend. . . . He convinced me that he wanted me worse than any man he has ever been associated with. . . . that he owed me a great debt of gratitude, and that he had failed me in his allegiance and loyalty to me. And he apologized for that.

Bakker's enthusiasm quickly faded; underneath, Bakker felt threatened by Moss. When Moss arrived at a Valentine's Day board meeting, he found a security guard blocking the door. One of Bakker's secretaries asked him to wait in his office. After 30 minutes, Moss was called in. Bakker wanted him to resign. Moss refused. As Moss recalled, Bakker warned the board he would resign—and leave the board to come up with the money to pay millions of dollars of debt—if Moss was not dismissed.

Bakker complained that his remaining vice presidents had objected to Moss's continued service; they believed that PTL with Bakker and Moss both in positions of power was a "two-headed monster," and one head had to go. Moss reminded Bakker that the vice presidents' assessment made Bakker a monster as well. "If that be the case, maybe both of us need to go," Moss said. Bakker didn't care for the suggestion. Bakker also suspected, incorrectly, Moss said, that he intended to profit personally from a separate advertising agency he was setting up. In fact, Moss said, any commissions the agency collected when it purchased air time for PTL would have gone to the ministry, not to him.

Inside the meeting room, Moss challenged Bakker. "Just you be a man and look me in the eye and say, 'Jim, you're fired' and I'll walk out of here." Bakker kept his eyes turned away. Then, Moss castigated the other board members for weakness. "I would have liked for them to stand up and say, 'Jim Bakker, this is the last time you are going to threaten to resign and leave the indebtedness to the board.' All they had to do was call his bluff."

Instead, the directors urged Moss to resign, and they agreed to give him a generous severance settlement. To director Forbes Barton, it seemed there was no chance for PTL to function with both Moss and Bakker working in the ministry. To remove Bakker would invite a pitched battle for control—after all, just two months before the board had essentially voted Bakker president for life—and the mass defection of his mesmerized TV audience.

Moss insisted on being fired. Moss, the sixth PTL vice president to leave in four months, spoke bluntly to reporters later that day. "He's afraid of me. He's afraid I want to be president . . . You couldn't give me the presidency of PTL."

As Moss departed, Barton, a surgeon in Charlotte who had come on the board shortly after Larry Hall was forced off, had reached the conclusion that Bakker was a paranoid surrounded by inferior people who would not threaten him. In early 1979, Bakker had recommended hiring an out-of-town consultant, but the board—leery of the man's background—refused to give their OK. As Barton remembered, Bakker hired the man anyway and told his staff not to tell the board. Barton found out, stormed into an executive staff meeting and called Bakker a liar. Several days later, Barton resigned from the board, convinced that PTL's situation was hopeless.

Early March brought more bad press. The *Observer* reported that PTL was helping a PTL vice president who owed more than $100,000 to skirt his creditors. PTL had kept the vice president's house in its name, protecting it from confiscation; the ministry made the monthly mortgage payments and then deducted the tab from the employee's paycheck. The vice president, who had produced at least one of the Bakkers' albums during their tenure at CBN, had incurred most of the debts in recording and gospel-singing businesses he owned before joining PTL. As he traveled around the country performing in telethons for PTL, the ministry began getting calls complaining about his unpaid debts. In its eagerness to accommodate a member of the inner circle, PTL was willing to flout the most basic standards of corporate integrity.

A few days after that revelation, PTL began laying off as many as one-fourth of its eight hundred workers and shelving its plans for a children's program, a comedy show, and a Christian soap opera—the alternative television that Bakker had for so long claimed he wanted to produce. PTL had begun operating its twenty-four-hour all-Christian satellite network nearly a year before, in April 1978. Although its technology was state-of-the-art, its programming remained little more than the traditional Sunday-ghetto shows.

As the next workweek began on March 12, investigators from the Federal Communications Commission arrived at Heritage Village. They had come to look into the allegations that PTL had misspent the money raised over the air to fund overseas TV programs. The investigators' mission was informal but serious. Federal law prohibits raising money over television or radio for one purpose and spending it on another. Breaking that law can cost the owner of the TV station his broadcast license and his freedom.

At first, PTL assured the FCC that it would cooperate. Soon it adopted a contrary posture, informing the investigators that no documents or employees would be available until PTL's board met on April 19. It was the sort of brush-off PTL could give an inquiring newspaper but a dangerous response to give the US agency empowered to regulate American broadcasting. The FCC became suspicious and telegrammed orders to comply; the agency wrote that its jurisdiction was "abundantly clear." The FCC had no direct means to control a company that merely produced TV shows, but it did have authority over a company, religious or secular, that owned an American TV station. PTL's holdings included WJAN, the TV station in Canton, Ohio. If PTL refused to cooperate, the telegram warned, the FCC might have to revoke its license in Canton.

Bakker rallied his forces. "If I ever leave the air and we're not there, I want you to know it's not because I wanted to," he told viewers that week. "PTL is in the greatest crisis of our lives." Bakker announced that he would march on Washington with a hundred thousand Christians "to demand the right to preach the Gospel of Jesus Christ without harassment."

He declared that he was innocent. "There has never been any intention of wrongdoing. Seventeen years of keeping my ministry clean is going to pay off." He claimed that the *Observer* had made exposing PTL its number-one goal for 1979 and that he had inside documents to prove it. He vowed to spend $1 million to fight the FCC, and he promised to write a book, *You're Under Investigation,* to detail his last six months of harassment. "It's a conspiracy," he said.

A year of crises and bad press and now the ominous threat of an FCC investigation had stripped away the new era of "maturity" Bakker had declared to viewers in early January. The raging child inside the middle-aged minister was laid bare: combative, paranoid, unwilling to admit his own failures, and quick to use his weapon—television—to lash out at authority. Under fire, Bakker's "reality" lost any reasonable relation to what occurred around him. He believed and believed fervently. In his impassioned hands, television, the medium of make-believe, authenticated his reality.

Though he might seem outlandish to a secular audience, Bakker had the Teflon shell with his followers that another skilled actor, Ronald Reagan, was soon to display in the White House. Bakker could make his partners believe in him as resolutely as he believed in himself. Good acting helped, as did his constituency's distance from Charlotte; scattered over the country, few ever saw the *Observer*'s articles documenting PTL's mistakes. Instead, they heard only Bakker's version, and it often sounded persuasive.

The full-gospel culture also strengthened Bakker's hand. Many Pentecostals had tasted mainline America's social and theological disdain for "holy rollers." Emotionally, they could believe in some conspiracy against their kind. The PTL world was trusting and hierarchical; for most partners, it was second nature to defer to the pastor and church leaders. And for many, the notion of Satanic attack was doctrinally sound and entirely believable. The Devil, just like scheming government agencies and newspapers, served as a convenient distraction for the shortcomings of PTL's leader.

With Bakker holding the flag, his troops counterattacked. Within days, the FCC was deluged with thousands of letters from PTL supporters and hundreds of calls from congressmen inquiring about the case. By the close of March 1979, Bakker had proclaimed the FCC inquiry a witch-hunt and announced that he would not acquiesce to the FCC's request for videotapes and financial records. Bakker said that he had nothing to hide but did not want to waive PTL's constitutional rights or risk hurting religious broadcasting. The National Religious Broadcasters didn't share his concern; the organization urged Bakker to cooperate.

On March 30, 1979, the five FCC commissioners unanimously agreed to open a formal, private investigation because PTL had refused to cooperate. What might have once been a routine inquiry was now to consume Bakker's attention for years.

Despite his claims of innocence, Bakker took steps to mend his reputation with PTL's missionary partners in Brazil and Korea. On March 20, he sent Robert McAlister a check for $25,000 and an apology "for any inconvenience that has been caused you by our cash crisis." He promised future support but said he could not guarantee when it would come. Three weeks later, he sent another $25,000, but asked McAlister not to cash the check for thirty days. By year's end, PTL would begin helping McAlister produce the Brazilian television show.

In May, Bakker drafted a letter to Cho. The night before, he wrote, the Lord had encouraged him to send a $350,000 check.

> Pastor, I want you to know I'm a man of my word. . . .
>
> I know that our delays have put you in an intenable [*sic*] personal situation. It hurts and shames me that PTL would be the cause of embarrassment for any ministry. I have wanted so badly for us to bless others. Especially, it is such a personal loss for me to feel we let down someone like yourself, who I have so admired. . . .
>
> Christian America has been so selfish. We at PTL have been trying to set a precedence of giving and generosity that will encourage other media ministries to do the same. In your eyes, I guess we failed. . . . But our intentions were good. . . .
>
> The Devil has tried to embitter me over this and at times I have felt that PTL would be better off avoiding Mission promises, but God has convinced me that is wrong.

On the suggestion of his advisers, Bakker never sent the letter. Instead, he gave the foreign-missions office of the Assemblies of God $350,000 to underwrite Christian TV in Asia. Bakker had finally fulfilled his impulsive two-year-old promise to Cho.

On the eve of the FCC inquiry, an incoming PTL board member named Richard Dortch approached an old acquaintance, Ed Stoeckel, at a church meeting in Memphis. Dortch served as district superintendent for the Assemblies of God in Illinois, a position equivalent to bishop in other denominations. Stoeckel was a layman in the denomination. Stoeckel's wife and Dortch had worshipped in the same church as children, and Stoeckel's family church east of St. Louis fell under Dortch's jurisdiction. PTL needed help, Dortch told Stoeckel, who had never heard of the Charlotte ministry.

The son of a construction worker, Stoeckel had grown up in Belleville, Illinois. After college and graduate school, he worked his way up the corporate ladder to a post in operations in Ralston Purina's consumer products division. Later he served as an executive on the engineering side for several big grain firms.

As word of the FCC investigation broke in the local papers, Bakker and Stoeckel met in Charlotte. Bakker found him "more reserved and dignified than the people I was used to." A week later, Stoeckel was summoned back. Though he had not yet accepted the job of executive vice president, he learned upon his arrival that Bakker had already announced he was coming. The PTL staff gave Stoeckel a prolonged standing ovation.

Bakker announced that he had decided to step "out of management" and was giving Stoeckel responsibility for all of PTL's daily operations. "I will become more involved with ministry and long-range planning." He had put too much faith in God, he said. "Every corporation reaches the point when, if the founder-manager doesn't allow others to take over, it will be a disaster." PTL had enough visionaries, Bakker said; now it needed someone to control the vision. If Stoeckel opposed a new project, Bakker said, "I wouldn't do it." He promised that PTL would live within its budget.

Stoeckel, fifty-four, described himself to the press as a firm businessman. "Jim has definitely said to me he doesn't want a yes-man. I would not come as a yes-man." The Lord's business—and money—required careful handling, Stoeckel said. PTL's bills now ran around $3.5 million a month.

As he began unraveling the mess, Stoeckel lived up to his own advertising. He proposed selling Heritage USA and possibly leasing back the buildings PTL needed—a proposal that put Bakker in a state of shock. He shut down Heritage Academy, the grade school populated largely by the children of Bakker's staff. Herb Moore, PTL's finance director and Bill Perkins's nemesis, was fired.

Stoeckel rebuilt PTL's image. He released an audit for 1977–78, which PTL had withheld the year before. Along with that audit, Stoeckel issued an August 31 balance sheet showing marked improvement. PTL pledged to release its audits annually. It applied for membership in a new accountability group, the Evangelical Council for Financial Accountability.

PTL's partners made Stoeckel's job easier. In March, April, and May, donors gave $5 million more than PTL needed to cover daily expenses. Stoeckel wiped out PTL's past-due debts. He put PTL on a $3-million-a-month budget. In July 1979, the *Observer* pronounced PTL on the road to recovery, thanks to Stoeckel.

Bakker sensed the change. "It's a more mature kind of morale than it's been in the past. Less euphoric and more solid somehow." But he acknowledged to an interviewer that he mourned the loss of total control.

> This corporation has grown up, and I'm not the father anymore. It's an adjustment, and I'm not totally adjusted yet. I designed every inch of all this. There's not a carpet on the floor that I did not choose the color of. But the change is good. We simply couldn't keep going the way we were.

He added that by forcing PTL to look at itself, the critical newspaper articles and even the FCC inquiry would help the ministry in the long run.

PTL caught a glimpse of what the organization could be without Bakker in absolute control. For a moment, it seemed, there was hope.

In a city of majestic government edifices, the eight-story home of the Federal Communications Commission is a homely presence. To former PTL missions director Bob Manzano, arriving the morning of June 22, 1979, the FCC's offices inside 1919 M Street seemed surprisingly spare. Manzano was to be the first witness before the FCC's investigators, led by government attorney Larry Bernstein. Swearing to testify truthfully, Manzano took a seat next to administrative law judge Thomas Fitzpatrick. The hearing room was perhaps twenty feet by thirty feet, with room for an audience. On this day, there was none; the hearing was closed.

As he spoke that day, Manzano pointed a gentle finger at Bakker. He had given his boss weekly reports of his activities, so Bakker knew the problems he was having. Bakker, he said, was a man without the intestinal fortitude to discuss bad news. He was with-drawn by nature too, Manzano said. "Just to be very frank, people just don't get to know Jim Bakker. He is a very closed individual. He's not the type of person that you can have a cup of coffee and get to know within fifteen minutes."

Manzano boasted about his qualifications: he spoke five lan-guages, he said, had traveled to eighty-six countries, and held a master's degree in theology and a doctorate—the degree he had obtained from the California correspondence school. Other PTL employees were not qualified for their work, he said, and no other executives were particularly articulate or well educated. Bakker, he said, did not know the Bible well.

Perkins was the FCC's second witness. He added little new infor-mation during his two-day appearance; his letters and memos had already told his story. As the date of Perkins's court appearance approached, Bakker had telephoned the former vice president to complain about comments Perkins had made to ABC's "20/20" news program. Bakker opened the call invoking Scripture: if you have aught against a brother, he said, you are to go to a brother. Yes, Perkins answered, but he had nothing against Bakker as a brother.

"Why are you trying to destroy me and the ministry?"

"I'm not trying to do either of those things, Jim."

Bakker pressed, complaining that he didn't understand Perkins's decision to talk to the media. Perkins reminded Bakker that the PTL president had himself given a ninety-minute interview to a local TV station. He had branded the newspaper's sources—includ-ing Perkins, by implication—as "tools of Satan," uninformed and "mentally ill."

> Jim said he was referring to a letter written by a mentally ill woman. . . . I pointed out that I was aware of who he was talking about, but that woman had written that letter nearly a year before, and the people who heard him on TV would never make the connection between that woman's letter and the current newspaper stories he was attacking which quoted the names of Roger Flessing, Bill Perkins, and Bob Manzano. I also pointed out that his own staff made comments to both myself and Roger Flessing about our being "mentally ill," in

jest of course. I told Jim that his charges of lies and inaccuracies notwithstanding, Roger Flessing and I both knew that the facts and figures in the news stories were accurate.

Bakker seemed eager to shake Perkins's resolve. He accused his former vice president of "playing God," suggested the documents Perkins had might have been stolen, and implied that he would question Perkins's management abilities during his upcoming interview with an ABC reporter.

"I'm not afraid of anything you say to . . . ABC or to anyone else." Perkins said.

"What should I tell Don [Farmer, of ABC] when he asks me about what you've said?"

"Just tell the truth, Jim, and neither of us will have anything to fear."

Bakker was worried that TV stations might drop the "PTL Club" if the FCC ruled unfavorably.

> If this happened, Jim said that I would be responsible for all the "souls" that went to hell because of not hearing the Gospel from the PTL TV programs. Needless to say, I told Jim that I refused to accept that, and pointed out that I had performed my responsibility nine months earlier when I tried to get his attention and he refused to even acknowledge receipt of my correspondence, let alone discuss the issues.

Moss, whom Bakker had forced out six months before, followed Perkins before the FCC. He testified that he had learned not to speak out on financial matters if he wanted to keep peace with Bakker. He prodded his boss in what he called a "love manner," not with derogation. "We had a statement at PTL that you fall 'out of favor' or 'out of grace' " with Bakker. Bakker was happiest when Moss used his talents as a salesman to produce or market Bakker's work, Moss said.

Moss's testimony was more supportive than Manzano's.

> I have never met a minister anywhere in the world that would give to projects like that. He might deprive his cameramen getting a raise, but he would never deprive a ministry of giving

what he committed to. . . . No matter how I disagree with Mr.
Bakker as an administrator and as a businessman, I will never
challenge his heart and his intention to meet every single one
of those commitments. I have said that since day one.

Moss had found Bakker particularly eager to help Assemblies of
God ministers like Cho. "He grew up in [the denomination]
. . . and I think he chose to impress them, and he wanted to be
accepted by his own denomination. . . . I think he wanted to impress
his peers."

Moss had seen Heritage USA become Bakker's top priority,
more important than ministering to people and converting souls,
the work to which Bakker had once seemed dedicated. Many partners had abandoned PTL because of Bakker's new direction, Moss
said. "I was the one who had to talk with them. He never did."

By fall 1979, prosperity gospel had equaled, if not surpassed, miracles of healing in Bakker's TV ministry. A thoughtful analysis of
Bakker in *Christianity Today* magazine captured the changes.

> [Bakker] flares up at people who blame America for oppres-
> sively contributing to the world's poverty, asserting that the
> original principles of America—such as the freedom of man
> and free enterprise—are biblical principles that naturally result
> in success. Bakker's Christianity is not a counter-culture; it is
> a superculture, a realization of the very best the world has to
> offer.
>
> How does Bakker handle such passages as the one where
> Jesus tells the rich young ruler to sell all he has? "Keep read-
> ing," he says. "Later in that chapter Jesus says everything we
> give up will be returned to us. What would have happened if
> the rich young ruler had given all to serve Jesus? I sincerely
> believe he probably would have moved up in his ruling class.
> Everywhere we turn Jesus was preaching an abundant, full
> life."
>
> In television Jim Bakker has found a perfect vehicle for his
> promises of health and wealth. . . . It is a miserable platform
> for discussing complexity and struggle, and hosts who try to
> represent life's complexity, such as Dick Cavett, are eventually
> relegated to the minority viewing audience of public televi-
> sion. Inevitably, a Christian faith tailored for a TV audience
> comes across as scrubbed-up, incomplete.

Suited for American television, Bakker's theology also made a tidy fit with the changing circumstances of his personal life and ministry. Six years earlier, Jim and Tammy Bakker had lived in a travel trailer and had driven from city to city hosting telethons at struggling TV stations. Now they resided in a 4,500-square-foot home with four bedrooms and 3.5 baths and owned a second home on a lake where Bakker could use his new houseboat. Once crammed into a tiny office, broadcasting on a single TV station, PTL now owned the picture-perfect Heritage Village and the retreat at Heritage USA and broadcast over a nationwide network of TV stations. If God got the credit for the transformation, then certainly He was endorsing PTL, Bakker, and his prosperity gospel.

On November 14, nearly five months after the FCC began taking testimony, Jim Bakker sat before FCC attorney Larry Bernstein for the first of a series of appearances over the next seven months. "I have absolutely nothing to hide from anyone," Bakker announced as he began. Bakker came with plenty of reinforcements: three lawyers and PTL's new finance director. Bakker seemed ill at ease. He couldn't remember the year he was ordained. "I'm not good at figures and dates," he explained. He needed help spelling Paul Crouch's name. "Spelling is not one of my better points, either," he said.

Bakker depicted PTL as a mom-and-pop business overwhelmed by its success. Yes, PTL had made mistakes—no research before his spontaneous, overly ambitious promises to other ministries, for one. No, he wasn't a businessman. "We were just a group of guys that got together with a vision. And so, in missions most of it was how we felt led of God. . . . I believed God could do anything." Now his ministry had budget controls, Bakker said, and it wasn't going to overcommit to any project.

That first day, the FCC's Bernstein, a one-time advertising copy-writer for whom law was a second career, pressed Bakker to describe what he had told viewers about the overseas TV programs. Had he ever said he would limit his support to Cho to what donors designated for the Asian programs? Before he committed to building Heritage USA, did he check one financial document, talk to one accountant or look at one piece of research to see if PTL could afford the project?

Bakker declared his good intentions; this time it was the FCC's turn to hear the squeaky-clean speech. "I'm an honorable man, and I would die before I would not follow through on a commitment. . . . I have always been very concerned about accountability to our partners and honesty in accounting of every dollar that comes into our ministry and wanting it to go where the people wish it to go."

Near the close of the day, Bakker began to blame Manzano. He accused his former missions director of insulting Cho and of negotiating the $150,000 agreement with McAlister without informing him. Manzano, he told the FCC later, had been terminated for "many, many causes . . . a long history."

Bakker returned the next day. The thirty-eight-year-old Bernstein pressed Bakker to explain his leadership. Bakker talked about faith—the supernatural notion that defied the rational judgments that Bakker sensed behind the FCC investigator's questions and had encountered from critics like Perkins and the newspapers.

> I don't think you totally understand faith, and everything we have ever done at PTL, we have never had the money in the bank. . . . God supplied all the money, and we have to look at things scripturally . . . the Bible tells us that "without faith, it is impossible to please him. . . . Faith is the substance of things not seen, the evidence of things hoped for." And so you can't measure faith in dollars and cents. You can't say "I've got it in the bank." . . .
>
> I know it seems ridiculous . . . perhaps you could understand that I am not a businessman. I am a minister, and faith is what motivates us, not fact.

Bakker acknowledged a preference for doing things fast. "I like to do things today," he said. "That is a flaw perhaps in my personality."

Two months earlier, the FCC had received more than two hundred hours of "PTL Club" tapes. With transcripts in his hands, Bernstein pressed Bakker to explain his optimistic statements on the air while preparations for the overseas programs encountered delay after delay. Had he ever told his TV audience that it might be quite a while before there was a Korean PTL? Bernstein asked. Bakker had not, of course. He told Bernstein that he had assumed that his staff was working on Korea to make good on his commitment.

Late that afternoon, the FCC lawyer pressed Bakker to enumerate the factual errors contained in a letter Cho had sent Bakker earlier that year. Bakker consulted his lawyer before answering.

> The Scriptures are very clear that we're not to call our brother a liar, and it's very dangerous before God. And I cannot in my own religious conscience and spiritual conscience answer that question, if it would be all right. . . . I'm finding it very difficult for me.

Bernstein explained that he was not asking Bakker to call Cho a liar, only to note any inaccuracies. The presiding judge pressed Bakker to answer. Bakker agreed, but reluctantly.

> Dr. Cho said in his message that he had built a studio just for PTL. . . . He said because we were slow in coming through, that he would have to tear down this expensive building. But the facts are, the building was already built.
>   And I have betrayed a brother.

At that, the hearing closed. Bakker was in tears.

That night, an associate of Bakker's told the press—with Bakker's OK—that Bakker had cried when asked to betray a Christian friend during his testimony. The associate, Doug Wead, declined to say who the Christian friend was. In a taped message to his viewers, Bakker called the session "the hardest day of my life . . . I hope to God I never have to go through what I went through today," he said, his voice breaking. "I think I would choose to go to jail."

If criticism constituted betrayal, Bakker had already "betrayed a Christian brother" with his testimony about Manzano. His comments about Cho were mild by comparison. If Bakker had betrayed Cho, it was by his failure to make sure that PTL fulfilled his promises on time. With his show of martyrdom, Bakker turned himself once again into the victim.

Soon, Bakker began openly challenging Bernstein. With Judge Fitzpatrick handy, he had someone to appeal to for help. "Your Honor, every time I try to explain it seems like the [FCC] counsel gets upset with me," Bakker said. Fitzpatrick warned Bernstein not to display his feelings, and Bernstein apologized. Bakker, acutely sensitive to the disapproval of others, explained his feelings to Bernstein.

> I really feel in my heart that the FCC attorneys don't really want to hear my side of anything. It seems like you have already made up your mind that I am a guilty man and you would like to see me hung.

Bernstein pressed Bakker to explain why he had waited eight months after meeting Cho in Korea to give the Assemblies of God the $350,000 donation for Asian television that Cho had turned down.

> Bakker: I don't have a reason why I waited. I am sorry.
>
> Bernstein: Was it because of the commission's investigation [that you made the $350,000 payment]?
>
> Bakker: No, it was not. . . . I am a busy man. I go on the air every day. I have much activity. I have world-wide activities.

Bakker couldn't seem to recall much about the Brazilian outreach. He couldn't remember raising money specifically for McAlister, as he had. He couldn't remember pledges coming in earmarked for Brazil, as they had. Pressed further, Bakker complained about Manzano. It had been Manzano's job to handle problems. Bakker had been busy, he testified, "building a college where I was out tramping around every day, laying out roads and buildings, and working day in and day out for the Lord."

Bernstein bored in. Why was Manzano unable to get checks approved to pay the $50,000 a month promised to McAlister?

> Bakker: I've always, always said pay missionary commitments right up top. They're important. It's part of our ministry. . . . I've had to change staff members, and we have rectified this situation.
>
> Bernstein: Well, who didn't carry through, Mr. Bakker? Dr. Manzano . . . tried to get a check paid. Apparently, the check wasn't paid, so who didn't follow through?
>
> Bakker: I did not sign check approvals. . . . I would have to look at the bank balance. . . . I would believe in the year 1978

we would have a daily average bank balance of . . . maybe $900,000 a day, so I would presume there was money in the bank accounts to pay those bills. . . .

Bernstein: Can you tell us then why Dr. McAlister wasn't paid in 1978? If it wasn't for lack of money, why was it?

Bakker: . . . There was a lack of communications from the missions department to accounting, I presume. They did not follow through on my directives to pay all missions accounts. We have memos backing that statement, and that is something that has always been my policy and will always be my policy.

His testimony over for the afternoon, Bakker emerged from the hearing room and condemned the FCC lawyers as "back-room bureaucrats [who] could put a black name on my ministry. . . . They are trying to trick me." Bakker appealed to the FCC to open the investigation to the public. "We like the truth, and we feel truth doesn't have to be hidden."

The next week, Bernstein began to challenge the PTL president more pointedly about his statements over the air. Again and again, using videotapes of Bakker, Bernstein showed Bakker deceiving his public. Why had he claimed on June 15, 1977, two days after he and Cho agreed to air a program in Korea, that Cho had a beautiful concert hall to house the show, when in fact Cho had only a gymnasium-auditorium? Bakker stumbled.

I believe everything I have said on the air is true, as I said it on the air. I have never made a false statement that I disbelieved on television in my lifetime. . . . If I said it on the air, I believed it.

Why, Bernstein asked, had he told viewers on June 21, 1977, that he planned to start the Korean program in thirty to sixty days? Bakker was unable to answer. The prosecutor continued.

Bernstein: Was it your practice to make statements to your audience without knowing the facts?

Bakker's lawyer: Objection, Your Honor. I think the witness has testified.

Judge: That will be overruled. Could you answer that?

Bakker reached for his Bible. At Bernstein's request, the judge intervened, asking Bakker to please answer the question and not to read aloud.

> Bakker: I am a minister. I am not a businessman. And I think when the FCC is investigating a minister it must understand the thinking and the philosophy and the spiritual tenor of what we do.

Bakker read from Scripture about faith, as he would do repeatedly during his testimony.

> "For verily I say unto you, that whosoever shall say unto this mount, Be thou removed and be thou cast into the sea, and shall not doubt in his heart, but shall believe that those things which he sayeth shall come to pass, he shall have whatsoever he sayeth." You speak in faith that God is going to do the work. And you must understand faith to understand ministries. . . . My whole life is built in faith.

Bernstein repeated his question: had Bakker made statements on the air without checking his facts? Bakker again insisted that at the time he believed everything he said on the air. "So," Bernstein asked, "the answer is yes to my question, is that correct?" Bernstein pressed on. What about the July 1977 claim that Cho had "given" PTL a building in Korea. Or the claim that same month that PTL had an ongoing ministry in Korea?

Bakker's lawyer, John Midlen, objected, complaining that the prosecutor was questioning his client about statements he had made as he prayed on the show. "I don't believe that is an appropriate subject to be part of this record."

Bernstein responded. "Your Honor, Mr. Bakker may be in prayer a lot, but I don't think there is any law that says you are not held accountable for things you say while you are in prayer." The judge sided with Bernstein.

After a break for the Thanksgiving holiday, Bernstein resumed his questioning. "What was the basis of your statement?" he asked repeatedly, directing Bakker to his own words from transcripts of the "PTL Club." In October 1977, Bakker had said that PTL was ready to ship cameras. In fact, the cameras had not been purchased.

Bakker said in October 1977 that it would be "just a matter of days" before the Asian programs began; this was also untrue. Bakker claimed in November 1977 that Korea and Japan were being reached and that the people of Brazil would receive the Gospel within a few weeks.

> Bakker: We were working on these [Asian] projects.
>
> Bernstein: Is that what "are being reached" means to you, Mr. Bakker?
>
> Bakker: I think you would have to review all the tapes in order and see what I am saying. I think to pull sentences really out of context of what has been said, you know, you just cannot give a full report.
>
> Bernstein: But your testimony is that you intended to convey on this date that this was simply going forward, not that it was actually happening?
>
> Bakker: Yes sir. . . .
>
> Bernstein: On November 23, 1977, had the Brazilian "PTL Club" purchased any time on any Brazilian stations to broadcast the program?
>
> Bakker: I cannot say. I do not know.
>
> Bernstein: Is it not a fact that when you made the statement about Brazil, that is the statement about the next few weeks, that there was no possibility of reaching 110 million people in Brazil within the next weeks with the "PTL Club"?
>
> Bakker: I believe the statement as I said it. I believed one hundred percent when I gave it on the air.

Bernstein pressed Bakker to explain his motives, asking whether he was trying to stimulate his audience to give PTL money with the "good news" he reported.

> Bakker: My intention is always on every telethon to share as much information about what PTL is doing around the world and in the United States to inform the people.
>
> Bernstein: Would you raise a lot of money for Korea if you got on the air during a telethon and said we have hit a lot of snags and we are not getting anywhere and there is a duty problem that we are not going to be able to, to solve, until we get a lot

more money and we still have got all these other problems, and you didn't give them any hope of a quick resolution? . . .

Did you ever recall getting on the air and saying, "Well, we really meant it could take as long as years to cover all of Latin America"? . . . Did you ever get on the air and inform your audience that the project in Korea was back on hold, that you were not moving full speed ahead? . . .

Bakker: It would be my general policy to inform the people on just about everything that was happening to our spontaneous program.

Bakker complained that his statements were taken out of context; Bernstein replied that the FCC had included every reference to missions it could find on Bakker's TV program. Bakker accused Manzano of being derelict in his duty. Bernstein, recalling Bakker's tears at "betraying" Cho, suggested a contradiction.

Bernstein: Why is it that you apparently don't feel the same kind of unhappiness about repeatedly, to use your word, "betraying" Brother Manzano? . . .

Bakker: When you state a fact, that a man did not carry forth the job that you expect him to do, is that dishonoring the man? You are asking me questions of what went on at PTL, and I am trying to the best of my ability, with all truth, to tell you exactly what I have in my heart and exactly what went on.

Bakker seemed to see no inconsistency. Perhaps he also wouldn't see the contradiction when, years later, he told his TV audience he had never lifted a finger to hurt his enemies in the FCC investigation, "never even testified against them. . . . I took all the blame, and I let it all fall on this ministry."

On November 30, the last of his nine days of testimony, Bakker had a second opportunity to articulate PTL's defense under gentle questioning from his own attorney. As testimony to his character, Bakker explained his ties to the Assemblies of God denomination.

Assemblies of God is known as one of the finest ministries. It is well known in our circle that you are a minister in good standing in America. . . . They have great church disciplines— there must be no false doctrines, any morals problems, scandals, any problems of any kind would be dealt with.

The attorney's words were designed to vouch for Bakker's integrity. Seven years later, they would take on a less friendly significance.

Four days after sending Bakker home, the FCC staff heard from former finance director Herb Moore, who opened one of the most puzzling chapters of the agency's investigation. The session began at 10:05 A.M. Judge Fitzpatrick asked Moore's lawyers to introduce themselves. Donald Trinen, a lawyer from Denver spoke first, identifying himself as present "for the witness." Then John Midlen, the Washington, D.C., lawyer who represented PTL, gave his name. Since the hearings were closed, Midlen had a right to be present only if he was Moore's lawyer too. "Your Honor, could we have representation that Mr. Midlen is representing Mr. Moore personally?" an FCC lawyer asked. Judge Fitzpatrick turned to Midlen. "You have been authorized to be one of his counsel in this proceeding?" Midlen answered. "That's correct."

The truth was more complicated than Midlen suggested. PTL's general manager, Ed Stoeckel, had fired Moore the summer before and then discovered that Moore had signed two PTL checks to lawyer Trinen without Stoeckel's approval. The checks totaled $7,500. One had been made out the day before Moore's ouster, one the day after. In his letter terminating Moore, Stoeckel—later described by a colleague as having a "deep and abiding dislike" of Moore, as had Perkins—ordered Moore to return the money. Otherwise, he warned, it would be removed from his severance pay.

During fall 1979, with the severance-pay issue still unresolved despite Midlen's efforts, lawyer Trinen told Midlen that he could no longer represent Moore since Moore claimed that PTL, Midlen's principal client, owed him money. This meant that Midlen could not witness Moore's testimony before the FCC staff.

PTL was eager to discover what witnesses were telling the FCC. It had obtained Perkins's transcript with his permission. It had offered to provide representation for a former manager from the PTL cashiers department subpoenaed by the FCC. It had even asked Moss and Manzano for their transcripts. Both had refused.

PTL's efforts had not gone unnoticed. In late October, the FCC staff chastised Midlen for PTL's failure to pay the $11,000 in severance promised Moss while the ministry tried to persuade the former executive to turn over a transcript of his testimony. The staff suggested that the move bordered on unethical or illegal conduct. Chastened, Midlen decided to drop his efforts to resolve Moore's severance pay until after he testified.

As Midlen told the story, he considered Moore a friend, believed Trinen too inexperienced to handle the FCC hearings, and felt that Stoeckel's position on severance pay was unfair. More comfortable with Bakker after weeks at his side, Midlen raised the issue of Moore's pay with Bakker the day that the PTL president finished his testimony in November. Midlen and several other members of PTL's defense team were discussing Moore's upcoming appearance.

"Just take care of it and handle it fairly," Bakker said. PTL should pay Moore's legal fees, he said. When someone brought up Stoeckel's opposition to the payment, Bakker replied, "I am running the company." Together Bakker, Midlen, and the others in the room agreed that Midlen could tell Moore that PTL would pay him three months' severance and drop its demand for the $7,500.

Midlen, Moore, and Trinen met the next Monday, the day before Moore's appearance. Midlen assured the visitors that PTL was not making Moore the fall guy. He was, he acknowledged later, eager to put Moore "in the best frame of mind that [he could], consistent with the truth." Trinen, aware that PTL wanted to be present for Moore's testimony, hoped to use his client's forthcoming appearance as an incentive for PTL to settle with him. But Midlen did not negotiate a settlement. It was only later that night, Midlen testified, that he shrugged off the "intimidation" of the FCC staff and decided to do what he thought was fair—to work out an agreement.

At half past seven the next morning, a ringing phone woke Trinen in his room at Washington's Mayflower Hotel. It was Midlen calling from the lobby; he wanted to talk. The two lawyers met in Trinen's room for fifteen minutes.

A few minutes later, Midlen encountered Moore by the elevator stop in the Mayflower lobby. Moore was on his way to meet Trinen for breakfast. Midlen told him that he'd just been with Trinen, "and he has something important to tell you." The two men stepped into the elevator and returned upstairs.

Trinen explained the PTL proposal and gave it his endorsement.

Midlen had agreed to pay ten thousand dollars—Trinen's calculation of what Moore was owed—if Midlen could appear as one of Moore's lawyers at the hearing, Moore later said in a signed, sworn affidavit drafted by the FCC staff. In return, PTL would forgive the two checks Moore had written. According to the affidavit, Moore was told that Bakker would call him later in the day and "make everything right." Moore, who felt he had been mistreated in his dismissal from PTL, had tried a half-dozen times to reach Bakker by phone. Bakker had never returned his call.

After eating breakfast together, the two lawyers and Moore walked to the nearby FCC office building. In his testimony that morning, Moore expressed none of Bakker's confidence that PTL had had the cash to pay for the overseas missions programs. "We didn't have the money to pay our bills. . . . We couldn't even pay our [air]time charges." Short of cash, he and his staff had had to decide

> whether we should turn off the lights or let them pull out the IBM equipment. . . . It was just a matter of what we had to do to get by . . . it was a matter of survival. . . .
> There were no funds in the general account at any time. . . . Funds were being deposited and paid out every day, but there were no excesses."

An FCC lawyer asked Moore about his recent conversation with Bob Manzano. Moore was tight-lipped by nature, but his response to this question was particularly reserved.

> FCC lawyer: Did you tell Dr. Manzano whether you were considering whether or not to sue Mr. Jim Bakker?
>
> Moore: I respectfully ask that, I decline to answer the question.
>
> Judge: All right, now I will direct you to answer the question.
>
> Moore: Decline.

In the hall later, out of earshot of Midlen, Moore explained to Trinen why he had refused to answer; he didn't want PTL to know that he was considering a suit against PTL for defamation. In his later affidavit to the FCC, Moore described the moment:

Mr. Midlen's presence in the hearing room adversely affected my testimony and caused me to answer some questions incompletely. In addition, when asked by Commission counsel whether I intended to sue Jim Bakker, I refused to answer the question. . . . One reason for my refusal was that I did not want Mr. Midlen, who is also Jim Bakker's attorney, to think I was considering a lawsuit against Jim Bakker and PTL for payment of wages and vacation monies due to me. Mr. Midlen's presence was intimidating.

After Moore's day of testimony, Midlen telephoned Bakker and reported on the former finance director's performance. Herb was kind, like a father, Midlen told him. He also told Bakker about the settlement with Moore. But for months afterward, Moore didn't get the promised call from Bakker.

Bakker's testimony had further aroused the FCC investigators' suspicions; Bakker might perform masterfully when he controlled the microphone, but he did not do well under cross-examination from a sharp, informed skeptic. Two days after Christmas, 1979, the government subpoenaed more PTL records and scheduled Bakker to return to Washington in January. Bakker refused. By late winter, the FCC and PTL were back in court. The FCC wanted the courts to order PTL to comply; PTL sued in Charlotte, complaining again that the FCC was infringing on its freedom of religion and speech. Bakker was back at war. A truce would not come until April.

As the FCC announced its intention to enforce the subpoena, PTL aired a one-hour "documentary" called "Under Investigation." A local TV critic called it textbook propaganda—full of testimonials, rousing music, and adroit manipulation of facts, narrated by the silver-haired Efrem Zimbalist, Jr., a new PTL board member known best for his crime-fighter's role in the TV series "The FBI." It was somehow fitting: Bakker was fighting real Washington with Hollywood's idea of a Washington good guy.

The next day, Bakker announced that PTL was in its best financial shape ever. He had added two new faces to PTL's "strong management team," including Gary Smith, a new vice president for corporate planning. Three weeks later, PTL acknowledged that Ed Stoeckel—the man widely credited for PTL's revival—had stepped down. The move was voluntary, announced a ministry spokesman, who said, "He's completely exhausted." PTL also announced that, after a vacation and leave of absence and if his health improved, Stoeckel would continue to work with the ministry on a consulting or administrative basis.

A few weeks later, Bakker finally placed the promised call to Herb Moore. He had fired Stoeckel, he said, and had told the PTL staff that Moore had been responsible for improving PTL's finances. He asked Moore to rejoin PTL's staff, Moore later told the FCC, but no one contacted Moore to pursue the offer.

Bakker returned to Washington on May 20 to give three more days of testimony. Internal PTL memos, given to the FCC a few weeks earlier, contradicted Bakker's earlier testimony. Asked before why Manzano had been unable to get ten thousand dollars for McAlister, Bakker had testified that he considered the commitment to McAlister a private pledge by Manzano, not one from PTL. But in May 1978, Bakker had told his viewers that PTL needed $50,000 to ship to Brazil immediately to meet its missions commitments. Bakker explained that he was simply repeating what Manzano had told him.

By spring 1980, FCC investigators had learned of PTL's severance-pay settlement with Moore on the day of his testimony. Bakker appeared to be stunned when Bernstein brought up his recent contact with Moore, who had signed the accusatory affidavit three days earlier.

> Bernstein: In the past four months, have you spoken with Mr. Herbert Moore?
>
> Bakker: I'm not sure. I don't—I may have talked to him for just a few moments. Let me think. It seems to me I talked to his wife, and I may have talked to him for a few minutes on the telephone, but I don't remember talking to him in detail at all since the last, since he left.

Pressed further, Bakker began to recall details of the conversation. He admitted that he might have told Moore that PTL was considering rehiring him but said that after reading a transcript of Moore's testimony, he would not consider employing Moore again.

Bernstein sought an explanation of the suspiciously timed settlement with Moore. Bakker denied trying to bribe him, saying that he had authorized severance pay for Moore, but that he had attached no stipulation that Midlen be admitted to the hearing room. Bakker expressed surprise that Moore had been offered money hours before testifying. "I think you are trying to build a bribery case or something here, and I am quite shocked by it," Bakker said.

The strange case of Herb Moore would end inconclusively. Moore later sought to discredit the affidavit that FCC investigators had drawn up after talking to him. He had been hospitalized with heart problems at the time, Moore said, and his "thought patterns" were not functioning properly. Yet golden handcuffs were an undeniable part of PTL culture. Cash and gifts were routinely used to cement strategic relationships. Those whom Bakker wanted to influence got fat honoraria or a chunk of ministry business or lavish Christmas gifts or, in the final years, free shopping trips in the mall at Heritage USA. There were no quid pro quos, but the effect was the same. The seduction was complete.

In September 1980, fifteen months after his first day of testimony and more than three years after Bakker's spontaneous offer to Cho for the Korean TV show, Manzano returned for two more days of questioning. FCC investigations normally span six months. With Bakker's resistance, the PTL inquiry had now stretched over eighteen.

Before his return, former missions director Manzano spent two days reviewing Bakker's testimony, which the FCC's Bernstein had shown him. Manzano recalled his reaction in a 1983 letter to Bakker. "I wept through many pages. I then testified with an anger towards you, trying to get even."

Bakker had approved the $150,000 commitment to McAlister, Manzano insisted. To suggest otherwise, he said, was a "total gross departure from truth on [Bakker's] part." One reason for PTL's failure to make good on its promise, Manzano said, was Bakker's lack of enthusiasm for paying McAlister, one of his critics during PTL's early years. Nothing had been kept from Bakker, Manzano said, because he was the man who could decide to make things happen. Bakker could have completed the Korean project within weeks if he had pushed it as a top priority.

Bakker had never told the public that PTL's support for the Brazilian program had been shelved, Manzano testified. Characteristically, "when [Bakker] had bad news, he had a tendency to keep it to himself. When he had good news, he told it to the public. ... It would have been disappointing for our public to have known that we ... weren't going to do what we said we were going to do."

Manzano said that he had not challenged Bakker's inaccurate statements on the air. "That would have only made the situation worse. One thing that Jim Bakker didn't care for was being called a liar." Once Flessing had accused Bakker of lying, Manzano said, and "I have never seen him get so angry." To get anywhere with Bakker, you had to play to his insecurities.

> I tried to learn how to handle Jim Bakker as far as getting things done. You could never force Jim Bakker to do anything. I tried to use a little child psychology with Jim Bakker by making him sound like it was his idea to do something, while Bill Perkins was very blunt and blatant . . . and only got negative response. . . .
>
> Whenever you pressure Jim Bakker to do something he would go the other way. He would become extremely stubborn, and you couldn't get him to move.

Line by line, Manzano contested Bakker's testimony. "Either Mr. Bakker is not telling the truth, or he has had amnesia." Manzano painted a man motivated as much by the demands of PTL's appetite for cash as by a sincere desire to help others.

> Jim Bakker would raise money for the projects that he was excited about at the time. Jim Bakker got very much missions-minded typically during a telethon, because he knew that missions would touch the hearts of people. People will give you more if you show a hungry kid on the air.

For months, Ed Stoeckel kept Bakker under control. It had been surprisingly easy; Bakker seemed to be resting, to appreciate having the worries lifted from his shoulders. Stoeckel had no need to please the boss, and he wasn't intimidated by Bakker. When Bakker told an engineer to draw up plans to add a library and balcony to his office in the Village, Stoeckel didn't bother to say no. He took the plans for the $60,000 renovation, put them in his office credenza, and waited for Bakker to say something. Bakker never did.

Stoeckel had halted all spending on buildings at Heritage USA. He believed that the core of PTL's ministry lay in TV and missions, not in the complex outside Charlotte. He also believed Heritage USA posed a long-term threat to PTL's cash supply. "Jim, look, I'm an engineer. It would be great to go ahead and build. But that isn't what we should be doing," Stoeckel told Bakker. He explained that it was one thing to raise the money to build a structure, but it was much tougher to raise the money to operate it.

Stoeckel wanted to sell Heritage USA but couldn't find a buyer. Bakker—haunted by the half-finished reminders of his past failure—wanted the bulldozers and carpenters back to work. Finally Stoeckel gave in, but he stipulated that PTL would raise the money first. Bakker agreed. Down deep, though, Stoeckel sensed that Bakker didn't want to wait.

After nearly a year, Stoeckel was exhausted. He spent twelve to fifteen hours a day on the job, commuting home to Memphis to rest on weekends. He had little affection for Bakker, and it showed. His subordinates remember seeing Stoeckel shaking his finger at Bakker as if he were scolding a youngster. Stoeckel thought that Bakker was a paranoid, spoiled child living in a fairy-tale world, unwilling to accept no for an answer, and at the same time a man with a pathological capacity for making his lies become the truth. Bakker seemed to cycle through different emotions, each seemingly sincere. He might be the innocent boy at one point then turn frightened, mean, repentant, or arrogant.

One day in March 1980, Stoeckel flew into Chicago and met Richard Dortch, the board member and Assemblies of God district superintendent who had recruited him for Bakker. After just a year Dortch was the most powerful member of PTL's docile board. Dortch had hoped to work out tensions between Bakker and Stoeckel, but there was no room for the sort of compromise Dortch wanted. As Stoeckel interpreted their conversation, Dortch believed that Bakker should get his own way. It was his ministry, and they shouldn't stir the pot.

Stoeckel agreed to oblige. The Lord had brought him there to do a job, and now it was time to go. Stoeckel got a generous going-away package, including six months' severance pay and ownership of his company car. Dortch helped him secure a job at North Central Bible College, where Dortch served on the board.

Stoeckel met with Bakker. The PTL president was very complimentary, and it seemed to Stoeckel that Bakker both didn't want to lose him and didn't want him in the way. On March 7, 1980, the newspapers reported PTL's sanitized explanation of Stoeckel's resignation. The ministry announced that Gary Smith, the thirty-three-year-old engineer and business consultant from Waco, Texas, would take Stoeckel's place and have as much power as his predecessor. Smith, too, would last less than a year. In truth, Bakker was determined never again to surrender control.

CHAPTER EIGHT

TAMMY FAYE

"I think my wife is having an affair"

Once the Bakkers had seemed inseparable, working side by side at the studio, decorating side by side at home. But success had cost Jim and Tammy dearly. As a two-headed TV personality, they seemed supportive and affectionate, a model couple, but they didn't get along away from the set. Now, with PTL's money or their own ample salaries, the Bakkers could pay others to take care of the children or renovate their home, responsibilities that had once drawn them together.

Tammy viewed Heritage USA with thinly disguised resentment. As Ed Stoeckel had searched for a buyer for the complex, she wrote later, she felt guilty "because I was almost happy it was almost over: the days and nights of worry, the horrible extra financial burden, the months of talking to a husband who never heard a word I said, the months of doing things all by myself."

As Bakker busied himself with building, he encouraged Tammy to throw herself into her music. There, she found a new friend and protector: producer-songwriter-singer Gary Paxton of Nashville. Paxton, eight months older than Bakker, was a big, friendly guy with a bushy beard and a fondness for red jumpsuits. He had won a measure of fame in rock 'n' roll, singing the song "Alley-Oop" and cowriting and producing the song "Monster Mash." Paxton was born again in 1971, rescued by the church from a life sullied by drugs and whiskey. In the late seventies, Paxton became a common face around PTL, appearing on Bakker's show and writing the theme song for the "PTL Club." He had been a friend to both Bakkers, introducing them to the world of stock-car racing and producing preaching records for Jim.

To Tammy, Paxton became a painful reminder of the things her husband was not. Paxton's world was music; Jim couldn't carry a tune. Paxton took time with Tammy, encouraged her music, made her feel like someone important; too often Jim treated Tammy as just another cog in a sprawling ministry. Paxton accepted Tammy's makeup and wigs, the weapons in Tammy's fight to overcome doubts about her beauty; Jim put her down. Paxton could relate to the common people; Jim preferred to relate to his rank-and-file partners through the camera. Tammy told friends that she felt more kinship with the common folk, the sort of people you'd meet at the Charlotte Motor Speedway, than for the politicians and celebrities to whom Jim seemed drawn.

By fall 1978, there were already whispers about Paxton and Tammy. That year, Paxton wrote the foreword for Tammy's biography. During Jim's trip around the world, Paxton helped Tammy host the show, and viewers noticed how cozy the two seemed on the air. Tongues wagged when Paxton and his wife, Karen, stayed with Tammy while Jim was away.

By early 1979 and the advent of the FCC inquiry, Tammy seemed more interested in spending time in Nashville, where she worked in Paxton's recording studio, than in Charlotte. Paxton's influence showed in other ways. He worked out regularly and preferred his women slim. Tammy started dieting and taking exercise classes. She shaved off thirty pounds, losing the baby fat that had accentuated her girlish manner.

With brows furrowed, Roger and Linda Wilson—close friends of the Bakkers from CBN who were now on staff at PTL—watched the Bakkers' marriage wane and Paxton's star rise. One day, with Bakker a captive audience on a trip up I-77, Roger Wilson warned him to pay more attention to his family. The ministry might be important, and who knew what would happen to it, but Bakker would have his family forever, Wilson lectured. Bakker, who had turned forty that year, sensed that something was amiss. He and Tammy didn't communicate like they used to, he told Wilson.

Linda Wilson was Tammy's secretary, constant companion, and

best friend. As she joked to Bakker, she also deserved a salary as the PTL president's analyst; he dropped in occasionally to ask her what was wrong with Tammy. Repeatedly, Linda offered the same advice: all Tammy needed was his time, his attention. Tammy needed to know she was the most important thing in his life. The message made Bakker defensive. He'd given her everything in the world she could possibly want, a nice house, two nice kids, he told Wilson.

In the early years in Charlotte, Tammy was one of the girls. She cried, giggled, and cut up with her friends. She had a quick, intuitive mind and an iron will. Her wit was biting and goofy. She could be bawdy, pulling her dress over her head and exclaiming to a friend, "Look how much weight I've lost!"

She could also be a genuinely empathetic friend. When a young volunteer working on PTL's first studio lost the diamond from her engagement ring—which her husband had spent a year buying on layaway—Tammy gave the young woman one of her diamond rings. She said that she had talked it over with Jim, and she felt that the Lord had told her to give it away. Two years later, Tammy's friend Carolyn Hall—the wife of then board member Larry Hall—suffered the death of her two-day-old baby boy. Tammy, who had given birth to Jamie Charles a few weeks earlier, cried and cried. On a family outing later that year, Tammy handed her infant son to Hall to hold. In minutes she realized what she had done. "I'm sorry, Carolyn," Tammy said, "but I want you to know Jamie Charles is as much your baby as he is Jim's and mine." It was a generous, if childlike gesture.

A little-girl, scatterbrained quality had become part of Tammy's stage personality. It was an act reminiscent of one of her early role models, Lucille Ball. To her admirers, Tammy was a welcome break from the sobriety of the church and the upright mores of the old-time Pentecostal world. Tammy was alive and human, a catalyst for the chemistry that made Jim and Tammy a success. She wasn't embarrassed to ask God for help with her pets, as she had in a letter published in a PTL magazine.

> I gotta talk to you! It's the guinea pig. Now, I thought he was a good idea. You see, we've tried dogs and they wet on the

carpet and our cats run away. I love my birds, but can't pick
them up and pet them: at least mine you can't, so I asked you
what would be just right and I thought I heard you say a guinea
pig. Well, Lord, as you know, the first one, "Teddy Bear,"
died and almost broke Susie's heart. "Why did he go do that
for?" she said. So I got another one, but Jim has a real hang-up
about him. He says it looks like a big rat . . . he squeaks little
happy noises, but Jim says it sounds like he's in the last stages
of dying, which I think he secretly wishes it would. Well, God,
what do I do?

To her detractors, Tammy was puerile, her message an uneducated
trivialization of Christianity. Tammy's thickening mask of makeup
violated the essence of traditional holiness standards, day-to-day
rules designed to put a wall between the saved and the sinful.

In early 1980, as Jim Bakker lurked in the doorway, a tight look
on his face, his chatty wife described her daily makeup regimen to
an interviewer from the *Observer*. The application took fifteen minutes each morning: a heavy coat of beige liquid base, dark V's of
contour powder to create cheekbones on her rounded "chipmunk
cheeks," a thick navy line around her eyes. That was just the start
for the eyes. Tammy brushed light shadow on her eyelids, up to the
crease. At the crease she drew a dark half-moon of brown powder.
Above that she put another half-moon of light shadow extending
to her eyebrows. The eyebrows were arched and lengthened. Instead of wearing lots of mascara, she used fake eyelashes, à la Lucille
Ball. "Some people tease me I wear too much makeup," she told
reporter Jody Jaffe. "But a person has to find a look unique to
them."

Tammy laughed, giggled, and shrieked. "One time I pulled all
my eyelashes out," Tammy said, recounting the hazards of replacing her fake eyelashes every three weeks. "I looked like a little,
naked chicken." Her security, she joked, was her four-inch spike
heels. "I don't go anywhere without them. I gotta make five feet
somehow."

She acknowledged that Jim—the Muskegon boy who once asked
his dates not to wear cosmetics on visits to his church—didn't care
for her heavy makeup. "Jim fought it. Jim still fights it. He says it
so much, and I just say, 'Oh honey.' . . . I know for sure love is blind
because he says I look better in the morning without any makeup."

To her friends and husband, Tammy's makeup was a barometer of her emotional equilibrium. If Tammy left her wigs at home, wore less makeup, and avoided outfits with plunging necklines, she was most likely in good spirits. On those days she didn't need so much help to feel good about herself.

Twenty days after Ed Stoeckel was replaced, PTL announced that Roger Flessing was returning to head PTL's broadcast division. Flessing had resigned just fifteen months before. Since then, he had worked first as program director at KXTV, the CBS affiliate in Sacramento, then as a $75,000-a-year producer for Oral Roberts in Tulsa. It was not a happy marriage in Oklahoma; Flessing felt that the Roberts ministry used television less for ministry than for marketing its university and City of Faith Hospital. Flessing couldn't see the evangelism in Roberts's seed-faith preaching and its promise of multiplied blessings for those who sent their dollars to Tulsa.

Flessing had sensed that he would be moving back to Charlotte; the news from PTL had been encouraging since Stoeckel's arrival. Ruth Egert, Jim's secretary, phoned, giving Flessing Bakker's unlisted phone number.

Bakker was contrite, telling Flessing that he was right, that they had had some problems. "We've made some changes. I want to offer you a job," Bakker said. Flessing's response was immediate. "And I want to take it." Bakker was surprised. "You do?"

The Flessings—Roger, wife Kathy, and their two young sons—arrived in Charlotte around April 1. They sensed that something was wrong with the Bakkers. They noticed the physical changes in Tammy—the recent breast implant to give her a more prominent bosom and, together with her familiar thick eyelashes, makeup caked on her cheeks and painted vividly around her eyes.

A few days later, Flessing and Bakker left Charlotte to attend the mid-April National Association of Broadcasters convention in Las Vegas. After they settled into the first-class section of the Delta jet, Bakker leaned over to Flessing. "I think my wife is having an affair."

One day, Tammy confided to Linda Wilson that she had fallen in love with Gary Paxton. She would rather live with him, she told her friend, than have all the comforts Jim had provided and no attention. She told Wilson about kissing and hugging Paxton, but assured her there had been no serious lovemaking. Years later, Paxton described the pair's physical contact as nothing other than what they had done on the air—a show-biz kiss on the cheek and an arm around her shoulders. "There never was any affair. There was never a romance."

Linda Wilson was staunchly opposed to any involvement with Paxton, and she let Tammy know how she felt, She reminded her friend that she was married, that she was a Christian. Scripturally it was wrong—she couldn't be involved with another man. Wilson's words seemed to have little influence.

Wilson had done her best to stay between Tammy and her friend, even accompanying Tammy on her trips to Nashville. But in April 1979, Linda Wilson gave birth to a daughter. She could no longer drop everything and take off immediately when Tammy felt the urge to go to Tennessee. Another PTL employee took her place. Still, Linda Wilson worried about romance and, lacking that, the appearance of sin.

One night, during one of Tammy's trips to Nashville, Linda Wilson called Paxton's home in Tennessee from Charlotte. The ringing phone woke Karen Paxton, already in bed for the night. Wilson asked if she could speak to Tammy, and Karen Paxton said she was next door with Gary at the recording studio. "Get to the studio," Linda Wilson implored. "Don't leave Gary and Tammy by themselves."

Karen Paxton refused. "Linda, that's ridiculous. First off, Tammy and Gary aren't going to do anything. Besides that, if they're going to, I'm not going to watch over a man."

Karen Paxton had sensed the affection between her husband and Tammy during their stay in Charlotte in fall 1978. By 1980, Karen Paxton was contemplating leaving her husband; she would do so that summer. Karen and Tammy were friends, and one day Karen Paxton asked Tammy if she ever felt like leaving Jim. Tammy admitted that she wanted to, that she had feelings for another man. But, she said that day, it is not God's way to leave your husband— the very message Linda Wilson had been pressing on her. Tammy didn't identify the man she loved.

In spring 1980, Linda Wilson decided to spell out to Jim Bakker what was happening to his wife. Tammy knew how Linda felt, and she was not listening to her. She told Bakker that Tammy was infatuated with Gary and that she might feel she was in love with him; Paxton might feel the same towards Tammy. "Jim, you've got to end this. You've got to get hold of your marriage."

Bakker was worried about prostate trouble and had scheduled a physical exam at a hospital in Palmdale, a small city in the high desert northwest of Los Angeles. Bakker and Flessing rented a Cadillac at the LA airport; after the stop at the Palmdale hospital, they planned to drive on to the convention in Las Vegas.

Six months earlier, Bakker had interviewed one of the hospital's owners on his TV program. Also on the air that day was a member of the hospital's staff, Fred Gross, talking about a Christian, or psychospiritual, approach to counseling. Bakker's physical exam eventually turned into an examination of his psyche. Bakker told Gross that Tammy was involved with another man. Gross asked Flessing for more information, and soon Flessing was ordered to get Tammy to California immediately.

Tammy was reluctant to go. Roger and Linda Wilson picked her up at the Bakkers' lake house, which the Bakkers had continued to use since their move to the donated house in Foxcroft. Tammy wanted to talk to Paxton before she left. The Wilsons waited in their car while the two talked in Paxton's car. Then the Wilsons escorted Tammy to the Bakkers' home in Foxcroft, she packed, and they took her to the airport. They watched her flight take off to make sure she didn't back out.

Kathy Flessing was drafted to accompany Tammy on the flight. It was a bad time for her to leave; her second son, six months old and still nursing, had to be weaned abruptly. But those around Jim and Tammy were accustomed to sacrificing for their unpredictable, temperamental friends and employers.

Tammy braced herself for the flight with a chip of a tranquilizer pill. She disliked flying and still needed help making it through a trip—despite the claims of her ghostwritten book about overcoming fear, *Run to the Roar,* which PTL was scheduled to release later that spring. On that April day, Kathy Flessing was warned to be sure Tammy didn't wander off under the influence. In fact, Tammy slept most of the way.

Roger Flessing picked the two up in Los Angeles and drove them to Palmdale. The Flessings took the room next to the Bakkers' suite at the Holiday Inn, the best hotel in town. The 123-bed Palmdale General Hospital was two miles to the east.

The Palmdale hospital was a friendly environment for charismatics. Lester Nichols, the hospital owner who had appeared on Bakker's program, and his wife, June, had steadily converted many members of the hospital staff to full-gospel Christianity and membership in the Church on the Way, a prominent charismatic church in Van Nuys, California. For several years, the hospital had offered the Christian Therapy Program under Gross's direction.

Gross, a month younger than Bakker, had earned a doctorate in clinical psychology at Indiana State University, taught at Louisiana State University, and served as staff psychologist at Camarillo State Hospital outside Oxnard, California, before joining the Palmdale staff. Raised a Baptist, Gross now attended the Church on the Way, pastored by the Reverend Jack Hayford. Gross credited the widely respected Hayford for inspiring his blend of spiritual principles and psychiatric treatment. Gross, a tall, pasty man who tended to speak in the abstract jargon of an academic, described his program to a reporter in 1977.

> The Bible . . . is the starting point for practical counseling. The Scriptures give an understanding of man as soul, spirit, and body "never fully taught in psychology courses," he said.
>
> Gross attested to what he believes have been "miracles of dynamic restoration" through prayer, Bible reading, and other spiritual disciplines, as well as by "direct intervention of the Holy Spirit."

At that time, Gross's program had room for fifteen in-patients served by a professional staff of ten. Patients rose in the morning to watch Pat Robertson's "700 Club" and had thirty minutes of devotions followed by group discussions, group therapy, and individual counseling.

For two weeks after Tammy Bakker's arrival, the Bakkers met daily with members of Gross's counseling team. The team prayed with the Bakkers; the Bakkers vented their resentments. Jim thought that Tammy's clothes were too provocative, Tammy wondered about Jim's tight pants. Tammy insisted that she and Paxton had not slept together. The counselors told her to repent because she had committed adultery in her heart. They pressed Jim to spend more time at home. Tammy told him that she didn't need a new fur coat or a new car, she wanted more of him. The Bakkers tried to agree on a schedule that would get Jim out of the office at a reasonable time.

During their first week in Palmdale, the Flessings served as the Bakkers' chaperones. The couples were out for pizza one night when a fan recognized Jim and Tammy. It struck Jim, after the two admirers had departed, that he liked the relaxed feeling of being just anybody, of having time to talk, of shopping idly at the local K-mart.

Roger and Linda Wilson flew out for the second week, bringing Tammy Sue and Jamie Charles. Jim was enthusiastic about the Christian therapy team and encouraged the Wilsons to undergo testing and therapy sessions. The Wilsons agreed. The counselors were especially interested in the Wilsons' insights into and experiences with the Bakkers.

The Palmdale team made its first of many appearances on Bakker's program in early May 1980. The Bakkers prodded Sam Orender, the TV man who had worked with them for seven years, to go through counseling with his wife Kathy, another PTL employee, while the team was in Charlotte. The Orenders had been separated for more than a year. For three days, the couple worked with the Californians. At week's end, on May 9, the Orenders renewed their marriage vows on television. It seemed to Sam Orender that the Palmdale team believed that making that commitment over the air would keep the Orenders from splitting up again. Later—after he and his wife had separated for the last time, the glow of the quick fix lost for good—Orender went to each member of the Palmdale team and told them that he thought they had done him an injustice.

Bakker had dispatched Gary Paxton from PTL after confronting him over the phone. "You slept with my wife, didn't you?" Bakker asked Paxton angrily.

"No, Jim," Paxton answered, "just the opposite, when I probably could have." Paxton had, on at least one occasion, encouraged Tammy to return to Bakker. Later, Paxton told his wife that Bakker had accused him of meeting Tammy at the Bakker's lake house. Bakker asked if Tammy had ever touched his genitalia. Paxton told

Bakker he should be ashamed for suggesting that Tammy would do such a thing.

Soon after the blowup, Paxton learned that Bakker and members of his staff had telephoned radio stations and churches and accused Paxton of sleeping with Tammy. In Paxton's eyes, Bakker had set out to destroy him. When Paxton wrote to Bakker asking that he forgive whatever trouble Paxton might have caused, Bakker mailed the letter back with a nasty note. For Gary Paxton, there was to be no forgiveness.

The Bakkers surfaced in Washington, D.C., after their two weeks in Palmdale. On April 28, they attended a reception given by First Lady Rosalynn Carter at the White House. The next day, Bakker spoke at a Washington for Jesus rally before two hundred thousand Christians gathered for twelve hours of prayer and fasting. "If we are to maintain the blessing of God today, we must honor the Lord. We have sinned as a nation. In many areas, we have recognized sin as a life-style and denied our Creator." The speech was Bakker's first public appearance since mid-April, when, PTL had told the local papers, Bakker had "checked into a California hotel on doctor's orders for rest."

Unlike Jerry Falwell and Pat Robertson, Bakker was not a political animal. In the pivotal election year of 1980, however, self-interest drew Bakker into the evangelical protest against big government. In his campaign to discredit his prosecutors, Bakker depicted himself as one of the many victims of a sweeping secular attack. He complained that Uncle Sam wanted to tell Christians how to live, prohibiting prayer in the school and permitting abortion. Now, with the FCC's investigation of PTL, it wanted to tell a ministry how to run its affairs.

Campaign aides for President Jimmy Carter and former California governor Ronald Reagan courted Bakker. Each candidate was eager to capture the born-again voter, and Bakker was a prominent undecided vote. The attention was the sort Bakker savored. He recorded his meetings with each candidate, reprinting lots of pictures and publishing excerpts in PTL's magazine. The Friday before Election Day, 1980, Bakker met Air Force One in Memphis, Tennessee, and rode with Jimmy Carter to Jackson, Mississippi. During the flight, the two men prayed together. Before he left, Bakker pocketed some napkins and matchbooks with the Air Force One emblem.

But Bakker endorsed no candidate, a noncommittal position PTL made clear after the plane ride with Carter. Privately, though, Bakker seemed most sympathetic toward Reagan.

The summer of 1980 was a tough one. The Bakkers' marriage was still shaky, and Tammy, though resigned to the reconciliation, was unenthusiastic. Bakker eased his work pace at first, but by summer he was staying into the evening supervising work on the Barn auditorium. The building was one of several left unfinished following PTL's 1978 financial collapse. With Stoeckel gone, Bakker had begun raising money to finish it, putting construction crews to work with a tight July 4 deadline. The building was not ready in time, and the construction drained the staff's energies throughout the summer.

The auditorium job was full of costly Bakker whims and turnabouts, the sort Bakker could justify as pursuing the best for Christians but that seemed, in truth, to reflect the highly personal needs prompting much of PTL's building. Bakker wanted the front of the stage built from the same wood that Oral Roberts had in his office. Later, the costly wood was ordered covered over. One day, Bakker decided he didn't like the Barn's $100,000 stucco exterior any more than he liked the original plan for an open air tabernacle. He ordered the outer walls covered with cultured field stone instead.

Bakker wanted to install a massive pipe organ in the auditorium. That summer, PTL spent hundreds of thousands of dollars preparing the building to house the organ. The instrument was another of Bakker's biggest-ever projects. "We're purchasing the old NBC pipe organ from old radio days," Bakker said. "We're putting three units together to build one of the largest theater organs in the world. It will be five ranks bigger than Radio City Music Hall's."

Gary Smith, Bakker's general manager, was leery of the price PTL was supposed to pay. He called around the country and learned that the organ's seller, an acquaintance of Bakker's from his days in California, was asking too much. Bakker told Smith to pay for the organ. Smith refused. Bakker would get his way a year later, after Smith's departure. Three years after that, PTL attorneys in California privately characterized the $330,000 PTL had paid for the organ as "outrageous." They estimated the organ's value at $50,000 and complained that the seller had committed fraud. PTL eventually sued but settled on terms that deeply offended its own lawyers. The organ would never be installed.

To veterans like Orender, it seemed that Bakker now saw PTL's future in the Heritage USA retreat center and not in the TV ministry that he had once termed his calling. Bakker talked about the day when the government would force his show, indeed all Christian programming, off the air. Then, he told his staff, they would have Heritage USA to sustain PTL.

When Orender, Flessing, and others pressed for new Christian programming—the carrot that Bakker had dangled before them for so many years—Bakker reacted as if they were threatening his show. An earlier proposal for a show patterned after "Saturday Night Live" had languished. Orender and Thurlow Spurr, PTL's music director, had produced a series of fifteen-minute segments on themes such as love and helping people. The segments began to get popular, and Bakker intervened. Eventually, Orender suggested half-seriously at a vice-presidents' meeting that PTL save money by canceling its TV contracts and broadcasting Bakker's show by radio. He felt that if television didn't make creative use of the visual image, it was little more than radio anyhow.

That summer, Bakker made a change on his program to make Tammy feel more a part of PTL. Tammy moved into the co-host's chair next to her husband, and Bakker's longtime co-host, Henry Harrison, was relegated to a guest's chair. Once a guest arrived, the fifty-two-year-old had to move onto the set's sofa. Harrison understood that Bakker wanted to placate Tammy, but he was hurt that a producer, not Bakker himself, had told him of the new arrangement. Uncle Henry, as Harrison was known, was a guileless fellow with a fondness for punning and an unswerving loyalty to the Bakkers. Stout, with thinning hair, Harrison was a dinosaur at PTL, a good old boy in a ministry gravitating discernibly toward the famous and flamboyant.

One of those celebrities was the Reverend Bob Harrington, a onetime insurance salesman with a ministry in what he called "the Devil's boot camp," New Orleans's Bourbon Street. He was a funny man, easily spotted by his trademark red tie, red handkerchief, and red socks. Bakker turned his back on reports that Harrington had had an affair; one PTL employee had complained that she found Harrington embracing his young secretary. As Bakker's secretary, Ruth Egert, remembered it, Bakker refused to believe office scuttlebutt he heard about this person or that—PTL was rife with such reports, and Bakker was the target of many himself. Eventually, Harrington, who had preached about making marriages work, acknowledged he was separating from his wife. He quickly faded from the PTL scene.

By 1979, Bakker had enlisted a new crony, a traveling faith healer named John Wesley Fletcher. Fletcher had grown up in North Carolina, one of ten children of a tobacco-factory worker. He dropped out of high school after spending two years in ninth grade and two years in tenth. Known as J. W., he took a job driving an ambulance for funeral homes (as an evangelist, he would claim that he had been a funeral director), and he moonlighted as a clown at hospitals and birthday parties. He helped sew up bodies and clean up after autopsies at Duke University Medical Center (he later would claim that he had attended Duke for two years). He also claimed that he owned a café, catering service, and topless restaurant or nightclub. The truth was ever-changing in Fletcher's hands. One of his former aides remembered him as "the con artist of all con artists."

For a time, Fletcher attended an Assemblies of God church in Durham, North Carolina. By 1970, he had left town, owing $3,800. He had been convicted five times for passing bad checks. The next year, he married in Iowa. Soon he was holding faith-healing revivals. Fletcher became an Assemblies of God minister in 1974, the year of Bakker's arrival in Charlotte, and was ordained in 1977. He first appeared on Bakker's program in 1976, and returned six times in 1978 and 1979. In 1980, he became a regular, appearing thirty-four times.

PTL employees were troubled by Fletcher's emergence. They thought he was an opportunist, the sort for whom Bakker had always had a blind spot. Fletcher could be abrasive, and he told off-color jokes. He liked to drink; his favorite in those days was Benedictine and brandy. He seemed preoccupied with the money he brought in and eager to make a show of the money he had. One night, he bought Flessing a seven hundred dollar bottle of wine.

Fletcher was a convincing performer; even some of his detractors felt God was using him to heal. Before services at the outdoor amphitheater at Heritage USA, he would sequester himself in a trailer, reading the Bible, crying, and begging God to move him. His healing services had a theatricality that bordered on the bizarre. Once, a woman collapsed and Fletcher lay on top of her, ostensibly to heal her; Bakker's security chief, Don Hardister, ordered him off. The woman was rushed to the hospital. A few days later, she died.

In a July 1980 service, Fletcher summoned from his audience a young man weak from melanoma. He had refused medical treatment for the cancer. You have a disease attacking your entire body, Fletcher said, but you have been steady in your faith. Healing is taking place. As Fletcher touched him, the young man fell into the arms of those behind him. He had been "slain in the spirit," supposedly knocked down by divine power transmitted through Fletcher's hand. Bakker came forth, asked the man his name, and invited him back on the show in forty-five days. "You'll be fat and sassy," Bakker told him. The audience laughed.

Soon the man was dead. Bakker later responded to a reporter's inquiry about the case.

> All I can do is pray for healing and leave the results to the Lord. I feel the tragedy is not that this brother went to be with the Lord because, that is the ultimate for every Christian. . . . I personally do not profess to heal anyone, nor does any of the ministers I associate with. [This happens] through prayer and sometimes with the help of the medical profession.

By summer 1980, Fletcher was Bakker's frequent companion. The two men, born just twenty-two days apart, began to look more and more alike. When Bakker collapsed one day from the heat in PTL's amphitheater, it was Fletcher who stayed with him all day as he recuperated in one of PTL's lakeside chalets. And Fletcher became a shoulder for Bakker to cry on as his marriage began to fall apart again.

Heritage USA was catching on with PTL's partners. Eight hundred visited on a typical day, and the on-site accommodations for one hundred ran eighty-five percent full. Bakker predicted two to three thousand visitors a day within a year. "I think the sky's the limit. But we don't want to overcrowd it because the idea is to minister in person and to have more of a personal touch than television."

With workers finishing the $2-million, three-thousand-seat Barn auditorium, Bakker announced that PTL was financially the strongest it had ever been. He declared the FCC battle over and won, though the investigators had yet to hear their last witness, Manzano. On Labor Day, Bakker orchestrated a Jim Bakker gala: a victory parade, appearances by Christian celebrities, a dedication speech in the Barn by Oral Roberts. Bakker's childlike faith, Roberts said, had made the building possible. "What Jesus needs . . . is the little boy, and the little girl, in all of us."

After the dedication, the Bakkers flew to Acapulco for a vacation with their two children. Secretary Ruth Egert and her husband, Phil, now Bakker's administrative assistant accompanied them. But the Bakkers were unhappy in Mexico, and they soon flew to Los Angeles and settled into the Bonaventure Hotel downtown. Bakker telephoned Flessing and suggested he fly out for the weekend to talk business. Flessing rushed home, packed some clothes in a carry-on bag, and drove to the Charlotte airport. He parked in short-term parking, figuring he'd be back in a few days. He was gone for three weeks. Bakker was given to such unpredictability. A one-week trip could sprawl into a month; a two-week trip might end after a day.

Bakker had decided that Tammy needed to record a new album. PTL staff members flew to the West Coast to help. With Paxton gone, music director Thurlow Spurr produced the record. Out flew an art director and layout experts to design the cover, writers to draft the liner notes. Flessing considered the album Bakker's grand gift to his wife—at PTL expense—for the late nights and weekends he had spent supervising the latest round of construction at Heritage USA. Back at PTL, Gary Smith felt as if Bakker had abandoned PTL. For four weeks, the ministry relied on canned shows.

Thurlow Spurr had joined PTL's staff three years before. For the past twenty years, he had been hiring fresh-faced young men and women to travel around the country performing contemporary, often Christian, music. Press profiles described him as the dean of contemporary gospel choir music. Six years older than Bakker, he was a private person with a smooth stage manner. Like Bakker, he was a master salesman, the type, one former employee remembered, who would have made the million dollar round table if he sold insurance.

Spurr had made it big in Detroit with a group called the Spurrlows. In the early sixties, he convinced Chrysler Corporation to sponsor a tour by the group to high schools around the country, where they would make a pitch for safe driving and spread the good name of Chrysler. At night, the same group often performed Christian music at churches. Spurr's gift was not so much in performing or directing, but in booking engagements and convincing gifted performers to work for his company, Splendor Productions. His business grew to include rock bands, a choral church group, and eventually groups that played in hotel lounges and in Las Vegas.

One of Spurr's first tasks at PTL was to create a resident band of twelve musicians and a singing corps of six vocalists for the "PTL Club." By early 1978, the PTL Band and PTL Singers were in place. They would become a fixture, their upbeat music adding to the professional polish of Bakker's TV program.

In June 1978, a few months after Spurr's arrival, PTL added David Taggart, Spurr's twenty-one-year-old administrative assistant, to the PTL staff. Taggart was a Detroit native, just three years out of high school. He had studied music in college, played keyboard part time for Spurr, and done administrative work for Spurr's company. He was close to Spurr, traveling with him and living in his home.

Taggart's gift was not so much playing piano as arranging his boss's daily schedule and frequent trips. Spurr traveled most weekends, working out-of-town jobs as a church music director. Bakker had seen Taggart at Spurr's side during his impromptu September visit to Los Angeles and was impressed. He asked Spurr if young Taggart could come to work for him. Spurr agreed, reluctantly. "If it's for you, then OK."

Taggart and his older brother, James, who soon followed him to PTL, had expensive taste. They wore pricey designer clothes and expensive jewelry. The brothers had grown up rich, or so David led his friends and colleagues to believe. "Daddy has been really good to me," he liked to say. As David told it, Daddy was a Cadillac dealer.

Bakker had already adopted a tonier style himself. Always crisply dressed, he had begun to gravitate toward designer labels. One summer day in 1980, an *Observer* reporter saw Bakker wearing a Christian Dior T-shirt, smoothly pressed Calvin Klein jeans, and fine leather Western boots. Bakker looked "cool, classy, and even continental—a type who would blend in easily along the Croisette at Cannes or the quay at Portofino."

David Taggart's "wealthy" parents were a shadowy presence in their sons' PTL lives. When the brothers spent a weekend in the Hyatt Regency in Dearborn, taking a suite and inviting a fellow PTL executive along, they didn't take time to visit their parents, who lived in nearby Livonia.

The Taggarts' friends in Charlotte would have been shocked to see Henry and Jane Taggart's home. Henry Taggart had been born in Belfast, Ireland. He was a drill-press operator when he married in December 1952, at age twenty-seven. His bride, a native Michigander six years his elder, was a supervisor according to their marriage license. In 1957, the year of David's birth, his father worked as a salesman at a Chevrolet dealership in Detroit. Later, he rose to the position of service manager. Eventually he retired, disabled by a bad back. He owned no Cadillac dealerships.

David and James Taggart had spent most of their childhood in a one-and-a-half story, two-bedroom, one-bath duplex on the northern edge of Detroit. Jane Taggart's parents lived in the other side of the duplex. The Taggarts seemed a good Christian family, attending church regularly.

By the late sixties, the neighborhood had begun to deteriorate. In 1972, with James apparently headed to a local institute of technology to study interior design, Henry and Jane Taggart bought a new, 1,378-square-foot ranch house in the western suburb of Livonia. The three-bedroom home cost $34,990. Interstate 96 ran at the end of their street.

David transferred to a nearby high school, completed his final three years of education, and graduated in June 1975 in a class of about eight hundred. For the next two years, he studied music at Schoolcraft College, a two-year community college in Livonia. Later, he chose not to mention the school when asked about his education. He left without obtaining a degree and enrolled in January 1978 at Detroit's Wayne State University. He majored in music but stayed only six months, departing about the time he appeared on PTL's payroll. Later, in program notes for an unusual on-stage piano performance after his move to Bakker's staff, Taggart described himself as a keyboard student since 1970. "While attending Wayne State University, he studied under the skillful mastery of professors in the classical arts."

Gary Smith chose to give Bakker more freedom than his predecessor Ed Stoeckel had, to "let Jim be Jim." Smith believed that Bakker wanted to do right, and he tried to steer PTL along the path of professionalism and fiscal accountability that Stoeckel had followed. He funneled key decisions into a committee of executives to restrict Bakker's free-spending ways. If Bakker insisted on one of his plans over Smith's objections, Smith obliged. Unlike Stoeckel, Smith favored keeping Heritage USA.

Early in his tenure, Smith flew to Norfolk to see Pat Robertson at CBN. He wanted to know why he never saw Bakker and Robertson and their ministries talking to one another. Robertson was not encouraging. Good luck, he told Smith. If you can do something good with Jim, you'll be the first. As Smith remembered, Robertson told him that Bakker was two people. He did not explain further. Smith interpreted the comment to mean that Bakker had everything going for him—lots of talent, a successful TV program—and yet he was never content and always driven to have and accomplish more.

After eight months, Bakker was weary of Smith and all the problems he kept bringing up. Smith had reported possible wrongdoing at the Canton, Ohio, station and in PTL's Canadian office. And PTL's lawyer in Ohio was worried that PTL might face legal action for failing to make good on its promise to build a studio at WJAN, a victim of mismanagement and PTL's financial troubles. Bakker had become more and more distant since Smith had come to him with a bizarre story about one of PTL's ghostwriters who had suggested that Bakker had had a homosexual encounter as a teenager. Bakker told Smith one day to "quit turning over rocks" in the ministry. He seemed to avoid talking to Smith, who was dismayed at the see-no-evil position.

Soon three of Smith's colleagues informed him Bakker wanted him to step down and take another position at PTL. Instead, he drafted a one-page letter of resignation.

I can not suppress, compromise, or violate ethical business principles; especially possible fraudulent or unlawful acts. Since our policy has seemingly been not to generate and deal with, but rather a desirous decree to elude or destroy any data or testament to this type material, I have attached . . . a twenty-eight page letter from Mr. Paul H. Chappell dated April 9, 1980 to illustrate my numerous concerns.

I have intentionally not referred to matters that apparently exist or which have been known to exist which are of a more serious nature for my motive is not one of vindication.

Chappell was PTL's tax attorney, and the letter mentioned by Smith had warned PTL that it could be jeopardizing its treasured tax-exempt status with its disregard of federal tax regulations. Smith sent a copy of the package to board member Richard Dortch. He wanted to make sure that the board was aware of the continuing problems at PTL.

In late 1980, Tammy talked about her life and her marriage in an interview with a writer for the *Saturday Evening Post.* She spoke wistfully, the interviewer wrote later, as she described her changing relationship with her husband.

We used to be more alike than we are now. Jim's more laid back and quiet than I am. Sometimes I wish he'd talk more . . . sometimes I wish he were more nutty. But I guess if there were two nuts in the family, the world couldn't take it. It's good he's like he is. He calms me and keeps me in perspective. We complement each other.

The interview with the sympathetic *Saturday Evening Post* was classic Tammy. "Every time I get into a bathtub with hot water and bubbles, I say, 'Thank you, Jesus!'" A hot bubble bath was a reminder of how far Tammy had come from her humble childhood home in International Falls. She talked about her unpredictable hairstyles, from a black, Spanish-looking wig to a red Lucille Ball hairpiece to the short brown hair that was indeed hers. She said that women should keep themselves interesting and not fall into a rut with their husbands. "Jim says he's lived with me for nineteen years and doesn't know me. I say I'm going to keep it that way."

Tammy acknowledged that she and her husband had had their

share of problems. "But thank God we've straightened them out. You've got to talk. Even if you're screaming at each other, you've got to get it out." People didn't try hard enough anymore to avoid divorce, she said. Instead, they "see an easy way out and they take it. You've got to work at a marriage. If you don't, it will fail."

But the Bakkers' marriage was failing, despite the quick-fix counseling in Palmdale and the recording sessions in LA. Soon, even the cosmetic emblems of success the Bakkers held before the public—the declaration of strong finances, the grand opening of the Barn, the ride on Air Force One, and the claims of a happy home life—couldn't cover the rot beneath.

CHAPTER NINE

INDISCRETIONS

"Make sure . . . I don't ever move into a strange position again"

The sunny, seventy-degree weather in Clearwater Beach, Florida, was a welcome break from the winter descending on Charlotte that Saturday, December 6, 1980. At the pool of the Sheraton resort on Sand Key, Jim Bakker sunned in a white terry-cloth swimsuit. Across the broad beach of white sand lay the unbroken blue expanse of the Gulf of Mexico.

Bakker had flown to Florida to help WCLF, a Christian TV station outside Tampa, with its fund-raiser. The station carried his show locally, and his friend, John Wesley Fletcher, served as one of its corporate officers. It was a rare telethon trip for Bakker: where once he had traveled from city to city to raise money for PTL, he now relied on telethons broadcast nationally.

Fletcher had joined Bakker, as had Sam Orender and Bakker's ten-year-old daughter, Tammy Sue. The trip was one of Bakker's first without Phil Egert, the older, married ex–military man who had served as his administrative assistant. Bakker's new traveling companion was David Taggart, the young, single assistant Bakker had recruited from his music director.

Late that morning, Fletcher had left the hotel for the Tampa airport a half hour away to pick up a friend from Long Island, a twenty-one-year-old named Jessica Hahn who worked as a church secretary in Massapequa, New York. The two arrived at the Sheraton at lunchtime, and Fletcher escorted Hahn to her room on the fifth floor. Soon after, Bakker left his daughter at the pool and disappeared into the hotel. Taggart stayed with young Tammy Sue.

Later that day, Fletcher invited Sam Orender to Hahn's room on the fifth floor, three flights below the rooms of the PTL contingent. The two men had often worked together at PTL. Orender, who was not one for shows of piety, knew Fletcher's carnal side, the foul language, the taste for liquor. Even so, he was surprised at what he saw.

Fletcher introduced Hahn. He explained that she had baby-sat for his kids years ago when he had preached a revival at her church. Hahn was lying on the bed, wearing a dress. Fletcher sat in a chair and talked. After a few minutes, the evangelist slid onto the bed and began to wrestle playfully with the young woman. Hahn seemed to be enjoying herself—and not to care how it looked to Orender. As Fletcher and Hahn rolled about, Hahn's dress hitched up enough to expose her panties.

Orender sensed—from what he saw and from what Fletcher had told him—that this young woman had joined Fletcher on the road before. She hardly seemed an innocent; Orender thought she might be a prostitute. Orender also sensed that Fletcher had invited this girl to Florida as a favor to Jim Bakker.

Orender had been in the room perhaps twenty minutes when Fletcher and Hahn decided to leave. The three walked into the hall together. As they parted, Fletcher pledged to send the woman to Orender's room later. Years later, Orender was unsure what he would have done if Hahn had paid him a visit. She was, he thought, a very attractive girl.

Later that trip, Fletcher apologized to Orender that he and Jessica hadn't returned in time to come to Orender's room. They had gone for a walk on the beach, Fletcher boasted, and screwed three times.

On December 10, four days after that Saturday in Clearwater, PTL's board of directors met at Heritage Village. Bakker, A. T. Lawing, and Richard Dortch were there. So were two newcomers to the board, both Assemblies of God ministers. One was a woman prison chaplain from New York City, Aimee Garcia Cortese, whose brother, Robert Garcia, had been elected to Congress a few years earlier. The other was a longtime friend of Dortch's, Charles Cookman, the veteran district superintendent for North Carolina. Board member Efrem Zimbalist, Jr., was absent.

The board quickly turned to a gloomy subject: what would happen to PTL if Jim died. Bakker was haunted by the specter of his own mortality, a worry made more pressing by his oldest brother's death at age forty-five. Now, with his marriage failing, Bakker was eager to make sure that his wife wouldn't take over PTL if something happened to him.

PTL's directors agreed that Dortch would step in as president and board chairman. The board would choose a new host for the TV program. "If ever a stalemate should come about, on any situation, or if liquidation should occur," the minutes read, "Mr. James O. Bakker would want the 'PTL Club' program and [PTL] to go into the hands of the Assemblies of God." The board agreed unanimously.

Before the meeting ended, Dortch suggested that the board award Bakker the equivalent of one month of his $79,000-a-year salary as a Christmas bonus. The directors agreed. They also approved, again at Dortch's suggestion, a $16,000 increase in PTL's annual contribution to Bakker's retirement account.

During his encampment in Los Angeles, Bakker had decided to hold a world prayer conference after Christmas for PTL partners in Honolulu, gathering PTL's foreign TV hosts and taping his show ocean side. The Bakkers left Charlotte on December 14, stopped in Los Angeles to spend the night and shop, and flew on to Honolulu. They were to be gone for four weeks. It was to be a month of scenes carved deeply into PTL's collective psyche.

The Bakkers occupied the $350-a-night Presidential Suite on top of the Ilikai Hotel, the spot where Jack Lord stood at the opening of the TV police show "Hawaii Five-O." All hope for the Bakkers' marriage seemed to vanish in this idyllic setting. Tammy told her husband that she didn't love him any more, she wasn't going to live with him, and she wanted a divorce. She wasn't going back to Charlotte. Around the hotel pool, Tammy complained to other PTL wives. "Anybody who really knows Jim wouldn't blame me for leaving him," she told them. Tammy confided that she wanted to stay in ministry work but with a different, unnamed partner.

Bakker struck back in kind, telling her he didn't love her any

172

more either and ordering his wedding ring melted into a charm. "This is your twenty-year service pin," he told Tammy. He felt sad and hurt, he said years afterward, and so he had lied about his feelings.

Bakker, usually so driven, had little enthusiasm for his work. The night before the three hundred partners who had signed up for the conference were due to arrive, Bakker considered flying home to Charlotte. At one point, he summoned four aides—Flessing, Orender, Taggart, and Spurr—for advice. He told them that his marriage was falling apart. "I think that there's no hope, and we're going to have to get a divorce. What do you think we should do?"

Roger Flessing urged Bakker to walk away from the pressures of work to help save his marriage. He doubted that PTL could survive a divorce between Jim and Tammy. "I think you shouldn't be on the air. I think you ought to take three months off and just get your head back together," Flessing said. Spurr disagreed, telling Bakker to stay on the air. Bakker seemed to want to hear Spurr's advice, and he took it.

Listening to Spurr that day, Sam Orender was amazed. For weeks, he and others around Bakker had noticed that Spurr seemed to be taking Gary Paxton's place as Bakker's rival for Tammy's affections. Tammy had once so disliked Spurr that she had urged her husband to fire him. Her attitude had changed by the night of Reagan's November 1980 landslide victory over Jimmy Carter. On impulse, the Bakkers had decided to hold a party at their home. Spurr and Tammy Bakker had spent an hour together that night, talking by the stairway.

The Hawaiian conference proceeded, painfully. The Bakkers' suite acquired the somber mood of a morgue—when the Bakkers weren't shouting at each other. Bakker slept discreetly in a separate room. On the bad days, he drank piña coladas to cut his anxiety. In public, the Bakkers and their staff put on their best faces. Tammy looked distant, so PTL's cameramen and directors filled the programs with close-up shots of Jim. One day, Tammy refused to share the stage with her husband. Instead, she spent the program in the audience. Most everyone there sensed that something was terribly wrong.

One day, while he shopped near Waikiki Beach, Bakker pulled Sam Orender to the side. "That girl in Florida, did you have her too?'' he asked. No, Orender told him. Bakker talked briefly about Jessica Hahn. She was beautiful, he told Orender. And her breasts were firm but real, unlike Tammy's surgically enhanced chest. It was the only time the subject had come up between the two men. But now Orender knew that, yes, the woman had been intended for Bakker's pleasure.

On the matter of sex, the adult Jim Bakker behaved very much like a teenager in the locker room, eager to boast to male friends about his latest heterosexual gymnastics. At CBN, he and Tammy would disappear conspicuously into Jim's office, evidently to make love. He gave one CBN colleague a case of Trojans for Christmas, a gift the friend thought peculiar coming from a minister. At PTL, Bakker told friends how he had made love to Tammy in a park and how passersby had reacted to their passionate grunts and groans. He recommended that friends try vibrators, as he had with Tammy; he said that they had saved his marriage.

All of Bakker's exhibitionistic talk of marital passion did not silence quiet speculations about his sexuality. Some of those close to him were particularly troubled by the swift rise of David Taggart and the frequent visits of John Wesley Fletcher. If Bakker was engaging in sexual activity with other men—and by 1989 the evidence would be convincing, despite Bakker's denials—then the PTL president had no choice but to build a wall around that private truth, just as he so often did with the "facts" about PTL that he shared with his audience.

With his stylish clothes, jewelry, and prim and proper ways, young David Taggart left a distinctly effeminate impression. Members of Bakker's staff had even warned Bakker that his proximity to Taggart was creating at least the appearance of wrongdoing. Bakker told one PTL executive not to worry, because David had sworn on a stack of Bibles that he wasn't homosexual. Indeed, Taggart acknowledged to heterosexual friends and colleagues that people thought he was gay, saying that really, he wasn't, that his manner was just the result of his upbringing.

There were louder protests about Fletcher's sexuality. As the faith healer became more prominent on Bakker's broadcasts, PTL began fielding complaints that Fletcher had engaged in homosexual acts while on the revival circuit. Bakker's staff sent routine replies sidestepping the accusations but declaring PTL's opposition to homosexuality. Soon, Bakker ordered his publications director not to address the issue at all, saying that he was endangering the ministry and making PTL vulnerable to a lawsuit from Fletcher.

Bakker had condemned the homosexual life-style in his early years at PTL, but he soon adopted an attitude of forgiveness. In 1978, he and Anita Bryant had each spoken at a charismatic conference in Pittsburgh. Bryant had also appeared on Bakker's program. In an interview that year, Bakker alluded to Bryant's fight against a proposed ban on discrimination against homosexuals in Dade County, Florida.

> I think we ought to love [homosexuals]. I think we ought to welcome them in our churches, and we ought to pray for them, and we ought to love them because we're not gonna reach the homosexual for Christ by segregating them off to the side and preaching hate.
>
> Now, if I can love the alcoholic and tell him that Christ is the answer, if I can love the adulterer . . . if I can love the prostitute, I can love the homosexual. And I believe the church's job is to love people. God's job is to judge them, and everybody wants me to be the judge. I'm not God.

But, Bakker added, the homosexual act was without question a sin, much like adultery, murder, hatred, and gossip. Nevertheless, Bakker said, he would hire a homosexual if he told him, "Jim, I'm gay, I'm asking God for deliverance. Would you help me, would you give me a job?"

> The thing is, and I'm gonna be misunderstood unless you guys write this portion very carefully, but why should somebody have homosexual [sic] in his past be any more of an impossibility for God than a man who was an alcoholic in the past. If the Gospel that I preach is true, then I have a God of miracles, I have a God that changes lives.

Before his October 1980 departure, general manager Gary Smith had encountered suggestive but ambiguous evidence that Bakker was bisexual. Smith was firing an employee with a drinking problem when the man declared that Smith could not go ahead because the employee had "been with" Jim on his houseboat. He didn't explain further, and Smith moved ahead with the dismissal. At three in the morning, Smith was woken by a ringing phone. It was Bakker. "Gary. . ." Bakker paused for what seemed like three minutes. "Don't fire him."

Within weeks of Smith's departure, and just one month before his trip to Clearwater, Bakker had taken a spur-of-the-moment vacation to Bermuda with Taggart and Fletcher, flying there on the jet he had chartered to meet Jimmy Carter and Air Force One in Tennessee. It was in Bermuda, John Wesley Fletcher alleged in a 1989 *Penthouse* article, that he had discovered Bakker and Taggart in bed together.

Such a scene should have been no surprise to Fletcher. On three occasions, Fletcher alleged in the same *Penthouse* article, he and Bakker engaged in oral or anal sex. Their sexual relationship began, Fletcher claimed, when he gave Bakker a backrub in the ministry sauna at Heritage Village. The first advance, he said, was Bakker's.

In a final effort to avoid a divorce, Tammy agreed to undergo further counseling in Palmdale. David Taggart and her secretary escorted Tammy back to Palmdale, rented a car for her, and moved her into an apartment, paid for by PTL, next to the Palmdale hospital. PTL told the press that Tammy was in California "under doctor's orders to relax" because of a "temporary spell of exhaustion."

In later years, the Bakkers talked periodically about their separation. Neither acknowledged adultery, but Bakker told his audience that both had made "horrendous mistakes."

As Tammy explained it publicly in late 1981, she could no longer face life. She was paranoid and disenchanted and spent most of her time sleeping. "I imagine I was on the verge of a nervous breakdown." The FCC investigation had made her life miserable. She felt neglected by her hardworking husband and "less a part of PTL than the PTL Singers." Tammy sensed, too, that the staff put up with her only because she was the boss's wife.

> So I went away for about five or six weeks. I didn't think I was
> ever going to come back because I couldn't face what I felt
> everybody thought of me in my heart. I felt I'd failed, and I

thought I can't go back and face everyone, that they only love me cause I'm Jim's wife anyway

Separated from his wife, Bakker walked through his days in a pained daze. At one point, he contemplated suicide—for Bakker, the ultimate act of self-pity.

One night, when I hit bottom so bad, and I really wanted to end my life, I couldn't. I said how can I go back on television? My life is through. It's over with. I tried to find somebody, and I drove through the town of Charlotte, North Carolina, not knowing what to do or where to go. I needed help so bad, and I was a preacher. Where does a preacher go when he's dying?

Finally he stopped at the home of an Assemblies of God pastor.

They came out of bed and they cried with me for hours. . . . I needed someone to cry with me. I needed someone just to get the pressure off me. . . . I didn't care what happened to Jim Bakker any more. I really didn't. I didn't care whether he lived or died.

Bakker did not confess his adultery to his wife, but in early 1981 he did recount his version of the event to Fred Gross of the Palmdale therapy team. Six years later, after the public learned of his encounter with Jessica Hahn, Bakker authorized the psychologist to describe his three-hour confession.

[Jim Bakker] was in absolute agony . . . when he mustered the courage to tell me he had an indiscretion in his life just a few weeks before. A one-time incident—something that happened real quickly, in a time of real need in his life.
He was sobbing when he told me. He was shaking so violently that I had to hold him. He was so totally distraught and out of control that he was racked with pain and guilt from the head to his toes. And in that moment in time I, like many of you here, had to ask myself, what do I do? . . .
I looked at Jim Bakker and I knew that he was in a process of release. And I knew that he was honest and open. And together we knelt on the carpet, and then within ten minutes we were prone on the floor. His face was buried in the carpet,

sobbing. He was kicking the floor. He was writhing. He was retching.

And I led him before the throne of God to seek the mercy of Almighty God because God asked us in our time of need to come to Him and ask, plead for mercy, and then to confess our sin. . . . Jim Bakker asked God to forgive him, he confessed his sin in detail. He apologized to God. He was absolutely so honest that I hurt for him. . . .

I said to him that night, I remember it so very well, I said, "If God be with you who can be against you? Now I tell you before God, Jim Bakker, that you have been forgiven of God."

Bakker told Gross to be vigilant—a declaration reminiscent of his "squeaky clean" speeches to his finance staff. "He said, 'Fred, stay with me. Make sure that I'm on track. Make sure that I walk the right road, that my heart is clean before God. That my motives are clear. That I don't ever move into a strange position again.' "

Bakker's big house in Charlotte's Foxcroft section held too many memories of a marriage gone sour. Bakker moved himself and his two children into a double-wide trailer next to his studio at Heritage USA. His first Saturday back in North Carolina, Bakker and a real-estate agent scouted properties on Lake Wylie, southwest of Charlotte. During the day, the two stopped by the Bakkers' old house on the lake.

That night, Bakker telephoned Flessing at his hotel room in Washington. Flessing had gone to the capital to prepare to televise Bakker's participation in a Sunday prayer service marking Ronald Reagan's inauguration.

"Is anybody in the room with you? Is anybody listening to this phone?" Bakker asked his aide. Flessing assured him he could talk freely.

"I found out. I found out what's happening with Tammy."

Bakker had walked into his lake house and felt God telling him to look in the garbage can. He looked in several and finally, in the bedroom, found a letter that had been torn to pieces. Painstakingly, he pieced the letter together. It took him hours.

Bakker read the letter to Flessing. As Flessing remembered it, the author was Tammy, Spurr the intended recipient. The letter writer had declared, "I can't wait until we can get away and be together."

The letter alluded to Tammy's concern that she would be Spurr's only woman. Spurr was married.

Bakker showed up at Roger and Linda Wilson's front door at eleven that night. Linda was in her nightclothes, ready for bed. After blowing the whistle on Tammy's relationship with Paxton, Linda Wilson had been transferred from her job as Tammy's secretary and escort. Friends with the Bakkers for more than ten years, the Wilsons had not seen the Bakkers socially in months. The picture of their infant daughter, Kristy, had disappeared from the wall of Bakker's office. It was the quintessential Bakker freeze-out, an experience shared by many who got close to the Bakkers: best friends one minute, strangers the next.

As the Wilsons listened, Bakker told them about the torn-up letter. He seemed to need an audience, and they were available. They told him what they had said many times before, that he was so wrapped up in his ministry that he neglected his wife. Bakker didn't want to hear the bad news. He left.

A day after his talk with Flessing, Bakker arrived, by chartered jet, in Washington. Bakker had suggested earlier to Vi Azvedo, a counselor on Gross's Palmdale therapy team, that Tammy join him at President Reagan's inaugural ball. Tammy agreed, flying in from California with Azvedo. Jim watched his wife and Spurr together, but he said nothing. After the inaugural events, Tammy returned to California.

A few days after his return from Washington, Bakker summoned Spurr to his office. He asked Flessing to join them as a witness.

"I found out what's going on with my wife," Bakker said. Spurr said nothing; Bakker fired him immediately. He expressed his disappointment in Spurr, a man he had treated well in months past, giving him a vice-president's title, a six-thousand-dollar PTL boat, and a pay raise to $37,000.

Spurr denied nothing. He told Bakker he loved Tammy, that she was quite a woman and that he ought to take better care of her. It wasn't Spurr's fault that Bakker neglected Tammy.

Spurr departed, and the Bakkers' marriage continued to hang by a thread. Some at PTL expected Spurr to fly to Las Vegas, divorce his wife, and marry Tammy. Instead, Bakker flew to Palmdale for more counseling with Tammy. As had become routine, PTL paid the tab; the three-day trip by chartered jet cost $11,400.

Tammy soon returned to Charlotte. Life in California wasn't as glamorous as Tammy had expected, Jim Bakker later told his TV audience. Tammy told one of her friends that she wasn't sure where her interest in Spurr might lead.

Bakker rewarded Tammy with a $340,000 present, a Balinese-style home in the private Tega Cay development on Lake Wylie. The PTL board agreed to buy and redecorate the home, and the Bakkers moved in by month's end.

The work began immediately. Until the Bakkers moved out six years later, the house seemed under constant renovation. A new roof. New decks outside. New carpet. New plumbing. New wiring. An enlarged master bedroom with a wall of windows looking out on the lake. A new atrium and a new garage. A TV viewing room, later converted into a rehearsal room with mirrored walls, hardwood floors, and enough track lights to make a miniature studio. An adjoining exercise room, with mirrored walls, weight-lifting equipment, a padded door, marquee-type flashing lights along the walls, and track lights overhead synchronized with the music from the stereo system.

The house contained seven thousand square feet when the Bakkers picked it out; when they left in 1987, it sprawled over ten thousand. By then, PTL had invested $1 million in the home—or parsonage, as it was called for image and tax reasons—far more than PTL could hope to recoup if the home was sold. No expense was spared. The main kitchen was full of big-name appliances: Sub-Zero refrigerators, a Thermador oven, a Jenn-Air grill. Eventually the L-shaped room became two kitchens, one built to commercial standards, the other suited for a single family. A third kitchen was added downstairs to service the heated outdoor pool.

Flessing jokingly called it the Winchester Mystery House, and other visitors found it a curious jumble of choppy rooms linked by long hallways and confusing stairwells. In a sense it mirrored its principal resident. The house felt like a fortress, an impression compounded by the elaborate security system installed by PTL—surveillance cameras, an access gate atop the driveway, and guards stationed around the clock in a freestanding utility room at the foot of the drive. The house was an escape from the outside world and, with all its crannies, from those inside the house as well. Like Bakker, the house in Tega Cay guarded its secrets well.

Bakker justified his move to the PTL board as an effort to enhance security, but his new house seemed nearly as vulnerable as the old. It was exposed to boat traffic on the lake and to strangers from the houses on the hill above. PTL set out to make the house more secure. Within days of the move, Bakker began approaching owners of neighboring homes, asking them to sell. He hoped to create a compound of houses and perhaps, eventually, to wall off the entire complex.

Bakker suggested to one neighbor, a certified public accountant, that the man could net $120,000 for his house if he had a letter from PTL saying that he had donated a portion of the selling price. To do that, the neighbor would have to claim to the IRS that the house was worth $140,000, $20,000 more than its market value. He declined the offer.

Cost would be no barrier in pursuit of Bakker's plan for a compound at Tega Cay. By the start of summer 1981, PTL had purchased three more houses at a cost of more than $340,000. The next year, the ministry bought its fifth house for $139,000. A sixth house was added in 1985. For the most part, the houses were poorly constructed and worth less than PTL paid. As PTL remodeled one home, workers discovered a crack more than an inch wide running across the floor; the front of the house was sliding down the hill. The repair cost more than $14,000.

PTL bore the expense of another cocoon for Bakker—the battalion of maids, security guards, and groundskeepers hired to meet the Bakker family's whims. The retainers did everything imaginable. Security guards changed the kitty litter, shined Bakker's shoes, stocked coolers with soda, checked every light bulb in the house, turned the air conditioning off and on in the houseboat, and washed Bakker's car each morning.

Bakker's domestic staff performed the most personal chores, with orders often issued by Bakker through his office staff. They bought hair coloring and British Sterling aftershave and collar stays and a new toothbrush for Jim, Clairol curlers for Tammy Sue, fresh corn on the cob for the house. They were told to get rid of the Tab soda, program new numbers into the telephone, deflea the dogs.

Without including the cost of security, IRS auditors found that PTL had spent nearly $54,000 a year during the first two years on housekeeping, grounds, and maintenance of Bakker's home. During each of Bakker's final four years, the cost rose to close to $70,000.

After Bakker's return from Hawaii, his TV program changed its name and its home. In January, the "PTL Club" became simply "Jim Bakker." Publicly, PTL said it wanted to reduce confusion with Paul Crouch's "Praise the Lord" show in California and to capitalize on Bakker's name recognition. Privately, Bakker had complained to his staff that viewers could find other evangelists but not him. The new name also put a strategic distance between the program and Tammy Bakker at a time when her return to the air was very much in doubt.

To some PTL veterans, the name change seemed another step away from PTL's roots. The ministry had been founded on a dedication to Jesus and a commitment to minister to its viewers. Now, it seemed more and more to function for the glorification and comfort of its leader, Jim Bakker.

By May, Bakker was broadcasting his program from the Barn auditorium, leaving behind the well-designed five-year-old studio set at Heritage Village. With the move to larger quarters, PTL hoped to have room for the big summertime crowds Bakker's show drew.

On Sundays, the Barn doubled as a church. Bakker had opened a church at Heritage USA the September before in a further departure from PTL's original stated purpose of steering viewers into local churches and from Bakker's pledge to local ministers not to found a competing church. As he opened the church, Bakker explained that he had been troubled by television's impersonality. "The older I get, the more I see the need for a church. The more I want to be a part, the more I need the brethren. They can offer a kind of instant barometer on what I'm doing."

Starting a local church had another, more tangible benefit as well: it strengthened PTL's claim to the protection from government that churches receive under the US Constitution. As a church, PTL could avoid state regulation of its fund-raising, limit its property-tax bill, and avoid filing the annual tax returns that the IRS requires of most tax-exempt organizations. Once filed with the IRS, those Form 990s—and their disclosure of top executives' pay—would become available for inspection by the public and the press, a potential public-relations disaster for PTL as Bakker's compensation grew.

PTL had stopped filing Form 990s in 1977, shortly after the board amended PTL's corporate purpose to include establishing a place of public worship. The board had also renamed the parent corporation Heritage Village Church and Missionary Fellowship. But the early church services at Heritage Village had been a half-hearted exercise, and by 1980, the IRS was seeking evidence from PTL that it in fact qualified as a church. It was perhaps no coincidence that at this time Bakker opened his new, more organized church at Heritage USA.

More important than PTL's qualifications as a church was its claim to exemption from income taxes. Under the US tax code, organizations operating exclusively for religious, charitable, or educational purposes may apply for tax-exempt status. The privilege of tax-exemption, so critical to the financial survival of a TV ministry, comes with strings attached. One is the prohibition against spending the tax-exempt group's money on "nonexempt purposes," such as the benefit of the organization's leaders. In tax law, this violation is known as private inurement.

Tax-exempt groups are allowed to pay their officers, employees, and outsiders what the IRS considers reasonable compensation for goods and services rendered. There are no hard-and-fast scales for unreasonable pay. The IRS makes its judgments case by case, applying a series of standards to safeguard against abuse. Is an insider with the power to control the organization reaping benefits? Is an employee with a high salary getting other compensation as well? Are there other family members on the payroll? Are insiders getting loans from the organization? Is the organization paying for personal gifts to friends and relatives of those in charge?

As PTL's financial interests grew indistinguishable from Bakker's, PTL's legal advisers recognized the growing risks to the ministry. In April 1980—days before Jim and Tammy began their first round of marital counseling in Palmdale—tax attorney Paul Chappell had warned PTL that it was creating "private inurement problems" that might cost PTL its tax-exempt status, much as similar violations had cost L. Ron Hubbard's Church of Scientology.

Chappell's confidential, twenty-eight-page letter itemized specific transactions that he feared could cause PTL trouble in the event of an IRS audit. He was worried, he wrote, about PTL's use of travel-expense money.

> I seem to recall an instance in the latter part of 1976 or early 1977 in which Jim and Tammy and a group of PTL employees took a weekend trip to Nashville, Tennessee, at a cost of approximately ten thousand dollars for the purpose of accompanying Tammy in preparing a record for production at the Gary Paxton Studio. The cost of this trip was paid for by PTL.
>
> Moreover, I understand that it was Jim's practice at one time to draw down a substantial sum of money, *e.g.*, twenty-five hundred to five thousand dollars, for Tammy to use to go shopping with for a week when they were out of town on a telethon. I would suppose that such checks would have been issued either to "Cash" or to Jim and Tammy individually who in turn would endorse and cash them. . . .
>
> A somewhat similar incident occurred in 1978 following Jim's world missionary trip. After the entourage returned from this trip I understand that all of Jim's travel money was accounted for except five thousand dollars. Herb [Moore, finance director,] was informed by Ruth Egert that Jim intended to retain five thousand dollars of unspent travel money. I believe this amount was set up on the PTL books in 1979 as a loan receivable reflecting an obligation on the part of Jim to the corporation. If the "loan" remained unpaid at the end of 1979, it was Herb's intention to reflect the five-thousand-dollar amount on a Form 1099 so that Jim would report it on his 1979 income tax return.

Chappell wrote that PTL must be prepared to show that the travel-expense money was not diverted to the Bakkers' personal benefit. PTL should find out if the Bakkers reported any of the diverted travel money on their individual tax returns in the years they got the money. If not, he wrote, they should file amended returns.

Chappell was worried that PTL was supporting two houses at once for Bakker—the house in Foxcroft and the Bakkers' personal home on Lake Wylie. Not only was PTL paying for substantial renovation, improvement, and interior decoration at Foxcroft, including at least $15,000 spent in fall 1978, but Chappell said he believed PTL was paying the mortgage, taxes, and utilities for the home the Bakkers owned. "It seems to me that if this situation were discovered on audit, an examining revenue agent would determine that the PTL payments that were made with respect to *one* of the residences was for the personal benefit of Jim and Tammy."

Despite the seriousness of Chappell's letter, little was done. The lawyer was being replaced, another in a long line of PTL attorneys, and the document was interpreted at PTL as a CYA—cover your ass—letter. Finance director John Franklin concluded that many of the specifics Chappell cited were in fact rumor, and he believed that Bakker's secretary, Ruth Egert, had been diligent in seeing that Bakker reimbursed PTL for his personal spending. Though concerned about the issue of inurement in years past, Franklin was more worried about what PTL was doing now.

A year after Chappell's warnings, PTL was still bending IRS regulations on private inurement to the breaking point. In April 1981, the Bakkers celebrated their twentieth anniversary—the anniversary that almost wasn't—with a dinner at Cafe Eugene, one of Charlotte's finest restaurants. As always, the Bakkers traveled in the safety of a crowd; Bakker's top executives came along, as did PTL's outside directors who, seven weeks earlier, had heard Bakker's assurances that all excess spending was being cut. All in all, twenty-three people attended the dinner. The event carried the stamp of David Taggart and his brother James, who often dined at Cafe Eugene. They had arranged for elaborate ice carvings and gorgeous floral decorations; truffles were even flown in from Europe for the soup.

When the evening was over, PTL paid the $8,500 tab. Four years later, IRS auditors cited the party as further evidence that Bakker had profited personally from PTL, in violation of federal law. Their report also would cite Bakker's $350-a-night hotel room in Hawaii, the $11,400 chartered jet ride to Palmdale, and the hundreds of thousands of dollars PTL had spent on the Tega Cay home.

By summer 1981, several key figures from the early years of PTL had left Bakker's side, partly out of frustration with Bakker and disenchantment with the changing moral climate at PTL. Ruth Egert quit, along with her husband, Phil, who had served as Bakker's photographer and executive assistant. Bakker had stopped listening to their advice. Phil Egert, appointed operations manager in late 1980, had recommended that Bakker slow the pace of construction as high interest rates and rising unemployment squeezed PTL's donors at home. Bakker decided to move ahead anyway. The Egerts were uncomfortable, too, with the sort of people who had ingratiated themselves with Bakker, most notably John Wesley Fletcher and David Taggart. To the Egerts, these men were fundamentally secular, using God and the church for their own ends.

Weary of PTL, Tammy's former secretary, Linda Wilson, also resigned. PTL gave her a going-away party, and Tammy came, squired by Vi Azvedo from Palmdale, as she had been since her return to Charlotte. Linda and Tammy had lunched occasionally, and Tammy seemed resigned to her fate. PTL wasn't what Tammy wanted to do with her life, but she saw no alternative. At the party, Tammy gave Linda a teardrop necklace and hugged her. In that moment of intimacy, Tammy confided to her former best friend, "I wish I was leaving instead of you."

A week after his wife's departure, Roger Wilson was laid off. His supervisor was gentle, saying that he was sorry to do this, that it wasn't a reflection on Wilson's work, but that because of budgetary restraints, PTL no longer needed his position. Wilson figured that Bakker was tired of his readiness to disagree. He had known the PTL president long enough and well enough to talk to him man-to-man, without the deference Bakker now received from most of his staff.

Roger Wilson had orchestrated the conversion of PTL's pyramid, the three-story building Bakker had started as a home for Heritage University and which had been transformed into PTL's executive office building. Wilson had disagreed with Bakker on how to outfit the pyramid, formally called The World Outreach Center; Wilson suggested a practical approach, while Bakker preferred more extravagant and costly alternatives. Bakker hadn't liked the look of the planter that separated his third-floor office suite from the building's atrium. He ordered it redone, didn't like the new one any better, and had it redone again. It wound up looking much like Wilson had wanted it in the first place.

After nine years with Bakker, Sam Orender had lost his enthusiasm. In the early years, he had given PTL one hundred dollars a month. For years now, he had given nothing. He wanted to leave but lacked the fortitude to surrender his job.

In early 1981, Bakker had ordered Orender to draw up plans for a second annual Christmas trip to Hawaii for PTL partners. Bakker wanted the second tour to be bigger and better. Instead of three hundred, Bakker wanted one thousand people. After two months of hard work, Orender had persuaded United Airlines to schedule three jumbo jets for the group. He had also negotiated approval to shoot from the same ocean-view spot that PTL had used in 1980, over the stubborn opposition of local Hawaiians.

In a staff meeting one afternoon, Orender presented his plans to Bakker. He told his boss that United Airlines required a deposit six months in advance for the aircraft. With a quick verdict—"no, no, let's just cancel the whole thing"—Bakker pushed aside Orender's paperwork. The meeting moved on, and Orender's efforts were wasted.

A few months later, a member of Bakker's newest executive council told Orender that he would have to step down from his vice-president's post because he had separated from his wife again five months earlier. Orender was told that, according to Scripture, his marital problems rendered him unsuitable to serve as a deacon of the church. Orender smelled hypocrisy. What about Jim's drinking wine, as Orender knew Bakker had been doing for several years. Didn't that contradict the Bible too? Offered the chance to return to directing, Orender decided instead to quit.

If Bakker's memories of Clearwater weighed on his conscience, he showed no evidence of bitterness towards evangelist John Wesley Fletcher, his go-between with Hahn, the facilitator of what Fletcher would later describe as an effort to make Tammy jealous. On Bakker's TV program two days after that Saturday in Florida, the two men had prayed together and talked of faith and God's love. Fletcher joined Bakker in Hawaii. There Don Hardister, Bakker's security chief, heard the men plan for Fletcher to fill Tammy's place on the show. Fletcher was at Bakker's side on television for four days in January, another four in February, two in March, five in April, and four in May.

But that summer, Fletcher made a mistake that cost him his lucrative alliance with Bakker and PTL—and that set the stage for the upheaval six years later that would cost Bakker his ministry.

A PTL counseling intern who moonlighted as a security guard accused Fletcher of propositioning him. Fletcher had invited the young man to his room in Heritage Village and offered him a job. Eventually, Fletcher tried to hug him. The young guard reported that Fletcher had invited him to spend the night.

Flessing laid the evidence before Bakker in a brief meeting. Bakker appeared to be shocked. "Let the elders handle it," he said; he didn't want to get involved. The board listened to both accuser and accused. Fletcher was evasive, never categorically denying that he had made the advance. The elders recommended that Fletcher not appear again on Bakker's program.

Fletcher was banished from PTL, but word of the incident was evidently never passed along official Assemblies of God channels, even though there is no graver sin for one of its ministers. But other accusations soon sealed Fletcher's fate with the Pentecostal church.

At about the time Fletcher was forced out of PTL, Richard Dortch, the Assemblies of God official with jurisdiction over Fletcher, learned of accusations that Fletcher had gotten drunk and propositioned another man. Fletcher admitted drinking, and in October 1981 Dortch decided to dismiss Fletcher from the ministry for that conduct. Dortch and the Illinois district presbyters also agreed that Fletcher would have to face the more serious charge of homosexuality if he sought to return to the Assemblies pulpit after completing a mandatory two-year period of restoration.

Dortch met Fletcher at the St. Louis airport to deliver the news. As he read Dortch's letter, Fletcher, with tears in his eyes, looked up and asked, "What are you going to do about Jim?"

"John," Dortch answered, "you would be a very poor witness against anybody." Dortch chose not to pursue the matter of Bakker's conduct any further.

Fletcher soon violated the terms of his two-year restoration, returning prematurely to the evangelical circuit. Accusations of homosexuality continued to dog him. In 1985, he sued a Missouri couple, complaining that they had spread rumors at a revival in Cape Girardeau that he was a homosexual, a liar, a drunkard, and out to defraud the faithful. The suit was settled out of court.

Two years later, within weeks of Bakker's resignation, an Oklahoma man sued Fletcher. During a March 1986 business trip to Atlanta, the man charged, Fletcher had subjected him "to mental anguish as well as physical liberties unbecoming a normal person, never mind a 'man of the cloth.'"

* * *

Taboo in the Pentecostal world, male homosexuality was incomprehensible to many PTL partners and staff members. Some of the men at Bakker's side were also hard put to understand their boss's peculiar sexual conduct. Instead of labeling it homosexual, they tried to explain it away as the symptom of sexual frustration in an unhappily married man or tension in an overworked executive.

On a Friday afternoon in March 1981, a few weeks after Tammy's return from California, Bakker asked one of his aides for a backrub. Bakker sat in the barber's chair in his dressing room, unclothed save for a towel around his waist. The aide, a married man who often traveled with Bakker, stood behind him, rubbing his shoulders.

As the aide looked down, Bakker opened the towel and began masturbating. The aide, stunned, turned and walked out. Bakker emerged soon after. "I'm sorry," he said, "I'm so sensitive." The employee interpreted Bakker's words generously—he was so starved for love that just the touch of another human aroused him sexually.

But the scene was replayed again and again over the next three years. Each time the aide walked away, turning the lights out as he left, while Bakker aroused himself. Bakker's conduct infuriated the aide, but he liked his job, with its unlimited budget, travel, and the sense of divine calling. He was proud of his ability to serve, to be an employee the boss could rely on. So he continued to give Bakker rubdowns, blowing off steam afterwards to David Taggart and Vi Azvedo, who was now on PTL's staff. Azvedo told the aide to call her each time the masturbation happened.

CHAPTER TEN

A PROSPEROUS PRESIDENT

"We intend to be good stewards with God's money"

The four directors agreed: PTL had been blessed by a miracle. How else to interpret the deluge of $9 million in donations in a single month? "To God be the glory," Jim Bakker told his fellow board members. The August 1981 offerings had been so big that some days PTL's staff couldn't finish counting all the money, Bakker said. The signs that day, September 22, 1981, pointed to continued success. Indeed, donors would give another $7 million in September.

Like many of Bakker's money-raising triumphs, the "miracle" of that summer was born in a crisis exaggerated, if not manufactured, by Bakker. In August, the company holding the mortgage on the central tract of land of Heritage USA warned PTL that it might foreclose if the ministry failed to make its overdue payments. The day the letter arrived, PTL paid up.

But Bakker, recognizing the drawing power of calamity, was not finished. He read the letter on the air and mailed a copy to four hundred thousand partners. He pleaded for one thousand supporters to give one thousand dollars each. PTL was fighting for its life, he said. "They're not going to take Heritage USA away from us. It will not be sold at auction on the courthouse steps."

Thanks to Bakker's jeremiads, revenues for PTL's summer quarter ran $6.8 million over expenditures. PTL needed the good news. Despite record donations in the fiscal year ending May 31, 1981, PTL's current liabilities on that date totaled $17.2 million, more than seven times the $2.4 million it had in current assets. PTL's problem was not how much money it was getting but how wildly it spent what it got.

The vast sums spent on Bakker were the most outrageous examples of corporate profligacy. The September 1981 PTL board meeting demonstrated the willingness of PTL's directors—trusting cheerleaders led by Richard Dortch—to condone a rich-man's lifestyle for Bakker. Once its justification had been Bakker's hard work. Now, the board seemed anxious to protect Bakker and his fragile home life.

As Dortch proposed, the board approved. A $50,000 bonus, evidently Bakker's biggest ever. A study of how to give Bakker the Tega Cay house while PTL continued to pay for its maintenance, remodeling, decorating, and utilities. An increase in Bakker's salary from $79,000 to $102,000. A company Cadillac or Lincoln. A company-paid vacation for Bakker and a search for a residence in Florida that the PTL president and his family could use as a retreat. If there was any question left that the board had domestic harmony on its mind, the board voted to double Tammy Bakker's salary to $52,000 a year and inform her, officially, that the board, "thank[s] you for who you are."

Later, in a confidential talk with the accountability group to which PTL belonged, board member Charles Cookman explained the board's vote to buy a Florida residence. The Bakkers' marriage had come under strain, he said, due to "the high visibility and the intensity and perhaps some other things too."

> We know, as a board of directors, that if Jim Bakker falls, if his marriage collapses publicly, that these are the kinds of things of which disasters are made. . . . PTL is down the tube, it's gone. It's his vision and burden. . . . One of the things that I feel is a very important responsibility [is] to help protect him. He is a workaholic.

The board continued playing mother-protector at its meeting the following December. Bakker seemed tired, they thought. Cookman suggested that Jim and Tammy go to Pinehurst, North Carolina, for a rest. Dortch proposed that Bakker consider installing a recreational facility in the Tega Cay home. The board endorsed Dortch's idea. Then they voted each of the Bakkers a five-thousand-dollar "love offering."

That night, December 10, after a staff Christmas party at Charlotte's Civic Center, the board members and PTL executives—ninety persons in all—dined at Cafe Eugene. The affair cost nearly one hundred dollars a person.

The year 1981 was a watershed for the rationalization of greed at PTL. With the board's generous pay raises and bonuses, Jim and Tammy Bakkers' income began to mushroom. They earned $115,899 from PTL that year, more than $420,000 the next, and over $675,000 in 1983.

But the Jim Bakker who kept his ministry teetering on the financial brink was not a big saver. With PTL's deep pockets so readily at his disposal, he saw little need for prudence. In early 1982, as Bakker toured the boat show in Charlotte's downtown convention center, he fell in love with a fifty-eight-foot houseboat priced at more than $90,000. He told friends that it would be a cozy getaway, an intimate contrast to the rambling Tega Cay home. Soon after, David Taggart telephoned PTL's fastidious finance director John Franklin. Taggart wanted a check for more than $50,000—a loan, he said, so Bakker could buy the boat, adding the trade-in on the houseboat that had caused such a fuss in 1978.

"We can't do that," Franklin told Taggart. Franklin, the thirty-three-year-old CPA from Indiana who had replaced Herb Moore as finance director in 1979, knew the IRS rules on private inurement. Three or four days later, Franklin was summoned to the third-floor executive offices in the World Outreach Center. Dortch was there, as was Taggart. Dortch pooh-poohed Franklin's concerns, telling him that it was done all the time, that Jim would pay the money back. He told him not to worry, that everything was fine, that they were a church and allowed to lend money to their pastor.

"I'm just not going to do it," Franklin answered. Dortch insisted that Franklin comply; Bakker needed the money the next day.

Dortch was in Charlotte to attend the latest board meeting, timed to coincide with the Bakkers' wedding anniversary. The minutes of the session reflect no discussion of the loan or the new houseboat. But the board did agree to maintain Bakker's houseboat and provide "new furnishings, incidentals, and refurbishing" as needed, all because board members and PTL associates supposedly used the boat "frequently." The board also voted Bakker another raise, this time $12,000. Later, as Franklin learned from another PTL executive, Dortch returned to the board meeting and suggested that Franklin be fired for insubordination.

Franklin avoided a showdown with Dortch. The morning after their confrontation, a bank that had much of PTL's banking business agreed to make the $50,000 loan immediately. Franklin considered the intervention divine, but emerged from the experience troubled by the board's growing willingness to appease Bakker. It was an attitude many attributed to Dortch.

Roger Flessing was with Bakker the day the new boat arrived. The Somerset was fifteen feet longer than Bakker's old boat and fourteen feet wide. It carried twin 170-horsepower MerCruiser inboard-outboard engines, an electrical generator, two air conditioning–heating units, an electric oven, refrigerator with icemaker, wet bar with icemaker, AM-FM radio, queen-size bed in the stateroom, two beds in the bunk room, and a sleeper sofa. Flessing was impressed.

But Bakker, always envious of the greener grass on the other side of the fence, told Flessing that he had found another boat. "You won't believe this one, it's seventy-five feet long."

Later that month, Flessing decided that it was time for him to leave PTL. He had returned two years earlier, still an idealist. He walked away a tired old man, as close as he had ever been to a physical breakdown. Daily television was an all-consuming enterprise; once the day's show was over, you had just twenty-three hours to prepare for the next. Bakker's unpredictability compounded the intensity. Flessing was also unhappy that Bakker was backing out of an agreement to let him produce a series of thirteen televised concerts with ABC's gospel-music subsidiary. After six concerts were broadcast over PTL's satellite network, "More than Music" was canceled. Bakker seemed jealous of Flessing's time, as he had been of Orender's.

Flessing's mother had encouraged her son to stay in the executive vice president's post, reminding him that he had a $60,000 salary, a company house (one of the homes in the growing Tega Cay compound), and a stable home for his family. Besides, she liked to see her son on television.

But Roger Flessing had seen the enormous amounts of money flowing through the hands of Taggart and the Bakkers. He felt that things were not right. "If I stay here," he told his mother, "someday I'm going to jail."

Finance director Franklin had been shopping for another job for months. Like Flessing, he was tired. He felt that he was having little impact. He hoped to give PTL a reputation as a stable and honorable corporation. He might agree with a vendor on a payment schedule—something he had to do to get goods and services, given PTL's poor credit record—only to have Bakker tell him to back out. Bakker would say PTL needed the money more in other places, and the vendor had made a lot of money off the ministry. "Just tell them we'll pay," Bakker said. In Bakker's mind, if PTL paid someday, it had lived up to its obligations.

Franklin's insistence on playing by the rules had irritated Bakker, who would share his feelings with Taggart and Flessing. The finance director was anxious that his boss comply with federal tax law on his personal income-tax return. He told Bakker that he should report as income the salary of the PTL employee tutoring his children and the money PTL spent on his children's travel. It wasn't advice Bakker wanted to hear. He thought that moral concerns were coloring Franklin's advice, that he didn't want Bakker spending so much of PTL's money. Franklin told Flessing that Bakker could get whatever he wanted; Franklin was just trying to keep him out of jail.

In August 1982, David Taggart and Vi Azvedo informed Franklin that Bakker wanted him to take over PTL's operations in Canada. Instead of replacing Franklin with a single, all-powerful finance director, Bakker divided Franklin's job among three staff members—his sister, Donna Puckett, his new finance director, Peter Bailey, and his budget director, Porter Speakman. Inside PTL, the trio was jokingly known as Peter, Porter, and Puckett.

Franklin had been eager to see PTL set priorities for using its money, an essential step toward stable finances. By May 1982, it seemed that PTL finally had the mechanism in place to do that—an elaborate budgeting system that had taken the staff seven months to create. Budget director Porter Speakman was proud. He considered the creation the Rolls Royce of accounting systems, a fitting match for a ministry that had taken in $52 million in contributions in twelve months. Now, at least in theory, each department could spend the money in its budget without having to have each purchase approved by someone in finance with a stack of yellowing purchase orders on his desk.

Speakman had been hired as budget director in October 1981. Like many on PTL's staff, he arrived flush with idealism and confident that PTL would be the perfect place to work. Raised an Episcopalian, Speakman had been a plant accounting manager for DuPont in New Jersey and a closet alcoholic when his wife, Joanne, accepted Christ as her personal savior. Speakman noticed a joy and peace in her life. She stopped nagging him about his drinking, entrusting the problem to the Lord instead. She played lots of Christian music and watched Billy Graham and the "PTL Club" on television. Soon a renegade charismatic and member of their church told Speakman about the peace Jesus could bring to his life.

Three days later, on December 17, 1978, the thirty-three-year-old opened his refrigerator and reached for his trusty companion, a six-pack of Budweiser. He stopped, asking, What am I doing? I don't even want this. And he didn't take another drink. He had tried many times to quit but was too proud to admit he had a problem. The credit for his sobriety, he believed, belonged to Jesus.

Two years later, the dark-haired man with a gentle, genuine manner felt the Lord calling him to enroll in PTL's counseling program. One day, the PTL personnel office called. Did he have some experience running budgets? they asked. Yes, he answered, and the ministry had its new budget director.

The new computerized system was impressive, and Bakker bragged about it to visitors. But he did not support the system behind the scenes. He never looked at or approved the budgets his staff proposed. Without Bakker at the wheel, the Rolls Royce could go nowhere. Department heads were reluctant to trim their inflated budget requests, and budgets became lead weights around managers' necks. The staff worked around the new rules, circumventing the purchasing and finance staff to get what they needed. Nothing had changed.

The top priority at PTL was getting the job done the way Jim wanted, regardless of consequences, and it would stay that way for years. The man at the top set the tone for the organization. Bakker was notorious for breaching protocol to expedite his pet projects. As others followed his lead, bills for equipment ordered or services rendered often arrived while the purchase order sat—unapproved —on a desk in finance. At best, PTL's new budget system became a source of information. But it offered none of the spending control PTL needed.

With the Barn and World Outreach Center complete by early 1981, Bakker continued thinking up new buildings for Heritage USA; more and more, he was using bricks and mortar to entice his partners to give. A reconstruction of the Upper Room, the site of Christ's last supper with the apostles, for prayer. A ninety-unit motel. An educational and family-counseling center.

Where once PTL had been dedicated to bringing the unchurched to the Lord, it now emphasized catering to the needs of the Christian faithful. Bakker's original justification for Heritage USA—as a community of soul-winning counselors working from telephone hookups at campsites and retirement apartments—was forgotten. Instead PTL emphasized healing Christian marriages, families, and psyches. Bakker's ministry had become a reflection of Bakker's own experiences and interests.

An article in the PTL magazine—once called *Action,* now renamed *Together*—described the new family-counseling center as an outgrowth of Bakker's "vision to help troubled families."

> People need to learn how to become better husbands and wives, how to make their marriages work, and how to train their children. Proverbs 22:6 tells us to "train up a child in the way he should go," but just how do you do that? We want to show people how.

That how, Bakker believed, could be taught at intense two-and-a-half day workshops directed by Palmdale's Fred Gross and Vi Azvedo at a cost of seventy-five dollars a person. The first workshop was held in January 1983. It was dedicated to what the team called personal growth—understanding one's emotions and learning to change one's behavior. Then followed workshops in marriage enrichment, parenting, pastoral counseling, sexual relationships, and inner healing of memories and past traumas.

In the two years since they had first patched up the Bakkers' marriage and became privy to the most intimate details of Jim Bakker's life, the Palmdale team had become a powerful force inside PTL. Their dual role—counselors and business associates— was troubling to some of Bakker's subordinates.

Like Bakker, psychologist Fred Gross was very much the entrepreneur. In summer 1980, Gross had asked PTL general manager Gary Smith to put up $1 million from PTL to open a mental-health hospital in Charlotte that would be run by Gross. As Smith remembered, Gross wanted a retainer of $90,000 a year and first-class airplane tickets whenever he flew to and from his home in California. During his stays in Charlotte, he wanted to be put up in the mansion at Heritage Village. He told Smith that he had Jim's OK. "Well, you know Jim's office is right next door to me," Smith told Gross. "When he tells me to do all that, then I'll talk to him about it." For now, Gross got no hospital, but a similar idea would surface several years later.

Gross also began participating in management decisions, at one point earning a weekly thousand-dollar consulting fee. Even more powerful within PTL, however, was Gross's one-time subordinate, Vi Azvedo. Azvedo looked like an elementary-school martinet and was a force to be reckoned with. Unlike Gross, she had no known educational degrees or training for counseling; she had run a restaurant earlier in her life. But Azvedo was a close friend of June Nichols, the wife of hospital owner Lester Nichols and a vital force in the creation of the Palmdale team.

In Palmdale, Azvedo had specialized in spiritual healing, suggesting Scriptures to patients and praying at their sides. She was a mystic of sorts, given to extracting prophecies from her own dreams; where a Freudian might have seen the inner workings of the psyche, she heard the voice of God.

After his reconciliation with Tammy, Bakker hired Azvedo as staff counselor with a $30,000 salary and a broad charge to address troubled relationships among the staff, be it helping top executives cope with stress or finding the best mix of employees for the organization. When she wasn't serving as traveling companion, babysitter, or peacemaker for the Bakker household, Azvedo tried to probe the secrets of staff members. Some appreciated and respected her work; others felt that her paramount concern was not them but Bakker. They felt uneasy sharing confidences with her. She seemed most eager to control behavior that threatened the ministry's stability.

Azvedo was controlling by nature, the sort of person who answers a question with a question, who has a hard edge that keeps people from getting too close. She was a tireless worker, determined and willing to act behind the scenes. Soon, Azvedo had Bakker's ear, and she kept it, something that few PTL executives would ever accomplish.

While Bakker put his energy into building, his staff pressed to spend a bigger share of its millions on charitable works. Bakker reluctantly agreed to set aside ten percent of PTL's gross income, a traditional tithe, for missions, but he warned his colleagues that it would be their fault if PTL went broke.

PTL's decision paid dividends in good publicity. In a year's time, PTL spent $5.5 million on charitable contributions and missions, a level the ministry would never exceed. In the past, PTL's efforts at charity typically ended with aid for its employees and individual partners and grand, costly gestures that Bakker made at the spur of the televised moment. For the first time, with gifts like the $60,000 it sent to the Salvation Army, PTL appeared to be saying that it felt an obligation to Charlotte and its needy.

PTL also began expanding its programs for the down-and-out. In April 1982, Bakker opened PTL's first People That Love center, offering first-time walk-ins at least three days' food and all the clothes they needed with no questions asked. By the close of 1982, nearly two hundred families were visiting the center each week. PTL began helping more than 850 churches open People That Love centers in their cities. Many were already among the four thousand local churches that made follow-up visits to new believers for PTL and intervened when PTL phone counselors learned of a possible suicide or crisis.

The love-center network sounded great at telethon time, and

Bakker could be counted on to trot it out, making little effort to avoid viewer misunderstanding about PTL's financial contribution to the affiliated centers. PTL provided manuals, signs, and advice on fund-raising to those interested in starting a center, but rarely did PTL donations underwrite the start-up or operating costs. Occasionally, Bakker's staff fielded calls from centers complaining that viewers mistakenly believed that PTL, not the local churches, subsidized them. In fact, the love-center program cost PTL little, perhaps $150,000 at its peak. By comparison, CBN's older Operation Blessing cost Pat Robertson's ministry $18.7 million, or eleven percent of the organization's budget, in 1986–87.

PTL also inexpensively bolstered its image with a prison ministry. Founded in late 1977, at its peak the program had a staff of about five employees, fifteen hundred volunteers visiting prisoners, and thousands of pen pals writing to prisoners. It put up satellite dishes at prisons so that convicts could watch PTL's network, and it distributed at least one million pieces of literature a year.

The program's budget for staff and hardware never exceeded $250,000, although PTL did spend as much as another $750,000 on Bibles, books, and other material given to prisoners. The prison ministry struggled constantly for money as PTL's finance office tried to offset overspending on Bakker's pet building projects by borrowing from the modest prison-ministry budget.

By late summer 1982, PTL was back in financial crisis, slowing construction and laying off workers from its payroll of 750. Privately Bakker ordered his staff not to write checks "unless the wolf is at the door." A PTL spokesman blamed the crisis on the economic recession and credited PTL's response to an efficiency study. "The whole ministry is determined to knuckle under to its best financial advisers," the spokesman said. For his part, Bakker assured his staff, "We intend to be good stewards with God's money."

With Franklin sentenced to exile in Canada, the troika of Peter, Porter, and Puckett took over finances. The three-way split was classic Bakker management. Bakker constantly juggled job responsibilities, staff titles, and the assignment of office space. From moment to moment, it was well-nigh impossible to discern who was a vice president or who had what authority over this department or that. Whether by design or by accident, Bakker fostered systemic confusion in management. Amidst the chaos, his control was secure.

Bakker showed contempt for his finance staff, thumbing his nose at those with more training and education. One day, Bakker gushed about his next building project in a meeting attended by his financial troika. Someone asked where the money would come from. Bakker snapped back, "Financial people will never be visionaries."

Later that day, budget director Speakman pulled Peter Bailey aside. "I could dream as good a dream as anybody," Speakman told his colleague. "How can you dream when you're dealing with what we're dealing with every day? It's hard to see above the rim when you're down in the crevasse."

In August's crevasse, Bakker "discovered" the budget that Speakman had been working on for nearly a year. He had told a top aide that PTL needed to get some budgets. The aide informed him that PTL, in fact, had a budget and a budget director. "We do?" Bakker answered.

The next day, the PTL president appeared at Speakman's door. "Are you Porter Speakman?" he asked. "I want you to show me the budget." Speakman pulled out his reports and explained the new computerized reporting system. Soon after, Bakker summoned his managers, introduced Speakman, and told the group that it was going to follow his budgets. Speakman was thrilled; he finally had the endorsement he needed.

As he had nearly a year before, Speakman asked each department to draw up a budget. On his show, Bakker started talking about budgeting and getting PTL's house in order. Internally, the managers got excited, thinking that now they might be able to get purchase orders filled promptly. An excellent month of donations helped: PTL tallied $7.1 million in September.

But Bakker did little to curb his own spending. In early fall, he toured the Middle East and Europe with his wife and two children, Vi Azvedo, David Taggart, and five others. The entourage stayed overnight at the Grand Hyatt in New York, flew on the Concorde to Europe, and then jetted to Israel. They stopped in Rome and in the Swiss Alps. Taggart took along $26,000 in cash advances for the trip.

The spending continued when the Bakkers returned. On October 25, 1982, Taggart—as always, Bakker's proxy in matters of money—purchased a Florida condominium for Bakker's use, fulfilling the board's year-old mandate. To disguise the transaction from the press, the condo was not recorded in PTL's name.

Bakker had resisted the board's initial offer of the vacation retreat, objecting for financial reasons, board members later said publicly. Privately, board member Cookman explained that Bakker was motivated, at least in part, by fear of bad press. "One of the things he said was, 'If the Charlotte *Observer* ever gets hold of this, they'll make something out of it.' "

The unfurnished condo overlooking the ocean near West Palm Beach cost PTL $390,000. That fall Taggart, now vice president of the executive office with a new salary of $35,000 a year, and his brother, James, spent another $202,000 of PTL money for furniture and fixtures.

The unplanned expenditure hit the fledgling PTL budget hard. To pay the bills in Florida, finance pulled money already budgeted for other uses, including $222,000 for payments to companies supplying the gifts that PTL used to reward donors. As always, the needs of PTL's creditors came after Bakker's.

In late November, Bakker, Taggart, and Bakker's secretary spent another $25,000 of PTL's money during a two-week trip to California for plastic surgery. Both Bakker and Taggart went under the knife. Taggart had his jaw built up and his nose trimmed back. Bakker, who had already had the gap between his front teeth narrowed, returned to Charlotte with his ears pinned, the roll of skin under his chin trimmed, and the wrinkles lifted from his face. Before leaving, Bakker treated his plastic surgeon to a meal out, courtesy of a PTL credit card.

Tammy, who had stayed home to host the show, was taken aback at her husband's appearance. Bakker's face looked so young and so different that Don Hardister, his security chief, told his boss that he didn't know how to read the new face. Bakker's TV audience had to content itself with the official PTL explanation for his absence—recuperation from surgery for a herniated neck.

The FCC's investigation of PTL, now nearly four years old, had languished within the agency. Investigators had taken their final testimony in September 1980. Two months later, Ronald Reagan crushed incumbent Jimmy Carter at the polls. Soon, Reagan was naming new members to the commission, and there was a tacit understanding within the agency that a matter as constitutionally sensitive as the PTL case could wait until the full Reagan commission was in place.

By fall 1981, PTL had begun seeking a way for both the ministry and the FCC to bow out gracefully. Its solution was to sell WJAN, the station in Canton. If it got permission from the FCC, PTL could escape an entanglement that had proven a financial and managerial nightmare. Once PTL no longer owned its one and only TV station, the FCC would no longer have jurisdiction, since it regulates holders of TV-station licenses, not companies that produce TV programming. The FCC would be obliged to end its investigation of PTL. PTL's broadcasts, meanwhile, would continue to run on purchased airtime and over its cable network. Bakker was eager to make the move, even if it meant essentially giving away a broadcast license with a potential value of millions of dollars.

In April 1982, PTL announced that it had a buyer, a little-known Tulsa-based missionary organization, the David Livingstone Missionary Foundation. The foundation received generous terms. PTL agreed to give WJAN in return for the foundation's promise to pay off PTL's remaining debt of less than $1.4 million. PTL also agreed, privately, to give the buyer a contribution of $25,000 each month for a year.

The David Livingstone foundation was a curious choice. It had no roots in Canton and no experience running TV stations. Its reputation was questionable. It had been founded in 1966, part of the ministry of conservative anticommunist Billy James Hargis. Ten years later, Hargis resigned in disgrace, accused of having sex with five students at his college, including four men. His bisexuality was exposed after two students whom he had married confessed to each other on their wedding night that they had each had sex with Hargis.

In 1978, two years after Hargis stepped down, the second of the three incorporators of David Livingstone also resigned. He complained that donations to the foundation were not being used honestly. The sole remaining incorporator, a onetime motel owner named Lonnie Rex, now controlled the organization, and it was with Rex that PTL negotiated the sale. Rex lived flamboyantly, driving a Lincoln and buying a Rolls Royce as an investment for his ministry—which operated, theoretically, as a charity to aid the world's sick and needy.

The foundation had not been PTL's first choice. Bakker offered it to Moss when he forced him out; Moss refused. A PTL lawyer recommended giving the station to the Full Gospel Business Men's Fellowship. Bakker offered WJAN to John Gilman, his former colleague at CBN, but Gilman declined the gift. "I don't have the organization or the financial backing to pull that off," Gilman told Bakker.

The two men talked for five hours one day on Bakker's houseboat. Bakker wanted Gilman to come to work for PTL. Gilman sensed enormous potential in Bakker's ministry, but as they talked, Gilman wondered if Bakker wanted him for his creative ability or to pluck a choice plum off the CBN tree. In the end, he decided both had influenced Bakker's offer.

On the houseboat that day, Gilman laid out for Bakker his plans to evangelize in India and Africa with films about Christ. "You're as crazy as I am, aren't you?" Bakker asked him. "I don't know," Gilman answered, "but this is what I feel God wants me to do." Bakker was very kind. He could be charming when he shed his customary aloofness, looked you in the eye, and became engaged in what you were saying. Afterwards, Gilman told his wife that he felt as if he had stepped near a big, dark hole.

PTL was generous to Gilman's ministry, eventually contributing about $120,000. But Bakker promised Gilman more than he delivered. Over the air one day, Bakker declared that PTL wanted to underwrite the entire project in India—one of his spontaneous on-air gestures that fostered excitement among his partners. Gilman had a massive plan in mind and proposed to Bakker that PTL send $50,000 a month. PTL sent $5,000 a month instead. After a year, the checks stopped.

PTL's initial 1982 effort to transfer WJAN to David Livingstone Missionary Foundation foundered. The FCC refused PTL's request to handle the matter without a face-to-face meeting of the commissioners. A decision was put off.

When they met on December 8, 1982, the five commissioners had before them the latest version of a report by lead investigator Larry Bernstein. Bernstein's work had been shortened and tempered on orders from his superiors. Still more than a hundred pages long, the report detailed the testimony and evidence collected by investigators. It closed with a legal brief proposing that a second, public round of hearings be scheduled. The FCC investigator believed he had found "substantial and material questions of fact" indicating that federal law or regulations had been broken.

Though diluted, Bernstein's report carried the mark of its author. It was brimming with suggestions that Bakker had misled viewers and testified untruthfully. Footnote after footnote alleged lapses of memory, illogic, and contradictions in Bakker's testimony. Bernstein believed that the investigation had convincingly demonstrated Bakker's unwillingness to tell the truth, both on the air and in the witness box.

In the final weeks of 1982, Bernstein had taken a leave of absence to write a novel. One day, his office telephoned saying that he was needed downtown, that the commission was going to make a decision on PTL. The caller told Bernstein that the vote would probably come in four-three in favor of public hearings. Bernstein was eager to orchestrate the trial-like proceeding, thinking that he could get into the open all he had learned during the confidential investigation.

As predicted, the vote that day broke down four to three. But the majority, all appointed or reappointed by Reagan, had swung to the other side. The FCC agreed to allow PTL to transfer WJAN to David Livingstone Missionary Foundation. The FCC's inquiry was over.

The commissioners did not absolve PTL, as Bakker would often claim in the future. Instead, they passed the buck on the hard questions. They agreed to forward "relevant information" about the FCC inquiry to the Justice Department, which was responsible for pursuing criminal allegations like fraud and perjury. The commissioners also voted to send information about the last-minute settlement with witness Herb Moore to the District of Columbia bar. (The bar later dismissed the FCC complaint.)

The majority gave no public explanation for its decision. One of the four, Stephen Sharp, issued a brief statement saying that they had made their decision in good faith. Sharp challenged the "innuendo and mischaracterization" of two members of the minority.

Those two, Joseph Fogarty and Henry Rivera, filed a joint dissent, eight strident pages complaining about the "stench" of the majority's decision.

> To characterize this action [by the FCC majority] as "arbitrary, capricious, an abuse of discretion, [and] otherwise not in accordance with law" is to pay it a gratuitous compliment. . . .
>
> It is plain that the record raises substantial and material questions as to whether PTL engaged in fraudulent solicitation of funds over the air, whether PTL breached its fiduciary duty, whether the president and chairman of the board of PTL gave false testimony to the commission, and whether witnesses before the commission were corruptly influenced.

The two men termed the commission's decision a "rude and cynical insult" to its responsibilities. While they understood why PTL wanted the inquiry ended, they wrote, "we find it difficult to understand on what legal or policy basis the majority so magnanimously but surreptitiously accepts its total surrender."

Commissioner Anne Jones, a 1979 Carter appointee and the third member of the minority, embraced the substance, but not the tone, of the Fogarty-Rivera dissent. Her comments offered the greatest insight into the majority's thinking. The majority wanted to maintain a low regulatory profile for the FCC consistent with the Reagan administration's philosophy. They were also concerned about the cost of public hearings. And, practically, they recognized that PTL's proposed transfer would mean that PTL no longer controlled a TV station; from their point of view, the ministry was out of broadcasting.

Three months after the FCC's decision, the Justice Department ended its review of the FCC investigators' work. It chose to take no action. Bakker again proclaimed that he had been vindicated. In its notification to the FCC, the Justice Department wrote that it had "determined that, based on the underlying facts and circumstances, prosecution should be declined." A Justice Department spokesman explained that Justice didn't find enough evidence "to show a violation of the federal criminal statutes or that it will be a prosecutable case."

Bernstein, who had spoken to Justice Department lawyers during the review, was not surprised that Justice had declined to act. His FCC inquiry had ended once he determined that "substantial and material questions" about Bakker's conduct existed. There was no point in his going further for the time being; any evidence he collected in the initial investigation would not be admissable in the public hearings he expected to come next.

In the public inquiry that was never to be, Bernstein had planned to go further afield. He had been especially eager to explore accusations that Bakker was personally enriching himself at PTL. Disgusted with the FCC's decision in December 1982, Bernstein soon quit his job.

A few weeks after the announcement from Justice, word surfaced that the IRS was interested in the FCC material. As was its duty under law, the IRS refused to confirm that it was conducting an inquiry. But Bakker complained to his TV audience that the IRS was checking on him. IRS agents "are like vultures," he said. "They're going to see if they can pull Bakker apart now."

Little more was said. For now it seemed that Bakker had dodged the bullet, spared by his shrewd campaign to discredit the FCC, the relatively small sums of money involved, the vagaries of communications law, the politics of deregulation, and the political clout of America's religious right.

Nine days after the FCC's December 1982 decision, Bakker, Dortch, Cookman, Cortese, and Lawing gathered for another board meeting. David Taggart was present to take the minutes. Earlier in the year, Taggart had replaced another PTL employee whose minutes Dortch considered too revealing.

Taggart's minutes made no mention of the presence of John Yorke of Charlotte, one of PTL's outside lawyers. Nor did they indicate that Yorke was asked to leave the meeting. They did record a motion from Richard Dortch that an attorney was not needed at the directors' meetings. "Reverend Dortch stated that board meetings should be times when the board unites together in prayer and agreement with the president and seeks God's direction for the ministry for the future." Cookman seconded the idea, and the board agreed.

With the lawyer gone and other items out of the way, Richard Dortch once again pressed for more money for Jim Bakker. At its July 1982 meeting, Dortch had successfully proposed a $50,000 bonus for Bakker, the second of its size in nine months. Today, he proposed that PTL's contribution to Bakker's retirement fund with the Assemblies of God rise from 30% of his pay to 50%, a change worth $40,000 a year. The board agreed. PTL contributed money to two other retirement accounts for Bakker; together, PTL now paid a total of 81.7% of Bakker's salary into the three accounts. Cookman proposed a bonus, and the board agreed. The minutes did not record its size—$75,000—because the board agreed that day to stop putting that sensitive information in the minutes; instead, it agreed, the information would be kept in files on the third floor. Cookman then recommended Bakker's salary be raised 91.2%—an increase that put his pay at $195,000 a year. Dortch suggested that Tammy's salary be increased 53.8% to $80,000. Both motions passed.

Dortch then informed the board that the Florida condominium had been found. On Dortch's motion, the board agreed to pay for its furnishings and staff costs—expenses PTL had already incurred. It agreed to pay the Bakkers' cost of traveling to and from the condominium and to buy a car for their use there. The directors suggested that Bakker go to the condo twice a month "for rebuilding and for rest." Later that month, the Bakkers would do just that.

Near the close of the meeting, Richard Dortch—who had helped look for the condo and who himself had a vacation home in Florida—suggested the board hold its next meeting at the ocean-front retreat.

CHAPTER ELEVEN

RICHARD DORTCH

*"When you bless the man in the pulpit, you
will be blessed"*

Like Jim Bakker, Richard Dortch had grown up poor and Pentecostal in the Midwest. He was born in October 1931 in Granite City, an Illinois steel-mill town across the Mississippi River from St. Louis. Dortch's father, Harry, had lost his first wife when a train rammed into a truck carrying his family and other parishioners to church. While Harry Dortch recovered from a fractured skull, five families each volunteered to look after one of the widower's five children.

In one of those homes, Harry Dortch found his next wife, sixteen years old, less than half her husband's age. Two years later, the marriage produced its only offspring, a son named Richard. The Dortch family struggled during the Depression, more than Raleigh and Furn Bakker did in Muskegon. Harry Dortch rose early to bake small pies, supplementing the meager pay he got in a WPA job. When the pies were finished, his children sold them for a nickel apiece.

As a boy, Richard Dortch tasted both sides of the Pentecostal experience. In Granite City, his family attended the Full Gospel Tabernacle, a forward-thinking church with five hundred members and pastors who commanded respect in the community. One, Thomas Zimmerman, later ran the entire Assemblies of God denomination. But when the Dortch family moved to Collinsville,

Illinois, another St. Louis suburb, they joined a fifty-member congregation that met in a church building that was nothing more than a basement. The congregation worshipped with high emotion and grand theatrics in classic "holy-roller" style. As the pejorative term suggested, these Pentecostals got little respect. It was a commodity that would be very important to Richard Dortch as a grown man.

In December 1947, sixteen-year-old Dortch listened in awe as Oral Roberts preached a Sunday-night service. Roberts had a commanding presence, and Dortch—a zealous sports fan whose heroes in those days were athletes, not preachers—was one of five young men who came forward that night to accept Christ. He lost interest in school and dedicated himself instead to the ministry. The church's only serious competition was baseball; Dortch, a catcher and sometimes second baseman, loved to play the game.

Dortch became a pastor's understudy and then enrolled at North Central Bible Institute in Minneapolis, taking a high-school equivalency exam to assure his admission to the Assemblies of God school. In Minneapolis, Dortch sold shoes, dispatched calls for oil deliveries, and served as night watchman at North Central to pay his way. He dropped out of school in 1952 after two years, much as Bakker would later, to become a traveling evangelist.

Soon Dortch was pastoring at churches in Watertown, South Dakota, and Garden City, Kansas. He then served as a missionary in Belgium for five years. From there he was called to pastor the Edwards Street Assembly of God in Alton, Illinois, the largest and most progressive Assembly in the area and an ideal assignment for an ambitious pastor. Three years later, in 1967, the Assemblies of God ministers in Illinois elected Dortch to one of the top positions in the Illinois district. He quickly rose to the top job, becoming district superintendent of one of the denomination's largest districts. He was also chosen for a seat on the denomination's thirteen-member executive presbytery, its national governing board.

From his headquarters in Carlinville, a city of five thousand a long hour's drive north of St. Louis, Dortch oversaw seven hundred ordained and licensed ministers. They were spread across the state, in small congregations in coal-mining towns in the south, in eight-hundred-member churches in the farmlands of central Illinois, and in the bigger, affluent Assemblies upstate. He traveled constantly, preaching, dedicating new sanctuaries, and installing new pastors.

The work was not always joyous. A board of deacons might be fed up with a pastor, or a pastor might have sinned. In the role of mediator, Dortch acquired a reputation as a deft politician. He could adopt the sophistication of his affluent northern-Illinois constituency one day, the down-home attitude of the southern congregations the next. As a judge, Dortch was known as a caring pastor who tempered discipline for ministers with mercy.

Dortch was more steadfast than Bakker in his adherence to the strict moral code of the Pentecostal denomination. He opposed smoking and drinking. When he learned that the out-of-town boyfriend of a secretary in his Carlinville office had spent the night in the girl's district-owned apartment, he decided to fire her, although a witness confirmed that she had not slept with the man. To Dortch, even the appearance of wrongdoing was a serious breach. Her boss pleaded with Dortch, and the girl repented. Eventually Dortch rescinded his decision.

Dortch preferred to be addressed as "Doctor," a glossy cover for his spotty education. He had earned no doctorate, just an honorary degree bestowed by North Central during his tenure on the school's board. He had no degree from an American college either. Other than two years at North Central, Dortch's higher education consisted of completing a night-school program in French during his stint in Belgium.

Dortch was considered a progressive district superintendent. He urged churches to raise pastors' salaries and retirement stipends, as he was later to do so zealously behind closed doors at PTL. He set up a program to expand training for pastors. He started three radio stations, creating a network he hoped would someday blanket the state. He recruited bright young men to his staff, including several with theological and management training superior to his own. Jim Cobble, who coordinated the continuing-education program for ministers, had earned a doctorate in education at the University of Illinois. Mark Burgund, the son of a pastor in Dortch's district, served as business administrator—one of the first in an Assemblies district office—after earning a master's in business administration at Southern Illinois University. In 1976, during Dortch's sixth year as superintendent, he recruited Al Cress, a Bible-studies student at

Central Bible College in Springfield, to be his administrative aide.

As district superintendent, Dortch developed Lake Williamson Christian Center, the district's 350-acre retreat, into a model successor to the traditionally humble church campground—an effort not unlike what Bakker had undertaken at Heritage USA. The center housed a two-story, forty-eight-unit hotel, an air-conditioned auditorium with two thousand seats, and a brick office building for Dortch and his staff. Dortch and some of his staff members lived in homes scattered around the edge of the forty-acre lake.

For two weeks each summer, Dortch staged family camp at Lake Williamson. He invited big names in the Assemblies such as C. M. Ward, David Wilkerson, and Jimmy Swaggart. Swaggart was the traditional closer, performing on the last three nights. The Baton Rouge evangelist drew the biggest crowds, packing the auditorium so tight one summer night that the fire marshal ordered that no more people be admitted. A few female fans persevered, climbing in through the bathroom window.

By the mid-seventies, Dortch's star had risen high in the Assemblies constellation. His ascent could be charted every other August when ministers in the Assemblies of God gathered for their national convention, or general council. In 1975 in Denver, Dortch was nominated for the post of general secretary, one of four top jobs at the national headquarters in Springfield, Missouri. Dortch was young and progressive, the sort of man that some believed should succeed the top man in Springfield, Dortch's boyhood pastor, Thomas Zimmerman. But Dortch withdrew his name from consideration, a move some regarded as a sign that he was interested only in being number one, not in service to the denomination.

In 1981, the general council convened in St. Louis, Dortch's backyard. Many expected Zimmerman, then sixty-nine, to step down. With the general superintendent out of the running, Dortch—presumably backed by the large contingent of ministers from neighboring Illinois—would have been unstoppable. But Zimmerman did not resign. From the pulpit, Zimmerman told the gathering that he had planned to do so, but he had decided on impulse to accept another term.

With his growing stature, Dortch was a valuable commodity for Bakker, who picked him for PTL's board of directors in early 1979.

The flamboyant Bakker was suspect within the restrained ranks of the Assemblies. Not only was Dortch admired—and Bakker had always appreciated the value of a well-known name—but he was a staunch ally. When his own staff expressed doubts about the Bakkers, Dortch pointedly asked, "Have you ever met these people?" Usually the answer was no. "Well then, how have you become an authority on the way they live?" After a few such exchanges, Dortch's staff—including those who considered the Bakkers flaky and their program theologically shallow—kept their feelings to themselves.

Bakker also found Dortch willing to cater to his thirst for the trappings of celebrity. Here was a church leader who not only didn't disapprove of Bakker's life-style, but who eagerly sanctioned it. Dortch had pushed for the Florida condo, the houseboat loan, a higher salary, and unparalleled bonuses. When Jim and Tammy came to Lake Williamson to speak at family camp in 1980, the first of their two appearances there, Dortch made sure that the Bakkers got royal treatment. It seemed fitting that Bakker talked of ministers' pay as he preached at the lake.

> I'm so pleased to see churches that take care of their pastors. When I was younger, the pastor at my church drove a Cadillac. Some people had cardiac arrest when the pastor drove down the street in a Cadillac. I was proud to be able to point to him and say, "That's my pastor."
>
> I think we ought to want the best for our pastor. I believe a pastor should live at least, *at least,* as good as the wealthiest member of the congregation. When you bless the man in the pulpit, you will be blessed.

In late January 1983, Jim and Tammy Bakker joined the PTL entourage at the annual National Religious Broadcasters convention in Washington. The NRB had been formed thirty-nine years before, an arm of the newly formed National Association of Evangelicals dedicated to assuring that mainline Protestant churches did not monopolize access to radio and television. As religious broadcasting proliferated in the seventies and early eighties, the NRB's membership rolls swelled. By 1983, the NRB counted 1,045 radio stations and 79 TV stations carrying mostly or only religious programming. Another 600 organizations produced religious radio programming, and 365 organizations, including PTL, produced TV programs or films.

PTL served as the convention's official TV network that year, and Bakker produced his daily program from Washington for the entire convention week. Among his guests was the venerable evangelist Billy Graham, who had been born and raised in Charlotte. Bakker's staff asked Graham to grant a five-minute interview. Instead, it lasted for twenty-three.

This interview nagged at the Graham ministry for years. PTL rebroadcast a clip from it at least twenty times as part of a montage of celebrities saying kind things about Bakker. In the Graham excerpt, the evangelist seemed to endorse the PTL president and his wife. "Jim and Tammy both, I love you with all my heart," Graham said with a smile. "I watch you so often, my goodness, I feel like I am a part of your family."

Three years later, T. W. Wilson, one of Graham's associates, expressed the Graham ministry's frustrations to a supporter. "Since that meeting," Wilson wrote, "they have run it and rerun it and rerun it, and we have no control over it. Mr. Graham has tried to be cooperative with all groups everywhere, and it is unfortunate when some use his name to promote their own cause. . . . His integrity has been without question over these many years."

Graham was hardly inclined to serve as Bakker's character witness. Later that winter, in a three-page article in *TV Guide,* Graham conspicuously omitted Bakker's name from a list of TV evangelists he admired. Graham took a swipe at religious broadcasters who asked constantly for money for buildings.

> I watched one program recently in which the speaker spent nearly half of his show pleading for donations. Such preachers bring reproach to the Gospel, and damage all other religious TV programs. . . . Giving to religious programs should be, at least in part, God-inspired. If a religious program is not prospering financially, I would take that as a portent: perhaps it is not *supposed* to succeed. . . .
>
> The vast majority of TV evangelists and pastors are moral, ethical, and worthy of our trust. However, a minority may attempt to mislead us—or themselves—into believing that God intended all our contributions to be buried in mortar and concrete.

On February 6, 1983, as the convention ended, the *Observer*'s Sunday-morning edition broke the news of Bakker's Florida condominium. For years, the newspaper had written about mismanagement and deceit at PTL. Now, for the first time, the *Observer* painted a detailed picture of the life-style Bakker had adopted at PTL's expense. The front-page story recounted the Bakker family's costly trip to Europe and Israel. It reproduced an invoice for plumbing supplies for Bakker's new studio dressing room, which had gold-plated fixtures and a built-in $11,678 Habitat capable of simulating a sauna, sunroom, rain forest, or a warm, breezy day.

The article documented $81,000 in decorating costs, including $22,000 for floor-to-ceiling mirrors in the three-bedroom, two-bath, seventh-floor condominium overlooking the ocean in Highland Beach, Florida. The owner of the mirror company remembered the job well. Decorator James Taggart "spent as if money were no object. I think it's the most luxurious job we've ever done." In fact, the newspaper's $440,000 estimate for PTL's total cost was conservative. The getaway had actually cost $592,566.

For the first time, too, David and James Taggart stepped into public view. The brothers had picked the condo for Bakker. David had signed papers to complete the purchase. The Taggarts and their friend and PTL colleague Sandi Watson had stayed at the nearby Boca Raton Hotel and Club as they decorated the condo, their rooms costing PTL at least $195 a night. Over a month, the three and other PTL staff members spent $12,780 on lodging, food, and other expenses.

Bakker had refused to talk to *Observer* reporters Allen Cowan and Tex O'Neill before publication. The Monday after the story appeared, he began his efforts to blunt its effect. He started with his constituency at PTL, with the employees whose willingness to submit to his authority was so vital to PTL's equilibrium. At eleven o'clock that morning, usually showtime, Bakker talked to his staff inside the TV studio in the Barn while the ministry broadcast a taped show. A smattering of partners joined them, sitting in the tiered blue theater seats.

Toying with a gold-plated fixture, Bakker tried to cut the tension with a joke. "I've been in my dressing room taking the knobs off. I've decided since they're all twenty-four karat gold I'd have them melted down." He tossed the fixture to Henry Harrison. "By the way, [the fixtures] are not twenty-four karat gold. I was just kidding about that."

Bakker's rallying cry to his troops was reminiscent of the speech he had delivered to his staff after his 1978 houseboat purchase. "I'm not going to respond to the newspaper." The audience of four hundred burst into ten seconds of applause. "I believe in all my heart, it's time God's people reject the call of the enemy. . . . We can choose to accent the positive, or we can choose to live like buzzards on dead flesh. I believe God has called us to higher things and better places." We must, he said, "get our eyes off bathtubs and condominiums" and get back to work for Jesus Christ. "This is the greatest hour of growth in the history of this ministry. . . . You know, sometimes we live so close to a miracle we can't see it. . . . I am more encouraged by what God is doing than at any time in my life, and I choose to live on the mountaintop and not in the valley."

Bakker's board stood behind the PTL president, issuing a statement complaining of an unwarranted attack. Aimee Cortese publicly questioned the *Observer*'s juxtaposition of the October 1982 condo purchase with PTL's layoffs in August 1982 and the fall 1982 PTL declaration that the ministry was in a "financial crisis." "Putting the two issues together is what suits [the newspaper] at this time. I don't see it that way," she said. Cortese acknowledged that the board had put no limit on the spending for Bakker's Florida getaway.

The viewers' reaction was more negative. Three weeks after the article was published, PTL's finance director, Peter Bailey, informed Bakker by memo that donations for the month were the worst in a year. The latest week's income had been the lowest in more than two and a half years. "We are continuing to hold fast to a tight financial policy; only absolutely necessary expenditures are being paid for," Bailey wrote.

As it defended itself, PTL avoided admitting that donors' money had paid for Bakker's luxury condo. Bakker preferred to say that the board of directors had purchased the unit. Bakker also distanced himself from the work the Taggart brothers had done. "I did not pick the condominium. I did not decorate it. I did not see it until it was completed," he said. "I would prefer that the board had not perhaps gone as beautiful in the apartment. But in the area of Florida, the apartments are that price, they're expensive."

Bakker adopted a similar defense for the money spent on his new dressing room. In a sympathetic interview with a charismatic-Christian magazine, Bakker said that he had not had the time or energy to pick anything for the room. "They did it, again as a labor of love," he said, without identifying who "they" were. Bakker dismissed the $11,678 Habitat as a "one-man steam cabinet."

Bakker quickly decided to sell the condo; it had lost its appeal as a private retreat. Never again, Bakker said, would he expect PTL to make such a purchase. "What Tammy and I and the children will have to do is to, just for privacy, we'll have to keep moving because we know the press will never leave us alone." Within the next four years, he would in fact purchase three more vacation homes. The issue of Bakker's regal life-style was not going to go away.

A few days after publication of the Florida-condo story, a middle-aged man with a gentle Southern accent telephoned the new religion writer at the *Charlotte News,* the *Observer*'s sister newspaper. The caller claimed to hold a position of fame in the Christian world, but he did not identify himself. Sixteen months had passed since his dismissal from the Assemblies of God, and John Wesley Fletcher—the unidentified voice at the other end of the line—was bitter at what he considered the "lack of compassion and understanding for people who had fallen from God." He was angry that PTL appeared to be actively discouraging pastors from inviting him into their churches.

As Fletcher talked, reporter Terry Mattingly took notes. Mattingly had started his first full-time reporting job the summer before. As he listened, Mattingly wondered if the caller might be Oral Roberts's son, Richard.

> My name is synonymous with religion. I don't think there is a household in America that wouldn't know my name. . . . I've got to talk to somebody, somehow, someday. I'm scared to death. It's a moral thing to me. . . . My nerves are gone. I've had my problems, but I don't have them now. . . . Today I feel so low—for my friends. . . . [Jim Bakker] gets tight with one person, then he throws them down. . . . I never knew a more

corrupt man in my life, period, than Jim Bakker. Now I see
him for what he is.

Fletcher suggested that the reporter telephone board member
Richard Dortch and ask whether Dortch had pushed for the Florida
condo over the objections of other board members. Fletcher gave
Mattingly the home number of Efrem Zimbalist, Jr., in southern
California and the name of the actor's maid. He suggest asking the
actor—with whom Fletcher had been close—when he had last at-
tended a PTL board meeting. Zimbalist had attended the board's
July 1982 gathering but was absent from most meetings.

The caller also mentioned the Taggarts. The brothers were living
in Jim's first home on the lake, which Bakker still owned. Why? the
caller asked. Because David, he said, was Jim's "lover."

Fletcher added an unfamiliar character to the puzzle. "Just remember this name," he said, "Jessica Hahn." Mattingly recorded
the suggestion, spelling the last name Hann. Fletcher called her an
"ex-girlfriend" of Jim's and said Bakker's PTL cohorts had a damaging letter and a picture of Jim and Jessica.

"I tried to pray this thing through and tell God to clean it up,"
Fletcher said before hanging up. "Maybe the *Charlotte News* and
[the] *Observer* are going to have to clean it up."

The caller telephoned twice more in the weeks that followed, still
refusing to give his name or telephone number. He did, however,
suggest that they meet in a neutral setting. Mattingly consulted his
editors, who wanted a meeting closer to home, in North Carolina.
The man stopped calling.

For now, the secret of Jessica Hahn was safe.

Jim Bakker recognized that his success in television and mass ministry hinged on his ability to break down the distance between himself and his audience, to exploit the technological intimacy of
television. He fostered his image as his partners' friend: he was Jim,
not the Reverend James O. Bakker. Tammy, well, she could never
be anything but Tammy. The Bakkers laughed, cried, and lived like
real folks, or so it seemed. Bakker's newest set was designed to
resemble the Bakkers' living room. Replacing the runway and
flashing lights of the glitzy Nashville look PTL had used in 1981,

the homey set gave Bakker's show a warmer, more relaxed feel. Bakker routinely opened his TV shows walking out from the audience, like a man of the people. In the later years, even as he put further distance between himself and his partners offstage, he routinely used the studio audience as an auxiliary set. Tammy sang standing amidst the audience, Jim interviewed his guests sitting in the theater seats, and members of the audience stood to give their testimonies. If the Bakkers' on-screen lives had become a living soap opera, then PTL's partners could feel that they were members of the cast.

That ersatz familiarity nurtured donors' dedication to the Bakkers and their generosity to PTL. It is easier to dig into your pocketbook for a troubled friend than for an impersonal institution. PTL's efforts to raise money took an increasingly personal turn, mimicking the self-centeredness that was corroding the Bakkers' ministry. In 1982, Bakker had raised money by sending out cards for Tammy's fortieth birthday and confiding to partners about Tammy's tiring days of work for PTL. A year later, a letter with Tammy's signature sought twenty-two dollar contributions to honor the Bakkers' twenty-two years of marriage and ministry.

> I want [Jim] to see how many friends we have who love and appreciate us. . . . After the anniversary celebration on TV, Jim and I will take all the cards home so we can read the personal notes and pray God's blessing on our special friends. . . .
>
> Right now Jim could use a little extra love and encouragement. He works so hard. Anytime there is a problem, misunderstanding or criticism, he has to handle it.

The bond between preacher and partner made the Bakkers' surfeit of self-pity an effective shield against criticism. While outsiders might become suspicious of the Bakkers' oft-repeated cries of victim, PTL's partners felt the Bakkers' pain. Their sympathy engaged, they could not see how Bakker had manipulated their sense of right and wrong.

Not all PTL partners, however, submitted to Bakker's reconstructed reality. Richard Robbins of Oak Ridge, New Jersey, had been a faithful partner and strong contributor for years. As the condominium story spread, Robbins began to wonder. His brother-in-law chided him for giving money to a phony. Robbins wrote PTL with his questions.

He didn't get answers. Upset, he telephoned PTL and threatened to eat Easter dinner at PTL with *Observer* reporter Allen Cowan, who had become Bakker's bête noire. He talked to David Taggart, who told him that Cowan wasn't allowed on the grounds. Robbins told Taggart that he had a problem. "I don't care. I'm coming."

Later that day, Bakker telephoned. He wanted to know why Robbins was upset. Out of the blue, Bakker invited Robbins to have Easter dinner with him, an unusual gesture for a man who steered clear of his critics. The next day, Bakker's secretary called to say that Robbins would be staying on the grounds as Bakker's guest. For the past month, Robbins had been told that there was no room. The red-carpet treatment made him more suspicious.

Robbins and his wife, Edith, were put up in a lakeside time-share suite. Robbins was a tough Yankee, a thirty-year veteran substation operator for a New Jersey utility company. Until his Christian rebirth in 1970, he had lived a hard, carousing life. With that worldly background, he knew how to ask tough questions.

But Robbins's dinner with Bakker was anything but private. The dining room was loaded with people—guests from that day's broadcast and Bakker's relatives—and Robbins was embarrassed to ask hard questions in front of the crowd. After dinner, Bakker slipped out with his bodyguard, leaving Robbins with little more than a photo. He had gotten food and celebrities, but no answers. In his Jersey lexicon, Bakker had soft-soaped him.

For an organization so totally dependent on the goodwill of its fans, PTL knew surprisingly little about its partners. It had conducted occasional surveys but developed no comprehensive, integrated body of research.

One of its biggest studies, a detailed look at more than three thousand questionnaires returned by PTL partners in 1985, documented PTL's interdenominational appeal. While the most, twenty-one percent, belonged to the Assemblies of God, fifteen percent of the partners were Baptists, eight percent were Pentecostals, eight percent Methodists, and another eight percent claimed no denomination. Bakker's support was geographically well distributed too, with his strongest support coming from California, New York,

Ohio, Florida, Michigan, Texas, Illinois, and North Carolina, in that order.

Bakker's audience, at least those willing to fill out and return a questionnaire, tended to be older. The average partner was fifty-one years old. Nearly half were over sixty years old. Slightly more than half watched Bakker's show each day, and four out of five planned to visit Heritage USA.

Earlier PTL surveys showed that the ministry's donors tended to be female, slightly less educated than the average American, somewhat more likely to own their own home, and significantly bigger spenders on home entertainment. The PTL partner tended to be someone who bought country-western records, life insurance, and gifts by mail order.

Partners were also inclined to donate by mail, and PTL pursued their gifts through a steady stream of mass mailings. For about $70,000 in 1981, PTL could reach about eight hundred thousand homes with a mass mailing. The return on each solicitation could exceed $1 million. PTL's offer of gift premiums—an album of Tammy's or a book of Jim's—was an integral part of its appeals. In 1981, for instance, PTL mailed 956,000 gifts; slightly more than half were rewards for donations. In all, the gifts attracted more than $18 million in 1981.

PTL relied most heavily on its core of repeat donors. In 1981, for instance, 164,274 of PTL's donors were newcomers. They gave $11.3 million. Another 103,458 contributed for a second time, generating $12.5 million. But half of PTL's $50 million in donations came from 138,844 loyalists with a history of at least three years' support, many of them partners faithfully donating fifteen or twenty dollars a month. These donors gave more money than the other contributors: $186 each over the year, compared to the $69 average of new donors and the $121 average of those renewing their gifts for the first time.

By 1983, ominous patterns had begun to emerge in PTL's internal counts of donors and their giving. Fewer people were giving, and total contributions—far and away PTL's principal source of revenue—were leveling off. In 1980, 496,000 people had contributed to PTL. At the close of 1983, the count had declined twenty-two percent to 385,000. Only a jump in the size of the average donation and a slight rise in average number of gifts per donor per year had sustained total contributions at PTL's plateau of $50 million. By then, Bakker had begun to look for ways to command a bigger slice of the evangelical pie, as it was being carved into smaller and smaller pieces by the growing numbers of religious broadcasters.

While PTL defended the Florida condominium purchase in public, it was taking steps internally to protect itself against an IRS attack on its tax-exempt status. As the IRS showed increasing interest in PTL, the ministry identified a series of perks for Bakker and his relatives that could strengthen an IRS assertion of private inurement. PTL checked its records for evidence that the ministry had paid the Bakkers' personal expenses. Between 1980 and 1982, the internal review found that PTL had furnished $149,591 in payments for clothes, dry cleaning, gas, charges at Heritage USA, and various personal expenses. None had been reported as income on Bakker's W-2 Form. PTL deemed seventy-five percent of the wardrobe and dry-cleaning costs to be ministry expenditures and subtracted their cost. That left Bakker owing PTL $75,908.57.

During the April 11, 1983, board meeting, Richard Dortch raised the subject of Bakker's finances. He felt that Bakker was under financial pressure, and he invited the directors to suggest ways to help their minister. The minutes describe the discussion that ensued.

> Reverend Bakker then stated that his first priority was the ministry and that he did not desire any further assistance from the board. Each board member stated that it was their responsibility to take care of the needs of the leader of the ministry and felt that they were under a mandate from the Lord. . . . It was decided that no additional assistance would be provided at this time, but that the board should review this matter at the next meeting.

The minutes did not mention the reason that Bakker was under financial pressure, but nine days later, Bakker paid PTL the $75,908.57, apparently drawing the money from one of his PTL-funded retirement accounts. The board had showed unusual restraint in awarding no bonus. But in July 1983, the directors voted a $100,000 bonus for Bakker and $50,000 for Tammy. Minutes of that meeting include no reference to the earlier discussion of Bakker's financial problems, but the combined $150,000 bonus produced enough after-tax income to make the Bakkers whole.

During the April 1983 board meeting, Bakker announced that David Taggart had resigned, effective that day, after two-and-a-half years' service. Bakker explained that David was leaving to finish his education. The departure came "on the best possible terms," Bakker told the board, and Taggart "had served the ministry well, always being kind and considerate and having the welfare of the president and the ministry uppermost in his mind."

Taggart's terse letter of resignation did not explain his reasons for leaving. Years later, under oath, Bakker suggested that Taggart was exhausted; he had been doing the work of at least three people. Bakker also said that Taggart was eager to go to The Juilliard School in New York City to study music. James Taggart quit his PTL job as well, and Bakker sent him a warm letter of thanks.

> I would highly recommend you for any position in the future, and I wish you all the success in the world. You have all the necessary qualifications for success—enthusiasm, persistence, compassion, uncompromising dedication, the ability to communicate and bring out the best in people, an excellent background, and so much more. . . . We look forward to a continued association with you.

The brothers moved to Florida, leasing a $252,000 three-bedroom condominium a half-mile from the condo they had picked out for Bakker a few months earlier. There, David Taggart would say later, he spent time rehearsing for an audition at Juilliard.

At PTL, some wondered whether the *Observer*'s embarrassing coverage of the Taggart brothers' central role in the Florida condominium purchase had necessitated their swift exit. Taggart himself considered the reason for his departure sufficiently sensitive to assert his Fifth Amendment right against self-incrimination during a 1988 deposition.

At least one board member, actor Efrem Zimbalist, Jr., had heard rumors of a relationship between Bakker and David Taggart. At a golf tournament in Florida, Zimbalist had fretted about confronting Bakker; after all, he was only a new Christian. Dortch would be more suited to the task, but apparently he had done nothing.

Joe Bakker, Jim's paternal grandfather

Armilda Irwin, Jim's maternal grandmother

Raleigh and Furnia Bakker on their wedding day in 1926, fourteen years before the birth of their youngest son, Jim.

The Bakker family in the forties. From left: Norm, Raleigh, young Jim, Bob, Furnia, and Donna.

Jim Bakker (at right) in December 1958, outside Muskegon High School. Miss Michigan of 1959 was the star attraction of Bakker's third and final high-school variety show. (Photo courtesy of Terry L. Gibson)

Jim and Tammy, shortly before their marriage in 1961, ride the train in matching North Central Bible College shirts.

Jim Bakker during his first year in college. Bakker portrayed himself as a former rock 'n' roll disc jockey who had found Christ.

*Jim and Tammy Bakker pose
with a church congregation in
Falling Waters, West Virginia,
in 1962, during their career as
traveling evangelists.*

*Jim and Tammy with the family
of puppets from their children's
show at CBN. At far left, Allie
the Alligator and Susie Moppet.*

*Bakker and Pat Robertson flank
faith healer Kathryn Kuhlman
(left of Robertson) during a CBN
telethon. Kuhlman would influence
Bakker's early style of ministry.*

Bakker with Jan and Paul Crouch (both to left of Bakker) on the Trinity Broadcasting set in Santa Ana, California, during their short-lived collaboration in 1973.

Bakker inside PTL's Independence Boulevard studio in Charlotte, with Jim Moss (left) and co-host Henry Harrison (right).

Tammy during the early years in Charlotte, wearing one of her many wigs.

Bill Perkins, one of the few PTL executives who stood up to Bakker.

Roger Flessing worked for Bakker in California and became one of his most valued associates in Charlotte.

Ed Stoeckel tried to set PTL on a path to financial stability in 1979–80.

Bob Manzano, the missions director who challenged Bakker's veracity during the Federal Communications Commission investigation.

John Franklin, one-time finance director, pressed Bakker to follow the rules. He was eventually exiled to a position in PTL's Canadian operations.

Bakker, John Wesley Fletcher, and Efrem Zimbalist, Jr., play golf at a Clearwater Beach, Florida, course. Thirteen months later Bakker and Fletcher would return to Clearwater to have sex with Jessica Hahn.

Bakker with Fletcher, who appeared monthly on Bakker's TV show until summer 1981, when he was accused of making homosexual overtures to a PTL security guard.

Music director Thurlow Spurr, on the set with Jim and Tammy. Suspicious of his wife's friendship with Spurr, Bakker later forced Spurr's departure from PTL.

Gary Paxton and Tammy Bakker performing together. In 1980 Bakker would suspect that Paxton and Tammy were having an affair.

Jim and Tammy on the outdoor set in Hawaii in January 1981, flanking PTL director Efrem Zimbalist, Jr. During this trip, a few weeks after Jim's encounter with Hahn, the Bakkers decided to separate.

Vi Azvedo and psychologist Fred Gross of the Palmdale Christian therapy team helped rescue the Bakkers' troubled marriage.

In 1981 Azvedo joined PTL's payroll. She became a ubiquitous presence around the Bakkers, a referee for their arguments and a helping hand in their household. In fall 1982 she joined the Bakkers and their children, daughter Tammy Sue and son Jamie Charles, on a PTL-financed trip to Europe and the Middle East.

The Palmdale team's workshops became an integral part of Bakker's ministry. In May 1980, soon after the Bakkers emerged from marital counseling in California, PTL staff members Sam and Kathy Orender agreed to similar sessions with the Palmdale team in Charlotte. At week's end, they renewed their wedding vows on Bakker's TV show. Despite the grand gesture, the Orenders' marriage would not endure.

Bakker's longtime friend Doug Wead heard Zimbalist at the tournament and decided to broach the matter with Bakker on his next visit. Inside the mirrored windowless exercise room at Bakker's house, Wead related the rumors to Bakker as Taggart listened silently. Wead suggested that Bakker find Taggart a job in another department for appearance's sake. Bakker was angry. "I'm very hurt that you would believe this," he said.

After he resigned, Taggart's duties fell into several hands. Speakman, frustrated with the repeated failure of PTL's budget, had agreed a few weeks earlier to move to Bakker's office as a troubleshooter. He was responsible for managing Bakker's personal finances, paying personal bills from the president's personal checking account, withdrawing cash from Bakker's accounts when Bakker needed money, opening an IRA account for Bakker, and gathering information for his tax return.

Speakman saw the magnitude of Bakker's compensation. He found the salary understandable, but the bonuses overwhelmed him. He knew how tight money was on the ministry's front lines and how unpleasant relations were between PTL and its creditors. He had seen Bakker's sister, Donna Puckett, leave work in tears. In charge of accounts payable, she lived under constant pressure from creditors. She refused to let her colleagues tell callers she was Bakker's sister. Armed with that information, creditors were sure to say, Oh, you can get it from Jim. Puckett, though unshakably loyal, seemed to dislike her brother's free-spending ways. Like her parents and brother Norm, she lived modestly. When Jim quit in 1987, Donna Puckett was living in a mobile home in the South Carolina countryside.

With a wife and children at home, Speakman could not perform Taggart's duties as Bakker's valet—buying clothes, packing for trips, and traveling at Bakker's side. Bakker chose several men from his staff to be his new escorts. Among them was Jay Babcock, a twenty-five-year-old member of his TV staff.

Babcock, the son of a truck driver, had left his hometown of Corning, New York, in 1978 to join the first class admitted to PTL's Heritage University. Later, he took a job cutting grass for PTL. He soon jumped to a job as a writer on the producers' staff, and by mid-1983, he was producing Bakker's show.

Babcock had divorced in spring 1983 and overhauled his physical appearance, fixing his teeth, wearing a shorter haircut, and replacing his wardrobe. It was shortly thereafter that Bakker invited Babcock to join his entourage on a vacation trip to Bermuda.

The night before their departure, Bakker's secretary called Babcock at home. She told him that Bakker was at Tega Cay by himself and that he hated to stay there alone. Tammy and the kids were on vacation in Orlando and were planning to meet Jim in the Atlanta airport for the flight to Bermuda. Babcock took his bags to the Bakkers' house at Tega Cay and dined with Bakker.

That night, Bakker asked his young employee for a massage. Babcock had given Bakker rubdowns in the dressing room, and he had seen others do the same. Bakker lay down on his bed, and Babcock worked on his shoulders. After fifteen minutes or so, Bakker seemed to drift off. As Babcock rose to leave, he felt Bakker's hand on his leg. The gesture scared Babcock, he said later, but he dismissed it as something Bakker had done unknowingly in his sleep.

A few weeks later, Bakker surprised Babcock in the dressing room, extending another invitation to travel with him. "Are you packed?" Bakker asked. He wanted Babcock as his companion on a week-long vacation in Hilton Head. Babcock was pleased. He was eager to climb the PTL ladder, and he recognized that proximity to Bakker could dramatically speed his ascent.

Babcock spent that weekend in a hotel at Hilton Head. At the beginning of the new week, Tammy returned to Charlotte to host the show, leaving her husband behind for a week of rest. Babcock moved into the house, taking a second bedroom. Bakker's cook slept in the third.

Bakker was busy reading *Megatrends* and *In Search of Excellence.* Babcock screened calls for the PTL president and organized the material he highlighted. Bakker, given to bursts of enthusiasm for his latest discoveries, was eager at the time to create a new Japanese-style corporate culture at PTL, doing away with PTL's hierarchical management and giving employees the chance to challenge their bosses.

Tuesday night, Bakker asked Babcock for another massage. Babcock rubbed his shoulders and back while they talked shop. Then, without explanation, Bakker rolled over and reached for Babcock.

This time Babcock didn't move. Bakker began undressing Babcock and put the younger man's hand on his penis. In silence, the two men brought each other to orgasm. There was, Babcock recalled later, not a word said during or afterwards.

The next day, Bakker told Babcock that he wanted his managers to spend the upcoming weekend in a management retreat at Hilton Head. It was, Babcock thought later, as if Bakker wanted him to be too busy to think about what had happened between them. Bakker wanted not only the forty managers, but their wives and children as well—106 people in all. Babcock began looking for rooms at the resort and ordering flowers and fruit baskets for each room. Some rooms had complimentary bottles of wine as well.

That Wednesday night, as he lay in his darkened room, Babcock realized someone had entered. It was Bakker. Briefly, he explained that he was there to return the massage and Babcock's other favors. Again, in silence, the two men masturbated each other.

The management retreat was impromptu but hardly inexpensive. Each guest's room cost forty-eight dollars a night. Babcock had arranged activities for the kids, a dinner on a chartered boat, and free food for the guests at the resort's restaurants. PTL paid for the wives to go out shopping—picking up the tab not only for transportation but for their purchases as well. Bakker offered his managers cash if they showed up on time to his morning and afternoon meetings. It was a trial run for his new emphasis on the benefits of incentives.

With the return of Tammy and the Bakker children, Babcock moved to a Hilton Head condo. But Bakker had found a willing sexual partner. The quiet exchange of masturbation continued, off and on, behind the closed doors of Bakker's TV studio dressing room until November 1986.

After David Taggart left, Bakker ardently courted director Richard Dortch to join PTL's staff.

For years, Bakker had bounced in and out of handling PTL's day-to-day operations. During the Stoeckel era, he had seen the dangers of putting too much administrative power in the hands of a single executive. But Bakker felt confined within the glass walls of his roost in the World Outreach Center. He disliked most nitty-gritty details, but PTL needed someone who could handle them if the ministry was going to survive Bakker's reckless leadership. Bakker preferred to throw himself into projects he cared about— usually his latest building project—and to manage by wandering, holding impromptu meetings on the grounds or in his car.

Bakker thought that Dortch was qualified to take over day-to-day management responsibilities; he had also demonstrated repeatedly that he was willing to defer to Bakker's authority. Dortch would also provide a commodity that Bakker increasingly coveted: respectability in the church world.

By the time of the Assemblies of God's biennial general council in Anaheim in early August, Dortch had already talked to some of his closest aides about taking a job at PTL. In Anaheim, Dortch showed what he could do for Bakker's stature in the church, arranging for Bakker to fill in as a speaker. Bakker's talk pushed all the right buttons.

> If you don't believe in this denomination, I do. God put us together and made us all different. Some of you say, "I sure wouldn't do things your way, Brother Jim." Well, I sure wouldn't do it your way either! But thank God, together we can win the world!
>
> I am so proud of what our denomination is doing. You know what? . . . We have decided we are not going to be a denomination that divides but one that brings God's people together.

In a letter a few weeks later, Dortch congratulated Bakker and praised his "strokes of genius" in the speech. "I was so proud of you. God used you in a wonderful way! Be assured of my love, concern, and prayers for you. I am here to serve you and want to do anything that I can to be a blessing to you."

Dortch recruited new faces for PTL in Anaheim. He introduced Bakker to Roe Messner, a church builder from Wichita, Kansas, whom Dortch had known for thirty years. He considered their union a "marriage made in heaven"—Bakker the relentless builder and Messner an Assemblies of God layman and the self-proclaimed leading church contractor in the nation. "Both of them are pow, pow, explosive in what they want to do," Dortch said a year later.

Bakker and Dortch also courted Sam Johnson, a regular speaker at Dortch's family camp, a Bible-school acquaintance of Bakker's, and the younger brother of Dortch's Bible-school roommate. Johnson was a missionary for the Assemblies in Europe; he would decide to remain there for another year. At a Saturday morning prayer breakfast in Anaheim, Johnson told Jimmy Swaggart about PTL's interest.

"Oh man, there's trouble out there," Swaggart told Johnson. He warned broadly of sin and corruption inside Bakker's ministry. "Sam, stay clear of that."

The featured speaker at that morning's breakfast for four thousand was Secretary of the Interior James Watt, a layman in the Assemblies of God. Watt denounced abortion, saying that those who didn't speak out against it were much like the church folk in Germany who failed to stand against Hitler's extermination of the Jews. Pat Boone entertained the crowd that morning; as he sang, Swaggart walked out. While Pat Boone was Jim Bakker's cherished on-air guest, he represented the sinister influence of Hollywood to Swaggart.

That fall, before leaving his post in Illinois to join PTL, Dortch claimed one more trophy for Bakker. He proposed to his fellow directors at North Central Bible College that the school award Bakker an honorary degree and name him its 1984 graduation speaker. Two years earlier, Dortch had made the same proposal, but the board had declined. This time, the vote was contested, but the board finally accepted Dortch's recommendation.

Dortch pressured his key staff members to follow him to Charlotte. He defended Bakker as a man of integrity, a man who did not judge others. Dortch considered Bakker an admirable contrast to what he considered the smallness of spirit among the Assemblies leadership in Springfield. The church hierarchy seemed ossified, Dortch complained, and the city's isolation made it hard to attract leaders with new ideas. As for Tammy—whose silliness and industrial-strength makeup were widely ridiculed within the denomination—Dortch argued that she was reaching people the church was not, as indeed she seemed to do. He contended that those who criticized her might in fact be jealous.

Dortch acknowledged to aides Cobble, Cress, and Burgund that PTL had its problems. He appealed to their idealism, telling them that they could reshape the ministry, be forces for good. Instead of criticizing what was wrong with PTL, why not try to help?

Cobble agreed, with reservations, to make the move. He believed that Dortch earnestly wanted to recruit good people to make order out of the chaos at PTL. Cobble also saw promise in the Charlotte area. The city had a reputation as a safe, clean, family-oriented community with a lush canopy of trees. Its white-collar economy was thriving on banking, sales, and distribution dollars. It was the largest city in the Carolinas, with a population of 325,000. Charlotte, its home county of Mecklenburg, and the six counties around it contained a million people.

For weeks, Dortch cajoled and teased the reluctant Cress. "Oh, Al, you're going to love PTL," he said. Cress agonized. He had seen Bakker and his entourage close up in Anaheim and was nauseated by the bodyguards and self-important whisking to and fro. Where was the spirit of God in them? he wondered. Everything seemed to reek of the flesh.

Cress was an intense man. He grew up Roman Catholic in Trinidad, Colorado. As a sixteen-year-old, he converted to the Assemblies of God against his family's wishes. His dad checked meters at the steel mill in Pueblo. His mother, a woman of Mexican descent with a strong sense of morality and an intuitive sense of people, raised Cress, his six older sisters, and two younger brothers. Cress served four years in the navy as a personnel-office supervisor before enrolling in Bible school, where he met and was hired by Dortch.

Finally, Cress gave in. He made the choice out of trust—not in Jim Bakker, but in Richard Dortch.

Dortch's successor in Illinois tried to persuade Mark Burgund to stay, suggesting that the business administrator call Ed Stoeckel, the former executive vice president. "Dortch thinks he can change Bakker," Stoeckel told Burgund. "I'm sure he can't. There's absolutely no financial control. You are not going to be able to have any when you get there either." But Burgund, like his close friend Cress, placed his trust in Dortch; his boss would not be going if it was that bad at PTL. Besides, Burgund believed he had what he called a "ministry of helps" to the Reverend Richard Dortch. Dortch had told him he wanted to work together until he retired; Burgund felt that their fates were intertwined.

While Dortch gave Bakker respectability, Bakker and PTL offered Dortch a broader pulpit than he had enjoyed in Illinois and arguably even more influence than he could have had if he pursued the top job in the Assemblies, one of the fastest-growing denominations in the world. And PTL, always willing to pay its top executives generously, offered financial security to Dortch, a man who seemed particularly concerned about his personal finances. He had seen ministers retire with little property or money; he didn't care to make the same mistake.

Bakker committed to Dortch for a minimum of five years. Recognizing Bakker's fickleness, Dortch drafted a memo that fall, without signature or date, recording the agreement and protecting himself. Dortch's salary was set at about $135,000 a year, $25,000 more than he had received in salary and benefits in Illinois.

The new job would mean a great deal more for Dortch financially. Within days after his hiring was announced, PTL began renovating a lakefront home for Dortch later conservatively valued by tax assessors at $256,000. Dortch's divorced daughter joined PTL's payroll, as did Dortch's wife, Mildred, and his son, Rich. The younger Dortch, a financial specialist respected by his colleagues at PTL, later acquired an MBA from Duke University with thousands of dollars of tuition support from PTL.

By PTL's 1985 budget year, Dortch's first full fiscal cycle, his salary, housing allowance, and retirement contributions totaled more than $213,000. By his final year at PTL, his total compensation had climbed to $530,377 on the strength of $240,000 in bonuses and a $50,000-a-year increase in retirement contributions. Years later, the IRS contended that Dortch had been paid over three quarters of a million dollars more than he reasonably should have been.

PTL's board never considered or approved Dortch's compensation arrangement with Bakker, a further indication of the extent to which the two men ruled the board. During its September 26, 1983, meeting, Bakker had explained that he needed an administrator to help run PTL. He suggested Dortch, and the other board members present—Lawing, Cortese, and Dortch—agreed. Dortch was given an unrivaled collection of titles: co-pastor, senior executive vice president, and corporate executive director. For a man of Bakker's paranoid suspicions, the decision to concentrate so much power in another man's hands was a sign of remarkable trust.

A week after the board meeting, PTL announced that Dortch had accepted the number-two job. "Pastor Dortch's coming to this ministry has been the answer to a longtime prayer by Tammy and myself. He will certainly be a great asset," Bakker announced. For his part, Dortch vowed in a news release, "I will, under God, do everything I can to take your burden and assimilate it into my spirit. And together we can see this ministry become what God wants it to be."

At PTL, the announcement raised hopes of greater stability and maturity inside the ministry. It would take time for the staff to see what some of Dortch's associates in the Assemblies of God had already recognized: Dortch's gift was playing diplomat and fire fighter, not administrator. Though he looked the part of the wise pastor, the Richard Dortch who emerged at PTL was a politician, willing to bend the rules and the truth to serve the interests of his boss and the PTL ministry. In an era of spin control, Dortch, like his boss, was a master.

Heritage USA took its biggest step yet from rustic retreat to religious resort in 1983 as PTL erected a ninety-six-unit motel. The Heritage Inn dramatically expanded the on-site lodging PTL offered. Bakker's supporters not only wanted to visit Heritage USA, they wanted to live there year-round. That spring, nearly ninety condominiums had been completed or were under construction. During the summer, construction crews began laying the foundation for the first of three hundred detached single-family homes. Bakker's plans for a Christian city were taking shape.

On July 4, 1983, Bakker dedicated PTL's new thirty-five-thousand-square-foot, fifteen-hundred-seat TV studio, which had been built next to the older Barn auditorium. A few months later, Bakker announced that PTL would build a home for forty to fifty unwed mothers, coupled with an adoption agency. He had spoken out vigorously that summer against abortion, displaying pictures of aborted fetuses and prompting some of PTL's affiliated stations to censor PTL's programming. Now, Bakker wanted to provide an alternative to abortion, both a place to bring pregnancies to term and, if the mothers chose, a Christian agency to adopt their babies.

But the home was soon dwarfed by a series of building projects that forever shifted PTL's center of gravity from TV evangelism and charitable ministry to the task of erecting and running a vacation center for Christians. Publicly, the buildings set the stage for Bakker's crowning moments at PTL. Privately, they compounded the institutionalized patterns of deception, disdain for law, financial strain, and mismanagement in the ministry—a legacy that Dortch would not be able or inclined to change.

During September's board meeting, Bakker rattled off proposals for building after building for the directors' approval. Bakker wanted to move Billy Graham's boyhood home from Charlotte, where a developer planned to raze the structure, to Heritage USA. Board minutes give no indication that the board was told that PTL had already spent $9,500 on the project. The board voted its OK. It also sanctioned construction of the home for unwed mothers and a new welcome center, purchase of new trams to move people about Heritage USA, and acquisition of a miniature train that Bakker wanted to circle the lake adjoining the Heritage Inn. The minutes include no evidence that the board was given the projected cost of these projects. No mention was recorded, either, of another project on Bakker's list: a water amusement park that he would soon research at trade shows in Kansas City and New Orleans.

Bakker informed the board that the new Heritage Inn had fewer rooms than PTL needed. The board agreed—unanimously, as always—to seek an architect and to secure money from a "reputable lending company" for a project Bakker called a new "motel/convention center/Downtown USA."

First public word of that project filtered out in early November, in the weeks following the announcement of Dortch's hiring. Bakker confirmed that he planned to open a $25–$30 million complex that would include a hotel, shopping mall, cafeteria, and meeting area. Inside PTL, there once had been talk of simply adding two hundred rooms to the Heritage Inn. But Bakker told his vice presidents that God had told him that now was the time to build a larger hotel. He began to sketch what the complex should look like: a five-hundred-room hotel and a street of shops enclosed under a pitched glass roof with a cafeteria at one end. He called the hotel the Heritage Grand.

Bakker declared publicly that the complex would open on July 4. He had chosen the fast-track schedule, he said, because visitors had complained that Heritage USA didn't have enough lodging. Thousands looking for rooms had been turned away, he wrote later, and many had promised not to return until PTL had more lodging. "We knew then that we had no choice—we must fulfill the

FORGIVEN

vision that God has given us for the PTL ministry, or the vision would be destroyed."

Marlene Way—the Elvis impersonator Jim had befriended in Muskegon as a teenager—had not seen or heard from Bakker since she left Muskegon in 1958. A letter she had written during the sixties had gone unanswered. Way now lived in Florida, and during the fall of 1983 she persuaded her husband to make the drive north to meet Jim Bakker. She arrived at the World Outreach Center unannounced.

"Is Jim Bakker in today?" she asked. The receptionist looked at her with an odd expression, answering that yes, he was. Bakker's staff was accustomed to forming a wall around him, protecting him from avid fans who mistakenly thought that he was as approachable as he seemed on the air.

Way explained who she was and said that all she wanted to do was say hello. The receptionist telephoned upstairs.

The answer was blunt: I'm sorry, he's very busy, he has a conference today, you can't see him. Way was heartbroken. She knew that if she were ever famous—and once Way had been certain she would be—she would never be too busy to see a friend. She wondered if Bakker's secretary had told him that she was downstairs, in the same office building. If she had, Way couldn't believe that Bakker had not at least sent a note down. She left a brief note and her home address.

On October 13, Bakker answered the note with a letter impersonal enough to have been written by his secretary.

> It was so nice to hear how you are doing and what has been happening in your life. Many things have happened since our days in Muskegon. I am sure we never expected to be where we are, but when we are willing to be used, He will direct our paths.

That fall, Bakker telephoned David Taggart in Florida and asked him to come back to work. He missed Taggart's efficiency and dependability. Taggart agreed to return, and, as Taggart remembered it later, Bakker offered him a $100,000 salary. The sum was nearly three times what Taggart had received a year before.

Dortch, handling the particulars, agreed to a starting salary of $80,000 with a raise to $100,000 in January. PTL also paid $6,000 in moving expenses, including the cost of mirrors and vinyl shelves Taggart had installed in his Florida apartment and the limousine rides he took on trips back to Florida in early 1984.

In late October, Taggart reappeared on the third floor. Sitting in his office, a step away from Bakker's, Porter Speakman fumed as Taggart helped the PTL president reorganize his corner office. Speakman had heard that Taggart was going to return, but Bakker—the quiet, private man to whom Speakman had never gotten close—had not bothered to mention that Taggart would replace him. Speakman waited until half-past six that evening for Bakker to approach him. Finally, Speakman walked out.

There had always been limits to Speakman's allegiance. He and his family had stopped attending church at Heritage USA, even though Speakman—like other PTL executives—knew their presence was expected. Each Sunday, Bakker had kept him busy with chores doled out from his dressing room. Sunday was no longer the Sabbath for Speakman; he could not worship in peace of mind, he could not replenish his store of spiritual strength. He found the love, spiritual climate, and wise pastor he needed at another church.

A day after his reappearance, Taggart told Speakman that Jim wanted him to serve again as budget director. David was nice about it—Speakman had always found Taggart friendly and kind, as did most who worked closely with the young man—but Speakman wanted to hear it from Bakker himself. He vented his frustration to Vi Azvedo. She was blunt. Shape up, she told him, you've got to pray through it.

PTL's board met for an unusual third time in four months in the week before Christmas. Bakker presented Taggart to the board, which agreed to name him to a vice presidency. That same day, Taggart was given a $10,000 Christmas bonus. For the third time in its last four meetings, the board voted a $100,000 bonus for Jim. In six months' time, the Bakkers together had been given $460,000 in bonuses.

As the new year approached, Dortch's administrative assistant, Al Cress, drove from Illinois to Charlotte to start work at PTL. He felt no joy, no excitement at the new $53,000-a-year assignment. His first day of work, January 2, he knew that he had made a mistake. He hated PTL. The people were not friendly. Mornings, before he would walk into the office, Cress would sit in his car, dazed. As he'd slip out and walk toward the pyramid-shaped World Outreach Center, tears would well up in his eyes.

CHAPTER TWELVE

LODGING FOR A LIFETIME

"You cannot find a better investment opportunity anywhere"

Though Bakker gave the credit to God, his vision of Heritage USA owed much to the genius of Walt Disney. Bakker read books about Disney. He hired people who had worked for Disney's company. He visited Walt Disney World regularly after it opened outside Orlando, Florida. Bakker may have been a creative mastermind, as most around him believed, but he was not an especially original thinker. Instead, he adapted secular commercial successes to his Christian world. Disney's Fort Wilderness campground in Florida was a model for the Fort Heritage campground at Heritage USA. The Main Street shopping mall at PTL was patterned after its namesake in the Magic Kingdom. Bakker liked Disney's green wrought-iron fencing, and it soon appeared at PTL.

But as Bakker entered the big-money resort business, he and his ministry clung to the practices of a mom-and-pop operation: poor planning, impulsive decision-making, and inadequate financing, trademarks of Bakker's first decade in Charlotte. PTL was a $66-million-a-year corporation now, with a payroll that had climbed as high as nine hundred and assets that soon reached $86 million. PTL's inspiration might be divine, but the ministry needed sound, down-to-earth corporate management to prosper. Even Bakker recognized it. You are making million-dollar mistakes, he told his executive staff in a March 1984 meeting. "We can't run it sloppy any more. . . . We've built a national ministry with a local mentality. . . . We need to be on the cutting edge. We need to be the best."

There was little basis for optimism during the final weeks of 1983 as PTL began its massive Partner Center project, the five-hundred-room hotel, shopping mall, and adjoining cafeteria and conference center. Even though $30 million or more was at stake, PTL once more moved ahead with little preparation. It had no master plan for Heritage USA, merely Bakker's fantastic wish list. Little or nothing had been done to review the tax implications for PTL, even though the IRS had just started a formal audit of the corporation. And it was not until after construction had begun that PTL commissioned an outside market study of the hotel, a step that logically should have been completed months before. The study, like PTL, was optimistic. The outside analyst concluded that the hotel was marketable; with occupancy of seventy to seventy-five percent, PTL could expect to clear close to $4 million before paying debt service and income taxes.

PTL had ordered the study to help acquire financing for the project, but that too remained unresolved as construction began. Through the fall and winter, Bakker's staff shopped for loans of as much as $100 million to pay for the hotel/shopping complex and other projects.

As he announced the Partner Center on November 1, 1983, Bakker said that he didn't expect to ask viewers for money to build it. Instead, he suggested, financing institutions would provide the capital. The project, he claimed, would pay for itself.

That changed quickly. At a small staff meeting three days later, Bakker said that he and the partners did not want to pay tens of millions of dollars in interest. Bakker spelled out his alternative: seek thousand-dollar contributions from twenty-five thousand supporters whom he called "lifetime partners" and promise them in return three nights' free lodging a year for the rest of their lives. Half of the hotel's rooms would be set aside to fulfill the promise, but PTL wouldn't have to borrow and pay millions in interest. Money from paying customers would cover all operating costs.

As the new year began, PTL showered its partners with a three-page mass mailing explaining the Partner Center. Bakker wrote that television alone couldn't meet the need of Christians to assemble together in the final days before Christ's return. The mailing explained the offer of free lifetime lodging with an adman's enthusiasm: "You cannot find a better investment opportunity anywhere." The mailing claimed that lifetime partnership privileges would be worth almost $20,000 after forty years. "Stay Here Free . . . For the Rest of Your Life," a flier promised. On the other side, Bakker included a note warning that "Time is running out . . . Only 25,000 Lifetime Partnerships are available, and they are going fast!"

This was not just another free Bible or Tammy Bakker record or opportunity to add your name to a plaque on a new building. The risks for PTL had multiplied. With the promise of a lifetime of free lodging, PTL had committed itself to offering hotel rooms sixty, seventy years into the future, long after the last penny of partnership money had been spent. It had given the IRS new cause to question PTL's claims to be a church and a tax-exempt corporation. And it had put Bakker at greater jeopardy should he bend the truth in his TV appeals, as he had in his foreign missions appeals in the late seventies. Then he had misused perhaps $300,000 or $400,000 and angered a few evangelists overseas. The stakes were higher now; he meant to raise tens of millions of dollars from thousands of US and Canadian partners.

The lifetime partnerships also changed the expectations of PTL's donors at a pivotal time for the ministry. In recent years, Bakker's genius for raising money had relied increasingly on more valuable gift offers. Once the premiums for donors had cost ten cents for each dollar PTL received. By the early eighties, PTL spent as much as twenty-six cents for each dollar contributed. Bakker was now offering partners a premium conceivably worth much, much more than the donor had ever given. Like children fed too many sweets, PTL's donors began to show less and less enthusiasm for donations that didn't offer free pieces of Heritage USA in return.

The lifetime partnerships took an immediate toll on contributions to PTL's general fund. From a high of nearly $51 million in 1983, contributions dipped to $44.8 million. By 1986, they would decline to $35 million.

Lifetime partnerships would more than make up the difference. In 1984, PTL recorded taking in nearly $51 million in partnerships, and in 1986 $61.4 million. But lifetime partnerships were beyond the reach of many in Bakker's audience. In the first half of 1984, the number of donations to PTL dropped 17.7%, and the total count of donors declined 11.6%. PTL now would have to stretch the lifetime money far enough to pay not only for the lodging Bakker had promised but also for PTL's day-to-day operating deficit, the legacy of shrinking donations to the general fund. PTL soon found itself surviving on the lifetime partnerships.

Nearly six years had passed since Bakker stood before the towering white satellite dish at Heritage Village and proclaimed PTL's new satellite network "one of the most historic developments in the entire church history." Though hardly that, the satellite network had become an essential source of viewers and dollars for PTL— and now a valuable tool for marketing the lifetime partnerships.

As corporate America realized there was money to be made in cable TV, black coaxial cable became a common fixture on America's utility poles. In cable television's early years, local systems needed programming to fill their broadcast menus, and PTL's network offered a mix of TV preachers of all stripes. PTL now dubbed its twenty-four-hour offering for cable the Inspirational Network to help distinguish it from the industry's leader, CBN, which now offered more family entertainment than religious programming. Eventually, about thirteen hundred cable systems serving 12 million homes would agree to use PTL programming.

That base enabled PTL to get its flagship program, "Jim Bakker," into homes across the country, live in the morning and taped in mid-evening, without paying the steep fees that local stations charged for such prime time. With the spread of cable, mainstream America discovered Jim and Tammy Bakker.

PTL still bought airtime on local TV stations, both to reach TV sets not tied to cable and to provide a second path to those receiving cable. Changes in the commercial TV industry had given PTL access to better broadcast time. Competing network programming had pushed PTL out of the sunrise spot on ABC affiliates that it had relied on heavily in its early years. But independent TV stations had proliferated in small and medium-sized markets like Memphis and Rochester, giving PTL a less costly way to air Bakker's show live at eleven in the morning. By 1987, PTL broadcast on 165 local stations covering eighty-five percent of the national TV market.

As Kansas contractor Roe Messner began the Partner Center, Bakker and his staff put together plans to build the water park Bakker wanted in operation by Memorial Day, 1984. Bakker saw the park as a showcase attraction for the young and the young at heart, giving Heritage USA more pulling power beyond PTL's older core constituency. Instead, the project became a costly monument to how little Bakker and PTL had learned about management.

First, PTL hired a Wisconsin firm to design the water park and an Ohio company to provide wave-making equipment. Since time was precious, the Wisconsin firm threw its staff into the job, building a $15,000, one-hundred-square-foot model based on sketches approved by the PTL executive in charge of the project. Then a second PTL executive, Jim Swaim, took over the project. Swaim, a former executive producer of Bakker's TV show, had Bakker's creative spirit and a relentless drive to please his boss. Swaim concluded that the Wisconsin company's work lacked creativity and ordered the company to halt work. After the firm threatened suit, PTL paid them $60,000.

Swaim also sought other manufacturers of wave-making equipment, eventually signing a contract with a California company whose machines made more sophisticated waves. But PTL failed to cancel its contract with the Ohio firm, in part because no one had read the contract PTL had signed. The Ohio firm sued PTL and later won its full claim of $225,840. Without a shovelful of dirt being moved, PTL was already nearly $300,000 in the hole.

In his search for a new company to design and build the water park, Swaim found Don Barcus and Terry Zinger, owners of REC Associates, the Burbank firm that had managed construction of the Raging Waters park in San Dimas, California. In late February, Barcus and Zinger toured the proposed site. With three months to go before the start of the summer season, the Californians wanted to know what barriers they might encounter if they took the fast-track job. The PTL executive escorting them assured the two that local building inspectors were flexible and would even allow work ahead of permits. He predicted that state health authorities would give similar cooperation and pledged that PTL had the water and sewage-treatment capacity the water park required.

After lunch, Swaim described Bakker's ideal: a natural-looking structure without the erector-set towers that marred roadside water parks. Swaim acknowledged that Bakker's desires might be unrealistic but, he cautioned, Bakker didn't react well to what he didn't want to hear. Bakker was the boss, Swaim said, and he got what he wanted if it could be done.

REC's Zinger pressed for assurances that PTL had the money to pay for the project—a must to finish the project on time. Zinger pressed and pressed until Swaim seemed irritated. Swaim assured him that money was no problem.

That afternoon, in the private dining room at the Wagon Wheel restaurant overlooking the lake at Heritage USA, Barcus, Zinger, an architect, and several others huddled with two illustrators to create a design. They came up with one in five hours, a dissonant mix of ornate Victorian outbuildings, intended to blend with the adjoining Partner Center, and the centerpiece volcano of artificial rock that Bakker wanted. The mountain was supposed to evoke images of old religious movies and serve as a stage for fireworks displays.

Bakker approved the design, and Barcus, Zinger, and several others worked through the night figuring out what the park would cost. At seven o'clock the next morning, they had a price tag of $6 million, $2 million more than PTL had planned to spend. The session had been so rushed, they realized later, that they forgot to include their management fee of $421,000. They told Swaim, and he thanked them for being honest.

Bakker was sold. No matter what, he told Dortch and Swaim later that day, he wanted the country's most beautiful water park. At one point Bakker turned to Dortch. "Can we afford this thing?" he asked. Dortch was confident. "Oh yeah, we can put it together some way."

In fact, PTL was struggling mightily under the weight of Bakker's renewed zeal to build. In December 1983, PTL had asked Messner to hold one of its payment checks for two weeks. In mid-January, finance director Peter Bailey had informed Bakker that PTL owed $13 million in accounts payable, $9.4 million of it past due. "I respectfully suggest that we curtail as much future spending as possible for the next two months," Bailey wrote. "We are not able to make commitments to anyone as our income is far less than our current spending (approximately $500,000 per month). All savings accounts have been used." The picture would not improve in the weeks to come.

After PTL committed in writing to build the water park, and work began at the site, it took nearly three weeks for Bakker's board of directors to be asked to approve the $6 million project.

To those on the outside, it was obvious that PTL's board was ill-suited to oversee the large corporation that PTL had become. The Evangelical Council for Financial Accountability had questioned the board's vigilance on the matter of the Florida condominium. Not only had the board set no price limit on the purchase, ECFA learned, but the $11,678 Habitat sauna in Bakker's dressing room had been installed without the board's knowledge. It had been a surprise from one of Bakker's aides to her boss.

In an October 1983 letter, ECFA executive director Art Borden told Bakker that ECFA recommended that PTL's board grow in size and diversity, meet more often, and approve and monitor budgets for all major projects. Then, in April 1984, Borden informed Bakker that ECFA had put off approving PTL's 1984 membership until it received evidence that PTL's board was a responsible one.

IRS agents had raised similar concerns. John Yorke, one of PTL's local attorneys, urged Bakker to expand the board to twelve or fifteen and to assure that it became more familiar with the ministry's projects and finances. He also repeated his advice that one and perhaps two lawyers attend all board meetings. "Many of the problems of the past could have been avoided with a little advice up front."

But Bakker had little incentive to change. His compliant board— Dortch, Cortese, Cookman, and Lawing—believed that what was good for Jim Bakker was good for PTL. It would take time for Bakker to find more board members with the same attitude. Meanwhile, the board continued to compound its mistakes.

On March 13, 1984, the board voted Bakker a $390,000 bonus, only three months after the Bakkers together had been voted

$160,000. This bonus represented Bakker's single largest payment to date from PTL—a lump sum roughly equivalent to what he had earned from the ministry in all of 1982.

As always, Bakker made a show of his fiscal responsibility, recording a vote against the bonus. In fact, he needed the money. The Bakkers had gone house-hunting during a January trip to Palm Springs, California. They had found the house they wanted on a mountainside overlooking the nearby resort city of Palm Desert.

At about twenty-six-hundred square feet, the three-bedroom, three-bath house was small compared to Tega Cay. Inside its front gate, visitors walked through an Oriental garden with shallow pools, a decorative waterfall, and plants set amid natural stone. The former model home was furnished in upscale Oriental style—black lacquer cabinets, a Coramandel screen across one wall, an Oriental rug on the living-room floor. Out back, surrounded by an iron fence, there was a V-shaped swimming pool and a small outdoor spa. The view was spectacular. The Indio Hills loomed across the desert floor; mountains with names like Haystack, Indio, Asbestos, and Sheep stood guard in the distance.

The house cost $449,000. In early May, the Bakkers secured a $300,000 mortgage. Shortly afterwards, PTL wired $190,000—Bakker's $390,000 bonus, less withholding taxes—into Bakker's bank account. Years later, Bakker said that he couldn't remember the reason for the transfer; in fact, the money arrived just in time for Bakker to make the $149,000 down payment and pay what were likely more than $30,000 in closing costs.

Even as his projects proliferated back in the Carolinas, Bakker hatched grand plans for the southern-California market. He had first tapped it during his brief alliance with Paul Crouch, and it had continued to supply strong support to his Carolina ministry. In fall 1983, Bakker talked to his board about creating a base in California. The PTL president envisioned West Coast seminars by the Christian therapy team and a wintertime home for his program. He could get fresh faces on the air, save on transportation costs, and serve the California partners, who outnumbered their counterparts in the other forty-nine states. Eventually, Bakker thought he might replicate Heritage USA, much as Disney had expanded from Anaheim to Orlando.

* * *

During the winter of 1984, Roger Flessing decided to leave the Dallas ad agency where he produced Billy Graham's TV crusades. Flessing wanted eventually to return to his native California. That would take time, but PTL could help with the transition. A decade before, coming to PTL had been an act of commitment for Flessing. Now, it was an act of convenience.

Returning to the ministry, Roger and Kathy Flessing found a radically different PTL. In two years, the staff had mushroomed, but it seemed less optimistic, and the atmosphere was colder. Once the staff had joked that life would be better once PTL moved into the new building—there always was a new building. Now even that jesting hope had faded.

By March 1, Flessing was back at work. He met that day with Bakker, Taggart, and Dortch. He recorded highlights of the meeting afterwards in a log.

> 1. JB wants show to look more professional.
> 2. Tammy may be on or near a nervous breakdown.
> 3. Tammy addicted to ———.

Flessing did not record what Tammy was addicted to. After Bakker's resignation, Mike Richardson, one of the Bakkers' bodyguards, wrote about Tammy's 1984 troubles.

> Tammy was taking serious amounts of Valium that year, "for her nerves," and we all knew it. She had both blue ones and yellow ones. I personally saw her take Valium more than twenty times—and I wasn't with her all day long the way I was with Jim.
>
> At least twice while I was at PTL, Tammy was taken to California by Vi Azvedo—because she was sick, Vi said. But David [Taggart] said that the Valium was getting to her and she needed to "dry out" some.

Richardson also saw Taggart give Valium to Bakker. Occasionally Taggart would use them himself. "You don't *know* what I've been through today!" he would exclaim.

Those who had known Tammy could see that something was wrong. Once the more stable of the two Bakkers, she now often became irrational and over-emotional over insignificant foul-ups.

She had a reputation for pressuring her husband to fire staff members she didn't like. When she used the tranquilizer Ativan—a sister drug to Valium and the drug her friends remember her taking most, a quarter of a pill at a time—she mellowed. But the next day, one of her friends said later, she would claw your eyes out. Afterwards, Tammy seemed without remorse, as if she didn't realize what she had done.

On April 7, six days after the Bakker's twenty-third wedding anniversary, Bakker radioed one of his executives to meet him at his Tega Cay home. It was Saturday, and the man was out shopping for cars with his wife. Late that afternoon, the executive found Bakker outside at his pool watching the PTL satellite network. Bakker said that he wanted to talk about TV programming for kids. But when they went inside, Bakker asked for a backrub. He lay down on his bed, and the executive began massaging Bakker's back.

Then Bakker complained that his leg hurt. He rolled over, reached up, and pulled the visitor's hand towards his crotch. He reached for the man's zipper. The executive froze, much as Jay Babcock had the summer before at Hilton Head.

The sun poured in through the wall of windows at the end of Bakker's bedroom. "Why don't you close the curtain?" Bakker suggested. Stunned, the executive stammered back, "No, I've got to go, my mother's here for dinner." He left abruptly. That night, he said nothing to his wife about the incident, and he tried to put it out of his mind. He and Bakker never spoke about that day, but their relations became strained. Soon, the executive resigned.

The first weeks on the water-park job had been sobering for Don Barcus, co-owner of REC. Barcus learned that local and state inspectors were not the willing partners PTL had described. The ministry had taken advantage of their flexibility too often—water and sewer mains had been built at the Partner Center without a building permit—and now the inspectors insisted that REC go by the book. As it turned out, REC would not get the permit to build the water park's pool until late August 1984, close to the end of its planned first season. REC could not obtain permits for water and sewer lines because, contrary to what Barcus had been told, PTL had to expand its sewage-treatment capacity first—at a cost of $1 million. PTL also needed a new well and water tower.

To compound matters, PTL began changing its plans—the consequence of a job hastily conceived for a fickle executive like Bakker. The ministry's poor planning puzzled Barcus and Zinger. Had this been Disney, the project would have taken five years, they thought—two for design and more for architectural work, cost studies, cross checks with other departments, and competitive bidding on the construction contract. They asked why PTL had not done a feasibility study, at least to decide the park's optimum size and admission fees. Even a nonprofit corporation had to clear enough money to support itself.

They were told not to press the subject; Bakker got his inspiration from God, and that was sufficient cause for PTL to move ahead. PTL seemed confident that the audience for Bakker's TV program, the stream of visitors to Heritage USA, and the lifetime partners would generate the necessary traffic.

REC had made its own mistake: it had miscalculated the cost of the park it had agreed to build. From the start, its chief subcontractor warned that REC had not asked enough; you've got $2 million in underground utility work alone, he said. He estimated that the project would cost $10 million. The water park was shoe-horned onto a small site, with extensive rock work and costly details like an underground viewing room and a restaurant on top of the wave machine.

After a week of work, Barcus began to realize that PTL had misled him with its claims to have the water park financing in place. PTL's first payment to him came up $9,000 short of the agreed-upon $165,000, even though Barcus saw new projects and more spending—large and small—going on all around him. PTL brought in a carousel, began a warehouse office building, and overhauled its outdoor amphitheater to create a set for its passion play. Bakker was eager to begin a nursing home/medical center and a $3.7 million, five-thousand-seat auditorium. It all seemed preposterous, but it was what Bakker wanted—and so it was what Bakker's staff set out to get.

A consultant working for PTL at the time later described the pattern he saw in 1984:

> If Mr. Bakker says he wants something, his employees dare not
> question Mr. Bakker or other PTL management about fund-
> ing. Generally, a contractor or other outside vendor is hired
> with the worry of payment put off to a later date. If severe
> resistance is encountered in securing these payments, memo-
> ries, concerning how firm the commitment to a vendor was,
> become soft.

Money never seemed an issue with PTL until a supplier wanted a
bill paid, the consultant wrote. Then the delay began.

PTL's Jim Swaim delivered the bad news to Barcus in early May:
Swaim was having trouble getting approval to pay the contractor's
bills. Dortch and finance director Peter Bailey wanted to delay the
project. Three days later, Swaim managed to extract $50,000. He
apologized for the small check; PTL still owed more than $1 mil-
lion. Soon, PTL paid another $281,527, but Swaim warned Barcus
that he didn't know when he could get more money. Bakker's plan
for a summer of grand openings was unraveling. On May 22,
Barcus laid off his construction crews. The park would not open on
July 4.

The Partner Center wouldn't open on time either. By mid-May,
it had already drained $13 million from PTL's bank accounts. With
PTL owing another $8 million, contractor Roe Messner had slowed
the work. PTL blamed the delay on heavy winter rains.

Peter Bailey had been warning Bakker for weeks about the
deteriorating state of PTL's general fund. PTL couldn't meet its
payroll or make critical payments to suppliers. Each day deepened
the crisis; Bailey expected a $1 million monthly deficit in March and
April. On March 30, Bailey's frustration bubbled over.

> I spend countless hours dealing with our cash flow crisis. We
> (management) need to face our problem and decide now what
> we are going to do about it. I feel that we must face temporary
> stoppages on projects until our partner base is built up to
> sustain $5 million to $6 million cash outflow each month.

That same day, with Bailey listening, Bakker told ten of his top
executives that PTL's managers were spending too much time with
Bailey. "Finance is running this place. . . . The most damaging
phrase is 'We're out of money.' . . . Don't live in the negative." To

prosper, Bakker suggested, PTL needed creative management and creative ideas.

Bakker was able to persuade himself that PTL didn't have any serious financial problems. He felt that real-estate sales, handled properly, could pay for the new buildings, and long-term financing could enable PTL to stay within its budgets. No longer would he have to risk being the "national beggar." If needed, PTL could turn to the partners. "If I have a genuine problem and it's not overused, the partners will bail me out every time."

The same day that Barcus laid off his workers, Bakker painted a cheery picture of ministry finances for his board. Income for the last three months was excellent, some of the best in the corporation's history, he said. The minutes show no evidence that Bakker passed along the warnings of his finance director.

Dortch offered a similarly optimistic appraisal of PTL's budget. "Management has been supportive of the budget system," the minutes record him as saying, and "efforts are being made to look at every area of the corporation to see where necessary cuts could be made."

Budget director Porter Speakman also saw the worrisome patterns that prompted Bailey's complaints to Bakker. Undesignated gifts in April and May had averaged $3.75 million a month. That could pay for salaries, TV airtime, utility payments, and interest payments, but it left PTL short another $2 million a month for vital expenses—including gas for its cars, travel for employees and guests, postage for its mass mailings, gifts for its donors and maintenance of the grounds.

In early June, Dortch asked Speakman to recommend places to cut PTL's budget. On June 8, Speakman replied with an ominous three-page memo.

> We must take immediate and decisive action if we are to avoid a potential disaster.
> I would like to recommend the following:
>
> 1) All programs, projects, capital expansion, etc. that is not absolutely vital to the daily operation of this ministry be stopped immediately.
>
> 2) A hiring freeze on all new employees be implemented immediately *throughout the ministry.* This would include all employees from executive level on down.

3) An immediate meeting be held between Mr. Bakker, the vice presidents, and yourself to discuss the current crisis. . . . Hard decisions should be made as to which programs to eliminate, which ones should be delayed, which can be reduced, etc. The decisions of that group must be implemented immediately with *no exceptions.*

4) Lean and strict budgets be developed and *tightly* adhered to.

5) Constant monitoring and updating on the financial crisis be done by finance and reported regularly to executive management.

Finally, I believe it is time we faced the crisis of what I feel is the deepest and most dangerous financial crisis we have ever experienced. I also know that our God is able to deliver us from this crisis and we must seek His wisdom in making the very hard decisions necessary for the survival of this ministry.

Just four days later, Bakker assured ECFA, the accountability group raising questions about PTL's internal operations, that he believed in a strictly controlled budget and was putting one in place. Bailey and Speakman, however, saw little progress in that direction all summer.

Two weeks after Bakker's letter to ECFA, Bailey reported that planned budget cuts were not being made. "We are still traveling, hiring new people." By mid-July, Bailey reported that Swaim and his staff—the group in charge of Heritage USA—were spending as if PTL had no crisis.

I have grave concern for the size of our payroll. We cannot keep going. We pay for street actors and actresses, which does not seem to be a priority, allow unlimited spending for the passion play while we struggle to cover basic expenses such as payroll, indebtedness, and utility bills. We need to have a realistic budget in force for us to use as a management tool.

Bailey continued to write memos. Speakman asked for a transfer. Instead, Dortch offered severance pay, and Speakman agreed to leave. Later, he wondered why he had stayed so long. He deplored the Bakkers' extravagant life-style and the vast sums PTL spent to support it. Like so many at PTL, he believed that God had called him there for a reason. He didn't work for Jim Bakker, he worked for the Lord. Yet Bakker had charisma, PTL was an exciting place to work, and Speakman had seen the ministry touch people's lives.

The third floor was virtually immune from the ups and downs of PTL's bank balance. While Bailey proclaimed crises, Bakker and his entourage spent freely on the road. Bakker, Tammy, their two children, Azvedo, Taggart, and a bodyguard settled into a suite atop New York City's Waldorf-Astoria hotel for a week of shopping. The trip burned up a ten-thousand-dollar cash advance. A few weeks later, the Bakkers were off again, this time for a two-week visit to the Bakkers' new house in Palm Desert. Bakker's entourage flew to and from the West Coast by chartered jet. For this trip, the jet service had cost PTL more than $100,000. There was also more shopping—a California wardrobe for Tammy, thousands of dollars in Frederic Remington bronzes, and new dishes for the house and new glassware for the breakfront. They bought so much that a truck had to follow them home from the store.

Jim Bakker also went shopping for cars. He acquired a new Mercedes coupe for nearly $46,000. He flew by chartered jet to Orange County's John Wayne Airport at a cost to PTL of three thousand dollars. There he purchased an antique 1953 Rolls Royce for $58,884. With PTL money he bought a 1939 Phantom III V12 Rolls to use at the new Heritage Grand Hotel. The car cost $27,438 but stayed at the dealership for an expensive overhaul.

Within days of Bakker's return, the board voted more money for the Bakkers. Jim Bakker's pay climbed to $250,000. PTL was contributing another $125,000 to his retirement account each year. Less than two months had passed since the $390,000 bonus. A few days after the meeting, Jim Bakker received a new bonus check for $100,000, Tammy Bakker one for $50,000.

The Bakkers returned to California in August, flying on PTL's new $965,000 Sabreliner jet. After Bakker had been gone for a few days, he called back East, eager to have his staff come see the two thousand acres he had found for just under $2 million. The land was in the mountains across from Red Skelton's ranch; perhaps the proximity to a celebrity validated the find. "I didn't want to leave without finding the property because I've looked so long," he told Flessing over the phone. A few days later, Taggart purchased a four-wheel-drive, $13,582 Jeep for PTL to use exploring potential sites for Heritage USA West. The two-thousand-acre site didn't pan out.

Watching the early morning PTL broadcast had long been a sport for the ladies at Mr. Kenneth's Hair Design, a salon along Palm Canyon Drive in downtown Palm Springs. The clientele scoffed at weepy Tammy and indignant Jim. One day in walked Tammy, whom one regular remembered as a "cute little gal with these brief shorts." Tammy had befriended Jolie Gabor, the mother of Eva and Zsa Zsa, and the elder Gabor patronized Mr. Kenneth's. Tammy was taken with the very gay salon owner. She posed for pictures with him. She kissed him. She told him she prayed for him every night. She began visiting daily to have her makeup applied or her hair styled. Ken told her she didn't need all the makeup; it was advice she often heard and never took.

Even to the monied regulars in Palm Springs, the Bakkers' spending was memorable. The chauffeured limousines, the hotel suites used during their early trips, the tens of thousands of dollars spent at the local auction house—much of it courtesy of PTL. Tammy, who preferred to talk on the air about her fondness for discount stores, was seen at Saks Fifth Avenue, I. Magnin, and tony Laykin Jewelers, where she had asked for a security guard to watch over a particularly expensive transaction. At the salon, she spent what seemed like more than a thousand dollars in three days on cosmetics. She never asked what anything cost. She customarily paid for her purchases with what one bystander described as a roll of hundred-dollar bills that would choke a horse.

By late July, Bakker had begun to acknowledge publicly the difficulty his finance and budget directors had identified months before. He announced that PTL's regular monthly giving had suffered with the rush to lifetime partnerships. It was time for a crisis.

By now, crises were routine at PTL, not as predictable as the July 4th parade or the Labor Day all-night gospel sing, but every bit as much a part of the landscape. Though Bakker might say that he was tired of being the nation's beggar, he recognized that it was in a crisis that he did his best fund-raising. There had long been a fundamental misrepresentation in Bakker's crisis appeals: PTL's gravest difficulty was not earning too little money but misusing what it already had. Now, as Bakker's consumption grew more conspicuous and millions poured in to PTL from lifetime partners, Bakker seemed to bend the truth even further to motivate his donors.

On August 1, 1984, the Bakkers appealed for help to pay for TV time. Without it, they said, PTL stood to lose its network of affiliates—the lifeline into viewers' homes. Bakker finessed the obvious question of how there could be a financial crisis when PTL was reporting record revenues from the lifetime partnerships. His answer was a pledge that no regular contributions were being used to pay for the Grand; regular partner donations were paying PTL's other bills. Tammy spoke up with a similar point about the lifetime partnerships. "Thousands and thousands and thousands of dollars that these lifetime members have given is being used to build the Grand. It's not being used to pay the bills. So now we need some paying-the-bills money."

PTL did indeed need money to pay the bills. It had needed it for months and, contrary to Tammy's statement and despite Bakker's failure to correct his wife, it was using the lifetime partnership money to pay operating expenses. Her husband knew it but had skillfully avoided saying so. Bakker could manipulate information deftly, creating an impression very different from the truth. Tammy, a spontaneous talker with little of her husband's inside knowledge, strayed from the literal truth more often.

That same day, Tammy stretched the truth again for the cause. She sobbed:

> You pay for the foreign missions [PTL's overseas broadcasts]. Jim and I can't. We've given everything we have, and literally we have given everything. I have offered to sell everything I own because things really don't mean that much when it comes to getting the Gospel of Jesus Christ out. But if I sold every single thing I owned, Jim, it would probably keep us on the air one more day.

Jim chimed in, "Oh no, it wouldn't be that long."

The tale of unrestrained generosity might be effective television, but it was untrue. Just a week before Tammy's emotional declaration, the Bakkers had sold—not donated—a car to PTL for $9,967.

Just three weeks had passed since the Bakkers claimed $150,000 in bonus money. Bakker had taken another $390,000 a few months before. If the Bakkers had given "literally everything," they had overlooked their handsome new home and cars in California, subsidized with those timely bonuses from PTL and valued at more than $550,000.

Bakker was proud of the lifetime-partnership idea and defiant towards the naysayers who had discouraged him. "I knew people would say, Jim, you're crazy, you're absolutely crazy. You can't do this." But the Lord had shown him, he said. "One morning I woke up and in fifteen minutes the total plan for this whole thing was there." It was the greatest fund-raiser ever, Bakker told a visiting friend from CBN.

Anxious to refill its coffers, PTL continued to issue lifetime partnerships in the Heritage Grand long after Bakker's announcement that all twenty-five thousand partnerships had been issued. By the end of July, PTL had taken in $29.7 million in lifetime partnerships. Bakker said at the time that he had, at most, 150 left, but PTL recorded another $1.3 million more in August.

That fall, Bakker acknowledged that he had increased the numbers. In his words, the partnerships were "overgone."

> I told you we're going to go for twenty-five thousand. Well, we really had room for thirty thousand. . . . I thought well, I'll just stop at twenty-five thousand, and then it will just kind of trickle over, cause we can't go over thirty thousand in the Grand. And you know what, it not only trickled over the thirty now, it's avalanched over.

In early September, Bakker told his viewers that he didn't know how PTL would make it through financially. Thirteen days later, he unveiled his solution to the money problem and the heavy demand for lifetime partnerships—another hotel. The twenty-story, five-hundred-room Heritage Grand Towers was the high rise that Bakker had talked about with contractor Messner as early as February. Bakker said that PTL planned to open it in a year. Bakker recited his gospel of growth, the same explanation he had used for the Partner Center nearly a year earlier. "If you don't expand, and you don't keep growing, you can't go forward. And we've turned people away from this place too many years."

In fact, PTL could not afford not to raise more lifetime partnerships. Unable to trim operating costs or generate needed revenues from general contributions, the ministry had to rely on the Towers to bring in the money to finish the Partner Center and make ends meet. Bailey looked on the Towers as PTL's financial salvation, even as Bakker promoted it primarily as an effort to make more room for visiting partners. The new offer was a vivid, if risky, illustration of one of Bakker's favorite private sayings: "New projects pay for old projects."

Unbeknownst to the TV audience, the Towers was also PTL's salvation from a grave public-relations and fiscal threat. PTL's outside auditor, Deloitte Haskins and Sells, had informed finance director Bailey that its next audit might not sanction PTL as a going concern able to pay its debts. The accounting firm was worried about the broad gap between PTL's $28.5 million in current liabilities and its $8.6 million in current assets.

Such a finding would tarnish PTL's image and place the ministry in further difficulty by alarming suppliers and scaring away lenders. Four days before Bakker unveiled the Towers project, Bailey informed him of Deloitte's concerns. Bailey had eased the auditor's worries, he wrote, by spelling out PTL's plan to raise $30 million for the highrise. The finance director genuinely believed that the Towers could pull PTL out of its chronic crisis.

> When we get current on all our bills with the funds from the Tower promotion, it will be a different world with less time on everyone's part in hassling over payments, getting better discounts, better credit ratings, more efficient use of our time, better morale, happy vendors, etc.

Given PTL's growing dependence on the lifetime money to pay its bills, Bailey expected Bakker to promote the Towers with only a broad description of PTL's purpose for raising the money. The finance director had seen the millions raised for the first hotel diverted, leaving too little to pay Messner for its construction. The hazards of that course were readily apparent to anyone who had lived through the FCC investigation.

In fact, Bakker did not free himself from all promises on how the Towers money would be used. As he unveiled the Towers project on September 17 and pitched partnerships in subsequent broadcasts, he did spell out how PTL would spend the money. He said that PTL needed 30,000 people to give a thousand dollars, but that the offer would stop there. PTL would use $10 million of the $30 million raised to finish the Partner Center. Bakker told his audience that he expected three hundred rooms of the Heritage Grand to open by Thanksgiving, even though he had told his board five days earlier that he expected the hotel to begin opening by Christmas. Bakker also told his audience that the Towers would cost $15 million, a "bargain price" thanks to Messner, "a Christian man who believes in working with me." So, Bakker said, "The Tower will be paid for, even before it's done."

By his own reckoning, Bakker would have $5 million left to spend. That sum, he said, "will pay every TV station in America current" and keep the network from crumbling. His dream, he said, was to accomplish "the miracle" before December 1.

Charlotte had never been a comfortable match for the PTL president. It was, at its heart, a banker's town, and Bakker was a banker's nightmare. Charlotte was proud of its top bond rating; it was a city that could be trusted to pay its debts. Charlotte's leaders worshipped at moderate, mainline churches where pastors preached social responsibility and avoided conspicuous shows of wealth. There was little tolerance for a man of God who behaved like a Hollywood star.

As he worked on PTL's water park, contractor Don Barcus found few folks around town with much good to say about the ministry. He was surprised. Heritage USA seemed the sort of place of which a city would be proud. But too many vendors and builders had been taken by PTL. They might have been paid for their work, but the money often arrived late, and the companies suffered. By 1984, many local contractors were playing it safe. When PTL's payments for water-park work remained erratic, a plumbing contractor bowed out. So did a local electrical company. Building-supply houses demanded that Barcus pay cash up front. Others asked him to guarantee his credit personally.

With local banks reluctant to lend money on terms that PTL

could accept, the ministry turned to a throng of loan brokers representing domestic lenders and shadowy investors overseas. PTL wanted an enormous loan, both to eliminate high-interest debts in a period of declining interest rates and to supply the capital needed to build Bakker's dream without drying up its operating cash. Even as PTL turned to its supporters for $30 million to build the Partner Center, it had continued the search for loans.

By summer, a Greensboro broker had found a savings and loan in Texas interested in lending PTL $22.5 million. In mid-August, Bailey notified Bakker that the thrift had stated, in writing, its intention of giving PTL a loan. Bakker didn't share the good news with his audience. Word of a big loan could only hamper his fundraising, robbing him of the precious leverage of crisis talk. In a plea for donations on August 24, Bakker complained, as he often had about loans that had been promised but that never materialized. "Lending institutions had promised money . . . so we could spread the payments of building the Grand out and the other things. They did not come through. We still have the promises."

Even after the lender's commitment letter arrived and his finance director began planning how to spend the money, Bakker continued complaining about recalcitrant lenders. In mid-September, Bakker turned to Messner during a broadcast. "We didn't get a penny from a bank, did we?" Messner, who himself was charging PTL interest on its unpaid balance, answered in the negative. Bakker railed on about banks that financed dictators overseas who didn't pay their debts instead of lending inside the United States. If PTL had gotten a loan, he told viewers, it would have taken on a fifteen-year mortgage that would have consumed the revenue from half of the hotel's rooms. Instead, he said, the partners were getting that half, and there was no mortgage to pay. "So it's better for the partner." Henry Harrison cheered Bakker on with a "Praise God."

The Texas thrift and PTL would never complete the loan. But seven weeks after Bakker lauded the merits of foregoing a mortgage, PTL quietly consummated a substitute $10 million financing package with a Maryland savings and loan. PTL put up the new Partner Center and other PTL property as collateral. The loan was the biggest in PTL history. Not only did it require the very interest payments Bakker had talked of with such disdain, but it also subordinated the partners' lifetime claim to free hotel stays to the security interests of the lender. In its search for loans, PTL even privately produced a letter from its lawyer affirming that point so as to reassure the lender that it could freely foreclose on the hotel. After preening about the miracles of partner financing, Bakker chose to say nothing about the new mortgage.

PTL issued no written contracts to cement Bakker's promise of a lifetime of free lodging, though none in the ministry doubted the commitment. It was a measure of the deep trust that Bakker's flock had for the PTL president. For the partners in this new marriage, a prenuptial contract seemed wholly unnecessary.

CHAPTER THIRTEEN

A DESERT HIDEAWAY

"It's not really a secret"

We approached our prey with caution that afternoon, shooting the first photos from our rented car so as not to arouse attention in the hillside development in Palm Desert. There were two of us inside, huddling over the feeble air conditioner: myself, a reporter at the *Charlotte Observer* for the past seven years, and fellow investigative reporter John Wildman. That morning, we had traded the steamy Carolina summer weather for the torrid, low-season heat of the California desert to ferret out details of Jim Bakker's other life in California.

The Summit was a new subdivision, its streets dotted with unsold lots and half-built houses. Late August was a slack time of year in the desert, and we soon realized that we had the street to ourselves. We walked cautiously to the head of Bakker's driveway, then into the empty parcels of land that sat on each side, where we snapped photos. To a passerby it might have looked very ordinary; to us, the picture-taking that day seemed a thrilling breakthrough.

The *Observer* had dogged Bakker on and off for years, chronicling his management troubles and questioning his use of donors' money. By 1983, reporter Allen Cowan had thoroughly antagonized Bakker. Cowan was gifted at getting inside information; the well-documented story of Bakker's Florida condo demonstrated his talents. After five years of intermittent reporting on PTL, Cowan knew enough to be deeply cynical about the institution and its president. But Cowan's relations with the editors at the *Observer* were strained; like many investigative reporters, he chafed at authority, including that of his bosses. In addition, the *Observer* editors had grown uneasy with Cowan's methods and more cautious in their approach to the highly sensitive PTL story. In summer 1983, Cowan left the newspaper, frustrated at his editors' restraint.

Watching Cowan work the PTL story in the office and listening to him talk about it after work, I was convinced that PTL remained one of the most compelling and important stories for the *Observer* to pursue. In early 1984, Wildman and I were given responsibility for investigative reporting. That summer, we had convinced our supervising editor, Jeannie Falknor, to put us on the PTL story.

In August 1984, as Bakker prepared for a trip to Palm Desert, a former employee told us about Bakker's new home and new cars in California. Just two days before, I had listened to Tammy declare that she and her husband had given everything to PTL to keep it alive.

By phone, we found the address of the house on Palm Desert's Greenbriar Lane. It was in the Bakkers' name; there had been no attempt to hide ownership of the property from anyone who knew where to look. But we still hadn't found evidence of the two cars, and we needed photographs, public documents, and some interviews before publishing our story about deceit and the fruits of the Bakkers' burgeoning income.

With our pictures of the house being rushed back to Charlotte by Federal Express, Wildman and I worked for a week, combing records in Palm Desert, Riverside, and Los Angeles and looking for people who had met the Bakkers. We found pictures of Bakker's house in its initial incarnation as a model home. We learned that Bakker had been shopping for other homes in the area, apparently for his associates. We found documents recording Bakker's purchase of the Mercedes and the Rolls. At the Rolls Royce dealership in Palm Springs, where Bakker had looked at cars before flying to Orange County, a salesman remembered Bakker's complaint that he would be "crucified" if he drove a Rolls in North Carolina, as he had done years before in a Rolls donated to PTL. It was a common point of contention for Bakker, who considered his partners and the press parochial on the subject of luxury cars. At the dealership, the salesman and his colleagues laughed at the evangelist's choice of words.

By the time we left, John and I were confident that PTL knew we had been in Palm Desert asking questions.

For Bakker, a good offense was the best defense against a damaging newspaper story, or even the threat of one. This philosophy displayed itself in many forms. Among the most subtle was his tendency to talk of family or staff health problems. Consciously or instinctively, Bakker recognized that his ample supply of self-pity could elicit partners' sympathy at strategic moments. In mid-September, Bakker told viewers that Tammy had been put on a heart monitor because she had been under such stress. On September 28, two days after the *Observer*'s first request for an interview about California, Tammy was absent from the show. Bakker asked his audience to pray that his wife got well.

> She has good days and bad days. And I just literally have had to make her stay home. There are so many rumors going around. They got a rumor up in Canada that she's had a heart attack, and we've had rumors all over. . . . Of course then the real nasty people probably think we've separated or something because she's not been on the show this week. . . .
>
> Tammy is exhausted. Tammy has not rested in twenty-five years. She is one of the hyperest ladies in the world, and I am doing my best to get her to slow down. The doctors tell her that there is no way she is going to be better unless she rests, that there's no shot, no pills, nothing, but she's got to rest. Did you ever tell a stick of dynamite to rest?

By October 2, PTL was waging its counterattack on several fronts. That day, Dortch informed PTL's viewers about the ministry's new jet, a subject raised in a list of questions we had just submitted to PTL. Dortch also dictated a letter to the *Observer*'s publisher and top executive, Rolfe Neill, inviting him to see Heritage USA and "discuss matters of mutual concern." Dortch was trying an end run.

> Your reporters did not get the questions to us until about 11 A.M. last Friday morning. . . . Mr. Bakker began his long-planned vacation immediately after the program last Friday, at

noon. We will discuss these matters with him when he returns
next week.

In fact, PTL was already well into the execution of a preemptive
strike.

At work editing videotape at Heritage Village, Bobbie Garn, a
thirty-year-old director, was ordered to hurry to a meeting with her
bosses, Dale Hill and Paul King. They told her that she was going
on a trip the next day. Everything had to be hush-hush; if she said
anything, she could lose her job.

It was four o'clock in the afternoon. Garn was ordered to be at
the airport by half-past five. She raced home and packed without
any idea where she was going. Before she and her fellow travelers—a cameraman and an engineer—boarded PTL's Sabreliner,
they were each handed a brown bag of cash. PTL had collected the
money from the cash registers of its stores at Heritage USA, a ready
source of money for top-priority missions.

The jet touched down in Oklahoma City, and the cameraman
thumbed through $1,300 in small bills to pay for fuel. During the
stopover, when he was far enough from Charlotte to feel safe
sharing the secret, the pilot told Garn that they were flying to Palm
Springs. He had done his part to maintain secrecy, filing a flight
plan for Arkansas so the air-traffic controllers in Charlotte wouldn't
know where the plane was headed.

The contingent arrived in Palm Springs late that night. The next
morning, Vi Azvedo telephoned Garn. "The king wants to talk to
you."

Garn thought that Azvedo meant Paul King, but Bakker picked
up. "Jim," she asked, "why was I flown to California?"

"Well, you are going to shoot with me in a few minutes," Bakker
told her.

"Where are you, Jim?" The afternoon she left, Garn had seen the
PTL president at the front gate of Heritage USA.

"I'm just down the street from you," Bakker answered. He had
flown on a commercial airline while the TV crew took the PTL jet,
he explained.

By nightfall, the Bakkers and the TV crew had produced videos
of the house, the new cars, and contemplative trips into the desert,
all starring the "vacationing" Bakker. That evening, the crew

climbed aboard the Sabreliner and flew home. The footage had to be ready to be aired at eleven o'clock on the morning of Thursday, October 4.

The morning of the fourth, *Observer* editor Falknor telephoned the PTL public-relations director. She was told that Dortch still hadn't decided whether to answer our questions.

Ninety minutes later, Falknor, Wildman, and I sat huddled around the computer inside the office of Mark Ethridge, the *Observer*'s managing editor. Ethridge was editing a draft of the story Wildman and I had written as we waited for word from PTL. A few minutes after eleven, I slipped down the sunny private hallway leading into editor Rich Oppel's office. Oppel was on leave that fall, and we used his office television set to watch the daily PTL show. I wanted to make sure that PTL was saying nothing that day about our story. As the fuzzy TV image came into focus, I made out Jim and Tammy Bakker inside their home in the Summit. Our wait for an answer was over.

As PTL often did when Bakker was under fire, that day's show began with a string of video testimonials from celebrities: President Ronald Reagan, frequent TV guest Dale Evans, fellow Christian TV preachers Robert Schuller, Oral Roberts, and Rex Humbard. The 1983 clip of Billy Graham's "endorsement" was also included.

The Bakkers appeared first at the entrance to the Palm Desert home. They were cheery and hospitable, offering no hint of the gravity of their task.

> Jim Bakker: Hi, everybody! Welcome to the desert. We're glad you're here. . . . Tammy and I are taking a little rest, and we're here at our home in the desert, a place where we come occasionally.
>
> Tammy Bakker: Once in a while.
>
> Jim Bakker: Not as often as we would like, and not as often as Tammy's doctor would like us to do right now, but we're here resting. And we thought during this time that we would just like to say "Thank you." . . . We'd like you to come on into our house and see a little bit behind the scenes in the life of Jim and Tammy Bakker.
>
> Tammy Bakker: You know, Jim, I think the most personal thing a person can do is bring someone to their home. And we

are really glad to be able to bring our partners right into the house with us. I think that will be nice. I'll even fix you some fudge. OK?

The tape continued from the Bakkers' living room.

> Jim Bakker: You know, it is so wonderful to have a place that we can escape to, and have a little privacy. I think the problems that we have faced over the last few years is that we haven't taken a real vacation. . . . Every vacation we have really is a working vacation. And we always end up preaching or having a workshop or doing something of that nature. And so when we go to a hotel, there would always be so many hundreds of people around. . . . We knew that we just had to have a little place of our own. So we found this house in the desert, and it's just a marvelous hideaway. . . . It's not really a secret.

Of course it had been a secret, until the secret became a liability. The performance was masterly. Bakker, not the newspaper, had broken the news. He had put his spin on the revelation. He down-played the acquisition, talking about a little house in the desert and not a new home that cost nearly half a million dollars. The televised visit with the partners seemed testimony to Bakker's transparency and fondness for his audience. "We always said it would be won-derful to have all our partners at our house," Jim said, "but of course that's physically impossible." To underscore their "genu-ine" hospitality, Tammy added the folksy touch of making a batch of fudge. Jim sweetened the confection. "I wish we could give everybody at home some of Tammy's famous fudge."

We published our story the next day. The opening contrasted the Bakkers' acquisitions in California and Tammy's August 1 claim that she and her husband had given "virtually everything" to keep PTL afloat. The story raised the question of the Bakkers' pay. Five years earlier, in its last public disclosure, PTL had said that the Bakkers earned $72,800 a year in combined salary. Now Jim and Tammy were earning enough to afford a $150,000 down pay-ment and buy $550,000 in homes and cars for use on occasional vacations.

The Bakkers returned to the air by videotape the morning our story appeared. The previous day, they had made no mention of the new Rolls and Mercedes. This time, Jim and Tammy appeared alongside Jim's Rolls, his "pride and joy," he called it. Bakker avoided calling the car a Rolls, though, and the camera avoided showing its telltale profile. Tammy did her part to downplay this purchase. She joked that she wouldn't ride in the car because a door handle had broken off in her hand. Besides, she said, the car reminded her of the embarrassing old Pontiac her father had driven when she was a girl. Bakker climbed into the car without her and drove into the desert, a PTL camera recording the journey. Bakker recalled that once, when he was in the desert, God had reminded him how easily people were distracted from His voice. Bakker seemed blind to the irony of a modern-day prophet seeking God in his Rolls Royce.

The *Observer*'s morning mail brought a news release from PTL, apparently prompted by our questions about Heritage USA West. PTL announced that it was considering expansion in the West Coast, Canada, and Europe. The release gave no hint of Bakker's determination to move into California. Later that month, Bakker would return to the state to set up a Palm Springs office and secure land and property. In November 1984, the PTL board would endorse a plan to buy the 180-unit Village Racquet Club in Palm Springs for $2 million down and another $19 million in financing. The club was to serve as the West Coast base for PTL's family-counseling workshops.

On October 8, PTL broadcast a third and final video from California showing a cheery Tammy visiting the hospital in Palmdale for tests on her heart. Director Garn and her crew had taken the Sabreliner back to California to tape the trip to the hospital where the Bakkers had undergone marital counseling. Jim Bakker told his audience that Tammy's heart condition was more serious than they had first thought—her heart was racing at 170 beats a minute at times. A Charlotte doctor had diagnosed the problem as an erratic, accelerated heartbeat known as paroxysmal atrial tachycardia. "We need people to pray for us," Bakker said.

The doctors in Palmdale concluded that Tammy needed rest. "Tammy's just going to have to stay out of the controversy, stay off the television for a little while and rest," Bakker said. The tape had been made on a Friday. That weekend, Tammy went shopping with Azvedo and Garn.

For weeks afterwards, PTL sought to soften the impact of the newspaper's revelations with more shrewd manipulations of the truth. Dependent on their partners' trust and generosity, the Bakkers could not allow suggestions that their life-style came at donors' expense. As it had after the 1983 Florida condominium revelation, PTL announced that its church congregation, not the TV ministry, paid the Bakkers' salary. In one program, Dortch even said "the television audience does not pay any of Jim Bakker's salary or expenses or Tammy's." Of course, Dortch did not specify what Bakker's pay, perks, or expenses cost the church congregation.

At the *Observer,* we doubted whether the statement was true, but we had no access to ministry records to prove otherwise. In fact, the church contributions during PTL's 1984–85 budget year had totaled just $1.9 million. During the same twelve months, the Bakkers' total benefits exceeded $2.1 million. Even if the church had paid nothing for its other staff, operating costs, and overhead, it still wouldn't have been able to foot the entire bill for the Bakkers' life-style.

The gap was to get worse in years to come. By Bakker's final year at PTL, the church took in just $852,955 in contributions. That same year, IRS auditors found that PTL spent more than $3.4 million for the direct benefit of Jim and Tammy Bakker.

During the show, Dortch also tried to minimize Bakker's wealth. "You know what the net worth of Jim Bakker is? It's . . . the pension that he has, plus the amount of money that he just recently paid down, which he got from selling a house recently," Dortch told the TV audience. The description gave Bakker's finances a reasonable scale, particularly since Dortch avoided attaching a value—$150,000—to the down payment. Dortch used the same explanation in a letter the next day to the Evangelical Council for Financial Accountability. "The Bakkers have used their own money that PTL nor Heritage Village church have been involved in." Dortch could hardly afford to disclose that Bakker had obtained enough cash for the California down payment in a single, curiously timed bonus granted by a board that Dortch and Bakker dominated.

Each time Dortch cited the sale of the prior home, he avoided saying how much the Bakkers had cleared. Their Lake Wylie home had been sold eleven months earlier for $100,000, $21,000 more than the Bakkers had originally paid. That profit, plus Bakker's original down payment, yielded less than $41,000 in cash, a fraction of the California down payment. Dortch also chose not to elaborate on the balance in Bakker's fat retirement accounts. In Bakker's final seven years, PTL would pay $665,950 into those funds.

Dortch, the church figure who supplied the respectability that Bakker needed so badly, testified to the Bakkers' generosity and motives. "Jim and Tammy do not care about material things," Dortch told the TV audience. "These folks have walked away again and again from things that they have acquired, possessions. You know what they've done with them? They've given their car away. They've given things away like no two people I have ever seen in all my life."

To cement the Bakkers' image of selflessness, Dortch revived the notion that Jim and Tammy had given PTL millions in royalties from their books, records, and tapes. "Just in the last two years, Tammy Bakker has given just about $3 million of royalties to this ministry. . . . There would be nothing wrong for her to earn by the sweat of her brow. . . . But she has chosen because of her love for Christ to lay down all that she has before the foot of the cross."

The donated-royalties defense had been a favorite, and it would remain so for the Bakkers long after their departure from PTL. As with so many of their assertions, the truth was much more complicated than they claimed. For one, the Bakkers had accepted some royalties from PTL. Tammy had taken $2,000 in 1976–77 on her records, purchased mostly by PTL for use as donor premiums. The next year, the Bakkers together got $18,363 in royalties for books and records, more than three times what they had donated to PTL. Again, most of the books and records had been sold to PTL. In 1978–79, the couple's royalty total dropped to $6,407; in 1979–80, to $1,186. In 1979 and 1980, several years after signing over the royalty rights to his autobiography to PTL, Bakker received $50,000 from an outside publishing house for the publication rights to a book PTL used as a premium.

What PTL depicted as an act of generosity was, in fact, a case of following legal advice. Paul Chappell, PTL's tax lawyer in the late seventies, twice warned the ministry that it was courting disaster if the Bakkers took royalties. In an October 1977 letter to Bakker, Chappell noted that PTL had paid the ghostwriters who wrote

Bakker's first, second, and third books and had financed production of Tammy's albums. At that time, PTL expected Bakker to receive royalties from his second and third books and Tammy to do the same from her albums.

> I understand that PTL has been the largest single purchaser of your first book as well as the largest single purchaser of Tammy's recordings. Consequently, it appears that by far the largest percentage of the royalties received by yourself and Tammy have been (and will continue to be) generated by sales of books and records to PTL.
>
> If it were not for the sensitive corporate and tax implications involved, these royalty arrangements could be an appropriate method of supplementing your income. However, since you are the principal officer of the corporation, as well as chairman of its board of trustees, these self-generating royalties could cause serious difficulty for PTL. . . . As a fiduciary, a trustee of course is required always to act in the best interest of the corporation and not to use his office in a manner that would create personal benefit. . . .
>
> Accordingly, I would recommend that you and Tammy assign all your existing royalty rights to PTL. In my opinion, such an assignment would prevent the IRS from attempting to use the royalty arrangements as grounds for attacking PTL's exempt status. . . . I believe it would be in the best interests of PTL to simply increase your compensation in the amount you and Tammy expected to receive from future royalties.

Bakker chose not to take that advice. Nearly three years later, Chappell remained ill at ease about the threat the Bakkers' royalties posed to PTL's tax-exempt status. He issued another warning in his April 1980 letter, the correspondence that general manager Gary Smith had attached to his resignation. Chappell felt that the IRS could conclude that by paying production costs for the Bakkers' books and records, PTL had diverted corporate funds for the Bakkers' personal benefit. Such diversion would put PTL's tax-exempt status for 1978–79 at risk.

> I have . . . heard that the production costs on the first of Tammy's records produced by Gary Paxton ran from $50,000 upwards to possibly $75,000. Also, I have heard estimates that the production costs on the other four or five records ranged from $20,000 to $50,000 apiece.

Several months after Chappell's April letter, PTL's audited financial statements disclosed that PTL had adopted a new royalty policy. All employees were required to agree that they wouldn't receive royalties on items purchased by PTL.

After his "vacation" in California and his return to the air in mid-October—an event greeted with a staged celebration, cascading balloons, and placards reading We Love You—Bakker took up his own defense. For a full hour one day, Bakker answered questions from three staff members in a mock news conference. Dripping with self-pity and emotion, manipulating the truth, Bakker tried to explain away Tammy's August claim that the Bakkers had given virtually everything to help their struggling ministry.

> I checked Tammy's checkbook myself . . . to see what on August 1 was happening. . . . Her checking account was almost empty. Tammy had given all she had to give. She didn't know what else to do. She had given her royalties all of her life. . . . That very day, Tammy with tears in her eyes was so concerned about the affiliates [local TV stations broadcasting PTL programs], she said . . . "I want you to take my jewelry and everything I've got and sell it and pay bills at PTL." I said, "Tammy, we won't get anything for your jewelry." . . . We'd come up really with a few hundred or a few thousand dollars at the most of all that she had. . . . She gives every month. She gives thousands of dollars every year to this ministry. . . .
>
> Just before that broadcast, in that month before, we had decided to sell Heritage Village in town . . . she almost died. She said, "No, honey, that's our birthright. We can't sell Heritage Village." . . . She was exhausted. She's been on the verge of a nervous breakdown for weeks . . . for a long time. I didn't want to talk about it. But the press has forced me to just talk about it. . . .
>
> I said, "Tammy, we're going to sell the parsonages. PTL owns several parsonages." . . . Do you realize that in all of our life Tammy Faye and I have only lived in a house for a year at the most? When I told her we were going to sell the parsonage because of the overhead and the expense and we were going to consolidate everything at Heritage USA, she said, "But Jim, this is the first home that you and I and the kids have had and we've been in that home over three years now . . . the kids love this house." And the kids just cried. They said, "We don't want to leave the house. This is our home." And they had the first sense of security that those children have had in

their life of . . . following their father in these ministries. . . .

So in her mind, we're selling Heritage Village, the place we loved and built. I've told her we're going to sell the parsonages. . . . She had given her royalties. She had given her book. She had given her funds. And when she got on the air, she didn't know what else to give. She didn't know what else to do.

With that introduction, Bakker ran the tape of the August 1 program. Tammy's words were as they had been recorded in the *Observer*. Tammy's statement, Bakker declared confidently, had been taken out of context.

A month before, PTL had announced that it was selling Heritage Village, the twenty-five-acre site that had been PTL's home in the late seventies. No asking price was announced, but privately PTL hoped to get $13 million for the property and equipment. PTL still operated its satellite network, taped foreign missions programs, and edited videotape from the site.

Bakker made no mention of his plans to replace the Tega Cay parsonage that Tammy and the kids wanted to keep with an even more elaborate home on the grounds of Heritage USA, far from the jeering boaters who occasionally pulled into his cove on Lake Wylie. In September 1984, PTL's board had agreed "it is in the best interest of the Church that a parsonage be built on the grounds of Heritage USA when desired by our pastor." Later that month, Bakker had reviewed blueprints for the new house. As one Bakker friend remembered it, the complex included a lighted tennis court and a bowling lane. It would never be built. The Bakkers would remain at Tega Cay.

Tammy returned to the air on November 8, three weeks after her husband. Her heart problem, that well-timed magnet for viewer sympathy, had turned out to be a case of bad nutrition, viewers were told. Her heart was strong, but the doctor wanted Tammy to stop consuming so much sugar and caffeine. "She's one of the few people I know that starts her meal with a piece of pie," Bakker said. A few weeks later, Tammy, a fiend for diet colas, acknowledged that she was drinking soda six or seven times a day to stay "revved up." She claimed that without enough rest, she would sometimes hyperventilate. She said that she was rearranging her life.

Several weeks earlier, a Charlotte TV reporter had pursued a tip that Tammy was in California for treatment of a chemical dependency. Through a spokesman, Bakker denied the story. He was, the reporter was told, outraged at the question. The TV news broadcast no story.

Later that winter, though, Tammy seemed to speak from the heart as she talked on the air about the dangers of addiction to medicine. As she spoke, tears welled up in her eyes.

> You know, even prescription drugs are so terribly dangerous because you get up, you say, "Well, I'll just take one or I'll take a half of one, just to help me through this stressful time." And before you realize it, you can't stop taking them. You need another one to get you through that stress . . . until you find yourself living every single day and there has to come—and then you need more than a half of one, you need a whole one, you find, to get you through that stress. . . .
>
> And before you know it, there's no way you can get off it yourself. And that is drugs that the doctor prescribes, that is, seems so innocent. The doctor . . . says take it when you feel like a stress is overcoming you and you can't take it anymore, take a little bit of it . . . it will calm you down a bit. Be careful. Be careful. It's that one little bit, it's that first one that leads to destruction. . . .
>
> A little innocent-looking pill can be literal hell on earth until you think your body is going to, the inside of your body is going to destroy itself trying to get off of it.

For now, Tammy Bakker was still a prisoner.

That fall, Bakker's TV program seemed little more than an hour-long commercial for Heritage USA. With building projects and construction costs mushrooming, marketing, once a small part of Bakker's show, had now eclipsed evangelism. Bakker's natural passion for the entrepreneurial had overshadowed his obligatory interest in the spiritual. Bakker routinely showed off a model room inside the unfinished Grand, displaying what he called the "little details that people are going to appreciate"—remote-control TV, custom furniture and rug, and Corian marble countertops. It was all prosperity—and little gospel.

As he unveiled the Towers lifetime partnerships that fall, Bakker said he was sure that some people were saying that he was conning people. "Well, I'll tell you. If this is phony, if this is counterfeit, don't wake me up. It works. God's people are getting blessed."

Days after Bakker's October return from California, finance director Peter Bailey issued a stern warning. His optimism of late August had vanished. In one month, PTL had issued $5.2 million in lifetime partnerships in the Towers. Already, Bailey had been forced to spend $900,000 of it to meet payroll and pay bills at the water park—expenses that Bakker had not included in his televised explanation of how the $30 million in Towers money would be divvied up. From the start of the Towers project, Bakker had raised money for certain purposes and allowed it to be spent for others— the very violation of federal law that had prompted the FCC's investigation. In a single month, PTL had diverted nearly three times the sum at issue in the earlier federal inquiry.

Bailey expected to need more of the Towers money to pay for day-to-day expenses. "To me, we are in a false euphoria," he said. "We must cut back on spending or continue to use Tower funds to maintain operations." Bakker chose the latter course.

The partners were given only good news about the Towers partnerships' effect on PTL's finances. Bakker reported a steady decline in PTL's back TV debts, which he had predicted would be eliminated by the Towers money. On October 25, he announced that PTL had paid seventy-five percent of its airtime bills in all fifty states. "I'm determined that we're going to get out of the red, be current, and then we won't have this tragedy all the time. . . . Once we're current we have budgeted so we can stay current."

The Towers partnerships and receipt of the $10 million loan in November 1984 left PTL briefly flush with cash. By month's end, PTL had paid Messner at least $4.5 million. REC, the water-park contractor, got nearly $2 million, enough to clear PTL's bill. But in that same month, just a year since Bakker had boasted that Heritage USA was completely self-supporting, PTL's retail-store, restaurant, and real-estate divisions all lost tens of thousands of dollars. Operating costs ran $4 million over gifts to PTL's general fund.

Bailey was particularly galled by the Christmas City lights display, which Bakker had expanded dramatically in 1983. A breathtaking sight, the display wreaked havoc on PTL's finances. In November 1984, it required a $550,000 subsidy from lifetime partnership funds. Bailey complained to Bakker in a December 5 memo.

> At present, PTL has 175–200 employees either working in the Christmas City department or working in Christmas City as a second job. I don't feel anyone is aware of this.
>
> There is very little control on costs as some people are working up to 122 hours just on overtime plus their regular eighty hours for two weeks. That's over fourteen hours a day, seven days a week. . . .
>
> I know of people who volunteered to sell records and were not used because they were too short for the costumes. Surely, they could have been used. We presently have 1,388 employees on the payroll.
>
> I know Jesus is in control, but we are held responsible to Him how we use the funds entrusted to us.

A few weeks later, Bailey pressed his argument further, this time in response to Dortch's request for advice on eliminating the chronic check-bouncing that had cost PTL $20,000 in bank fees in a single month.

> Ever since I have been with PTL (almost six years) checks have been written on future deposits. This is what is called "float." This is a common practice especially with Christian organizations. . . . If contributions fall or emergencies come up (which is continually) then the chances of bouncing a check becomes stronger. . . .
>
> In order for PTL to guarantee that no checks bounce . . . PTL's top management must have the financial integrity to stop approving expenditures that continually exceed our income. That is the root of our problem. No system will work unless top management assumes its responsibility of financial integrity.

PTL's top management had approved weekly spending of $1.2 million, but PTL was taking in just $700,000 without the lifetime partnerships.

> This negative cash flow of $500,000 a week has been funded by the hotel and tower account over the past few months. This must stop. This is not financial integrity. I agonize daily over this and the lack of action taken by top management to

resolve this critical problem. We have the water park to finish as well as plans to build a five-thousand-seat studio and a nursing center. Nursing centers do not pay for themselves. We cannot afford to keep financing projects such as more television equipment, the water park, a nursing home, or maybe even the West Coast operation. On paper, the West Coast will make money, but funding the project until it is running is questionable. . . .

My main concern is the financial integrity of PTL or the lack of it. We constantly buy from local vendors knowing we cannot pay for it on time. Our system rewards those at PTL who get the job done whether or not it leaves PTL in the eyes of our vendors as being irresponsible.

Through the fall, Bakker had talked of raising the price of a Towers partnerships to $1,500. At first, he said that the change would occur in thirty days, but he extended the deadline again and again. Bakker's deadlines, like his reality, were plastic, bending this way and that to inspire a sense of urgency among the partners and serve his ravenous ministry. Bakker also held the threat of shrinking supply and cascading demand over his uncommitted supporters. "We can't have any more memberships than we physically can have people in the hotel," he said.

Bakker's sales pitch hit high gear. "The deal of a century," he called it, and on the surface it was. Once Bakker had talked about a $20,000 return for lifetime partners. Now PTL calculated that the value of the free lodging over an average partner's lifetime was $80,000. Bakker said it with passion; it was like him to believe the story with every fiber of his being. It was also like him not to wonder how PTL—so wasteful with its money, so starved for cash day in and day out—could possibly return eight thousand percent on the thousand-dollar investments to as many as 30,000 people.

The partners didn't ask the questions either, and Bakker's salesmanship was breathtakingly successful. In December alone, PTL recorded more than $10.5 million in new lifetime partnerships; another $3 million in donations flowed into the general fund. PTL had never had a month like this in all of Bakker's eleven years. In a year's time, sale of the lifetime partnerships had raised nearly $51 million.

By December 21, the day before the Heritage Grand's opening, Bakker announced that the outpouring had gone "beyond our wildest dreams of our whole lifetime, of anything that's ever happened to us." He gushed about new Heritage USAs springing up all over America. "This is the beginning of a new phenomenon all over America, that there's going to be Christian centers built for fellowship like filling stations all over the country for people to come and to be filled up with the presence of the Holy Spirit."

Bakker took a few moments that day to inform his partners, in an offhand way, that the lifetime partner mathematics had changed. The partnerships for which he had hoped to collect $1,500 had been taken at $1,000. The remaining ten thousand would cost $2,000. From then on, he said, PTL had to use the partnership money to finish paying for the Towers. Three months earlier, Bakker had predicted that his back airtime bills would be wiped out with $5 million in Towers money. He proclaimed no such victory now. Instead, he said, PTL would have to rely on other donations to pay for airtime. He did not say that only $1.96 million of PTL's first $18 million in Towers partnerships had gone to pay television bills.

Alluding to the new two-thousand-dollar price tag, he said, "Please help me to be honorable with that. I've got to do that because I can't pay for the whole thing if I don't."

Bakker avoided details. Had he spoken forthrightly, the partners would have learned that PTL thus far had set aside little or none of the Towers partnership money to "pay for the whole thing." By January 10, PTL had spent its first $18 million on other bills. Bakker's new hope was to raise a total of $42 million by issuing the last nine thousand memberships at two thousand dollars each. This supplementary $18 million, plus $2 million in unspent partnerships, would supply the money Messner said PTL needed, Bailey told Bakker on January 14, 1985.

> Because of this, I will no longer approve any further expenditures from the Tower unless approved in writing by Jim Bakker, David Taggart, or Richard Dortch. What this means is that no longer will we be able to cover payroll, our loan maintenance costs, utilities, television time, or partner expenses at the present level.

Bakker had painted PTL into a corner. It either had to cut operating costs dramatically or dip deeper into the lifetime reservoir, jeopardizing its ability to finish the very projects Bakker had used to lure tens of millions of dollars from his audience.

CHAPTER FOURTEEN

JESSICA

"I need to know I am still a man"

The first call came after dinner on December 3, 1984, a mysterious tipster interrupting the daily procession of undertakers telephoning obituary information to the *Charlotte Observer.* The caller was a young woman, speaking with a sharp New York accent that distinguished her from the funeral-home workers with their softer Southern tones. Clerk Gerry Hostetler sensed a story behind the call, and she took a few moments to compose a note to my editor, Jeannie Falknor.

> I received a call from a woman (no name, of course) who was very vague. Says she has inside, documented information about:
>
> December 6, 1980, at Clearwater Beach (Fla.) hotel incident involving Dr. Dortch, vp of PTL, John Wesley Fletcher, and Jim Bakker.
>
> She wants us to call Dortch, mentioned date and place, and she says he will tell us what happened. Another person involved was David Taggart. . . .
>
> As I said, she was vague, but I got her to promise to call you tomorrow, Tues 12/4. She promised that if we made the call, she would give us the rest of the story. I gathered that she was involved in whatever incident it was, and she referred to "they made a promise and didn't keep it. I kept my end of the deal." She says if this paper doesn't do something, she'll try another one and if nothing works, she will take it to court.

She sounded more like an axe-grinder than a looney, by the way. Actually, she could be an insider because she gave me the number, said Shirley Fulbright, [Bakker's] secretary, would likely answer the phone tomorrow.

The woman telephoned the *Observer* newsroom again later that week. She wanted to speak to someone about PTL, and I was at my desk working on an article about the soon-to-open Heritage Grand Hotel. The woman didn't want to identify herself; I suggested we agree on a pseudonym, and she selected Jennifer. As she explained her reason for calling, I remembered the note from Hostetler, which my editor had passed along earlier. I scribbled notes on a yellow legal pad, shunning the nearby computer terminal for fear that a clicking keypad might make the woman uneasy.

Jennifer said that a friend, a woman, had been forced to sign a false statement that protected PTL from legal action. "Now, she wishes to reveal enough evidence to protect herself from accusations. . . . This is an inch away from going to court. The media is more effective than court." The friend had signed because she had been warned that otherwise her family might be affected.

Jennifer sketched her "friend's" story, offering the sort of precise detail that reporters use to gauge a source's credibility. On December 5, 1980, Fletcher had invited the woman to Clearwater Beach, Florida, to see Jim Bakker in a telethon. She flew there the next day. She had stayed in room 538 at the Sheraton Sand Key Resort. It was in that room, Jennifer said, that Fletcher had introduced the woman to Bakker. There, Jennifer said vaguely, the woman had been "brought into a situation in which she had no control."

I had a hard time believing that Jennifer's friend was anyone other than Jennifer herself. Ten minutes into the call, I voiced my suspicion. Yes, Jennifer admitted, "I'm the girl." I brought up the name Jessica Hahn, and she acknowledged, "That's me. I just don't want to be hurt any more," she said. "All I want is my protection. . . . I'd swear in front of any judge that what took place is the truth."

I had heard the name Jessica Hahn for the first time that fall. Fellow investigative reporter John Wildman had talked about PTL to religion writer Terry Mattingly, a member of the recently merged staff of the *Observer* and the *Charlotte News*. Mattingly shared his notes of the 1983 anonymous calls that, I later learned, had come from Fletcher. The mysterious reference to a Jessica Hahn attracted our attention. That fall, I checked for a telephone listing in New York City for a Jessica Hahn. There was no one listed by that name. Now, by what seemed incredible good fortune, she had dropped right into our laps.

Hahn continued her story. She had been led to act against her better judgment, to do something she was not mature enough to do. She read from a legal-sounding document that described her in the third person. At the Sheraton in Clearwater, she read, Bakker "then did disrobe, seduced, and sodomized her . . . did then physically enter the private recess of her body with his genitals . . . this girl continues to be talked about . . . she has been through a tremendous shock. She hasn't been sane since . . . her job may be at stake. She is unable to perform her duties at the same level of productivity as before. . . . She is unable to respond to and sustain any romantic attachment. . . . Please locate the source of the information that continues still to be talked about and have it stopped . . . [obtain] an apology from Mr. Bakker. Third, Miss Hahn's family is to be protected from any future embarrassment."

We talked for more than an hour that morning, and Hahn agreed to talk again. A few days later I reached her at the walk-up apartment in West Babylon, N.Y., that she had moved into a month before. We discussed the events of the last four years again, in finer detail. Hahn explained that she had jotted down the details a few years back to preserve her memories. She had also kept evidence: an airplane ticket, the key to her hotel room. She had followed PTL gossip closely in the intervening years. "I know a lot about it," she said, "because after this I made it my business."

Jessica had grown up Catholic, but at age fourteen she embraced the community she had discovered at a Pentecostal church on Jerusalem Avenue, a few blocks from her home. The pastor there, then affiliated with the Assemblies of God, was a Brooklyn-born faith healer named Eugene Profeta, a swarthy man with deep-set eyes a few years older than Jim Bakker. That summer of 1974, an evangelist named John Wesley Fletcher conducted revivals from a tent in the church parking lot. During his stay, Jessica took care of Fletcher's two children. In 1977, two months after she graduated from high school, Hahn was hired to work in Profeta's office. Eventually she became Profeta's personal secretary.

Hahn told me that she had come to revere Fletcher. But she had sensed a physical attraction on his part, noticing him watch her during services. During a visit to the church in February 1980, Fletcher told Profeta, "Well, she's really grown," as she listened. She sensed a come-on but said that she tried to ignore it.

Ten months later, Fletcher telephoned. "Jessica, I can't talk too long. Look, I've got a surprise for you. I'd like you to fly to Florida. I'd like you to meet someone very special."

At the time, Hahn told me, she was a Jim Bakker fan, a loyal fifteen-dollar-a-month partner. Knowing how close Fletcher was to Bakker, she suspected that Fletcher was arranging for her to meet the PTL president. Fletcher told her to pick up a prepaid $129 ticket at the airport. She caught an Eastern Airlines jet to Tampa on Saturday morning, December 6, 1980.

Fletcher met her inside the Tampa airport. It was nearly noon. During their half-hour drive to Clearwater Beach, Fletcher talked of Bakker's problems—at home with Tammy, in Washington with the FCC. Three months earlier, the FCC investigators had taken Bob Manzano's second round of testimony. Two weeks later, the Bakkers' marriage would collapse altogether.

As they talked, Fletcher's words became more suggestive, and Hahn began to feel uneasy. He told the twenty-one-year-old how good she looked, he commented on the weight she had lost. He had wanted to see her for so long, he said. "You're a little Christian bimbo," he said. She didn't know what he meant. "I've learned a lot since then," she told me.

Fletcher drove his rented car past the hotels and motels of Clearwater Beach and turned onto the bridge that crosses Clearwater Pass. The car passed Sand Key Park and turned right into a parking lot. The eight-story Sheraton Sand Key Resort rose before them.

Fletcher asked Hahn to walk in front of him. "Just kind of pretend you don't know me," he said. Hahn answered with a question. "What's the big deal? We're not doing anything wrong." Hahn told me she was getting suspicious. They walked through the lobby and rode the elevator to her floor. Her room was halfway down the hall on the left.

Inside, Fletcher led Hahn to the terrace. She heard Jamaican music coming from the pool directly below. "Look, there's Jim," Fletcher said, pointing towards the thatched umbrellas bordering the pool. The PTL president was wearing a trim white terry-cloth bathing suit. Tammy Sue Bakker, Bakker's ten-year-old daughter, looked up. "John Wesley, who's that?" Fletcher answered, "Oh, it's one of our partners."

Fletcher left to get Bakker, and Hahn started to unpack. A few minutes later, Fletcher arrived with Bakker in tow. Bakker was still wearing his swimsuit. "This is Jessica," Fletcher said. "This is the girl I've been talking about."

As Hahn told it, Bakker, then a few weeks short of his forty-first birthday, was quite taken by her. At 5'5", she stood six inches taller than Tammy. Her hair fell around her shoulders; it was brown, like her eyes. She was big-chested, and she dressed to set off her figure.

"I didn't know girls from New York were so beautiful," Bakker told her. "I like your long hair. My wife's hair should be like that." He told her she should be a model. He asked about her flight that morning and asked what she did for a living; her boss, Gene Profeta, had appeared years before on Bakker's TV show.

Fletcher spoke up. "I've known her for seven years. Her father is president of a rubber company." Hahn asked him what he meant; Fletcher indicated that it was a joke. He was always joking, Hahn told me.

Fletcher turned toward the door. "Look, I told Jim a lot about you. I think you can help him." As he left, he set down a bottle of Vaseline Intensive Care Lotion. He suggested Hahn give Bakker a backrub. "Jim's been through hell."

Sitting on one of the room's two double beds, Bakker began pouring out his troubles. He complained about the FCC and his wife. "I feel like I can talk to you, and you can really help me." He tore the cover off one of the two beds. "I hate bedspreads."

Jessica interrupted her recitation. "I should have run out. I should have. But I was scared because I didn't trust John." Fletcher had said he would be waiting, but she didn't know where. "I should have done a lot of things. I wasn't sure what was going on."

She began to feel sick, like she needed to leave, she told me. "I started to cry. I said, 'I really don't want to be here.'" Perhaps, she wondered aloud to me, she was feeling the effects of something in the water Fletcher had given her earlier.

She returned to her story. Bakker spoke up, saying "I've come to the place where I need to know I am still a man." His wife had

279

been involved with someone, and he didn't see how their marriage could survive. He reassured her. "There's nothing to be afraid of. No one's ever going to find out about this."

Bakker pulled off his swimsuit and began untying her plum-colored wraparound dress. She could feel the sand on his skin. "I was crying, nervous." Bakker was quiet, she said, but very persistent.

Hahn interrupted her story again. "I know the story is hard to believe. I'd never had sex with anybody before this. I honestly didn't believe what was happening, even to myself. I just practically laid there. . . . I didn't know what he was going to do." Bakker was very interested in pleasing himself, she said. "He didn't waste any time. He wasn't at all considerate. I really couldn't believe this was going on anyway. . . . I just wanted the man out of the place. The man wouldn't give up. I couldn't stop him."

When he finished, Bakker got up and brushed his hair. "You really helped me in ways you'll never know." He left. He had been there, she estimated, for forty minutes or an hour.

A half hour later, Fletcher returned to Hahn's room. He told Hahn that Bakker was curled in a fetal position in his room, crying. He wanted to know if she was being taken care of, and he wanted to see her again. Hahn told him she wasn't interested. She wanted to leave. "If you don't let me leave, I will call the police." Fletcher reassured her. "Relax," he said, "you've done me such a great favor."

Later that afternoon, Hahn felt nauseous and dizzy. She called Bakker in room 836; his daughter answered. "He's in the shower. He can't come to the phone." Hahn left a message for Bakker to call. He never did.

That night, she said, she watched Bakker and Fletcher on Channel 22's telethon. Hahn ordered a burger from room service, but she was too sick to eat. The bellboy who brought the meal offered to call a doctor. "Forget it. I'll be fine."

Fletcher returned about eleven that night. As they talked, he ate her cold hamburger. He wanted her to go out for a drink with Bakker's producer. She didn't remember Sam Orender by name. "I guess [Fletcher] thought I was just going to keep going."

Hahn flew home early the next morning. She went to church that Sunday night, she said, and acted as if nothing were wrong. But two days later, she told Profeta, her pastor and boss, what had happened. "He wanted to kill them." Over the next months, she said, Profeta counseled her, helped her to recover. He didn't want her to be afraid to be involved with people her own age, she said. "I've grown up a lot since then."

Soon, Hahn said, a man began making harassing phone calls to her church. "He would just say, 'There are things I know. I could bury you both.' " She attributed the calls to Fletcher; she knew he had trouble with alcohol. Fletcher also told the story to several people. Word was out that Jessica was a party girl.

When the calls started, Hahn told me, she telephoned PTL. She spoke to David Taggart, who relayed her message to Bakker. That night, she said, Bakker telephoned her at home. She asked him to stop the harassing calls. Bakker was elusive, as if he were worried that she was taping the call. "I've been praying for you," he told her. Bakker promised not to talk to anyone. A week or so later, David Taggart called back. He assured her that no one was talking about the incident. He asked her for the same pledge. Taggart called occasionally after that, she said.

Dortch took over the prickly matter during his first months at PTL. Again, Hahn had specific details. Dortch had telephoned her on March 12, 1984. They talked for two hours; she yelled at him. Dortch offered to get Hahn a job in radio or television outside PTL. He said he wanted her to get counseling and he asked why she was so bitter and hard. He assured her that he loved her as he loved his own daughter. She thought he was afraid and a phony. "He kisses Jim Bakker's butt and covers up his dirt."

Dortch called again three days later. Hahn told him that she was considering hiring an attorney. Dortch tried to dissuade her. He called again on March 20, during his vacation, and said he wanted to meet her. They made an appointment for the last day of the month.

On Saturday, March 31, the day before Jim and Tammy Bakker's twenty-third wedding anniversary, Hahn and Dortch met in room 616 of the Holiday Inn at La Guardia Airport. Dortch had asked board member Aimee Cortese to accompany him. He had some papers he wanted Hahn to sign. According to Hahn, Dortch told her "If you don't sign these statements, I don't think you're ever going to have any peace." He said that PTL could protect her, that it would deny that anything had ever happened. "The man really does want forgiveness. He is sorry," she remembered Dortch's saying. Dortch told Hahn that he was worried that Bakker might have a nervous breakdown or blow his brains out.

Seven months later, at the same time he was trying to neutralize the *Observer*'s disclosure of Bakker's California purchases, Dortch telephoned Hahn at home. He told Hahn what a shame it was to have everything torn down at PTL by what happened on one afternoon. In this October 22, 1984, call, he also repeated his promise to protect her. Hahn told Dortch that she had consulted a lawyer, and he felt that an injustice had been done.

On November 1, Hahn met PTL board member Cortese in her church in a run-down section of the Bronx. There, Hahn told me, she had signed papers that "actually reversed everything, saying that I had initiated everything." I asked if she had copies. No, she said, Cortese refused to give her any.

I found Hahn's story compelling. She knew plenty of intimate details about Bakker and his circle. She showed no reluctance to answer my questions. And the 1983 anonymous call to reporter Mattingly tended to corroborate her story.

Still, her conduct made little sense. She wanted to end the rumors plaguing her, she said; that was why she was telling chapter and verse to a newspaper reporter. But certainly a newspaper story would only compound the problem. I asked her about the contradiction. "I don't really know my reason. I feel very unsafe, unsettled," she said. "I'm threatened, my job is threatened, everything around me is threatened." She resented Bakker's actions. "Whether I come out looking bad or good, it doesn't bother me. . . . He did this to me. I didn't ask for it. He is a minister. I was twenty-one years old. . . . He did this without ever knowing the girl. . . . It wasn't like I was sitting there laughing. I was crying, I was sick."

She knew that I would have to use her name, she said, but she preferred that I said that the newspaper had contacted her. We agreed to talk again in a few weeks, after I finished the hotel story and had finished a Christmas vacation with my wife, Jody, and one-month-old son, Ben.

I doubted that Hahn's story would pass my editors' standards for newsworthiness. The *Observer* was cautious by nature, and I knew that management would be reluctant to unveil Bakker's private sex life without clear evidence that his indiscretion raised compelling questions about his public role. The best hope for publication, I thought, was to prove that PTL had paid for Hahn's trip to Florida to satisfy Bakker's sexual needs. But Hahn didn't know who had paid her way.

I never had a chance to debate running the story with my editors. During my Christmas vacation, Hahn telephoned my home. I was out. My wife, Jody, also a reporter at the *Observer,* answered the phone. Jessica was hysterical. She said that everything she had told me was a lie. "Print any of it and I'll sue," she screamed. I decided to leave Hahn alone, to let her cool down; I could possibly revive the contact later. It was clear, however, that Hahn would be a weak witness if the *Observer* stuck its neck out on the story of Bakker's extramarital fling in Florida.

Despite all the details, despite our hours talking over the phone, Hahn had given me only part of the story; a pleasant person to talk to, she also could be a skillful liar. She had not told me that she and Fletcher also had had sexual intercourse the day of her arrival in Florida; she was too embarrassed, she explained years later. In 1988, Fletcher—who had denied having sex with Hahn—acknowledged it for the first time. He claimed, however, that Hahn had been a willing participant in the day's debauchery—the same claim Bakker would make about Hahn.

Hahn had told me only part of the story of her February 1980 encounter with Fletcher. Not only had she encountered him in her office, but she had gone to dinner in Manhattan with him. In 1988, Fletcher alleged that he and a willing Hahn had had sex in a New York hotel room that night, ten months before Hahn's trip to Clearwater. Hahn denied the claim.

Hahn made no mention of the money she had received from PTL in 1984. She told me later that in a Massapequa diner on April 24, Cortese had handed her two thousand dollars; on the package were the words "To gain my respect—Jim Bakker." Long after his departure from PTL, Dortch would characterize the money as payment for medical treatment and counseling. On November 1, 1984, in return for signing the documents she would complain to me about a month later, Hahn had taken ten thousand dollars from Cortese.

As Hahn remembered it later, Cortese handed over some advice at the same time: "Go get some counseling."

Dortch had borrowed the ten thousand dollars from Sam Johnson, the Assemblies of God missionary, and then dispatched it to New York with one of his trusted aides, Mark Burgund. "Just don't ask me any questions about it," Dortch told Burgund, "I can't go into detail what it is." Burgund had flown up and back in the same day, meeting Cortese inside LaGuardia long enough to hand her an envelope three-eighths of an inch thick.

Hahn had failed to tell me about her participation in earlier efforts to secure money from PTL on her behalf. Instead, she avoided the subject. When she read to me from the legal-sounding document describing her suffering, she omitted a portion of the text suggesting she be paid $100,000.

That document, five pages long and undated, had been sent to PTL in 1984, apparently in early March. The letter was unsigned, but it had been drafted by a woman friend of Hahn's who used an alias, Carla Hammond. As Hahn told the story later, she had not participated in drafting the letter. When her friend showed her the document, Hahn claimed, "I said to her that this was blackmail and would cause a lot of problems. . . . We're going to go to jail." Yet Hahn decided to play along with the letter, as she remembered. "I wanted to get their attention. . . . I hated Jim Bakker. The only way to hurt Jim Bakker was to hit his pockets."

The document was directed to David Taggart.

> I represent Jessica Hahn. Miss Hahn has advised me that she has attempted to contact you on numerous, separate occasions, and you, sir, and Mr. Bakker have failed to return her calls. So now I am contacting you because this is a final attempt.
>
> We do not, absolutely do not want any trouble. All we want is for you to listen. We have to discuss a matter of mutual importance, and I'm afraid we cannot put it off any longer . . . this conversation is in reference to the events of the afternoon of December 6, 1980, and an incident that took place in Clearwater Beach, Florida at the Sheraton Sands Hotel in Room 538. . . .
>
> There have been some problems, some additional problems, and to tell you the truth they are from your end. There's still talk. Comments about Miss Hahn are still being passed along in someone's casual conversations. Please find out who it is and

have it stopped, please! It seems to go on and on and she has tried to put up with it. We know it is coming from down there because it has gotten back to us. Everything here was kept quiet. . . .

I want you to be aware of the numerous effects and ramifications this has caused this young lady, and if I may remind you, I am talking about a twenty-one year old girl, who has never been married, who lives with her parents, and I don't know if you're aware of this, but her father is a police officer. . . .

In view of the fact of her young age, I believe Mr. Bakker led her into making a wrong decision. I contend that he enticed her and coerced her into making a wrong decision to act against her better judgment, on that afternoon . . . a decision which, at that time, she did not yet posess [sic] the essential emotional and physical maturity to make.

The writer then retold Hahn's version of her encounter with Bakker.

Now, perhaps he has never done this with a stranger before or since, but I'm led to wonder if he has, or if this is a common, every day occurance [sic] with him. And as if this incidence [sic] wasn't tragic enough . . . this girl continues to be talked about. Something is very, very wrong.

She has to be compensated for her injuries of being socially disgraced. The town in which she resides is a closely knit commmunity; the church community here is even more closely knit. . . . She has suffered spiritual damage as well. She was just at her strongest point in her walk with the Lord when all this happened to her. Furthermore, she has sustained permanent psychological and emotional damages. . . . It has cost her in her womanhood. . . . She doesn't even have the usual anticipation of marriage and a happy future.

The writer asked PTL to meet Hahn's four requests. Hahn had read the first three points to me: silence the continuing talk, get an apology from Bakker, and protect Hahn's family from embarrassment. But Hahn hadn't disclosed the fourth request.

Miss Hahn requires and deserves an opportunity to pick up the pieces of her life and rebuild it; to make a fresh start, and she needs the financial means to accomplish this . . . $100,000 is not excessive in view of what happened here. That amount would not seem excessive to you if it had been your daughter or my daughter who had been violated.

You must be wondering why Miss Hahn waited three years before coming forward. Well, quite frankly the pain doesn't go away. She has tried and tried to forget, but then someone else opens a mouth to gossip, and yet another lends an ear, and so it goes. It goes on and on and on with reminders at every turn.

The rambling letter closed with a warning: inaction would be met with the "massive public scandal [Hahn] so thoroughly dreads." If Bakker ignored the demands, the writer said, Hahn would inform the Assemblies of God of the incident, hire a lawyer and commence legal action.

> We absolutely do not want the press and network news media involved in any way. PTL has more at stake here than Miss Hahn if this information becomes public knowledge. At this point in time, it would be wiser for you to ease the mind of one person than to appease all the mainline churches and the entire public.

When she received a settlement, the letter said in closing, Hahn would swear to "absolute and total silence" and disclaim any association with Bakker.

The five-page letter was apparently sent to PTL a second time with a cover letter signed with a typewritten "Jessica." That letter asked that PTL give Cortese's church four hundred new chairs—a need Hahn had heard about from Cortese. "If you do not concede to my request/requests, you will endure many long, hard days ahead . . ." the cover letter warned.

The five-page letter was cited in one of the two documents Hahn had signed for Cortese on November 1, 1984. That disclaimer read, in part, "I also admit I was not raped or physically abused at any time." On a second disclaimer, Hahn agreed to "cease harassing" PTL employees and to "cease to write accusatory letters or make accusations of any kind against evangelists, musicians, or ministry guests of PTL. . . . I admit to making accusatory statements and putting blame on PTL . . . for my own mistakes." Should she break her word, the document read, PTL could take her to court for defamation of character, harassment and "lying with intent to harm with malice."

Hahn—who had described herself as a sexual innocent—also misrepresented her relationship with her minister, Gene Profeta. He had first kissed her in February 1978 after he took her out for a drink, she said later. Heavy petting continued until July 1981, seven months after her encounter with Bakker, when she claimed she and Profeta had sexual intercourse for the first time. They then began a full-fledged, six-year romance, she said.

Despite that admission, Hahn would continue to insist in later years that she had been a virgin when she met Bakker in the Florida hotel room. She had never traveled with Fletcher before, she said. Though she remembered an uneasy Sam Orender standing in her hotel room as Fletcher suggested she spend some time with the PTL producer, she denied ever taking a walk with Fletcher on the beach, as Orender remembered, or coming to Florida expecting to have sex with Bakker, as Orender had inferred.

When Hahn became a household name in 1987, one-time friends would surface with damaging accusations. Co-workers described her to the press as a volatile woman who looked at life in terms of male conquests and enjoyed telling friends in detail about her adventures in lovemaking, including her sexual encounter with Bakker. One friend and fellow church member said he and Jessica had made love in 1978—two years before Bakker supposedly took her virginity—while his pregnant wife slept in a nearby room. Another woman suggested that Jessica had worked as a prostitute. Hahn issued angry denials. She blamed her troubles on Profeta, with whom she had had a falling out in the summer of 1987.

During their relationship, she and the minister twenty-two years her elder had met clandestinely every Tuesday night, she said in 1989. They went on trips to Atlantic City to gamble. He discouraged her from working after 1984, but continued to send her a check from the church each week. Indeed, according to a later indictment of Profeta, the minister used church funds to pay Hahn's rent and car payments and to pay for fur coats and jewelry.

In the final years of their relationship, Profeta would become obsessed with her, she said, and she would begin to feel trapped. Profeta hired private detectives to watch her and installed a phone in her car to keep track of her. He rented a post office box for her, and there he had intercepted the letter I sent her in mid-December, after our telephone conversations. He hadn't known about our conversations, Hahn said later, or about the money she had gotten from Cortese in November. "What's this about?" he asked her as the *Charlotte Observer* envelope settled on her kitchen table. "You call them up and tell them you're going to sue." She obliged with the frantic call to my home.

Hahn was a man's woman—she never seemed to get along with women—and yet she reserved her greatest fury for the men who mistreated her. The pattern was set early on. She had been born in Brooklyn in July 1959, the youngest of three children. Before she was three years old, her father and mother divorced; later her mother told of beatings. Jessica's father, a handsome utility splicer, disappeared from his daughter's life. Three years later her mother—who is also named Jessica—married a New York City cop named Eddie Moylan who would serve as a loving, if strict, father. In Jessica's ninth year, the family moved out to a modest cottage near the cul-de-sac on Massapequa's Massachusetts Avenue. Though her home was intact, her psyche was not; Jessica grew up feeling like an ugly duckling and an outsider.

In Fletcher, Bakker, and Profeta, Hahn found men who seemed, perhaps only for a moment, to fill the void her natural father had left. Inevitably, though, they let her down.

As Bakker walked into her hotel room in Clearwater, Hahn recalled in 1989, "I felt as if I knew him, and everything about him. I loved him and I loved what he represented. . . . I was really open-minded. . . . I thought, 'Well, good, he's comfortable.' " She was eager to please Bakker by listening to his personal complaints. "I don't want to turn somebody off. I don't want to become an outsider. They've let me into their life."

But as Bakker came on to her sexually, she became fearful, she said later. She felt as if she was in that hotel room to feed this man's habit. "All of that shining glory that was above him was no longer there." Afterward, Bakker left without a touch of consideration, Hahn thought; she might have treated him more kindly afterwards, "if he would have acknowledged [me] and not made it like, I'm God and you're mine, you're some piece of meat. . . . I've got her, she trusted me, I can do whatever I want and just walk away."

Two days after my second interview with Hahn, I tracked down Roger Flessing at the St. Moritz Hotel in New York, where the former PTL executive was traveling on business. I trusted that Flessing would tell me if he had heard the story of Jessica Hahn. "I know nothing about that," he said. "I do know that Fletcher was in thick at that particular point with Mr. Bakker."

Bakker did go to Clearwater periodically for telethons, but Flessing doubted Hahn's story. "I don't think anything like that ever happened. Jim is too much into the entourage. The group does everything." But some details did ring true. The Sheraton was Bakker's preferred lodging in Clearwater. The PTL president loved rubdowns, but usually, Flessing said, by a man, not a woman. And he had five or six white terry-cloth bathing suits—revealing swimwear that Flessing considered more appropriate for a teenager than a minister.

Flessing had left PTL three months earlier. Dortch had shown no interest in his research-and-development work. Bakker, though willing to boast on the air about his backdoor association with the esteemed Billy Graham, was unhappy with Flessing's periodic departures to produce broadcasts of Graham's crusades. Flessing was unhappy with how little support there was at PTL for new ways of doing things. One day during the summer of 1984, he had scribbled down the PTL malcontents' latest theory on Bakker—that Jim was against abortion, but he was killing more ideas than he was hatching.

Ten days before his trip to New York, Flessing had attended services at Calvary Temple, a large Assembly of God in the Dallas suburb of Irving. Dortch was speaking that day, and he joked about ministers in the loosely knit Pentecostal denomination. The only thing two Assemblies of God ministers could agree on, Dortch said, was what a third person should give in the offering.

Afterwards, Dortch told Flessing that PTL was soothing the waters with the *Observer,* that they had met twice with the publisher, Rolfe Neill. Dortch invited Flessing to attend the opening of the Heritage Grand Hotel, scheduled for December 22. "Jim just needs a friend right now," he told him.

Dortch was eager to polish PTL's tarnished image in Charlotte; he couldn't do so without reaching out to the *Observer.* With the furor over the story about the Bakkers' California home subsiding, PTL agreed to a lunch meeting between Bakker and Rolfe Neill, who wanted to get to know Bakker personally so he could deal directly with him on future stories. Furious at the newspaper's repeated inquiries into his private life, Bakker had ordered his security chief, Don Hardister, to get the "dirt" on the *Observer.* Despite searches through local records and hours of clandestine surveillance, Hardister had found little for Bakker to use. During the lunch, to let Neill know that PTL was watching him, Bakker mentioned in passing that he knew that Neill was divorced, lived in an apartment behind *Observer* editor Rich Oppel's house in town, and owned a home on nearby Lake Norman. Neill told Bakker the surveillance hardly seemed consistent with what PTL preached. Bakker replied that he was simply fighting fire with fire.

Next, a delegation of *Observer* editors visited Heritage USA for lunch and a tour with Bakker. "We met with some of the nicest people [from the newspaper] that you'll ever meet," he told his audience on November 22. That week, the *Observer* published a generous spread on PTL's annual Christmas City lights display, which now included 1.4 million lights.

Finally, on December 13, three days after my second interview with Hahn, the Bakkers and Dortch lunched with several editors in downtown Charlotte. Afterwards, they visited the *Observer*'s fourth-floor newsroom and sat down to talk with John Wildman and me. It was the first time I had met any of the three. Tammy seemed friendly but nervous, Bakker aloof. He seemed irritated at my blunt suggestions that PTL needed a professional PR operation that would turn out truthful answers to press inquiries, not the run-around we had gotten that fall. With Bakker dressed in his formal business clothes, sitting a few feet away from his wife, I could hardly visualize the adulterer in a skimpy swimsuit whom Hahn had described a few days before.

To further the détente between PTL and the *Observer,* PTL agreed to allow an interview with Bakker about the Partner Center. Five days from opening, Wildman and I met Bakker in the unfinished lobby of the Heritage Grand Hotel. Bakker was wearing designer jeans and cowboy boots. His fourteen-year-old daughter, Tammy Sue, stood beside him. With the dust, the clatter of hammers, and the roar of power saws filling the cavernous four-story atrium, it looked and sounded as if Bakker had a month's work to go. He seemed to enjoy his creation nonetheless. "Standing in the lobby makes me hyper. I almost think my blood pressure goes up."

Bakker led us around the lobby, down the Main Street shopping mall, and into the cafeteria and conference center. Then we stepped outside. Suddenly, Bakker commandeered the miniature C. P. Huntington train circling the lake outside the hotel. He motioned the driver aside and took the controls. If Heritage USA was Bakker's playground, the train was one of his favorite toys. We slid into the front passenger car, and Bakker played tour guide. He was in control and loving it.

Our trip around the lake complete, we ducked into a hotel room for the interview. Bakker sat on a bare mattress and began talking. A few minutes later, he asked Hardister to close the door. In the calm of the room, his fatigue began to show.

> I'm very, very tired. So it's very hard for me to—you know I'm really straining because I've got so much out there I need to be doing and my mind is just trying to figure out how I'm going to cover this so forgive me if I'm not—I'm really, really tired. I'm just at the breaking point almost.

Aside from this glimpse of self-pity, Bakker kept his distance. He was not the sort who bothered to call reporters by their first names, to inquire about their past, to get to know them as human beings. Though his stage was distant, his performance was impressive. Bakker had a knack for communicating his ideas in everyday, human terms, reducing his arguments to vibrant, easily visualized images. We could see how absorbed he was in his work. His identity seemed to flow from the buildings, the fatigue of overwork, the constant demands for his decision on this or that.

So too, Heritage USA flowed—in truth or after-the-fact packaging—from Bakker's personal experience.

> Ever since I was a kid I would always say, why can't Christians have something this nice? . . . Why is it we can almost enshrine a mouse, a Mickey Mouse or a Donald Duck? I mean, you hear the Mouseketeers' song . . . it's almost sung like a hymn. And I thought, why can't we have something where young people will be connected to Jesus Christ? . . .
> I believe that the Christian family needs a place where they can not only have a good vacation, but their family's needs will

be met, their marriages can be put together, teenagers can find help with whatever problems they have. . . .

Jesus said, basically, that we were to be fishers of men. And with some of the bait that we have used in the church—I call it dill-pickle religion—I've never seen anyone catch a fish with a dill pickle and sourpuss religion. . . .

The thing that I have resented in the past is that somehow there is almost an unseen force that says religion has to be boring and dull and dreary. And I rebel against that. I think true religion is a relationship with Jesus Christ. . . . It should be beautiful, it should be creative. You are in touch with your Creator so you should actually be more creative. But somehow we're letting people in, say, Las Vegas build creative buildings, beautiful gambling casinos. . . . I think we should be on the cutting edge and not apologize. There is no shortages in heaven and God's able to do all. . . .

The secret to success has always been find a need and fill it. There's a great need for what we're doing. And we're filling that need and God is honoring it. I believe this is . . . really a model for something that's almost going to become a phenomenon over the next few years because of the Scripture, "Forsake not the assembling of ourselves together." . . . Those who are born-again Christians believe that we are living in the last days and that He has told us to assemble together.

Here and there, Bakker talked about himself. He went out rarely, he said, partly because he never knew if he would be hugged or insulted.

I'm very bashful by nature, very, very bashful. Most people don't think so, seeing me on the air, but I really am. And a one-to-one confrontation is something that I would avoid probably at all costs. I just don't like them.

After Bakker left for his next appointment, Dortch drove us around the grounds. He was more relaxed with us than Bakker, talking freely and apologizing for his harsh comments after the California story. The tour over, the three of us sat in his car outside the hotel and talked for well over an hour.

Dortch acknowledged PTL's past shortcomings. Without seeming boastful, he presented himself as a maturing influence on the ministry's bullish future.

We're seeking in everything we do not only in buildings but in our ministry, in our programs, that we want something that's going to last, something that's got substance to it. I think we can say that without being necessarily critical of the past.

One of the interesting things to me in coming to PTL a year ago was the fact that this is largely a ministry of young people. . . . We need desperately the vision of young people, but we need the wisdom of maturity. I think we have a good balance here in that. . . .

I'm fifty-three years old. I'm not threatened. I know who I am. I'm not running for anything or from anything. And so I'm comfortable . . . I am more pleased and more excited by what I see in this ministry than I've ever been. . . .

Where we need to give attention is in the matter of business. That's basically where we're looking for help.

Dortch alluded to the 1978 mass suicide–homicides of Jim Jones's People's Temple congregation in Guyana.

One thing we have to face continually is Jonestown, that cult mentality. . . . I want to be careful people don't think we're a bunch of religious nuts. You know what I'm saying—that we follow our leader. Well, that's rubbish. . . . We don't want to stick a thermometer in anybody to test them, whether they're this or that. That's not the kind of world I want to live in.

As the sky darkened, the talk ranged more freely. Dortch asked our advice on hiring a new spokesman for the ministry. We asked about the Rolls Royce that Bakker had planned to use at the Grand, purchased the summer before in California. "If you take away the car, you take what is Jim Bakker away," Dortch said, alluding to Bakker's creativity. "Don't write this—I'll kill you—what rational person would do this? You gotta see an old Rolls Royce to do something with it. The juice that flows. It's all part of the same package."

My notes that day contain no reference to Jessica Hahn, but Dortch seemed keenly aware that we might encounter her story, as we already had. In passing comments to me and my editors, Dortch spoke of his encounters in Illinois with publicity-seekers who falsely accused pastors of sexual impropriety. Without saying so explicitly, Dortch implied that there was no truth to Hahn's story.

Dortch also underscored Bakker's willingness to submit to the oversight of his church.

> Jim Bakker is the only television minister in the country with two state superintendents of his denomination on the board [Dortch and Cookman]. . . . If I were going to try to pull some shenanigans, two of the last people I would try to get on my board are two district superintendents. It would be dumb to do that.

The next day, Jessica was on Dortch's mind again. His assistant, Al Cress, recorded Hahn's address in his notepad on December 18. "Copy of those people," he wrote next to it. Years later, Cress could not remember the task Dortch had given him that day.

If Hahn hadn't already told him, Dortch found out on December 22 that the *Observer* knew about Jessica Hahn. Roger Flessing had arrived at the hotel that afternoon as workers set flowers in place for the night's grand-opening festivities. Near the front desk, Flessing spotted David Taggart. "I got a funny call from someone at the *Charlotte Observer*," he told him. "The reporter told me Bakker had an affair with someone in Florida in 1980. Wouldn't I have been on the trip?"

Taggart stared blankly. "That didn't happen. No way. They're just looking for anything." He walked away.

A few minutes later, Dortch walked over to Flessing. The pleasantries were brief. "I understand you got a phone call from the *Observer*," Dortch said. Flessing retold the story. "Well, they're just looking for anything they can find. They've been out to destroy this ministry from day one," Dortch told Flessing. "But if you hear anything else, would you mind giving me a call?"

Dortch and Bakker had not shared the Hahn troubles with the board, and Cortese had kept quiet. The board had met on November 20, nineteen days after Cortese's meeting with Hahn in the Bronx. Near the close of the meeting, the board agreed to "recognize the leadership" of the Bakkers and Dortch. The recognition came in the form of dollars: $150,000 for Jim Bakker, $50,000 for Tammy Bakker, and $50,000 for Dortch. It was Dortch's first bonus from the board.

Within two weeks of that meeting, Bakker ordered checks drawn for the board members, apparently acting on his own authority. Cortese, Cookman, Zimbalist, and Lawing were each given ten-thousand-dollar bonuses. Ernie Franzone, a new board member, received a thousand dollars.

Bakker had primed his audience in case PTL lost control of Hahn. The day after Dortch's October 22 telephone call to Hahn, Bakker told his audience how he had hit bottom in his marriage as he spent too much time doing the work of the Lord and too little time with Tammy.

> Tammy and I went through hell. I went through a period where I didn't care if I lived or I died, I didn't care if I served God, I didn't care if I preached another sermon, my life was gone. . . . Our love seemingly died somehow, and there was no hope. And yet people are living in that position right now. And we wait until a minister falls or makes a mistake or something and then we kick him out of the church instead of reaching out to say we want to help you.

Three days later, PTL rebroadcast a 1981 show in which the Bakkers detailed how their marriage had almost ended in 1980, the year of the Hahn encounter. Bakker talked of forgiveness and the dark days of 1980 again in a church sermon broadcast October 28. "[Tammy] hurt me so bad, and I hurt her back so bad. I remember when she told me, 'I don't love you, and I never loved you.' 'Oh,' I said, 'I don't love you any more.' "

Jim Bakker looked like a winner as the Heritage Grand Hotel opened the night of December 22 with an evening of live broadcasting from the lobby. Eleven days later, Bakker staged another made-for-television black-tie party at the hotel, celebrating his forty-fifth birthday for six hours under the TV lights. Bakker wore a tux that night, Tammy wore a low-cut white lace dress with a heart-shaped pendant necklace and white choker. Bakker's birthday cake stood six layers high, a frosted monument to a birthday boy who wanted the biggest and the best.

Bakker was eager to form a bond in his viewers' minds between this hotel and traditional evangelical goals. God had told him that he couldn't win the world without a broad base of support in the United States, he said. So God instructed him to build a daily TV show, the satellite network, and a center that would make him immune to government restrictions on raising money over the air. He picked up this theme during his birthday broadcast. "This Partner Center is our base," Bakker said. "This is the beginning of an impact around the world. Our goal is to tell more people than ever before that Jesus loves them."

Dortch predicted good times. "With joy we are your co-laborers. The best is yet to come for this ministry."

The day after Bakker's birthday gala, Jessica Hahn sat in Gene Profeta's office in Massapequa. Profeta was there with Paul Roper, a forty-one-year-old businessman from California who had spoken the year before at Profeta's Full Gospel Tabernacle. Roper had a reputation as a man willing to stand up to big-name preachers, and Profeta had called and asked him to talk to a young woman who had had some problems with TV evangelist Jim Bakker.

Roper turned on his tape recorder as Hahn, crying off and on, told her story. Her words paralleled much of what she had told me four weeks earlier, but details had changed and been added. According to Hahn's amended story, while they were driving to the hotel, Fletcher had predicted that one day he and Bakker would be partners, sharing billing on the PTL show. Once they had arrived in her room, Fletcher had offered her wine, not the glass of water she described to me. He told her the drink would help her relax.

She described her subsequent incapacitation more vividly. "What was in my head wouldn't come out of my mouth. I couldn't do it. By then if John had told me to stand out on the terrace and jump I probably would have done it." She told Roper that she had kept the bottle of Vaseline lotion that Fletcher had given her. As Bakker lay on top of her, he had assured her she need not worry about getting pregnant. "Oh, I've had an operation." Hahn described having sex with Bakker more explicitly, detailing a lengthy encounter of sexual intercourse and oral sex. "Once wasn't enough. He had to keep finding new things to do."

She now said that she had confronted Fletcher when he returned to her room after Bakker left. "Why didn't you tell me what you were planning?" she recalled saying. Fletcher responded, "Just think how many people you are helping. He is a shepherd, and when you help the shepherd, you help the sheep." Then, she told

Roper, Fletcher tore off her robe, ordered her to the floor and began making love to her. "He was very, very, very rough. He was swinging my body any way he could. He wouldn't stop. He threw my legs up and just went crazy. He had a look on his face that to me looked like the Devil."

She described Fletcher's visit with the unnamed PTL producer—Sam Orender. "While the producer talked, John ate my cheeseburger. I told John I wanted to feel better and asked if we could go for a walk on the beach and talk so I could understand why it all happened. He just shrugged his shoulders and said he had to go see his wife, maybe I should go for a walk with the producer. I told him no way."

Hahn supplied more, and slightly different, details of the phone calls that followed the Clearwater encounter. According to her, Bakker had called a few days afterwards to ask her forgiveness and get her assurance that she would keep their secrets. Fletcher had done the same, warning that her family might run into trouble if she talked. "I was given code names to use when I was to return a phone call—like Jennifer Lee or Elizabeth Anderson. The secretary would answer the phone and then David Taggart would get on or Dr. Dortch." Taggart, she said, had given her his address and told her to contact him in case she wanted to do anything. She had become nervous, upset, and emotional, she said, and had lost twenty pounds.

"Once Dortch called and told me . . . he wouldn't allow John [Wesley Fletcher] into the Assemblies of God and because of that John is fighting back and causing a lot of trouble. . . . Dortch thought John was a drunk and a homosexual. He also said John was merciless and I should be careful. He asked me if I was taping his conversations."

Hahn was asked if she had told anyone this story. She lied, a choice she blamed years after on Profeta. "No!" she answered. Had she talked to the newspaper? "They called me and asked me about it, but I denied the whole thing. I didn't admit anything. I haven't talked to anyone." So whoever talked to the papers wasn't her? "That's right," Hahn replied, "but someone is talking."

As he listened, Roper had trouble believing that a woman who seemed so worldly-wise could have been a virgin at twenty-one, but Profeta vouched for Hahn's innocence. Hahn said nothing of the

297

money she had already taken from PTL or of the letter asking for $100,000. Roper suggested to Hahn that she see an attorney. She had already done so, she said, but the lawyer wanted a lot of money and wanted to file a lawsuit. Roper, a second-semester law student at Western State University in Fullerton, agreed to see if he could resolve the matter.

After his return to California, Roper tried without success to get through to Bakker. Next, he approached a friend, John Stewart, for help drafting a complaint, a document stating the claims that Hahn would make if she sued. Stewart, a former pastor, had finished law school and was studying for the California bar. Roper hoped that sending PTL the draft complaint would get the ministry's attention without necessarily forcing the matter into litigation.

The eight-page complaint named seven potential defendants: Bakker, PTL, Richard Dortch, the Assemblies of God, Aimee Cortese, Cortese's church, and the Sheraton Sand Key Resort. The suit claimed $12.3 million in damages for assault and battery, intentional infliction of emotional distress, false imprisonment, and negligence. Attached to the document was a rough transcript of Roper's session with Hahn and a January 14 cover letter from Roper giving PTL one week to answer.

CHAPTER FIFTEEN

A SECRET
SETTLEMENT

"God is still captain . . . you're safe in his arms"

Paul Roper's mailing arrived first at the Bronx church of PTL board member Aimee Cortese. On the afternoon of Sunday, January 19, 1985, Cortese flew to Charlotte to speak at Sunday-night services at Heritage Village Church. Dortch was out of town, but his assistant, Al Cress, was running the evening session. Later that evening, Cortese discreetly handed the package to Cress to give to his boss.

Cress routinely screened Dortch's mail. That night, in the bedroom of his home at Heritage USA, Al Cress read the papers with disbelief and disgust.

> On or about December 6, 1980, defendant James Bakker assaulted and battered plaintiff [Jessica Hahn] in her hotel room in Clearwater Beach, Florida, by advancing upon her and forcing her to engage in sexual intercourse and oral copulation. Said advancing occurred when plaintiff was weak, nauseous, and sedated due to defendant's actions in drugging plaintiff's drink.

The draft lawsuit seemed authentic: it resembled other legal documents Cress had seen, and it was neatly typed and largely free of the misspellings Cress had seen in the earlier five-page letter. The mass of detailed evidence in the transcript impressed Cress, who knew only bits and pieces of Dortch's dealings with Hahn the year before. How, he wondered, could this not be true?

The next morning, Cress noticed a similar package on his secretary's desk—the copy Roper had sent to Dortch. The contents were identical. Cress reached his boss in Springfield, Missouri, at the national headquarters of the Assemblies of God. He told Dortch that the papers named the denomination as one of the defendants. Dortch said that he would check to see if a package had been sent to Springfield.

Paul Roper's deadline passed. Four days later, on January 25, Dortch telephoned. He told Roper that he was sorry he had taken so long to respond, but that he had been sick with Crohn's disease, a chronic intestinal inflammation. The two men agreed to meet in California on February 7.

Dortch also tried to arrange a meeting with Gene Profeta. Years later, Dortch said that Profeta had been abusive and threatening; the two men would never meet. On orders from Dortch, Cress located John Wesley Fletcher at a church in Virginia. Fletcher agreed to talk with Dortch, the man who had dismissed him from the Assemblies of God three years earlier. Before Dortch's departure for California, the two men met at an airline lounge in the Charlotte airport. Dortch showed Fletcher the draft lawsuit. Later, Fletcher said that he had told Dortch that the accusations were true.

In fact, Dortch already knew that Bakker and Hahn had had a sexual encounter. Dortch had first considered Hahn's story—with what he remembered as an allegation of rape—to be preposterous, and for two months he had said nothing to Bakker about his efforts to placate the woman. But one day, as the two men sat in Bakker's office in the World Outreach Center, Dortch told his boss "I'm dealing with a woman who says you raped her." Bakker denied raping anyone but asked who the caller was. Jessica Hahn, Dortch answered. Dortch recalled Bakker's response. "He stood looking out the window, not moving for a long time, probably five minutes. Then, he turned to me and said, 'There is a problem. . . . I'll give Dr. Gross permission to tell you the story.' " It was to Fred Gross, the head of the Palmdale therapy team, that Bakker had confessed within weeks of his encounter with Hahn.

Bakker may not have raped Hahn, but the PTL president had admitted to a moral indiscretion. With that knowledge, Richard Dortch confronted a dilemma: to adhere to the moral code of his church or protect the evangelist on whom he had staked his future. As an executive presbyter of the Assemblies of God, Dortch was obliged to bring Bakker before the church for discipline. He knew that such a step would result in public censure, leaving PTL traumatized by bad publicity and donor defections. If Bakker wanted to remain in the Assemblies of God, he would have to stay off the air for at least a year and would lose his ministerial papers for two. Moreover Dortch, who had been chosen to assume the ministry if Bakker should leave, might be suspected of having stolen another man's pulpit.

Should Bakker decide to leave the denomination in the face of such punishment but remain in his PTL ministry, PTL's image would still suffer, as would support from the partners, twenty-one percent of whom belonged to the Assemblies. Remaining at PTL would create other problems as well. If Bakker left the Assemblies under a cloud, each Assemblies of God minister on his staff—Dortch included—would have to choose between their jobs at PTL and their affiliation with the denomination.

Dortch had another, less painful alternative: silence. Admit nothing to PTL board member and longtime friend Charles Cookman, the North Carolina district superintendent for the Assemblies, the man who would be responsible for investigating any allegations that were brought against Bakker. Admit nothing to the executive presbyters of the Assemblies of God, the twelve men with whom Dortch met regularly to approve the disciplinary measures taken against other ministers in the denomination. And do everything possible to assure that Jessica Hahn said nothing more.

At quarter-past seven on the morning of February 7, PTL's Sabreliner jet took off from the Palm Springs airport for a twenty-five-minute flight to Los Angeles. Richard Dortch was the sole passenger. It was apparently that morning that Dortch, squired by psychologist Fred Gross, visited Los Angeles lawyer Howard Weitzman to get advice on how to handle Roper and Hahn. As Gross and Dortch drove to Weitzman's office, the psychologist asked Dortch if he realized the chance he was taking with his own position in the Assemblies of God. Dortch acknowledged that he did. Gross joined Dortch as an advisor for the meeting with Weitz-man.

Bakker always wanted the best, and Weitzman was one of the country's hottest criminal-defense lawyers. He was a curious choice, though, since Bakker was under no threat of criminal prose-cution on the four-year-old matter. The summer before, Weitzman had persuaded a federal jury to acquit carmaker John DeLorean of conspiracy to smuggle cocaine. The verdict of not guilty was a stunning achievement. Federal prosecutors had hours of secret videos and recordings that seemed to show DeLorean participating enthusiastically in a scheme to sell millions of dollars of cocaine. Weitzman discredited federal agents and prosecutors, convincing the jury that the government was prepared to use any means to get his client. Soon, Weitzman's name was everywhere—representing actor Sean Penn, rock singer Ozzy Osbourne, and Cathy Evelyn Smith, imprisoned for injecting a fatal drug dose into comedian John Belushi.

Later that day, Paul Roper met Dortch at a hotel near the John Wayne Airport in Orange County. He drove him to a borrowed office in Newport Beach, where they talked. Dortch performed well, talking about his post on the executive presbytery of the Assemblies, his work as a district superintendent, and his confi-dence that Hahn's accusations were untrue. Roper thought Dortch was charming, one of the finest men he'd ever met.

Dortch had no firm answers for Roper that day. Bakker would not meet with him, as Roper wanted. Roper suggested that they settle the matter through a Christian conciliation procedure. He would name one person to a panel, Bakker would pick another, the two would pick a third, and the three would render a binding decision on Hahn's claim and demand for damages. Dortch was noncommittal but agreed to get back in touch.

At half-past five that afternoon, after giving Roper a tour of PTL's corporate jet, Dortch flew back to Palm Springs. The next afternoon, again the only passenger, Dortch flew home. Bakker—whom Dortch had described as despondent over the Hahn mat-ter—left his vacation home in Palm Desert for Charlotte the next day. On February 11, Bakker and Dortch returned to the air after weeks of reruns.

As he drove home from his meeting with Dortch, Roper realized the significance of Dortch's passing comment that Hahn was not the innocent she claimed to be but an experienced professional. How would Bakker know this, Roper thought, unless he had had sex with Hahn? Roper wasn't especially troubled by Hahn's questionable claims of virginity; Bakker had no business having sex with Hahn no matter what.

By phone, Dortch informed Roper that Bakker had rejected the proposal for Christian conciliation because it was not a procedure recognized by the Assemblies of God. Dortch talked about his pastor's heart and his concern that Hahn not be damaged emotionally. He told Roper that he had hired Howard Weitzman—not to fight the case, which would mean the very publicity PTL was desperate to avoid, but to settle.

The evening of February 19, Dortch caught a commercial flight to Los Angeles, accompanied by his wife, Mildred. The next day, he checked into a sixteenth-floor room in LA's Century Plaza, around the corner from Weitzman's office. He and Roper met over lunch in a hotel restaurant to settle Hahn's claims once and for all.

Each man made an offer. Roper started high, Dortch low. They agreed, finally, on $265,000. Dortch told Roper that Bakker's salary was modest, that he would have to sell a house to raise the cash. The two agreed that Bakker would pay partly in cash, partly in a twenty-year trust fund, a compelling incentive for Hahn to adhere to her pledge never to talk about the case again.

A few days before the Heritage Grand's December 22, 1984, opening, Bakker and his family moved into their new suite on the top floor of the hotel. As always, PTL spared no expense for its president. The company had paid Roe Messner $139,000 to frame up rooms in the suite before ordering PTL crews in to finish. In September 1984, eleven days after publicizing the new Towers partnerships, Bakker accepted a $250,000 "bid" from David Taggart's brother James for furnishings, labor, and consultation on his presidential suite and two honeymoon suites. Not content, Bakker would later approve another $450,000 for James Taggart to do further work and improvements to those suites. His fee included $161,000 in furniture and $7,364 in silk trees.

The suite's kitchen, just off the living room that overlooked the water park, had the finest brand-name equipment: a Sub-Zero refrigerator that retailed for more than two thousand dollars, a Jenn-Air range, a Sharp microwave, and a Thermador dishwasher and trash compactor. When the Sub-Zero's compressor broke down that first winter, PTL couldn't wait for an ordered part that would have been free under the warranty. Instead, PTL bought a new compressor.

Bakker said nothing about the suite to viewers as he raised money to pay for the hotel that fall. Tammy assured her audience that the Partner Center was not for Jim and Tammy, because they already had a house. Bakker told viewers that the furniture in the hotel's rooms would be as good as any they would find in a hotel's presidential suites—but it was not good enough for Bakker himself.

There seemed to be little joy for Bakker that winter. Late on the night of February 21, as Tammy Bakker attended an awards banquet at the Beverly Wilshire hotel in Beverly Hills and began a week-long trip in southern California, Bakker strolled through the lobby of the Heritage Grand. Bakker was "going through some very difficult trials," as he wrote in a fund-raising letter that spring, and he couldn't sleep. He heard Mike Murdock, a Dallas evangelist and favored guest on his show, playing the grand piano in the hotel lobby. "Mike Murdock and I both hit the bottom of the valley at the same time."

That night, Bakker and Murdock wrote a song, "God Will Outlast Your Storm." The lyrics were testimony to the willingness of Bakker's God to forgive any trespass.

> The waves may be crashing around your battered soul,
> And your eyes may be blinded by tears.
> Oh, but through those darkened waters
> I see a hand reaching down.
> God is still captain—there's nothing to fear
> . . . .
> Sheltered, protected, you're safe in his arms.
> Oh, your night will pass, but God will outlast the storm.

The song made its debut on his program the next morning. His marriage—and the troubled days of 1980—were on his mind. "Tammy Faye has come through some valleys. Jim Bakker has come through some valleys, and we've come through some storms."

The broadcast that day caught the staff's attention. A crowd gathered in front of the TV screens inside the World Outreach Center. A PTL staff member later wrote, "something exciting was obviously happening in the studio . . . the Holy Spirit began ministering across the airwaves." Caught up in his own suffering, Bakker had touched the hearts of his audience in a way that he did less and less often.

Dortch was visibly relieved as he returned to Charlotte from his second meeting with Roper. But he still needed to come up with the $265,000. His solution was Roe Messner. He met with the contractor over lunch at the Hampton Court restaurant in the Heritage Grand lobby. Dortch told Messner that a woman from New York claimed that she had had an affair with Jim; she was going to the newspaper unless she has $265,000 within a week. Of that money, some would be paid up front, some would be put in a trust. Tammy knew nothing about it; she and Jim were separated when it happened. They couldn't trust anyone inside PTL to keep it confidential, so they needed his help. Messner agreed. Dortch told Messner where to send the money and, as Messner told it later, directed him to tack the sum onto his construction bill.

At 3:04 P.M. on February 26, $265,000 was wired from Messner's bank in Wichita into Howard Weitzman's clients' trust account at the Bank of Los Angeles. Messner included the sum in his next invoice, adding it to the balance outstanding for labor and materials used on the set of PTL's passion play. Apparently, the irony was inadvertent. Messner listed Dortch as the person authorizing the billing.

The day after Messner's money arrived, Cress wired another $25,000 to Weitzman from a bank in Rock Hill, South Carolina, just south of Heritage USA. Dortch had directed Cress to make the transfer, apparently to pay the fees of PTL's lawyers. The $25,000 came from a confidential bank account accessible only to the highest-ranking executives with offices on the small third floor of the World Outreach Center—Bakker, Dortch, and Taggart. Dortch was obsessed with confidentiality. A year earlier, he had ordered several special accounts set up so that PTL's top executives could spend without risking leaks or having to answer to employees in finance. One account, administered by PTL's outside accounting firm, supplied salaries and bonuses for Bakker, Dortch, Taggart, and other favored executives. Another paid the bills for the homes Bakker and Dortch lived in; a third supplied money for a variety of disbursements—including the California legal bills.

A few hours after Cress's visit to the bank, Weitzman's partner, Scott Furstman, escorted Paul Roper and Jessica Hahn into an office ten floors above Pico Boulevard, a few blocks from the studios of 20th Century-Fox. Roper had spent the day giving Hahn a tour of the Los Angeles area. Profeta had joined them for the sightseeing but now stayed behind in the lawyers' waiting room.

Inside, Roper and Hahn met a former superior-court judge from Los Angeles, Charles Woodmansee, one of the retired local judges available for the private settlement of disputes in the Los Angeles area. Roper, only a law student, wanted some official sanction of the agreement. He was worried that the settlement might someday be portrayed as blackmail.

Woodmansee interviewed Hahn. He was thorough but courteous. He asked Hahn if she was happy with the settlement and Roper's representation. He asked Roper who he was. The questioning halted for a moment when Howard Weitzman arrived. Weitzman let it be known that he thought he could crush Hahn's claim if the dispute were fought in court; he told Hahn and Roper that it was a good thing the matter was being settled that night. After several hours, Judge Woodmansee gave his blessing to the private settlement. "This would pass muster in my courtroom," Roper later recalled the judge saying.

Before leaving, Hahn signed a five-page document labeled "Compromise and Settlement." Furstman signed on behalf of Bakker, Dortch, Cortese, PTL, and the Assemblies of God, which had never been notified of the threatened lawsuit. The agreement prohibited Hahn from discussing or doing anything to "otherwise disseminate" what she knew. She could not contact any media source about her allegation or settlement. If Hahn felt that the agreement had been breached, she could pursue relief only through private binding arbitration, not in public court.

Roper walked out with a check for $115,000, drawn on Weitzman's clients' trust account and made out to a bank in Yorba Linda. Nowhere did the check betray any tie to Hahn. Roper would keep most of the money, giving about $20,000 to Hahn and using another $15,000 to pay fellow law-student Stewart for his advice and to reimburse expenses paid by Profeta. Hahn would be the beneficiary of the agreed-upon twenty-year trust valued at $150,000. At the end of twenty years, the money was Hahn's. Until then, she would get only the interest off the principal.

With his secret apparently safe, Bakker behaved like a man freed from prison. His ministry began spending money as if it no longer had to hoard cash for a rainy day. On February 27, the day of the settlement meeting in Weitzman's law office, Bakker broke ground for the Towers. The next day, PTL obtained a $2 million loan to help build the water park. On March 3, PTL paid REC $1 million, more than it even owed the water-park contractor. A few days later, Bakker summoned his staff, declaring that everyone's pay would be going up by six percent. This across-the-board raise would be the last awarded by Bakker at PTL.

Bakker emerged from the tense winter with a new project for the needy—a gesture of generosity that some around him attributed to the humbling experience with Hahn. Bakker proposed building a home for the homeless at Heritage USA. He called it Fort Hope.

> Have you ever driven down the streets of a major city and seen how the "street people" of America live? I have . . . and I cannot forget them. I have seen them wandering the streets after dark, looking bewildered and confused. . . . God has given me such a heavy burden for the men and women who have been abandoned—many by their own families—and literally left on the streets to fend for themselves.

At the March board meeting, a month and a day after the Hahn payoff, PTL's board voted bonuses to Jim and Tammy Bakker, $200,000 for Jim, $50,000 for Tammy—a sum ironically close to the cost of the Hahn settlement. Bakker stepped out of the room during the vote. When he returned, he registered his token opposing vote.

With the price of lifetime partnerships up to two thousand dollars, the flow of lifetime money had thinned to a trickle, from December's $10.5 million to February's $63,000. In mid-April, Bakker reopened sales of the Heritage Grand partnerships, claiming in a mass mailing that he had been "shocked to discover" that PTL still needed more than nine hundred lifetime partnerships in the Grand to meet its goal, due to bad checks and credit-card charges. He claimed that partnerships would soon cost three thousand dollars, but the remaining original lifetimes were still available for a thousand dollars.

Bakker no longer talked openly about the maximum number of partnerships he would offer. PTL had already issued 34,203 partnerships in the Grand when Bakker reopened the offering. By May 31, 1985, Bakker's partners had doled out $47 million in partnerships for the Grand, in excess of fifty percent more than Bakker had once said he would issue. The take from Towers memberships already totaled nearly $20 million.

Contributions to PTL's general fund continued to lag. For PTL's entire fiscal year from June 1984 through May 1985, general-fund contributions declined twenty-one percent to $42 million. Total revenues on PTL's audited financial statements had grown nine percent, however, mostly on the strength of increased lodging and food sales and the first appearance of the money PTL had received from the lifetime partners. Though PTL had chosen to spend the lifetime money without setting any of it aside in a cash reserve, PTL's outside auditors insisted over PTL's objections that the vast sum of partnership money not be declared as revenue immediately, since PTL had received the money in exchange for a promise of free lodging years into the future. So PTL reported a portion of the money as revenue each year, using a scale that would amortize ninety percent of the entire sum over seven years. With little actual use of the half-finished hotel in fiscal 1985, PTL reported only $3.5 million of the $66 million in partnerships as revenue. So, despite a record-breaking year in cash receipts, PTL's books showed an embarrassing year-end deficit of $17.5 million.

Quietly, Bailey and Mark Burgund, Porter Speakman's successor as budget director, began to save money for the Christmas City lights display that had proven such a financial shock in the last two years. Without telling Bakker or Dortch, the two began setting aside $20,000 a day. One day that summer, as Bakker complained about the shortage of money, Bailey fessed up. Within twenty-four hours, the money was gone.

The overselling of the Grand continued into the summer of

1985, but Bakker dropped his talk of 900 partnerships. Instead, PTL issued more than 20,000 new partnerships, and thousands more Towers partners were allowed to transfer their free-lodging privilege to the operating Heritage Grand. By September 1, lifetime partnerships in the Grand totaled 63,300. An internal ministry report showed that PTL had issued enough lifetime partnerships to fill 103.7% of the Grand's capacity. Predictably, the soaring numbers compounded PTL's troubles by dramatically increasing the demand for rooms. The hotel had opened in late 1984 with only half of its rooms ready for occupancy. By July 1985, some eighty of its five hundred rooms still needed the fire marshal's approval to open. To make matters worse, PTL had done nothing to help partners spread their requests for "free rooms" over the entire year. Peak times sold out quickly, and those calling several months into the year often found their vacation dates filled. Some accepted an inconvenient or briefer stay. Others gave up altogether.

The complaints made their way to Bakker. By summer's end, he asked his staff to find out why so many partners were complaining that they could not get through to the hotel's reservations clerks. On the air, Bakker chose to blame the problem on partners who waited too long to make reservations. To placate his supporters, Bakker extended the 1985 "year" three months into 1986—a solution suggested by his hotel staff on August 13, the day that the lifetime partners booked the last of their 1985 allotment in the Grand. Privately, Bakker suggested that more partners be admitted on nights that the hotel had vacant rooms in the paying half of the hotel—a solution that would create its own problems for the financially strapped hotel. "I know it's going to be a little strain on us, but it would sure help save our neck."

The busy days of summer 1985 seemed to confirm the success of Bakker's vision of a national retreat center for born-again Christians. Bakker's show at eleven in the morning was so popular that the audience spilled from the new TV studio into the adjoining Barn. In the Partner Center, PTL offered dinner theater, sometimes featuring PTL talent, sometimes outside stars like Dean Jones. The passion play filled the amphitheater, live music was performed on an outdoor stage next to the lake. PTL staged events for teenagers and young adults, including performances by contemporary Christian musicians. The Partner Center offered restaurants and plenty of stores to shop in.

PTL still had none of the sophisticated rides of a theme park like Walt Disney World, but it offered bicycles, tennis courts, swimming pools, a petting zoo, the miniature train, and a roller-skating rink. PTL encouraged its partners to volunteer; some staffed the prayer phones, others helped in the mailroom. The center had a menu of more conventional religious activities—church services in the Barn, prayer in the Upper Room, Bible seminars, marriage workshops, and advice for those who wanted help with finances or staying off alcohol and drugs.

The sight of the happy visitors at Heritage USA sustained the idealism of Bakker's staff on days darkened by the failings of their leaders. The evidence that Heritage USA was working came in many forms. The couple whose marriage had been saved by one of the Palmdale team's seminars. The lady with the bad right knee who had mistakenly stepped into the healing line at the Upper Room and walked out without her cane. The homeless family put up for a few nights at PTL expense. The mother and daughter bubbling with excitement about the Bible seminars, nightly camp meetings, and other opportunities to deepen their faith.

If there were heroes in the PTL story, one employee suggested, it was these earnest partners and their counterparts in the PTL staff, the ladies who read the letters and the groundskeepers who whistled while they worked. They were committed to their God, passionately loyal to PTL, and far removed from the greed and deceit that infected the upper reaches of PTL management.

As Bakker's projects escalated in size, his habit of paying for old projects with the money for new put PTL deeper and deeper into the hole. Once this practice had meant falling tens of thousands of dollars behind; now it meant millions. Driven perhaps by an illusory sense of success, perhaps by the realization that he needed to continue pulling rabbits from his hat to keep his audience's trust, Bakker pursued a costly battery of new projects.

One such project was a reconstruction of biblical Jerusalem centered around Heritage USA's amphitheater, which PTL had remade to resemble an idealized scene from the Holy Land so that it could house PTL's new passion play. In July 1985, PTL hired a

Mississippi firm to develop detailed plans for a $40-million, thirty-six-acre Jerusalem theme park. PTL had already asked a second firm to develop a one-of-a-kind ride depicting heaven and hell. Bakker also wanted to build a nursing home designed with an Old West motif, "not putting them just on a slab somewhere with their mouths open and flies flying in . . . we're going to build a place where they're going to have fun, we're going to lift them up where they belong." He planned a 170-bed hospital, a new six-lane entrance road, and a newer welcome center right beside I-77. "There's so much going on here that we would overwhelm you if we told you everything," he told his TV audience in late August. This time, Bakker was telling the truth.

Bakker had also dispatched his vice president for real estate, V. J. Sherk, on a buying spree that deepened PTL's debt and aggravated its cash crisis. PTL had added occasional parcels of land to Heritage USA in the early eighties, but it escalated the pace of its purchases after December 1983 as Bakker worried that he, like Walt Disney in Anaheim, might be boxed in by adjacent development. In 1984, PTL spent $2.4 million on land. In the first seven months of 1985, PTL closed another $5.6 million in purchases, including one for 130 acres across U.S. 21 that cost $4.3 million, or $33,000 an acre. The land fronted on I-77. With it, Bakker had acquired close to two-thirds of the interstate frontage between two interchanges on the eastern side of the highway.

During summer 1985, Sherk targeted for purchase fourteen parcels spanning 925 acres, including virtually all of the remaining I-77 frontage. In at least eleven cases, PTL entered into contracts to buy. These contracts would also give PTL more than 400 acres of land on the western side of I-77, miles from the current borders of Heritage USA. Altogether, the fourteen parcels carried a price tag of $11 million.

That summer, PTL unveiled Bakker's most outlandish building plan ever. After spending $775,000 for steel and architectural plans, PTL had shelved a 1984 proposal for a five-thousand-seat auditorium. Instead, Bakker decided to create the Crystal Palace Ministry Center, patterned after the iron and glass Crystal Palace built in London for the Great Exhibition of 1851. As Bakker envisioned it, the structure would span 1 million square feet of floor space and hold up to thirty thousand seats. It would extend the length of three football fields and cost, as of summer 1985, $75 million. It was, PTL's public-relations man told me that summer, "a vision based on reality. The reality, what has happened on these grounds in the last seven years, gives tremendous confidence for the future."

Although PTL had already funded the Hahn settlement, Roper and Dortch still had details to resolve. The first was the wording of the Jessica Hahn trust itself. On July 1, 1985, Roper urged Scott Furstman, the lawyer handling the case for PTL, to resolve all details so the trust document could be completed. The next day, Furstman dispatched a letter to Dortch. He was having trouble getting through to Dortch by phone.

> I would appreciate you contacting me at your earliest convenience so we can discuss who to designate as the Trustor of the Jessica Hahn Trust.
> I have done additional research and am of the opinion that the Trustor can be designated as a corporation as opposed to an individual. Furthermore, I believe the trust agreement can be structured whereas the purpose is to discharge an obligation or a debt, as opposed to a gift . . . [so] there will be no gift tax consequences.

Cress, Dortch's assistant, had suffered a horrible spring and early summer. His mother was dying of pancreatic cancer. Unable to eat for three months, the heavyset seventy-four-year-old had lost a hundred pounds. With his work as Dortch's assistant and new role as executive producer of PTL's passion play, Cress juggled a crushing work schedule with twice-monthly trips to his mother's bedside in a Trinidad, Colorado, nursing home.

The Hahn payoff still troubled him deeply. Despite Dortch's representations that Hahn was a nut and her story a lie, Cress was convinced that Bakker had had sex with Hahn, an indiscretion that demanded ecclesiastical punishment. He sensed the tension in Bakker and Dortch as the third floor grappled with the pressure from Hahn. If the young woman was merely demented, as Dortch claimed, then why the special attention? He knew that Bakker would fight publicly when he felt unjustly accused. Why didn't he just go on the air and say that someone was trying to blackmail him?

Cress's disillusionment had deepened that spring as the result of a casual conversation with Taggart and Bakker's secretary, Shirley Fulbright. The thirty-five-year-old Cress was sitting in Taggart's glass-walled office a few feet from his own cubicle. The subject that day was job security under the unpredictable Bakker.

Taggart, in his fifth year as Bakker's aide, had no worries. "Oh, Jim Bakker will never get rid of us. We know too much," he told Cress. Shirley agreed.

"Like Jessica Hahn?" Cress asked.

Taggart and Fulbright looked at each other and laughed. The twenty-seven-year-old Taggart spoke for both veterans. "Oh, Al, we know stuff a lot worse than that."

Cress felt estranged from Dortch, his boss for the last ten years. He had seen a new Dick Dortch emerge at PTL, an opportunist willing to abandon old loyalties in his pursuit of membership in Bakker's inner circle, a man capable of mental gymnastics to justify his conduct. Had Hahn accused one of Dortch's ministers back in Illinois, Cress was certain that Dortch would have seized the minister's credentials. He remembered how eager Dortch had been to fire the secretary in Carlinville who had let her boyfriend sleep in her apartment.

A March 21, 1985, letter to Dortch from David Wilkerson, author of the best-seller *The Cross and the Switchblade*, had articulated the uneasiness Cress felt. Wilkerson, an Assemblies of God minister best known for his work with youth gangs and drug addicts in New York City, wrote to Dortch that he would not be coming to PTL, now or in the foreseeable future.

> My reasons are deeply prophetic, and I grieve because of them. What God has shown me about that ministry I dare not even put in print.
>
> I love you and I believe you are a man of God, but you are at a crossroads and stand on the brink of being deceived and blinded.
>
> You asked me what the sin is that I saw. It is fornication with wood and stone, and that is just the tip of the iceberg.
>
> If you are the man of God I believe you are and will take more time to fast and pray and seek God's face and not get caught up in the voice of the counsellors there—within two years, you will no longer be there. You will escape before it all comes down. . . .

What is going to happen will make the ears of all who hear
it to tingle.
I will share my whole heart with you, but only in private.

Dortch's move to PTL had not worked out as he expected.
Despite Bakker's early efforts to see that Dortch and his staff felt
welcomed, the new arrivals from Illinois could sense the suspicion
of the old guard. Some veterans at the World Outreach Center
considered Dortch two-faced. Dortch's growing cadre of executive
recruits—"Dortchites" as they were called behind their backs—
only compounded the suspicion. Vi Azvedo, whose power Dortch
had underestimated, detested him. Privately, Dortch reciprocated
the feeling.

By summer 1985, Cress saw that Dortch felt his aide had outlived
his usefulness. Dortch seemed to prefer having younger men at his
side, assistants who were in awe of him and tended to his needs
slavishly. On July 2, the day Furstman wrote Dortch, Dortch told
Cress that he thought it was time for Cress to leave, that he'd never
been happy there.

That night, Cress's brother called. The nursing-home staff
thought their mother was dying. Cress left at daybreak. At the
Denver airport, he learned that his mother had passed away while
he was en route. Cress returned to work on July 15 and left the next
Friday for a trip back to Illinois for the fiftieth wedding anniversary
of some friends. The next Monday, he felt ill and called in sick.
A friend brought over his mail. In it he found a Dear Al letter
from Dortch. Dortch had decided to put another employee in
his position. From what Cress could tell, he was now a glorified
receptionist.

That night, Cress drove to the World Outreach Center and typed
a brief resignation letter to David Taggart. He cleaned out his desk
and collected his files. He also stopped to check the folders where
secretaries put Dortch's incoming mail. In one, Cress noticed the
Furstman letter. It had arrived fourteen days earlier in Dortch's
private post-office box.

Without any particular plan, Cress photocopied the one-page
letter. He had kept a copy of the letter Taggart had received from
Hahn's anonymous friend the year before. He sensed that someday
he might need a copy of this correspondence as well.

* * *

On August 9, thirteen thousand pastors and members of the Assemblies of God gathered inside the San Antonio convention center for the second day of their biennial convention. It was time to pick their leader, the denomination's general superintendent. For twenty-six years, the post had been held by Thomas Zimmerman, a dominant figure within the denomination and a respected leader among evangelicals. But Zimmerman was now seventy-three years old; it was time for a fresh face. On that day's nominating ballot, Zimmerman failed to win reelection to another four-year term. The slender, white-haired Zimmerman stepped down gracefully. Dortch finally had his chance at the top job in the Assemblies of God.

Bakker had given Dortch the go-ahead to seek the post, telling his deputy that he could better serve PTL as head of the denomination. Bakker told one aide that he envisioned PTL becoming the loosely affiliated broadcast arm of the Assemblies of God if Dortch prevailed.

The Saturday session in San Antonio began with a prayer breakfast built around the theme Stand Firm in Integrity. By late morning, balloting for general superintendent had begun. With Zimmerman out, Dortch had a solid but unspectacular showing—325 votes and fourth place. The front-runners were the sitting assistant superintendent, G. Raymond Carlson, and an executive presbyter from New Orleans, Marvin Gorman. On the seventh ballot, Carlson prevailed.

Bakker had flown to San Antonio to make a show of support for Dortch, but the maneuver backfired. Bakker swept in with his entourage, including David Taggart, whose effeminate manner was the topic of much tongue wagging. Taggart wore casual clothes and plenty of jewelry, not the more appropriate conservative Sunday church attire. Bakker simply voted and left, showing little interest in the denomination's affairs. Soon, he was flying west to California for a vacation.

Undeniably, Dortch's move to PTL had cost him dearly in the vote for general superintendent. But he was optimistic that he could retain a seat on the executive presbytery, the thirteen-member national board. He was fighting the odds, though, running in the Southeast district, not in his home Great Lakes region, which had reelected him repeatedly. To win, he would have to unseat the Southeast incumbent—a rare accomplishment.

Monday night, the voting began. The Southeast incumbent, a district superintendent from Florida, led the field of thirteen with 709 votes. Dortch followed closely with 600. The winner needed 1,125. Dortch lost forty-nine votes on the second ballot, and the incumbent won on the third vote. The loss devastated Dortch. He had always been hungry for approval. Now, he had been rejected by the gathering that just a few years earlier had been prepared to make him its general superintendent. Dortch cried. At dinner that night with friends, he was subdued, not the characteristic center of conversation. By daybreak Tuesday, he had boarded a private jet for the trip home. He skipped the final morning of the convention.

In late August 1985, as Bakker returned from his vacation in California, PTL's house of cards was teetering again. In the first seven months of the year, PTL's payroll had climbed from 1,600 to 2,642. In the same span, general contributions had dropped from $31.8 million to $23.4 million. On August 19, 1985, finance director Bailey informed Bakker once again that PTL was not generating enough gifts to its general fund to pay operating costs. That same day, Bailey had received a written warning that PTL's slow payment of insurance premiums could prompt cancellation of its coverage and result in an "astronomical" rate increase. Bailey proposed eleven possible solutions to Bakker, including sale of real estate and an immediate forty-percent cut in payroll.

Bakker "discovered" the new crisis as he returned to the air. "From time to time it seems like we have a crisis develop that seems to come out of the blue," he told his audience on August 29. This time, PTL's mailing system was to blame. Bakker had been so busy preaching and building the Partner Center, he explained, that he had not directed his full attention to the job of answering PTL's mail and shipping gifts to donors. Some lifetime partners had not heard from PTL in six months. Offended donors had stopped giving. That, Bakker said, was jeopardizing PTL's network of TV stations—the same catastrophe Bakker had warned of twelve months earlier. This new crisis was PTL's worst ever, Bakker said. But if the partners gave PTL one more chance, Bakker predicted, PTL wouldn't suffer such a crisis again.

Bakker had never accepted responsibility for PTL's problems in anything other than an obligatory, rhetorical fashion. Like a young-ster uncertain of his parents' love, fearful that his failures might chill the little affection he received, Bakker concocted excuses and found scapegoats. Instead of blaming PTL management for the ministry's mailing troubles, he talked about mail theft and shipping damage and, as he often did, PTL's rapid growth. Later, apparently after postal authorities complained about being his whipping boy, Bakker acknowledged in passing that most of the problem was PTL's. Bakker couldn't afford to make an enemy of the US Postal Service.

In a crisis, Bakker played the role of hero. He declared he would not return to the air until he had sorted out PTL's mailing troubles. "I have totally made up my mind that I will solve this problem or I'll never got back on television again, and I mean that sincerely." Of course he never left the air. Whether it was the license that full-gospel Christians give to evangelists, the general pliability of truth on television, or the short attention span of the American viewer, Bakker was able to exaggerate and distort with impunity. "I've been working for thirty days, day and night, with our en-tire team" to solve the mailing problem, he said on September 4. If so, he had been working day and night during his vacation in California.

To underscore his commitment to PTL, Bakker made one of his patented grand gestures of generosity.

> God has always demanded of me that I take the step forward whenever there is a crisis, and I was trying to think what is my most prized possession besides my children and my wife and all because I believe in this ministry. I really don't care about anything else. And people accuse me of caring about material-ism, and, because I build so much, I care about people. . . . I would rather have Jesus than anything the world can offer.
>
> A couple years or so [ago] I bought an antique car. It was the dream of my life to own the car, and it's a big boy's toy. . . . It's something that I've been making payments on for a little while and would have to pay some more on. But I'm going to pay it off somehow, and I'm going to give that car to PTL today . . . my nicest toy I've got, and I'm going to give it to pay TV stations. I believe that that seed faith that I'm going to give is going to begin an avalanche of giving.

The antique car was the 1953 Rolls that the *Observer* had disclosed eleven months earlier. Bakker had been complaining about his monthly payments on the car, Dortch told me a few days later in an unusual moment of candor. Bakker was a man who tired quickly of his toys; he had driven the Rolls just five times, and the car had been driven fewer than eight hundred miles since its purchase a year earlier. Though Bakker was serious about giving PTL the car to buy airtime, it would never be used for that purpose. Instead, it would remain garaged on PTL property for another seven months.

One year earlier, Bakker had doused a late-summer financial crisis with money from the new Towers partnerships. Now, the executives on the third floor responded to Bailey's warnings with a serious, if belated, effort to cut costs. PTL's land-buying ended abruptly. On August 30, Sherk had executed a contract to buy thirty-three acres of land for $82,500. A day or two later, Dortch informed Sherk that PTL didn't have money to complete the pending $11 million in purchases. On September 1, PTL failed, for the first of many times that fall, to live up to promises it had made in its land contracts.

On September 9, less than a month after PTL's board had voted to pursue financing for the Old Jerusalem project, PTL notified the Mississippi firm developing the plans that the project had been put on hold because money was tight. The firm had already completed $36,000 worth of work.

Bakker's September 12 checklist, prepared from the orders he dictated each day into a small tape recorder, reflected his growing concern. Bakker ordered that every PTL spot used on the network promote a PTL product for raising money. He ordered his staff to instruct finance to control losses. The next day, he planned a mailing to his partners designed to resemble a telegram. He dictated the text, soliciting hundred-dollar gifts in return for leather-bound Bibles.

The water park felt the axe as well. It had been another summer of frustration at the construction site; PTL had missed its second summer season. Don Barcus and Terry Zinger, owners of the firm building the park, realized that they couldn't cut costs enough to offset the effects of bad weather, PTL's inability to pay as originally promised, the project's escalating scale and their own miscalculation. They wrote to PTL in July 1985, explaining that in the seventy-two hours they had taken to conceptualize and bid the job in February 1984, they had

> accepted the design of, and had made an irreversible commitment in execution of a level of aesthetic treatment (primarily rockwork scopes), more than four times greater in scope than was contained in our conceptual budget, and that the cost . . . would be so great as to bankrupt our firm. . . .
> It is our fervent hope . . . recognizing that our dilemma arises largely out of our commitment (apparently, at times, to distraction) to delivering the truly one-of-a-kind attraction that we promised, that you will find it possible to view favorably an increase in project funding.

Barcus and Zinger proposed that PTL authorize another $1.3 million in addition to the $6.9 million called for in their latest revised contract. On PTL's behalf, Jim Swaim agreed to the increase, but he told REC that he didn't know where the money would come from. A few days later, Bakker toured the water park. He understood REC's predicament, he said. He was happy with the workmanship—it was as good or better than anything at Walt Disney World, he said—and he would try to help get the money.

Bakker returned on August 3, saying that he wanted to get the project rolling again. If he had money, he asked, could Barcus finish by Labor Day? Barcus told him that it was impossible. OK, Bakker said, but PTL needed the park finished by fall so that it could produce advertising for the next summer. Barcus agreed, and Bakker promised him another $500,000 the next day. The money arrived four days later.

As PTL agreed to the new price, REC billed PTL for the miscellaneous loans, extra jobs, and courtesy purchases the firm had made on the ministry's behalf. The invoice totaled more than $102,000. PTL's finance office seemed surprised by the bill, and PTL's internal auditor studied the water-park contracts and spending. It was the first and only close look PTL had taken at REC, a company Bakker's staff would later conclude was not equipped to manage the project—just as it would realize Swaim was ill-suited to oversee the job for PTL.

Dana Cadwell, the internal auditor, reported to her bosses that she expected the water park to cost PTL $10 million when all fees and costs were included. An overrun of at least $1.6 million, she wrote, "could have been avoided if we had required change orders for all the changes made. . . . We should begin to implement change orders for all projects we undertake so we won't be in this predicament again."

Though Bakker had declared he wanted the water park finished that fall, Barcus learned by late August that PTL had no more money. PTL had promised another payment, but none came. On September 3, 1985, the builder halted work; REC had stretched its cash reserves to the limit. Barcus drafted a handwritten letter to Swaim, which ended with an apology. "I'm sorry that this action must be taken but REC . . . cannot continue to fund this project." PTL agreed to pay REC for "all work performed to date." REC valued that work at nearly $1.9 million. PTL decided to finish the water park itself, with help from REC's chief subcontractor.

The job would take nine months more.

CHAPTER SIXTEEN

THE IRS AUDIT

"The IRS is not in favor of success"

On a Saturday morning in June 1985, Jim Bakker and his daughter Tammy Sue walked into a Mazda dealership on the south side of Charlotte. Sitting in a brown, top-of-the-line RX-7 in the showroom, the teenager announced to her father. "This is the car I want, only I want it in black." Bakker tried to persuade her to consider a less expensive sports car, but she wanted the GSL SE, with a sunroof, stereo, graphic equalizer, eighty-cubic-inch engine, and a $17,000 price tag. Her bodyguard had leased an RX-7 a month before, and Tammy Sue—fifteen, with no driver's license or learner's permit—wanted one just like it.

Soon Tammy Sue was driving the new car around the Heritage USA grounds, her bodyguard in the seat next to her or in a car behind. A vanity tag on the front bumper carried her name. Her classmates and PTL's employees assumed that Jim and Tammy Bakker had purchased the car for their daughter. In fact, PTL had provided the money.

The transaction was a measure of how freely PTL's money and perks now flowed into the Bakkers' pockets. Bakker's corporate identity and private life were joined seamlessly. His daughter was not old enough to drive, but Bakker had deemed it proper for the ministry to provide a sports car for her to drive freely on the grounds, despite warnings from security that she posed a threat to visitors and a liability nightmare for PTL.

By summer 1985, Bakker was marshaling the ministry's resources to turn young Tammy Sue into a singing star. A few days after shopping for the Mazda, Bakker instructed David Taggart to have a PTL musician produce her work and to hire a Charlotte studio to record her first disc. A few weeks later, he told his staff that he wanted Tammy Sue performing live at Heritage USA. When Bakker discovered that his daughter wasn't getting the live backup musicians he had requested, he burst out angrily, "What do I have to do, quit my job to manage my own daughter's affairs?" At PTL expense, Tammy Sue traveled that summer to the annual gathering of Christian recording artists in Estes Park, Colorado, to get exposure to the gospel-music world. That fall, she began the studio work on her first album. PTL assigned a $16,500-a-year employee to be her manager. Eventually, Tammy Sue would quietly receive more than $50,000 in royalties from PTL.

That summer, PTL began adding another 1,168 square feet to the Bakkers' home on the lake, at a cost of more than $41,000. The addition included a new bedroom and bathroom and alterations in the master bedroom—a bay window with a seat, a fireplace of the finest-quality stone, a spa by the pool.

As the work began, a neighbor noticed a new trench cutting down PTL property next to Bakker's house. He telephoned the city of Tega Cay and asked if Bakker had a permit to build a water slide. He had none. At the house, a city inspector discovered a trench 327 feet long and three feet wide running from the top of a hill to the lake—the planned site of a fiberglass water slide. PTL had already erected a wooden deck at the top. After a story in the local paper and a warning from the city that it needed a building permit, PTL halted the project, covered the hole, and landscaped the site. As Bakker told it years later, the project had begun when his son played with a store-bought plastic water slide on a hill next to the house. Bakker and another neighbor had then decided to erect a more substantial slide. They were going to share the cost, Bakker said. Bakker could not explain why PTL had spent $8,500 on the project.

I asked Dortch about the water slide a few weeks after the building inspector discovered the open trench. "What is Jim Bakker worth to this ministry?" Dortch asked rhetorically. He told me that Bakker had done most of the work on the water slide himself in a show of commitment to his son. Then, Dortch said, "I think some other people said, 'We'll help. Let's make it something a little nicer.'" It was difficult to imagine Bakker dirtying his hands on such a job. He might pick up a hammer or shovel for the cameras, but off the air he preferred to bark orders or dream up new projects.

The Bakkers had given their children everything but time—"everyone else is raising my kids," Tammy complained one day—and to those around the Bakkers, the wreckage was plain to see. After her inaugural concert at Heritage USA in 1985, Tammy Sue sobbed to her young bodyguard, Beth Mills, "I can't believe my mom and dad weren't there. Beth, I feel as if you're my mom." As she entered her late teens, Tammy Sue experimented with drugs and dated an older boy who had been fired from his job as a Heritage Grand bellboy when he was caught in a room with a girl. Tammy Sue got the boyfriend rehired as a lifeguard at the water park.

The two Tammys fought. Tammy Faye seemed uneasy competing with another singer in the family. She was torn between giving her daughter the trappings of wealth and making her live more as Tammy Faye had lived in International Falls. Those were the days Tammy Sue got five dollars in spending money instead of a hundred, the days she was told she couldn't shop at Lillie Rubin or buy a $20,000 car.

Jamie Charles, nearly six years younger, could usually count on the hundred dollars, and he had come to expect the royal treatment he saw his father demand. He was accustomed to having security guards as playmates. Often, even if his mom or dad was home, it was up to a PTL employee to put him to bed. Sometimes in anger, sometimes in jest, and sometimes in what seemed a cry for attention, he would lash out at a guard who defied him, "You're fired! My daddy said I could fire you!"

The Bakkers were still no more successful at marriage than they were at raising a family. They showed little affection in private. Tammy seemed angry at Jim half the time, one friend remembered. They could agree on little. Tammy liked to eat fast, Jim liked to sit and enjoy his meals. She liked noise all the time, he liked quiet. Usually Tammy and her hot temper prevailed.

Bakker continued to turn to his male staff members for sexual release. One day in the summer of 1985, a Bakker aide discovered Bakker and Taggart together in Bakker's bedroom in his presidential suite at the Heritage Grand. Bakker was lying on the bed, nude. Taggart, fully dressed, was massaging Bakker's testicles. The sight made the aide sick to his stomach. Afterwards, Taggart pulled him aside, saying matter-of-factly, "If you tell, nobody's going to believe you." The aide didn't tell until long after Bakker's resignation, when a federal grand jury wanted to know what he had seen. It had been his job at PTL to help Bakker, not to spy on him. He suspected that Taggart was right, too; nobody would have believed, even if both men had accused Bakker of sexual activity with men. And the aide felt—and would continue to feel, long after Bakker's departure—a strong allegiance to his one-time boss, David Taggart.

The Bakkers relied on members of their inner circle to keep peace at home. Taggart fought fires. So did Vi Azvedo and, in the final years, gospel singer Doug Oldham and his wife Laura Lee. Oldham was an established figure in gospel music, a man who could enhance PTL's stature just as Dortch had. Fifty-four years old, Oldham was thinking about retiring, particularly after a cancer operation that had cost the heavyset man two feet of colon and four feet of small intestine.

One night in the winter of 1985, during Bakker's three-month stay in his presidential suite, Bakker padded down to the lobby in some dreadful-looking knitted slippers, an unusual glaring lapse of taste, to meet Oldham. A few months earlier, Oldham had suggested that Bakker start a record company at PTL. "You're the president of my record company," Bakker told him that night. Oldham laughed. "Hey, I can't even keep myself afloat. I've got an attorney and my wife handles all my finances, and I'm still in debt. I make a lot of money, but I don't know how to spend it."

Bakker told Oldham that he wasn't worried. "I can buy MBA's for $25,000 a year all day long. I want your name. I know your body isn't working well. I've been on the road. Nobody ever says thank you to anybody on the road." Soon, Oldham arrived with a salary of $155,000 and a generous package of perks—insurance, a house, a company car, and a staff job for his piano player. Oldham began work in May. In fine PTL tradition, the Oldham family—

Laura Lee, two of the Oldhams' daughters, and a son-in-law—were soon employed at PTL.

Little came of Oldham's association with PTL's record company. Instead, he and Laura Lee became the Bakkers' companions, the latest in a line of what some PTL employees called "paid friends." Laura Lee joined Tammy on her relentless shopping trips. In addition to his emerging role as Bakker's favored TV co-host, Oldham became a willing ear for Bakker's latest vision, be it a new ride at the water park or a new hotel built next to a smoking man-made volcano.

During PTL's 1985 Fourth of July parade, Dortch presented Bakker with a gift he said came from PTL's board—a replica of a 1938 Mercedes Gazelle that had cost PTL $23,270. As he listened to Dortch's presentation, Ernie Franzone was stunned. The board had never discussed such a gift during Franzone's service of nearly a year as a PTL director. Nearby, longtime board member A. T. Lawing grinned and smiled for the cameras. The gift was news to him too, and privately he wondered how much it had cost.

The board met the next afternoon. At Bakker's suggestion, the directors voted Dortch a $50,000 bonus and a vacation trip paid for by PTL. A few minutes later, the board was asked—the minutes do not say by whom—to consider bonuses for Jim and Tammy Bakker. The motion passed unanimously. Bakker got $200,000, Tammy got $50,000.

Despite his enormous bonuses, Bakker had successfully perpetuated the myth that his pay was modest. That summer, the editor-publisher of board member Charles Cookman's hometown newspaper published a glowing tribute to PTL after a trip to Heritage USA.

> You read outrageous stories about the amount of money [Bakker] makes.
>
> He's probably the most underpaid man in the United States.
>
> But a man in private business running a $150-million-a-year enterprise would probably get a salary of over a half million a year, plus perks worth another hundred thousand, or more.
>
> "Money itself and worldly things have little appeal to Jim Bakker except that it can help to provide things like Heritage

USA and help bring people to the Lord," pointed out Dr. Dortch. "He would walk away from everything here today without a dime in his pocket and tomorrow he'd be starting something for the Lord even bigger and better. That's the kind of man he is."

Think about it, a superstar like Barbara Walters gets over a million dollars a year. . . . Jim and Tammy Bakker are on television every day for an hour or two and get only a tiny fraction of what Barbara Walters earns. Yet, the liberal press has the gall to criticize him. Whatever Jim and Tammy Bakker get, they deserve even more.

In fact, Bakker had earned nearly $900,000 in salary, bonuses, housing allowance, and retirement contributions during the recently completed budget year. In the next year, he would break $1 million; other remuneration would push the IRS's tally of Bakker's total compensation over $2 million. Tammy's salary and bonuses added another $340,000.

Of course Bakker—so quick to jump on inaccuracies that showed him in an unfavorable light—did nothing to correct the newspaper's erroneous characterization of his pay. Indeed, Bakker jokingly suggested on the air that PTL might send the story from the Dunn, North Carolina, *Daily Record* to all its partners. "My staff wouldn't write that nice about me."

At dinner on September 9, 1985, the Bakker clan celebrated Raleigh and Furn Bakker's anniversary inside the elder Bakker's new home on the grounds of Heritage USA. A PTL staff photographer was summoned to take snapshots. When Jim's mother complained about the air conditioning and Bakker himself couldn't get it working properly, the PTL president ordered a security guard to summon a PTL maintenance worker. While other residents had to wait for help from the outside contractor, Bakker could snap his fingers and get instant service from the ministry; within minutes, a group of workmen descended. The next day, Bakker ordered his staff to see that the air conditioning was repaired, along with his parents' whirlpool bath. "Get that fixed right away."

After moving to Charlotte in mid-1978, Raleigh and Furn Bakker had volunteered at PTL as greeters, attending Jim's show and serving as surrogates for their elusive son. In 1979, PTL made much of the Bakkers' willingness to give their time to PTL "unto the Lord"—for free. "The elder Bakkers are not, nor ever have been, on PTL salary," a friendly magazine article asserted.

This situation changed, quietly, as Bakker ignored federal tax rules and further risked PTL's tax-exempt status by using his control over the ministry to benefit his parents. In 1980, Bakker ordered his staff to clean his father's car and gas it up "for when he's using it here at Heritage USA to do his tours." By 1983, the elder Bakkers were apparently using a PTL car and living in a PTL condo. Recognizing that the IRS might claim this arrangement was private inurement, PTL found other ways to accommodate the elder Bakkers. A car was leased to Raleigh Bakker, ostensibly at cost; in fact, the IRS later alleged, PTL subsidized nearly half the leasing cost. Jim Bakker bought the condo units where his parents and Tammy's mother and stepfather resided. Public deeds indicated that Bakker had paid $54,900 for each unit. In fact, according to the IRS, Bakker received a $18,548 discount off the combined price. Since Raleigh now had to pay rent to cover his son's costs, he was added to the payroll, joining Bakker's sister, brother, brothers-in-law, sister-in-law, mother-in-law, and several nephews and nieces.

PTL came to the rescue again in 1985 after Jim Bakker chose a new $94,750 house for his parents. Again, Bakker bought the property and rented it back to his parents. Four days after notifying his staff that he had picked the unit, Bakker ordered his mother put on PTL's payroll "at about $150 a week or something in that neighborhood." She was added the next day. By 1987, both of the elder Bakkers would be earning $17,000 a year.

Living alongside the Bakkers, it was easy to become a taker. The Bakkers could be terribly generous with their friends, often at PTL expense. A house on the lake, a PTL car, a big salary, very generous bonuses, and hundred-percent medical insurance helped cement loyalties and compensate for the Bakkers' around-the-clock demands. Perhaps, too, the perks hardened the Bakkers' companions to the excesses of the royal family.

Though not a social companion of the Bakkers, Dortch enjoyed the same pampered life that, as a board member, he had helped give Bakker. He brought with him from Illinois a $28,500 executive caretaker for his new PTL house. The caretaker's duties included washing, drying, and vacuuming Dortch's car each day, rendering the same service to his wife's and his daughter's cars, cleaning and gassing up Dortch's boat, and making sure his household was never out of Dole strawberry popsicles. The corporate jet gave Dortch easier access to his frequent speaking engagements, even though it made little economic sense for PTL; the chief pilot alone added a $50,000 salary PTL's payroll didn't need. As PTL aggressively cut costs in fall 1985, the ministry moved ahead with the addition of a room and deck to Dortch's PTL-owned lakefront home. Messner later submitted an invoice for $53,000. At the same time, the third floor purchased nearly $20,000 in furniture for Dortch's home.

The rest of PTL's enthusiastic board also did well by the ministry. Whether by design or by instinctive generosity, Bakker and Dortch further compromised the board's independence. They began paying board members larger sums for their work, apparently without the board's approving the compensation. They also rewarded the faithful in other ways. In July 1985, PTL donated $50,000 to Cortese's church in the Bronx in gratitude for her help with Hahn. During 1985, PTL paid the tuition of Cortese's daughter, a former PTL employee, at North Central Bible College. PTL had given a son of Charles Cookman a $28,000-a-year job, though he would later be released after a conflict with Bakker, and the ministry generously supported the North Carolina district of the Assemblies of God. For years, PTL rented warehouse space from A. T. Lawing at an annual cost as high as $32,400. Though Ernie Franzone had no church and no warehouses, he was picked for a seat on the board after PTL hired his employer, Brock Hotel Corporation, to manage the Heritage Grand. Should Franzone rebel, he would realize later, he might jeopardize Brock's interests.

In the loose moral and managerial climate Bakker fostered, where reckless initiative was more important than playing by the rules, it was inevitable that some individuals dipped into the tremendous river of money flowing through the ministry. In 1985, PTL's internal auditor discovered that a PTL executive and a member of his staff had been steering music royalty payments to themselves for several years. The two staff members were quietly let go, but PTL had lost tens of thousands of dollars.

* * *

A man with little patience for the minutiae of finance or law, Bakker was obsessed with the aesthetics of Heritage USA. He ducked into bathrooms and found broken hand dryers. He visited PTL's carousel and fumed about burned-out bulbs. He observed the piano player in the hotel lobby and complained about the ugly kitchen fan cooling her off. He drove the roads of Heritage USA and spotted signs with peeling paint. He walked up the Main Street mall and rebelled at the coin-operated The Day You Were Born robot.

Bakker's daily checklists—the transcript of his recorded orders which his staff converted into a stream of memos to offending staff members—illustrated how thoroughly consumed Bakker was by his job. The checklists reek with the scent of irritation, sometimes with the stench of rage. On a particularly bad day, August 5, 1985, Bakker found enough complaints to fill seven typewritten pages; Heritage USA was not living up to his Dutch standards. Bakker, the man who hated to hear bad news from his staff, had nothing but for them that day.

> I am very dissatisfied with the condition of that [drug]store—the lack of merchandise and the crumminess of the counters. It is not a Heritage USA standard and something must be done. We may have to either negotiate them out of the contract or force them to get the quality put into the store that is the PTL standard here. This looks like Carowinds [a theme park just a short drive away from Heritage USA], not Disney World. . . .
>
> Send a memo to all the store managers to try to cut down on the junk and boxes piled in the stores. Get that trash taken to the dumpsters. . . .
>
> There has been filth outside of the side entrance door next to the water park. . . . Ice cream cones and filth have just been laying there for days. Maintenance and cleaning has got to be improved. . . .
>
> The lawns in front of the chalets by the water—the grass is about 2–3 feet tall. It needs to be mowed. There's some paper and trash in the lake. They need to police the lake and around the lake side. Also, in the petting zoo area there are some cans—trash, pop cans. . . .
>
> Send a memo to the Producers of the Sunday-morning TV show. . . . Be very careful about their close-ups. They're get-

ting so many people frowning and talking to each other. Use wider audience shots from the back and front. Use wide shots and broad shots and then varied shots of the pulpit and the church service itself. It looks so bad to see people picking their noses, people talking to each other, and people frowning. It doesn't encourage people at all. . . . If we're going to get close-ups, make sure . . . they're going to get bright, happy people. And try to balance with youth as well as old people so that there's a variety of people, so people will feel some connection with their age group no matter what it is.

Perhaps correcting these cosmetic problems gave Bakker a sense of control over an institution that more and more defied anyone's command. Perhaps Bakker's anger helped avert his attention from his responsibility for many of the problems he found.

While bulbs were changed, signs painted, and trash picked up, PTL's internal systems suffered. The people, procedures, and equipment that enable a corporation to function smoothly lacked the cosmetic impact Bakker cared about so dearly. There was often not enough money for daily expenses. Upper-level management meddled constantly, often to please Bakker, sometimes to compensate for its own inadequacies. Department heads who knew how to save money and steer clear of operational problems rarely had a chance to shape Bakker's projects. Little concern was shown for the staff. That fall, a middle-level manager complained by memo.

Upper management is so concerned with pleasing the partner that they forget about the front line employee who is "busting his fanny" every day in order to do a good job. . . . As it now stands PTL views its employees as expendable and without individual merit. PTL's position is, "if they don't like what's going on, there's the door." Thus you have a high turnover rate, huge discontent among the staff, and a real sense of disloyalty or dissension. . . .

This ministry has more specialized talent in the form of personnel than any company I have ever worked for. There are people here with talent and ideas that are being wasted. . . .

I feel that the strongest trait in this ministry is the dedication and love that the PTL staff has for our Lord Jesus Christ. Without this commitment to the Lord, PTL would crumble under the weight of its own inefficiency.

The *Observer* and PTL had continued their efforts at détente in 1985. A busload of *Observer* staff members toured Heritage USA. The newspaper published a routine article about the PTL girls' home. In a tougher story, the paper got PTL to explain why social-services agencies in the area complained about poor people who came to Heritage USA expecting work and ended up relying on the local agencies for food, shelter, and tickets home.

In spring 1985, Dortch invited me to lunch. He enjoyed meeting over a meal as much as Bakker disliked it. In Illinois, he had often gathered his top-level staff members and big-name guests like Swaggart and Bakker for meals inside the Lake Williamson center's Fireside Room. At PTL, Dortch held court at lunchtime in the hotel's elegant wood-paneled restaurant, the Hampton Court.

Dortch seemed eager to ingratiate himself. He was a master, cheerful and talkative, with a way of packaging his words that made you feel he was speaking from the heart, really leveling with you. Later, I wondered whether he hoped, by winning my trust, to improve the odds that I would not pursue the story Jessica Hahn had told me that winter.

That day, Dortch wanted to introduce me to Neil Eskelin, PTL's new vice president for public relations. Eskelin had spent seventeen of his forty-six years on the staff of Evangel College, an Assemblies of God liberal-arts school whose board Dortch had chaired for nearly a decade. He was a short, friendly man with a smile that could survive the rainiest day. During the fifties, Eskelin, his mother, father, and sister had toured the country as the Musical Eskelin Family. Out of graduate school in 1961, Eskelin joined Pat Robertson's new TV station in Portsmouth with a salary of forty dollars a week. He left CBN before Jim and Tammy Bakker arrived, traveling the circuit of high schools and churches as a speaker before taking a job in 1967 teaching broadcasting at Evangel in Springfield, Missouri. Eventually, he took the post of director of development.

After lunch, Dortch orchestrated a small press conference in the hotel lobby, announcing that PTL was buying transponder time from Home Box Office on Galaxy, the premier cable satellite. Dortch refused to disclose the cost, which was nearly $208,000 a month. With this second satellite—PTL was already transmitting on the older RCA Satcom III at a cost of $140,000 a month—PTL's satellite network was now available to every cable system in the country. PTL shared that good news, but it chose not to reveal that the added cost would at least temporarily push the network into a monthly operating loss of $100,000.

Nearly a year had passed since the first push for Towers partnerships, and once again Bakker spoke ominously about losing stations. In early 1985, I had talked with a local TV broker frustrated by PTL's failure to cut its airtime debts as Bakker had promised when he unveiled the Towers project. "What galls me is they keep asking for money from these people, and they never pay off on time," the broker complained.

To gauge the gravity of PTL's problems, my editor and I recruited several reporters and contacted more than 110 of PTL's 170-plus broadcast stations. The hint of renewed scrutiny upset PTL. Bakker complained on the air that our phone calls had nearly caused a run on the bank—immediate demands that PTL pay back debts—even though we were simply following up the apocalyptic statements Bakker himself had been making to his viewers.

On September 9, Dortch, Eskelin, and Walter Richardson, the man in charge of PTL's network of affiliated broadcast stations, answered my questions in a conference room at the *Observer.* I asked Dortch why PTL had not retired its airtime debts with the Towers money. His answer suggested that PTL's problem was the growing cost of the Towers, not diversion of the Towers partnership money.

> We want to make sure we're keeping our commitment to our partners . . . that we built that thing as we said we were going to do.
> Well, no building ends up costing what you say it's going to.
> . . . I don't care whether it's your house or the Partner Center.

Dortch claimed he didn't know how much PTL had raised in lifetime partnerships. In fact, his staff issued regular reports.

The article on airtime debts was published the next weekend. "PTL, dogged by money and management problems in past years, is again facing questions about how it operates, this time from TV stations." Some TV stations had expressed skepticism at PTL's claims that it had no money when the ministry was spending millions on new construction. I quoted an Oklahoma City station official who had just canceled Bakker's show. "It's a religious runaround. It's my opinion that a Christian organization pays their bills first and foremost. They shouldn't have gone into this building program if they couldn't pay their bills."

The article gave ample play to Dortch's apology for any commitments to its affiliated TV stations that PTL had not honored. Eskelin called to say that PTL considered my news story balanced and fair, though PTL was offended by a critical editorial several days later. Despite Eskelin's praise, Bakker represented my story to his TV audience as another hatchet job. The article—magnified the size of a living-room rug and hung prominently on a wall of the set—was the centerpiece of the PTL "Brink of a Miracle" telethon that opened on October 7. Bakker complained about the headline, which Eskelin had told me would be a big help in PTL's fund-raising. Bakker evidently agreed. "For some reason, the press is very anxious for PTL to die . . . when I built the Heritage Grand we didn't get a headline like that on the front page."

The next morning, the Bakkers sailed through a gentle interview on ABC's "Good Morning, America" show. ABC's David Hartman asked if Bakker found it difficult to be criticized. "I grew up as a very bashful boy, and I think the inferiority complex of your youth, somehow when you hear criticism, it reinforces that feeling from your childhood." Bakker worked the same theme on his program. "If you say you like criticism, I think you're strange." Speaking to singer-producer Jeanne Johnson, Bakker asked, "Jeanne, would you like someone to come up and say 'Jeanne, you're ugly'?" Bakker asked for a show of hands from those who agreed. As always, Bakker got the chorus he needed so badly. *"Charlotte Observer,* none of my partners like to be criticized either. So there."

The telethon, with its pitched talk of us against them, made for a healthy October. Nearly $6.7 million in general contributions flowed into the ministry, the best monthly tally of the year and a sweet complement to the previous month's take of nearly $5 million. Lifetime partnerships had bounced back up as well. After two slow months, PTL took in close to $2.4 million in partnerships in October. For now, finance had a little breathing room.

From the start, PTL had been a round peg in a square hole for the Evangelical Council for Financial Accountability, an organization set up in 1979 to promote good financial practices in Christian ministries. When PTL applied for membership in fall 1979, ECFA asked that PTL's board of three be expanded to at least six and preferably nine members. Three directors were added, but ECFA put off accepting PTL's membership while the FCC continued its investigation of PTL's fund-raising for overseas missions. Finally, in April 1981—several months after an initial, confidential five-to-four vote to decline PTL's bid for membership—ECFA accepted PTL.

ECFA required its member organizations to meet several standards for "responsible stewardship." Members had to disclose audited financial statements to anyone who asked, including the press. They had to adhere to "the highest standards of integrity," avoid conflicts of interest, and ensure that appeals for money clearly identified the way the money would be used. Members were also required to make sure the donations were used for those purposes.

The ECFA seal displayed at the close of Bakker's program conveyed the squeaky-clean image that Bakker wanted to promote. PTL used its ECFA membership to maximum advantage, declaring it proof of the ministry's accountability. But behind the scenes, PTL's performance as an ECFA member had been anything but exemplary.

After Bakker's Florida condominium was discovered in early 1983, PTL failed to satisfy ECFA's worries about internal management and the performance of the board of directors. Later that year, ECFA suggested that PTL enlarge its board, call board meetings more often, create board committees to oversee major aspects of the ministry, and require board approval for budgets for all major projects. In early 1984, despite assurances from Bakker and the newly arrived Dortch, ECFA decided to shelve PTL's annual membership application until it got "accurate, complete, and current information" indicating that PTL was expanding its board and taking control of the ministry's budget, consistent with an ECFA standard requiring governance by a "responsible board."

In a June 1984 response, Bakker told ECFA executive director Art Borden that PTL expected to add two board members by year's end. Bakker defended PTL's heavy spending on buildings, a sticky point with ECFA. "It is the express concern of the [PTL] board that we be sensitive to the Holy Spirit's ministry in attempting to meet people's needs here at Heritage USA and not to try to predeter-mine the percentage of total income that we spend for these specific needs—because we believe it is all ministry."

Bakker told ECFA that his ministry had put a budget into opera-tion on June 1, 1984. "We do believe as strongly as you do that a well-defined operational budget and capital budget, with strict controls, is a 'must,' and we are already on track in this matter." In fact, budget director Speakman had encountered little more than frustration. Just four days before Bakker's letter—but after the June 1 date cited by Bakker—Speakman warned Dortch by memo about a pattern of deficit spending. "Lean and strict budgets [must] be developed and *tightly* adhered to," he wrote.

Bakker's June 1984 letter quoted an excerpt from the minutes of the PTL board's November 1983 meeting. ECFA had asked for evidence that the directors had authorized the initial offering of twenty-five thousand lifetime partnerships at a thousand dollars apiece. In fact, the official minutes didn't document any such autho-rization. They said only that "a tentative proposal for raising the funds was presented to the board." But the "minutes" quoted in Bakker's correspondence presented the picture ECFA wanted to see:

> Proposal was made for the raising of the funds for the [hotel] project. The plan shall be that twenty-five thousand Lifetime Partner Memberships shall be offered at one thousand dollars each for the securing of $25 million towards the building and payment for the project. The details of the program shall be committed to the Executive Committee.

In August 1984, PTL secured ECFA's uneasy approval of its membership application, but disclosure of the Bakkers' home and cars in California prompted further scrutiny from ECFA. Dortch—then in the midst of his efforts to suppress the Jessica Hahn threat—railed against the *Charlotte Observer* in a letter to ECFA. "If any of us would have been under the microscope as the Bakkers have in this community, I am sure that some big revelation would have come out that could have hurt any of us."

As Dortch negotiated the $265,000 settlement with Paul Roper in February 1985, ECFA's board again voted to hold PTL's annual membership application in abeyance. Executive director Art

Borden's March 25 letter informing PTL of the decision showed ECFA's growing frustration with the gap between PTL's rhetoric and its actions.

> [We] have frequently heard from PTL that financial account-
> ability and integrity are important issues, yet little real substan-
> tive progress appears to have been made.

Too much money was still being used to solicit donations and pay management and general expenses, prompting "serious questions about whether donations are used for the purposes for which they are raised," Borden wrote. PTL had added only one board member in 1984, not the two Bakker had pledged. ECFA wanted the board expanded to eleven.

PTL's problems with ECFA worsened in early June 1985. A Christian TV station in Lima, Ohio, complained to the accountabil-ity group about Bakker's chronic late payments—the very issue the *Observer* would take up a few months later. The station, WTLW, also belonged to the accountability group.

> At this point, Jim is eight months late with his payments or
> $28,135 behind in his commitment.
>   Ironically, I took a loan in December for $33,000 to pur-
> chase three new cameras and paid it off last week with $1,700
> in interest charges. . . .
>   I don't think it's fair for one Christian organization to oper-
> ate on another's capitol [sic], unless permission is granted.

ECFA also learned that Franzone, the sole board member added in 1984, was an executive for Brock Hotel Corporation, the firm PTL had hired to manage its hotel. In a letter dated July 12, 1985, ECFA again raised questions about PTL's conduct.

A month later, the four ministers on PTL's board—Bakker, Dortch, Cookman, and Cortese—met in a hotel in San Antonio, where they had come to attend the Assemblies of God general council and to support Dortch's unsuccessful bid for a place in the denomination's national leadership. A month remained before the deadline for a response to ECFA's queries, but the third floor had another solution. Board minutes recorded a brief discussion of ECFA.

> Reverend Dortch proposed that Heritage Village Church and
> Missionary Fellowship, Inc., withdraw from ECFA. A motion
> was made, seconded, and passed unanimously.

Though its board had voted PTL out of ECFA, PTL did not
disclose the decision to the accountability group. In fact, ECFA
heard nothing from PTL at all. On October 15, ECFA's standards
committee recommended that PTL's membership be terminated.
The next day, ECFA's board met in Chicago. For two years, the
board was told, the council had been trying to bring PTL into
compliance. The board agreed, unanimously, to drop PTL and
decided not to report the decision as a less embarrassing "non-
renewal." Within days, a Charlotte TV station began asking PTL
about the status of its ECFA membership.

Saying nothing about their August vote to withdraw, Bakker and
Dortch protested to ECFA. Dortch asserted that he had mailed a
partial response to ECFA's inquiries the summer before. PTL
claimed that Dortch's assistant had failed to mail the response.

ECFA's board agreed to give PTL a reprieve. Executive director
Art Borden, a well-meaning man with a natural trust in and protective instinct toward his member organizations, refused even to
confirm that the board had voted to terminate. "We are a Christian
organization dealing with other Christian organizations. If we've
got to go the extra mile, we'll go the extra mile." Borden released
a statement saying ECFA and PTL had been "in discussion" about
full compliance. He would not specify PTL's problems. Bakker told
the press that ECFA "simply [had] a need for more accounting
information" and wanted a larger board of directors. In fact,
ECFA's concerns were far more profound.

Faced with a public-relations disaster, Bakker counterattacked.
He sought to discredit a local TV report suggesting that PTL had
been booted out of ECFA. Bakker told his viewers that the report
was "the most hyped-up stuff that you ever saw in your life . . . it's
just unbelievable, unstory story. . . . It's not even a story, and it was
built on rumor really." Bakker railed at ECFA in a letter and in
private calls to Borden. He complained that a "vicious" ECFA
board member had leaked word of the Chicago meeting at the
worst time for PTL, "just when I am endeavoring to pay all my bills

current." The ECFA executive director later drafted a memo excerpting Bakker's comments over the phone.

> All the media wants to do is to try to get one Christian against the other. . . .
> It has been reported to me by a number of Christian leaders that ECFA is just set up to protect Billy Graham. I know that it is reported that he gets a salary of only $50,000. I also know that he receives over $1 million a year from other corporations set up to receive . . . other income. . . . I don't see why ECFA is picking on me about my house.
> We just had the best telethon that we have ever had and our accounts payable should be current in about thirty days.

Bakker told Borden he was leery of putting just anyone on PTL's board.

> Jim is paranoid (his term) about getting people on the board that just want to use him and take advantage of the privileges and prestige of being on the PTL board. He admits that his contacts in the business world are so limited that he does not know where to turn to get the kind of help that both he and we realize that he needs.

Even as Bakker put ECFA on the defensive, he also moved to placate the organization. A day after writing to Borden that the board planned two more meetings in 1985, Bakker ordered Taggart "to schedule a board meeting as soon as possible. And we need to make sure we're having an adequate number of board meetings." The board met three weeks later.

By then, the board had hurriedly acquired two more members, though not the three or four Bakker had described in a letter to ECFA. The choices assured that the board would remain under the control of Bakker and Dortch. One new member was J. Don George, the respected Assemblies of God pastor at whose Irving, Texas, church Dortch had preached eleven months earlier. Dortch had known George for years. Bakker had spoken at dedication services for George's new five-thousand-seat church in April 1985. Looking at the barren site, he had offered to pay for landscaping. But PTL did not send the $100,000 to cover the work until a week after Bakker announced George's appointment, long after the church had hoped to have the cash.

On November 12, Bakker welcomed a second newcomer, the Reverend Evelyn Carter Spencer. Spencer, a former nurse now serving as co-pastor of the 250-member House of Truth in Oakland, California, was a regular guest on PTL. She was also black, an indication of PTL's interest in strengthening its interracial appeal. During the late seventies, Bakker had given Spencer a PTL Cadillac. "We've loved you for years, and now you can tell me what to do," Bakker said on his show as he introduced Spencer as his newest board member. "Now you're my boss, isn't that wild?"

Two hours later, the board met on the third floor of the World Outreach Center. The minutes recorded a discussion of ECFA and a vote undoing the August decision to withdraw.

> Mr. Bakker stated that the National Religious Broadcasters was in the process of organizing an association for accountability for broadcasters. Mr. Bakker requested that the Board consider a recommendation that, to keep the Corporation under the covering of an association for accountability, we withhold withdrawal from ECFA at this time. A motion was made, seconded, and passed unanimously.

As the third floor worked to contain the ECFA tempest, it faced a far greater threat—an IRS audit. For two years, the Internal Revenue Service had studied PTL's records. Now it was auditing Bakker's personal return as well. The PTL president was about to reap the harvest of his indifference towards federal laws governing tax-exempt charities.

After its first year studying PTL, the IRS had questioned the "reasonableness" of the Bakkers' compensation. In late 1984, the ministry's latest tax lawyers, the Charlotte firm of Caudle and Spears, warned in a memo:

> So long as Reverend Bakker and his family (and others), receive substantial compensation and benefits from the church with a "controlled," directly or indirectly, board of directors, the issue of private inurement will continue to threaten the tax-exempt status of the church.

The IRS had also raised a second issue: whether many of PTL's quasi-commercial activities had a "substantial relationship" to PTL's tax-exempt purposes. If the IRS could show they did not, PTL could lose its tax exemption and eventually face an enormous bill for back-taxes on the tens of millions of dollars taken from lifetime partners.

The IRS had been looking aggressively at tax-exempt organizations that had expanded beyond their traditional activities to compete with for-profit companies, the businesses that generated tax dollars for the federal treasury. Tax law already required that exempt organizations like PTL pay taxes on "unrelated business income." Too much unrelated business income—ten to fifteen percent of gross receipts was a commonly accepted threshold—could jeopardize an organization's tax-exempt status.

Concerned that the IRS might find PTL's hotels—and the planned $60 million in lifetime partnerships—to be unrelated business income, Deloitte Haskins and Sells recommended in fall 1984 that PTL seek an IRS ruling on the exempt status of lodging at Heritage USA. The accounting firm and PTL's tax lawyers also proposed that PTL lease its new hotels to an outside firm to reduce the percentage of income PTL derived from potentially unrelated business activities. Deloitte Haskins and Sells recommended immediate, "critical" changes in PTL's organizational structure. It urged PTL to look ahead next time before it leaped.

> Since tax rules . . . are extremely complex and failure to meet these rules can place the exempt status of an entire organization in jeopardy, we recommend that the tax structure of any future organizations or any future expansion be considered before funds are solicited or construction has begun.

Loss of tax-exempt status could be disastrous for PTL. Donors would no longer be able to claim a charitable tax deduction for their contributions, eliminating a key incentive for giving to PTL. The publicity could sully the ministry's image. The financially fragile PTL would have to pay taxes on its entire income, not merely the portion from unrelated activities.

PTL chose to ignore several crucial recommendations from Deloitte Haskins and Sells and its tax lawyers. The ministry didn't seek a ruling from the IRS and didn't lease the hotel. The accounting firm was soon replaced, as the lawyers would be. On January 1, 1985, PTL transferred its lodging business, the lifetime-partnership monies, and other quasi-commercial activities from its for-profit subsidiary to the non-profit mother corporation. Instead of hedging its bets, PTL had decided to fight for the position that virtually everything it was doing at Heritage USA related to its tax-exempt purposes.

Fight was precisely what PTL would have to do. By October 25, 1985, the IRS had informed PTL that the government would propose revoking PTL's tax-exempt status for the full audit period, from June 1980 to May 1983. The IRS also said that it would likely take a similar position in later years, compounding PTL's financial exposure. Soon, the IRS was at work auditing records from June 1983 through May 1985.

In its report on the 1980–83 audit, the IRS asserted that auditors had found "numerous expenditures and transactions" that benefitted Bakker and other PTL officers personally and did not fulfill PTL's exempt purposes. The IRS had also found "numerous expenditures" that lacked proof of an exempt purpose.

The confidential document detailed numerous examples of Bakker's profiting personally beyond the IRS's standard of reasonable compensation. In the twelve months ending May 1983, Bakker had received $638,000 in various forms of compensation. The IRS considered $121,000 defensible. The IRS questioned specific expenses paid by PTL on Bakker's behalf, including the Florida condo and the flowers, newspapers, and decorative items bought during Bakker's 1982 trip to California for a face lift.

> Many of the expenditures appeared to be lavish or extravagant and, even if made in carrying on an exempt activity, would not meet the "ordinary and necessary" requirement [of the tax code], thus becoming a private-benefit expenditure.

The IRS reported as evidence tips as high as 119%, the two costly dinner parties at Cafe Eugene in 1981, Bakker's $350-a-night hotel suite in Hawaii in December 1980, and the purchase of various travel items for Bakker, including an $800 briefcase, a $70 address book, a $74 Gucci toilet kit, and a $120 Gucci pen.

PTL had defended the spending on Bakker's behalf, the IRS said.

> They do not agree with any issue raised in the report. They
> have presented no documentation but contend that all expen-
> ditures questioned were expended for exempt purposes. They
> further contend that the compensation paid to James O. Bak-
> ker was reasonable because he is the guiding light of the minis-
> try and is the key to PTL's success in fund-raising.

The IRS report raised an alternative set of issues, in case PTL was able to retain its tax-exempt status on appeal. PTL, though a religious organization, was not a church, the IRS claimed. PTL's partners had no vote within the organization. Its membership was not affiliated with any denomination (only the Heritage Village Church, not the entire corporation, was associated with the Assemblies of God). PTL's "worshippers" were scattered across the country and had no established relationship with their minister. And PTL's activities included promotion of the for-profit activities of Heritage USA.

Should PTL lose its status as a church, it would have to meet stringent record-keeping and reporting requirements. One of those reports would make Bakker's compensation—by now a carefully guarded secret at PTL—a matter of public record.

The IRS also challenged PTL's handling of its quasi-commercial activities. PTL clearly had had a thousand dollars or more in gross income from business unrelated to its tax-exempt purpose such as advertising, Christmas catalog sales, and sale of time on its satellite network, the IRS said. Once past that threshold, PTL was obliged to file returns or pay taxes on the unrelated business income. It had not.

The IRS report vindicated critics of Bakker's life-style. The IRS had concluded that Bakker lived lavishly at PTL expense. It had also found that PTL was breaking federal laws and regulations. The federal government, which had cut short its earlier inquiry into the conduct of Bakker's ministry, was now taking advantage of its second opportunity. The IRS report, however, was secret. PTL had the right to appeal, and appeal it did. When Bakker resigned seventeen months later, the contents of the IRS report remained a closely guarded secret, and PTL's appeals continued to work through IRS administrative channels.

* * *

In case the IRS story leaked out, Bakker had primed his staff and his TV audience subtly for bad news from the IRS. He framed the events without adhering to either truth or context, controlling damage to his image and authority and preserving the allegiance of his staff and partners. Able to blind himself to his own irresponsibility, he was able to condemn his accusers persuasively.

On October 11, Bakker summoned his top staff together to rail about the government and to take measures to strengthen PTL's defenses. As his employees listened, Bakker set out a plan for recasting PTL's image. For Bakker, image became reality.

> I am going to be a tad blunt this morning because you've got to start understanding the gravity of the situation. . . .
>
> We must never advertise this ministry as a resort, as a commercial entity. Every ad—and I've said it over and over again—must have the statement under Heritage USA, "An inspirational park." . . .
>
> The government is not a friend to the ministry—any ministry. . . . The federal government is pitted against us and all major ministries. I'm not talking off the top of my head; I'm talking from twenty-five years of experience . . . they are not after a slap on the hand, ladies and gentlemen. They want to get one big one and close it down as a precedent so they can continue their onslaught against ministries. . . .
>
> We are going to create our own reputation, and *we* must put out the facts ourselves of what *we* are. . . . I want a new sign made at the gate. . . . We tried to stay away from religious buzzwords. Now we're going back to religious buzzwords. Here's what this will say: "Welcome to Heritage USA, a 21st Century Christian Retreat Center." . . .
>
> The sign that says, "Heritage Grand Hotel—luxurious rooms," that sign must come down this week. Don't you ever advertise a luxurious hotel or anything concerned with hotel. We are not running a hotel. It is not a hotel. . . . I'll fight as long as I have breath in me to preserve the right to build a quality Christian center. . . .
>
> Labeling is everything. . . . Use ecclesiastical language on anything you write down. Today, for instance, your notes. . . . We cannot use the language of the world here. . . . If you want to know good terms, go to the Catholic terminologies. . . . They've got a word for everything—for every building, every action, and every deed. And the government is not about to close the Catholic church down.

Bakker complained about the tangle of tax rules PTL had to follow.

> I just want them, Brother Dortch, to understand a little of what we face. It's like trying to open a can of worms and getting them all to lay down in lines or something without wiggling. . . .
> And attorneys make the world go 'round. . . . I'm sure the lawmakers are all lawyers and they have done it to propagate their own business. . . . Life could be very simple if we had basic rules, but they're all open for interpretation. . . . We must be, as I said earlier, wise as serpents and harmless as doves. . . .
> One of the key things we must have is a booklet, a brochure, that says what this ministry is . . . we are a total church ministry. We minister to the total man. There really isn't a good broad term to say what we are. If you want one label, we are a church. Say that out loud—church.

So the IRS took its place alongside the *Observer,* the FCC, and local building inspectors as the forces that, in Bakker's words, "glorified littleness." Without explaining the background of his complaints, Bakker whined to his TV audience and church congregation about the ills of big government.

> As you grow up and you begin to try out your wings, you find out society doesn't really want you to achieve.
> You'll find out that as soon as you become big the IRS is very interested in you, and they're going to do everything they can to stop you, and they're going to take every loophole where a man can make money in America and close it up quick if they can. We find out the IRS is not in favor of success. . . .
> The larger a ministry grows, the more you become an enemy of Satan. . . . The government agencies seemingly are anti-Christ and anti-God and they try their best to find mistakes or something wrong in Christian ministry so they can come in to harass them and close them down. Do you all know that almost every preacher of a major proportion in this country literally lives with the federal government inside its organization looking every month for something to harass them about?

Soon the sign reading 21st Century Christian Retreat Center appeared at the entrance to Heritage USA. Bakker began planning a coffee-table book touting the ministries of PTL; privately he referred to it as "the IRS book." A November 17 video spot describing the Heritage Village Church boasted, "The heart of a pastor is evident in Reverend Jim Bakker every Sunday morning as he preaches to a congregation of over twenty-five hundred members, as he brokenheartedly presides over a funeral or joyfully joins couples in holy matrimony." In fact, Bakker was an evangelist by nature, not a pastor. He thrived on the high of celebrity, the rush of constant change. He didn't have the personality for the week-in, week-out grind of running a church. He kept his distance from the rank and file—one of his executives later said that Bakker loved crowds, but not people—and he usually disappeared behind his curtain of security when services were over. He lacked the depth and schooling to be an effective teacher of Scripture. He had had little wisdom to offer as a counselor.

Sunday services inside the Barn were a two-hour TV spectacular. The PTL Singers performed, as did the star singers from Bakker's weekday show. Bakker preached occasionally, but the congregation often listened to sermons by Dortch or a visiting star evangelist like Rex Humbard or Oral Roberts. The church, like PTL itself, was built on entertainment, not a solid foundation of teaching, soul-winning, and commitment.

In March 1985, Bakker received a three-page letter from Springfield, Missouri, writer and public speaker Doug Wead, the friend who had warned him years before of rumors about his relationship with Taggart. Two years earlier, Wead had tried to excite Bakker about the presidential candidacy of former Florida governor Reubin Askew. Askew "is moving up fast. He would love to be on PTL, and you could have the tape in the can in case he's elected president or vice president. . . . Sometimes helping somebody out early in the game pays huge dividends later. Anyway, he's born again, and a presidential contender. It would lend even more prestige to PTL and you."

As Askew faded from the race, Wead joined the camp of Vice President George Bush. The relationship would work out well for Wead. From a position on Bush's presidential-campaign staff recruiting support from religious groups, Wead took a White House staff position as special assistant to the president for public liaison after Bush's 1989 inauguration. Four years earlier, in a March 13, 1985, letter, Wead took up Bush's cause to Bakker.

> It is extremely important to PTL and the Kingdom of God that you have a good relationship with the president of the United States, and there is a very real possibility that George Bush could be that man . . .
> Now is the time to build a relationship before it looks too expedient. I sure would love for the vice president to get down to Heritage Village, stay in the hotel, and see how much bigger the evangelical movement is . . . Quite frankly, the predominating impression is of the well-scrubbed, closely cropped hair, students of [Jerry Falwell's] Liberty Baptist College.

Two months later, Wead arrived with two of Bush's political confidants, Pete Teeley and Ron Kaufman. Wead was eager to see PTL make a good impression. He arranged for PTL to fly the men in first class, and in an advance call to the third floor, Wead passed along word that Teeley and Kaufman were "Bush's closest friends and advisors" and should be put up in a plush suite. After talking with Wead, a secretary in the executive offices wrote, "Mr. Kaufman is Jewish and would be the blockage to V.P. Bush's coming to PTL, so he needs to be impressed with everything at PTL."

Teeley had served as Bush's press secretary for six years, leaving the vice president's staff in March 1985 to start his own Washington public relations firm. Kaufman held the title of political director for Bush's political action committee, the Fund for America's Future; after Bush's inauguration in 1989, he would become deputy White House personnel director. Both men would serve in the 1988 Bush campaign for president.

The morning of May 24, Teeley and Kaufman talked to an audience of one hundred upper- and middle-level managers at PTL. Employees at the meeting would remember talk of Bush's sympathy for evangelicals and PTL and suggestions that Bush would make a good friend for PTL if he succeeded Ronald Reagan in the White House. Teeley would recall talking about politically active ministers like Jerry Falwell; Teeley believed that religious leaders should stick to the work of their ministries and shy away from politics and controversial public-policy issues.

Before they left that afternoon, Teeley and Kaufman were each given a check for $5,000. Told about the payment years later, several of Bakker's former subordinates reacted with surprise at so generous a payment for what seemed to them a campaign speech; the sum seemed to demonstrate the third floor's willingness to use PTL's cash to curry favor with power brokers. To Teeley, PTL's payment was reasonable pay for a day's work, as were the bracelets PTL gave each man to give his wife. To explain the $700 spent for the jewelry, Taggart—who had confided to a colleague that he hoped one day to work in the White House—described Teeley and Kaufman on an internal PTL document as "White House Contacts."

On November 13, nearly seven months later, Jim Bakker notified his finance office that Teeley had agreed to be a consultant for PTL in Washington. Teeley held the position quietly until Bakker's resignation, offering advice on marketing, the IRS audit, and a new communications lawyer. Teeley was paid a monthly retainer of $5,000 and, later, $10,000. All in all, he would receive about $120,000 from PTL—not unusual pay for the work he did, Teeley said in 1989. Never, he added, did PTL ask him to lobby George Bush.

On November 8, 1985, shortly before Teeley's hiring, Bakker met with the vice president during Bush's politicking swing through Charlotte. The encounter inside a Charlotte office building lasted twenty minutes. Afterwards, Bush characterized it as a "very enjoyable, very friendly, no-agenda kind of meeting. . . . It was almost a social meeting." A Bush spokesman told the press that the two men discussed their Christian beliefs, the expected candidacy of Pat Robertson, and PTL's Heritage USA headquarters. Bush told reporters that he watched the PTL show "from time to time." Later that month, Bakker sent Wead a thank-you note for setting up the meeting with Bush.

> It was a very pleasant meeting. He is a warm and kind man and I felt the time together was beneficial to us both. Your advice was helpful in letting me know some of his interests and I thought he was receptive to the things I had to say.

Four days after Bakker's meeting with Bush, PTL's board met at Heritage USA. If there was any question about whether Bakker's pay would be trimmed to protect PTL from IRS claims, it was resolved in no uncertain terms on that day. Over Bakker's token opposition, the November 12 minutes show that the board voted bonuses for the Bakkers totaling $300,000. The IRS's formal audit report was mailed to PTL the next day.

CHAPTER SEVENTEEN

SECRETS REVEALED

"Tammy, they will not give up until they destroy us"

The Jessica Hahn cover-up began to unravel on December 11, 1985. I had first learned about Hahn's accusations from Hahn herself. Now, one year later, the ringing phone on my desk in the *Observer*'s newsroom signaled a second stroke of good fortune.

The caller identified himself as John Stewart, from Orange County, California. He told me he had information that made him question Jim Bakker's integrity. Without giving names or precise details, Stewart began to recount Hahn's story. "Bakker had his way with her, much to this gal's detriment," he said. Yes, I told Stewart, I knew about it. I gave him Hahn's initials to demonstrate how much I already knew.

Then, in general terms, Stewart told me what had happened after Hahn's frantic call waving me off the story. A friend of his, an "upright individual in California with no love lost for Bakker," had learned of the incident, interviewed Hahn, and asked Stewart to help draft a lawsuit. Stewart would not identify the friend, and another thirteen months would pass before I first heard Paul Roper's name. Stewart said only that the man had helped expose Ralph Wilkerson, pastor at Melodyland Christian Center in Anaheim. Stewart told me about lawyer Howard Weitzman's role, about Dortch's trips to California, about the settlement before an unidentified retired judge. About $300,000 had changed hands, Stewart estimated.

We talked for a half hour, and again at greater length two days later. With experience, a reporter develops the instincts to weed out improbable tales. I was impressed with Stewart. The thirty-four-year-old's voice was self-assured, he had details, and his story fit neatly into what I already knew about Hahn. It might even explain her abrupt decision to stop cooperating with me. Stewart had sketched his background for me: he had pastored a church in Ana-heim for six years, attended law school at nearby Western State University in Fullerton, was assistant dean and a faculty member at a young Christian law school in Orange County, and hosted a religious radio show.

According to Stewart, Dortch had told his friend that Bakker was using his own money to pay Hahn, raising the cash by selling a house. The sacrifice had seemed an appropriate act of contrition. As he mulled it over, though, Stewart had grown suspicious of the claim; it seemed odd that Bakker could raise so much money so quickly.

When Stewart told me the house-sale story, I laughed aloud. I explained that Dortch had already "spent" Bakker's profit from the home sale months before the settlement with Hahn. In his October 1984 effort to explain Bakker's home purchase in California, Dortch had claimed that the down payment had come from funds Bakker had received from a recently sold home. To render the explanation even more incredible, Bakker's $40,000 profit from that home sale was a fraction of the money that Stewart said had been paid to Hahn.

If he had been wary when he first telephoned, Stewart soon seemed willing to cooperate in a search for the truth. He had not been directly involved in the settlement and so, he thought, he might not be bound by the confidentiality provisions of the Hahn trust. I was exhilarated with my luck. The Hahn story, once des-tined to be insider gossip, now appeared to be a story explosive enough to topple Bakker and Dortch.

I telephoned Stewart on January 7, 1986. He asked if it was possible for me to document the true source of the payoff money. It wasn't. Two weeks later, we talked again. Stewart had talked to his friend. "He didn't see any way I could be involved in a story," Stewart said. "He tried to point out that in no uncertain terms we would jeopardize the trust if we disclose the terms of it."

I was disappointed, but not surprised. The story was too devastating to be so easy. Stewart and I agreed to keep in touch.

After taking over as budget director in summer 1984, Mark Burgund had encountered the same roadblocks that had frustrated his predecessor, Porter Speakman. Managers didn't care about producing budgets for him. Pleasing Jim was their first priority—it had to be, for survival's sake—and doing so meant breaking budgets with regularity. After all, Bakker never ran his building projects past finance for approval. PTL's money managers had to cope with the boss's unanticipated demands for millions on top of the ministry's already unpredictable cash flow. The departments that Jim didn't care about—mailing, magazines, missions—often watched helplessly as the money they had been told they could spend was reallocated to pay for his whims.

Receiving little background information from the departing Speakman, Burgund had been unable to get a hold on the elaborate computerized budget system Speakman had installed. It didn't matter, anyway—he didn't have the staff to enter the data required to make the system work. Without a computerized budget and accounting system, budget and finance knew only how much cash they had, not how much of that cash had been committed. One day, Burgund was asked to approve the purchase of a $57,000 piece of heavy construction equipment. He was prepared to say no until he was told PTL had had the machine for three months.

As PTL emerged from its October telethon and the tiff with ECFA, Bakker entered another of his occasional periods of intense interest in budgets. He had read another book on management excellence, and he'd suddenly realized that he needed a budget if he wanted to be a good manager. By mid-November, signs of acute financial strain had reappeared. PTL's $500,000 check to Roe Messner had bounced, PTL owed Messner $7 million, and Messner said that his banker was losing confidence in PTL.

Burgund was summoned to Bakker's office for a rare face-to-face meeting. Bakker told him that he wanted Burgund to speak up if the PTL president did anything to break the budget. It was Burgund's turn to hear the "keep me squeaky clean" speech that Bakker had made to his past finance executives.

Burgund agreed, with a proviso. "I'll tell you, Jim, if you promise not to shoot the messenger." Burgund, a loyal soldier to Dortch for years, had been too direct, too threatening. Bakker went blank. His secretary, Shirley Fulbright, walked in the room, and Bakker said nothing more, not even good-bye. Burgund realized he had stepped over the line, the same line his boss Dortch had trod so gingerly.

On November 18, Bakker ordered a memo sent to Bailey, Burgund, and Dortch demanding a firm plan for trimming the payroll. "We cannot wait any longer. Budget controls must be put in. Our payroll is so big and it is getting further behind every week. There is just no way we can continue this."

Bakker's checklist that day included a string of orders and ideas for cutting costs. Use volunteer workers at PTL's People That Love Center. Put Jim Swaim (who was $75,000 over budget on the Christmas lights display) under Peter Bailey's control. Find out how much each department is losing or making.

The answer to that order was not encouraging. Out of nineteen "income producing areas," thirteen had lost money. Food, accommodations, and transportation had run a $2.1 million deficit in fourteen months. Bakker told Bailey and Burgund to get control of spending.

Bakker now felt pressured to suggest that he and his buddies make some sacrifices. He ordered Taggart to arrange for Vi Azvedo, her husband Eddie, Dale Hill, the Oldhams, and singers Howard and Vestal Goodman to pay for upkeep of their PTL-owned homes near Bakker's, and he complained a few weeks later when he saw a crew working on Dale Hill's house. He told his staff that his family would have to make do with a housekeeper, a cook, and a single security man during the day.

Bakker also ordered Taggart to see to it that he and Tammy did not get a Christmas bonus. "The board can just put it on their minutes that they will not grant any bonus at our request until the ministry is in the financial place where they can do so. I feel very strong about this." The "sacrifice" was hardly painful. Just twelve days had passed since the board's approval of $300,000 in bonuses for the Bakkers.

Before PTL's latest boom had turned to bust, the ministry had expanded the homegrown programming offered on its satellite network. Now Bakker ordered programs canceled or put into reruns to save money. Most of the shows had been in production for less than a year. One was Tammy's latest woman's show, "Tammy's House Party." PR man Neil Eskelin had hosted a show similar to "Nightline" each weeknight. Oldham emceed a Saturday-night gospel-music show. Henry Harrison, Bakker's former co-host, ran a show called "In the Upper Room," broadcast amidst the prayer phones in the basement of the Upper Room—the same phones that had once been a main attraction on Bakker's talk-show set. When Harrison's show was unveiled in spring 1985, Vi Azvedo claimed that it marked a return to "what is in Jim Bakker's heart."

Once, TV professionals like Flessing had hoped to use PTL's satellite network to evangelize, to make the gospel unavoidable. Bakker now embraced a new philosophy. He saw live television at Heritage USA as a way to entertain partners on the grounds. With all that activity—after all, Americans love a TV taping—the partners would keep coming back and keep giving, Bakker believed. At eleven o'clock each weeknight, partners could gather in the lobby of the Heritage Grand to watch Eskelin interview a newsmaker on the air. Television, once a tool for saving souls, had become another cog in Heritage USA's entertainment apparatus.

Bakker's list of cost-cutting orders included an abrupt end to Fred Gross's contract with PTL. To those who worked with him, it was apparent that Fred Gross, Bakker's psychologist from Palmdale, was as interested in assuring his financial security as in healing the souls of hurting Christians. In 1985, Gross presented PTL with a plan to run sixty Christian therapy workshops nationwide under the ministry's sponsorship. With the plan came what one associate considered an outlandish request for money. PTL said yes to the counselor, who a few months earlier had helped Dortch with the Jessica Hahn matter. In the August 1985 contract, PTL agreed to reimburse Gross's company $35,000 a month—$420,000 over a year's time—and to pay him an additional twenty percent of the gross revenue from each workshop.

By fall, Bakker had had second thoughts about the deal, and word spread that he considered Gross greedy. On November 19, Bakker informed Dortch that Gross's contract with PTL was null and void. Instead, Bakker wanted Gross to get a fee for each visit he made to Heritage USA. During Bakker's final year in office, Gross would receive a $12,000 check each month. He would also propose that PTL join in a lucrative joint venture to sell insurance to the elderly.

The Friday before Thanksgiving, PTL executed a major staff layoff. The next week, the Charlotte paper reported the cuts, describing them as the latest sign of "mounting financial troubles" at PTL. Bakker encountered a local TV news crew at his kickoff of PTL's annual Christmas City lights display. As always, he doctored the truth, claiming that such cuts were routine. "We always cut back in the wintertime, and we look at everything. . . . Otherwise I can't keep funding everything and all the outreaches of the world."

Soon after, Dortch received Jim Cobble's resignation. Like Al Cress, Cobble had followed Dortch to PTL from Illinois despite his deep doubts about PTL. Dortch was proud of Cobble, a thoughtful, restrained man who had one of the most impressive intellects on the PTL staff. Cobble's tenure had been deeply frustrating. After his arrival, PTL had boasted about the new Heritage Institute Cobble would direct. It would offer seminars for PTL workers, retreats for pastors, and a hot line for pastors who needed personal counseling. The purpose, PTL said, was to fulfill "Jim Bakker's vision to serve and assist Christian pastors."

Whether part of Bakker's vision or not, Cobble's work interested only Dortch. Soon, Cobble found it difficult to get even Dortch's attention, as did several executives nominally under Dortch's supervision. Cobble's programs languished; several were canceled, others attracted no more than a handful of participants. Cobble began to feel like an ornament, hung out to beautify PTL's image.

Cobble's letter of resignation was blunt. It alluded to the recent layoffs.

> There are some things that I do care strongly about such as how our faith in Christ is expressed in our daily relationships reflecting both love and commitment. I know that you feel the same way too. . . .

The current cutbacks, while obviously necessary, are nevertheless being conducted in such a way as to create feelings of institutional disintegration and personal disillusionment. Sensitive people cannot help but to see a great dissonance between the fund-raising appeals on TV to sustain a ministry dedicated to helping people and the personal pain, confusion, and turbulence that exists among the staff. The picture is sobering. . . .

I perceived a growing disparity between my understanding of our biblical mission and corporate responsibilities as the people of God and the daily reality of working at PTL. Furthermore, the problem is not simply administrative. More fundamentally it is spiritual. . . .

There are points in an individual's life where he must act in harmony with his understanding of God's rule regardless of personal consequences. . . . I feel that I've been on a diet of spiritual junk food for two years and my system is just starting to get cleaned out.

Cobble's protest, however discreet, was the sort that PTL could never take to heart. Dortch never answered the letter.

As his Thanksgiving Day broadcast neared to a close, Bakker announced that he was going off the air to rest and cut PTL's budget. Already, he said, he had cut $15–$20 million. "We're turning things around."

Bakker made a second major announcement that day. Many of those who had promised to take Bakker's latest lifetime offer had failed to make good on their pledge. Without that money, Bakker said, PTL would have to stop building the Towers. From Thanksgiving to Christmas, PTL would offer thousand-dollar memberships in the Towers and thousand-dollar "Silver" memberships entitling the partner to a lifetime's free use of the water park and other recreational facilities at Heritage USA. Again, Bakker did not say how many lifetime partnerships PTL had already sold. By now, the tally for both the Heritage Grand and the Towers had climbed close to $90 million, half again as much as the $60 million Bakker had talked of just a year earlier.

That night, cars streamed into Heritage USA for the official opening of Bakker's Christmas City lights display, which now encompassed a stunning 1.25 million lights. The attraction had

become a must-see even for the most cynical resident of the Charlotte metropolitan area. Traffic backed up for miles, and PTL's
neighbors had trouble getting to and from their homes.

Bakker was eager to have the water park pool full of water for
the Christmas City display. In early November, Bakker told viewers
that the park would be finished within the month and would open
for Christmas City. "It's finally coming about." It was in fact months
from completion; privately, Messner had told Bakker that work was
progressing slowly and wouldn't be complete until May. But PTL
kept up the make-believe, just as Bakker had done with his Korean
TV program eight years before. Now that Bakker had added free
recreation to his lifetime-partnership package, the long-delayed
water park had become an even more crucial drawing card. It was
the most marketable recreational facility at Heritage USA. Without
it to help attract interest from donors, Bakker's latest appeal could
founder.

With the new year came more cost cutting. Bailey reported to
Bakker that PTL's payroll—not including costly executive pay—
had dropped fifteen percent in a single month, from more than $1
million to $877,000. But Bailey wanted it trimmed further. More
employees were laid off, and by January 20, PTL said publicly, it
had cut its payroll by twenty-five percent. To those who survived
the cuts, the future did not look cheery. A middle-level employee
telephoned me at home. "Morale in the past year has dropped
tremendously. People are very disillusioned. They wonder if they
will have a job tomorrow. Communication is very poor."

Taking finance's suggestion that PTL hold a TV auction, Bakker
announced a fund-raiser for Fort Hope, the home for street people
he had unveiled weeks after the Hahn payoff, saying that God had
given him a "heavy burden" for America's street people. Nine
months later, Fort Hope was again a Bakker priority. "We must get
open in the next few days, we must, we just have to do it in the next
few weeks," he declared. The project wouldn't open until late
summer 1986.

As he had done with his Rolls the summer before, Bakker made
a grand show of sacrifice. This time, he declared he was giving
away the Mercedes replica Dortch had presented to him on July 4,
1985.

I tried to figure out what I had. And this car was given to me as a love gift when I finished the Heritage Grand, and I said well I can't drive this car because the press would put me in the front page and ridicule me . . . and so I'd already given my other car away, my antique car that I had [the Rolls]. And so I decided that I would give this car away for Fort Hope.

Jim's "gift" became a refrain on PTL broadcasts in the days before the auction, but Bakker and his colleagues carefully avoided saying who had given him the car. Bakker described the "love gift" as coming from "some folks," Tammy said that the car had come from friends. To hear them, it sounded as if Bakker was giving away his property. In truth, money for the "gift" had come from PTL and, despite the show Dortch had put on the summer before, the car had remained in PTL's name. With great fanfare, PTL was giving itself a car.

The Bakkers played a similar charade with daughter Tammy Sue's Mazda. Five days before the auction, Bakker ordered the Mazda offered for sale. "Have it taken to the television studio and have the Tammy Sue license plate taken off." The car had been getting little use. Sue's manager-companion, Doug Oldham's daughter Dee, was driving the teenager in her own sports car. Tammy Sue told friends that she was getting another luxury car. Tammy Faye would intervene, insisting that she hadn't driven a $20,000 car when she was a teenager and that her daughter didn't need to either.

The day after her husband's order to auction the Mazda, Tammy Bakker found herself in the awkward position of pitching the car to viewers. The staff was instructed not to treat the car as Tammy Sue's on the air. Tammy Faye stuck to that story, pretending she had never seen the black auto. "Here's another car that's just been donated for the auction. I don't—what kind of car is it?" A Mazda RX-7, PTL's auction director explained. "This is a cute car. I like this. I wouldn't mind having one like that." Tammy even sat in the car on the air, explaining that she wanted to see if it was made for shorter people.

On the air the next day, Jim Bakker sidestepped the question of the car's origin. "What is that?" he asked, looking at the Mazda. He asked how many miles the car had on it. A member of the PTL

Singers looked inside and told him thirty-three hundred. "It's like brand new." In fact, Bakker knew it was new, "fully equipped, it is deluxe, it is—beautiful, it is beautiful."

In 1985, PTL donors had heard much about PTL's overseas missions work, the international TV programs underwritten by the ministry. Missions had been the theme of the February 1985 telethon. "Missions has always been a vital part of life for Tammy and me, and for this ministry, from the very beginning of PTL, we have made a commitment with our lives, our programs, and our giving to reach those overseas with the Gospel. This year, our outreach will be more powerful than before," Bakker wrote to his partners. In a September 1985 employee newsletter, Bakker expressed similar enthusiasm.

> In the hustle and bustle of Heritage USA, sometimes it is easy to forget just how powerful the worldwide impact of PTL is. But when I sit with my international hosts, and receive letters and testimonies from all over the world, it becomes an exciting reality. . . .
> PTL is broadcasting into a total of fifty-two countries. We can only estimate the millions of lives every day that the PTL ministry is touching with the message of Jesus Christ . . . we are definitely on the brink of a miracle. That is why I am convinced it is time for us to do MORE, not less!

During the October 1985 telethon, Bakker urged his supporters to help save broadcasts in countries like Italy, the Philippines, and Thailand. "We have to pay the bills around the world."

Overseas missionary work remained an attractive drawing card to evangelicals in PTL's audience—and a less costly inducement to donors than the offer of free lodging or recreation. In late August 1985, Bakker told his TV audience that PTL had been given "the rights and privilege to print the Holy Bible in mainland China. This has not been allowed in forty-five years. . . . They're going to allow us to print over 10 million Bibles and distribute them throughout China." Dortch announced that the Chinese Bibles could reach a billion people. "This is all for real . . . this is really going to happen," Bakker's deputy said. "The [Chinese government] sports federation has said . . . 'You can do this. You can print 10 million

Bibles. You do them on our presses. You can even be there to see the distribution.' "

Bakker told his audience that he needed five thousand people to send a thousand dollars each, for a total of $5 million. He called it the Reach Out With Love Club. If all five thousand donors came forward, Bakker said, PTL would also have enough money to bring its TV debts current—the same promise he had made the year before as he raised the first Towers partnership money. "You're not just sponsoring Bibles, you're paying airtime around the world." According to the plan Bakker's staff had devised, PTL would pay just thirty cents for printing and distribution of each New Testament.

Bakker had grossly exaggerated what PTL could accomplish if all went well. A Christian leader in China had already planned a mass printing of Bibles inside the country; PTL's plan was not a first. In an interview a few days later, I asked Dortch about Bakker's claims. Dortch corrected his boss, saying that Bakker hadn't intended to say that the money for the Chinese Bibles would enable PTL to pay up all its airtime bills. Bakker also hadn't meant to say that the distribution was unprecedented, Dortch said. Instead, he should have said that it's very difficult to distribute Bibles there. "I haven't listened as closely as I should," Dortch said. "It's the first time we have had the opportunity to distribute Bibles."

That, of course, was distinctly less of an inducement to donors. In the weeks that followed, PTL's hyperbole managed to avoid clear falsehoods but did little to correct Bakker's early claims. "For the first time in forty-five years, the Chinese government has given the PTL ministry the privilege of printing the Bible in the Chinese language," bragged a letter to partners. The PTL ministry hadn't been around for forty-five years. This first for PTL was hardly a breakthrough; it was merely the first time PTL had tried such a program.

In late October, Assemblies of God missionary Sam Johnson—the Bible-school classmate of Bakker's and family friend of Dortch's—took over as PTL's director of world missions after being courted by PTL for years. He found the situation sobering. There wasn't enough money to pay for light fixtures or to have the drapes in his office cleaned. At his first vice-presidents' meeting, executives were asked not to cash their paychecks right away. His staff had great trouble getting money to pay for international airtime, and many host stations had pulled the PTL-sponsored foreign programs for lack of payment. PTL was no longer on the air in all fifty-two countries.

In the early days of January 1986, Bakker quietly disclosed his plans to phase out PTL's overseas missions programs—the outreach that was once supposedly the heart of his ministry. "The Lord really dealt with me about sixty days ago, and he said, 'Jim you cannot fund the whole world.' " Bakker packaged the development as good news, a new vision from God, not an effort to cut costs and ease the financial pressure generated by his building program. "We're starting a new missions program . . . the greatest missions outreach I believe in the history of the world," he said, alluding to plans to underwrite communications majors at North Central Bible College and a second Assemblies of God Bible college.

> We're getting ready to turn most of our foreign missions over to the countries and to the hosts. We're going to build for each host. We're going to give them their own ministry, that they can begin to build, not dependent on us any more. But we're going to build ministries all over the world. If God gave us a dream and a vision, instead of us funding the whole world, as one of the missions groups gets big enough, we're going to give them the ministry . . .

Bakker said that the overseas TV ministries would now become self-supporting and would no longer be subject to his control. "It will be totally indigenous. That's a wonderful word."

Bakker had made the decision to cut missions without consulting Johnson. Johnson was not deeply troubled. The Assemblies of God encourages missionaries to build indigenous structures that can survive long after the outsiders leave. PTL's overseas missions had relied too heavily on PTL's deep pockets; PTL had created no framework for independence. Without PTL's support, it seemed to Johnson (and would later prove to be the case) that most of the programs would disappear. Johnson's goal was to develop PTL as a place to train foreigners, who would then return home to build their own ministries.

For some veterans on Bakker's staff, the decision to withdraw support from overseas TV programs was the latest sign that PTL had strayed from its divine purpose. The employees had watched Bakker's TV program drift from focusing on the testimonies of ordinary folks to a fascination with celebrities. They had watched the prayer phones disappear from the set and seen fund-raising and marketing of Heritage USA usurp more and more airtime. If the missions were shut down, the veterans thought quietly, the Lord likely wouldn't honor anything happening at PTL.

In November 1985, as the IRS finished its 1981–83 audit, the FCC finally agreed to give the *Observer* access to the records of its closed investigation of PTL. The material was voluminous—forty-five hundred pages of testimony and scores of documents. Citing the federal Freedom of Information Act, the newspaper had been seeking access to the records since the FCC's decision to end its inquiry in 1982. The FCC had put the newspaper off, first because of Justice Department and IRS reviews, and then because the transfer of PTL's Canton, Ohio, station had been challenged in court. That legal battle had ended in the fall of 1985.

I flew to Washington before Thanksgiving, scanned the transcripts and documents, and ordered hundreds of pages photocopied. In early December, I began sifting through the material and preparing stories detailing the FCC investigators' findings and the behind-the-scenes picture of PTL presented in the FCC records.

On Wednesday, January 22, I telephoned PTL's PR man, Neil Eskelin, and asked for an interview. As always, Eskelin was professional and amicable, despite the latest chill in *Observer*-PTL relations. Disgusted with our critical editorial and editorial cartoons, PTL had pulled $100,000 a year in advertising and had banned sales of the newspaper at Heritage USA beginning in November. It had also refused to comment on stories we were preparing to publish, including a late-November story disclosing the ministry's millions of dollars in land purchases.

After Thanksgiving, Dortch had taken his case to the *Observer*'s publisher, Rolfe Neill, in a private letter that exemplified PTL's inability to accept the painful realities of public life, from unkind cuts in the press to close inspection of personal life-style:

> I am sitting here . . . with a very heavy heart.
> I am writing to you to appeal to your sense of fairness.

. . . From the first time I met you, I felt you were a sincere person trying to be fair; even with the tough task of doing your sometimes unpleasant job of exposing what you believe to be wrong or worthy of press coverage.

Twice, he complained, the *Observer*'s editorial cartoonist Doug Marlette had taken aim at PTL with "degrading cartoons." In October, after Bhagwan Shree Rajneesh was arrested at the Charlotte airport trying to flee the country, Marlette had sketched Bakker's Rolls Royce colliding with the Bhagwan's. Marlette had also drawn Bakker holding a credit card labeled American Excess.

When we have disagreed with you, Rolfe—we have never mentioned your name on the air. We've never said an unkind word about Rich Oppel as a person—It's always been "The *Observer*"—your paper attacks Jim Bakker as a person—Why? Always a frontal attack. Would it be fair for us to get on national television and talk about what we would believe to be your personal excesses? . . . You let it happen consistently! Again, and again you do it. Why are your people so bitter and mean? . . . Will you grant [Marlette] liberty to keep doing it until total malice comes through? The case for malice to me is already clear, by "The *Observer*'s" constant harassment.

Rolfe, I mean it kindly, as a Christian gentleman. You are not being fair. You are letting meanness reign in your newspaper. Are you in an organized, designed plan of putting down Pentecostals? Are we upsetting to your people because we worship differently? . . . Don't we fit the preppy, establishment mentality of the editorial and management staff of "The *Observer*"? It does make us wonder if there is an element of bigotry or just plain meanness toward this ministry.

If there is a wrong assessment on my part, then why with such frequency, do you let this happen? Are you in control? . . .

The Bible tells me to live peaceably with all men. I really want to do that.

Neill responded with a suggestion that the two meet for lunch after the New Year.

When I spoke with Eskelin nearly two months later, he informed me that PTL was still not granting interviews, at least not until Dortch and publisher Neill could talk face-to-face. I offered to tell PTL about the topic of my story at noon on Friday, two days later. We didn't want Bakker to preempt us, as he had in October 1984.

Left in the dark, Dortch apparently considered the worst scenario—that the *Observer* was going to disclose the Hahn story. Shortly after I talked to Eskelin, Dortch telephoned Roger Flessing—the former PTL executive who had asked Dortch about the Hahn episode after my call in late 1984. Dortch told Flessing that he was calling to see if Flessing was interested in some TV work PTL needed done. Dortch was flattering. He then asked Flessing if he had heard from the *Observer* recently. Flessing had not.

That afternoon, Eskelin telephoned back, saying that Bakker wouldn't do an interview. He said I could speak with Dortch the next morning. "It may result in an interview. It may not."

Bakker had already begun preparing his viewers for more bad press, bringing his customary technique of misstatement into play. "Just yesterday the local newspaper reporters called our office," he said that morning, "and [they] said 'we're going to basically try to destroy PTL again. We're coming after you this time. We're going to destroy you.' This is basically the interpretation that I got from our staff. Well, there they go again . . . they won't be content until either God deals with them or I'm gone." Of course, I had told no one that the *Observer* was going to destroy PTL, and we certainly did not expect to do so. We knew how volatile Bakker could be. My editors and the newspaper's lawyers had agreed that we needed to exercise caution in our public and private statements.

At midday on Friday, Dortch and Eskelin telephoned me. Unbeknownst to me, they were sitting in Bakker's office, and Taggart and Bakker were listening to the call. I spelled out the stories I had prepared, including the lead story reporting that FCC investigators had concluded that Bakker misled viewers repeatedly while he had raised money for PTL's Korean and Brazilian TV shows in 1977 and 1978. The two men said they would consider responding. At three that afternoon, Eskelin telephoned with a seven-paragraph statement.

> We are deeply disappointed in the latest attempt by the *Charlotte Observer* to defame PTL, its leadership, employees, and hundreds of thousands of supporters by the publicity of this story. . . . The PTL organization, its leadership, and employees have been completely vindicated by the United States Justice Department of any wrongdoing whatsoever. This latest series

raises legitimate questions as to the intent of the *Observer* regarding PTL.

That afternoon, Dortch appealed to the *Observer*'s editor, Rich Oppel to hold the story so that PTL could produce receipts, cancelled checks, and other evidence that would refute the FCC findings. Oppel offered to spend the thirty-six hours before publication going over PTL's material and to include PTL's rebuttal material in the article. Dortch didn't take him up on the offer.

A few weeks later, in a letter to PTL partners, Tammy Bakker described her husband's reaction to the news that the FCC story was being revived.

> His first words to me were, "Tammy, they are going to do it again. I just don't know if I can go through it again." My heart stuck in my throat as I said, "Jim, who is going to do what again?"
>
> He gave me a one-word answer: "Newspaper."
>
> "What more can they do?" I screamed, before I realized I was screaming. He said, "Tammy, they will not give up until they destroy us—not only us personally, but the whole PTL ministry."
>
> Almost together, we said, "Let's just give it all up. It is not worth the hurt to our children, the hurt it will cause our employees, the hurt it will cause our faithful partners, and the hurt it will cause the unsaved in that it will be yet another attempt to get them to distrust this wonderful Jesus we preach about."

That night, the letter said, Jim had tossed and turned in his sleep, while Tammy had cried her eyes out.

CHAPTER EIGHTEEN

ENOUGH IS ENOUGH

"We are people who want you to know the truth"

A day after the Space Shuttle *Challenger* exploded in the skies over Florida, Tammy Bakker opened PTL's first live broadcast since publication of the FCC stories. Her grief that day in January 1986 was not for the dead astronauts. "We have been through a pretty bad couple of days . . . probably the most hurt we have ever been in our whole life," she said. Dortch, her co-host that day, spoke up. "Tammy, I know the difference between people who are nice and people who are mean. . . . [The *Observer* articles were] really one of the meanest, vicious, cruel attacks that I've ever known in my life that has been made, without foundation."

Three days earlier, the lead FCC story had appeared splashed across the front page of the Sunday *Observer*. "Bakker Misled PTL Viewers, FCC Records Show," read the headline. On two inside pages, separate stories profiled the fate of PTL's missions programs in Korea, Brazil, and Cyprus. A fourth story detailed allegations contained in FCC documents that the Bakkers had used PTL money for personal purchases—accusations much like those PTL's tax attorney had described in 1980. The next day's paper carried another two pages of articles, which contained descriptions of Bakker and PTL's internal operations drawn from the extensive FCC record.

The stories got quick response. An anonymous caller phoned my home on Sunday morning and told my wife, Jody, that God would punish us. The wire services picked up the articles, and they appeared, in much shorter form, in papers across the country. Letters and phone calls streamed into the *Observer;* most were negative. A PTL partner from Guymon, Oklahoma, wrote to editor Rich Oppel.

> You will have boils, tumors, scurvy, and itch, for none of which there will be a remedy. You will have madness, blindness, fear, and panic will come over you. You will watch as your loved ones are taken by dope, booze, or maybe prostitution. You will eat the flesh of your sons and daughters in the days of siege ahead. This is not something I thought up. It is the Word of God.

At PTL, Bakker and his staff worked long hours putting together a rebuttal; it would take until Friday, January 31. The resulting hour-long program was unusual, in that it was a formatted broadcast. Bakker, who performed best when he was free to be spontaneous, was uneasy under the pressure to squeeze certain information into sixty minutes.

The program began dramatically, without PTL's customary cheery theme song. Jim and Tammy appeared side by side. "Tammy and I are undergoing the most vicious attacks in the history of this ministry," Bakker said. "Today we're going to talk to you and give you the documented facts—not gossip, not somebody said that somebody said."

Bakker was surrounded that day by members of his staff. He invited viewers to summon their friends to watch. He then spoke the words that would become PTL's slogan in the months that followed: "Somebody said, 'enough is enough.' And I think this ministry has had enough." Soon PTL partners' cars sprouted PTL bumper stickers proclaiming Enough Is Enough, and Tammy Bakker sang a song by that name comparing PTL to David and its tormentors to Goliath.

Bakker's defense of his handling of the overseas missions sounded persuasive. He held aloft canceled checks to demonstrate that he had paid Bob McAlister in Brazil. He didn't, however, call attention to the dates on the checks, which had been written in 1979, a year after PTL was supposed to pay McAlister the

$150,000. On the show, Dortch evoked memories of his years as a European missionary. "There are times when people made commitments to Mildred [Dortch's wife] and me, and it just didn't come at the right moment that Mildred and I thought it should come," he said.

Bakker introduced Elias Malki, the missionary who wanted to build a radio transmitter on Cyprus. Malki confirmed that he had been paid, but he said nothing about the fate of the money, much as Bakker said nothing about his aides' advice in 1979 that he shouldn't pay Malki because the money would be wasted.

When Bakker raised the subject of Korea, Dortch attested to the complexity of putting projects together overseas. "It would be impossible to do in a moment everything we aspire to do," Dortch said. He and Bakker made no mention of the FCC staff's findings that Bakker had repeatedly claimed on the air that the Korean studio was being built and the Korean show was being broadcast. The claims had been false and an embarrassment to the Koreans, who found themselves explaining to visitors why the studio the Americans thought they had helped pay for did not exist.

Bakker read a wire-service story from 1983 reporting the Justice Department's decision not to pursue the FCC inquiry further. The UPI story incorrectly portrayed the decision as a vindication, using language such as "there is no evidence" and "allegations . . . were unfounded" that was inconsistent with public statements from the Justice Department and the opinions filed by the FCC's dissenting members.

Bakker's strongest complaint concerned the story published on an inside page of the *Observer* about personal misuse of PTL money. At issue were a mink coat Bakker had purchased for Tammy, the Corvette that Bakker had ordered bought in 1976, and the houseboat he had purchased in summer 1978. It was difficult to ignore the suggestions from government investigators that the Bakkers had misused donors' dollars for their benefit. But these allegations were thinly documented, unlike the rest of the FCC staff report. My editor, Jeannie Falknor, and I had decided not to do extensive additional reporting but rather to report the contents of the FCC record as if we were covering a trial.

During the rebuttal program, Bakker blamed the *Observer* for bomb threats, death threats, and a display of girlie magazines left in front of his house years before. "We almost got a divorce," Bakker said, alluding to the dark days of 1980–81. "We separated, and Tammy couldn't really take it any more. Something snapped inside of her and said, 'I can't face it anymore.' "

As he closed the program, Bakker acknowledged that PTL had made mistakes—honest mistakes, he called them. He said PTL was accountable to its auditors and to ECFA, "and we are people who want you to know the truth." The hour ended with the scroll of video testimonials from past programs—Rex Humbard, Art Linkletter, Oral Roberts, and a snippet of the Billy Graham interview, which PTL had run in full the day before in a bid to build legitimacy for the rebuttal program. Then Pat Boone, a regular PTL guest who was attending a long-planned conference at Heritage USA, delivered a parting message. He opened with a quote from Teddy Roosevelt that PTL would use to defend Bakker from his critics.

> Theodore Roosevelt once said, "It's not the critic who counts. . . . The credit belongs to the man who is actually in the arena." Friends, Jim and Tammy . . . continue to stand firm in their commitment to their call, encouraging, ministering, reaching, building, offering hope to countless lives with that simple message, "You can make it." . . . I know there are millions . . . who are willing to stand with Jim and Tammy as they offer a message of love and hope to a world that is hungry for good news. . . . Let's show them we're all in this together. And together we will make it.

The special report, as PTL called it, was a sterling illustration of Bakker's manipulation of the truth. The program testified, too, to the power of one-sided television to shape public opinion. There was no instant analysis from critical onlookers, no shrewd questioning from reporters as there would have been if Bakker were a government official running a $100-million bureaucracy or an executive in a public corporation. The propaganda did its job.

A few days later, a Madison, Wisconsin, man penned an angry letter to the *Observer.* He attached a letter to Bakker. In his letter to the newspaper, Robert Toomey complained that the *Observer* had published unfounded material. "Jim is giving his side of the story, and it is one that is hard to deny." Toomey wrote to Bakker that he had recently sent PTL one hundred dollars for a Bible, on top of his monthly gift of twenty dollars.

> I fully and completely trust PTL. You are a member of the ECFA. You are open and honest about everything. Ninety-nine percent of the time, the television doesn't lie, meaning that one can tell that you and Tammy are honest, humble, caring, and loving people by watching your program. . . .
>
> There have been times when I felt down and lonely, but I watched your program and was uplifted emotionally and spiritually.

PTL now began to fight back behind the scenes as well.

Bakker's security chief, Don Hardister, hired a Charlotte private detective, Ron Guerette, to investigate Manzano and other former PTL executives, looking for information that would discredit the FCC witnesses. Police records and credit-card records were checked. Guerette telephoned Manzano posing as Ron Bouchard, an independent writer for UP. Guerette read from my articles, and Manzano confirmed their accuracy. Guerette asked him about his marriage (Manzano had divorced), his educational background (Manzano commented that Bakker made a big deal that his degrees were fake, but that "I personally don't see what that has anything to do with anything"), and his current work (loan broker, but Manzano refused to disclose the name of his companies). The next day, Guerette prepared three pages of scuttlebutt for his client.

Bakker also commissioned Doug Wead to write a book about Bakker's battle with the FCC and the *Observer.* Bakker alluded to the book in ominous but vague terms, promising that it would shock America. Wead, who had coauthored James Watt's *Courage of a Conservative,* said later that he offered to help PTL without asking his going rate of $135,000. But, he said, Bakker insisted on paying, and he eventually received about $75,000.

That spring, a Concord, California, writer and Assemblies of God minister contacted the *Observer* saying that he needed some information for a book he was writing on PTL, the FCC, and the *Observer.* I asked the man if he had any connection with PTL, and he assured me that he did not. I argued, unsuccessfully, to my editors that we should answer his questions. Apparently, their instincts were better

369

than mine. Wead had hired the man to help on the PTL-financed book. He had shared his plans to do so with Bakker.

> It will do much to heighten the drama and controversy of the manuscript. It is important to get some of these questions through, before the *Observer* is on to me. . . . There is a substantial risk that Shepard and any other spokesman at the *Observer* will recognize my name.

In early March, Bakker telephoned Roger Flessing at home. He wanted Flessing to talk with Wead about the FCC investigation. Bakker claimed to have tapes of *Observer* reporters describing him as a crook and to have hired private investigators to find out who had talked to the newspapers. He read to Flessing transcripts of comments by Moss, Manzano, and former general manager Gary Smith. Manzano had told Guerette (in his incarnation as reporter) that he didn't trust Flessing. "Roger just cannot basically bear to keep his mouth shut. . . . He tells everything he knows. And what he doesn't know he invents." It seemed to Flessing that Bakker wanted to pit his former staff members against one another.

Bakker's televised special report marked the opening salvo in his public counterattack. The volleys continued for months. Bakker's defense consumed him. He suggested that the US Senate should investigate, he invited charismatic-Christian writer Jamie Buckingham to look over PTL's books, he suggested that the Christian community create its own antidefamation league. "If we were Jewish, you couldn't do this to us. . . . It's time that the church stand together and say we're not going to put up with the trashing of God's people." Bakker's call for such a group was picked up in mid-April by Jerry Falwell, the TV minister from Lynchburg, Virginia. "The time has come for us to join hands and fight together or hang separately," Falwell said.

Bakker acquitted himself by creating the notion of a conspiracy against evangelicals. He said that PTL was the nose cone of the rocket, catching the heat first. He cited a newly released series of critical articles in the *Tulsa Tribune* about the city's most famous TV preacher, Oral Roberts. "I think they've found some whipping boys because they know the preachers want peace . . . and say,

'Well, we can rip these people apart because they probably won't sue us. And they surely are not going to put a hit man on us. . . . They don't have enough political clout to get the government to come after us.' "

As my stories appeared in the *Observer*'s sister newspapers in the Knight-Ridder chain and in other papers that used the Knight-Ridder news service, PTL portrayed the spreading coverage as evidence of a corporate plot to get PTL. The Bakkers suggested boycotting the newspaper and its corporate parent. Bakker threatened to file lawsuits if the press didn't clean up its act. PTL issued at least four mass mailings to press its case, and ads appeared in the *Observer* and in selected newspapers across the country. One featured a letter signed by PTL board members saying that inside the ministry, "we [board members] express ourselves forthrightly and candidly in a manner consistent with our fiduciary trust."

Bakker's quest for credibility got a boost from writer Buckingham, whom Bakker represented, incorrectly, as an "investigative reporter." Buckingham, an occasional guest on Bakker's program, published a friendly account of PTL's defense in his *Buckingham Report* newsletter and in *Charisma* magazine. But Buckingham did not endorse all he saw at PTL, and his words reflected the lingering distrust of Bakker felt in his own religious community.

> The problems I unearthed at PTL have to do with differences in style—not ethics. I, for instance, have a hard time understanding this fetish many Pentecostals have about gold to decorate themselves. One recent guest for the show was wearing a gold Rolex watch, as well as two gold bracelets on the same wrist.
>
> I wince over Bakker's emotive behavior on TV. I shudder at his fund-raising techniques. And I have a hard time trying to sort out the mixture of God, commercialism, high fashion, and entertainment at Heritage USA.
>
> Yet . . . as my wife pointed out, "What's wrong with having a first-class, decent family park where Christians can come at reasonable prices for clean, wholesome fun and entertainment?" She's right. Jim and Tammy are doing a good thing. They deserve our blessing and support. PTL has grown—and Jim Bakker has grown with it. He no longer makes snap decisions on the air. He has learned to submit to wise men. . . .
> Bottom line: It's time to put an end to this civil war and unite

our forces against the common enemy who wants to divide us
into little chunks so he can easily devour us. . . .
 If the bell tolls for Jim Bakker, it also tolls for me.

Within days of its special report, PTL also began to attack my
integrity. By phone, Dortch told publisher Rolfe Neill that PTL
had videotapes of witnesses questioning the conduct of *Observer*
reporters. In a letter to editor Rich Oppel, Dortch said that PTL
had obtained signed affidavits from people accusing reporters of
misconduct. "I felt the honorable thing was to discuss it with you
prior to doing anything else," he wrote. Dortch suggested a meeting on March 13. He did not name the reporters.
 The day of Dortch's letter to Oppel, Bakker described for his
audience the reporters who wrote about PTL. They "are always,
almost always that I know, as far as I know, are the new guys, the
young guys who have never established a reputation yet, and they
hire them as their paid killers to come out and do the job." Bakker
did not say that I was thirty-one years old, had been at the *Observer*
for eight years, and was considered one of its more established
reporters. The next day, Bakker said that he wouldn't want the
reporters in his living room. "They're unkept, they're unclean, they
would sit in beat-up cars in front of our house. I don't think they
washed their hair for months, it looked like." Bakker hinted that
the *Observer* was offering bribes. "They have enough money they
can pay somebody to testify against [us] a million dollars if they
need be to destroy us. . . . They have the money to buy anything
they want. And I have documents and records and videotapes of
witnesses who will testify that they have been offered money to lie
about this ministry." Bakker paused and looked solemnly into the
camera. "I have not used it, but we may have to."
 On March 3, 1986, as I ate lunch at my desk, a clerk connected
a caller to my phone. The voice was a man's, probably in his thirties.

Caller: My name is Jim Wright. I work at WALE TV in Alabama. . . . The reason I was calling . . . we were just recently
purchased by Knight-Ridder Corporation. [Knight Ridder had
in fact recently purchased several TV stations, including
WALA in Mobile, Alabama]. . . . The reason I was calling was
to ask you a question. We've been getting a lot of calls. . . .

> Could you give me some firsthand information on [PTL] that
> we can give the people who are writing in to us?

I gave the man some background about the stories.

> Shepard: Bakker has been talking and his cohorts have been
> talking ad nauseam about it ever since. And they've cooked up
> this Knight-Ridder plot to get PTL. . . .
>
> Caller: You don't know what type of weirdos I've got calling
> me. . . . Of course a lot of this is off the cuff, between the two
> of us, because I need to know what I'm dealing with. . . . What
> do you think of Bakker himself?

I told the man I didn't have an opinion, that we had simply been
reporting past events. The caller pressed me, saying that I must
have an opinion. "Do you think he's another one of these phony
evangelists running the airwaves?"

I was already puzzled by the man's clumsy language. When I
heard the question, I hesitated. His questions were becoming too
leading. "Jim, let me call you back. My editor just signaled at me.
What's your number there?" Wright gave me a number. I didn't
recognize the area code, which turned out to be for New Jersey.
Before I hung up, Wright pressed me again. "Can I ask you a
question first, before you go hanging up on me?" He asked me
again if I thought Bakker was a phony. I didn't answer.

After I hung up, I tried the number the caller had given me. It
was out of order. The same number with an Alabama area code was
also nonworking. I drafted a note to my bosses saying that I was
being set up. Soon the tape of my conversation was in PTL's hands.

Earlier that week, the same man had talked to Joe Sovacool, the
afternoon clerk who manned the newsroom phones after three
o'clock. Again, the caller identified himself as station manager Jim
Wright. Again, he offered assurances that the conversation was
confidential. Wright asked Sovacool his opinion of Bakker—from
a station manager to a newsman. "Personally I think he's a phony,"
Sovacool said. "I can't speak for the newspaper."

"What do you think Charlie thinks about all this?" the caller
asked. Sovacool said he was hesitant to speculate. The man pressed

him, and Sovacool answered, "Let me put it this way, I don't think we would be going after these people in the way that we're going after them and the way that we've historically gone after them if we didn't suspect something was amiss down there."

The caller pushed for more. "Between you and I do you want to see him off the air? . . . Between you and I do you think Charlie Shepard wants to see these people off the air eventually? I'm just asking you for your opinion." Sovacool said he didn't have an opinion of what others thought.

Later that spring, PTL mailed a *Reader's Digest*–size glossy magazine to its partners. The cover story—called "The Anatomy of a Smear," which was PTL's working title for Wead's book—quoted Sovacool's "something is amiss" comment. Sovacool was identified as "one of the employees of the giant Knight-Ridder . . . [speaking] from his position in the newsroom." No mention was made of the private detective's report to PTL that suggested, accurately, that Sovacool's duties included answering telephones and taking obituary information from funeral homes.

If Jim Wright had failed to get the goods on me, PTL thought that it had a smoking gun in the person of a drifter named Janet Brady. On February 3, she came forward and accused the *Observer* of improprieties. Her statement was captured on audio and then videotape. On March 6, three days after the bogus call from the Alabama station manager, Dortch dictated a short letter to Rolfe Neill. Dortch still wanted to meet with the *Observer* publisher, he wrote, but "I wanted to let you know that because of the repeated printing of the stories you ran several weeks ago by the newspapers in the Knight-Ridder chain, we feel we must release the stories told us by concerned people. We must let our partners know what it is we are facing."

Shortly after eleven the next morning, Bakker appeared on the air from the garden of his Palm Desert home.

> This desert just a few years ago was nothing but sand. And today this is like a garden. . . . It is so easy to destroy, it's so easy to tear down. But it takes something to build up.

Bakker held up a single red rose, an example, he said, of planting, growing, and cultivating.

There are those who will plant. . . . But then today there are those who will take a beautiful rose like this and just crush it and tear it apart. There are those who will just take the beautiful things of God and just petal by petal tear it apart, trying to destroy, tearing down the very work of the hands of others.

The camera pulled in tight for a shot of Bakker's stubby fingers grabbing the rosebud. It then cut to the image of the blood red petals falling to the ground.

PTL, Bakker said, was under examination by people looking for the one wilted flower,

> ignoring all the beauty, ignoring all the good, and trying their best to find the evil. What a shame. PTL is under probably the greatest attack ever in the history of its ministry. And every day now more and more is surfacing . . . that this is not just an accident. But there is a design, there is a plan to destroy PTL.

Then Bakker introduced Brady, "a lady who this ministry helped [who] came forward to tell us . . . how she was approached to try to destroy and hurt PTL." A sitting room appeared on screen. A PTL employee was on one side of the picture and an unfamiliar short, heavyset woman of about thirty-five sat facing the camera. The woman was rough looking, not one of the well-coiffed, precisely dressed personalities who populated PTL's TV world. She wore a blue work shirt. Her eyes were hidden behind tinted glasses. She spoke with little expression in her voice or on her face.

Janet—no last name was given—proceeded with her story, her most damning words appearing in text superimposed on the screen. She had lived for six weeks in a trailer at PTL's expense, she said, and had kept a journal about her experiences.

> It's natural when you're out of work and your husband's got a broken wrist, you get depressed, you know. And, you know, things that I was hearing people say and things that I was feeling . . . I was taking and writing them down.

One day, she said, another resident of a PTL trailer had appeared with a stranger. The new arrival identified himself as Charles. He was, she said, a "representative" of the *Charlotte Observer.* Somehow, she claimed, this man had gotten a copy of her notebook. He returned a second time, she said, and offered to help pay her rent and utility bills in exchange for her journals. Her story continued:

> You don't go stab your brother in the back, you really don't. You know, how they say, you don't, you don't bite the hand that feeds you and PTL has fed us for I guess three months there. . . .
> I think that he was, you know, trying—the word's not blackmail, but more bribery. You know, pay for something that I've written, you know, and then gonna turn it around and feed it backwards to other people to make them think, Look how horrible Jim Bakker is.

The words "to make them think, look how horrible Jim Bakker is" flashed on screen.

Bakker and the Palm Desert scene reappeared.

> I know this testimony is shocking to many God-fearing people. But this is just the tip of the iceberg. The things that have been told to us in the last few hours will shock you. . . . Yes, I believe there has been a consistent, concise effort to destroy and to smear the ministry of PTL.

Soon the broadcast returned, live, to the studio. Bakker's colleagues added their condemnation. Doug Oldham, looking sullen, his voice breaking, evoked memories of Adolf Hitler's march through Europe and his father's warning that the churches would be Hitler's target after the Jews. PR man Eskelin praised Brady for not bending to the paper's offer. "She stood up and she said, 'My goodness, I'm sick and tired of this. I don't believe this is right.' . . . And she came to us."

I learned of the broadcast minutes after it ended from a former PTL employee who knew that Brady was not to be trusted. The employee told me Janet's name. I had never met, talked to, or heard of her, but I began to get information from others who had. The *Observer* assigned another reporter, Elizabeth Leland, to pursue background information. Brady herself had disappeared.

Speaking of Brady and the man she described as her husband, Brady's former landlord in Colorado Springs told Leland, "They

will lie and cheat. . . . They are professional tenants and mooches."
Court records in Colorado Springs showed that a Janet Brady had
been charged with three counts of welfare fraud, including one
count of making a false statement. Authorities there had been unable to find Brady to arrest her. The Bradys' landlord in Rock Hill,
South Carolina, said that he had felt sorry for Brady after she cried
and told him she had no place to go. PTL paid the Bradys' first
month's rent of $250 and their hundred-dollar security deposit, but
the Bradys failed to pay later months' rent or their heating-oil bill.
After the landlord filed eviction papers, Brady's husband charged
the landlord—falsely, the landlord said—with assault, much as they
had done earlier in Colorado. The couple and their nine-year-old
daughter soon moved out, taking mattress covers, light bulbs, a
vacuum cleaner, a new set of flatware, an electric toaster, and a food
mixer of the landlord's. "They are the nastiest, filthiest, sorriest
people I've ever had in my house," the landlord told Leland.

The afternoon of Bakker's broadcast, a crowd gathered in editor
Oppel's office to watch a tape of the Brady interview that PTL had
furnished to the newspaper. I was amazed by PTL's irresponsibility.
Soon after, another reporter called Eskelin for comment. "We went
to a reasonable effort to ascertain her credibility," he said. "We are
using the same standard the *Charlotte Observer* has used for ten years.
It's the testimony of one individual. . . . I'm sure the *Charlotte
Observer* felt she was a credible person also or they would not have
met with her three times and offered her money for her story as she
alleges." Two days later, PTL ran the program again on a Charlotte
TV station.

The *Observer* decided to ignore the allegation; my bosses did not
want to get in a shooting match with PTL, making the *Observer* the
center of attention along with PTL. Oppel sent a low-key letter to
Dortch telling him "you've got legal problems with the allegations." Oppel asked for Brady's full name and current location.
PTL never responded. Because there was no public reaction from
the newspaper, Bakker's employees and TV audience knew none
of the facts about PTL's reckless disregard for the truth.

PTL began getting calls from other victims of Janet Brady. Private detective Guerette was dispatched to investigate PTL's star
witness. His report was not encouraging. Brady's older brother, a
prison guard in Texas,

stated Ms. Brady uses people continuously, mostly church people . . . his sister continuously uses the system and people by
crying, begging, and making them feel like heels. . . . He states
her psychological profile is such that when things get hot, or
she is about to get caught in a lie, she will move out as quickly
as possible.

Her brother also listed nine aliases used by his sister and said that
she was wanted in three states for writing worthless checks. Another brother told Guerette that Brady "goes under so many different names, he cannot keep up with her." PTL realized that it had
been had, but it ran no retraction, issued no apology.

A week after the Brady broadcast, I received a letter from a "PTL
Club" viewer in Bossier City, Louisiana.

> To buy testimony to try to destroy a ministry of a man who
> loves the Lord is even lower than the terrible journalism which
> prints lies and slanders beautiful people, is more than I can
> understand.
> I hope you don't have a wife and children for it must be a
> daily embarrassment being married to you or having you as a
> father.
> May God forgive your miserable sinful soul.

A familiar face was missing from the set on the day of Janet Brady's
appearance. Actor Dean Jones had hosted all week for the absent
Bakkers. Jones had a gentle, thoughtful manner, in stark contrast
to the combativeness of Bakker and his cohorts. Jones had appeared
on Bakker's show before and had been friends with the Bakkers for
seven or eight years. He was struck by the way the public treated
Jim and Tammy Bakker as if they were soap-opera stars.

If the pastor was treated like an actor, Jones the actor acted like
a pastor. Bakker had characterized Jones on the air a few months
earlier as more spiritual than many preachers he knew. The comment was intended as praise, though Bakker occasionally mocked
the pious. To Bakker, "super spirituality" went hand in hand with
an unwillingness to forgive and a propensity for righteous judgment. "The most scary people on earth are the super-religious
people," he told his congregation. "Religion kills. . . . My God says
he gives you the desires of your heart. If you want a phony pastor,

then you go find yourself a real religious pastor. Religion crucified Jesus Christ."

Though nominally out of town, Bakker remained a presence on his daily TV show during Jones's stint as guest host. On the actor's first day, Bakker appeared by videotape to complain about the *Observer*. Afterwards, Jones urged those on the set to speak positively. "I think it would . . . serve our friends Jim and Tammy if we helped them through this and we say, 'Jim and Tammy, let's reach out . . . to that high calling in Christ Jesus without becoming bogged down in this pit.' "

Though it mirrored the sentiments of many PTL partners and employees, Jones's effort to keep to 1996high road infuriated Bakker. Don Hardister had never seen Bakker so mad at a guest host. At eight each morning in California, Bakker rose to watch the program. He complained that Jones was acting too spiritual. Bakker wanted the fire stoked. Jones had planned Friday's show to focus on the gifts of the Holy Spirit, including talking in tongues. But Dortch informed him the program would focus instead on fund-raising. Jones decided to leave. His absence the next day spoke eloquently of Bakker's absolute loss of perspective.

PTL had managed to convince ECFA to reverse its October 1985 decision to oust the ministry from its membership. PTL produced a five-year cash-flow projection that claimed PTL would pay all its overdue bills by May 1986. Its application for membership categorized the IRS audit of PTL as "routine." Indeed, on January 27, 1986, Dortch assured a four-man contingent from ECFA that he expected the IRS audit to be resolved favorably in the near future. The ECFA group was also told that PTL was under tight budget control. In a meeting with his own board the next day, Bakker reported that ECFA would be renewing PTL's membership.

In fact, the accountability group was still uneasy. After studying PTL's November 1985 financial statements, an accountant working with ECFA reported his ominous assessment on February 11:

> The financial statement appeared to be very poorly prepared. . . . The income and expense has no breakdown at all by project. It is not possible to determine whether PTL is operat-

ing at a profit or loss either on a project basis or overall. It
seems strange. . . .

I believe that the financial condition of Heritage is much
more critical than was represented to us during our visit.
. . . PTL must be under tremendous pressure from its creditors.

The completion of the Heritage Towers appears to be completely dependent on future donations, unless financing is obtained. . . .

I suspect that the tax situation will not be resolved as easily
as Mr. Dortch indicated to us. . . .

I do not think we should be overly surprised if certain of
PTL's operating companies are forced into bankruptcy by its
creditors in the near future . . . it would be particularly cata-
strophic for PTL in view of its commitment to provide future
services (lodging and other facilities) for a substantial number
of people. . . . Consideration ought to be given to the effect
on ECFA if my prediction of financial disaster comes true.

In late February, a month after the visit to PTL, ECFA's board
agreed that PTL was in compliance with the organization's standards. But the board decided to warn PTL about its marginal financial condition. After learning of ECFA's decision to renew PTL's
membership, Bakker announced it to his viewers, claiming that
reports in the *Observer* had been misleading.

We are saying to the world today that there are people that
look us over, that every time these newspaper articles are in
the newspaper . . . they come and look at us to see if the
charges that are made against us are really true. . . . People
are looking at us closely, closer than maybe they need to. But
they do. We're accountable to the government, we're accountable to the FCC, we're accountable to the Justice Department. . . . We're accountable to our partners. . . . I think
you have a right to know what you're giving for and I want
you to know that when you put your money with PTL it is
going to go for exactly what you have committed it for. And
I feel good about that.

Two days later, ECFA sent its warning letter to Bakker. Executive director Art Borden wrote that PTL had made "commendable
progress" in achieving compliance with the council's standards. But
his words conveyed a message very different from the image Bakker had left with his viewers.

The Board wants to communicate its deep concern regarding PTL's apparent precarious financial condition. . . . The Board believes it would be remiss to ignore signs of apparent persistent and substantial financial difficulties such as chronic under capitalization, over spending, or cash-flow shortages. PTL's current liabilities are significantly in excess of liquid assets. In terms of non-fixed assets and liabilities from a strict accounting standpoint, the organization is technically bankrupt. In other words, the organization's continued financial viability is largely dependent upon the forbearance of its lenders. . . .

For any organization to be able to represent with integrity to its donors that their contributions will be devoted to the purposes for which they are solicited, there must be sufficient financial viability to offer reasonable assurance that the organization will not dissipate those funds in bankruptcy.

The *Observer-*FCC crisis supplied Bakker with another opportunity to raise some much-needed money. "Here we are fighting for our very life in this ministry and then to have this kind of thing circulating all over America, it is just devastating us. And so unless our faithful partners stand with us we are on the brink of a disaster, not a miracle." Hiding behind this smoke screen, Bakker renewed his mass sales of lifetime partnerships in the Towers. Fifteen months after his first offer of free lodging in the proposed building, only the skeleton of eight of the hotel's twenty-one stories had been erected. On New Year's Day, Bakker had told his viewers that PTL didn't have the money to finish the building. "But I have faith, and I've counted the cost."

As he had done so many times before with remarkable impunity, Bakker suddenly "found" enormous numbers of available lifetime partnerships. In early January, he had warned partners that the supply of Tower partnerships was running low. But on February 7, that report was a faded memory; Bakker now told his audience that he had learned from Dortch that PTL had about twenty thousand Towers partnerships left. Bakker and Dortch still clung to their past promise to commit half the Towers's rooms to PTL lifetime partners. As he had done so many times, Bakker represented the February 1986 offering as the last. "When they're gone, they're gone," he said on February 10. He predicted they would sell out by April 1.

Three days before the announcement of the remaining twenty

thousand partnerships, Bakker had gotten bad news from Bailey. Two major lenders—including PTL's largest secured creditor, Fairfax Mortgage Corporation the Baltimore, Maryland firm holding mortgages on the hotels and water park—were threatening to foreclose. "Because of payroll, utility bills, and emergency payments, we cannot meet the growing list of emergencies," Bailey wrote. "I do not foresee being able to meet our weekly commitment to Roe Messner until contributions pick up considerably." Messner was getting frustrated. In mid-January, he complained to Dortch about Bailey's refusal to pay him.

> Peter . . . always uses the excuse that he has to get a call from third floor before he can give me a check. I just don't understand because I know millions have been raised on the Tower and I can't get the $300,000.00 a week that you promised . . .
> [My banker] thinks I am crazy to keep working and mortgage everything I have, when PTL won't even keep their word to me. Something has to be done.

Bailey sounded another klaxon in his February 11 report to Bakker. PTL now owed Messner $7 million. "Many people in the ministry are not happy with not getting my attention. All it means is they can't get money." PTL needed more than $800,000 a month merely to make good on its promises to repay debt. The ministry's total expenses were running close to $1.6 million a week. Dun and Bradstreet listed PTL's financial condition as unbalanced.

Bailey's dire warnings bore little resemblance to Bakker's public pronouncements about PTL's efforts to cut costs. "We are budgeting, controlling overhead. We are making people turn the lights out in every building." The budget director's office had been moved next to his "forever," Bakker said. With the budgets trimmed, "every dollar is going to be like giving ten dollars to us. So when you give this thousand dollars to us, we're going to bring all of our bills current. We've got such structure. I told our budget director, I said you're a policeman. . . . You will not allow us to spend any more than the budget allows."

Bakker sanitized his repeated failures to see that PTL stuck to its budget. "We started a budget process, believe it or not, five years ago. And every time we would get to the point where we would get it in budget and control, the old systems were antiquated," Bakker told his audience. Tammy assured viewers that "the dream of Jim's whole lifetime I believe is to be able to keep the bills of PTL up-to-date and keep them current." Once her husband could cut PTL "down to a roar, a dull roar, and get the right amount of people here and get everything, it will work the best it's ever worked."

I had been eager to see PTL's latest audited financial statements, a document PTL was obliged to release as an ECFA member. A footnote in PTL's 1984 statements had disclosed that the IRS was auditing PTL, but the note had provided no details. On February 27, 1986, after ECFA's decision to renew PTL's membership and with it PTL's obligation to release its audit, Dortch released a copy of PTL's 1985 audited financial statements to the *Observer.* In tiny print in footnote ten, the document disclosed that the IRS audit was over and that the IRS had "proposed various alternative tax positions which may, if the IRS prevails, result in the assessment of taxes to the Ministry." The disclosure carefully avoided any suggestion that the IRS wanted to revoke PTL's tax-exempt status.

The audit also disclosed that the South Carolina Tax Commission was claiming taxes on the money PTL had raised with its lifetime partnerships. The audit did not say what the agency wanted in dollars, but a total was easy to derive. The state's sales and hotel-room tax was seven percent. PTL had raised $66 million in partnerships in 1984 and 1985.

The twin tax claims had cost PTL an unqualified audit. In its one-page auditors' report, PTL's new outside accounting firm, Laventhol and Horwath, warned that the federal and state tax claims could have a "material" impact on PTL's finances. The disclosures were unquestionably news, but I had precious little additional information. The IRS, bound by rules of secrecy, could say nothing about the case. PTL had little to say. I asked PR man Neil Eskelin if PTL was concerned that it might lose its tax-exempt status. "We're just not commenting on that possibility," Eskelin said.

The tax story appeared in mid-March. Bakker struck back using more deception. "Now the new story is they're trying to get another agency to come in and investigate us," he said. "Here's a story about a tax agency that we have not commented on, and the IRS said they didn't comment on. So how could they print a story that they have no comments on from anybody involved?" Bakker never acknowledged what his own audited financial statements had revealed—that the government agencies had long ago come in to investigate. Dortch skillfully turned the story into an attack on PTL's partners, the constituency whose minds PTL hoped to seal. "The *Charlotte Observer* is once again expressing its contempt for God's people who have been ministered to and helped by PTL."

Weeks after Dean Jones's efforts to calm the rhetoric, Bakker was still obsessed. He complained to his staff that he had asked repeatedly that Enough Is Enough bumper stickers be handed out at the entrance to Heritage USA, but he had never seen it happening. He wanted the city of Charlotte saturated with one hundred thousand more stickers. The order backfired. Soon Bakker complained to his staff that bumper stickers had been sent to each pastor in Charlotte—an embarrassing move, Bakker said, because many didn't cooperate with PTL.

After a visit from author Doug Wead, Bakker told his staff that he wanted Wead's book finished by the end of April. After a few days, he complained that Wead hadn't been contacted. "I have been asking for days. . . . It's something that has to be done now, or it's going to be dropped." (Wead wouldn't finish his work until late June—his early drafts were deemed too soft on the *Observer*—and PTL would tell Wead then that it did not want to go another round with the newspaper. The book would never be published; PTL had wasted another $75,000.)

On April 14—the first day of a two-week telethon dubbed "Enough is Enough"—Bakker told his staff to see if Jamie Buckingham's report on PTL could be sent to all active and inactive names on PTL's mailing list. Bakker also wanted ten thousand copies sent to Christian leaders and magazines. He suggested that PTL billboards around town carry a picture of Tammy Faye painting the words "Enough is Enough," and soon they would.

Bakker's staff had had enough of enough is enough, and cable systems carrying PTL programming had begun reporting a drop in viewership to Bakker's staff. Some days, sitting in his dressing room before the show, Bakker promised to heed his staff's advice to cool it. But by the end of his hour before the camera, as he sat and stewed about his perceived victimization, he would unleash more accusations. The newspaper had caused the ulcers in his son's stomach. The newspaper kept paid informants. The newspaper's lawyers—he did not name them, of course—had been overheard in a country-club locker room joking that they didn't even read *Observer* articles before publication because Bakker would never sue.

Jim and Tammy Bakker's twenty-fifth wedding anniversary on April 1 offered momentary relief from the monotony of Bakker's attacks on the newspaper. The day's TV show began with a testimonial from Oral Roberts. Roberts spoke in tongues, a display of the gifts of the Holy Spirit highly unusual on Bakker's program. He also offered a prophecy which would be mercifully forgotten a year later. "You're going to come into that fullness of your ministry that you know, that you know, that you know, that you know God calls you to and by word and knowledge I call it forth, and so it is."

Bakker's staff had wrested control of the show from Bakker for that one day. "I'm usually in control. I'm not and I'm nervous," he confessed to his audience. Usually, Bakker's producers' staff fashioned a plan for each day's show, identifying a theme from its list of expected guests and proposing music to enhance the message. Each night, a three-page timed format was sent home for Bakker's perusal. Usually, Bakker rewrote the plan. He made changes during the broadcast as well, dispatching orders during music breaks.

Bakker usually arrived at the studio at about ten in the morning, Don Hardister notifying producer Sandra Sims that "unit eighteight"—the number of Bakker's portable radio—was in the dressing room. Bakker would take a seat in his antique barber's chair. One of Tammy's former secretaries, now the proprietor of a beauty salon in the Main Street mall, applied Bakker's makeup. From his seat, he might ask to see new video spots that had been prepared for the show, watching them on a nearby monitor. Sims reviewed the day's guests and the proposed format with him.

Occasionally, Bakker would summon other staff members to the dressing room, though he preferred to avoid getting bad news before the show. Sometimes he would sit silently, lost in the private universe to which he often retreated. Even on the telephone, he could remain silent for what seemed like minutes.

There was a big cake on the day of his anniversary and a syrupy "we love you" message from Dortch with the mail he'd been soliciting for the event. The show's feature was a reunion with Bill Harrison, Bakker's journalism instructor from Muskegon High School, whom Bakker described as "the one man who had touched my life so dramatically," giving a shy kid who skipped class confidence in himself.

Bakker had not seen Harrison in twenty-five years. "I'm scared to death."

"You think he might not approve, honey, or what's the problem?" Tammy asked.

"Yeah, yeah," Bakker answered. "I mean, it's just like your teachers and your mom and dad always are such special people and you want their approval."

The festivities continued that night with a dinner for Jim and Tammy, carried live on the PTL network and rebroadcast during the next two days. Wead, a frequent speaker on the Amway circuit, delivered an extended joke about the TV evangelists.

> It sure ain't boring being Jim Bakker, that's for sure, being Tammy Bakker. Did you hear the story about everybody got to heaven and Saint Peter called all the television evangelists . . . into a side room and he said, "This can't get around, but you guys will appreciate the jam we're in, we've oversold heaven. . . . You guys have been through hell before, and we're gonna have to send you to hell for just, hey, just for a couple weeks." . . .
>
> A few weeks later, the Devil calls Saint Peter, and he said "You've got to get these people out of hell. Rex and Maude Aimee Humbard are going around everywhere putting 'You are Loved' pins on the imps. . . . Kenneth Hagin is going around telling everybody this isn't really fire, it just feels like fire. . . . Jimmy Swaggart's going around telling everybody good to see you here, good to see you here. And Doug Oldham and the Happy Goodmans have eaten all the devil's food cake. . . . Pat Robertson keeps telling me how to run hell on a scriptural basis. . . . Oral Roberts is getting everybody healed. Jerry Falwell is getting everybody registered to vote. And Jim and Tammy Bakker are raising money to build a water slide and air condition the place."

Wead got a big laugh.

Afterwards, the Bakkers invited friends and PTL executives to the Presidential Suite. They walked up Main Street on their way to the private party. Bakker's staff had booked ten rooms overlooking the enclosed street to shoot balloons and a thousand pounds of confetti on the anniversary couple. Looking on that night in the enclosed mall, Henry Harrison, Bakker's one-time co-host, saw that Bakker had recaptured the exuberance Harrison had seen in him years before in Virginia.

Late that night, as the suite was being cleaned, the Bakkers relaxed with Roger and Linda Wilson, the couple who had been close friends with the Bakkers until Linda Wilson warned Jim about Tammy's feelings for Gary Paxton. Jim and Tammy were struck at how young, rested, and peaceful their friends looked. The Bakkers suggested that the Wilsons, who now worked at a Christian TV station in Pittsburgh, spend the night in the suite. David Taggart arranged for them to stay as long as they wanted. Linda Wilson couldn't imagine anyone living in such splendor, in room after room of fine appointments. To the Bakkers, it was routine. To Linda Wilson, it seemed like "Life-styles of the Rich and Famous."

In their days together at CBN, the Bakkers and Wilsons had shared Sloppy Joes for dinner and joked about remembering each other when they got famous. Now, Linda Wilson realized how little the Bakkers understood the real world—what it was like to work for what you have, to struggle to pay your mortgage and utility bills, to balance your checkbook. Amidst the plenty, the Bakkers didn't seem to have enough. On her occasional trips to Charlotte, Linda Wilson had joined Tammy on her daily afternoon shopping forays. Tammy didn't seem to give a thought to how much she spent. Shopping filled the void within. Tammy assured her that she had never been happier, her marriage had never been better. But Linda Wilson sensed that Tammy was trying to convince herself that it was true.

After their return to Pittsburgh, the Wilsons discovered a huge box on their driveway. Inside, they found a letter from Tammy. Just wanted you to know we are thinking about you, we care about you, she wrote. Underneath, the Wilsons discovered jewelry, lipstick, makeup, and women's shoes and clothes, many with price tags still attached. Some had apparently been bought for Tammy, others had been purchased in Linda Wilson's size.

* * *

Bakker spent hours showing his high-school teacher Bill Harrison around the grounds. Bakker enjoyed displaying what he had accomplished, and his visitors invariably came away impressed. Harrison, an agnostic, was no exception.

Heritage USA invariably surprised the first-time visitor: the bucolic entrance, with its grassy fields, grazing horses, and quaint condominiums; the isolated World Outreach Center where Bakker had his offices, where Bailey struggled with too many debts and too little money, and where the earnest ladies on the first floor processed the enormous sums of cash that came in twice a day in tray after tray of mail; the bustling Partner Center, with its cavernous hotel lobby full of casually dressed partners and the curious sight of a formally dressed pianist playing a black grand a stone's throw away from a swimming pool that doubled as a baptismal font; the picture-perfect Main Street under its cyclorama ceiling; the unfinished water park, a sprawling mass of man-made rock; and, across the lake and along a winding, wooded road, more lodging, campgrounds, the amphitheater, the stucco Upper Room, and the TV studio–Barn–Total Learning Center complex where partners could see Bakker tape his show or preach a Sunday service before the TV cameras. Altogether, the complex left a ubiquitous sense of constant activity and surprising promise.

Bakker's gentle comments to the pregnant girls at the home for unwed mothers especially impressed Harrison that day. Bakker explained to his former teacher that he had done everything he could to preserve each girl's dignity. Harrison had gone to Heritage USA wondering if PTL wasn't taking advantage of the stereotypical little-old-lady donor. After his visit, he thought that lady was getting good value for her gifts to PTL.

But Harrison cautioned Bakker to stop fighting the newspapers. And he warned Bakker to stop building and consolidate, to shelve his long list of projects. "I think you're in danger of running right from under yourself. You've arrived, whether you know it or not." Bakker listened, respectfully.

CHAPTER NINETEEN

IN PURSUIT OF
THE TRUTH

*"Knight-Ridder . . . [is] harassing people
related to this ministry"*

A month into the Enough is Enough campaign, I telephoned Roger
Flessing in California to talk about PTL and the FCC. Flessing was
a friendly, talkative man who had none of the suspicion of the press
that afflicted Bakker and his palace guard. Flessing was troubled by
the recent layoffs—"bloodletting," he called it. After his return
from a 1984 trip to Russia with Billy Graham, Flessing had been
struck by the similarity between the Soviet Union and PTL. Each
was run by a small bureaucracy that made all the money, held all
the privileges, urged the rank and file to sacrifice, and used misinformation to manipulate the internal and external media. The layoffs had been a reminder that at PTL, individuals were expendable,
that everything existed for the good of the state. The Enough Is
Enough campaign had demonstrated how effective PTL propaganda could be.

I asked again about Jessica Hahn, as I had fifteen months before.
"I keep running into that story all over the country," Flessing said.
"The one you really need to talk to is Al Cress." Dortch's former
assistant had telephoned Flessing in fall 1985 at his home in the hills
above Sacramento. Cress was fuming over what he had witnessed

at PTL. He had called Flessing because, among PTL's staff, Flessing had a reputation as someone who sympathized with the disaffected.

Cress had asked if Flessing knew about the payoff to a woman named Jessica Hahn. "Wait a minute, Al. I've heard that name before," Flessing answered. He told Cress about my call in December 1984, when Flessing had dismissed the possibility that Bakker might go to bed with another woman. Cress told him about the draft lawsuit Cortese and Dortch had received—"the most vile thing I ever read," Cress called it. Cress alluded to the events that followed, concluding with the payoff. "Dortch arranged it all."

Flessing encouraged Cress to tell somebody. As Flessing hung up, he realized that Dortch and Taggart had lied to him the day of the Heritage Grand opening. Yes, he realized, Jim Bakker had had sex with Jessica Hahn.

As Flessing and I talked five months later, I asked if Cress would be willing to answer my questions. "You have to understand Al," Flessing said. "He is an intensely spiritual person with a strong sense of right and wrong. He doesn't know what to do about it. He's been bombarded by PTL propaganda—if you do anything to cause PTL to come crashing down, then you are guilty. . . . Al is churning inside, a time bomb. He's ready to tell somebody something." Two weeks later, I telephoned Flessing again. He had talked to Cress, who was somewhere in Illinois. Flessing told me that Cress was very upset but probably not ready to talk.

I began looking for Dortch's assistant. I checked for a forwarding address. Cress had left none. I looked at the deed transferring his home at Heritage USA. It offered no clues. I checked voting, property ownership, and telephone records in Carlinville, Illinois, where Cress had worked for Dortch. I came away without a lead.

I had already collected a few circumstantial facts corroborating the story that John Stewart had told me in December. The John Wayne Airport in Orange County had recorded a takeoff by PTL's corporate jet at 5:34 P.M. on February 7, 1985—about the day Stewart placed Dortch's first meeting with Hahn's representative. I learned that Scott Furstman, Weitzman's law partner, had written a letter for PTL in December 1985 complaining about a Florida TV documentary about evangelists. I found out that Hahn had purchased a new car, a black two-door Oldsmobile Toronado, in mid-

July 1985. It was, I thought, the sort of acquisition you might expect from someone who had just come into money.

The day after Bakker's anniversary, PTL's directors heard the latest round of assurances the IRS audit would be resolved favorably. The board had been told little more about it. In fact, the directors as a rule heard little bad news from their leaders. To believe Bakker and Dortch, board member Charles Cookman later testified, "there would have been no reason to assume other than that things were going well." In its 1988 indictment of Bakker and Dortch, a federal grand jury would accuse the two men of failing to inform the board of PTL's poor financial condition, severe cash-flow problems, and overselling of lifetime partnerships.

The board believed in its leaders with the naiveté of the most complaisant PTL partner. Contrary to the on-air claims of Bakker and Dortch, it was the directors who had submitted themselves to PTL's top executives, not the other way around. "I trusted Jim Bakker, I trusted Richard Dortch, and I don't regret believing in people, believing in the goodness of people," J. Don George said in the days following Bakker's 1987 resignation. "Jim Bakker is a generous man. He is a man with a true, loving heart. I truly believe it was his vision to build Heritage USA as a ministry center to people. I think Jim and Tammy are great people."

The Texas pastor never knew what Bakker received in base salary. He had assumed something on the order of $50,000 or $75,000, a guess that missed the mark by $200,000. George had been led to believe that Bakker led a hand-to-mouth existence, living from one paycheck to the next. If Bakker did live from check to check, it was a reflection of the Bakker family's staggering ability to spend money. Franzone, the board member who occasionally worshipped at George's church, thought Bakker's salary was $45,000. In his eyes, that modest sum made the board's periodic bonuses legitimate.

The board members apparently knew little about the bonuses they were approving. The bonus totals were no longer included in the official minutes shown to the directors during their meetings. Instead, the bonuses were recorded on separate addenda drawn up by Taggart or Shirley Fulbright and kept on the third floor. After

Bakker's resignation, at least four directors would express surprise at the sums paid to the Bakkers and Dortch. Some remembered approving smaller sums, others remembered meetings when no figures were discussed. The bonuses were routinely awarded in net-of-tax amounts, and each director had his or her own sense of the extra money PTL had to pay to cover Bakker's taxes.

With the board so completely out of touch with reality and failing so totally to perform its oversight role, its actions acquired an absurd flavor. In its April 2, 1986, meeting, it voted a $200,000 bonus to Bakker for his efforts to control PTL's budget. Tammy Bakker and Richard Dortch each got $100,000. The board voted another perk for Bakker worth nearly $200,000 a year, resurrecting a proposal Dortch had made in 1981. With its customary unanimity, the board agreed to transfer title to their PTL-owned homes on Lake Wylie to Bakker, Dortch, and Bakker's neighbors in Tega Cay—Vi Azvedo, Doug Oldham, and singers Howard and Vestal Goodman. The transfer would be spread over several years, they agreed, and PTL would pay all taxes on the transfers. The board decided to wait for advice from its accountants and lawyers on how to make the transfers.

Three months later, without further board action, Charles Cookman—who had spoken with concern about pastors retiring without a home—signed a "certification of action" on the board's behalf ordering the transfer of the PTL homes Bakker and Dortch lived in.

> Whereas, the history of the Assemblies of God in regard to parsonages has produced some awkward and embarrassing circumstances by leaving ministers homeless in their senior years and. . . .
> Whereas, the N.C. District of the Assemblies of God has gone on official record as favoring the personal home ownership of its ministry rather than the parsonage system,

PTL's board resolved to give Dortch and Bakker full ownership of their parsonages in equal increments over a ten-year period, the document read. Should they retire or die earlier, it continued, the homes would be transferred to them or their estates in their entirety.

The latest round of executive perks was endorsed without the vote of board member Efrem Zimbalist, Jr. During January's meeting, Dortch had announced that the actor had resigned in November citing "a heavy motion-picture and television schedule." The board balked at accepting the resignation and agreed to let its one secular celebrity know that the board could excuse his absence until he had more time to give. In February, Zimbalist said thanks, but no thanks. The Lord had directed him to resign from all ministry work and rebuild his career, Zimbalist wrote.

It was hardly a propitious time for the board to pay massive bonuses, in cash or in kind. Twelve days before the board's April 1986 meeting, finance director Peter Bailey reported expenses still running over general contributions. Seven days before the meeting, Bailey had told Bakker that PTL's bank balance was nearly $1.7 million in the red.

Bailey's weekly reports continued to warn of fiscal danger through the spring. Bakker had his reward for cutting the budget, but PTL was slipping closer to the abyss ECFA had warned about.

April 7: Bailey wrote to Bakker saying if PTL didn't make a $582,309 bond payment on April 25, a $5.7 million issue of church bonds used to finance an earlier building project "will be in default and the SEC [Securities and Exchange Commission] will become involved." PTL could hope to make the bond payment only if it could close a large loan by April 15. By coincidence, that day was also PTL's deadline to pay $306,737 to the company leasing telephone-switching equipment to the ministry. If the firm received no money, it planned to sue.

Bailey told Bakker that PTL's retail stores—supposedly a cog in the money-making machine subsidizing PTL's evangelism—were losing money. Since the ministry opened the stores, they had cost PTL $388,348. The subsidiary that handled records, tapes, and books had lost about $39,000. "This is contrary to the information you receive," Bailey wrote. "If we didn't have these companies, [PTL] in fact would have a better cash flow."

April 16: The major refinancing loan Bailey was expecting had not closed, and Bailey needed more than $2 million to make eight "real emergency" payments. PTL needed $275,000 to settle a lawsuit filed over a broken land-purchase contract, and it had promised the ministry's tape supplier $200,000. "We can have all the financial controls in the world, but if we don't live within our means it doesn't mean anything."

April 21: "I am not writing checks this week unless it is an extreme emergency. I already am having difficulty with team members cooperating," Bailey wrote. "We need to quit blaming finance for our difficulties and bite the bullet by cutting expenses and new fund-raising ideas. We must survive!"

April 28: General contributions for the previous week had totaled $500,000, but PTL had spent $1.2 million. "We are surviving because of the lifetime partnerships. . . . We need to cut back our projects until we are within our means. . . . I know this is not what we want to hear. But there are many, many vendors, TV stations, and loans that are close to legal action. . . . As you know, we all are working hard to obtain financing." Bailey closed with his customary statement of confidence in Christ's power. "Whether we get [financing] or not, Jesus will see us through it all and He is coming soon!"

May 5: PTL had $2.2 million in outstanding checks written against future deposits—more than twice the $1 million level Bailey considered safe. Staff members continued to circumvent PTL's financial controls. Bailey complained that he had found folding chairs, phone lines, carpet, and other unapproved staff purchases in Roe Messner's April 1986 bill.

Bailey's blunt memos were a contrast to his usually meek demeanor; he reminded one co-worker of Bob Cratchit, the clerk in Dickens's *A Christmas Carol.* Slight of build, bespectacled, and a bit hunched, he looked the part. Bailey was a devout man, taking time at work to read the Bible and to share with friends the story of what Jesus had done in his life. Unfortunately, he was not a dynamic leader. He was shut out of major decisions about PTL's financial future; he had not been involved in structuring the lifetime-partnership program. He got little response to his blunt memos, which were his principal communication with Bakker, aside from conversations with the more accessible Taggart. Bakker treated Bailey with little respect, dismissing him in staff meetings as a "bean counter." If it were up to finance, Bakker would say, PTL would still be in tents. "Yes," Bailey muttered under his breath, "but they would have been paid for."

Bailey had seen where stubborn adherence to the rules had gotten his predecessor, John Franklin. He did not speak forcefully to Bakker in staff meetings, but no one who valued their position did. As a result, staff meetings were usually a drawn-out Bakker monologue. Only in private conversations did Bailey sometimes blow off steam about his frustration with Bakker's freewheeling spending. Bailey and his staff felt estranged from the executives in the offices one floor above them in the World Outreach Center. In a January 1984 memo to Bakker, Bailey complained:

> Finance is looked upon as being in the way of progress by many in the ministry. . . . Whenever my finance people try to do their jobs to enforce financial procedure, they are stopped from doing so by the third floor, especially in the area of cash advances and emergency check requests.

A CPA since 1967 with a bachelor's degree from the University of Bridgeport, Bailey had a knack for the mechanics of the finance operation, supervising the accounting staff and straddling the gap between PTL's debts and bank balance. The job of juggling creditors consumed most of his time. If he was a plodder, as one coworker put it, or weak, as another suggested, he also gave Bakker the loyalty the PTL president demanded, despite Bakker's open abuse. He made occasional suggestions about Bakker's personal finances. If Bakker wanted something done, Bailey could be counted on to do it. His bosses rewarded him for his loyalty with a $16,000 1985 Toyota Cressida, an unsecured, no-interest $30,000 loan, and, during a twelve-month span beginning in February 1986, bonuses of $63,000.

In late April, the *Observer* published my detailed story about PTL's failure to make good on the millions of dollars in land-sales contracts that V. J. Sherk had arranged on Bakker's orders in 1985. The story also mentioned PTL's continuing dispute over the money claimed by REC, the water-park contractor. PTL had been unable to close on eleven contracts. I quoted a real-estate broker who represented one of the jilted sellers. "The whole history of this thing has been the failure to perform, failure to communicate, failure to be businesslike, failure to reply to proper inquiry. . . . The way this thing has been handled has been unconscionable."

PTL's decision to back out on the purchases had landed the ministry in court. The owners of a 131-acre horse farm had begun selling their breeding stock after agreeing to sell. PTL missed the October 1985 closing on the $1.6 million deal, and the owners sued. On April 14—with a trial approaching and a subpoena for sensitive financial documents pending—PTL settled out of court. PTL refused to disclose the terms. I could uncover no additional details at the time. PTL had, in fact, paid $275,000 to put the blunder behind them. In February 1986, PTL had agreed, in confidence, to pay $120,000 to settle a second suit over a 117-acre, $1.2 million deal that it had failed to close in October.

As it had with the March tax story, PTL now misled its audience with semantic manipulations. My story had opened with the words "PTL has been accused in court of breaking contracts to buy hundreds of acres." Bakker, appearing furious as he sat next to an indifferent and distracted Tammy, read the words and turned to Dortch on the set. Dortch wore a similar look of disgust.

> Bakker: Reverend Dortch, you're the executive . . . vice president of this ministry. Have we been accused in any court of . . . breaking contracts?
>
> Dortch: Never. Never.
>
> Bakker: It's never happened.
>
> Dortch: There has never been a court proceeding where PTL ever appeared and responded to anything. We've never been brought to court.
>
> Bakker: No court, no court has ever accused this ministry of these things. This is the front page of the *Charlotte Observer.* It is a lie. It is not even any truth to it.

It may have been true that PTL had never been in a court*room.* But PTL had in fact been named as defendant in four lawsuits—formal, written accusations filed in courts in York, South Carolina, and Charlotte.

Bakker called on Roe Messner to testify that he had been paid for the Partner Center. "How come they keep saying I did not pay bills, and I paid you $42 million in one year?" Bakker asked Messner. "You must be lying or we are all liars." Bakker blamed the *Observer* for PTL's trouble getting loans, for banks' reluctance to cash PTL checks, for the health problems of his staff. According to Bakker, most of PTL's long-overdue bills were for jobs where there were disputes over work of low quality. "I will always pay what I owe anybody. But I want to know, for sure . . . [we're] not being cheated and robbed."

Bakker was eager to see his staff limit the damage. Six days later, he instructed his staff to see that Sherk talked to the jilted sellers "on a regular basis and see what we can do to help them. . . . Communication is the key." He urged Bailey to make sure he talked to people calling to complain about debts.

Nearly five months had passed since the John Stewart call that had alerted me to the Jessica Hahn payoff. I was eager to pursue the Hahn story, but first I wanted to talk to Dortch's former assistant, Cress. On April 23, I called Roger Flessing hoping for another lead. I was in luck. Since we had talked last, Cress had sent Flessing a résumé with an address. Since October 1985, Cress had been living in Robinson, Illinois, a town near the Indiana border. "I've got a feeling he's staying with an elderly relative, aunt or something. My understanding is he hasn't told anybody at PTL where he is."

The night of April 28, I dialed the number on Cress's résumé. An older woman answered, and asked who was calling. I gave my name. Cress came to the phone. I could tell he was shaken. He told me he was busy, to call back in a few minutes. I agreed and thought maybe there was hope after all. I dialed back in a few minutes, but no one answered. I kept calling but got either no answer or a busy signal. Obviously, Cress did not want to talk to me. Late that night, my editor, Jeannie Falknor, and I agreed that I should leave the next morning for Robinson. I didn't expect to win Cress's trust about such a sensitive matter if I was only an unfamiliar voice over a phone line. If Cress had been watching Bakker's daily program, he would have every reason not to trust me.

Late the next morning, I rang the front doorbell of Mel and Gladys Carey's modest home on East Clearwater Street in Robinson. No one answered. I went around back, passing Cress's car in the driveway. No one answered at the back door either. As I waited on the back stoop, seventy-two-year-old Mel Carey approached from a neighbor's backyard. Carey, a retired custodian, had one glass eye and failing sight in the other. I introduced myself politely, telling him I'd come to see Al Cress.

Carey returned in a minute. "He's not available." I pressed further, asking if I could just see Cress to explain why I was there; I'd come all the way from North Carolina. Then, Mrs. Carey emerged and took over the conversation. "He's not available. . . . He has nothing to say. . . . He is a man of few words." I pressed her. Eventually, she shut the door.

I spent the afternoon sitting in my car hoping for an audience with Cress should he step outside. I felt alternately sinister and foolish staking out a house in the modest working-class neighborhood. Occasionally, I knocked on the Careys' door or rang their bell. I left a note in the mailbox appealing to Cress to talk to me. In mid-afternoon, while I was away calling my office, Cress's car disappeared. When it had not returned by dinnertime, I gave up. The day had been terribly frustrating, tempered only by the unbroken blue sky and the spring sun warming the air. As the golden sunlight fell over the rolling farmlands of western Indiana, I drove back to Indianapolis.

I had never told the Careys or Cress why I wanted to talk to him. When I got back to Charlotte, I wrote to Cress and expressed my appreciation for the Careys' patience. "I don't enjoy ringing doorbells or sitting in cars," I told Cress. I heard nothing from him.

But two weeks later, Jim Cobble, Cress's friend and colleague from Illinois and PTL, telephoned. He wanted to know why I had called Cress. I was evasive; I wasn't ready to show my hand on the Hahn story for fear PTL would cover up the evidence. Cobble and I chatted about PTL. He divided PTL's staff into two groups. One included skilled employees eager to end the battle with the *Observer* and to see PTL achieve excellence and financial integrity. According to Cobble, Bakker found the advice of this faction threatening. At the other extreme were those employees who were insecure and incompetent but were willing to worship Bakker. According to Cobble, Dortch was caught with one foot in each world. He recognized PTL's need for competent staff, but his job demanded more management ability than he possessed and he was terribly eager to preserve his relationship with Bakker.

We talked about the Assemblies of God. Himself an ordained minister in the denomination, Cobble thought that the Assemblies leadership in Springfield viewed PTL skeptically. While the Assemblies of God might admire PTL's evangelistic zeal, Cobble said, the denomination's mainstream found the ministry superficial, gaudy, self-aggrandizing—and perhaps guilty of using religion as a cover for greed.

In late May, Bakker and Dortch gave the TV audience their version of my trip to Illinois. Certainly Dortch, if not Bakker, could recognize the risk to the ministry if Cress cooperated with the *Observer*. Cress knew about Hahn. The Janet Brady episode had failed to discredit me or my reporting techniques with my editors; this incident, spiced up in the retelling, offered PTL a second opportunity.

"The Knight-Ridder representatives are harassing people related to this ministry in such an unbelievable way," Bakker said. "They are going to the homes of our associates, our former associates. They're going to their businesses and are literally harassing them until they are making life hell." Dortch jumped in with details about the Careys. "These are elderly people, seventy-four, seventy-five, seventy-six years old. And here's a reporter . . . there in front of their house, knocking on the door, hollering, screaming, 'Let me come in, let me talk to you.' Now we're talking about eight and a half hours of that. They are absolute nervous wrecks."

The next day, Dortch pursued his complaint in a private letter to editor Rich Oppel.

> The largest issue on our minds now is the question of harassment and that you did not commit yourself to a proper manner of conduct by your reporters is of great concern. I fully expected an apology to be given to the elderly couple in Illinois. . . .
>
> We believe the question of what [Observer publisher] Rolfe Neill called "trolling" is still before us and that harassment of former employees and people not presently connected with this ministry is an issue we will have to give attention to until some proper understanding is arrived at by both of us.

Under Neill's leadership, the *Observer* had become a newspaper that bent over backwards to listen to its critics—sometimes so much

399

so that reporters, highly sensitive to any show of favoritism, worried that the newspaper's independence and news judgment were being compromised. I had been at the *Observer* since December 1977, long enough to know the newspaper's corporate culture and to accept the necessity of defending sensitive stories against outside complaints. That defense often became full-time work when we published a PTL story.

In his search for a way to stop the newspaper, Bakker agreed in April 1986 to meet with Knight-Ridder executives, including board chairman Alvah Chapman, in Miami. The May 13 meeting, arranged by an evangelist who knew Chapman and had encountered Bakker by chance, was an extraordinary, direct involvement of the national corporate hierarchy in local news coverage. Indeed, Oppel had argued privately that Miami's involvement would undercut him. But Chapman was troubled by the sustained nationally televised attack on Knight-Ridder's credibility. Neill suggested—and Chapman agreed—to include Oppel and Neill in the meeting. In conversations with other journalists interested in the battle between PTL and the *Observer,* PTL sought to portray the scheduled session as evidence that the *Observer* had lost Knight-Ridder's support. Once the meeting was scheduled, I set to work preparing explanatory memos and a video sampler of PTL's *Observer*-bashing.

At the last minute, Bakker backed out of the meeting, saying he had to remain with his son, who Bakker said was suffering from ulcers. Instead of flying to Miami, Bakker flew with his son to Walt Disney World for a vacation. Later, Knight-Ridder would be told that Dortch did not want the fight to escalate to network TV; ABC's "Nightline" was becoming interested in the story.

Nonetheless, Bakker sustained his fire, launching rounds from the TV screen and making no mention of Knight-Ridder's agreement to meet or his decision to cancel. On the air, he invited his TV audience to write to the newspaper chain's Miami headquarters. "It's time that Knight-Ridder have an investigation of their own people and find out what's going on. . . . They need to come down from their glass tower in Miami . . . and take a look," he said after his return from Orlando.

PTL's rhetoric continued to prompt self-examination among the Knight-Ridder management; we were not the monolith that PTL imagined. On May 14, Alvah Chapman telephoned Rich Oppel with some questions about the PTL matter. "Do you have any questions about what you've done? You know, you can almost always go back and say, 'Well, if I had to do it over again.'"

Oppel, the *Observer*'s editor since 1978, had no question about the content of the FCC stories we had published in January and none about the "play"—newspaper jargon for the location and amount of space given to a story. But if he had it to do over again, he told Chapman, he would have resolved his disagreement with Neill about the play of the FCC stories. Neill, like many readers and some of my colleagues, believed we had given the FCC story far too much space.

Neill, fifty-three, had worked as an *Observer* reporter and business editor early in his career. He had held management positions at the New York *Daily News,* and served as editor of the Philadelphia *Daily News* in the early seventies. In 1975, he was named publisher of the *Observer* and its sister paper, the *News.* As such, he had responsibility for all editorial and business operations. During Neill's early years in Charlotte, some reporters suspected that he had been moved into the job to make the traditionally liberal *Observer* more palatable to the conservative Charlotte community. Though executives in Miami denied it, Neill was forthright about his unhappiness with the *Observer*'s tone in the past. "One of the *Observer*'s problems still is that it's perceived, I think, by a number of people to be the village scold. You reduce your effectiveness when you become in people's minds shrill and then you are thought of as only tearing something down. . . . I think so many newspapers . . . are afraid to tell a city or a region that they love it."

By 1986, Neill had become very much an inside player in Charlotte's corporate community. In the *Observer* newsroom, he had acquired a reputation as a hardworking perfectionist with a fiercely dominating manner and strong influence over the editorial product. The *Observer,* though still capable of aggressive coverage, seemed less likely to challenge the status quo in its reporting columns. Sensitive stories were approached with considerable caution, although they did continue to appear; in 1981, the *Observer*'s coverage of "brown lung" disease afflicting Carolinas textile workers won for the newspaper the foremost Pulitzer Prize for journalism, the gold medal for meritorious public service. The newsroom's perception of undue influence would frustrate Neill; he challenged his critics to name one investigative story he had killed. But Neill acknowledged preaching extra care on stories where newspaper played "the executioner as well as the judge" and questioning the priority of costly investigative reports on PTL up against the need for more nuts-and-bolts coverage of the community.

A few days after Oppel's conversation with Chapman, Neill dispatched a memo to Oppel, sharing his thoughts and asking for Oppel's. "Where we go from here can have significant consequences for the *Observer*," Neill wrote. Neill complimented our PTL coverage for its professionalism. He agreed that PTL needed periodic scrutiny from the *Observer,* and he wrote that his concerns did not stem from the latest hostilities with PTL.

Neill listed a dozen observations. The complaints from PTL and Dortch's private appeals were hitting home.

> 1. For the first time, the *Observer* finds itself on the defensive regarding PTL coverage. This grows out of our January FCC stories. To me, they were overkill—too long, and more importantly, played in a way that opened us to questions of fairness: Had we dug up an old [story] and treated it as it were fresh? As you know, I am loath to make the final judgment call on matters such as this, believing those choices best belong in the newsroom. However, I ignored my instinct on insisting that this be reshaped before publication and I regret not intervening. . . .

> 3. We are not covering, nor have we for many years, the normalcy of PTL activities and the large project they have put together here. This aggravates the charges made against us in #1. Nor do we get into their theology from a religious point of view, concentrating as we do on the investigative side. . . .

> 4. Because we are focused so intently on the suspicion of wrongdoing in the PTL organization, we are often dealing with a shadowy group of ex-employees, disgruntled folks . . . this entails much cloak and dagger work.

> 5. Item #4 leads us to what Reverend Dortch calls *Observer* "espionage." That is, we leave PTL with the feeling that they [are] under microscopic, unending examination. There is no

surcease. . . . Can you imagine how we would feel under a similar cloud?

6. Many readers are largely bored with the subject. However, something like the cancelled contracts story would always be appropriate and readable.

7. Meanwhile, the manpower expended on PTL fishing expeditions and *Observer* record keeping could be usefully applied elsewhere on unreported or under-reported topics.

8. We have become preoccupied—perhaps even obsessed—with PTL in a way that is dangerous to our perspective. There is more evil incarnate surrounding us in some social problems than any shortcomings we have exposed in PTL. Nothing has a priority with us like PTL. That's excessive.

9. PTL's givers—the people our coverage is primarily intended to enlighten—have not shown us in any substantial way that they appreciate our revelations. Rather, they seem to endorse the show biz life-styles of the Bakkers and to admire the creation of Heritage USA. . . .

10. There is little left to show about the basic outline of PTL fundraising: *(a)* it's cyclical, lurching from crisis to crisis (with the [*Observer*] itself often the hostile rallying point for a new multi-million effort); *(b)* . . . The richness of PTL furnishings et al seems to be a positive for them; *(c)* PTL's send-us-your-money approach appears no different from any of the TV evangelists.

11. While it's not our fault that UPI put out an erroneous story based on our carefully written material [about the FCC], the fallout to PTL was instant and real. How would we feel if the situation were reversed? . . .

12. While we all know that each paper makes its own editing choices, circumstantial evidence—plus ignorance of our procedures and a very suspicious PTL constituency—all combine to give the appearance that the *Observer* is engaged in a vendetta against PTL. Add to that a fundamentalist conviction that the media are liberal and anti-Christian. We are dealing with impressions here and appearances. While we should not toady to our critics, neither should we be foolish. A newspaper only has so much to risk. . . .

We must disengage from our ceaseless thrall with PTL. Redirect those committed resources elsewhere. When something worthy of our attention presents itself, then do it. Meanwhile, gain credibility for having lifted the siege. (We don't announce it; just do it.) I think we largely had credibility concerning PTL coverage until the January stories. Our reputation for fairness has been stained by that one. You need ask no further than our own newsroom or division directors. . . .

If I believe our newspaper is unfair to someone then I cannot rest until that is set right. Right now, I think we're being unfair to PTL.

Your thinking is welcome. Thanks.

Oppel shared Neill's memo with Falknor and me. Jeannie and I thought we had good answers to the publisher's objections, and we had Oppel on our side. On May 30, Oppel responded with a diplomatic but firm memo reflecting his thoughts and some of ours.

I think it would be wrong if our action with regard to PTL takes the form of "backing off." . . . To characterize our activities now as "unremitting surveillance" is to pick up as fact PTL's assertions about espionage without choosing to hear what our editors and reporters are saying about what we're doing.

In summary, we've been accurate. And we've been fair. . . . I believe our PTL credibility problems begin—not end—if we back off the story. . . . The perception will gradually grow among our readers that PTL's efforts worked. Call the *Observer* people satanic forces long enough and they'll back off. . . . With the staff, there is a long-gathering belief that top management does not support the rank-and-file reporter. . . . There is also a feeling that top management doesn't support sensitive work. . . . [Your] support is seen as one of tolerance and not one of priority. The tough-nosed reporting is supported (but don't dare make a mistake), but it is not a priority, not one of the things that you believe is necessary for achieving greatness.

Furthermore, I think the consequences will be substantial and serious with . . . Jeannie and Charlie if we cannot continue investigative work on PTL for the balance of the year. If this project is shelved, it will be a long, long while before another with any bite to it—any chance of alienating a powerful person or group—is launched.

As he closed his memo, Oppel proposed that our PTL coverage continue, with Neill's direct participation. "Keep an open mind. We'll do so too."

A few days later, I joined Oppel, Falknor, and her boss, metro editor Foster Davis, in Neill's office. Neill, a movie-star handsome man with great charm, showed none of the fire that had prompted his memo. We agreed to continue pursuing a list of PTL stories. I was already at work on a story about PTL's water-park fiasco and eager to pursue stories about the apparent overselling of the lifetime partnerships, Bakker's compensation, the then little-known David Taggart and the Hahn payoff.

My call to Illinois had stunned Cress. First, he thought a friend was pulling a stunt. After he hung up, he began dialing. He relayed a message to Dortch through a friend. He reached David Taggart. The two men talked about Hahn and the payoff—the subject that Cress correctly suspected I was interested in. Taggart told him that Bakker felt that this was God's time for Heritage USA. "Nothing is going to stop us."

Still, Taggart wanted Cress to get on a plane to Charlotte immediately. PTL paid his way, and Dortch's wife and daughter met him at the airport, offering him a trip to Florida the next day. Cress—who had not seen Richard Dortch since his resignation—declined. He spent the night at a friend's condo at Heritage USA. The next morning, Dortch rang the doorbell; Cress didn't answer.

The next week, Dortch invited Cress to dinner at a Mexican restaurant in Charlotte. Cress found Dortch's transformation complete. He was arrogant and cocky. Cress felt no warmth from his former boss, though Dortch offered to get him a job at a church in Charlotte. Dortch complained about Cress's indiscretion in his final months at PTL, when he had shown Cobble and another PTL staff member the critical, prophetic letter from David Wilkerson warning Dortch he stood "on the brink of being deceived and blinded." Cress's actions, Dortch said, had communicated something to him about Cress's character and loyalty.

That night, Cress realized that he had to confront Dortch. He drafted a letter with Cobble's help, writing and rewriting for several days. He delivered the letter to Mildred Dortch on May 14 and cancelled his plans to dine with the Dortches that night.

One day, as Cress worked on his letter, PTL rebroadcast one of Bakker's sermons. The speech—a bitter diatribe against the *Observer* and a call for support from his congregation—seemed to be aimed at Cress.

> We must stand together. We must not let anything divide us. The only thing that will divide us around here will be pettiness, rumors, gossip, slander. . . .
> Rumors are noted for exaggeration and inaccuracy. . . . If you hear a rumor, the only place you have a right to spread it is to the person the rumor is about, privately, one to one. . . . Be a defender of the faith. Preachers wouldn't have to defend themselves, if you'll . . . stand with them.

In the days afterward, Bakker talked further of forgiveness, the shield he seemed to raise whenever the Jessica Hahn matter threatened. "We're living in a society that is so obsessed with investigations. . . . God says, 'Forgive, don't judge,' but our whole society now is built around judge and law."

Cress opened his letter to Dortch with an apology for his indiscretion with Wilkerson's letter. But he cut to the heart of the matter and bluntly recast the payoff as it would be interpreted by the public and press ten months later. "There are serious ethical, moral, biblical, and legal implications regarding the Jessica Hahn scandal." It was, he wrote,

> [a] religious "Watergate." . . . First, Jessica Hahn was paid to sign a document recanting that the event took place. In essence, PTL paid her to lie. Second, when that didn't work, a very large sum (over $200,000) was laundered in a covert way to "compensate her." The true motive was to keep Jim Bakker's public image clean. . . .
> How would you have handled a matter like this involving a pastor in the Illinois District? Would you have secretly permitted church funds to be used to "compensate" the teenage girl? Would you have allowed the pastor to retain his credentials, undergo no discipline, and remain as the pastor of the church? Would the matter never have been brought before the presbytery?? . . .
> Do we use one set of cards to deal with those less prominent and without access to large amounts of money and influence, and then use another set of cards to deal with those who can pay their way to cover up sin? . . .

The issue is not simply forgiveness. . . . True forgiveness is redemptive, it restores spiritual health, but It does not rational ize away sin. . . . God's money has been exchanged to cover this up.

Cress questioned Dortch's claim in a recent PTL fund-raising letter that "I know that for twenty-five years, Jim and Tammy have had impeccable, blameless lives and ministries." The things Cress knew hardly supported Dortch's assertion.

In his letter, Cress recalled Dortch's lack of compassion in 1985 when Cress's mother had been wasting away and he had watched PTL spend hundreds of thousands of dollars to cover up Bakker's sin.

On the one hand you were willing to overlook Jim's problem, and help him cover it up, and on the other hand you couldn't be compassionate enough to try to understand an error in judgment on my part. . . . Which Richard Dortch am I dealing with? The one who would reach out in love and compassion to Jim Bakker and help justify him for some gross immorality, or the one who alienated me after serving him loyally for nine and a half years and gave me the harsh cold treatment. . . .

My heart is an open wound. Each day I must deal with the pain. . . . My anger and animosity toward you is real and painful. And I confess it to you and I confess it to the Lord. I ask the Lord to help me deal with all of this because I desperately need His help in my life.

On Saturday morning, May 17, Dortch telephoned Cress, inviting him to talk over coffee. Inside the restaurant at the Marriott on I-77, Dortch tried to justify his actions. He seemed broken, not arrogant. He began to cry. "I can't believe that someone who's worked for me for ten years feels this way about me." Tears had always come easily to Dortch. This time, however, they seemed to be tears of fear, Cress thought. Perhaps Dortch had forgotten how much Cress knew about the payoff.

Dortch mounted his best defense. He said that he had been dealing with thugs, alluding to Hahn and Profeta. He felt that the girl's story was a fabrication—Dortch was still unwilling to acknowledge Fred Gross's confirmation of the incident—but he believed a public fight would cost PTL too much in bad publicity and lawyer's fees. Dortch told Cress that he had informed another elected official in the Assemblies of God about his handling of the matter; the official had sanctioned Dortch's approach. He did not say who that official was.

Cress shed no tears, and he didn't believe Dortch's tale. Dortch was a man accustomed to getting what he wanted from people, using what Cress called his "silver tongue." Cress felt that he was being used to serve Dortch's needs. He accepted the minister's invitation to go out for tacos that night. He also accepted the two hundred dollars Dortch pulled from his pocket, explaining that he had never given Cress anything when he had left PTL the year before. But Cress was not interested in the offer of the key to Dortch's house in Florida or a weekend trip on Dortch's boat or a seat in PTL's church on Sunday morning. The wounds of 1985 still festered.

Unbeknownst to Cress, Dortch was not finished with the Jessica Hahn trust. Though Scott Furstman had informed Hahn's representative, Paul Roper, in December 1985 that he hoped to "bring this matter to a rapid resolution," Dortch had still not decided details of the trust—most notably the thorny question who should be designated as trustor.

Dortch had been identified in a 1985 draft trust document as trustor. By late 1985, Furstman had proposed a new strategy, setting up a shell corporation to disguise PTL's involvement entirely. In a June 18, 1986, letter Furstman described to Dortch his latest plan to insulate PTL "from any connection or affiliation with the trust and/or Jessica Hahn." Furstman's office would serve as trustor and eliminate any references to PTL or Dortch. It would tell the IRS the trust was not a gift but the satisfaction of a debt or obligation, eliminating any tax liability for the source of the trust money. Furstman would not tell the IRS whose debt it was, citing attorney-client privilege. If the IRS pressed further, though, Furstman's firm could be subject to a large gift-tax claim.

Receiving no pressure from Hahn, Roper did not push for completion of the formal trust agreement, and none would ever be concluded. On July 15, David Taggart mailed Furstman two checks drawn on the confidential executive account and signed by Taggart and Dortch. One, for $50,000, would cover any back gift tax claim; it would be returned to PTL if the IRS made none. The other, for $10,000, would cover Furstman's costs of administering the Hahn trust for the next two decades.

CHAPTER TWENTY

VICTORY WARRIORS

*"The greatest weekend in giving in . . . all
history of Christian television"*

PTL had scheduled another auction over its satellite network for
Saturday, May 24, 1986, to help pay for the languishing Fort Hope
home for street people. At seven that morning, Jim Bakker telephoned his executive personnel director, Wanda Burgund, at
home. Get the phones staffed, Bakker said, we're going to have a
telethon. It was typical Bakker, a spontaneous change of direction
that disrupted the lives of his staff, this time on the Memorial Day
weekend. In short order, Burgund had to find at least eighty employees willing to come to work.

Just four weeks had passed since the two-week "Enough Is
Enough" telethon, and PTL still needed cash desperately. For
months, PTL had been searching for a loan of more than $50
million to refinance its high-cost debt and help finish paying for the
Towers. But the ministry had consummated none of the financing
packages presented by the loan brokers working on PTL's behalf.
Instead, the lifetime partnerships were carrying the ministry, as
they had for more than two years. But the thousand-dollar offerings
could only stretch so far. By April 30, PTL's debt to builder Roe
Messner had reached $8.4 million. A few days later, Messner in-
formed Bakker that his banker had cut off his credit completely
until he could repay some of the money he had borrowed to cover
PTL's unpaid debts.

On the day of the Fort Hope auction, PTL was one week away from the close of its fiscal year—the day that would provide the financial information for PTL's 1986 audit. Another discouraging snapshot of runaway debt could only compound PTL's problems with ECFA, the press, and the ministry's creditors.

Twenty-two hours before Bakker's call to Wanda Burgund, Tammy Bakker had arrived at a Charlotte medical clinic to have the fat sucked from her abdomen, as it had been removed earlier from her thighs. At home afterwards, Tammy's health deteriorated as the result of what eventually would be diagnosed as a severe staph infection. She was delirious for several days. Bakker didn't want to deal with her demands, her irrationality, her pain; he paid others to do it. Inside the Tega Cay home, Doug Oldham's wife Laura Lee stayed with Tammy, sleeping with her at night while Jim Bakker escaped to the bed in his office downstairs.

As Bakker told it on the air, he had decided to hold the weekend telethon because he had promised Messner $1 million of the millions he was owed. But, Bakker said, his studio audience had given only $400,000 that week in response to a special lifetime offer.

> I said, 'Well, Lord, I know I felt faith.' And so I went back to the Lord, and I woke up Saturday morning, the morning of the auction, and the Lord seemed to speak in my heart saying, 'Well, you're on television all day; just mention it to the satellite people, the need, and do the special that you were doing with the studio audience all week long, to be able to raise that million dollars.'

The studio special had been a fire-sale giveaway: for a thousand dollars, Bakker now offered three free nights a year in the Towers hotel for a lifetime plus a similar pledge of free recreation at Heritage USA. The same package had once cost three thousand dollars.

The offer represented yet another 180-degree turn by Bakker. In his mid-April telethon, Bakker had declared that just twelve thousand Towers memberships remained. He warned his audience that they were down to their "very last chance" to get a Towers lifetime partnership. By the end of April, PTL claimed that just 1,887 partnerships remained.

In his new, impromptu telethon, Bakker called his thousand-

411

dollar offer of free lodging and recreation the Victory Warriors Club. "Club" was a pet word at PTL, everyone wanted to be part of a victory, and the word "warriors" evoked the soldier-like allegiance and determination Bakker wanted to promote. He pushed the offer all weekend—in front of the water park during the day, in front of the Heritage Grand in the evening, from inside the model room at the half-finished Towers. He set deadlines to build the sense of urgency. Just one hour. We'll offer them until the phone calls stop, then we'll go home. I'll give you till midnight tonight. You must postmark your envelope by May 27. The one-hour deal spread over hours, then days, and finally weeks. The telethon would feed on itself. After the first round of fund-raising, PTL ran tapes of the weekend appeals. Privately, Bakker told his staff "let's make the miracle continue." The reruns prompted another wave of partnership purchases. Bakker then issued a new round of deadlines because, he claimed, some pledges had not been fulfilled.

Bakker's audience recognized a bargain, if not a financial risk, and the dollars flooded in. That first weekend, Bakker summoned worshippers out of church to answer telephones. He proclaimed the response "the greatest weekend in giving in . . . all history of Christian television" and said that it was vindication after months of persecution. Between May 19 and May 31, PTL took in $16.6 million, $11 million of it in just two days. Suddenly, there seemed to be hope that things really would get better. Creditors could be paid off, the Towers could be finished. Off-screen as well as on, they called it a miracle.

There were few voices of dissent. Bakker had manufactured a business with an adjustable moral compass; if the ministry did something, then it must be ethical. The critics had been forced out or silenced, and the cheering section reigned. Five days into the "Victory Warriors Club" telethon, Don Argue, the president of North Central Bible College, met at Heritage USA with two of Bakker's aides to discuss the communications major PTL was to sponsor at North Central. Argue was skeptical of the aides' triumphant talk. He suspected that PTL was running reckless, selling lifetime partnerships willy-nilly. The success that some interpreted as a sign of God's blessing could merely be the abundant fruits of slick marketing, he thought. How would PTL accommodate all the people? he wondered. He asked the PTL executives if anyone had determined the number of rooms PTL would need to fill the partners' demand. Argue was told that no studies had been done. He told them bluntly, "You're in big trouble."

By May 31, PTL had issued 16,500 Victory Warriors partnerships. On or about that day, the 1988 indictment against Bakker would allege, a PTL staff member warned Bakker that the partnerships had been oversold, that PTL could not accommodate all the Towers partners in the hotel. Bakker acknowledged the hazards as he pushed the Victory Warriors Club. He commented that he was making the offer against his good judgment. "We have to have some people pay . . . otherwise you're gonna sleep in a dirty room because we can't afford to pay the housekeepers to clean the rooms."

The more serious threat was that there would be no rooms at all. In early spring 1986, I talked in confidence with a disenchanted reservations clerk. She said that it was common knowledge among her colleagues that PTL had issued more than fifty-percent of the Grand's room capacity to lifetime partners. By mid March 1986, PTL had no three-night openings left in the Grand for the rest of calendar 1986, she told me. "They can't understand it," the reservations clerk told me, alluding to the lifetime partners. "They've been told four days, three nights. It's true, but it's not true."

To get their free rooms from then on, lifetime partners were obliged to check repeatedly for cancellations, to accept shorter stays, or to plead with reservations manager Joy Cole. Cole, thirty-two, could bend the rules to find space for people with terminal cancer and other hardship cases. But she had to say no to most callers; in one month in 1986, nearly three thousand eight hundred lifetime partners were refused space. She and her staff suffered through tirades from frustrated partners, many of whom seldom traveled and didn't understand how a hotel functioned. Her operators were told to be as nice as they could and to stay on the line. It was easier said than done. One day, after a twenty-five-minute harangue from an abrasive partner, Cole hurled her beeper against the wall.

Cole felt her heart plummet as she watched Bakker and Dortch issue more lifetimes when she knew she couldn't accommodate those they had already sold. She expressed her frustration to PTL vice president Steve Nelson, and Nelson offered her the justification that had gained currency within the upper reaches of PTL management: some lifetime partners had died, others from faraway states weren't using their privileges each year, and PTL would give refunds to anyone who was unhappy.

Indeed, by the time of Bakker's resignation, PTL had paid back more than $7.3 million to lifetime partners, subtracting the retail cost of any lodging already used before returning the money. With PTL's tight finances and flawed record keeping, getting a refund could be a challenge. Seventy-five-year-old Pauline Short of Beckley, West Virginia, got her thousand dollars back after she threatened to go to the *Observer*. Many—no one knows how many—gave up quietly.

When it had extra rooms, PTL bent its fifty-percent ceiling on lifetime-partner occupancy to meet the excess demand. Those around Bakker didn't doubt the sincerity of his desire to make good on his promise to finish the Towers and provide free lodging; he always seemed to care genuinely about the partners. But breaking the fifty-percent threshold—in 1986, fifty-four percent of the hotel's rooms were used free by lifetime partners—compounded PTL's financial troubles. Like many of PTL's quasi-commercial enterprises, the hotel had become a drain on the ministry, not the promised fountain of support for PTL's charities. To pay its way, the hotel needed to fill about forty percent of its rooms with paying customers. It hit that target only during its very best months. In 1986, the hotel's last year of operation under Bakker, thirty-two percent of the rooms were occupied by paying customers. PTL was forced to rely on donors' contributions to pay the hotel's phone bill, electric bill, and other expenses.

PTL's internal justification for overselling failed to acquit the ministry. Federal law—not to mention sound ethical practice—prohibits using false statements to raise money over the air or through the mails. The PTL executives had raised tens of millions of dollars in 1984 with the declaration that they would offer only thirty thousand partnerships in each hotel—the total number of three-night stays available if half the hotel's rooms were set aside for lifetime partners. Without calling attention to any change in policy, in fact by continuing to allude to the fifty-percent of hotel capacity set aside for partners, PTL issued tens of thousands more

David Taggart joined PTL's staff in 1978. Ten years later he would take the Fifth Amendment when asked if he had ever had sex with Jim Bakker.

Bakker speaks at the August 1983 management retreat in Hilton Head, flanked by Jay Babcock and Vi Azvedo. It was in Hilton Head, Babcock said, that he and Bakker had their first sexual encounter.

Jessica Hahn in the West Babylon, New York, apartment she moved into in November 1984, a few weeks before her first call to the Charlotte Observer. This picture was taken in May 1987, several weeks after Bakker's resignation. (The Charlotte Observer/Diedra Laird ©1987)

An aerial picture of frontier-style buildings
erected at Heritage USA in 1978. In 1984 the
land along the lake in the upper left became
the site of the PTL Partner Center.

The PTL Partner Center during Bakker's final months as PTL president. The Heritage Grand
Hotel is at the left; the Main Street Mall, cafeteria, and conference center at right. The unfinished
high rise is the Towers hotel.

PTL's water park
opened in 1986, two
years behind schedule.

Richard Dortch, on the air.

Builder Roe Messner of Wichita, Kansas, in May 1986.

Peter Bailey, Bakker's finance director.

Al Cress, Richard Dortch's longtime aide. Disturbed by Dortch's willingness to cover up Bakker's sin, Cress eventually agreed to help the author in his efforts to disclose the Jessica Hahn payoff.

Jim Cobble, Cress's friend and colleague.

Inside PTL's TV studio in the final years. Here Bakker interviews Pat Boone.

Tammy's spacious walk-in closet in the Heritage Grand Hotel presidential suite. This photo was taken by a PTL security guard offended by the luxury.

Richard Dortch, Jim Bakker, and contractor Roe Messner (right of Bakker) break ground for the Towers hotel on February 27, 1985, the same day Jessica Hahn formally agreed to a secret $265,000 settlement of her claim against Bakker. The Towers would never be completed.

Bakker and Ronald Reagan a year before Reagan's election to the presidency.

Bakker talks with then Vice President George Bush in Charlotte, November 1985. (© The White House)

Tammy Bakker with Richard Simmons, whose 1986 appearance on Tammy's TV show offended evangelist Jimmy Swaggart.

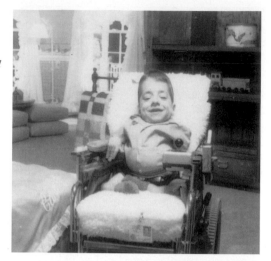

Keven Whittum, the handicapped adopted son of Bakker's cousin, in his bedroom in Kevin's House.

Members of PTL's board and the Bakker family eat lunch at Kevin's House on January 2, 1987. From left: J. Don George, Richard Dortch, Tammy Bakker, Jim Bakker, Jamie Charles Bakker, Tammy Sue Bakker, A. T. Lawing, and Evelyn Carter Spencer.

Aimee Cortese, PTL board member and Dortch's liaison to Jessica Hahn in 1984.

David Taggart, looking at Bakker, and secretary Shirley Fulbright help Jim and Tammy open a present—a pair of Jim and Tammy dolls —during a Christmas 1986 party at the Bakkers' Tega Cay home.

Jerry Falwell and Jim Bakker during a public appearance in the early eighties.

David Taggart (right) and James Taggart (with head bowed) flee the press on April 28, 1987, the day David Taggart and Richard Dortch were fired and Jerry Falwell's new board of directors thwarted Bakker's efforts to return to PTL. (The Charlotte Observer/ Bob Leverone © 1987)

Jim and Tammy Bakker in the California desert, March 1988. (The Charlotte Observer/
Mark B. Sluder ©1988)

partnerships worth tens of millions of dollars. Playing for much higher stakes, Bakker had repeated the pattern that had troubled the FCC investigators in 1979. He had made big promises to his TV audience, failed to make good on them off the air, and continued to suggest on-camera that he was living up to his word so as to maximize the flow of donor dollars into PTL.

As the Victory Warriors cash poured in, Bakker talked ecstatically about all that PTL could do with the millions. "Most all outstanding bills can be paid. . . . For the first time in my ministry, my TV stations will all be current, and all my suppliers will be current," he said. Finally, Tammy declared, they could minister to the audience. In truth, Bakker looked at the hoard of cash and saw future triumphs, not financial stability. He summoned his vice presidents to his dressing room one morning and announced that he needed them to help oversee a furious month of construction. The Fourth of July was coming, he said, and they had to get ready. PTL buzzed with the activity Bakker thrived on, the sort of tangible progress that said success to visitors, inspired enthusiasm from partners, and aroused the generosity of Bakker's board. "We're just building everywhere, things are happening everywhere," Bakker told his audience.

Things were happening alright—at the still-unopened Fort Hope; at the Towers; at the water park, which needed $2 million of work that spring; at Kevin's House, the home for hard-to-adopt handicapped children that Bakker had announced in April. Now, Bakker also began pitching his next menu of projects—Farmland USA, an idealized nineteenth-century Victorian village built around Kevin's House, and the massive Crystal Palace ministry center. To enhance the drama, Bakker scheduled three projects— the water park, Fort Hope, and Kevin's House—to open during the July Fourth holiday. He labeled the occasion a "triple-header victory day."

Kevin's House provided a classic study in the evolution of a Bakker project. It was born out of a highly publicized, ostensibly altruistic Bakker impulse that coincided with an internal cash crisis. It became a shrewdly promoted instrument for raising money and a well-disguised failure as a ministry program. Bakker announced his plans to his church congregation in a teary sermon on Sunday, April

6. He described the home as a "labor of love . . . perhaps the most vital project I have ever been involved with."

The project was named after Kevin Whittum, his cousin's seventeen-year-old adopted son, who Bakker said "has probably inspired me more than anybody else, in that he's made it." Kevin was a lamentable sight. He had the head of a teenager atop the torso of a toddler. He weighed twenty pounds and stood only twenty-nine inches tall, a victim of a condition known as brittle bone disease. Taken out of his motorized wheelchair and plopped down on the TV set at PTL, Kevin looked like a stray handbag.

Perhaps in Kevin, Bakker found some primitive identification with his own past, in exaggerated form. Bakker was short; Kevin was tiny. Jim was a gifted communicator; despite his physical handicap, Kevin was a bright, articulate young man. With Kevin's House, Jim had given Kevin the celebrity status and the trappings of success Bakker had longed for as a teenager—appearances on television, a new car, a Victorian house reminiscent of the lumber barons' mansions near Bakker's home in Muskegon. Talking on the air with Kevin one day, Bakker gushed about the unbuilt house. "Do you know, your room is so great. I just saw the plans, and you have like a big tower in your room too that goes way up high. And it's really neat." The finished house would sprawl over thirteen thousand square feet; had Bakker's staff not persuaded him to change his original plans, it would have been twice that size.

Bakker told his viewers that he had committed to the project on impulse after Kevin had cried when he contemplated returning home to Michigan after a visit to Heritage USA.

> I did something I said I wasn't going to do anymore. I made a commitment. On the spot. I said, "Kevin, I'm gonna build a house so you can come and live here at Heritage USA and you don't ever have to leave and for other kids." . . .
>
> Since our budget system does not allow me to do any projects that are not funded by themselves any more, so I can't get emotional and do a project any more, but . . . I told the directors of the ministry I will personally see to it that the funds are raised for Kevin's House. And I said if I can't get the funds I will personally take a loan out and I will build it myself and I will pay for it.

Kevin's House arrived just in time for Bakker's April telethon. From the start, Bakker played up the project's urgency. He suggested that PTL needed to open by July 4 because Kevin could die any day. "Thirty days will make the difference in little Kevin's life," Bakker wrote to his partners. "I really don't know how much longer Kevin has left." Kevin would still be alive three years later.

Even as Bakker drummed up his audience's sense of urgency, he also kept potentially embarrassing and discouraging information from his viewers. He avoided mentioning the family tie between himself and Kevin, a disclosure that might take the gloss off his gesture. And he didn't reveal the trade-offs PTL had accepted to meet his unrealistic building schedule. While Bakker packaged the house on the air as a group home for the handicapped, he learned from Messner that they couldn't get the required permits and complete the house by July 4 unless he represented the house to York County officials as a straightforward single-family home for Kevin, his adoptive parents, and other family members. Eager to sustain the excitement and undisturbed by the high cost of retrofitting, Bakker decided to wait until after the home was finished to make the changes necessary to qualify the building as a residential group home. On May 30, with no mention of any problems, Bakker broke ground in front of the cameras.

On Sunday, June 29, 1986, Bakker preached on "stubborn faith," the quality of character that he said kept him at the water park nearly sixteen hours a day. At his side, Dortch whispered the word that a government inspector had just given the go-ahead to open the water park that afternoon. Bakker announced that the park was finished. "We won again. Hallelujah!" Despite a cost overrun of one hundred percent and a construction schedule that had ballooned from four months to twenty-eight, Bakker declared victory.

Off-camera, PTL and its original water-park contractor were still fighting over who owed what. REC had taken its claim before an arbitration board, as required by its contract with PTL. REC claimed that it was owed more than $2 million. PTL filed a counterclaim saying that REC owed the ministry more than $2 million. It complained that REC had failed to use PTL's money to pay its subcontractors. After a closed hearing in April, the arbitrators awarded $559,000 plus interest to REC.

The arbitrators' ruling did not resolve the dispute between REC and PTL. REC said it didn't know how to divvy up the money among itself and its subcontractors. REC sued its chief subcontractor, and the subcontractor sued REC and PTL. A long list of smaller subcontractors and suppliers sought a piece of the $559,000. During summer 1986, REC—facing demands for more than $559,000—filed for protection from its creditors under the federal bankruptcy laws. The company soon closed down.

In late April, after the arbitrators had finished their work, PTL budget director Dana Cadwell sent a two-page memo to Dortch itemizing the lessons she had extracted from the water-park arbitration. The memo was dry and professional. Cadwell alluded to PTL's promises to REC in 1984 that it had the money to pay for the water park, when in fact it did not. Cadwell wrote that before PTL agreed to a contract next time, "we must have the funding in place that we are stating we have. In signing a contract we are saying we are 'ready, willing, and *able*' to meet the terms of the contract." And before PTL changed a fixed-price contract to allow for additional payments—as PTL had done repeatedly with REC—it should consult an attorney. "Ignorance," she wrote, "is not a defense."

The late summer of 1986 was a heady time for the Bakkers. The *Washington Post* carried a feature story on Heritage USA. *USA Today* ran a generous profile on PTL. *Newsweek* carried a two-page spread on Heritage USA, labeling it "A Disneyland for the Devout." Bakker finally seemed to have gotten respect.

By mid-July, I had drafted a detailed story about PTL's troubles at the water park. My editor, Jeannie Falknor, had taken a leave of absence, and I temporarily had no supervising editor, no advocate for my PTL coverage. The water park story had begun to sprawl. REC had failed to persuade the arbitrators to clarify their ruling, creating a cloud over the company's complaints. At managing editor Mark Ethridge's suggestion, we shelved the story.

Ethridge had a fresh perspective. He had just returned from a year's fellowship at Harvard. Falknor and I had arguably lost a measure of our perspective after nearly a year of intense PTL reporting. Ethridge had also picked up on Rolfe Neill's concerns. Ethridge believed we were writing the same story—mismanagement, shoddy business practices, pricey executive life-styles. He told me it was time to move on to another subject, saying that he—and the readers—would get interested in PTL again if I had a story that lifted the level of outrage another notch. We agreed, though, that there were few notches left. I disagreed with his argument—just because someone's committing the same crime doesn't mean you ignore it, I argued by analogy—but I was tired of PTL too.

I briefed Ethridge on the Hahn story. I had stopped pursuing Cress after Dortch and Bakker's public account of my visit to Illinois; I took their words as a sign that an interview with Cress was a lost cause for now. But I thought that with some luck, I could get the story. Ethridge was skeptical.

As I turned my attention to other stories, I winced at our daily stories about PTL. I had argued for the routine coverage of PTL that Neill wanted—we owed it to the ministry to provide the nuts-and-bolts coverage we gave other institutions in town—but our reports seemed too trusting. I began to hear whispers that the newspaper had been co-opted. Some originated at PTL, where a spirit of triumph reigned. The press, Bakker declared on the air one day, had stopped being cruel.

As he executed his "triple-header victory" dedication on July 4, Bakker pronounced Kevin's House complete save for its swimming pool. The house had been erected in five weeks, an astounding achievement as long as PTL said nothing about the inflated prices it had paid and the shortcuts it had taken to get the job done. "It is finished. It is beautiful. And the kids will all be moving in shortly. So keep on dreaming, America, for with God, all things are possible. . . . Kevin will be joined by other children, who we hope to bring out of institutions, who will come back into life, and realize there's people that love them." Bakker mentioned that it had taken three designs "before we got one we thought the state would approve."

In fact, government inspectors had not approved the house for the use Bakker had promoted, and the house was not even ready to be occupied by Kevin and his family. Fort Hope, which PTL also dedicated that day, also wasn't ready for occupation. Both buildings had yet to be connected to water or sewer service, another time-consuming process that PTL and Messner had chosen to delay during the pitched construction battles of June. Three days after the dedication, Bakker ordered his staff privately to get both buildings "finished and open."

Publicly, Bakker blamed the delay on too few donor dollars. In a mass mailing after the dedication, he announced that once PTL got enough money, it could "complete the dream for Kevin and so many other children" and open the doors. Bakker's April pledge to use his own money to make up for any shortfall had been forgotten. Still, he described himself as "hurt" to think of all the handicapped children unable to use the house. As the summer progressed, Bakker found others to blame: government inspectors, bad weather, underground rock, and a spring in the way of the underground sewer lines. Meanwhile, PTL used pictures of able-bodied children sitting in wheelchairs to put together a fund-raising brochure for Kevin's House.

PTL released no accurate information about the project's cost. It claimed a total of $700,000 at the dedication. The completed house would actually cost nearly $1.3 million. PTL spent another $300,000 on fencing, furniture, fixtures, and landscaping. The sums coming in to pay for Kevin's House were misrepresented as well. PTL told a reporter in early July that it had raised more than $400,000; the actual total was $700,000. Promoting the house into the autumn, PTL took in more than $3 million. Bakker had told viewers that he wanted to create a trust fund to support Kevin's House if PTL got more than enough to build the house. Instead, PTL assigned more than $1 million in donations to pay for TV time, production costs, and a man-made lake and roads near Kevin's House that Bakker needed for the adjoining Farmland USA development.

In early September, Kevin finally moved in, along with his adoptive parents and their adopted daughter, Carolyn, a twenty-one-year-old black woman who had been born with severe spina bifida, had had her legs amputated when she was a toddler, and now walked on her hands. Bakker's appeals never mentioned that the house was not ready to house other handicapped children. This situation would not change until late September, when the York County fire marshal—who suspected that PTL was trying to circumvent the law—confronted Bakker in his dressing room and reminded him that the house had been built as a single-family home.

Blaming the problems on red tape, Bakker then acknowledged on the air that the house had to be torn up to have sprinklers installed—a change actually demanded by Bakker, not the inspectors.

To meet code requirements for the sort of home Bakker had promoted, Kevin's House needed to have a stairway enclosed, exit corridors and bedroom walls made fire resistant, proper fire extinguishers installed, and the floor system changed to handle heavier loads. Bakker's staff, which had seen its initial design recommendations for Kevin's House subordinated to Bakker's aesthetic concerns, now had to persuade Bakker to relax his concern for appearances so that the house could qualify as a group home. PTL decided to seek certification as a foster home so that one or two children might be moved in by Christmas, a goal the ministry would not attain. PTL officials told the fire marshal that the ministry planned to obtain group-home status eventually, and Bakker's staff talked of making the changes needed so Kevin's House could become what Bakker's audience thought it already was. It would never happen.

The Victory Warriors money was spent as it arrived. In three weeks in June, $15 million was used to dispatch outstanding bills, including $160,000 to pay off the bank that had financed PTL's ill-considered corporate jet. The Sabreliner, purchased for $965,000, had been sold for just $460,000, less than the sum PTL had borrowed to purchase it two years earlier.

Peter Bailey hoped to save much of the Victory Warriors windfall to cover the remaining cost of the Towers, but PTL's operating deficit, now $1.4 million a month, ate into his reserve. Contributions to PTL's general fund totaled $2.1 million in August, the lowest monthly giving in five years, yet Bakker continued to spend millions on buildings and the grounds. To Walter Richardson, always quick with a joke or a metaphor, it even seemed as if PTL were buying birds to put in the trees being planted on the grounds. Richardson, the man responsible for PTL's purchase of airtime around the country, sensed the coming cataclysm. His mind lit on a few metaphors for PTL. Paris in flames. The life cycle of a house fly. The Titanic.

By late August 1986, PTL had spent the $15 million Bailey had saved, and Messner's estimate for finishing the Towers had climbed

$3 million to $18 million. Bakker still had ambitious plans. To his August 27 memo to Bakker, Bailey attached a four-page list of proposed building projects, property purchases, and other capital expenses. The bottom line was $191 million, including $100 million for the Crystal Palace with furniture and fixtures—a figure that had climbed $25 million with Bakker's decision to add a basement. In three months' time, PTL had soared to the summit and plummeted back towards the abyss. Should Bakker hold fast to his course, PTL seemed destined for financial collapse.

CHAPTER TWENTY-ONE

JIMMY SWAGGART

"Woe unto you that cast the first stone"

For a year, rumors had circulated inside the Assemblies of God that the Reverend Marvin Gorman of New Orleans had committed adultery. Gorman was an emerging celebrity in the Assemblies of God: a skilled preacher with a TV ministry, he served on the denomination's executive presbytery and had been runner-up in the 1985 election for general superintendent. In July 1986, church officials and Jimmy Swaggart, the other big Assemblies of God pastor in Louisiana, confronted Gorman with accusations that he had been involved with other women. Gorman would admit only to an immoral act with a woman in 1979. Swaggart insisted that Gorman surrender his minister's credentials and begin the two-year rehabilitation required by the Assemblies of God. Gorman refused. Instead, he resigned from his church and announced that he was leaving to focus his energies on his TV ministry. Soon he was dismissed from the Assemblies of God altogether.

On July 20, 1986, as word of Gorman's resignation spread, Bakker stood before his congregation at Heritage Village Church. Bakker was a dramatic pulpiteer, seasoning his sermons with more theatrics than he displayed to the broader audience watching his daily TV show. On this Sunday, however, Bakker spoke with extraordinary fury. If Kevin Whittum represented the hurting little boy Bakker had been as a child, the ousted Marvin Gorman embodied the condemned minister Bakker feared he might become. And Jimmy Swaggart symbolized all that Bakker detested in—and feared from—his own church.

> One of the great ministers of this country in a church of six thousand people, by evil devices, this man has just been destroyed. He has resigned his church. He is a man who is one of my dear friends.
>
> I want to tell you who destroyed him. You say, himself? No. The church. The church. The church. I don't know how much longer I can go on. I'm watching my brethren be destroyed one at a time, and the church isn't doing anything about it. All you do is gossip about them. . . .
>
> I'm supposed to go on and smile at the cameras. I can't smile. My brother is hurting. Where's Jesus? Are you all so perfect that we can go stone him today? If I was his congregation—and I hope someone tells them—I would not receive his resignation. I would say, "no, no, no more." . . .
>
> If this is the ministry, I don't want it any more. If we kill each other I don't want any part of it. . . . We drive our preachers until they break and then we kick 'em out. . . .
>
> We leave the unsaved in the pulpit. We kick out the good men who made mistakes instead of rebuilding them, instead of restoring them. My heart is broken. Woe unto you that cast the first stone . . . because honey, you got something in your life. And what you do unto others will be done unto you. That's not my word. That's the living word of God.

Bakker sounded the same theme for days on his weekday show. He complained about those who condemned Christians.

> I think we ought to bring stoning back. I really do. I'd honestly rather have some of you throw stones at me than tear me down by your mouth. At least we'd know who's throwing stones then. . . . It's time my denomination and every denomination start dealing with the scandalmongers as hard as they're dealing with those who've committed the sin. Because they're literally tearing up churches from coast to coast. The man who is destroying is the man who is pointing the finger.

Bakker never identified "the man," but the target of his virulent attack was unmistakably Swaggart.

Though they shared the title of TV evangelist, ordination papers from the Assemblies of God, and some of the same fans, Swaggart and Bakker represented antagonistic faces of the full-gospel world. Swaggart, the traditional Pentecostal, preached a legalistic Gospel, condemning sin and worldly influences with the fire of an Old Testament prophet and the style of an "old-fashioned camp-meeting preacher." Bakker talked of love, prosperity, and forgiveness without sweeping admonitions about the corrupting influence of modern culture.

Swaggart drew much of his support from the traditional Pentecostals, those who had grown up in established denominations like the Assemblies of God that believed Christians should remain apart from the secular world. Over the years, Bakker developed an appeal to charismatics, who shared the Pentecostal belief in the gifts of the Holy Spirit but usually came to the full-gospel church from a wholly different background. Many had grown up in mainline denominations, often with roots in the middle or upper middle class and little commitment to the orthodox prohibitions against movies, dancing, and flamboyant dress. Charismatics tended to show more enthusiasm in their worship and to adopt a more mystical, subjective relationship with their God. Prosperity gospel and other doctrinal fads were more likely to find a following among charismatics. While Pentecostals emphasized an eternal inheritance, charismatics pursued rewards in the here and now. In a sense, theirs was a me-generation expression of Pentecostalism.

Swaggart and Bakker had taken their ministries along different paths. Swaggart was a magnetic performer in front of a mass audience; Bakker preferred the artificial intimacy of a TV studio. The Swaggart ministry, generous contributor to overseas missionary work and an employer of scores of Assemblies of God ministers, had gained acceptance and a high profile in the denomination; Bakker's PTL ministry remained suspect. Swaggart had built a Bible college and a network of radio stations, which were valued, if conventional, accomplishments in the denomination; Bakker had failed in both areas, though his more novel emphasis on building lodging and recreation facilities for Christians had kept his ministry almost as large as Swaggart's.

Bakker had complained about Swaggart before, comparing him—anonymously—to the biblical figure Jonah, a "cruel prophet of doom and gloom." "We would turn the world upside down more than ever if we just stopped judging one another and started loving one another," he had said in November 1985. Even on his own cable network, Bakker complained openly, he saw preachers talk of a God with a big club who would knock a person's head off. How, he asked, could the church reach out to those it beat?

Swaggart had earned a reputation for brutal treatment of those with whom he disagreed. He had attacked PTL with little effort to disguise his target. In the weeks after Gorman's fall, Bakker challenged the still-unnamed Swaggart point by point. Bakker said that he wasn't embarrassed to mix with sinners, that he was proud of the entertainment available at Heritage USA, that people shouldn't judge PTL if they'd never been to Heritage USA.

Displeased with the escalating war of words, the executives of the Assemblies of God tried to make peace that summer. On July 30, while PTL rebroadcast portions of Bakker's Gorman sermon, Swaggart met with the Assemblies presbyters in Springfield. As Swaggart later remembered, he spent fifteen minutes of the four-hour session warning the presbyters. "What PTL stands for is not what the Assemblies of God stands for," he said. "I plead with you to distance yourselves from this organization because eventually it's going to explode." The presbyters acknowledged that they had heard many allegations against PTL, but they told Swaggart that they had no concrete proof to act on. To issue a critical statement without such proof, they believed, could cause serious problems.

Soon, Bakker made his visit to Springfield. Back in Charlotte, he ordered his staff to send notes to the denomination executives "thanking them for giving us time, and we pray that we can all work together in the Body of Christ in unity and harmony." In fact, the war was just beginning.

Inside PTL, Bakker and his deputies debated whether to pull Swaggart's half-hour show from its nine o'clock weekday-morning slot on PTL's network. Bakker often saw the program before he left for work, and he would often come into the office fuming. No one wanted Bakker angry at the beginning of the day. Walter Richardson begged Bakker and Dortch to keep Swaggart on the air. The evangelist was popular, and he was a good account, worth $40,000 to $50,000 a month to the financially strapped PTL. Richardson suggested that his bosses consider PTL and the Swaggart ministries to be like competing fishermen in the Bering Strait off Alaska.

There is plenty of fish for everyone. Dortch, you're the United States, Swaggart is the Soviet Union. . . . If you guys take Swaggart off the air, you will be starting a nuclear war that you will never be able to contain.

Six days after Bakker ordered conciliatory letters sent to Springfield, PTL informed Swaggart by letter that it was taking over his daytime slot, ostensibly to make room for its own programming. With the letter, PTL sent a copy of its new programming guidelines. Near the bottom, the document referred to Proverbs 6:19 and its admonition against sowing discord among the brethren.

Bakker had been angered by Swaggart's embrace of a book called *The Seduction of Christianity,* a frontal attack on the prosperity gospel and some of its advocates whom Bakker admired. A second broadcaster carried on PTL's network, a Baptist minister from Chattanooga, Tennessee, named John Ankerberg, had discussed the book on his point-counterpoint program. PTL had chosen not to air one of his shows, and Ankerberg had flown to Charlotte to explain his handling of the topic. He thought he had straightened out the misunderstanding. A few months later, PTL notified Ankerberg that the Wednesday-evening slot he had been offered—the only prime time open on PTL's network—had been assigned to another evangelist by a PTL executive. PTL offered him time at a later hour, but Ankerberg elected to wait for a better slot.

In the weeks after Swaggart's trip to Springfield, the Baton Rouge evangelist talked by phone to John Wesley Fletcher, the onetime Bakker intimate who had set up Bakker's encounter with Hahn. Fletcher told Swaggart about the Hahn incident. He related sketchy details of the Hahn payoff that he had picked up when Cress had telephoned him to find out if Hahn's draft lawsuit was true.

In the final weeks of summer 1986, PTL board member and North Carolina district superintendent Charles Cookman arranged a meeting with Swaggart in an effort to reconcile the two ministries. Swaggart asked Cookman to bring Dortch and Bakker. Bakker, who had met Swaggart only once before, during a Swaggart appearance on one of the early PTL shows, refused to attend. On September 22, Dortch and Cookman walked into a room at the Baton Rouge Hilton. Also present were the Assemblies district superintendent for Louisiana, Swaggart's co-pastor, Swaggart himself, and

Swaggart's wife Frances and son Donnie, who held ranking positions in Swaggart's ministry.

Jimmy Swaggart questioned Dortch bluntly. Cookman later described the conversation.

> "Dick, what about the girls?" to which Richard Dortch answered, "I don't know what you're talking about." And then he said, "Well, what about the boys?" to which he said, "I don't know what you're talking about." And he said, "Well, what about the lawsuit?" and [Dortch] said, "If there's a lawsuit against PTL, I don't know it," but he said, "There is the man's district superintendent. If you have any knowledge of any wrongdoing on the part of Jim Bakker, please tell him," after which I repeated the same thing.

As Swaggart remembered it, Dortch acknowledged hearing the rumor of a lawsuit against Bakker. He had told Fletcher that he had his Bakkers mixed up—the lawsuit had been threatened against a Jim Baker, not the Jim Bakker. No sexual encounter, no rape had ever taken place, Dortch said. Swaggart asked Dortch if any bribes had been paid. Dortch said that to his knowledge nothing like that had ever crossed his desk.

Swaggart was not finished. He chided Dortch about Richard Simmons's appearance on a PTL show a few months before. To Swaggart, having the effeminate exercise guru as a guest was symptomatic of PTL's willingness to condone the unholy values of Hollywood.

Back at PTL, Dortch's confidence seemed shaken. He had gone to Baton Rouge to mediate a truce, and he had not succeeded. He told members of his staff that he had felt insulted by Swaggart's questions about the boys and the girls. Bakker renewed his attacks.

Swaggart realized that something did not add up, even though he was inclined to believe the word of his old friend Richard Dortch over that of a defrocked minister like Fletcher. The day of the meeting in Baton Rouge, Swaggart's ministry notified PTL that it was pulling all its programming from PTL's network. Swaggart continued his harsh denunciations. Several months later, in a magazine article that appeared to describe the Baton Rouge meeting, Swaggart complained that Christian TV programming too often featured "got rich quick" schemes, psychological philosophies, rock 'n' roll entertainment, and all the way down to the exhibition of homosexual guests. . . . Why is it that our preachers can no longer differentiate between the world and God? Whatever happened to the spirit of *discernment?* . . .

The other day I asked an official of a major Pentecostal fellowship, "Do you have any idea what you are *doing?*" Worldly entertainers with scant claim to knowing Jesus Christ are featured on the television programs of a particular organization of which he is a board member.

"Don't you realize," I asked, "that when these performers appear on these telecasts that you are in effect saying to a whole Pentecostal generation that the nightclub circuit is now an acceptable part of the Pentecostal and Charismatic scene? . . .

He just stared at me; he had no answer.

I then went on to say, "An organization that *purports* to be a ministry of God is helping, by example, to fill the nightclubs, honky-tonks, and places of worldly amusement with our Pentecostal young people." God help us when church officials, pastors, and evangelists have sunk to the point where they can no longer discern right and wrong.

In another article, Swaggart acknowledged his reputation as a religious vigilante. The article began with a letter from an unidentified minister. "I have noticed an increasing reference to 'Assemblies of God pastors' and the inference is that they are doing things that are sinful. Just last week a report came to me that you had remarked, in some setting, that you had taken care of one minister, now you were going after the other." The unnamed correspondent recounted the instructions of Matthew 18—approach the individual privately, and, should that fail, take one or two witnesses along. If the individual still does not listen, tell the church. And if the accused ignores the church, then treat him like a heathen and expose him publicly.

Swaggart devoted nearly three pages to his reply, spelling out the arguments that would seal Bakker's fate within a year—and, ironically, framing the choice Swaggart himself would face a year later.

It is being strongly advocated in some Pentecostal and Charismatic circles today that when a pastor or an evangelist commits an immoral act, he is to be forgiven and allowed to remain in his position of leadership. My brother, if that would be the case, it would be tantamount to destruction for the movement. . . .

If a man in a bank is caught stealing and someone outside the bank finds it out, are you telling me that he should just go to the brother and tell him to quit stealing, and say nothing to the bank officers about it? . . .

The minister of the Gospel is in a very responsible position, and he is placed there by God. He is to set the example of righteousness. And if that example is not set, it will destroy the spiritual fabric of the church. And to allow a preacher of the Gospel, when he is caught beyond the shadow of a doubt committing an immoral act and then be allowed to remain in his position as pastor (or whatever), would be the most gross stupidity.

Cress had shared his story of the Jessica Hahn payoff with Cobble and other confidants in the Assemblies of God. By summer, word reached the executives in Springfield. On July 3, 1986, the general superintendent, Raymond Carlson, telephoned Cress at his brother's home in Colorado. Carlson wanted to talk about PTL. Cress agreed.

They met that fall at a private aviation terminal in Denver. Richard Hammar, legal counselor to the denomination, joined them. During the two-hour meeting, Cress detailed what he knew about the Hahn payoff. He showed the men a copy of the July 1985 Furstman letter, the earlier unsigned letter to Taggart purportedly from a friend of Hahn's, and Cress's own critical letter to Dortch in May 1986. But Cress was unwilling to sign an official complaint against Dortch. He knew the way Dortch operated, the way he could pull a rabbit out of a hat, and he feared the consequences for himself. He asked Carlson not to say where he had obtained the information.

Cress thought that the two men had believed his story. But Carlson was a gentle, cautious man, not the sort to crusade for justice. He was reluctant to take copies of the documents with him; if he couldn't handle the matter as denomination procedure required, he didn't want the papers floating in unofficial limbo. Cress believed that Carlson, like Cress himself, thought that the Hahn matter would surface at the right time.

* * *

On August 8, 1986, the Bakker family and an entourage of about ten left for what was supposed to be a three-day trip to the mountains of Tennessee and Virginia. Their itinerary included front-row seats for *Ten Little Indians* at the Barter Theater in Abingdon, Virginia, and a visit to a mountain festival. Paperwork for Bakker's five-thousand-dollar cash advance listed the jaunt as a "buying trip," while Bakker's secretary would remember it as an effort to research motels and hotels. Again, Bakker's public role as PTL president and his interests as a private citizen were indistinguishable. The Bakkers were avid shoppers on the road, using their PTL cash and credit cards to buy everything from antiques for Heritage USA and their church-owned home, to gifts for their employees and honored guests, to on-air wardrobes for themselves and other PTL talent. In fact, during the Virginia trip, Bakker's staff would arrange for a new company credit-card account for Bakker with a $100,000 credit limit.

The three-day trip stretched into a week, and by their return, the Bakkers owned a new $148,500 vacation home overlooking the tourist town of Gatlinburg, Tennessee. The 2,300-square-foot home was ten years old and located on a winding road in the city's prestigious Greystone Heights neighborhood. The real-estate listing promised "the best of everything"—two acres of privacy, a splendid view, three bedrooms, three baths, two fireplaces, and professional interior decorating.

Later, after word of his impulse purchase appeared in the press, Bakker explained. "This summer, the doctors told me, if Tammy Faye does not begin taking regular time off, her present heart condition will worsen and could prove fatal." As Bakker remembered it, the couple took a few days off to drive through the Smokies and fell in love with Gatlinburg. Jim, the quiet one, loved the serene mountains, and Tammy loved the shopping. They decided to sell their faraway home in California.

The Bakkers had moved quickly. They bought the house outright, without financing. Again PTL had supplied some timely cash. A month before, Bakker had received a bonus of $150,000 after taxes, and Tammy had taken home another $50,000. Before returning to Charlotte, the Bakkers began planning a massive renovation for the Tennessee home. Bakker summoned Roe Messner to

Gatlinburg. PTL would later be billed for Messner's $2,600 charter flight and for a second flight thirteen days later. The Bakkers gave him a picture from a magazine that captured the look they wanted: a country room with a country fireplace and beams across the ceiling. By mid-September, one of Messner's supervisors had obtained a permit to build.

The first project was a two-foot-thick wall of mountain stone topped with wrought-iron fencing. It eventually stood twelve feet high and ran 390 feet around the property. The townspeople dubbed it the Great Wall of Gatlinburg. Soon, Messner's firm was working on a swimming pool and an addition that included a master suite, new deck, and a pool house.

At a PTL board meeting in early November, Dortch raised the subject of Bakker's new home. The minutes record that the board was told inadequate security had "created a situation in which it is virtually impossible for Reverend Bakker to obtain the rest that he needs to escape the pressure of his duties at the church." The board authorized PTL to pay for a security fence around Bakker's home and a security gate manned by guards twenty-four hours a day. The minutes show no evidence that the board was informed of the $20,000 PTL had already spent installing sophisticated security equipment inside and outside the Gatlinburg house or of the nearly $41,000 in work already billed by Messner. Nor was there any mention that Bakker would furnish the Gatlinburg home, in part, with furniture he had ordered moved from the underused Kevin's House.

The board also agreed to pay for personal security for Bakker and his family when they traveled away from church premises— something PTL had already been doing for years. It then discussed PTL's responsibility to provide its pastor "the needs for seclusion and rest"—the impulse that had prompted the condominium purchase in Florida and the excuse Bakker had used to justify his California home. Charles Cookman proposed giving Bakker a bonus equal to the cost of building an addition to the Gatlinburg home. The board, minus the absent Bakker, agreed. By March 1987, Messner's staff estimated that the final cost of all the work being done at Bakker's house was between $400,000 and $500,000.

*   *   *

While Bakker assured his board that the IRS audit would find in favor of PTL, he prepared to snatch a public-relations victory from the jaws of defeat should PTL administrative appeals within the IRS not prevail. Making no mention of the IRS's pursuit of PTL's tax-exempt status, Bakker made an on-air offer to become the first minister to give up his church's tax exemption to save America from its growing national debt. A few weeks later, he warned again of an IRS assault on every major ministry, and he declared that he would die defending the ministries' freedom, if that's what it took. Enough, he said, is enough.

By then, Bakker had gotten sobering news from PTL's tax attorneys. The ministry had hired the Tulsa firm of Chapel, Wilkinson, Riggs and Abney in late 1985 to take over PTL's fight with the IRS. Partner Charles Chapel surveyed the case in a confidential July 9 letter to Dortch. He wrote that he believed PTL had a strong case against the revocation of its exempt status, but he had little doubt that PTL would owe some back taxes on unrelated business income. More threatening to PTL, he warned, was the issue of private inurement. "Keep in mind that *any* inurement is grounds for revocation," Chapel warned.

Chapel and his colleague, Fort Worth lawyer Michael Wigton, had resisted the IRS's efforts to audit PTL's records for two additional years, fiscal 1984 and 1985, contending that a second audit would be extraordinary, discriminatory enforcement and a veiled effort to shore up the 1981–83 audit findings. He had also tried to discredit the IRS auditors, contending to their superiors in Atlanta and Washington that they had been unreasonable. He hoped to hold off the 1984–85 audit, prevail on the 1981–83 dispute, and then dispose of the audit of later years altogether.

But his strategy might require a court fight that could reveal the tax dispute to the press, Chapel warned in his July letter.

> We have made a concerted effort to keep the proposed revocation confidential. If we get into court, there very well could be publicity. . . . The only alternative to fighting the proposed 1984–85 audit is to allow the commencement of the audit. . . . Prior to [our] entry into the case, the IRS pretty well had its own way with you folks. The IRS asked for something and you bent over backwards to help it. That did not work, and it will not work.

433

As he closed, Chapel reminded Dortch that to prevail "we need to work together in a team effort and have full confidence in each other."

Unwilling to risk public disclosure, PTL hired the Washington office of Baker and McKenzie and put that law firm in charge of its 1984–85 audit. Dortch gave orders to capitulate to the IRS demand for records. By early September, Chapel and Wigton were fed up. They were unsure which law firm was in charge of PTL's tax case. They believed that Dortch's capitulation order, which had enabled the IRS auditors to learn of the large sums paid Bakker in 1984 and 1985, had undermined their efforts to convince the IRS that his 1981–83 compensation was reasonable. On September 9—two weeks before Dortch's meeting with Swaggart—Chapel and Wigton notified Bakker they were withdrawing as PTL's counsel. They expressed frustration with PTL's halfhearted cooperation and continuing failure to recognize what the law required of tax-exempt organizations.

The lawyers wrote that they had told PTL that

> we could not achieve success without your cooperation and willingness to be tough, when needed, and to change, when necessary.
>
> We have received very limited and halting cooperation in gathering information and consequently have had to devote far more of our resources at more expense to the organization than would otherwise be required.

After protracted efforts, the lawyers had gotten Dortch's reaction to the firm's IRS submission, but nothing from Bakker, David Taggart, or PTL's other board members.

Chapel and Wigton had encouraged PTL to change its internal balance of power, making the ministry's executives truly accountable to the organization's board—a course that PTL's lawyers and auditors had been recommending for at least the past two years. The two lawyers had argued to the IRS that the board, and not a select few individuals, controlled PTL, but "it appears that Reverend Dortch is making all the decisions without consulting the board. . . . [We] have no indication that the board is aware of the specifics of what is going on. . . . How can we sustain that argument

before the national office [of the IRS] under these circumstances?"
PTL's best chance to save its tax-exempt status lay in creation of an
effective board and an oversight committee of financially independent persons, the lawyers wrote; that committee would serve without threat of dismissal and have authority to oversee all spending
by PTL executives.

Chapel and Wigton concluded that they had failed to convince
PTL how serious its tax problems were, especially for 1984–85.
They closed their six-page letter with a stern assessment of the
"accountability" and sound stewardship PTL had proclaimed so
proudly to its TV audience.

> You have been entrusted with the care, custody, and control
> of hundreds of millions of dollars. You have an extremely high
> responsibility, and we have not seen the kind of commitment
> required for us to continue to represent the Church. I know
> how busy you are; I know how many other things are on your
> mind; and I know how fast the church has grown and how hard
> it is. Believe me, I know and sympathize. But that is not
> enough. You have got to take charge and get your business
> under control. Otherwise, your church will be lost.

About the time the Chapel-Wigton letter arrived, Bakker hosted
more than one hundred relatives and guests at a family reunion
timed to coincide with his parents' sixtieth wedding anniversary.
For many in the Bakker clan, it was an all-expense-paid vacation,
courtesy of PTL. The relatives saw the passion play one night,
dinner theater the next two, and attended a gala black-tie dinner—
much like the anniversary banquet five months earlier for Jim and
Tammy—on the final evening.

The trip was a treat for cousin George Bakker, a regional director
for the Indiana State teachers union. A PTL limousine picked him
up at the airport, an unaccustomed luxury. For four days, he enjoyed a taste of a movie-star's life. On his way back home to Terre
Haute, George Bakker turned to his wife. "Does this mean I have
to drive my own car?" he joked. "Yeah," she said, "it's back to the
real world, George."

As they talked privately with their relatives, the elder Bakkers
and their famous son confided that all was not as happy as it
seemed in the Bakker family. The elder Bakkers complained that

they were never invited to their son's home. Once, when Jim was out of town and Tammy was hosting the show, Tammy's heavy makeup had so angered Raleigh that he had telephoned her at home and told her she looked like a French whore. Since then, the story went, the elder Bakkers were not given Jim and Tammy's home number.

Jim expressed his frustrations as well. His mother was cold, he felt, and his parents showed little interest in Tammy Sue and Jamie Charles. During the family reunion, Jim doted on his aunt, Florence Bakker, George's mother, a woman with a gentle face and kind heart, the sort of maternal figure Bakker seemed to need. Bakker lodged Florence Bakker in his presidential suite. He told her that she was staying in the same suite where celebrities like Art Linkletter had stayed. He spent an afternoon lounging on a bed there, reminiscing with Florence and her daughters.

George Bakker thought that his cousin had changed little from the teenager with whom he had double-dated thirty years before. As a boy, Jim had been eager to rise above the world around him, be it with sharp clothes, the imposing house on Webster Avenue, or the variety shows at Muskegon High. Now PTL supplied the facade of distinction. During an earlier trip to Heritage USA, George Bakker's daughter had been struck by how often her Uncle Jim mentioned what something cost—this camera was $75,000, this microphone $5,000. Bakker's point was not how tough it was to pay the bills. Rather, he seemed proud to be surrounded by these costly tokens of success.

Tax lawyers Chapel and Wigton had advised PTL executives to reevaluate their use of lifetime partnerships, the fund-raising device that had fueled PTL's building boom and papered over its operating deficit. The lawyers had learned from Peter Bailey that the Towers lifetime money was being treated as an undesignated gift to PTL, one the ministry could spend—and was spending—as it wished. In his July letter to Dortch, Chapel wrote:

> It appears that this could at least potentially result in difficulty. In the future, it would be helpful to clearly specify that all gifts from all sources shall be treated as general gifts to the ministry.

When Chapel and Wigton withdrew as PTL's counsel in September, they complained that their efforts to warn PTL about "serious and substantial legal issues" regarding the partnerships had met with inaction, even hostility. To their dismay, they had found that PTL had done virtually no legal research on these issues. The lawyers had been told that the matter was none of their business. In their letter severing their connection to PTL, the lawyers noted that PTL was now selling a new type of lifetime partnership.

Bakker called the new five-hundred-dollar partnerships the Family Heritage Club. These partnerships carried the promise of two nights' free lodging each year for life and free year-round admission to certain attractions. Instead of the oversold, unfinished Tower, PTL promised to provide lodging in rustic "bunkhouse" structures. On paper, the bunkhouses promised a windfall for PTL. In early September 1986, Bailey told Bakker that PTL expected to issue twenty-nine hundred partnerships in each sixteen-unit bunkhouse. He estimated that each single-story building would cost $400,000, leaving more than $1 million in extra revenue for PTL.

With the Victory Warriors money spent, Bailey relied on the Family Heritage partnerships to pay other bills. In late September, he withdrew $1 million to pay for work on the Towers. In late October, Bakker ordered his staff to use bunkhouse money to help prepare the Christmas City lights display for its November 1 opening. "We're committed—there's nothing else I can do," Bakker told Taggart. By mid-November, the bunkhouse account was empty.

One week later, Bakker unveiled another lifetime club. It was, he claimed, possibly the last ever—a familiar claim. The 1100 Club offered free stays in a country-inn farmhouse, mansion, bunkhouse, or a campsite with what Bakker called "country-club camping" in addition to certain free recreation during the partners' visit. To join the club, donors had to contribute $1100. In all, PTL would issue more than $11 million worth of Family Heritage and 1100 Club memberships. Of all the promised lodging, only a single bunkhouse would ever be completed.

Roe Messner's alliance with Bakker had proved lucrative. Virtually all his work at PTL had been performed under a cost-plus contract—

cost plus five percent overhead, with another ten percent of that total added as his profit. Messner made even more at PTL by using his own companies to supply windows, siding, designs, and other work. As Bakker and PTL altered and expanded their original plans and tossed in other jobs at Heritage USA, the cost of each project escalated dramatically. The original estimate for the Partner Center had been $22 million; final billings exceeded $41 million. By September 1986, Messner claimed a personal net worth of $32 million.

Messner's regular letters to Bakker were full of grand ideas, some of them his, many of them Bakker's. He wrote of subdivisions with million-dollar homes, a $3-million golf course designed by Arnold Palmer, a 270-bed hospital. As he gained Bakker's trust, Messner began proposing commercial profit-sharing ventures with PTL. In one letter to PTL, Messner described his company as "the goose that can lay the golden egg" for PTL. He sought control over PTL's thriving real-estate market, proposing in September 1985 to build condos that would house a community of fifteen thousand. PTL would get thirty percent of the selling price—an enormous sum—if Bakker could sustain demand for the units.

Messner was also a valuable backdoor source of capital. His money was not free; Messner charged PTL from ten to twelve percent interest on unpaid balances. With PTL owing $7 million or more from month to month, the costs mounted. In Bakker's last fifteen months at PTL, Messner charged the ministry more than $1 million in interest.

Messner preferred to do business on a handshake, and he and Bakker had developed an extremely close working relationship. A sinewy man with a steely manner, the fifty-one-year-old Messner recognized Bakker as the source of all power at PTL and he did his best to deal directly with the PTL president. This personal bond, coupled with Messner's leverage as a major creditor, meant that Bakker's staff had little room to challenge him.

On the air, Bakker claimed that Messner was providing high-quality work at remarkably low prices. Off the set, Bakker's staff had nagging doubts about the quality and cost of Messner's designs and construction. The roofs and exterior walls of the grand hotel leaked constantly; an outsider contractor would later estimate that it would cost more than $1 million to make them sound. The hotel's elevators were undersized. Its central-air-conditioning unit couldn't cool the lobby because the individual units in guest rooms had been vented into the lobby, not outside. Sewage backed up into the indoor swimming pool.

In summer 1986, PTL began a serious, if belated, effort to manage its multimillion-dollar construction budget more professionally. PTL hired a construction auditor and a professional engineer, tried to insist on signed, fixed-price contracts and formally approved change orders, and took steps to seek competitive bids.

Construction auditor Wally Stalnaker found that his new colleagues in PTL's finance department had done little to scrutinize Messner's invoices. Stalnaker—an outspoken sixty-nine-year-old with close to fifty years' experience in construction and construction auditing—was unimpressed with Messner's work. He discovered a six-lane road being built by a subcontractor without plans, specifications, or a permit. He was suspicious of huge discrepancies between Messner's original estimates and the bills he finally tendered. Stalnaker concluded that Messner had consistently billed PTL for a higher percentage of work than his crews had actually accomplished on the Tower's hotel.

Stalnaker received little support from his superiors once their initial enthusiasm faded and they realized how willing Stalnaker was to upset the status quo. Stalnaker challenged Messner's assertion that PTL owed him $660,000 in South Carolina sales tax; Stalnaker believed PTL had already paid the tax through Messner's cost-plus billings. One of Messner's aides took the matter to Taggart, and Taggart approved the payment on Bakker's behalf, together with another $700,000 item that Stalnaker had questioned. Messner could pretty much do what he pleased, Stalnaker joked years later, even if it meant building with straw.

Stalnaker's idealism had soured during his first week at PTL. He discovered what he would later learn was the money Dortch had laundered through Messner to silence Hahn. Dortch had commissioned Stalnaker to audit the Towers hotel project after May 31, 1985. But Stalnaker had strayed, his interest drawn to the millions of dollars Messner had charged PTL earlier for extra or miscellaneous work. On Messner's March 1985 invoice, Stalnaker found an unexplained $29,000 charge for work on PTL's amphitheater, the site of the passion play. He drove to the site and found no evidence to support the claim. A few days later, he discovered a second undocumented charge—this time for $265,000—listed against the amphitheater on Messner's April 1985 bill. A second trip to the site yielded no sign that any such work had been done since the amphitheater was renovated in mid-1984.

Stalnaker asked Messner for an explanation. Messner said that the $265,000 was between Dortch and himself and that he would make no change until he got word to do so from Dortch, Stalnaker remembered later. Bailey would recall being unable to get an explanation from higher ups; Stalnaker remembered hearing from Bailey that the $265,000 was actually for work done at the lakefront residence which PTL provided for Dortch. Stalnaker was unconvinced—he visited the house and found no evidence that work had been done in early 1985—and he would continue, without success, to try to figure out what had happened to the money. He was sure that he had stumbled onto a cover-up.

Meanwhile, Bakker's staff was still struggling with his voracious appetite for building. Despite the darkening financial clouds, despite the failure to complete the Towers after two years, the projects mushroomed. Work continued at Farmland USA, the nineteenth-century village next to Kevin's House; Bakker wanted the first bunkhouse finished so he could show it off in his November telethon. PTL ordered an enormous steel whale fabricated for its Christmas lights display. Bakker broke ground for an eight-thousand-square-foot Wendy's fast-food restaurant shaped like a giant sand castle. It was to be the world's largest Wendy's with room for three hundred diners. Bakker continued to order architectural drawings for future structures; by late September, Messner wanted $1.4 million for drawings for the Crystal Palace and the adjoining time-share tower. Bakker had given James Taggart orders to improve the quality and appearance of the Towers interior. By December, the decorating cost for guest rooms had increased by $1.5 million, and Bakker had authorized a $1.3 million marble foyer and staircase.

By the end of 1986, Messner claimed that PTL owed him $10.5 million. As he had done many times before, Messner asked Bakker for help. "I know you are trying, Jim, but I am getting desperate for money. My banker is insisting that I pay down my loan to $5 million before December 21." By month's end, PTL still owed him $10.3 million.

* * *

Bakker's occasional sexual encounters with Jay Babcock ended in November 1986 after what Babcock regarded as one of Bakker's most bizarre approaches. Bakker had taken a few hours off from PTL's latest telethon to sleep in the common room of his dressing-room complex. He dozed on one side of the U-shaped sofa, while singer and co-host Doug Oldham slept on the other. Babcock slipped into the room to wake Bakker; he had to return to the air within a half hour.

As he awoke, Bakker grabbed Babcock's hand and pulled it towards his genitalia. He was naked under the blanket. Babcock pulled away. "Look, I can't do this any more, and you need to get up and get dressed to go on the air." Bakker muttered his assent, and Babcock left. Oldham was still asleep. After more than three years of occasional mutual masturbation, the sexual relationship between Bakker and Babcock was over.

Though Richard Dortch owned the number-two title, insiders regarded David Taggart as Dortch's equal. Taggart was Bakker's alter ego: he organized Bakker's schedule, accompanied him on many of his trips, handled his personal finances, helped buy his clothes, and made sure the Bakkers got nothing but the best. Executives who wanted Bakker's ear approached Taggart. Bailey rarely got an audience with Bakker; he spent hours talking to Taggart instead. While Dortch might take months to make a decision, Taggart could be relied upon to give a swift yes or no. Taggart was proud of his efficiency, bragging to a co-worker about getting Bakker a passport in less than a day's time.

David Taggart was well liked by the Bakker family, and most of those who worked at his side shared that affection. He could be charming and generous with his friends—expensive meals on Taggart's tab were commonplace, and his gifts to close friends were sometimes worth thousands of dollars. He had given Shirley Fulbright a four-thousand-dollar full-length mink coat one Christmas and a two-thousand-dollar gold chain with diamonds another. Taggart had the sophisticated taste and knowledge of the world that seemed to confirm his stories of a silver-spoon upbringing.

Taggart had gone to great lengths to convince his friends and co-workers of his parents' wealth. He told of being cared for by nannies and taking vacations on the *Queen Mary*. One friend remembered Taggart saying that his parents had given him their $3 million art collection. He told another that the three-foot-tall jade sculptures flanking his fireplace were a present from his mother. The friend came away with the impression that the abstract figures were worth a quarter of a million dollars.

David Taggart worked very hard, and he was rewarded generously, earning $210,000 in salary and bonuses in 1986. But that sum was hardly enough to sustain his pretense of family money and his freewheeling spending on jewelry, designer clothes, travel, and fine food and drink. In fact, PTL money was flowing into the brothers' household from several other directions.

Bakker considered James Taggart "one of the best design decorators probably in the world," and when he wanted something prettied up, Bakker and his assistant David Taggart often turned to brother James. James had quit his PTL job after his brother's abrupt 1983 resignation. When David returned, so did James. Instead of taking a staff job, James Taggart opened his own decorating company—a firm in which his brother served as corporate secretary. Instead of a PTL salary, James Taggart was soon receiving hundreds of thousands of dollars from PTL for interior decoration, be it for the lobby of the World Outreach Center, or an overhaul of the Bakker's lakefront home.

In November 1986, James Taggart began to receive a second, steadier stream of money from PTL: a monthly retainer of ten thousand dollars, paid from the confidential executive payroll account. Bakker had ordered the payments as he accepted James Taggart's $100,000 bid for the interior-design plan for the Towers hotel. In all, James Taggart would receive more than $1 million from PTL between his return to Charlotte in 1984 and April 1987.

Over a four-year span, David and James Taggart also obtained $1.1 million from PTL to pay what a federal indictment later alleged to be the Taggarts' personal debts. Beginning in May 1985, David Taggart repeatedly used cash advances from PTL, ranging in size from $7,500 to $50,000, to pay the balance on the American Express account he shared with his brother. In May 1986, David Taggart used PTL credit cards to secure cash advances totaling $30,000, money he then allegedly used to cover purchases at Cartier in New York. The federal indictment, returned nearly two years after Bakker's resignation, alleged that the Taggarts had failed to report the money as income on their federal tax returns.

By 1986, the Taggarts were accumulating assets as befitted the children of wealth they claimed to be. In March 1986, David Taggart purchased a $640,000 one-bedroom condominium on the fifty-seventh floor of Trump Tower. The unit, two blocks from Cartier, cost nearly nine times what the Taggarts' Charlotte home had cost two years earlier. To secure the Trump condo, David Taggart paid $160,000 down and financed the remaining $480,000. In the weeks right before the closing, PTL had paid James $75,000. David had received $65,000 in cash advances and loans, money soon converted to a bonus.

The Taggarts also liked fine cars, driving Cadillacs and Mercedeses. Three days before Christmas 1986, the brothers bought each other Jaguars at a total cost of nearly $90,000. In the early months of 1987, the brothers began building a $317,000 house on a double lot in an exclusive Charlotte subdivision.

Like the boss whose proxy he wielded, David Taggart could have his way at PTL, even if it meant the most unabashed conflict of interest. In fall 1986, Taggart telephoned Bailey and said that he needed a quick $75,000 loan. Bailey telephoned PTL's bank and arranged for PTL to put up a certificate of deposit as collateral for the loan. After Bakker's resignation, the bank would have to claim the CD to regain its money. Not long after, again at Taggart's request, Bailey signed three blank checks that Taggart later used to pay $125,000 to his American Express account.

In December 1985, during the weeks that followed the arrival of the IRS audit report, David Taggart had played both employer and employee, orchestrating a highly generous employment contract for himself. Taggart's lawyer, who had also represented PTL, had drawn up the two-page agreement primarily to help Taggart secure a loan to buy the Trump Tower condo. The document promised Taggart an annual salary of $150,000—a figure suggested by his lawyer, Taggart said later, and more than he was actually paid—in addition to a bonus each December. The agreement also recorded two promises that Taggart later said he had gotten from Bakker: the guarantee of a full year's severance pay upon termination of his employment and a pledge to pay all costs if Taggart was hit with any claim for back taxes, interest, or penalties. Taggart's bosses had never approved the agreement. Instead, Taggart had taken it to his friend and office neighbor, Shirley Fulbright, and to Bailey, at best his equal on the PTL organizational chart, for their signatures. Bailey signed the third page without reading the other two. Had he read them, he might have noticed that the document twice mistakenly described Taggart as president of PTL.

The agreement's protection against back-tax claims was well timed. Taggart's spending of PTL money had attracted the attention of the IRS, as the November 1985 audit report made clear. By 1986, Taggart was defending his personal tax returns in an IRS civil audit. By early 1987, the IRS had claimed he owed $113,000 in back taxes for 1981 and 1982. Using the promises in his self-serving employment agreement, Taggart arranged his own $225,000 bonus to cover the back-tax claim as well as the taxes due on the bonus.

Taggart's spending habits had worried PTL's finance staff and outside auditors for years. By 1982, finance director John Franklin had expressed concern about Taggart's failure to document his expenses completely. In summer 1984, PTL's outside auditor advised PTL that some employee cash advances had been outstanding for more than six months without an accounting of how they had been spent. Taggart was a prime offender. A year later, Laventhol and Horwath, PTL's new auditor, recorded similar complaints in their annual letter to PTL management. The accountants had found no supporting documentation for large expenditures, and

> certain employees have not provided the ministry with supporting documentation for the use of [cash] advances. Certain employee advances outstanding at year-end are over one year old, and for one employee, total approximately $170,000.

The report did not name the employee, David Taggart. The firm recommended limiting the size of advances and requiring that larger purchases be paid for only after their purpose had been documented and approved.

But little changed on the third floor. Franklin's successor, Bailey, didn't control how the third floor spent the enormous sums flowing through its confidential accounts. In 1985, Bailey wrote off about

$200,000 in cash advances that Taggart had taken but had never documented. A year later, Bailey signed a letter at Taggart's request stating that Taggart had "adequate records" of how that money had been spent but kept those records on the third floor for confidentiality. The letter was then given to the IRS agent auditing Taggart's returns. Taggart's 1988 federal indictment listed this "misleading letter" as part of Taggart's alleged conspiracy to evade income taxes.

Taggart continued to assure Bailey that he had documents to show how he was spending the cash advances. Taggart's colleagues knew him as a fastidious record-keeper, and Bailey had seen his desk covered with receipts. The sums involved were stunning: in Bakker's final two years, Taggart or Bakker—in money matters, the two were often indistinguishable—withdrew more than $600,000 in cash advances on PTL credit cards. The IRS found another $126,000 in questionable purchases made through the executive checking account.

David Taggart was at Bakker's side a few days before Christmas as the Bakkers hosted a party for PTL's top executives at their home in Tega Cay. During the evening, Taggart helped the Bakkers unbox a pair of two-foot-tall dolls that resembled Jim and Tammy on the night of their twenty-fifth wedding anniversary nine months earlier. The miniature Jim wore a tux, the pint-sized Tammy a white lace dress. It was the sort of gift the Bakkers found terribly flattering.

As gifts for their guests, the Bakkers posed for pictures with them one by one. A PTL photographer took pictures, and the film was rushed out, printed, and the pictures returned to the guests before they left. PTL paid the tab.

Despite the worsening cash crisis at PTL, Bakker and his board doled out more than $1 million in bonuses in the final days of 1986. During the Christmas party, Bakker gave most of his vice presidents $10,000 bonuses. Shirley Fulbright was given $23,846 in bonus money that month, pushing her 1986 compensation to $160,750. Bailey—who had protested for so long against PTL's high operating costs but who would later say that he was underpaid—received $30,000. In all, Bailey was paid $115,368 in 1986. After approaching Taggart for help, he would receive another $54,000 bonus in January. Taggart was given nearly $30,000 in December

445

to complement the $125,000 he had received the month before.

The Bakkers and Dortch also did well. In its November meeting, the board had approved their Christmas bonuses. In its December meeting, it had approved Christmas gifts. All in all, according to records kept by Bakker's aides, the board had approved $150,000 in bonuses for Dortch and $650,000 for the Bakkers, in addition to paying for work on the Bakkers' new house in Gatlinburg.

A few days before the December board meeting, PTL secured three new $60,000 Mercedes SEL sedans—one for Dortch and one for each of the Bakkers. PTL also obtained a used Mercedes station wagon for the guards driving Jamie Charles; sixteen-year-old Tammy Sue would inherit the Mercedes coupe that an Alabama car dealer, a longtime friend of Dortch's, had lent Bakker in early 1986.

Dortch, the first to buy, ordered his staff to get the cash by bartering air time on PTL's satellite network. Though the car was rightfully PTL's, Dortch ordered the sedan titled in the name of the Alabama dealer's car-leasing trust so the *Observer* could not report that PTL had bought a Mercedes. When Bakker saw Dortch's car, he dropped his plans to get a new black Cadillac with gold-plated trim and ordered two more 560 SELs and the used station wagon. To some of Dortch's lieutenants, it seemed that Bakker needed to remind everyone that he, not Dortch, was in control.

The morning of December 23, the *Observer* telephoned me at home. PTL had called to say that it was releasing its annual audit, the document I had been awaiting for months. At PTL's suggestion, I met Richard Dortch and Neil Eskelin at Heritage USA for lunch. Dortch and I had had no cordial conversations in thirteen months, and he had been aloof during his last trip to complain to my editors. He kept his distance at this meeting as well, shedding his gloss of good cheer.

Joining us at the table in the Hampton Court restaurant was an older man whom I recognized but had never met and hardly expected to see—Charles Cookman, the board member and North Carolina district superintendent for the Assemblies of God.

"For the last four months," Dortch said, opening the conversation, "the board of directors has been reviewing our professional relationships." Among those, he said, was PTL's tie to ECFA. To remain a member of ECFA, PTL was required to release its audited financial statements—the document I had supposedly been summoned to receive. It was clear, from Dortch's opening words, that he was preparing to tell me that PTL was not releasing the audit.

"PTL has long sought peer relationships," Dortch said. "Lawyers belong to the bar association, doctors belong to the medical society. And interestingly, we think our focus is very, very clear as to what we are here—we are an Assemblies of God church." Dortch and Cookman gave me a few minutes of background about the denomination. Dortch continued. "Not one of the ten most-watched religious television programs in America belong to ECFA, and not one Assemblies of God church or ministry belongs to ECFA." Not Jimmy Swaggart, not David Wilkerson, not Lowell Lundstrom, Dortch said.

Deeply suspicious of Dortch, I wondered if he was manufacturing an argument. Certainly PTL had long known who did, or did not, belong to ECFA. The organization did have members with whom PTL could identify, if it so chose: Billy Graham's ministry, James Robison, numerous Christian TV and radio stations, and many evangelical organizations, including Campus Crusade for Christ, World Vision, and Youth for Christ. But Dortch was correct in saying that many of America's biggest TV ministries were not ECFA members. Pat Robertson's CBN was not; his board of directors was too heavily dominated by Robertson and his staff. Jerry Falwell's Thomas Road Baptist Church had withdrawn; ECFA had questioned whether Falwell supplied enough information about how donors' money was spent. I asked Dortch about Billy Graham, a founder of ECFA. "He's not a broadcaster, that's not his ministry. And he does not have a local ministry."

Dortch handed a letter across the table. "We have resigned as of today from ECFA," he told me. The two-page letter to ECFA recounted, diplomatically, much of what Dortch had already said. "We submit to the stringent code of ethics of the Assemblies of God and the National Religious Broadcasters," the letter read. "Having met their criteria . . . we have more than fulfilled our responsibility." Of course, Dortch said nothing to me of PTL's history of difficulties with ECFA. He made no mention in his letter, or to me, of the PTL board's 1985 vote to pull out of ECFA—a decision made long before its "review of professional relationships" but which had been shelved by the embarrassing publicity from ECFA in October 1985. He did not disclose PTL's discomfort with the tougher ECFA rules scheduled to take effect on New Year's Day, including requirements that members disclose the value of gift premiums and financial information on specific projects for which they raised money.

Dortch told me that PTL would continue to release financial statistics to anyone who asked. It expected to join a financial accountability group being proposed by the National Religious Broadcasters. But Dortch said that the financial statistics would not include the auditor's opinion or notes. That, Dortch explained, "is what our denomination and what any other broadcaster does."

I pressed Dortch, asking him if PTL was adopting this new policy because it was concerned about another embarrassing story like the one the *Observer* had printed based on the footnotes and opinion in last year's audit. Dortch lashed out. "That's an affront for me for you to even say that. It shows you have a preconditioned mind." I defended the question, but Dortch fumed. "When I look at the big picture, the material that was released last year was not offensive to me. It's not an embarrassment. Doesn't embarrass me in the least," Dortch said. "This change has nothing to do with the notes this year."

I had expected the new audit to disclose the status of PTL's appeal within the IRS. I was equally eager to see how many lifetime partnerships PTL had sold. By withholding the revealing footnotes, Dortch and PTL kept this and other highly sensitive information secret.

Dortch acknowledged that the IRS dispute remained unresolved. I asked when it might end. "Your guess is as good as mine," he said. "Obviously we feel we have a rationale for what we do. Whether it's the press or a government agency or people trying to understand this ministry, we have a constant educational process ongoing that we're involved in. We're not doing anything different from what's happening in the camp meetings. But because we're doing it in a more grand scale, what we do gets lost in the shuffle. . . . The questions are one of interpreting tax laws," Dortch continued. "It's not a question of"—and Cookman finished his sentence—"integrity."

* * *

448

Six days before my lunch with Dortch, a federal jury in Detroit acquitted John DeLorean of charges that he had embezzled $8.5 million from his failed sports-car company. As the verdict was announced, the sixty-one-year-old former carmaker wept. DeLorean, who had become a born-again Christian after his earlier arrest on a drug-smuggling conspiracy charge, cried out "Praise God" and embraced his attorney Howard Weitzman. For the second time in three years, Weitzman had saved DeLorean from a trip to the penitentiary, much as he and his one-time partner Scott Furstman had managed, it seemed, to put the matter of Jessica Hahn to rest for Bakker.

The next day, between requests for a staff member to hook up Tammy's new Coca-Cola telephone at home and a suggestion that PTL put a light atop the crane erecting a new condominium high-rise, Bakker dictated a brief order to his staff:

> Send a telegram to John DeLorean from Jim and Tammy, congratulating him on his victory in the courts yesterday.

CHAPTER TWENTY-TWO

THE COVER-UP UNRAVELS

"No weapon formed against you shall prosper"

The Crystal Palace Ministry Center was Jim Bakker's grandest project yet. It carried a price tag of $100 million and a three-year construction schedule. When complete, it would seat thirty thousand people. At 1.25 million square feet, it would be large enough to hold Charlotte's biggest shopping mall. As he broke ground on January 2, 1987, his forty-seventh birthday, Bakker was full of superlatives about the building he called the world's largest religious gathering place. "I've fallen in love with this building. It's an obsession. I will either build this building or I will die trying."

Behind Bakker stood a drawing of the proposed building on its forty-acre site a short walk from Kevin's House. The building would contain a five-thousand-seat TV studio, an auditorium with room for twelve thousand, an adjoining exhibit area with space for eighteen thousand seats, and various ministry offices. Bakker hoped to pay for the building by selling $170 million worth of time-share units in the adjoining thirty-story Crystal Tower. He talked, too, of 30,000 people paying $1,000 each to attend the grand opening.

The massive project, which Bakker and his staff had been discussing for more than a year, troubled many of those attending the groundbreaking. Raleigh Bakker thought that his son was foolish to erect a glass building. How could he heat it in the winter or cool it in the summer at reasonable cost? Dortch had tried to persuade Bakker to set the project aside. Bakker didn't budge, and Dortch, ever loyal, presented a united front. Finance specialist Mark Burgund thought they were breaking ground far too early. PTL's staff was just now getting the chance to say what it needed inside the building. Bakker wanted to begin construction, but his staff persuaded him to wait, to make sure the interior was right before Messner started putting up steel girders. There didn't seem to be enough bathrooms, enough meeting areas, or wide enough halls.

Construction auditor Wally Stalnaker refused to attend the groundbreaking. He was convinced that PTL would never have enough money to complete the structure. Otis Winters, a Tulsa oilman whom Roe Messner had recently recruited to manage his work at PTL, didn't consider the project serious. Winters didn't see where Messner had come up with the $100 million in projected profits from the Crystal Tower that would pay for the Palace, and he considered it ridiculous to think that PTL could get financing for the buildings and other planned projects. Costs for the Crystal Palace had already escalated in typical PTL fashion. Publicly, Bakker used the figure $100 million, but inside estimates had climbed beyond $110 million. Mark Burgund saw the bill soaring even higher if the TV engineers and Bakker got all the bells and whistles they wanted.

Coatless and shivering that winter day, Walter Richardson, the executive in charge of PTL's network of TV affiliates, had his doubts as well, but he had learned to believe that Bakker could complete even the most outlandish plan. Three years before, Richardson had been unable to envision the Heritage Grand Hotel. As he and Bakker ceremoniously cast tokens reading No Weapon Formed Against You Shall Prosper, a quote from a favorite Bakker Scripture, into footings at the hotel site in early 1984, he had told Bakker, "Jim, if we complete this hotel, I will never doubt you again." And Bakker had pulled it off.

As Bakker left the site that Friday afternoon, he noticed mud caked on his Ferragamo shoes. He suggested that a staff member preserve them as a memento. The shoes soon reappeared in the third-floor executive suite, enshrined in an $1,800 custom Lucite box, complete with a shiny gold plaque to mark the occasion. For now, the box was a monument to a celebrity's day of glory. Within weeks, Bakker's feet of clay would assume a darker significance.

The Bakker family and an entourage next headed to the Tennessee mountains and the Bakkers' new vacation home in Gatlinburg. As snow fell outside, Tammy Bakker's temperature climbed, and soon nearly everyone was sent home to Charlotte. Tammy stayed at the mountain home to recover, watched over by Vi Azvedo, on whom the Bakkers remained highly dependent. Jim Bakker returned to Charlotte to meet with the York County Council, the governing body of Heritage USA's growing home county in South Carolina.

The council had adopted zoning rules that curbed the unbridled freedom Bakker had enjoyed as he developed Heritage USA. On the night of January 12, Bakker was at his charismatic best, presenting a dazzling blueprint that promised York County more of the economic prosperity PTL had already brought. His audience was made up of mostly small-town folks, and they were impressed. Several came forward to ask Bakker to autograph the new coffeetable books about PTL that the ministry had given to the visitors.

From Tennessee, Azvedo reported that Tammy was getting worse. Her fever was climbing towards 104 degrees. Azvedo summoned Lester Nichols, the California physician, former owner of the Palmdale hospital, and Bakker family friend, whose wife was a member of the Palmdale therapy team. Nichols advised getting Tammy to a hospital immediately; Bakker later recalled being told that Tammy would have died had she waited one more day for help. Instead of taking Tammy to a local or regional hospital, however, PTL chartered a jet out of New Jersey to fly Tammy from Knoxville to California, where she was admitted to the Eisenhower Medical Center, near the Bakkers' home in Palm Desert. The plane ride cost PTL $36,920.

At Eisenhower, doctors confirmed that Tammy had pneumonia. They also diagnosed another, chronic condition—drug dependency. It was no surprise to those close to Tammy. She loved playing doctor, recommending medicines to ailing friends and prescribing drugs to herself. They had noticed how Ativan affected Tammy. Frank Marklin, a member of the Palmdale therapy team and himself a recovered alcoholic, had noticed Tammy walking around in a daze. Marklin expressed his concern to Vi Azvedo and Jim Bakker. He got little more than rationalizations.

Tammy had been taking several medicines to fight her latest illness: aspirin, three at a clip; Aspergum for her sore throat; over-the-counter cold remedies and nasal sprays. As the Bakkers told it later, a physician had also prescribed antibiotics. Her system flooded with drugs, Tammy began hallucinating, first mildly, then uncontrollably. She saw demons and visions of hell, bugs inside the plane taking her to Palm Springs, and, while in flight, a cat sitting atop the jet's wings.

While Tammy was spirited to California, Bakker began to acknowledge the scope of her drug problem to his staff. The Bakkers' retainers had discovered drugs everywhere—in Tammy's nightstand, her purse, her cabinet. Bakker was worried that Tammy's brain might be damaged, that she might emerge a vegetable. That day, Bakker talked privately with Wanda Burgund about his insecurities, his drive to build, and the resentment Tammy still felt about his obsession with Heritage USA and PTL.

Back home in Bethalto, Illinois, Wanda Burgund had been working her way toward a job as school superintendent when her husband, Mark, agreed to follow Richard Dortch to PTL in 1984. She had grown up in a working-class Assemblies of God home, and she had emerged with a driving ambition to prove what a girl from the wrong side of the tracks could accomplish. She had earned bachelor's and master's degrees in psychology at Southern Illinois University, begun work on a doctorate, and served for seven years as school psychologist for the thirteen-hundred-student Bethalto school district. She and her husband represented the new generation of Pentecostals, better educated, more affluent, part of mainstream America.

Dortch had given Wanda Burgund a job as PTL's executive personnel director, and Bakker found that he could rely on the determined aide to get jobs done at Heritage USA. When he would arrive at Heritage USA, Bakker would often radio for Burgund to meet him at the studio or on the grounds. There he would rattle off long lists of ideas and must-dos. Burgund was proud of her ability to deliver, despite Bakker's impersonal treatment. Others saw her adopting Bakker's attitudes, growing overly demanding and flush with the power she wielded by proxy.

Wanda Burgund did not regard Bakker as her equal in intellect or management ability, but he brought out the protective instinct in her, as he did in many of those around him. He was the fragile visionary who needed protection, mostly from himself. Like many of Bakker's employees and partners, Wanda Burgund believed at the time that Bakker was fulfilling the will of God. He might not do it efficiently, but Heritage USA seemed to attest to the essential goodness of his vision. Given enough time, Burgund believed that she and the other professionals who had arrived during Dortch's tenure could turn PTL around.

On January 13, sitting in Bakker's sterile office with its white desk and white carpet and white drapes, Burgund had her first—and, as it turned out, only—chance to counsel her boss. She had long felt that he would profit from such a talk. "Jim, if you lose your wife, these other things"—Bakker's work on TV and Heritage USA—"will mean nothing to you," she said. "Those that we love the most tend to take the most emotional abuse from us because we know we are safe with them. But there comes a point in time when no one can continue with that type of neglect and hang on to those relationships. There comes a point in time when there is nothing there."

Burgund's message was hardly new to Bakker; he had heard the same refrain from Roger and Linda Wilson seven years before. But now, Bakker was willing to listen. That day, he flew west to join his wife in California.

Returning from lunch on Monday, January 5, I found an electronic message logged into my computer: "A man called and wouldn't leave his name but said you need to talk to Jim Cobble about PTL because there are a lot of things going on there and Jim could tell you about them."

Earlier that day, Cobble and Cress had talked by phone, Cobble from his home in a Charlotte suburb and Cress from his third-floor apartment in Denver. The eleventh paragraph of my story on PTL's exit from ECFA, published on Christmas Eve, had angered them both. The paragraph reported Dortch's claim that PTL "will continue to be accountable to two organizations—the Assemblies of God denomination and the twelve-hundred-member National Religious Broadcasters. Meeting their standards, he said, fulfills PTL's responsibility." Cobble and Cress knew this was not true PTL, they believed, had set itself above the denomination's standards.

Late that afternoon, I phoned Cobble. I knew that he was my best chance to get through to Cress. When Cobble and I had talked in May 1986, I had been deliberately evasive about my interest in Cress. Now, I was eager to move the Hahn story off dead center. I decided to take a chance and take Cobble into my confidence.

I told Cobble that I had information that Jim Bakker had had a sexual encounter with a woman named Jessica Hahn in December 1980 and then PTL had paid her to remain silent. I showed a command of precise details—the white terry-cloth bathing suit, the hotel's name, the sizeable trust fund—that surprised Cobble. I emphasized that I wanted to get the facts straight. Cobble spoke guardedly. He was uneasy talking to a reporter and unwilling to trust me immediately, but he was also anxious to see PTL forced to justify its handling of the Hahn matter. "The information that I have is no longer really private. Quite a few people are aware of it," Cobble said. "I have friends who work at PTL. I don't have a desire to do anything harmful to them. On the other hand, I feel that there's a public accountability that the leaders have but don't take seriously."

Cobble had pieced together a similar story of PTL, Jim Bakker, and Jessica Hahn, much of it from talking with Cress. What Cobble had heard fit neatly into the stories John Stewart had told me thirteen months earlier and Hahn had alleged twenty-five months before. Stewart knew the events on the West Coast, Cress knew what had happened on the East Coast.

Cobble had seen Cress's photocopy of the July 1985 correspondence from Scott Furstman to Richard Dortch, the letter that explicitly mentioned the Hahn trust. Cress had described to Cobble the draft lawsuit written by Stewart and mailed to PTL. Cress had witnessed the use of PTL funds; at Dortch's direction, Cress had told Cobble, he had wired PTL money into a bank account in February 1985 to consummate the arrangements Dortch had made with lawyer Howard Weitzman. Cress told Cobble that he believed builder Roe Messner had served as the conduit for Hahn's trust-fund money. Cobble himself had talked with Fred Gross about the payoff in 1985. The conversations had been veiled, each man assuming the other knew what had happened. Cobble had wondered aloud why the payments weren't considered blackmail. As Cobble remembered it, Gross said that he didn't know what else to call them either.

I asked Cobble why his friend Cress had been so elusive during my April 1986 visit to Illinois. "I think at that time he was still pretty ambivalent about what he should talk about and who he should talk with. . . . I know that Al has communicated the information to people he feels should be aware of it," alluding to Cress's meeting with the officials from the Assemblies of God. "I think that the people he shared it with were greatly concerned. Their legal advice at this particular point in time is they don't have enough evidence to do anything."

Cobble said that the Assemblies of God leadership probably knew a trust fund existed, but, he added, they didn't know for sure the fund's purpose. "They don't make a practice of picking on ministers and forcing them to prove charges they don't have evidence for." Cobble thought that Dortch, his former boss, had decided to deny that any sexual encounter had occurred between Bakker and Hahn. Dortch had told Cress that the trust was set up because a public fight would be extremely damaging, whatever the outcome.

I asked how I could contact Cress; Cobble told me that he was in the Denver phone book. I asked about Cress's personality. "He's outgoing, very friendly, caring, responsible, hardworking, and thoughtful. He functions differently than I do. He's more intuitive, more likely to act on gut instinct."

I telephoned Cress the next night from my home. He spoke with passion. "PTL will do anything and will pay any amount to keep Jim Bakker's public image clean. . . . You are dealing with barracudas." Cress, like Cobble, did not want his name in print. "You know yourself what Jim Bakker will do to me. He will do everything he can to assassinate me." Cress considered Bakker's power at PTL as absolute as Hitler's. "They talk that PTL is totally responsible to the Assemblies of God. The national headquarters doesn't want that honor. . . . Nobody has the guts to tell Jim Bakker what he's going to do—nobody." Cress believed that membership on PTL's board had compromised Charles Cookman, the district superintendent overseeing PTL. He found it ludicrous that PTL claimed to be a local church, yet no member of its congregation sat on the parent corporation's board of directors.

Cress was candid about his resentment toward Dortch for pushing him aside two weeks after his mother's death in July 1985. "There is a side of me that I don't know that I will ever by able to forgive the man for that."

I asked Cress to walk through the events leading to the Jessica Hahn payoff with me. For the first time, I learned the name of Paul Roper, Stewart's friend and the man who had represented Jessica Hahn. Cress confirmed that he had wired $25,000 from PTL into a California bank account controlled by Weitzman; that payment, apparently for legal fees, was my first hard evidence linking PTL money to the Hahn settlement. "I have a hard time with that," Cress said. "Jim Bakker did not get on the air [raising money] saying, 'Folks, I have a young lady who has accused me of having an illicit affair with her.'"

On January 15, two days after Jim Bakker's departure for California, former PTL executive Roger Flessing stopped at Heritage USA to have lunch with Dortch. Flessing was in the Carolinas to produce a TV version of Billy Graham's spring crusade in South Carolina's capital city of Columbia, an hour's drive south. Flessing watched the day's PTL show from the control booth, as viewers were told that Tammy was sick in California with pneumonia and suffering what Dortch called a severe reaction to her medicine. Flessing felt nothing for the ministry he had left three times. "This place is sicker than ever," he muttered inside the control room. "I love coming back here because I remember why I left." A microphone in the control room spread his disgust to every crew member wearing a headset.

"I'm here because you have something against me," Flessing told Dortch as they sat face to face in the Hampton Court restaurant that afternoon. He related the comment Cress had passed along, that Dortch had warned that Flessing couldn't be trusted. Dortch was quick with a denial and a flash of charm. "Oh, I never said anything like that. We're buddies. You're the best guy in television in the country. We would do anything to have you back."

Dortch said that Cress was bitter. Then Dortch, speaking in

veiled terms, touched on the matter of Jessica Hahn and the documents Cress had shared with the Assemblies of God. He commented that Cress thought that he had seen some information that he really knew nothing about.

Dortch dangled work before Flessing, telling him that PTL was looking for someone to make a video of Heritage USA. "You're a TV genius," Dortch said, "and we'd like you to make it." Dortch gave Flessing his private post office box and asked him to send some estimates. Flessing would send nothing. As he left Heritage USA, he felt only disgust. He knew Dortch had lied to him.

After three years on the job, Dortch had lost much of his respectability. Too many of those who worked under him believed that he couldn't be trusted to tell the truth. Some had even given his dissembling a name: "Dortching." Dortching was telling a shrewdly crafted lie, perhaps technically accurate, but essentially deceptive. Jimmy Swaggart had been Dortched in Baton Rouge when Dortch had told him he knew of no lawsuit by a woman accusing Bakker of moral failure. Of course, there never had been a lawsuit filed, just a draft lawsuit sent to the accused, so Dortch was technically telling the truth. Now, without naming Hahn or explicitly accusing his former aide, Dortch tried to lead Flessing to believe that Al Cress had contrived the tale of Jim Bakker's accuser.

The deceptions might work with PTL's ignorant TV audience or its more trusting uninformed staff members, but Dortch's ability to manipulate was only as certain as his exclusive access to the facts. Once others began to acquire bits and pieces of the truth, the protective wall Dortch had erected around Jim Bakker and the PTL ministry began to crumble. Flessing had heard too much from too many. He had talked to Cress and knew him to be a man of his word. He had talked to me days after my first conversation with Hahn in 1984. In fall 1986, he had talked for the first time with Sam Orender, his former colleague, about Bakker's December 1980 trip to Clearwater Beach. Orender had told Flessing about the young woman who had been invited by Fletcher—and about the passing compliment Jim Bakker had paid her firm breasts a few weeks later in Hawaii.

On January 18, I flew to Los Angeles, my first visit to California since my August 1984 trip to report the story of Jim Bakker's new home in the desert. I felt the same thrill I had then, but this time, the stakes were extraordinary.

I spent Monday morning reading newspaper clippings in Orange County, looking for information about Roper and Stewart. I found plenty to establish Stewart's credibility and to flesh out the character Paul Roper. Both men had surfaced in reports of trouble at Melodyland Christian Center, Ralph Wilkerson's nondenominational church across from the entrance to Disneyland in Anaheim. Stewart had taught at Melodyland's theological school and had pastored a church formed by disaffected members of Melodyland in 1983. Roper had grown up on a Crow Indian reservation in Montana, the son of missionaries in the International Church of the Foursquare Gospel, a Pentecostal denomination. As a student in the late sixties, he had attended services at Melodyland. In 1979, Roper, now described as a real-estate developer and import-export dealer, took over as business manager as Melodyland foundered financially. He cut payroll and other operating expenses and helped the church secure needed cash.

But Roper and others eventually discovered evidence suggesting that Wilkerson had profited personally at the church's expense. He pressed the issue within the church, he said years after, and others prompted police and IRS investigations of Wilkerson. It was Roper's willingness to stand up to Wilkerson, a leading figure in the charismatic community in southern California, that had apparently led New York pastor Gene Profeta to seek Roper's help in the Hahn matter. In April 1983, as he left Melodyland, Roper declared that he was starting Operation Antichrist, a campaign to expose TV preachers and evangelists who "sell their theology for money. . . . They are their own God, their own boss, and they make their own rules."

Eager to keep a low profile, I had decided not to approach Roper on my trip to California. On Tuesday morning, I met Stewart at his home in Orange, California. He was thirty-five, tall and slender, and bore an uncanny resemblance to Dodgers pitcher Orel Hershiser. Stewart seemed relaxed, friendly, and interested in the truth. In his study, he showed me the yellow notepaper on which he had begun to draft the complaint that, in its finished form, Cress had seen in January 1985. He showed me the photostat of the $115,000 settlement check Roper had given him as a souvenir. At the close of our conversation, I told him that I knew Roper's name.

That same morning, singer Doug Oldham delivered PTL's first detailed report of Tammy's illness to the TV audience: the flu-turned-pneumonia, the 104-degree temperature, the call to Dr. Nichols, the flight to California. But PTL was not ready to disclose Tammy's drug problem any more than the Bakker family had been willing to admit it to themselves, and so her anticipated treatment for drug dependency was disguised as treatment for a less damaging illness. Oldham predicted that Tammy was in for a four-to-six-week siege. "We're just not getting the results we need." The next day, singer Vestal Goodman took the misrepresentation a step further. It was hard for Tammy to pull out of the pneumonia, she said, because she was so "worn out and run down and just totally exhausted." In fact, Tammy would be deemed well enough to leave the hospital within a week. It was her planned drug treatment at the Betty Ford Center that would take four to six weeks.

From Los Angeles I flew to Denver; Cress had agreed to see me. On the morning of January 22, I gingerly picked my way through the snow-covered parking lot of the Chestnut Ridge apartments. Cress lived in a lovingly decorated two-bedroom apartment on the third floor. He was a short, intense man whose face, accent, and dark hair reflected his mother's Mexican heritage. Though he had not been at PTL in months, he was well connected to the gossip that proliferated inside the ministry. He had heard of the Taggarts' new Jaguars, the third floor's new Mercedeses. His disillusionment was complete. "These guys have no sense of truth, no sense of integrity," he said that day. He wondered aloud why, if there hadn't been a payoff, did Dortch not dispute the contents of his May 1986 letter to him? Dortch had challenged only one fact—the age Cress had given for Hahn in his May 1986 letter.

I asked to see the daily steno pads Cress had kept in early 1985. Beginning on February 4, a familiar cast of characters emerged: Howard Weitzman, Paul Roper, Scott Furstman, John Wesley Fletcher, Aimee Cortese. On February 27, the day of the settlement, Cress had written down the name, account number, and bank location for Weitzman's clients' trust account.

When I arrived at the Denver airport that night to fly home, I was told that a rare heavy snowfall had closed Charlotte's airport. My flight was grounded. The airline agreed to fly me to Tampa overnight and home to Charlotte the next day. I was eager to see the Sheraton Sand Key Resort, where Hahn and Bakker had met. I spent a short night in Clearwater, rose early the next morning, and crossed the bridge to the Sand Key. I photographed the balcony from which Hahn claimed that she had first seen Bakker and the pool where Bakker had been lounging with his daughter. I walked through the halls outside the rooms where Hahn and Bakker had spent the night, three floors apart, after their first and only encounter six years and two months before.

Back in Charlotte, I began planning my next trip—to meet Hahn and John Wesley Fletcher. I wanted to approach each without warning, from me or PTL. These interviews could cinch the story. Fletcher could confirm the alleged sexual encounter in 1980, and Hahn could confirm the payoff. But I expected little cooperation— and from one or both, an urgent call to PTL. Soon, I thought, Dortch and Bakker would know I was chasing the story.

Tammy Bakker checked out of Eisenhower Medical Center on Monday, January 26. For another three days, PTL suggested that she was still inside—on the twenty-seventh, PTL even broadcast a videotape update from Bakker standing in front of the hospital entrance. Tammy would remain under doctor's care for several more weeks, he said, due to the side effects of prescription and nonprescription drugs for her illness. In fact, Tammy had checked in to the Betty Ford Center, located on the same site as the hospital. The Betty Ford Center is widely known for the celebrities who have graduated from its inpatient program for alcohol and drug addiction. But this was one celebrity experience Tammy Bakker could do without. She rebelled at the Spartan regimen and her loss of freedom. After one night, she left.

At Heritage USA, substitute host Tammy Sue Bakker wasn't sure what story to tell PTL's TV audience. On Thursday, January 29, the sixteen-year-old hesitantly acknowledged that her mother was out of the hospital. "She's doing a lot better. She, uh, I don't"—Tammy Sue interrupted herself, turned aside, and whispered quietly, "Can we tell them, tell outpatient?" It's OK, Doug Oldham assured her. Tammy Sue continued. "She's at home and can't shop. And she

461

can't go out and do anything, and she still has to go for the—to the hospital for periodic checks and things like that.''

By now, some on PTL's TV staff suspected that Tammy was receiving treatment at Betty Ford. On Friday, January 30, Dortch met with the production staff and reported that Tammy was resting at home. A band member asked if she would receive any further treatment. "This is the first I've ever heard about it," Dortch answered. Everyone laughed. They had been Dortched, more clumsily than usual. "Did I say something wrong?" Dortch asked.

After refusing the inpatient care, Tammy agreed to enroll in the center's outpatient program. It begins with six weeks of individual and group therapy, lectures, and films offered in four-hour blocks each weekday evening. Family members and some close friends participate in the sessions as well. The patient then begins a year of weekly group therapy. Jim, David Taggart, and Vi Azvedo participated in nightly sessions for co-dependents, and Jamie Charles and Tammy Sue attended occasionally too.

Meanwhile, the strain between PTL and builder Roe Messner had grown more pronounced. Messner was getting mixed signals from the ministry. Once in December and again in January, PTL staff members had instructed Winters, Messner's business associate, that Messner should not proceed on building projects without a written contract. But Bakker had written to Messner before Christmas confirming his instructions to move ahead on several projects for which no contracts had been signed. Winters presented Messner's dilemma in a January 26 letter to Dortch:

> Just what are we supposed to do? Go ahead because Mr. Bakker tells Roe to start work immediately or pull off the projects because you and your staff are telling me to do nothing without a signed contract and signed change orders. . . .
> For some time, Roe has acted as if he was your in-house building department. He has worked for PTL as if he were on their payroll, and he did whatever the boss told him to do. It seems to me that this relationship is deteriorating, and you want to do business with us only on a contractual basis.

Winters cautioned Dortch that working for PTL under a fixed-price contract, rather than the cost-plus arrangement Messner had been using, would be "very difficult and perhaps impossible . . . because the scope of your projects is continually changed." If PTL required signed contracts and change orders—as Bakker's staff had been advocating more and more forcefully since summer 1986—then projects would take much longer to finish, Winters warned. Winters was sure that Bakker would not sit still for such formalities if he wanted something done.

The Wendy's restaurant provided a "dramatic" example, Winters said. Messner had given PTL a $1.2 million fixed price for the sand castle–shaped building, but Bakker, forever changing his plans, had moved the site one hundred feet at the last minute to protect a view of the water park's mountain. That had put the restaurant on top of an old fill area, creating a significant added expense. But Bakker had told Messner to go ahead with construction, without a signed change order.

Winters was also deeply troubled by PTL's $10 million debt to Messner. "The pace of your construction is accelerating, and your schedule of payments is slowing down," he wrote to Dortch. That fall, Winters had warned Messner not to let PTL's bill run beyond $5 million. But PTL—worried about the consequences of stopping work on the Towers, the building PTL's lifetime partners had given enough to pay for several times over—urged Messner to continue. The contractor, his pockets deep and his faith in Bakker still strong, worked on.

On January 8, PTL made the only payment it could muster in January, $1 million. At PTL's request, Messner waited eight days to cash it. The check bounced. PTL was not able to make good on the $1 million until month's end. Now, Messner's cash-flow problems were critical, Winters wrote. If not paid, they would pull off of virtually every job at PTL.

> This will be devastating and very painful for both of us. . . . We are both heading down the drain if things do not change immediately.
> I believe with every fiber in my being that Jim Bakker and the rest of you have the call and the vision to build this ministry. However, I have to worry about paying the carpenters, plumbers, and suppliers who may not have the same vision and can only see the need to have a job that pays them for their work in order to feed their families.

The only simple solution was either to raise more money or defer some of PTL's building projects.

Winters wrote Dortch a stronger letter on February 16, prompting a meeting with members of the finance staff. Together, they agreed that PTL would pay Messner $75,000 each month until the Towers hotel was finished to compensate for the cost of the delays necessitated by PTL's fragile finances. PTL agreed to restrict its building to the Towers and several other major projects.

PTL had teetered at the edge of this precipice before. But this time, Jim Bakker was not available to orchestrate a miracle; he was busy in California trying to mend his family. Never before had PTL fallen so far behind in Bakker's old-buildings-pay-for-new-projects shell game. By now, the cost of the Towers had escalated to $26 million. The adjacent recreation center—which continued to grow in scope as Bakker asked for one hundred lanes in the bowling alley and 950 seats in the dinner theater—had now been turned into a separate project costing another $6 million. To finish the Towers by July 1987, Otis Winters told PTL, Messner would need $1.8 million a month for five months—on top of the $11.6 million owed through January 1987.

There was little reason for optimism. Lack of money had forced Messner to cut his Towers crew by fifty men in early February, and another hundred were laid off a week later. Winters warned that a complete shutdown was not far off unless Messner received a substantial payment soon. "The picture looks bleak at the moment, but with our Lord's strength, we, too, can do all things." Winters wrote to Dortch.

On Wednesday, February 4, I flew to New York to meet Jessica Hahn. First, I wanted to check her background. In the Nassau County offices in Mineola, I found no criminal charges or lawsuits filed against Jessica Hahn, not even a voter-registration card. All I could turn up was a document indicating that she had planned, but never followed through with, a lawsuit against a Long Island riding stable after a fall from a horse.

That afternoon, I spent more than an hour in front of Hahn's mother and stepfather's modest home in Massapequa, hoping to spot Jessica's car and catch her unannounced. I had no luck there or at Wednesday-evening services at the Full Gospel Tabernacle, the church where she had worked. The service offered plenty of music, upbeat and loud, the work of a small band and a succession of well-amplified soloists. The crowd was thin. Profeta wasn't there. Hahn's car—I still didn't know what she looked like—was not in the parking lot outside.

The next morning, inside an office in Massapequa High School, I got my first glimpse of Jessica from her 1977 yearbook picture, taken more than two years before her trip to Clearwater. She hadn't stood out in school. She had belonged to the Future Homemakers of America, Student Office Club, and Health Careers. At the public library, I found a 1979 newspaper profile of Hahn's minister, Gene Profeta.

> As he does not preach poverty, neither does he live with it. He unabashedly favors furnishings and clothing of the brocade-and-cut-velvet school. . . . The pastor wears two diamond rings and a watch with diamonds circling the face. His clothes are designer-labeled but showy; pointed shoes, in varying tones of gray suede, navy silk shirts, color-coordinated from head to toe. . . .
>
> Profeta is lunching on lobster tails and broiled mushrooms and takes a modest amount of a good Beaujolais. He is enjoying the pleasant surroundings, the good food, the pleasures of the day.

Halfway into the article, the author quoted a church staff member named Jessica Hahn.

Late that afternoon, I introduced myself to Profeta in the parking lot of his church. I had hoped that he might be prepared to confirm the existence of Hahn's trust fund. The interview went badly from the start. He led me to an office and, as I sat down, pulled a gun from inside his leather jacket. He matter-of-factly set the weapon on the desk. He offered no explanation, and I said nothing about it. Clearly Profeta wanted me to know he was in charge.

I explained the article I was researching. "I know nothing about it," Profeta said. "I'm not familiar with that story, anything of that nature happening. If anything of that nature happened, I'm sure no one's going to go telling people about it." His denials were unconvincing. No, he said, he had not put Jessica in touch with Paul Roper. Yes, he acknowledged a few minutes later, Roper has preached in his church. "Who are you helping out of this? Jessica?

465

Jim Bakker? Who are you helping?" he asked. He resumed his protestations of ignorance. I asked how long Jessica had worked at the church, when she had left, what she had done there. He refused to say, suggesting only that she had answered phones. I asked if she was truthful. "I wasn't that close with her. So I wouldn't know. I couldn't tell you. . . . I don't know her personal life." She had never told him of any encounter with Jim Bakker, he said.

Profeta spoke about Bakker without anger. "A tree is known by its fruit," Profeta said. "From the fruit that I see at PTL they must be doing the right thing. That's all I know." God forgives, he said. Man does not.

I walked out of Profeta's office, swung my car around the corner, pulled into a diner, and telephoned Hahn at her mother's home. I wanted to get to her before Profeta. Her mother took my name and number and said she would have Jessica call. The pay phone rang within minutes.

"I can't talk," Hahn said. "I was told not to talk to you." I assured her that I knew why, that I only wanted to talk to her, to tell her the story I was working on. She sounded intrigued. We agreed to meet in a half hour at the Starlight II, a diner in nearby Massapequa Park.

I arrived first and took a table in a corner. At 5:35, Hahn arrived. She was wearing a fur coat, high heels, and sunglasses and was more glamorous than she appeared in her high-school annual. Her brown hair had been highlighted, her fingernails painted red to match her lipstick. She had dressed to display her ample bosom. She was friendly but tense. As we talked, I found her believable, a good witness; it was a reaction that many would have when they first met her.

I read the twenty-seven-year-old a draft of my story. We had agreed that we were not talking for publication. She quarreled with a few phrases—she denied making repeated calls to PTL, even though she had, or complaining in writing about the 1980 incident to PTL—but she was surprised how much I knew. I pressed for a comment I could use in my story. Hahn authorized a few ambiguous quotes. "All I can say is I don't want it to go in the paper."

She seemed prepared if the news broke. If PTL attacked her, she would go public, she told me. But she fretted about the impact a story could have on the true believers at PTL, those whose faith might be shaken. She worried aloud about the impact on her own life, which she had been able to put back together. She worried that people would blame her for bringing down a minister.

We talked for three and a half hours. She commented on the players in the drama. She didn't really care for Paul Roper—he was sharp, a good negotiator, but he wasn't the kind of man you enjoyed having a cup of coffee with, she said. She seemed fond of Scott Furstman, PTL's handsome young lawyer. She told me that she had considered calling him to say that she didn't want the trust money any more. (In fact, she never confirmed the trust per se, but her words seemed to verify the substance of my story.) She didn't care for Dortch. He used his tears and his grandfatherly manner to manipulate, she thought. Fletcher was always trying to take over what other ministers had. He would experiment at anything, she said, without elaboration. Yet she thought—as a curious number of Fletcher's detractors had already told me—that he had the touch of God as an evangelist. Profeta was a loner, she said, and he was just being cautious when he talked to me.

I agreed to let Hahn know before we published anything. She gave me her unlisted phone number.

At daybreak the next day, I flew out of La Guardia headed for Oklahoma City. I wanted to find John Wesley Fletcher before anyone at PTL warned him not to talk to me. By late morning, I was standing outside the Fletcher Building, a single-story office building in the suburb of Bethany, Oklahoma. Fletcher's ministry had a suite of rooms in the back. There the signs of hard times were unmistakable. The suite was empty except for a single secretary. Only color photographs peopled the offices that day—Fletcher with George Wallace, a signed picture of Ronald Reagan, an apostolic blessing paper from Pope John Paul II. It was a celebrity lineup much like a visitor would find in the lobby of the World Outreach Center at Heritage USA.

Fletcher lived nearby, just over the city line into Oklahoma City on a corner lot in a comfortable subdivision. I rang the doorbell of his split-level. Fletcher, dressed casually but smartly, from his cowboy boots and blue jeans to his neatly coiffed reddish brown hair, answered the door. Without hesitation, he invited me into his small living room. It was almost as if he expected me.

"I'd prefer not to make any comments on that. It's a situation that's behind Jim," he said in answer to my first question. I kept talking, spilling out all I knew. Within seconds, Fletcher was in tears. For the next three hours he cried, on and off, his face stained with tears, his head rocking back and forth, occasionally knocking against the family portrait on the wall behind him. Like his onetime friend Jim Bakker, he was quick to pity himself. "You don't know what I've been through." Once, he said, Jim Bakker had called him America's greatest evangelist. "No man can take that kind of praise. You start believing it. You let your ego get ahold of you. That camera is so powerful."

Fletcher said that he had thought the entire incident was over. I had shocked him, knocked him off his feet, he said. "I just got caught by the system, and because I wasn't as big as the rest of them they told me I better keep my mouth shut. I'm honestly afraid to say anything, I just am." Dortch, he explained later, had told him to remain quiet.

We talked about Florida, 1980. Bakker had asked him to invite Hahn, he said. "He just had such a hold over people around him. You would do anything for him." Bakker had told Fletcher that Tammy was going to leave him, and he had nobody. Bakker was considering blowing his brains out. "I did it because I honest to God believed I was helping Jim," he said. "I had no other motive." Fletcher denied having sex with Hahn, as her draft lawsuit to PTL had claimed and as he would admit nearly two years later. Fletcher said that day that Hahn had threatened to make the accusation if he ever said anything about Florida.

Fletcher confirmed that he had told Dortch at the Charlotte airport in 1985 that Hahn's accusations were true. Yes, he said, he had called the *Charlotte News* anonymously years before and mentioned Hahn's name. It was during a time, he said, when PTL had shut every door open to him in the evangelical field. "They just thought they could crush me," he said. He had seen the big names, the ones like Bakker with celebrity and money to throw around, escape punishment from the Assemblies of God. There was, he complained, a double standard.

On the final day of January, the National Religious Broadcasters opened its annual convention in Washington, D.C. Bakker passed up the meeting to stay in California, bowing out of a scheduled

Monday-afternoon speech before the forty-two hundred assembled broadcasters. Dortch was there to represent PTL. Also in attendance were Jimmy Swaggart, Jerry Falwell, and John Ankerberg, the Tennessee minister who had lost the time slot he wanted on the PTL network in 1986. John Stewart, who cohosted a nationally syndicated radio talk show called "Bible Answerman," was in from California.

At lunch one day, Stewart joined Ankerberg, Ankerberg's assistant, and Stewart's colleague, Walter Martin, an expert on cults and founding host of "Bible Answerman." Martin knew about the Hahn payoff and my reporting through Stewart and Roper. As the men talked, Martin stunned Ankerberg with the news that Bakker had been involved in a sex scandal and payoff and that the *Charlotte Observer* was preparing to expose him.

Wednesday night, February 4, Jimmy Swaggart sat on the dais, waiting to speak at the convention's closing session. On the other side of the lectern sat Jerry Falwell. Ankerberg walked over and introduced himself to Swaggart. As the two men talked, Ankerberg confided in Swaggart that the *Observer* was preparing to expose immoral conduct by Bakker. Swaggart asked Ankerberg if his source was reliable. Ankerberg said it was.

The next week, Swaggart telephoned Ankerberg and asked for more information. Ankerberg's tip dovetailed with the accusations Swaggart had heard months before from Fletcher. But Ankerberg assured the Baton Rouge evangelist that his source had not been Fletcher.

On February 9, a woman calling the *Observer* anonymously was patched through to my phone. She had heard a rumor that the newspaper knew that Tammy was in the Betty Ford Center but couldn't publish it because Dortch had damaging information on one of the editors. I assured her that the paper was not being blackmailed. The woman told me that she had deep family roots in the Assemblies of God. Then she asked if I knew anything about a woman named Hahn, Jessica Hahn. If the Assemblies could get some facts, they would take Bakker's ministerial papers, she told me. "They've turned their back on it, they've ignored it," she said, because they didn't want to think badly of their own.

The woman told me that she was calling for another person who might be able to help. We agreed on a pseudonym for him—Joe.

Two hours later, Joe called. He was a lawyer from Tennessee, he said, and he had been asked by a group of Assemblies of God ministers to look into the rumors. He said that the Assemblies was ready to take action, but that it had little concrete information to go on.

The man was articulate, bright, and well connected, most likely my age. He clearly had heard secondhand what Stewart knew. He suggested that I talk to Fletcher; I didn't tell him that I already had. We talked of Dortch. The PTL executive had cultivated the impression that he knew nothing, but that guise wasn't working anymore, Joe said. "It's like the dam's fixing to break and his finger in the hole is not going to do the trick."

Over the next two months, Joe and I became warm telephone friends. He provided valuable perspective and suggested which principal players might talk to me. But he preferred to remain in the shadows; I could only guess who he might be and wait patiently for him to call.

For Jerald Ogg, Jr., family and the Jimmy Swaggart ministry were inextricable. His father, an ordained minister in the Assemblies of God, directed Swaggart's crusades. His mother edited Swaggart's magazine, and his brother had served as personnel director and pastor of the singles group. After a stint practicing law in the air force, Ogg joined Swaggart's staff as general counsel in 1983. Swaggart already had a trusted lawyer named Bill Treeby, so Ogg—who held a bachelor's degree in journalism and would later earn a master's in journalism—specialized in handling the press.

After her return from the broadcasters' convention, Jimmy Swaggart's wife, Frances, summoned the thirty-one-year-old Ogg into her office. Frances Swaggart was cut from different cloth than Tammy Bakker. While Tammy Bakker had little responsibility offstage, Frances Swaggart was arguably the most powerful executive in the Swaggart ministry. She was a woman of iron will, condemned by her detractors as ruthless, described by those more neutral as controlling and fiercely protective of her husband. She had decided to see to it that the *Observer* published the Jessica Hahn story, but she didn't know how to leak information to the paper. For that, she wanted Ogg's help.

Ogg was told that the Baton Rouge ministry had taken the biblical path; Jimmy Swaggart had confronted Dortch face-to-face in Baton Rouge only to be met with lies. Now they feared Bakker would fall and take the Assemblies of God and other TV ministries with him, wounding the work of men like Ogg's father. Ogg was uneasy working surreptitiously, but Frances Swaggart was anxious to protect the Swaggart ministry from accusations that it had attacked PTL for selfish competitive reasons. Ogg was unenthusiastic, but he did his duty.

He first told his secretary to call the *Observer* and get the name of the reporter pursuing the Hahn story. The secretary had been the anonymous woman who had telephoned me about Tammy and the Betty Ford Center and had introduced Joe—her boss, Jerry Ogg, Jr. On that first day, and repeatedly in the days that followed, Frances Swaggart doled out the fruits of her own reporting to Ogg. He scribbled the information on paper—much of it didn't make sense to him at first—so he could relay it faithfully. As I came to appreciate his access, he began jotting down the topics I wanted to know more about. Unbeknownst to me, he took my list back to Frances Swaggart.

The Swaggart ministry also began to put pressure on the Assemblies of God, which it feared would lose nerve in the face of PTL's intimidation. Calls to the Assemblies were the job of Jimmy Swaggart's co-pastor, Jim Rentz. After several weeks, Jimmy Swaggart himself surfaced in internal strategy sessions. From Costa Rica, he had placed calls to the assistant general superintendent of the Assemblies of God, Everett Stenhouse. Swaggart told him that a story was being prepared on Hahn and a payoff and that he feared that a second story would accuse General Superintendent Raymond Carlson of ignoring the evidence of the situation. Swaggart urged Stenhouse to see to it that Carlson put a better spin on that second story.

Jim Bakker had decided to get his wife a present for kicking drugs: a house. With help from James and David Taggart, Bakker found what he wanted on Vereda Sur East on the north side of Palm Springs. The Spanish-style estate had once been owned by a member of the Florsheim shoe family and was known locally as the Florsheim estate—the sort of famous-name association Bakker savored. It had empty lots on each side and sat on nearly an acre of land. The property included a guest cottage and a forty-six-foot pool and a main house with five bedrooms and three baths. The seller was asking $595,000.

Six months had passed since the Bakkers' had bought the house in Gatlinburg. Though Bakker had announced after the Tennessee purchase that he would sell his home in Palm Desert, there had been no sale. Now, with this new purchase, he owned three out-of-state vacation homes in addition to his three condo units at Heritage USA.

As usual, the Bakkers moved quickly. By February 23, a neighbor walking past the Palm Springs house spotted a Mercedes, two Cadillacs, a Chevrolet, and the huge motor home that served as a base for PTL security. As it had in 1984 when Bakker bought his home in Palm Desert and again in 1986 when he bought in Gatlinburg, PTL supplied a timely cache of money for the Bakkers. In February, PTL paid a bonus of $300,000 to Bakker and $170,000 to Tammy, her biggest bonus ever. The Bakkers netted $253,500 in cash after taxes.

There had been no board meeting this time. Bakker later described the money as the unpaid balance of an earlier bonus. Indeed, an undated memo signed by Bakker's secretary recorded a November 1986 bonus of $500,000. Bakker had drawn $200,000 that month, leaving $300,000 outstanding. The mathematics weren't so tidy for Tammy Bakker. She had taken $50,000 of a $100,000 bonus in November, ostensibly leaving another $50,000, not the $170,000 paid in February as she underwent treatment for drug dependency.

Bakker took another $150,000 from PTL, ostensibly as a loan. He used the money to help pay for the new California house. He had financed only $250,000 of the purchase price and needed more than $350,000 to close the sale. Later, Bakker would say that the loan had been authorized by Dortch. He eventually tried to repay it, he said, but a PTL secretary informed him that he still had that much due him in unpaid bonuses. PTL never got the $150,000 and the IRS would soon have further evidence of private inurement.

The counselors at the Betty Ford Center had encouraged Bakker to spend time with his wife, and Bakker's staff was instructed not to call him when he was on the West Coast. The family usually lounged around the swimming pool until late morning. From there they went their separate ways, Tammy to shop with girlfriends, Jim to knock around building sites with contractor friends, unless it was Thursday, the day set aside for a trip to an out-of-town flea market. The Bakkers and their PTL entourage customarily ate dinner out together. Then the Bakkers would leave for the Betty Ford Center.

Bakker continued to dispatch orders by phone, calling the third floor from California three times a week. He rose early, and often his call came in before eight in the morning—not yet five o'clock in California. During a call to Wanda Burgund, Bakker sounded as if he was getting the rest he needed. But his mind was on PTL. He had a new project that excited him. God had directed him to minister to others suffering the addictions Tammy had when he returned, he told Burgund. Just as Bakker's marital problems had fostered the marriage workshops at PTL, the trial of Tammy's drug dependency was to become the springboard for a new ministry within PTL.

As Bakker discovered his new home, I phoned Paul Roper, my next hope for the on-the-record confirmation my editors were insisting upon. I reached him at about ten o'clock the night of February 9. I told him who I was and described what I thought I knew. Immediately, Roper set out to undermine my confidence.

"The truth of the matter is there was no trust fund from PTL ever set up," he told me. I was stunned. "I know what you're talking about," he said, "but there was never any trust fund set up by PTL." I recovered, slowly, from the shock. Perhaps, I thought, Roper was denying an overly specific question. Perhaps it hadn't been PTL, at least directly, that had set up the trust fund. I asked a series of follow-up questions to test the alternatives, but there was no give in Roper's answers. "This story just doesn't comport with any facts I know about. There's a great deal of difference between conversations, proposals, negotiations, and fact."

Even so, Roper seemed to be sending signals that I should keep trying. "I don't have any particular love lost for any of these TV characters." We talked some about Operation Antichrist. He still gathered information on suspect evangelists, he told me. Small details dribbled out. Dortch had never represented himself as being from PTL, Roper said, confirming that Dortch had been involved. Dortch had never said that he believed Hahn was telling the truth.

That had made him uneasy. He couldn't satisfy himself that the event had occurred as Hahn had said, and he was unsure that any settlement had been reached.

It was a dispiriting conversation with an Alice-in-Wonderland quality. Nothing was quite what it had seemed. As I hung up, I wondered if I had just witnessed my story disappear like the Cheshire cat.

The next day, I telephoned Stewart in New Zealand, where he had flown after the NRB conference. I told him about my call to Roper. Stewart was still confident that a settlement had in fact been reached. He had helped to review drafts of a trust agreement. We talked about Roper's personality. Stewart acknowledged that Roper liked to be in control, that he might be choosing his words carefully.

Two nights after my first call, I was back on the phone with Roper, my natural stubbornness fueled by Stewart's reassurances. It was another exercise in frustration. We began with a chat on background; I gave him a chance to talk without being quoted so that he could speak candidly.

Roper suggested that the matter was still pending. "I am not going to push it unless she wants to push it." Then Roper offered a bone. Yes, he said, some expense money had been paid, but nobody, to his knowledge, had gotten $100,000. How much had been paid? Perhaps $20,000, he said. And another bone: yes, he remembered discussing a trust agreement. But if there had been a trust created with a stipulation that nothing could be said, Roper told me, he would have told me right off that he could say nothing.

Roper said he would confirm that he had made accusations against Bakker on behalf of a woman and that those accusations had prompted an inquiry by Dortch. He would not identify who had made the accusations; that, he said, would be a great injustice to the woman. Roper said that he believed Dortch had been conducting his own investigation. "If the allegations are true," Roper said, "I think Bakker ought to do something else . . . if you're going to be a preacher you ought to act like one."

Roper would make no comment about how much money had been paid as a result of his intervention. He said that he had asked for damages for the woman, including the creation of a trust account. But, to the best of his knowledge, no trust had been created.

The process was unconcluded, he said. Dortch or his representatives had promised to get back in touch with him.

Roper gave me the first confirmation that PTL knew I was on the trail of the Jessica Hahn payoff. Richard Dortch had telephoned, Roper said, and he wanted to know to whom the *Observer* had been talking. Roper told him he didn't know. But Dortch told him that someone named Al—Roper didn't remember Cress's last name—was the probable leak.

In fact, Dortch would talk to Roper dozens of times in those final weeks of winter. Dortch pushed all the right buttons, talking about the harm that could come to pass—to Jessica, to PTL's goods works and to those with faith in the ministry and their God—if the story got out. He warned, too, that the *Observer* and Jimmy Swaggart were trying to destroy PTL.

Roper had tried to dodge my questions, using nuances of language to mislead me without telling outright lies. But I knew more than Roper had expected. Soon, he would adopt a strategy of damage control, setting out to soften the impact of the the seemingly inevitable story on the woman he had represented two years before.

On February 23, I telephoned Neil Eskclin, PTL's public-relations man, to ask for an interview with Dortch. What's the story about? he asked. Jessica Hahn, I answered. Through Eskelin, Dortch agreed to an interview. He wanted the questions in advance, however. The next morning, I prepared a list of eleven questions. With help from Jon Buchan, the newspaper's lawyer and a former *Observer* reporter and editor who had screened most of my earlier PTL stories, I winnowed the list down to seven questions.

> 1. When did you first learn of allegations of a sexual encounter between Jessica Hahn and Jim Bakker?
>
> 2. What specifically did Miss Hahn accuse the Reverend Bakker of doing?
>
> 3. Did the Reverend Bakker have sexual relations with Miss Hahn?
>
> 4. What is the Reverend Bakker's response to Miss Hahn's allegations?

5. How much money have you, PTL, or PTL associates spent to resolve this matter? Please specify the source of money paid, the amount of money paid, and the recipients of money paid.

6. Please explain the terms of the Jessica Hahn trust, including its secrecy provisions.

7. Who at PTL made or has approved the decision to spend PTL money to resolve this matter?

At half-past eleven, I dictated the questions to Eskelin. He made no comment to me as he jotted down my words; PTL, he thought to himself, was never going to be the same. Two hours later, Eskelin telephoned back. He had given Dortch the list. "I assume you have an affidavit from Miss Hahn, that whatever you're alleging is true. Is that correct? We're not on a fishing expedition, are we?" I assured him I was not. I had a serious story, I said. Eskelin promised to call back. He told me that Dortch had not yet decided whether to grant the interview.

At three o'clock that afternoon, the hour of our scheduled interview, Eskelin phoned. The interview was off, but PTL had a statement. Eskelin dictated it to me.

> As a ministry, and as individuals, we have submitted ourselves to the oversight of our brothers and sisters in the Body of Christ. As responsible people, we take very seriously any allegations. The scriptural method of dealing with accusations is to bring the accusation before the church, or to go to the person who has committed an offense and correct them.
>
> Our denomination has a procedure to deal with any such matters. We are prepared to face our accusers before the church, which is what the Bible tells us to do.
>
> We refuse to be judged by the *Charlotte Observer,* whose record speaks for itself as the accuser of evangelical causes and ministries. We refuse to become bitter and respond to rumors, conjecture, and false accusations. We place ourselves and our ministry in the hands of those who have spiritual rule over us and submit to their disposition of any matters brought before them concerning us.

It was three paragraphs of obfuscation. It did not confirm or deny the story, but it left the impression that I was trading in falsehoods. I had shown my hand. Now, before Dortch reached them, I wanted to talk to those with at least nominal authority over PTL. I tracked down the North Carolina Assemblies of God district superintendent, PTL board member Cookman, at a hotel in Greensboro, North Carolina. He listened politely but thought that the allegations were fiction.

"Of course, as you know, there are a lot of things that are said about high-visibility people all the time. I have never received any official or even any kind of written information concerning any allegations about Jim Bakker," he said. Before he could investigate, he said, he needed a signed complaint. "The thing that is so amazing to me is . . . here is a man who is accountable and reportable to the district, and yet whoever it is telling has told everybody else but me. And I am the one person in the whole state of North Carolina who is charged with the responsibility of investigating it." He had received no documents from the denomination's national executives in Springfield, he said, and they had not discussed the matter with him. He had never been contacted by Hahn. Cookman said that he would not pursue the matter unless the accusations moved beyond rumor.

Cookman acknowledged that he had heard Hahn's name. "The people who gave it to me simply represented to me that it was a false accusation. No one ever has reported to me that any kind of immoral liaison ever happened." Cookman refused to say who had told him so, other than to say it was not Bakker. I asked if it was Dortch, the obvious choice. Cookman wouldn't say.

The notion of a trust fund, he said, seemed "absolutely bizarre," and he did not believe there was one. It was not unusual, however, for a church to make an out-of-court settlement, he said. What, I asked, if the woman had been paid not to pursue her complaint any further? "To me, that's as dishonest as anything can be. If the man is guilty of immoral conduct, then she owes it to us." I asked Cookman if his dual role as district superintendent/investigator and PTL board member troubled him. No, he said, his first responsibility was to protect the denomination. "I guess it does depend on my integrity. That's what it gets down to."

I telephoned the Assemblies of God headquarters in Springfield and asked for Carlson, the denomination's general superintendent and the official with whom Cress had met in fall 1986. Carlson was out of town. I talked instead to Stenhouse. Yes, Stenhouse said, he had heard these rumors. But he had not discussed them with PTL, he said. "We are not investigative reporters," he said. "That's not the business we're in . . . when facts are placed before [us], then of course we must look objectively at whatever is there. Until that time, we do not spend time trying to determine whether what is being rumored here or there is part of someone's fancy or not." I asked obliquely about the information Cress had shown Carlson. Stenhouse said that he was unaware of any documentation of Hahn's allegations and the payoff. The denomination would be interested in any payoff, he said, but he considered the notion "preposterous."

At half-past eight the next morning, Dortch gathered PTL's staff for a prayer meeting. He said nothing of Jessica Hahn, trust funds, or the threat of an explosive newspaper story. The talk that day was of dark clouds, fear, and trust in God in the face of such pressure. Dortch was ashen. An employee with whom I talked regularly told me that he had never seen the mood so bleak.

The *Observer* was just one of Dortch's troubles. Signs of financial distress were everywhere. Work on the Towers had slowed to a crawl, and two days earlier Dortch had failed to make the $1.1 million payment Winters had demanded if work was to continue. In finance, the stack of purchase orders waiting for approval was growing taller. Heavy rains had washed away the concrete wall holding the water in the small lake in front of Kevin's House. The spillway—built with improper materials and little or no advance engineering—needed rebuilding. The empty pond was a painful token of PTL's latter-day frailty.

Board member Ernie Franzone was present at Dortch's prayer meeting. He had heard rumors of the Hahn matter, and he and his wife, Tina, wanted the truth. Franzone asked if Bakker had been involved with Jessica Hahn. Dortch assured him that Hahn had denied any involvement with Bakker in writing, without acknowledging she had been paid ten thousand dollars for her signature. Franzone asked if a trust fund had been established for Hahn; Dortch said no.

That afternoon, I reached Roe Messner by phone at his office in Wichita. I wanted to find out if, as Cress remembered, Messner had been the conduit for the money used to silence Hahn. I asked if the story sounded familiar.

478

"No, it really doesn't," Messner said. But the contractor was not issuing a denial, at least not yet. "We transfer money to our different jobs and stuff every day. And so we do an awful lot of transferring money around. So we may or may not have wired $250,000. I'd have to find out." I asked if he had made a transfer for PTL to a third party. "I don't remember. But if it was supposed to be two years ago, I would have to do some checking." Messner suggested that I call his business manager in an hour; I telephoned him that afternoon. The business manager said that the transaction didn't ring a bell, but he would do some checking too.

That same day, Dortch and *Observer* managing editor Mark Ethridge talked by phone. They had struck up a friendship of sorts during the fall 1984 *Observer*-PTL rapprochement. The conversation was not for publication; Dortch was playing the misinformation game, as he had tried to do, rather clumsily, with Roger Flessing in January. Anything on the record might be used to trap him later. Yes, a flaky woman had made allegations, Dortch told Ethridge. But Dortch assured Ethridge that he stayed away from any involvement in the Bakkers' marriage. Fletcher and Cress were out to get him, Dortch said, and any documents or checks we had indicating that Hahn had been paid or was the beneficiary of a trust were forgeries.

Putting his twist on the story, Dortch tearfully confided in Mark and Wanda Burgund as he sat behind the wheel of his new Mercedes after dinner out with his longtime friends. "Something terrible is happening," he said. "You've got to really pray with me that this thing will never hit the press," Dortch said. Mark Burgund asked his boss to explain.

"Each time," he said, "I learned more." A woman had accused Bakker of raping her years before, he said. He had not taken it seriously—rape was not in Jim's nature—but the woman was causing trouble with calls to the office and threats to sue. "So finally I went out to California and met with some people out there and with Roe Messner. And he said, when we all got together, 'We're going to take care of this.' I got up and left." Fred Gross had been there too, Dortch said. He left the Burgunds with the impression that he knew no more, that Gross and others had handled matters from there.

Dortch said that he feared the story would destroy Jim and

Tammy, the ministry, and all that he and the Burgunds had worked so hard to build. The Burgunds assured him of their support and love. When they arrived at their home in south Charlotte that night, they prayed.

David Taggart broke the word to security chief Don Hardister more matter-of-factly. Taggart told Hardister that his boss had been "a bad boy." He described the sexual encounter, the hush money, the girl's promises to stay quiet. The next day, Hardister mentioned to Bakker that Taggart had told him, but the two men did not discuss the matter. Bakker seemed humiliated and deeply sorry for what he had done. Hardister was busy beefing up security at the house, preparing for a big story breaking in the press. He added three guards to his security force in Palm Springs and bought seven surveillance cameras.

Once the camera had been the emblem of Jim Bakker's remarkable success. Now, perched along the perimeter of the Bakkers' $600,000 home, Don Hardister's black-and-white RCA video units were a sign of the forces closing in on Jim Bakker. Only behind the protective walls and impenetrable hedges along Vereda Sur East could Bakker be certain that he would find a world where God and good Christian people were ready to forgive adultery, deceit, and misuse of church money and to restore him to his place behind the electronic pulpit.

CHAPTER TWENTY-THREE

THE RESIGNATION

*"I have no doubt God has a redemptive plan
for PTL and for Jim and Tammy"*

On television, behind the pulpit, and in private, Richard Dortch was working damage control. The night of March 2, 1987, Dortch telephoned Sam Orender, the former PTL executive who had traveled with Bakker to Florida in 1980. I had telephoned Orender the day before, hoping to hear firsthand the story he had told Flessing of the trip to Clearwater. Orender had declined to comment and had promptly called PTL.

Dortch tried to flatter Orender, suggesting as he had to Flessing that PTL might hire Orender to make a video of Heritage USA. Orender said he wasn't interested. He wanted to talk about his conversation with the *Observer* reporter. Dortch struck out at Al Cress, telling Orender that he was trying to destroy Bakker, Dortch, and PTL, and that he even falsified documents to do it. Orender told Dortch that he couldn't believe Jim would pay off Jessica Hahn. He told Dortch he was worried—the story was coming out.

Dortch feigned ignorance. He didn't know if Bakker had even spent time with Hahn—Jim had never said so, he said—and Dortch had an affidavit from the woman saying that nothing had happened. Orender cut through the smoke. He was certain that Bakker and Hahn had had sex. He asked about the evidence of a payoff—the money Cress had wired, the correspondence alluding to a trust for

Hahn—that he had learned of in conversations with Roger Flessing and others. Dortch dissembled, saying he remembered nothing like that. Before hanging up, Dortch asked Orender for his suggestions—and his prayers.

That morning, PTL opened a long-planned national conference on church growth that it had hoped would attract a host of celebrities. Charles Cookman was among Dortch's guests on that day's TV broadcast. Six days had passed since I had asked Cookman about the Hahn payoff. His presence on the set that day served as a reminder that Bakker and Dortch still had the trust of the church official in charge of investigating any accusations of moral failure. Next to Cookman sat Robert Schmidgall, pastor of an Assemblies of God church near Chicago and a member of the denomination's executive presbytery—the body ultimately responsible for ecclesiastical discipline. For those who missed the symbolism, Dortch drove the point home. "Jim and Tammy have a spiritual overseer in their lives, Dr. Charles Cookman," he said. Dortch asked Cookman to pray for the absent Bakkers. Cookman obliged.

> Our Father, we thank You for Your marvelous, marvelous grace that has put Jim and Tammy in the ministry. It is Your call, it is Your bidding. It is the gifts and talents that You've given to them, that for which they seek to glorify Your name, and they have poured their lives into Your work in spreading the Gospel throughout this world. We thank You for the vision and the burden that You've given to them, to touch this world with the Gospel of Christ. And now, Our Father, they need Your divine healing touch today.

The next day, Dortch began preparing PTL's supporters for damaging revelations in the press, whether about Tammy's drug problem or the Hahn scandal. "We are going to talk about the subject of forgiveness," he announced as the TV program opened on March 3. Though some may regard us as plastic figures, he said, those at PTL suffer anguish and heartbreak too. Dortch seemed to be speaking to Cress as well. "It may be that you are harboring things in your heart against your pastor. It may be that you really have not been able to let loose some of those things. . . . Jesus said that we have to forgive, in every situation, for every problem, Jesus says we have to forgive." Dortch chided those who harbored resentment from long ago, who "know what happened in the fall of 1956, on a Thursday afternoon at four o'clock."

The next day, March 4, PTL security swept the Dortch and Bakker homes at Lake Wylie for telephone taps and other listening devices. None was found. PTL then purchased four $3,200 telephone scramblers to guarantee that their phone calls would be secure.

At two o'clock that afternoon, Jim Cobble sat down with Dortch and Cookman inside a third-floor lounge at the Heritage Grand Hotel. Cobble wanted to make sure that both men knew the Hahn story was in increasingly wide circulation and that they eventually would have to respond to the allegations. Cobble had already gotten a call from Jim Rentz, Swaggart's co-pastor in Baton Rouge. Cobble hoped, too, that talking with Cookman would encourage the Assemblies of God to deal with the matter of Jessica Hahn and the payoff.

"I want to share what I know about the alleged sexual relationship between Jim Bakker and Jessica Hahn," Cobble told them. As he spoke her name, Cobble saw a startled Dortch jolt with surprise. Cobble proceeded, step by step, through the events of 1985 and recent months. He told them about my contact with him, saying that I knew more details than he did.

Dortch wanted to clarify matters. Yes, he said, he had met with Hahn, but he had done so with Aimee Cortese present. The woman had charged Bakker with rape, Dortch indicated, but had said later that the incident didn't happen. Dortch said that he regretted not taking Cress with him to New York. "If only Al had gone with me, you would see what they really were like," he said.

Dortch acknowledged there supposedly was a letter in existence from Scott Furstman to him about Hahn. But, he told Cobble, "I have looked through my files, and I have had Mildred look through them, and we cannot find anything." It was a blundering defense, one of several that prompted Cobble to conclude that his former boss was lying to him. Cobble had not told Dortch all he knew. He had seen Cress's copy of the Furstman letter. He knew that Orender had told Dortch just days before that Bakker had had sex with Hahn, yet Dortch continued to deny the allegations. He knew that Dortch had justified the payment of money to Hahn in his May 1986 conversation with Cress. Cookman might not know how to find the money trail—the board member had commented that none could be found—but Cobble was confident that Dortch did.

Cobble's statements seemed to move Dortch. "Jim, I can live with it if the *Charlotte Observer* doesn't believe me. But I can't live with it if you don't believe me." Dortch tried to discredit me. He brought up our lunch the December before, when he had informed me that PTL was withdrawing from ECFA and I had angered him with my suggestion that PTL was worried about another embarrassing story about its audit. I had been rude, Dortch suggested, and Cookman—who had sent me a book with a kind inscription just a few days after the lunch—stood up for Dortch.

That evening, Cress telephoned Cookman in his room at the Grand. Cress was forceful. "PTL is arrogant, proud, and a stench in the nostrils of God," he told Cookman. Some reporters, he said, were more trustworthy than PTL. Cookman seemed eager to acquit Bakker and Dortch. He talked about the attacks on public figures in this country; Bakker, he suggested, was a victim of rumors just as John Kennedy had been. He asked Cress whether he had given documents to the *Observer* and Jimmy Swaggart. Cress had not done so, and Cookman suggested he tell Dortch that by letter.

Cookman had pleaded ignorance about the Hahn matter, but the more Cookman and Cress talked, the more it seemed that Cookman did know about it. At one point, according to Cress, Cookman made a surprising admission: "Well, Al, expenses were paid." When Cress quoted that phrase back to Cookman in a letter, a flustered Cookman called one of Cress's friends and relayed word that "Al Cress has made a terrible mistake." Cookman had not said that expenses were paid, he told the friend, but had merely suggested that they might have been paid. Later, Cookman asked Cress to strike the line from his letter. Cress refused and stood by his story.

In the days after his talk with Cookman, Cress drafted a searing six-page letter to the North Carolina district superintendent.

Brother Cookman, if the church doesn't have integrity, who does? If the church doesn't declare righteousness and character, who will? The Scriptures say that we are to "live above reproach that those who are of the outside will have no evil thing to say of us." The day you and I fear a reporter from the *Charlotte Observer* more than we fear the Bible, that's the day we have problems. . . .

As I mentioned to you on the telephone, I don't place loyalty above truth. . . . I am sorry, Brother Cookman, but I cannot and will not be a part of anything that is a lie. I will not be an accomplice of anything that has not been "wrought in God." When the work of God conducts its affairs in covert, Mafia-style tactics, that is when I wipe my hands of the matter.

I was talking to Joe, the anonymous caller, almost daily. Springfield was receiving lots of calls, he said, and the Assemblies general superintendent, Raymond Carlson, had acknowledged seeing a document that suggested that the Hahn story was true. Dortch was accusing Jimmy Swaggart of pursuing PTL and Bakker out of professional jealousy. Swaggart, the story went, couldn't tolerate that any ministry should be as large as his own. Joe's most explosive news was that J. Don George, the Texas pastor and PTL board member, had resigned from the board. In addition, director Ernie Franzone had told confidants that his resignation was in the mail. His wife, Tina, was livid at Dortch, Joe told me; she felt that she and her husband had been deceived. Franzone had asked Dortch for an opportunity to telephone Bakker, but Dortch told him that he didn't have Bakker's phone number.

Joe had urged me to call Don George. He'll talk to you, he said. When I telephoned George's church in Irving, Texas, late on the afternoon of March 3, the Reverend Don George seemed to be expecting my call. Yes, he told me, he had asked Brother Dortch about a rumor he had heard, a rumor that resembled the story I had just told him. Dortch acknowledged that a woman had accused Bakker, but, as he had told so many others, he said that the woman had fabricated the story. "And Bakker was not involved with her in any way, in any type of immoral relationship," George recalled. What, I asked, if money had indeed been paid? "I just feel wrong in my spirit, to pay somebody not to divulge the truth about a situation seems to be an attempt to cover sin, and sin cannot be covered by man . . . [only] by coming to the cross and confessing sin and allowing the blood of Jesus Christ to cleanse and forgive," the fifty-year-old minister said.

George, whose church had forty-five hundred members, told

me that he had handed his resignation to Dortch on January 18. He felt that he had been unable to interject his own convictions in fifteen months on the board. It seemed to make more sense for him to stay close to his church, where he could make a contribution. George—who was privately unsettled by PTL's relentless fund-raising and by its heavy reliance on lifetime partnerships—declined to elaborate.

A few days later, the Reverend Don George telephoned Dortch and told him about my call. He said that I had told him that there were documents to support my allegations. Was there any truth to it? Dortch dodged; no, he said, not to his knowledge. But Dortch left himself an out. PTL had two thousand employees, he said, and he couldn't always know what others were doing. George drew the inference Dortch intended; perhaps, he thought, something had happened that Dortch didn't know about.

The day after my call to George, I reached A. T. Lawing, the good old boy from Charlotte who was second only to Bakker in seniority on PTL's board. I described what I knew. Lawing, now in his mid-sixties and retired from running a company that sold and repaired service-station equipment, said that he had never even heard rumors about Hahn or a payoff. I was, he told me, barking up the wrong tree.

> He's not that type of guy. Jim is a dear friend of mine, and I'm a Charlotte boy, and I've helped him all I could from the beginning. I love him, I'll always love him and be with him. He is not that type of man. He is a great man of God.

Two hours later, Raymond Carlson—the man who held the position that had once seemed Dortch's destiny—telephoned me from a hotel in Buffalo, New York. He was polite and willing to answer more questions than I expected. The Assemblies of God might have turned its back on the charges for months, but the ostrich had now pulled its head out of the sand.

Carlson described himself as an honest, transparent person. "I'm not trying to be evasive. But really, we're at a point that we don't have information. We don't have any documentation. Now, I've heard rumors, yes." He explained that he needed documented charges to proceed. "We don't go around digging up things unless we have written proof. . . . We at our headquarters have nothing available to us for which we could take any action." I asked about the documents Cress had shown him that fall. "I saw a copy of part of one letter, but it doesn't really give any proof to me," he said. He was not even sure the letter was legitimate.

What have you shared with Charles Cookman? I asked. Only that there are rumors, Carlson said. What about Cookman's conflict of interest? After all, Cookman the district superintendent was also Cookman the board member. "I have faith that people deal ethically with any decision," Carlson said.

On Friday, March 6, Oral Roberts appeared as Dortch's guest on the show. That winter, Roberts had caused his own sensation with the declaration that God would "call him home" on March 31 if he was unable to raise $8 million for medical missionary scholarships. During the PTL broadcast, Roberts announced that God had told him that "never again will Satan be able to harm PTL, Heritage USA, no matter what anybody says—persons, news media—it doesn't make any difference. The harm has been lifted."

Dortch urged PTL's audience to watch the next show for a "very special report" from the Bakker family. As it did occasionally, PTL taped the next day's program that afternoon. As the studio audience listened, Jim and Tammy Bakker acknowledged in a taped segment that Tammy Bakker had been receiving treatment for drug dependency in California. Sitting in the audience was *Observer* reporter Linda Brown, a young staffer from our York County bureau whom PTL had invited to attend the taping. The ministry was expecting my article to appear that weekend. The Bakkers' tape would give PTL an opportunity to curry sympathy and blunt the Jessica Hahn story without making any specific admissions about moral indiscretion or backroom settlements.

The tape opened with the entire Bakker family sitting on a single sofa, Jim and Tammy at the center, Jamie Charles and a withdrawn Tammy Sue at either end. The Bakkers were inside their new home but chose to say nothing about the new acquisition.

The doctors had asked both of the Bakkers to stay off-camera, Jim Bakker explained, and that's why they hadn't reported to viewers for weeks. "So many times in our life I've put the ministry first. I've been on television twenty-one years, and always going back to the cameras, always going away even when Tammy was having a baby or whatever was happening, I would have to leave her. And I said, 'This time, I'm not going to leave Tammy Faye.' " Together, Jim and Tammy recalled the drama of January—Tammy's high fever in Gatlinburg, her hallucinations, the trip to California, two weeks in the hospital, the room full of flowers sent by ministers and PTL partners. Then, the Bakkers introduced the touchy subject of Tammy's drug problem.

> Jim Bakker: We had to face some realities that Tammy Faye had been taking a lot of medications for a long, long time. . . .
> Tammy Bakker: I just had no idea, Jim, that you couldn't mix over-the-counter drugs—I had no idea of that. You know, you think if you go buy it at a drug store, it's alright. But it's not alright.

For now, the Bakkers made no mention of the prescription tranquilizer, Ativan.

Doctors had urged him to get help for his wife, Jim Bakker said, and he had.

> Jim Bakker: It's taken many weeks of detoxification to get Tammy free from all of this medication. And it's been very, very difficult—it's not been an easy thing.

Together, the Bakkers offered their confused version of the genesis of Tammy's drug problem. Nearly every day, they said, she had been taking Allerest, nasal spray, and other over-the-counter treatment for allergies, a habit dating back to attacks of hives she had gotten when she was pregnant with Tammy Sue. The allergy medicine had chemicals in it that made Tammy tense and nervous. So, she said, the doctors had prescribed tranquilizers—she did not say which ones or for how long—to help her sleep.

> Tammy Bakker: I'd break a half or one milligram in half, and they said the problem was I never really took enough—I just would take just a little teeny bit.

The doctors had told her that those pills were making her hyperventilation attacks more frequent, and eventually she began hyperventilating on the air. Phlegm clogged her throat; she felt as if she were choking.

> Jim Bakker: So she was taking a little bit more medicine and her doctor told me that, they said Tammy Faye for years has been in a constant state of withdrawal. . . . It is painful and it makes you want to do more and take something to keep solving that problem.

Bakker did not identify the center the Bakkers had chosen for Tammy's drug treatment. He said, though, that they had learned much about medicine and a lot about themselves; one counselor had even told him that he needed help more than Tammy Faye. On this day, Bakker said, they were graduating from the program and moving into after-care. Bakker did not say so, but Tammy's after-care would mean periodic trips to Alcoholics Anonymous meetings at the Betty Ford Center. There, with a bodyguard at her side, she would stand and declare, "My name is Tammy, and I am an addict."

As he addressed his TV audience, Bakker was hopeful, full of the enthusiasm that his staff had noticed. "It's been one of the greatest experiences of my life. I have felt so happy and content and thrilled with what we have seen, the help that we have gotten for our lives, how to live without these pressures is wonderful." Tammy vowed that the next twenty-five years of her life would be pill-free—she had even made it through three hyperventilation attacks and a couple attacks of hives. Bakker pledged, "We're coming back to you, I think a new family, determined to help you more than ever before."

As the end of the tape drew near, Bakker alluded to the Bakkers' past marital troubles. If Dortch had laid the foundation with his recent talk of forgiveness, Bakker was taking the opportunity to give some veiled explanations for his 1980 adultery.

> You know, seven years ago, Tammy and I went through a very severe marriage problem. Our marriage collapsed, our lives collapsed. And during that time, we hurt, we both hurt. We both made terrible mistakes. But we're so thankful that we serve a God who forgives and forgets. And God forgave us of our failures, and God put our marriage back together. . . . We

have learned to forgive ourselves, we have learned to accept the grace of God for our own lives.

We published the story of Tammy's confession the next day, as she celebrated her forty-fifth birthday. We had asked PTL when Bakker would be back: by month's end, we were told.

Bakker had addressed the prickly issue of the unfinished Towers hotel in his video appearance, steering clear of details but suggesting that there was cause for optimism. "We have lost some partners during this time—people said, Well, the Tower's not completed, and boy, it's going up though. And they say, Where is Jim and Tammy? . . . Everything's going forward. We have almost two thousand people that work at PTL. Pastor Dortch has been helping and assisting me and making the ministry flow beautifully. Our team is working together."

In truth, all was not so promising at Heritage USA. Dortch had come up with only a paltry $200,000 for Messner in February, and on March 2, Messner's associate Otis Winters told Dortch by letter that he didn't believe that PTL could actually pay Messner. "We have now shut down all projects at PTL except Mulberry Towers [a high-rise condominium], Wendy's, and the Heritage Tower Hotel. . . . We will reduce our work force to twenty men [on the Towers] if we do not have the $1 million within a few days, and then we will have to shut down completely." Winters complained that Messner had not been paid for the work on Bakker's Gatlinburg home, even though David Taggart had promised prompt payment.

With such a large debt owed by the ministry, PTL's builder had more and more of a stake in how his chief customer ran its business. Winters told Dortch that he wanted tangible progress in addressing PTL's chronic operating deficit. He had been given PTL's sixty-day plan to reduce expenses by fifteen percent, he wrote, but he was disappointed to see no plans for a substantial payroll cut.

I told you it was not fair for us to have to let 175 men go, which is fifty percent of our work force, and you not make a corresponding cut in your work force. I noticed you are presently constructing another warehouse on the grounds, and I would like to know where the money is coming from to pay for that building.

Dortch and his staff had been working for much of the winter on an enormous refinancing package. They had ordered photographs of buildings that were to serve as collateral and pictures of the officials the lender would be trusting with its money. In early March, PTL received a commitment for $60 million in title insurance—the approximate value of the loan it was negotiating with a middleman in England who claimed to have funds in Switzerland. Of that sum, $36 million would pay off loans and leases, $18 million would complete building projects, another $4 million would pay for Messner's architectural fees for the Crystal Palace and the Towers, and $5 million would be put in a "sinking-fund deposit."

In mid-February, Dortch had promised Winters that PTL would begin pushing lifetime partnerships again in early April, timing the promotion for the Bakkers' return and the opening of the water park. By early March, it was evident that PTL couldn't wait that long. The day that word of Tammy Bakker's drug dependency appeared in the nation's newspapers, Dortch opened a weekend telethon, pitching heavily discounted Family Fun lifetime partnerships. They were much like the Victory Warriors offers Bakker had pushed with such success nine months earlier.

Bakker's prolonged absence had stalled PTL's efforts to reap more revenue from Heritage USA and PTL's new quasi-commercial ventures. In October 1986, Bakker had complained to his staff that Heritage USA was underpromoted. "We don't sell ourselves," he said, "we need people here who market and sell." In December 1986, PTL had hired a marketing specialist to put together a TV home-shopping service patterned after the successful commercial programs on the nation's cable systems. Bakker had told his staff that such a program could be a "gold mine" for PTL, despite staff concerns that the enterprise was too commercial and was starting too late in the boom-bust cycle of TV shopping networks. The ministry expected to market eighty or ninety religious products and companion merchandise, like a VCR and television for playing a video tape of Christmas City. The marketing specialist also entered into negotiations to sell corporate sponsorships in an effort to reduce PTL's reliance on Bakker's fund-raising talents. Kodak was interested in exclusive rights to the PTL market. K-mart was talking about a joint catalog sales program.

In December 1986, Washington liaison Pete Teeley drew up suggestions for a marketing plan for PTL. Bakker's staff had told Teeley that PTL had five hundred thousand core partners and another three hundred thousand occasional donors. First, Teeley said, PTL needed to know something about the enormous pool of people who watched Bakker's show but who had not signed up as partners. Teeley proposed that PTL's advertising budget grow from its "woefully inadequate" $100,000 to at least $500,000. He suggested inviting travel and religion writers to the PTL complex to promote stories on Heritage USA as a place to come for a "clean, first-class, wholesome atmosphere that is filled with entertainment, religious, cultural, and recreational opportunities. . . . We want publicity to help us attract people to Heritage [USA]."

On March 10, I learned from John Stewart, who had just returned from New Zealand, that Jimmy Swaggart and a TV minister named John Ankerberg were seeking more definitive information on the accusations against Bakker. They planned to confront Bakker themselves, following the injunctions in Matthew 18. Ankerberg and Swaggart had talked about enlisting other religious broadcasters— Jerry Falwell and D. James Kennedy of Coral Ridge, Florida, among them. I talked to Roper that night as well, and he told me that there was talk of a meeting with the high-profile ministers. Both he and I would be invited, he said.

Several days earlier, Jerry Falwell had contacted Ankerberg for information about the rumor that Ankerberg had evidence of moral failure by Bakker. Ankerberg asked Falwell to join him in a face-to-face confrontation if Ankerberg could substantiate the charges. Ankerberg hoped to hold the meeting—or at least approach Bakker—before my story was published.

On March 11, Ankerberg sent Swaggart and Falwell a copy of the letter he proposed to send to Bakker.

> According to biblical admonition and the spirit of Christian love, we come to you as representatives of the Body of Christ and of Christian media. We are aware of certain well docu-

mented facts, plus additional allegations involving Jim Bakker, PTL, and an unmarried woman from New York state. . . . Given the serious nature of the above mentioned offenses, given the high profile of Jim Bakker, we come to you urgently requesting a meeting to discuss the matter. Our purpose is to seek a biblical solution. We trust you'll allow us to meet with you.

Ankerberg proposed that he, Swaggart, and Falwell sign the letter. If Bakker confessed, he thought, then the three could stand with Bakker and help the ministry recover. Ankerberg raised a question to both men. What should they do if Bakker took them to court? As Ankerberg remembered later, Falwell responded, "I've never walked away from a fight in my life, but let me check with my lawyers. At least I can tell him which fight we're going into now." This remark would soon take on a particular irony.

On the morning of March 11, Bakker appeared on PTL's daily broadcast—again by videotape—to engage in further damage control. We can't change those who want to reject us, he said. Only God can do that. "We want to be honest. . . . We know we've made ourselves vulnerable to our enemies who always wait to capitalize on anything." I've changed, Bakker said. I've learned to accept those things that I cannot change—be it Tammy Faye or the rain that falls on a parade at Heritage USA. We must trust in God. We must forgive.

Even while he preached his doctrine of forgiveness, Bakker spoke of his enemies with thinly disguised spite.

> Their works will boomerang. . . . I've watched those who have plotted against our ministry. . . . I've watched them turn to naught. I've watched their lives, literally, disappear. Most of the enemies who have come against me over the years . . . their whole lives have disintegrated, their families have disintegrated. Everything they've touched has turned to negative. Why? Because when you touch God's anointed, when you touch God's work, you're not touching that individual. The Bible says you're touching God.

Bakker read from the Bible, Psalms 37:32. Jimmy Swaggart's condemning presence hovered over Bakker's words; Bakker was obviously being kept abreast of Dortch's suspicion of Swaggart.

"Evil men spy on the godly, waiting for an excuse to accuse them, and then demanding their death." You know, there are those today that are walking in evil, in evilness, walking in the ways of Satan, Christians looking for others to fall. You know, I know of ministers, even, who have gotten so wrapped up in digging evil out of everyone's life that they have just become specialists in evil. And they send their spies out. They collect all the filth and all the material they can. Just like the reporters of the day do, working all the time trying to collect material, trying to destroy the people of God.

Like a corporate executive preparing stock analysts for a discouraging earnings report, Bakker seemed to be priming his audience for the day the Jessica Hahn story broke.

You know, there's newspapers that have written about us over the years, and they consistently have somebody spy on us. . . . We realize that we can't change the press. We can't change what they do to us. We can't change what other ministers feel about Jim and Tammy. We can't change what you think about us. We can only change us. . . . We can only say, "God, forgive us our sins. God, forgive me of what I have done."

Bakker put in a final word before sending the viewers back to Dortch and guest host Dale Evans. "Yes, we're flawed people. Yes, Jim and Tammy have made some mistakes. Yes, Jim and Tammy have problems. But thank God today, I have a God that's bigger than all of my problems. Thank you. Back to the studio."

The broadcast was to be Bakker's last as PTL's president.

Roper suggested in early March that it was unfair for the *Observer* to publish Hahn's name. That we were willing to do so raised questions about our motives and credibility, he said. Roper said he feared that any newspaper story could destroy Hahn. The next night, I telephoned Roper again with my managing editor, Mark Ethridge, on the line. I knew that any decision to withhold Hahn's name would require Mark's approval, and I wanted Roper to see that the newspaper was not taking the story or its consequences lightly. I wanted Ethridge, the ranking editor overseeing the story, to talk directly to one of the major players. That, I hoped, would enhance internal support for my story. Roper acknowledged that he would be more inclined to tell Hahn's story if we spared her from public humiliation. Retaining her anonymity was not without precedent; the *Observer,* like most American newspapers, routinely omits the name of rape victims. But we reached no firm resolution on the issue.

At lunchtime on March 11, I telephoned Roper and read him a copy of my latest draft. It didn't name Hahn. "It is as you told it in your story. I have no quarrel with what you said," he told me. Roper agreed to confirm, for quotation, that he had met with Howard Weitzman in front of a California superior-court judge and had received the $115,000 check on Hahn's behalf. I had the on-the-record confirmation my editors had been demanding.

Three hours later, Joseph Flower, general secretary of the Assemblies of God, and Assemblies counsel Richard Hammar placed a conference call to Cress. Cress had sent Springfield a copy of his February 6 letter to Cookman. Hammar now felt that the Assemblies of God had enough proof to act, and he and Flower were anxious to get more information before my article appeared. They expected it to be published on Sunday, March 15, as did I. Cress drove to a nearby church and typed a nine-page letter addressed to Cookman detailing the facts that he knew in much greater detail. He was now ready to step forward and accuse Richard Dortch and Jim Bakker.

By the next morning, Swaggart had decided not to sign the letter to Bakker. He telephoned Ankerberg, but the Tennessee minister had worked late the night before and couldn't be reached. So Swaggart, about to leave for Dallas, dictated a memo. Swaggart's intelligence network—including Joe, Swaggart's general counsel Jerry Ogg—had done its job. Swaggart knew how far I had gotten in my reporting and what was happening in Springfield. He also knew his adversaries. Swaggart's words to Ankerberg would prove prophetic, a script for the turmoil to come.

John, I know how the minds of Bakker and Dortch work. They will take that letter and show it over television, deleting the part they do not want read. They will say, "We had to take these two men off television, and then they went on a 'witch hunt' to hurt us."

Furthermore, I have already approached Dortch, gave him the evidence, and he lied to me about the situation. I even told him I would like to meet with Bakker, but all to no avail.

As far as I am concerned, Matthew 18 has been satisfied with these people.

Last of all, if any of this should ever go to trial, they would use that letter in any way they could. The *Charlotte Observer* will do its part. The Assemblies of God has finally started to move on this, and they will do their part.

Please believe me there is absolutely no chance of Bakker and Dortch stepping down for any type of rehabilitation. First, they will try to lie their way out of it, but the documentation should be irrefutable. Then they will pull out of the Assemblies of God. Their last step will be to institute a barrage, which has already begun, to elicit sympathy from the general public. That will be their modus operandi.

If there are severe difficulties and problems I will bear the brunt of it, not anyone else.

I realize that your course of action is correct. However, you do not know these people as I know them . . . it really will not work, and I will be surprised if Falwell will allow his name to be used for obvious reasons.

In Lynchburg, Virginia, Jerry Falwell had already begun his research. He telephoned PTL singer Doug Oldham, who had once worked on Falwell's staff. Laura Lee Oldham answered the phone. "Let me tell you what I'm calling about," Falwell said, "Someone's told me they have something on Jim and a lady." Laura Lee laughed. "Jerry, Jim's as straight as you are. It's a joke."

Falwell told Doug Oldham what he had heard. Oldham said he knew nothing, but he jotted down a note. Later, in a dressing room at PTL's TV studio, he approached Dortch. The two men had never gotten along; Dortch's aides suspected Oldham wanted the number-two job. Dortch played it cool. "Oh, I know all about that. This was taken care of a long time ago," he told Oldham. But Oldham noticed something peculiar. On his way to the TV studio, Dortch took Oldham's note and wadded it up, but didn't throw it away. Instead, he slipped it into his pocket.

Warren Marcus, a former CBN employee whom Dortch had tried to recruit for PTL three months before, sat in as Falwell and his aides deliberated the puzzling matter of Jim Bakker. Marcus was doing freelance work for Falwell. Marcus suggested getting PTL's side of the story—he couldn't believe that Jim Bakker, whom he had met a few months before, had raped anybody—and showing Dortch Swaggart's memo to Ankerberg, which Ankerberg had given to Falwell's staff during discussions of the proposed letter to Bakker.

Marcus telephoned Dortch. He was out. He told Dortch's secretary that the call was urgent. Dortch returned the call from Florida. He was on his boat, he explained, and if the connection skipped it was because he was talking on a cellular phone. Marcus explained why he was calling. "I already know all about it," Dortch answered. "Jimmy Swaggart is trying to take over our ministry. He's been after us for months. It's horrible."

Marcus asked Dortch if he knew about the *Observer* story. Yes, Dortch said, they've been threatening to publish an article every weekend. PTL thought Swaggart was behind it. Marcus asked if Dortch wanted to meet with some of Falwell's staff, but Dortch declined. When Marcus mentioned the note from Swaggart to Ankerberg, though, Dortch perked up. Could he fly down tomorrow? he asked. PTL would pay for the flight. A meeting in Tampa was set up for the next day.

Late on the afternoon of March 12, Marcus, Falwell's young PR man Mark DeMoss, and one of Falwell's newest executive recruits, Jerry Nims, met Dortch at the Thurston Aviation terminal in Tampa and closeted themselves in a private office. They talked for four hours.

As Falwell's staff remembered the meeting, Dortch talked of Jimmy Swaggart's plot to take over PTL in league with the Assemblies of God and the *Charlotte Observer.* Swaggart was on a personal vendetta, Dortch said, but he didn't know why. Ninety minutes into the meeting, Dortch broke down and cried. His sobs lasted for five, ten minutes. His audience was disarmed. Marcus draped his hand on Dortch's shoulders to reassure the fifty-five-year-old.

Hahn had called and called, pressing for hush money, Dortch said, but PTL had made no payment. He didn't believe that Bakker had raped Hahn. He acknowledged talking to Hahn and holding some discussions about the problem. But, for the most part, Dortch left the three men with the impression that he stayed out of the

Bakkers' marriage. That was for Bakker's counselors, Gross and company, to handle, he said.

Dortch fingered Cress. He suggested that his former aide had taken the stationery of a PTL lawyer; presumably he needed to explain the Furstman letter, which had been typed on the firm's letterhead. Dortch said that Cress had also had access to the ministry checkbook; he needed to explain the $25,000 Cress had wired to California. The trio from Virginia commiserated with Dortch. They wondered if another source of PTL's leaks might be the Texas auditor PTL had shared with Swaggart. PTL had pulled the auditor off its tax case just days before.

Nims, a shrewd businessman and a pugnacious adversary, suggested that PTL hire an intimidating attorney to scare off the *Observer,* at least temporarily. Nims recommended Norman Roy Grutman, an attorney from New York who had represented Falwell. He was an attorney who liked a fight.

The Virginians left Tampa convinced that a hostile-takeover attempt by Swaggart was underway, a religious version of the intrigue that had grown so common in America's for-profit boardrooms. Dortch had performed masterfully. On the flight home that night, Nims told DeMoss that Dortch seemed a sincere and lonely man.

I spent most of that Thursday, March 12, huddled over a newsroom computer with my supervising editor, Ken Friedlein, editing the latest draft of the Jessica Hahn story. Ken had spent weeks playing intermediary, juggling an impatient reporter and cautious editors. Once Paul Roper had agreed to go on the record saying that he had received the $115,000 check on Hahn's behalf, Friedlein agreed we had a publishable story.

I still had a final round of calls. One was to Roe Messner. I wanted my first story to identify PTL as the source of the payoff money. Messner's business manager had failed to return my call despite repeated messages; that day, I finally reached Messner. He had checked his records. "We don't have any record of that at all," he told me. I followed up with other questions. He continued to insist that he had no record or memory of such a transfer.

Neil Eskelin had telephoned earlier in the week, ostensibly to tell me that he couldn't answer several questions I had posed as I worked on the story of Tammy's drug problem. A few minutes into the call, Eskelin asked when the Hahn story would appear. I told him it would be published that weekend. The *Observer* traditionally publishes its major stories on Saturday and Sunday, when readership is highest.

March had been a frustrating month inside the office. Each time I completed what I considered a publishable draft, my editors told me I needed more proof. I had started to blow off steam to friends in the office, complaining that we would need a signed confession to publish the story. The *Observer* moved with great deliberation on stories that might damage reputations, careers, and businesses and expose the newspaper to costly lawsuits. To compound matters, the controversial FCC articles of 1986—the stories that our publisher, Rolfe Neill, had considered excessive—were, in my opinion, coloring the newspaper's handling of the story of Jessica Hahn.

Rich Oppel, editor of the newspaper and the man who had taken the brunt of Neill's criticism of the FCC stories, wanted to convince the readers with tangible evidence, not with our reputation. We knew our sources—we had tested their credibility, we had looked at their résumés. But several key players—including Cress, who feared reprisals, and Stewart, who feared jeopardizing the Hahn trust—didn't want to be identified by name. Oppel had set a high standard—on-the-record verbal confirmation and/or indisputable written confirmation. I thought this threshold would be impossible to attain, and I expected Oppel to relent as we got closer to publication. He didn't.

The night of March 12th, metro editor Foster Davis—Friedlein's boss and a former correspondent for CBS News—glanced at the story on the newsroom computer system. Unable to confirm the existence of the trust—Roper had denied that it had been consummated—I had opened the story with the $115,000 payment.

> PTL lawyers paid a New York woman and her representatives $115,000 two years ago as the TV ministry sought to keep private allegations that she had sexual relations with the TV ministry's president and senior pastor, Jim Bakker.
>
> The alleged incident occurred December 6, 1980, at a hotel in Clearwater Beach, Florida.
>
> The woman, then a twenty-one-year-old church secretary, complained that a Bakker associate arranged her flight to

Florida and got her a room in the hotel where Bakker was staying. She said she expected to meet Bakker and watch him do a TV show.

The afternoon she arrived, Bakker came to her room and had sex with her, she said. She later said the incident had scarred her emotionally.

A California businessman, Paul Roper of Anaheim, confirmed Wednesday that he received the money from the Los Angeles law firm that represented PTL in negotiations over the complaint.

Bakker, forty-seven, did not respond to requests for an interview. . . . The next highest ranking official at PTL, executive director Richard Dortch, declined to discuss *Observer* questions about the charge and whether PTL or its associates paid the woman.

According to an individual familiar with events at PTL, Dortch led the ministry's effort to keep the woman's charges from becoming public.

The story read well, Davis told Friedlein by computer message; they would talk about the evidence tomorrow. Oppel glanced at the story and told Friedlein his "gut instinct is that it will work." Still, Oppel said, he wanted to "go over *every sentence* for attribution, fairness, etc. Will want to know name, documentation for each source."

At midnight, as Friday, March 13 arrived, managing editor Mark Ethridge pulled up the story on the computer terminal in his home study. In the next thirty-five minutes, he sent Friedlein seven messages. His final one, which I saw the next morning, was encouraging. "We're close. Good work. . . . One worry: we sound too sure about things we're really not sure about. We have just one source on $25,000 (and say that), but the language leaves no room for hedge. Can't be that strong on one source."

Eleven hours later, I walked across the newsroom to Mark Ethridge's office. Our lawyer, Jon Buchan, was scheduled to meet with Ethridge, Friedlein, and me to walk through the story word by word—a routine test for sensitive investigative articles. Buchan and Ethridge were already talking when I arrived. I immediately sensed that things were not going well. Buchan, a former *Observer* reporter and editor, was worried. He pointed out what he considered weaknesses: Roper, for example, had declined to say precisely what had happened to the $115,000, and we had not been able to say absolutely that the money had come from PTL. Hahn had retracted her description of events in Florida with her hysterical call to my home. If some fact in the story was untrue, Buchan said, he thought we'd get sued. The FCC stories of 1986, he felt, had created the impression in Charlotte that we were out to get Jim Bakker. What if the money wasn't PTL's but Bakker's? That, he said, might weaken our claim that the matter was of public interest. Even if our story was defensible according to the letter of the law and court precedent, the newspaper could lose a trial before an unsympathetic jury. Juries in PTL's home state of South Carolina could be especially unpredictable.

I was stunned. I have great respect for Jon, and I had expected and wanted his tough questions, but I hadn't foreseen such a strong negative assessment. I directed my arguments to Ethridge. In nine years at the *Observer*, I had seen editors listen to a libel lawyer say, it's awfully risky, and then decide to go ahead and publish. It was a lawyer's job to tell a newspaper what chances it was taking, as Buchan was doing; it was an editor's job to decide which risks were worth it.

As I saw which way the meeting was going, I stepped out to pick up a replacement paragraph I had written to strengthen the story. Cress had agreed, at my urging, to be identified stating that he had wired $25,000 from PTL to Weitzman's clients' trust account in February 1985 as the Hahn settlement was consummated. He had also said, for quotation, that he had described his actions and concerns in two recent letters to Cookman. As I returned to Mark Ethridge's office, I was confident that the additional on-the-record information would clinch my case. I was wrong.

Ethridge and I butted heads. I pleaded my case, arguing that the story was one of the most solid I had ever reported for the newspaper. We had documents. We had several people centrally involved in the events talking to us on the record. We had impressive, willing witnesses in case someone took us to court. We were dealing with a public figure, whose protection was limited under American libel law. I believed that we could persuade any jury that our stance towards PTL was simply adversarial, not malicious.

Ethridge wouldn't budge. I flashed arrogance and anger. "Mark, I cannot work at a newspaper that will not print this story. I'm an investigative reporter, and this is the sort of article I work here to publish." Mark stood his ground, telling me I was out of touch. After what felt like two hours, each of us left for our respective corner, the story no longer a candidate for weekend publication. I was furious. Friedlein and I retired to his office. I told him I was going home—and that I was ready to resign. Friedlein felt lousy and went home a short time later. In his glass cubicle, Ethridge felt awful, and wondered whether he was being too cautious.

Before I walked out of the newsroom, I noticed a 12:55 P.M. message from John Stewart on my computer screen. I returned the call from home. Stewart had exciting news. Ankerberg had told him that Cookman had resigned from PTL's board and was beginning a formal investigation. With Cress's second letter, Cookman—and his more vigilant bosses in Springfield—had documentation they couldn't ignore.

I was confident that Cookman's resignation and investigation would be big enough news to persuade my editors to go to press. In minutes, Ken Friedlein telephoned. A lawyer from New York City named Grutman—"the famous Roy Grutman," he had said— had telephoned Ethridge, telling him he represented Jim Bakker, Richard Dortch, and PTL. With characteristic bombast, Grutman threatened the *Observer* with legal action if we published any PTL story that weekend. He said the facts we had been given were false and had been disavowed by "the principal source upon whom you have relied," apparently Hahn.

It was clear that Grutman was new to the case. He told Ethridge that we had proceeded without giving PTL a chance to tell its side. He was surprised to learn that we had presented Dortch with written questions three weeks earlier. Grutman had sent the *Observer* a letter by fax that had spelled Bakker's name with one *k*.

Grutman's call, even more than word of Cookman's investigation, set the Hahn story back on the path to publication. In exchange for our promise not to publish a story that Ethridge had already decided to hold, Grutman promised Ethridge what we had wanted for weeks—an interview with Bakker and Dortch. Clearly, it made sense to hold our story as long as word of Cookman's investigation didn't leak.

That evening, I worked the phone from home. Cobble had heard the news about Cookman and understood that the Assemblies of God had prepared a statement. At nine o'clock that night, I reached Cookman at a church in Concord, a small city a half hour's drive northeast of Charlotte. He was meeting with the two top executives from the North Carolina district of the Assemblies of God. They were still in the middle of things, he said, but he had a statement.

> The denominational leaders of the Assemblies of God having become aware of allegations in recent weeks concerning PTL have contacted PTL in order to seek an explanation of these allegations.

Cookman was still protecting PTL and his friend Richard Dortch. He refused to say whether he had resigned, though he had in fact decided to do so. He was reluctant to acknowledge that his inquiry was a formal investigation, though it was. "If I seem reluctant now, it has nothing to do with candor." The problem was, he said, the facts they had were "changing before our eyes."

At lunchtime on Saturday, Cookman telephoned me at home. His meeting in Concord had ended at one o'clock that morning, he said, more than ten hours after it had begun. He had reached his home in eastern North Carolina at four in the morning. He wanted me to read to him the story we were going to publish. I explained that we were not printing anything the next day. Cookman, fifty-nine years old and in his twenty-first year as North Carolina district superintendent, asked for my help. Gene Profeta, Jessica Hahn's minister, would say nothing to him, he said. Roper wouldn't help either. "I need for you to help me with Jessica Hahn, so I can talk to her personally about this matter." I declined.

Cookman was frustrated. He wasn't a lawyer, a policeman, or an investigator, he said. "I'm just a nobody doing my job, trying to help people know the Lord and bless people." He didn't want to appear to be judging or condemning anyone. He was, he acknowledged freely, Dortch's longtime personal and professional friend. "Our whole process is a process of redemption. I don't want anything to sound as if I am presuming guilt."

A sense of relief pervaded the Bakkers' home in Palm Springs on Friday night. Bakker had spoken in vague terms of a plot against him to some of the PTL staff members. He mentioned John Wesley Fletcher. He said people were bringing something up from the past, from seven years ago. That evening, as he and Tammy met with a PTL writer flown in to prepare a letter to the partners about Tammy's drug dependency, Bakker talked of Roy Grutman's intervention as a divine gift.

Bakker seemed uncharacteristically peaceful. It finally looked as if he was accepting the reality he had kept at bay for so long. He recited the serenity prayer that he had talked about on the air a few days before.

The next day, David Taggart and the PTL writer flew back to Charlotte. Earlier, the writer had asked Taggart if Bakker had had an affair. Taggart nodded. "There was a rumor there was a child," Taggart added. Was there? the writer asked. "No." During the flight home, Taggart said no more.

Dortch had telephoned Lynchburg on Friday, March 13, with word that Bakker was willing to meet with Jerry Falwell, and Falwell alone. On Monday afternoon, after talking on that day's broadcast about forgiveness, gossip, and those who cast the first stone, Dortch flew to Lynchburg. Grutman, whom PTL had paid a $50,000 retainer, arrived on a separate flight. The two men, along with Falwell, Nims, and DeMoss, took off in Falwell's jet for Palm Springs. When they arrived, they discovered that the jets of Swaggart and Oral Roberts were there as well; both men had vacation getaways in the area. Just days before the beginning of what would be called the Holy Wars, the four major protagonists were within a few miles of one another.

Falwell and Bakker met on Tuesday morning, March 17, inside a suite at Maxim's hotel in Palm Springs. For an hour, the two men huddled inside the bedroom. Bakker talked of his encounter with Hahn seven years before. As Falwell remembered it, Bakker told him that he had spent only fifteen minutes with Hahn. He had not raped her, he said. Hahn had known all the moves, and he had been so frightened he couldn't get an erection.

The two men talked about the efforts of Swaggart and Ankerberg. Later, Bakker and Falwell would disagree over who had proposed the theory of a hostile takeover, though the evidence was compelling that Dortch had advanced the notion before Falwell was drawn into the dispute. Bakker was shown Swaggart's note to Ankerberg, which he took as a smoking gun—irrefutable evidence of a plot. Bakker claimed later that Falwell told him that day that if Swaggart wasn't stopped he would destroy Falwell's ministry next.

For several more hours Bakker, Dortch, Falwell, Grutman, Nims, and DeMoss talked in the suite's living room. Nims heard Dortch talk incessantly about the *Observer,* Cress, and Swaggart, whom he suspected had planted informants inside PTL; Bakker seemed gentle and sweet. A few days later, Falwell described Bakker as "very warm, very sincere, very loving and kind to me." Bakker seemed relieved at the opportunity to clear his conscience. Falwell had been the first minister to bother to come talk to him personally, he said (of course, Swaggart had tried seven months earlier) and now, Bakker wanted to know if Falwell would step in and help save his ministry. "You are the only preacher I trust right now," Falwell remembered Bakker saying.

The two men agreed that Bakker would someday return to the ministry, but they remembered the terms differently. Falwell expected an appropriate period of restoration. If Bakker's story was true, he recalled saying, then he wouldn't stand in his way. Bakker expected to be back in power within a couple of months. The PTL president recalled that Falwell had pledged not to touch or manage his ministry and that Dortch would act as president and TV host.

Eventually, Bakker and Grutman left to tell Tammy that Jim was going to resign. For her health, Bakker said, we cannot carry on, Nims remembered. Later, Bakker described the trip to the house as a twenty-five-minute opportunity for him to make the final decision whether or not to step down.

As Bakker remembered it, his new lawyer, Grutman, had pressed a Bakker resignation as the best strategy for mitigating the harm done by Hahn's accusations. There was talk that Ankerberg and Swaggart planned a class-action lawsuit to execute their hostile takeover, and Grutman warned that PTL's board members might be personally liable in such a case. Bakker later claimed that Grutman had warned him that a lawsuit might force a shutdown of Heritage USA.

Tammy told Jim not to resign. Standing out in their yard in Palm Springs, Grutman told her that he had to. It had been a tough few days for Tammy. She had only just been told about her husband's infidelity with Hahn. Fred Gross from Palmdale had broken the news to her and then had spent several days helping her cope with her feelings, she told a friend. To compound matters, the Bakkers' daughter, Tammy Sue, had slipped out the week before and caught a flight back East, leaving a note pinned beneath the windshield wiper of David Taggart's car.

During her January stint as substitute host, Tammy Sue had introduced viewers to her twenty-four-year-old boyfriend, a slight, sandy-haired young "good old country boy" named Doug Chapman. A few weeks earlier, Chapman had purchased a diamond engagement ring for Tammy Sue. PTL's security staff was eager to sever the relationship. Don Hardister had caught Chapman with marijuana, and his security staff reported that Tammy Sue was using cocaine. With discreet help from PTL, the York County Sheriff's Department had begun an investigation of allegations that Chapman was dealing drugs. In early February, after a warning that the police were close to an arrest, Hardister hustled a reluctant Tammy Sue to California. Three days later, police raided the trailer where Chapman lived. They discovered less than an ounce of marijuana, and Chapman was charged with simple possession.

In April, Tammy Sue would surface in Charlotte and announce to employees at PTL that she had married Chapman. In 1989, the nineteen-year-old would give birth to Jim and Tammy Bakker's first grandchild.

As Jim and Tammy remembered their talk with Grutman, the New York lawyer pledged that he would give the Bakkers the signed resignations of the new board so that Bakker could return at any time. Jim Bakker recalled assurances that he could pick people he trusted for the new board—familiar, unthreatening people like Pat Boone and Dale Evans from his broadcast guest list. In fact, Falwell wanted the resignations of the old PTL board so that he could be confident that he controlled the ministry as long as he was taking the risk of running it.

As the Falwell jet flew back East, the transfer of power was hardly a certainty in the minds of the Virginians. Nims doubted that Bakker could deliver a unanimous vote from his directors. He didn't realize how docile the board was that Bakker had created. At the Bakkers' home in California, Doug Oldham assured the PTL president he could trust Falwell, that Oldham's former boss wouldn't hurt him. Later, Oldham remembered a comment Bakker made in those tense days in Palm Springs, as he talked about giving up his ministry. "I might not have been able to keep her afloat beyond March, anyhow."

At nine o'clock on the evening of Wednesday, March 18, the PTL board gathered on the third floor of the World Outreach Center. The entire board was there except for Bakker. Around the table sat Cortese, the New York prison chaplain whom Dortch had used as a courier to Hahn; Spencer, the longtime Bakker friend who had served on the board for less than two years; Lawing, the senior outside director; and Franzone, who had recently decided against resigning. Shirley Fulbright took the minutes. David Taggart was there along with a newcomer, Roy Grutman. Dortch chaired the meeting and began it with an explanation.

He opened by saying that they were there primarily because of a forthcoming story in the *Observer.* He gave a history of the story and described, according to the minutes, "what irreparable harm would flow if corrective action were not taken to address the problems." Jim had decided to resign, asked that Jerry Falwell replace him as chairman, and said that a new board should serve under Falwell. "Unless such action were taken," Fulbright's minutes read, "in the opinion of Reverend Bakker, the ministry's mission would be seriously imperiled."

Dortch asked the board to amend PTL's bylaws to allow meetings by telephone conference call, which would allow Bakker to join in from California. The board then considered the resolution that it had adopted on December 10, 1980, four days after Bakker's interlude with Hahn, which specified that the Assemblies of God would take over PTL if Bakker could not serve. It was through this option, Bakker and Dortch feared, that Swaggart might execute his takeover, using his considerable influence over the Assemblies leadership. "In the view of Reverend Dortch, it would be appropriate for the Board to consider annulling said resolution." The board agreed by its customary unanimous vote.

Bakker then addressed the board through the speakerphone and resigned as president, CEO, general manager, and board member. The board voted Falwell in as his replacement. Falwell, who had just finished Wednesday-night church services in Lynchburg, accepted the position over the phone and listened to the final fifteen minutes of the meeting.

The board members then stepped down, one by one, each departure prompting the election of a replacement to sit on the Falwell board: Ben Armstrong, executive director of the National Religious Broadcasters; Sam Moore, president of Thomas Nelson Publishers; Nims, who held the title of chief executive officer of Falwell's "Old Time Gospel Hour"; the Reverend Charles Stanley of Atlanta, respected former president of the Southern Baptist Convention; James Watt, former US Secretary of the Interior and an Assemblies of God layman whose son, Eric, worked at PTL and was close to Dortch; and Rex Humbard, evangelist, Bakker friend, and frequent PTL guest. Only Dortch remained from the old board.

"Reverend Dortch then expressed the sincere appreciation of Heritage for the loyal and devoted services of those Members of the Board who had tendered their resignations at this meeting and wished them success in all of their future endeavors," the minutes read.

On Thursday afternoon, Bakker telephoned Paul King, the ranking executive in charge of television at PTL. Bakker told him to hang in, to keep the team together. The next few months would be tough, but Bakker would be back. Bakker didn't explain further but King guessed that he was going to resign.

Bakker also telephoned Charlotte Whiting, the fifty-eight-year-old who had started at PTL setting tables for lunch guests at Heritage Village. Bakker found that he could rely on her to do what he wanted, and she eventually became vice president in charge of Heritage USA with a $54,000 salary. In the final days, Whiting had become Bakker's second set of eyes and ears on the grounds and a caretaker for his parents. As he talked that day, Bakker told Whiting that he wanted her to know how much he'd appreciated her. He was about to release a statement to the *Observer,* he said; in a few moments, the whole world would know. He had promised, he said, to say nothing until the interview. But Brother Dortch would meet with her shortly and explain. "Just remember, we love you."

* * *

A few minutes after two that afternoon, a group of *Observer* staffers began to gather in Rich Oppel's office in the newsroom. The rectangular office is a fishbowl, exposed to the sprawling newsroom by an unbroken wall of glass. Ethridge and Grutman had agreed early in the week to an interview by telephone. We knew by now that the interview would be momentous. Grutman had told Ethridge we would come away with a national front-page story. We just didn't know what that story would be.

I commandeered Oppel's desk so I could take notes, either by hand or on a nearby computer terminal, and monitor the tape recorders we had set up for the occasion. We expected to take the call by speakerphone so that all of us could participate. Oppel was there. So was Ethridge, who had grown more enthusiastic about the story through his chess game with Grutman. My editor Ken Friedlein, lawyer Jon Buchan, and publisher Rolfe Neill completed the group. I felt like I was onstage. I didn't care to work in front of an audience.

The phone rang at half-past two. Ethridge and Grutman handled the introductions. Ethridge asked who was with Grutman. Grutman told him part of the truth: Dortch and Eskelin. In fact, David Taggart and Shirley Fulbright, armed with a tape recorder to capture the exchange, had taken positions inside the Presidential Lounge, the oval chamber overlooking the Heritage Grand lobby where two weeks earlier Cobble had talked to Dortch and Cookman. Builder Roe Messner, the man who had denied being a conduit for the Hahn trust money, was also inside the lounge. A guard stood at the door to keep others out.

As he introduced Bakker from his home in Palm Springs, Grutman asked that the PTL president be allowed to read his statement without interruption. After we agreed, Bakker came on the line.

> Thank you. As you know, for many years, Tammy Faye and I and our ministries have been subjected to constant harassment and pressures by various groups and forces whose object has been to undermine and to destroy us. I cannot deny that the personal toll that these pressures have exerted on me and my wife and family have been more than we can bear.

Time froze. Listening to the disembodied voice of the man whose TV image had become so familiar over the last three years, the man whose instinct was to fight the newspaper to the end, I realized, my God, Bakker was going to resign.

> In fact, as our friends are all too well aware, my and Tammy's physical and emotional resources have been so overwhelmed that we are presently under full-time therapy at a treatment center in California. . . . I have decided that for the good of my family, the church, and of all of our related ministries that I should resign and step down immediately from PTL.

The accusations were true, I thought, and the article was going into the newspaper. Within moments, one of my editors had stepped out of the room and had begun mustering reporters and editors to chase other parts of the story.

> I have also today resigned from the Assemblies of God. I am not able to muster the resources needed to combat a new wave of attack that I have learned is about to be launched against us by the *Charlotte Observer,* which has attacked us incessantly for the past twelve years.

The fighter still had his gloves on. The words cut with Roy Grutman's polysyllabic rapier, but the combativeness was Bakker's as well.

> I am appalled at the baseness of this present campaign to defame and vilify me.
>   I categorically deny that I've ever sexually assaulted or harassed anyone.
>   I sorrowfully acknowledge that seven years ago, in an isolated incident, I was wickedly manipulated by treacherous former friends and then colleagues who victimized me with the aid of a female confederate.

Gradually, I could make out the familiar sound of blame being assigned to others. Bakker had found another conspirator to join the *Observer,* the FCC, the IRS, and Jimmy Swaggart. He had not identified them by name, but Fletcher and Hahn were now at center stage. Without question, our story would have to name Hahn.

They conspired to betray me into a sexual encounter at a time of great stress in my marital life. Vulnerable as I was at the time, I was set up as part of a scheme to co-opt me and obtain some advantage for themselves over me in connection with their hope for position in the ministry.

Next, Bakker began to sound the theme Dortch had been chanting for weeks—forgiveness.

I have sought and gratefully received the loving forgiveness of our Savior who forgives us of our sins. I have told Tammy everything and Tammy, of course, has forgiven me, and our love for each other is greater and stronger than it has ever been.

A minute later, Bakker forgave those who had borne false witness against him.

Up to this point, Bakker had said nothing of the $115,000 check or the trust fund set up in Hahn's name. But we soon had a partial confession to what we regarded as the most damaging allegation in our story: not that Bakker had had extramarital sex, but that Hahn had been paid off to stay silent. Bakker was evasive about the source of the cash, and PTL was not eager to encourage anyone to follow the money trail.

In retrospect, it was poor judgment to have succumbed to blackmail. But when extortionist overtures were made, I was concerned to protect and spare the ministry and my family. Unfortunately, money was paid in order to avoid further suffering or hurt to anyone, to appease these persons who were determined to destroy this ministry.

I now, in hindsight, realize payment should have been resisted, and we ought to have exposed the blackmailers to the penalties of the law. I'm truly sorry for all this.

If we had already been stunned, Bakker's next sentences left us breathless.

I cannot undo the past but must now address the future. I have no doubt God has a redemptive plan for PTL and for Jim and Tammy. . . .

I've asked my friend, Jerry Falwell, to help me in my crisis.

The PTL board of directors has accepted my resignation, appointed Jerry Falwell as chairman of our board of directors, requesting him to designate a new board of directors. . . .

I ask the prayerful support of our friends and foes for the preservation and advancement of God's work and the future of PTL.

God bless you and good-bye.

With that, Bakker hung up. Across the continent, inside the Presidential Lounge of the hotel her boss had opened with such triumph two years earlier, Shirley Fulbright cried.

Grutman spoke up. Reverend Dortch had resigned from the Assemblies of God, he said, and PTL had withdrawn its church from the denomination. Dortch said nothing. With that, Grutman introduced Falwell. The familiar booming voice sounded surreal. I had watched PTL closely since 1984, and Falwell was not among the regulars or even occasional live guests on Bakker's show. In the weeks that followed, I learned more about the doctrinal chasm that existed between the fundamentalist Baptist from Virginia and the Michigan-born Pentecostal with a heavily charismatic following.

Falwell, whose weekly church service was carried on the PTL satellite network, explained his decision to take Bakker's post. He feared a backlash that could hurt every gospel ministry in America, he said, and he wanted to help Bakker. He recalled his decision two years ago to help a troubled church in Bangor, Maine. "I am convinced that the PTL ministry must not be allowed to suffer damage or in any way to, as a result of this dilemma, close its door." He wanted to assure that the vision of PTL and Jim and Tammy Bakker "continues in health, strength, and viability."

Falwell said that he had selected a new board and would make PTL's financial information available publicly. The board would meet in a week, he said.

They all have promised to continue in prayer for the complete healing and restoration of Jim and Tammy Bakker and with the prayer that God somewhere down the road has another fruitful and effective ministry in store for them somewhere.

Falwell, like Bakker, was not ready to talk about Bakker's return to power.

We were given a few minutes for questions. Oppel, a former reporter, leaped to ask the critical unanswered question. "How much money was paid, and was it paid by PTL out of PTL funds?" Grutman spoke evasively.

> I will answer that question within the limitations of what can be said. The money that was paid [to] which Reverend Bakker referred was meeting the demands of the lady in question. It was paid under a covenant of confidentiality. We believe that in honor you were bound and are bound to respect that confidence. If the lady or her representatives want to abrogate and breach the commitment that they made, you go get that information from her. And that's all that we're going to say on that subject.

Oppel tried to follow up, but Grutman sternly interrupted.

> Mr. Oppel, I have investigated the matter and am thoroughly satisfied that there was *no* illegality in connection with the payment.

Oppel pressed again. Was it PTL money?

> That's all I'm going to tell you.

As Oppel continued to press, Grutman carved out the high road for his clients.

> You may have an interest in that. I can tell you as a lawyer. I represent that I have looked into this with great care. I am completely satisfied that the transaction is free from any taint of wrongdoing. But more than that, it was a matter that was handled by attorneys, nobody was doing it in a corner or in the dark, although it was being done under confidentiality.
> My clients . . . apparently have a higher respect for the commitments that they make in the name of honor. They are not going to walk away from those commitments even though you may say that the press or some other snooper would like to have more details.

The woman's claims had been an exaggeration designed to misrepresent the event, Grutman said. The victim was not the lady, he said, but Reverend Jim Bakker.

Oppel pressed on. He had seen enough of Bakker and PTL to know that what seemed to be often was not. Was Bakker's decision irrevocable, or will the board ask him to reconsider? The question scored a direct hit on Bakker's strategy. Grutman remained gruff.

> Mr. Oppel, all that I can tell you is that he has resigned. There are no conditions, it is not a sham, word is that he has resigned and stepped down. Period. End of report.

It was my turn now, but Grutman instructed us that we had just eight minutes before he and Dortch had to leave to inform the staff. I asked Grutman to elaborate on the role Weitzman and Furstman, PTL's lawyers in California, had played in paying what Bakker now termed blackmail. Grutman dodged the question, characterizing the payments as a "shakedown."

I asked Dortch to describe his role in the payoff. Dortch remained silent, Grutman spoke instead. "Money was paid, and nobody's denying it. It was probably poor judgment, in retrospect." Did PTL's board approve the payment of the money Bakker had referred to? Grutman dodged the question. As the interview ended, Grutman assured us that no other media organizations knew about the resignation. "You've gotten the exclusive, but it is not a story that can be kept under wraps . . . the cat's out of the bag now." From Lynchburg, Falwell spoke up with encouraging words. He said that he would cooperate with our newspaper. "It's my intention in the next thirty days the *Charlotte Observer* and PTL are going to be friends."

I moved quickly to my desk to begin rewriting the Hahn story. I telephoned Hahn at her apartment in West Babylon, New York, as I had done regularly since our meeting, keeping her informed and hoping to elicit more of a statement. I told her what Bakker had done and said. She was ready now to speak on the record, although she refused to say whether she had been sexually assaulted.

> There was no blackmail, no extortion. In fact, I did not even set up the meeting. . . . I did not request a lawyer, I did not request Paul Roper.

She said that Profeta had engaged Roper, and Roper had originated the lawsuit.

> Jim Bakker is obviously trying to protect himself. That's how I put that. He is protecting himself. If he resigned on account of this, then if that's what he had to do, fine. . . . I know what the truth is. . . . I don't want Jim Bakker to leave PTL. I don't want to live with that.

We continued rewriting and editing the story late into the evening. There was only room for a fraction of what we knew; more would follow in days to come. The PTL revelations sold more than twenty thousand extra papers the next day. The presses were restarted three times on Friday morning and early Friday afternoon to meet the demand from merchants and to fill empty newspaper racks. Only the death of Elvis Presley had had such a dramatic effect on *Observer* sales.

As I rewrote my story, the PTL staff gathered inside the Barn auditorium. David Taggart sat next to Shirley Fulbright, his head bowed. Dortch introduced Grutman, and the lawyer read the statement Bakker had just given to the *Observer.* Falwell spoke from Lynchburg. The staff was shocked; the silence was funereal. Tears rolled down cheeks throughout the audience.

Fifteen minutes before the meeting had begun, Vi Azvedo had summoned Bakker's relatives into her office. Raleigh and Furn Bakker, his brother and sister-in-law, Norm and Dorothy, his sister Donna, and Tammy's mother, Rachel Grover, who worked in PTL's mail room, were present. Rumors had circulated about a damaging article coming out in the *Observer,* but Dorothy Bakker couldn't imagine that anything would be more damaging than the admission of Tammy's drug dependency.

Azvedo walked in wiping tears from her eyes. "I'm not going to be very good at this," she said. "Jim and Tammy have resigned." The family was shocked. Raleigh spoke up with characteristic disdain. "What do you mean resigned? Why did he go and do a dumb thing like that?" Azvedo explained Bakker's mistake seven years before, the payoff, the pursuit of the story by press and by the Assemblies of God. She told them that Falwell was taking over.

But Azvedo confided that they expected Jim and Tammy back. The doors were open for their return when they were ready. For now, she said, PTL was stressing that their resignation was legitimate. She warned the family not to tell anyone that Jim had not really resigned. "If people ask," she said, "just say we're hoping they'll be back."

CHAPTER TWENTY-FOUR

FORGIVEN

"What you are embarking on will truly start
. . . a 'holy war' "

Richard Dortch began laying the groundwork for Bakker's return the morning after Bakker's resignation. He spoke to the PTL TV audience with the syrupy, patronizing tone that had become familiar during his three years at PTL.

> Good morning. My name is Richard Dortch, and I'm going to spend a few moments with you this morning. And I want to talk to you about two people that you and I love very, very much—Jim and Tammy Bakker. Most days, you and I spend moments together with Jim and Tammy on this program, and in these moments together that we share, we talk about all the kinds of things that happen in life. That's what made Jim and Tammy Bakker so wonderful and so real, is the fact that when we have these visits with Jim and Tammy, we talk about all kinds of things.
>
> We remember the joys and the sorrows, those wonderful moments here at Heritage USA, we've had so many wonderful moments together, haven't we? Well, Jim and Tammy, right now, are going through the crisis of their lives. And I believe that you and I are going to stand with them, and support them, and say to the Lord and to them that, We love you and we're praying for you.

As he had done in early March, Dortch orchestrated a TV show that gave the theme of forgiveness center stage. "Jim Bakker is a hero. He's a man that came from nowhere and shook the world for God," one guest said. "But Jim Bakker . . . is a man just like any of us," capable of human failings.

That morning of March 20, PTL ordered its printer to resume printing Bakker's latest letter to the partners, an account of Tammy's illness and drug problem. By phone, Bakker and a PTL writer drafted a second letter to enclose with the first. The new note was handwritten on lined yellow paper.

> Since I wrote the enclosed letter I have had to make the most difficult painful decision of my life. . . . I am very sorry for what has happened in the past. . . .
> We know that God has forgiven us, and we hope that others will be able to forgive us also. I am very sorry if I have hurt you in any way, and I ask you to forgive me.

The PTL writer had included a reference in the letter to PTL's new directors, calling them "a board of righteous men." Bakker asked her to omit the word righteous. "You don't really know if people are righteous or not."

Within two weeks, the effort to cleanse the Bakkers of the taint of scandal had blossomed into a full-fledged public-relations campaign. One year after the Enough is Enough campaign, PTL had a new slogan—Forgiven. The word was written in flowers outside the PTL Welcome Center, visible to all who entered the front gate. PTL dispensed lapel pins that read Forgiven. Baseball caps were printed with the word. Dortch promised to hand out Bibles with Forgiven written across the front, and he urged viewers to buy a full-page ad in their local newspaper reading Forgiven. On the back wall of the PTL set, Forgiven was emblazoned atop a stylized heart. Scores of letters from partners fluttered underneath, evidence that yes, the partners would forgive.

On the set that morning of March 20, it might have seemed that PTL's strategy of limited confession and an alliance with Falwell, the leader of the Moral Majority, would work. In fact, like so many of Bakker's decisions at PTL, the maneuvers of March 1987 appeared to be executed with much impulse and little forethought.

\

By resigning, Bakker lost his greatest weapon— unbridled access to live television. Stepping down might provide a much-needed semblance of repentance, but without television, Bakker could no longer reach and manipulate his supporters as he had done so deftly in past crises. Bakker may have thought he had the ideal front man in Jerry Falwell—a respected evangelical and a man with his own ministry to run and a base of support so unlike Bakker's that he hardly appeared to be a threat. But Falwell was too much of an outsider; he hadn't been compromised. And, like the dreaded Swaggart, Falwell and his aides were inclined to play the role of a godly morals squad—condemning with the pious fervor Bakker found so threatening.

By turning the matter into high drama, PTL attracted the very attention it could ill afford. The media and public were soon captivated by a story PTL should have allowed to pass quietly from the nation's front pages and TV screens. Bakker and Dortch had much to hide. They couldn't afford to have details released about Dortch's role in the Hahn payoff. Nor did they want to admit that the Hahn payoff cash had been PTL's, laundered through its building contractor. Should there be too much attention focused on PTL, someone might raise questions about PTL's acute financial crisis, the overselling of the lifetime partnerships, the IRS audit and the enormous sums being paid Bakker and his deputies. But the men at PTL were lost in their righteous combat, unable to see the depth of their own wrongdoing.

Instead of playing a low-key role as custodian, Jerry Falwell quickly found himself called upon to sort out right from wrong.

Roper had agreed to meet Jimmy Swaggart on Friday afternoon near Palm Springs, where Bakker's new house would soon be surrounded by reporters and TV cameras. Roper and his wife, Cindy, drove to the desert resort, as did John Stewart and Walter Martin. John Ankerberg and his wife, Darlene, flew in. All six met for lunch, joined by Jimmy Swaggart's son Donnie. As the group talked, they questioned Dortch's fitness to serve as president and TV host for PTL.

Afterwards, Donnie Swaggart led the visitors to the condominium in Indian Wells where Jimmy and Frances Swaggart were vacationing. Bill Treeby, Swaggart's attorney and one of his board members, was there as well. Spread out in the living room, the group listened to Roper's January 1985 tape of Hahn describing what had happened in Clearwater Beach. The audience found her tale credible. Roper had come with documents that supported allegations of a cover-up—the complaint sent to PTL, the draft trust agreement, letters from Furstman to Roper, at least one of which had been copied to Dortch. Treeby studied the material. Swaggart was now convinced that Dortch had been the bagman.

Around dinnertime, someone switched on the television so the group could hear a report on Bakker's resignation on the evening news. They wondered what would happen to PTL. Most considered Falwell's tenure temporary. Swaggart told his visitors that he wasn't interested in running an amusement park. He and Ankerberg fretted about the effects of the Bakker scandal on the image of the electronic church. They could hardly imagine how bad it would turn out to be.

My attention had now shifted to Dortch. I had been surprised by his emergence as PTL's president and leading public representative under Falwell, given his role in the Hahn cover-up. I pressed Falwell for an explanation during an interview on Friday afternoon. He was sitting outside a Roanoke shopping mall in his GMC Sierra Classic, speaking to me from his car phone while his wife, Macel, shopped inside. His accessibility and loquacity impressed me; a deft man with the press, Falwell was the opposite of the reclusive, insecure Bakker. PTL needed a transition person, Falwell explained. "I knew very little about any of the matters in the case before I read [the *Observer* Friday morning]. I had only heard rumors." His embrace of Dortch was restrained, at best.

The next day, I wrote an article predicting that Dortch would now face scrutiny for his role in the Hahn matter. The article furnished details omitted from my original story—Dortch's meeting with Fletcher in early 1985, the July 1985 letter from Furstman to Dortch discussing a trust for Hahn, and Dortch's misleading answers to board member Don George's questions during the last year.

Friday afternoon, Roy Grutman began a counterattack intended to neutralize Swaggart. He telephoned Swaggart's co-pastor, Jim

Rentz, and asked for an immediate face-to-face conference with Swaggart. Grutman also talked to reporters about a second conspiracy, a "hostile takeover" by an unnamed evangelist. Grutman loved a fight, and events seemed to oblige. Soon, Grutman began escalating the battle, talking publicly about the dirty laundry in the unidentified evangelist's hamper.

Bakker played his part. That weekend, he and Tammy taped what would turn out to be their final appearance on the TV show they had dominated for thirteen years. If Grutman's comments had been a warning shot, Bakker's broadcast attack at eleven o'clock on Monday morning constituted a declaration of all-out hostilities. The Holy Wars had begun.

After an obligatory apology, Tammy opened with a crack at the *Observer.*

> I can't believe that a newspaper has the right to bring something up that has been seven years old . . . totally settled between you and me, you know, a husband and wife problem.

Bakker then explained his infidelity. It had not been a love affair— some press accounts had suggested that, incorrectly—but an effort on his part to make Tammy jealous and recapture her love.

> I made a mistake, and it was wrong. . . . I confessed my sins and they are under the blood of Jesus Christ. And if I cannot receive forgiveness and redemption, the message I have preached all of my life then simply is not true.

He talked of the toll the events had taken. Bakker had always been one for sharing his suffering with the viewers. "We've already cried so many tears, I don't know how many tears we can cry. We've already felt the pain of the stabs in the back. We've already felt the rejection and the hurt." Bakker was changing himself from adulterer to victim.

Bakker said that he had resigned not because of his indiscretion but because of an outside scheme to take control of PTL.

> They were going to use, yes, this material to blackmail us. Yes, they were going to use this story to begin their evil plot.

The conspirators made a mistake, Bakker said. They had called too many honest ministers—apparently an allusion to Falwell—and those men had contacted PTL.

> The complete game plan of those enemies of PTL fell into our hands. Not only the game plan, but ministers and friends began to call from all over the nation, for this man and his staff and group who were planning the downfall of PTL literally called and warned people of the very hour they planned the destruction. And not to come to PTL. Not to be there when it was to fall. In this plot, our attorneys have the documents, the papers.

The *Observer* article was the conspirators' opening move. Blown out of proportion, Bakker said, it would grab the public's attention. The conspirators had "manipulated church leaders, putting into their hands accusations, which I must say, no one ever contacted me with." In fact, Swaggart had tried to confront Bakker in 1986. And former director Charles Cookman had written Bakker more than a week earlier, informing him of the allegations and asking him to meet with top officials in the North Carolina district.

Bakker bathed himself in forgiveness, ticking off the calls he had received from TV preachers and born-again Christian stars—a who's who in the church world, he called it with pride, people saying, " 'We forgive Jim and Tammy of all of their sins.' And we're so thankful that God has forgiven us. We don't know what the future holds. But, I can assure you, Jim and Tammy, some day, will be helping people again, because we must help people, because God has helped us so very, very much." One of those Bakker listed, Oral Roberts, had taken to the air that morning to echo Bakker's conspiracy theory. The conspirators were a newspaper, ministry, and major denomination, Roberts said, and their unnamed victim was a "young prophet of God."

As he closed the videotape, Bakker promised his viewers that "the sun will shine again." There, from the porch of the guest house of their new $600,000 home, Tammy Bakker sang a song by that name. Back at the studio, the audience rose in tribute. A few minutes later, the crowd applauded a second time when Vi Azvedo declared that she wanted to see the Bakkers back on the set. Eskelin reported that PTL's phone lines had been swamped with callers saying, We love Jim and Tammy, We forgive them, We want them to return.

Though neither Grutman nor Bakker had named the mastermind of the hostile takeover, I knew from my conversations with Joe that PTL had fingered Swaggart. I had already begun to suspect that Joe had close ties to Swaggart. That weekend, I pressed for a chance to talk to the Baton Rouge evangelist. At half-past four on Monday afternoon, Frances Swaggart telephoned from Indian Wells. She laughed about Bakker's accusations—"it's quite funny," she said—and she handed the phone to her husband.

I asked Swaggart if he believed Bakker was talking about him that morning.

> I know beyond a shadow of a doubt that it's me they're talking about. It is a well-known fact that I've been opposed to the direction that PTL has been headed or has directed itself almost from its inception.

Swaggart enumerated all that offended him at PTL—teaching of the prosperity gospel, the multimillion-dollar water slide, rock 'n' roll music, the "Hollywood syndrome" of Christian actors and actresses who worked in the secular entertainment world and appeared on PTL's religious broadcasts.

Swaggart said that he had never considered trying to take over PTL. "I gravely suspect that the problems, financial and otherwise, that are attached to PTL are enough to drive anyone crazy." Why, I asked, had Bakker leveled this charge?

> It's my estimation that they are trying to do this as a smoke screen to get people's sympathy to raise more money. I think they want to get the people's minds off of Dortch and Bakker.

Swaggart reviewed what he had known and done in the last year—his trip to Springfield, his appeals to the Assemblies to distance the denomination from PTL, the call from Fletcher tipping him off about Hahn, the meeting in Baton Rouge with Dortch, the tip from Ankerberg at NRB, the proposal for a meeting with Bakker, and the smoking-gun memo he had sent to Ankerberg.

Swaggart said that Grutman had called Treeby, his lawyer, that

523

weekend to suggest that he would expose scandal in Swaggart's past if Swaggart did not back off. In reply to Grutman's request for a meeting, Treeby proposed a gathering that included Falwell. As Swaggart related it, Grutman answered by saying that such a meeting probably couldn't be arranged.

> I was greatly shocked. Here was a man [Falwell] I have held up and respected, and we have worked together, and then he's having his lawyer to call me and threaten me. That hurts.

We talked about Marvin Gorman and Bakker's emotional sermon in July 1986. PTL had blamed him for exposing Gorman's indiscretions, Swaggart said. "One bank robber doesn't like much to see another bank robber exposed." Swaggart used the same image to dismiss the notion of Bakker's returning to PTL. "They keep saying, We've got to forgive. Well, we do forgive. Even though a man who works in a bank may be caught stealing and may repent of hisself and even may try to make restitution, certainly you would forgive him. But you do not put him back in his same position."

That night, the tale of Jim Bakker became a national story about conflict, deceit and hypocrisy in an industry that most of the country found fascinating and incomprehensible. That night, Grutman appeared on ABC's late-night news show, "Nightline," with his veiled accusations against the unidentified evangelist. That same evening, I had spoken to Grutman in New York. He had acknowledged that he was talking about Swaggart. "I want Mr. Swaggart to call off his dogs," he told me. "I want him to go about his crusade against sin and evil and other abstractions without fastening for his own purposes on the flesh of my client."

That night, Dortch and Mark Ethridge talked again by phone. The minister agreed to give me his version of the September 1986 meeting in Baton Rouge. "He asked me if I was aware of a lawsuit against PTL concerning some woman. I told him that I had been a board member of PTL for years, and I had never known of any lawsuit filed against PTL concerning any woman. It's that simple, and that's the truth." His was hardly a powerful defense.

Soon the wires carried word that Robert Schuller, the Orange County minister with a nationally syndicated TV worship service broadcast from his Crystal Cathedral sanctuary, had taken Bakker's side, Pat Robertson spoke up, calling Bakker's resignation a "housecleaning"; despite his eagerness to please his old boss, Bakker had failed to win Robertson's enduring respect. That Monday—in a move well-timed for his old friend Richard Dortch—defrocked Assemblies of God minister Marvin Gorman sued Swaggart and other church leaders for $90 million, complaining of a conspiracy to defame him.

PTL continued its efforts to redeem Bakker. On Tuesday morning, psychologist Fred Gross recounted his version of Bakker's confession seven years earlier. Bakker had asked Gross to "tell my partners, because I love them so much, I want you to be very honest and very open because you're the only man alive that could tell this story—this story when I confessed to you my shortcomings," Gross said. As he finished the story, Gross proclaimed that Bakker had "met the biblical conditions of confession. He asked for mercy. He asked for love. And he asked forgiveness. God gave it to him that night, in an instant, because God's word says that."

Dortch spoke in his own defense that day, but stuck to generalities. "I have been a part of conflict and difficulties for many, many years. My background for the last twenty years is to try to be a mediator and to try to get people's voices a little lower, try to bring people together. . . . I'm foolish enough to believe, in this situation, we can all win."

As the evangelists' diatribes captured the country's attention, I chased bits of the Hahn story I had not yet been able to document. I was convinced that a trust existed, despite Roper's sphinxlike denials, and I wanted to establish that the money had come from PTL, as Cress believed. For several days I had elicited promises from sources that I would soon see the documents I had heard so much about—the draft lawsuit, the attached transcript of Hahn's conversation with Roper, the proposed trust agreement, and correspondence from Furstman on the Hahn trust. Wednesday afternoon, a source told me to fly immediately to Springfield, Missouri, if I wanted the information.

I missed my four o'clock TWA flight to Springfield, and my editors dispatched me and a photographer by chartered jet at a cost of four thousand dollars. When I arrived, I learned I would have to wait. I got the information I was waiting for a few minutes before midnight. An early-morning collaboration of editors and the *Observer*'s production staff got the story on the front page of our final edition.

Thursday morning, as reporters from all over the country gathered for Falwell's first board meeting, they learned from the headlines that Hahn had received not $115,000, but $265,000. The public now knew about the $150,000 trust fund.

Earlier in the week, Swaggart had told me that he didn't trust Charles Cookman to pursue the allegations against Bakker and Dortch. "He was on the board of PTL, and he still to me seems to be trying to defend Bakker." Cookman had done little to dispel Swaggart's concern. He had appeared at the March 19 announcement of Bakker's resignation to PTL's staff and praised Dortch for his loyalty to Bakker, a PTL staff member told me afterwards. In our conversations, Cookman showed no interest in investigating his longtime friend the former district superintendent. He was content to let the issue remain narrow: the single infidelity of Jim Bakker.

Cookman was eager to see Bakker restored in spite of Bakker's resignation from the denomination. "With his ability, his charisma, and his great following with millions of friends, I fully believe and expect him to rise to the top again," Cookman told his hometown paper. Cookman took up the case in a press conference on Tuesday, March 24, inside his modest one-story brick headquarters in Dunn. Twenty-three years earlier, Bakker had been ordained in this town forty miles south of Raleigh. Cookman had spoken to Jim and Tammy Bakker for nearly an hour, he told reporters, and Bakker had agreed to give prayerful consideration to Cookman's request to return to the Assemblies—a step that would require Bakker to undergo the two-year process of restoration. Cookman also confirmed that he had not investigated charges that money had been paid to Hahn. That issue, he said, was not within his purview.

Wednesday evening, reporters in Springfield waited with cameras and klieg lights outside the Assemblies of God's national headquarters, known to local wags as the Blue Vatican. Inside, the executive presbyters had gathered to listen to Paul Roper give sobering details of Jessica Hahn's allegations and the settlement negotiated by Dortch, their former colleague. Roper, who worshipped at an Assemblies of God church in Orange County, played the Hahn tape and presented documents. The Californian had not come alone. Ankerberg and Walter Martin were there. So was Swaggart's attorney, Treeby.

Cookman had also flown in for the meeting, and several executive presbyters were visibly upset with Cookman for what they regarded as his failure to act on the information he had received. The meeting lasted more than seven hours. The next day, the Assemblies' executives emerged with a public statement.

> First, we want the public to know that we as church leaders are deeply saddened, ashamed, and repentant before God for the problems that have developed in our own church family, as well as in the evangelical church world. . . .
>
> We have not tried either to expose anyone or to cover up any story. . . . Our love and compassion for Jim and Tammy Bakker remains strong. More than anything else, we want to be redemptive in our action. It must also be understood that when ministries hold credentials with the Assemblies of God there are high standards by which those ministers must conduct their lives and their ministries. When these standards are violated, there must be an accounting. . . .
>
> The evidence seems to indicate that effort and money have been expended to cover moral failure. We are deeply sorry to have to say this.

If overly circumspect during the preceding months, the ranking executives in Springfield would acquit themselves admirably in the weeks that followed. They handled the press openly, pressed Cookman to broaden the scope of his inquiry, dealt firmly with the misdeeds they discovered, and stood firm for the denomination's standards of pastoral conduct.

As Swaggart fired back at his accusers on national television, calling Bakker "a cancer that needed to be excised from the Body of Christ," Falwell backed away from any endorsement of the hostile-takeover scenario. "I knew at that moment that I had been deceived," Bakker recalled later. Even as the Oldhams and others reassured him, he said, "I knew. My heart broke. For seven months [that followed] I didn't care if I lived or died."

Wednesday, March 25, one day before the first board meeting,

Falwell told an audience in Cocoa Beach, Florida, that Bakker's return would complicate the new board's job. "I hear rumors that he wants to come back. I have no intention of having a legal battle with anyone. I am there for one reason only, and that is to do what I believe Jim Bakker wanted me to do, what I believe God asked me to do. That is to try to be a healing, cohesive influence during a very difficult, tumultuous time. . . . The board cannot be a caretaker board, or it will get nothing done."

But Falwell was not ready to discard Dortch. Thursday morning, the new board introduced itself to PTL's TV audience. At one point, Falwell was asked a question from the audience: will the new board replace staff members? The board had ratified his decision to select Dortch as president, Falwell said. "The rest of the question, you have to answer, because you're in charge," Falwell said to Dortch. And Dortch replied, "I want to assure you the same staff is going to stay here, so rest in peace."

Falwell announced that PTL would continue to pay the Bakkers' salaries, though he said he did not know what those salaries were. Falwell also disclosed that board members would look into PTL's finances and the payments to Hahn and report back in a month.

Flying home that Thursday morning from Springfield, I spotted Roe Messner at a pay phone in the St. Louis airport. We had never met before, but Messner was a familiar face on Bakker's show, a wooden, unadorned figure amid the PTL glitz. We were scheduled to take the same flight into Charlotte. I introduced myself. Standing in an empty corner of the concourse, I asked Messner again if he had been the source of the payoff money. Messner's eyes locked on me. "I'll tell you the answer," he said, "if you tell me who told you I supplied the money." Messner suspected someone, but he didn't say who. Behind his poker face, Messner appeared furious. "I can't say; I have promised confidentiality," I said. Like Dortch, Messner was eager to consider the Jessica Hahn story a closed book. Several days later, Messner told his hometown paper "They had an affair, and he paid her some money. That's the story."

Bakker began disseminating a sanitized account of the payoff himself. After meeting with Bakker, charismatic-Christian writer Jamie Buckingham quoted Bakker saying that a group of people around him, including Dortch, had offered to take care of the matter. The money had come from an anonymous donor Bakker had said that he himself didn't know who it was. As Buckingham told it, Bakker specifically made the point that the money had not been laundered through PTL. It was a curious denial: at that point, no one had publicly suggested such a covert transaction.

With his appearance before the executive presbyters behind him, Roper agreed to talk more openly for publication. On Friday, March 27, a week after our front-page report of Bakker's resignation, the *Observer* published my most detailed story of Dortch's role in the Hahn negotiations. We now knew that Dortch—who had led so many to believe that he knew nothing of a payoff or trust for Hahn—had personally negotiated the $265,000 settlement over lunch in a Los Angeles hotel. His involvement had continued: Roper had contacted Dortch several times when Hahn's trust-account payments had not arrived on time, and Dortch had received a year-end accounting of the 1986 interest payments Hahn had received from the trust.

That morning, Dortch struck out at the *Observer*. He took issue not with my story, but with an editorial cartoon by Doug Marlette that portrayed Falwell as the snake in the Garden of Eden. The paper's real target, Dortch declared, was not Jim and Tammy Bakker or Richard Dortch or even Jerry Falwell. "It's God's work." A few days later, Dortch told his TV audience about his solution to the Holy Wars controversy—turn off the television and ignore the newspapers.

But Dortch's role could not be ignored, obscured by conspiracy theories, or excused as poor judgment. Government agents began preliminary inquiries, contacting Roper for information. Though nominally waiting for Cookman's renewed inquiry, Assemblies of God officials continued their investigation. On April 2, John Wesley Fletcher appeared before the leaders in Springfield and accused Bakker of homosexual conduct. The executives heard more accusations—including anecdotes suggesting homosexuality—from Gary Smith, PTL's former general manager. Former board member Franzone also came to Springfield and complained he had been misled. On April 6, he sent Charles Cookman specific allegations of Richard Dortch's deceit.

* * *

PTL again needed cash desperately. The gap between its current liabilities and the assets available to pay those debts had grown steadily since the exuberant days of the spring 1986 "Victory Warriors" telethon. By the end of March 1987, PTL owed $36.8 million but had just $9.4 million available. To raise the much-needed cash, Dortch staged a telethon on April 11–12 hawking Family Fun lifetime partnerships.

With each offer, the deal for the partners seemed to get better. At several times during that weekend, Dortch offered the new partnerships in the Towers, with free access to other attractions, for just nine hundred dollars. He also tossed in a raft of premiums: the PTL picture book once offered at one hundred dollars, a silver medallion, a PTL tape or record, an extra night in the hotel to early callers, and a book of discount coupons to those using a credit card. In March and April, PTL took in $3.5 million from forty-six hundred would-be Family Fun lifetime partners.

Dortch could hardly ignore the continuing frustration of those who had secured Towers memberships as far back as 1984, when Bakker had talked about opening the high-rise hotel in just one year. Now, he told his audience that PTL had made some changes in the hotel—an enclosure for the elevator, a shift in the mix of banquet and guest rooms, a concourse—and so it was costing PTL a lot more than it had anticipated.

In fact, these three design changes were hardly the reason why PTL had not finished the building or why the ministry still needed money to pay for it. Bakker and Dortch could hardly admit that PTL had used tens of millions of dollars in Towers membership money to pay other bills, leaving too little to pay Messner. Just $13 million had been spent on the Towers itself.

By mid-April, Falwell aide and new PTL board member Jerry Nims had grown deeply suspicious. Nims had brought some consultants in to PTL; they had been received, as he put it, like they had scales. The kindly, white-haired Dortch was disarming, but Nims felt that Dortch's answers to his questions were misleading. Falwell had asked Nims to find out what Bakker earned; a reporter had given Falwell evidence that Bakker had received $1.2 million in 1985. Nims left a confidential briefing on the top officers' salaries in shock.

Nims also found it odd that executives' pay came through PTL's outside accounting firm, Laventhol and Horwath, not through routine ministry channels. Nims had been briefed on PTL's fight with the IRS and was stunned at PTL's failure to comply with federal regulations. He had asked about PTL's books and had found the finance system in disarray. He was also worried that the lifetime partnerships might be illegal. On April 10, Baker and McKenzie advised PTL to halt the offer, warning that the ministry could be violating South Carolina time-share law.

What had once seemed a simple knight-in-shining-armor rescue had become something much more ambiguous and ominous for Falwell. The Virginians were beginning to grasp the unique character of Jim Bakker, a man who, Nims said later, could create his own value system, his own logic.

If Dortch had any doubts that he was in trouble, he knew for certain on April 17. That Good Friday afternoon, the new PTL board gathered at a hotel in West Palm Beach. David Taggart and Shirley Fulbright were both present. The press was not told of the meeting.

Falwell surprised the board members with a passing reference to the reporter's tip on Bakker's salary. Dortch offered no explanation. Instead, he devoted his energies to persuading the board to continue offering lifetime partnerships. He claimed that PTL lawyers had certified the partnerships' legality. Nims called a lawyer who established that PTL had been cautioned it might be violating securities laws. Grutman leaned over and whispered his changing assessment of Dortch to Nims: "The man's an unmitigated liar." The board voted that day to halt sales of lifetime partnerships. It also terminated the Forgiven campaign.

Dortch left the meeting subdued, his image tarnished. The board had just seen how willing Dortch was to shade the truth.

Bakker and his aides received their fatal wound on Saturday, April 18. The headline across the top of the *Observer* that morning read "PTL '86 Payments to Bakker: $1.6 Million." Underneath were pictures of Jim and Tammy Bakker, Richard Dortch, David Taggart, Shirley Fulbright, and Peter Bailey, together with their approximate salaries and bonuses for 1986 and the first three months of 1987.

The third floor had learned of the story the night before when

I had telephoned for comment. Dortch was eager to find the source of the leak; there was no secret more sensitive than the executive payroll. That night, the former Bakker aides talked about administering lie-detector tests at Laventhol and Horwath. Later, they focused their suspicions on the members of PTL's new board.

Early Saturday morning, Dortch summoned his top aides to a nine-thirty meeting in the World Outreach Center to talk about damage control. Taggart and Fulbright and Bailey were there; none displayed any remorse. Their colleagues were stunned. Some felt misled, others felt humiliated. Vice president Steve Nelson worried about facing his employees on Monday; Dortch was worried what the congregation might say Sunday morning. Dortch tried to explain away his pay. He only took home $3,900 a month, he said; the rest went into his retirement account. He even suggested that Mark Burgund stand up and offer that explanation to the church. Burgund and the others told Dortch the worshippers wouldn't buy the explanation. They had to live on much less than that, and they didn't have PTL covering so many of their day-to-day expenses or paying their spouse what Mildred Dortch had received in 1986—a $22,700 salary and $10,500 in bonuses.

Sam Johnson faced the wrath of his friend, Pennsylvania road builder Al Hamilton. Hamilton was building a six-lane expressway at Heritage USA; his bills represented more than $500,000 of PTL's ballooning debt. Hamilton was livid about the executive pay. On Easter morning, after Johnson had preached the seven o'clock sunrise service, Hamilton, Johnson, and their wives met for breakfast at a restaurant in Rock Hill. Hamilton wanted to know what Johnson was paid. Johnson told him $53,000. Hamilton left to telephone his sons-in-law, returning a few minutes later. They're relieved, he told Johnson, to find out you're not on the take.

Later that morning, Johnson returned to PTL for the regular Sunday-morning service. Dortch was in Bakker's dressing room having his makeup applied. He asked Johnson to take the offering that morning. Both men knew it wouldn't be a good idea for Dortch to pass the plate. Even with Johnson as the front man, the congregation wasn't in a generous mood that day.

Falwell led the public chorus of outrage. His words were front-page news on Easter morning. "I don't think any reasonable person could believe these salaries are acceptable. In my opinion, no ministry in America pays pastors and staffs at this level . . . the compensation is horrendous. . . . They cannot be defended by reasonable people." Falwell said that the board would study the numbers during its April 28 meeting.

As he would do repeatedly in coming months, Falwell declared that the Bakker disclosures were a reminder that TV evangelists could regain their credibility with the public only through total forthrightness and accountability. He answered my questions about his own income: a salary from the "Old Time Gospel Hour" of $100,000, plus royalties from books and speeches. He had contracted with Simon and Schuster to produce an autobiography for a $1 million advance. His 1986 income, he said, had totaled about $435,000, including a $250,000 share of the publisher's advance.

Monday morning, Shirley Fulbright walked into the third-floor executive suite with her head hung low. She set down her purse and jacket. When she had left on Friday, her co-workers had thought she was a $26,000-a-year executive secretary. Now, they knew she had earned $160,000 in 1986.

"It's not what you think," she said. One of the junior secretaries—a young woman whose mother was dying of cancer—burst into tears. She spoke up, "To think that I've scrimped and saved and given to the ministry and to have this happen!" Shirley offered a lame explanation. "I had a need," she said, "and the ministry helped me." "That must have been some need," the secretary retorted.

As Fulbright faced her co-workers' wrath, Johnson called his staff of fifty together, declared his shock at the newspaper story, and announced that he was going to speak to Brother Dortch in the spirit of Matthew 18. Johnson found Dortch outside the Upper Room. During that day's broadcast, Dortch had solicited hundred-dollar donations with an offer to inscribe donors' names on a Walk of Faith outside the Upper Room.

As the two men walked through a parking lot towards the Barn, Dortch cautioned Johnson that it was not the time for bold statements, not the time to call the staff together; the uproar would die down within a couple days. Johnson told Dortch nothing of the meeting he had just concluded—he was not one to rock the boat, and he had never confronted Dortch in all their years of friendship. He shared his feelings diplomatically, "I don't think I can stay in this ministry any longer. I can't accept what I read in the paper."

As they talked, Johnson cited the example of Lee Iacocca of Chrysler, who had taken one dollar a year in salary until he had turned the car company around. Dortch was appreciative. "Sam," he said, "you really helped me." The next day, Johnson found out just how. As Dortch pitched the Walk of Faith from an outdoor TV set, he shared a revelation with viewers.

> I have not spoken to anyone in this ministry, and no one is aware of what I am going to do now. . . . It's so easy at a time like this to point fingers and make comments. But I want you to know that God has dealt with me. God doesn't deal with all of us the same way. But I have to answer to God for what He does in my life. . . .
>
> Yesterday, I was made to know—I've never heard the voice of God, but there have been times in my life when I was made to know—and as clearly as I knew that God called me to preach as a boy, yesterday, I was made to know. . . .
>
> I am advising my executive payroll department for the next twelve months, I will not accept any salary whatsoever from this ministry. I will not do it. I will continue to live in the parsonage of this ministry, and obviously, I'm gonna have to pay my taxes this year, Social Security, and insurance. But I will not accept any salary whatsoever, nor pension benefits or any other benefits.

Dortch expressed concern that his "sacrifice" not be interpreted as a criticism of anyone, presumably Bakker most of all.

The gesture was clumsy, and Dortch's friends in the ministry winced. Dortch was under tremendous pressure and was showing the effects of fatigue and overwork. One of his secretaries noticed how pale and drawn he looked. "Are you all right?" she asked. He assured her that he was and gave her a friendly kiss on the forehead. "Jesus is with us."

On Tuesday morning, April 21, Sam Johnson telephoned a friend in the Assemblies offices in Springfield. He said that he was thinking about quitting, but not until next Tuesday's board meeting. The friend counseled Johnson to resign immediately. Johnson decided he was right. He called his brothers, Dan and Joe. Dan, Dortch's close friend from Bible-school days, had just come to work at PTL, and Sam had asked Joe to drive to Charlotte from St. Louis to counsel him. They borrowed the key to a room in the Heritage Grand. There, with the television tuned to the daily show, the three brothers drafted an innocuous letter of resignation for Sam.

Dortch had taken that afternoon off to appear before the South Carolina Tax Commission in Columbia. PTL was still fighting the commission's demands for sales and accommodation taxes on the lifetime partnerships. Sam Johnson was happy to avoid Dortch; he was worried that he would talk him out of leaving. Johnson left the letter of resignation with a message that he'd be out of touch for the weekend. He bid a few friends good-bye and went home to mow the grass and wash his car. With a week to go before the second publicly announced PTL board meeting, Dortch's remaining support was beginning to crumble.

By April 22, Nims had begun identifying the staff members Falwell should fire. Dortch was at the top of the hit list. If the new PTL president didn't go at the April 28 board meeting, Nims decided, then he would quit and recommend that Falwell pull out also. "You lay down with dogs," he told one confidant, "and you get up with the fleas." Nims wanted to bring in Harry Hargrave, a Dallas amusement-park consultant, to run the organization. He was also prepared to replace Laventhol and Horwath—the accounting firm that had been handling the executive payroll and checking account—with the Big Eight firm of Arthur Andersen.

On the morning of April 22, the *Observer* published the results of interviews about Bakker's pay with former PTL board members Franzone, George, and Lawing. The three said that they hadn't known what Bakker was paid and didn't remember approving the enormous bonuses he had received. Cookman later testified that the size of the bonuses had astonished him.

That Wednesday night, a group of PTL alumni gathered at a hotel in Chattanooga, Tennessee. Cress was there, as were Roger Flessing, Gary Smith, and Ed Stoeckel. They had been summoned by John Ankerberg, who hoped to undercut Bakker's escalating efforts to regain his ministry. The next morning, the four men visited the office of Ankerberg's attorney in Chattanooga. Each one told the lawyer what they knew about PTL's operations under Bakker. Later that day, they flew by private plane to Nashville, where Falwell had just finished meeting with the four top Assemblies of God executives from Springfield.

With the church leaders gone, a catered lunch was served in Falwell's hotel suite. Again, each PTL alumnus took his turn telling Falwell and Nims what he knew. The Virginians were looking for damaging information. They knew they had lost the vote of board member Sam Moore and were eager to retain Jim Watt's support. Gary Smith shared two suggestive but ambiguous stories that indicated Bakker was bisexual. Ankerberg mentioned that he was going to accuse Bakker of homosexuality on Cable News Network's "Larry King Live" broadcast the next night. Later, Falwell would say that he had not known about Ankerberg's plan, but several of those present in the hotel recalled Falwell's enthusiastic reaction to Ankerberg's strategy.

The day of the gathering in Nashville, Bakker sent a telex to Falwell. He was doing so, he wrote, because he had been trying, without success, to reach Falwell by phone. Bakker now realized that PTL was slipping from his control. He was making his play.

> Due to the unrest in the charismatic world and also among the charismatic leadership, I feel that it is time now for you to turn the PTL ministry over to charismatics, appointing James Watt as chairman of the board, with Rex Humbard and Richard Dortch remaining. Others will be added.
> I'm recommending that a strong COO [chief operating officer] be appointed by this charismatic board. . . . I am going to submit to a large group of elders in the charismatic church world, and I will return to PTL when they feel it's God's time.

Bakker restated his recollection of the Palm Springs meeting in March, including what Bakker described as Falwell's pledge to return the ministry when Bakker asked him to.

> I will not fight you if you ignore my wishes, but I must let you know that what you are embarking on will truly start what the press has labeled a "holy war."
> Please let brotherly love continue and control what we do, and let us not allow the world to have any more opportunity to wag their tongues at the cause of Christ. Let us get back to our first love and calling, winning souls for the Kingdom.

Bakker gently threatened Falwell with exposure. He had given a Christian writer and a secular journalist "documentation on what is being done on both sides of this issue," he wrote. "I've sworn them to secrecy unless something happens."

There was more maneuvering behind the scenes. Falwell learned from Dortch that Tammy Bakker had requested a camera crew be sent to California. Dortch refused. As Falwell recalled Dortch's account of the incident, Tammy Bakker had informed Dortch that the Bakkers would go on the air at Trinity Broadcasting—the network run by Paul Crouch, Bakker's onetime partner—if they couldn't get access to a PTL broadcast. Nothing came of the threat.

At nine o'clock on Friday night, April 24, John Ankerberg appeared on Larry King's call-in TV show on the Cable News Network. "So, there are other things that [Bakker] has to confess to before he gets repentance and forgiveness?" King asked Ankerberg. "Yes," the Chattanooga minister replied. Then he rattled off, as fact, the allegations he had heard in Tennessee: mismanagement and diversion of funds, employees taking money through phony invoices, firings of those who spoke up, Dortch's deception on the matter of Jessica Hahn. Bakker had committed other moral transgressions as well, Ankerberg suggested. A prostitute said that she had serviced Bakker. He drank liquor. And, Ankerberg said, witnesses have seen Bakker involved in homosexual experiences.

Later that night Ankerberg appeared on national TV again, this time on ABC's "Nightline." Once again Ankerberg accused Bakker of homosexuality, one of the gravest transgressions for a Pentecostal preacher. For years, Bakker had demonstrated the potential for rank irresponsibility in live television, misrepresenting facts and recklessly attacking individuals and institutions. Now, in his battle for control of the ministry, Bakker himself had been wounded by a clergyman wielding the devastating power of an instant national broadcast.

With breathtaking speed, Jim Bakker and Richard Dortch had lost the protection that PTL's power, success, and money had afforded them. They now reaped a harvest of ill-will cultivated through years of deceit, arrogance, and self-serving leadership. In their time of deepest crisis, they had fewer and fewer friends willing to come to their defense. This was a high-stakes contest, played on many fields—national television, newspaper and magazine headlines, the pulpit, and clandestine meetings like the session in Nashville. In Falwell and his aides, Bakker and Dortch encountered adversaries who played hardball like seasoned veterans, who seemed to savor the fury of competition for its own sake. More and more, the Virginians were propelled by righteous indignation; they were not about to be Bakker's patsies or to cover up the outrages they had found inside PTL. Faced with such adversaries, Jim Bakker and Richard Dortch were simply overwhelmed.

Earlier in the week, I had secured a copy of PTL's complete audited financial statements—the document that Dortch had refused to make public in December when PTL had announced it was pulling out of ECFA. For nearly a year, I had suspected that PTL was overselling lifetime partnerships and that PTL would one day collapse under the weight of Bakker's building projects and grand promises. I had suspected that Dortch wanted the financial statements' footnotes withheld from the press and public for fear that the lifetime partnership tallies would prove a major embarrassment. Dortch's private motives remained his secret, but my instincts about the numbers had been right.

On Saturday, April 25, the story about the lifetime partnerships appeared on the front page of the *Observer*.

> PTL has raised nearly twice the money needed to build its $26 million Towers hotel, ministry records show, but by last month the TV ministry had paid just $13.5 million on the unfinished high rise and owed its builder $7.5 million. . . .
>
> Previously undisclosed pages from PTL's 1986 audited financial statements show PTL raised $49 million with "lifetime partnerships" in the Towers hotel between 1984 and last November. . . . The total . . . is well above the $30 million [PTL officials] once said they intended to finance through Towers partnerships.

The rationalizations of PTL's upper management—that some partners had died, others lived far away and didn't use the privilege each year, and excess demand could be met with the campground and the older Heritage Inn—could not justify the staggering totals. The *Observer* story covered only the partnerships issued through May 31, 1986. By the end of the "Family Fun" telethon eleven months later, PTL had issued more than $73 million in partnerships in the Towers hotel and more than $64 million in the Heritage

Grand. PTL had sold millions more in partnerships in its recreational offerings, undermining PTL's chance to generate revenues to pay for projects like the water park. All told, the lifetime partnerships had generated $166.6 million. More than 114,000 individuals had trusted Jim Bakker enough to buy at least one lifetime partnership.

In church on Sunday morning, March 26, Dortch did what he could to blunt the latest bad press. He explained that PTL's board had approved the bonuses, and he showed board minutes to two PTL pastors to get their corroboration that the board had approved the payments. After the service, Dortch summoned Don Hardister to his dressing room. He told the security chief to go to California. "Tell Jim I've opened the door for him to come back as wide as I can open it. I can't do more than I've done." He gave Hardister a tape of the talk to carry to Bakker.

In California the next day, Hardister found Bakker in the California mountains near Big Bear Lake north of Palm Springs. He relayed Dortch's message and played the tape in the cassette player of his car. The sermon angered Bakker; he thought that Dortch had made himself look good at Bakker's expense. Hardister told his boss that he thought Dortch and Taggart—Bakker's only line to his power base—were going to get fired. Bakker was convinced it wouldn't happen.

Hardister had arranged for a plane to fly Bakker to Charlotte so he could be at Heritage USA by the time the board meeting began. "It's just something I feel," Hardister told Bakker. "If we don't get home, there's not going to be any need for us ever to go home."

As Hardister made his way to Big Bear, Jerry Nims and lawyer Roy Grutman met in Atlanta with Cress, Gary Smith, and a third former PTL executive, the man at whom Bakker had made a pass during a massage at his home in April 1984. Jim Watt, whom the witnesses were expecting, didn't show up.

The former PTL executive who had been approached sexually by Bakker had good reason to believe Ankerberg was right about Bakker's sexual appetite. Concerned that Ankerberg's other evidence of homosexuality was flimsy, the executive had decided to describe Bakker's advances towards him, a story he had shared with no one. He told Ankerberg and his lawyer, and they urged him to tell Grutman. With a few minutes left before he had to leave to catch a plane, the former executive recounted the story into Grut-man's tape recorder.

Monday, April 27, had been an intense day at the *Observer*. I needed to finish three stories for Tuesday morning's paper. PTL's board was meeting on the 28th, and I wanted the directors—and the public—to know what we knew as they decided PTL's future.

For weeks, I had been trying to cajole Messner into confirming that he had supplied the money for the Hahn trust. He continued to refuse. He said that he had promised Roy Grutman that he would say nothing while Grutman investigated the payoff. I had found others who had learned details of Messner's role—details Falwell himself had learned firsthand from Messner during that weekend in Lynchburg. On Monday afternoon, as I completed a story saying that the Hahn payoff money had been PTL cash laun-dered through Messner, Falwell confirmed the account. "I am per-sonally convinced that Roe Messner is an honorable businessman with a long and impeccable business record. In my opinion, his chief error in the Jessica Hahn affair was lack of information and bad judgment." Falwell said that he planned to ask Messner to bid on the construction of a new ten-thousand-seat sanctuary for his church in Lynchburg.

I had also written a story about another damaging document I had obtained—the November 1985 IRS audit report. The report revealed that the federal tax authorities wanted to revoke PTL's tax-exempt status for 1981–83. The IRS had concluded that a sub-stantial amount of PTL's earnings had gone to benefit Bakker, his family, and other PTL officers, in violation of federal prohibition of private inurement by the officers of tax-exempt organizations.

I had long been eager to see the *Observer* profile the shadowy Taggart brothers—especially their life-style of wealth and the con-flict between their claims of family wealth and their parents' modest means. My colleague John Wildman, the investigative reporter who had worked on PTL in 1984, had taken over that story.

We carried a fourth PTL article that day—the latest counterattack from Falwell. He had said that he would announce Tuesday whether he was staying or resigning from PTL. Falwell showed less and less restraint in his criticism of Bakker. Should Bakker return to and take over PTL, Falwell said Monday afternoon, "he will simply preside over the funeral of the ministry. . . . It sounds to me like he's having some severe emotional problems. He has my deepest sympathy and prayers. I suppose the last seven years have been a living hell for him."

The night of April 27, Dortch glowed with confidence as he presided over dinner at the Hampton Court restaurant with board member Jim Watt. Dortch expected Falwell (who was hosting other board members for dinner in Lynchburg) to decide to pull out and leave the public controversy and alien charismatic ministry behind. Dortch planned that Watt would take over as board chairman while he held the president's post. To one of Dortch's top aides, the miscalculation was pitiable. "Granddad's sitting in the wheelchair, and he's convinced he's going to be playing ball with us next spring," Walter Richardson later told his colleagues. Dortch seemed to be the only person who didn't know that his days in the field were over.

By dawn on Tuesday, Dortch had seen the *Observer.* On the top half of the front page, there were three stories—one describing how Dortch used Messner to funnel money to Hahn, another detailing PTL's tax troubles, and a third carrying Falwell's warning that Bakker's return would mean the end for PTL. The Taggart profile appeared inside.

At six o'clock that morning, Dortch telephoned Messner. "Roe," he said, "we've got to get together and get our stories straight. Where did the money come from?" Messner told Dortch what he had told Falwell that weekend: It came from the ministry. "I put it on the end of my bill, and PTL paid it. We have nothing to talk about."

Tuesday, April 28, 1987, was a partly cloudy day on the cyclorama ceiling arching over Main Street. The board had closeted itself in the living room of Bakker's presidential suite on the top floor of the Heritage Grand Hotel. Most of the TV cameras and reporters present for the climax of a month's intrigue waited five minutes away inside the ballroom where Bakker had celebrated his twenty-fifth wedding anniversary thirteen months before. A handful of journalists had established a beachhead on the third-floor balcony overlooking Main Street, at the foot of the private stairway leading to the suite. We could see PTL security officers upstairs pacing back and forth in the corridor outside the suite.

For more than an hour, there was no sign of what might be happening upstairs. At 10:18 A.M. came the first evidence that things were not going well for Dortch. An ashen Rex Humbard, accompanied by his son Rex junior, swept through the double glass doors, past the press, and into his nearby hotel room. He didn't want to talk.

Inside the suite, events were traumatic, even for the determined soldiers from Lynchburg. Falwell announced that he was staying. As he spoke, Nims noticed David Taggart's face turn pale. Roy Grutman delivered his report on the Hahn payoff, producing an invoice showing that the $265,000 had been billed "per Richard Dortch." Dortch, who had denied his involvement for so long, now acknowledged it, but he refused to resign and fought for his job. Finally Falwell and his loyalists voted him out. Only Watt voted that he stay. Dortch was escorted out by his son, Rich. He slipped out a side door to avoid the press.

Under the portico of the Heritage Grand Hotel, a stony-faced David and James Taggart walked swiftly through the crowd of tourists waiting for a glimpse of the celebrities in their midst, perhaps even Bakker, whose return had been widely rumored. A couple of TV cameramen and reporters caught sight of the brothers. The TV crews closed in on the Taggarts' Jaguar. The two brothers picked up their pace, forced their way into the car, and drove off.

Ten minutes later, from a perch on the third-floor balcony, I spotted Jerry Nims in the lobby of the Heritage Grand. Nims had slipped out of the board meeting and eluded the waiting reporters. He stood among a dozen men dressed in conservative business suits, giving directions to the World Outreach Center more than a mile away. Listening to Nims were Harry Hargrave, PTL's new chief operating officer, a cadre of accountants from Arthur Andersen, PTL's new accountant, and several plainclothes security guards the Virginians had brought along in case the takeover turned ugly. Their instructions complete, the men scattered. Nims turned, strode between the grand piano and the fountain in the center of the lobby, and took the elevator back upstairs.

As the glass-walled Otis climbed above the lobby, Nims scanned the floor. His eyes locked on Hargrave, a handsome, self-assured thirty-eight-year-old Presbyterian from Dallas. Hargrave, a wry smile on his face, raised his arm in salute. The new era at PTL had begun.

In California, Don Hardister dialed the Palm Springs house from a pizza parlor near Big Bear Lake. He wanted the latest on the board meeting. Vi Azvedo's daughter April, a security guard and tutor for Bakker's son, told him that the board had fired Dortch and Taggart. When Hardister returned to Bakker's chalet, Bakker had heard the news on the television. He was sobbing.

Hardister was irritated that Bakker's room didn't have a phone. Bakker suggested that they use the phone at the home of some PTL partners Bakker had met in the area. When Bakker and Hardister arrived, the partners turned on a tape of Tammy's songs. As Bakker's wife began singing "The Sun Will Shine Again," Bakker lost his composure. Hardister told him to cry it out. Soon, Bakker and his son, Jamie, were headed back to Palm Springs in Bakker's Mercedes.

After five hours in the suite and the loss of two of its members, the PTL board emerged for a press conference in the ballroom. Two hundred seventy members of the press listened, and CNN carried the session live. Grutman confirmed the *Observer's* report on the Hahn trust. PTL would no longer make the trust payments, he said. Falwell announced that PTL had halted sales of lifetime partnerships, and he gently announced Dortch's departure, making it sound as if Dortch had resigned. He also told the press that David Taggart had been dismissed and that Hargrave and the Arthur Andersen firm had been hired. The Bakkers would no longer be paid, Falwell said, and Bakker's "ministry here has ceased."

Falwell took a question from the floor: have Bakker's efforts to return to PTL damaged your efforts to restore the ministry's credibility?

> You know, Tammy Faye said something to Macel, my wife. She said, "Try to put yourself in our shoes. If the coin were reversed, what would your husband be thinking, what would he be doing?" That's how I try to think, really, I have from the

543

beginning. No, I am not frustrated. I think human emotion is the same for everybody. This is not just the Bakkers' ministry, it's their life. Right here. We're all aware here, we're not dealing with property and buildings. God have mercy, this world's full of them. We're dealing with human beings.

But we also feel, beyond our responsibility to Jim and Tammy is our responsibility to 120,000 lifetime partners out there and Roe Messner and dozens of other vendors whom we owe money and little widows out there who put their life savings in this ministry. We are more committed there because we feel that if God will enable us to salvage all of it, and they lost nothing at one time, somewhere down the road we'll be able to look in each other's faces and say, Well done, and perhaps hear the Lord say, Well done.

CHAPTER TWENTY-FIVE

CODA

"God loves you, He really, really does"

It was a Thursday morning, ten days before Christmas. The clock read 10:00 A.M., the hour that Jim Bakker's chauffeured car customarily slipped into the executive garage behind PTL's TV studio. Ten o'clock was time for makeup, time for a planning session with the crew, time to wind up for the sprightly walk down the aisle with Tammy, greet the folks at home with a big grin, and exclaim to the studio audience, "Oh what a wonderful crowd we have today!"

Jim Bakker had dressed in his best, his gray pinstripe suit complementing the gentle gray of his hair. Richard Dortch was at his side, a few feet away. David Taggart sat a few rows back with brother James, blending, as always, into the background. But Bakker didn't speak to Dortch or Taggart this day, December 15, 1988. The audience sat in solemn silence on wooden pews, not in blue theater chairs. The man at the head of the room wore a black robe. He had come not to pray with Bakker, but to inform him formally of what Bakker and the world had known for ten days—that Bakker had been indicted by a federal grand jury.

With its oak-paneled walls and forty-foot ceilings, the chamber had a traditional stateliness that Bakker and David Taggart might have appreciated on a better day. But the august surroundings, the federal marshals' stern faces, and the presiding judge's warning that Bakker could go to jail for 120 years if convicted served as sobering reminders of the gravity of the charges against Bakker and his two former lieutenants.

Bakker's life had pitched wildly from peak to valley in the twenty-one months since he had sobbed to the sound of "The Sun Will Shine Again" in the California mountains. With Dortch and Taggart gone, Jerry Falwell and his aides continued their campaign to discredit Bakker, struggling to earn the allegiance of the PTL partners and venting their frustration and outrage at the mess they had inherited. They led reporters on a tour of Bakker's opulent presidential suite, condemned the fiscal and management practices of their predecessors, released a damning audit of executive salaries and expense accounts, laid off most of PTL's top executives, and talked, erroneously, about $90 million of PTL money the auditors couldn't find.

On May 6, 1987, the Assemblies of God defrocked Bakker for his confessed encounter with Hahn and for allegations of bisexual activity. Dortch—whose transgressions his old friend Charles Cookman had tried so hard to ignore—was dismissed for conduct unbecoming a minister, including concealment of Bakker's immoral conduct and apparent deceit about the Hahn payoff. The denomination's executive presbyters called for a day of confession, repentance, and prayer. At Heritage USA, Sam Johnson returned to take over as pastor of the Heritage Village Church at the request of Jerry Falwell. Johnson's longtime friend, Richard Dortch, severed all ties with the man he now considered a turncoat; Johnson denied that his April resignation had been part of a secret deal with Falwell for the PTL pulpit. Johnson would eventually inherit the job of presiding over what remained of the PTL ministry, which had been spun off into a new tax-exempt corporation and renamed Heritage Ministries. PTL's daily TV show would survive as "Heritage Today," its hosts two former members of the PTL Singers.

After a board meeting on May 27, 1987, Falwell disclosed to reporters the wish list for his future support that Bakker had sent by envoy Roe Messner: a $300,000-a-year lifetime salary for Jim, $100,000 a year for Tammy, rights to their books and records and ownership of the remaining inventory of their books and records, a secretary, maid and phone service for a year, the Tega Cay parsonage complete with furniture, two cars, security, and legal fees for IRS problems. "I don't see any repentance there," Falwell said as he finished. "I don't see any concern for the welfare of this ministry in that kind of request. I see the greed. I see the self-centeredness. I see the avarice that brought them down."

That night, the Bakkers appeared live on "Nightline," drawing the highest ratings in the history of the show. Bakker tamed interviewer Ted Koppel, taking the position that he would often embrace afterwards—that his motives were sincere and his chief error had been his failure to control his staff. Asked about his large bonuses, Bakker acknowledged "we should have said, 'No.' And we did say 'No' many times, but our board cared about us, and they would tell us that Jim and Tammy, you earn every penny that we give you." Bakker's self-pity was never too far from the surface.

> I think I've been selfish because I've—I've just let things happen. I should have been more attentive to more details, but I had a vision and a plan, and I was a man with a fire inside of me to do something for the Christian world. And six million people last year visited Heritage USA, and it was an exciting thing to see people putting their—getting their marriages back together and the families coming together. And to see that dream gone, it hurts. It's been living death. It would have been kinder for these men to assassinate us than to do what they've done to us . . . we do things flamboyant. And that's Jim and Tammy. I mean, do we have to kill people 'cause they're different? Jim and Tammy are a tad flamboyant. . . . I dream, I dream. I have to work. And I dream of building another city, maybe in California. And I dream about maybe going back on television someday. . . . It's up to the people. It's up to God, first of all, but it's up to God's people.

At one point, Koppel asked what David Taggart had done to deserve his one year's pay of more than $350,000. Bakker dodged the question. Just four days earlier, David and James Taggart had purchased more than $203,000 in jewelry and silver from Cartier, including a platinum and diamond watch for $95,000 and a jeweled pocket watch for $63,000. A year later, the New York jewelry store would sue, claiming that the Taggarts had failed to pay nearly $158,000.

On June 10, 1987, the Bakkers flew home to Charlotte for the first time since their departure for California and the Betty Ford Center five months earlier. Two days after their highly publicized return, Falwell's board of directors voted to seek bankruptcy-court protection for PTL while the TV ministry reorganized and drafted a plan to pay creditors the $70 million it owed. Falwell's deputies complained that Bakker had mortgaged PTL's future, erecting building after building to cover his "fiscal sins."

The cozy relationship between the new PTL leadership and Roe Messner quickly broke down. Messner, PTL's largest unsecured creditor, demanded $14 million, and PTL began to accuse the Kansas builder of shoddy construction and padded bills. The dispute soon went to court, where it remained as of June 1989. The unfinished Towers hotel and Wendy's restaurant stood as ghostly reminders of what Heritage USA might have been.

On September 21, 1987, a federal grand jury convened in Charlotte to hear the first testimony in a sweeping investigation of Bakker and his former lieutenants. Its first witness was Jessica Hahn, who had just agreed to tell her story and bare her breasts to *Playboy* magazine for a reported $1 million. For weeks, federal agents, mostly from the IRS and US Postal Service, had poured over reams of documents eagerly handed over by the new PTL leadership. For one week a month over the next sixteen months, the grand jurors listened behind closed doors to leading actors and bit players in the Jim Bakker story. Among them were John Wesley Fletcher, Paul Roper, Vi Azvedo, Jay Babcock, Mark Burgund, Al Cress, Sam Johnson, Shirley Fulbright, Don Hardister, Aimee Cortese, Ernie Franzone, J. Don George, and finally Roe Messner.

On October 8, 1987, after twenty-nine tumultuous weeks at the helm of the ministry Jim Bakker built, Jerry Falwell and his board of directors abruptly resigned. They were weary of the struggle to fend off Bakker, keep PTL afloat financially, and placate their wary charismatic and fundamentalist constituencies. Falwell attributed his decision to a US bankruptcy-court judge's willingness to allow PTL's creditors and contributors to file a competing plan for reorganizing PTL. The Lynchburg Baptist predicted that Bakker would return to power. "My convictions would not allow me to sit down at the table with the person who caused the problem," he said. Echoing the words of Jimmy Swaggart six months before, Falwell complained that Bakker had made PTL "probably the greatest scab and cancer on the face of Christianity in two thousand years of church history." Doug Oldham, who had allied himself with Falwell, soon joined his staff in Virginia. From the mountain home in Gatlinburg—transferred to Roe Messner, who hadn't been paid for hundreds of thousands of dollars in construction at the site—Jim Bakker announced, "We are ready to go anytime, anywhere, to restore our baby."

In fall 1987, Johnson would face his own Jessica Hahn crisis as he acknowledged first to Mark Burgund, his church business administrator, and later to federal investigators that he had lent $10,000 to Dortch—the money paid to Hahn in November 1984. As Johnson later described it publicly, Dortch had explained he needed help solving a problem with a "kook." In October 1987, as word began to spread in the media of a theretofore undisclosed $10,000 payment, Johnson told Burgund privately about the 1984 loan. Within days, Burgund resigned; he had seen Johnson declare a new day of openness from the pulpit, but then the pastor had failed to go public with his own involvement or to talk promptly to federal investigators, as Burgund advised. Burgund also was troubled by what he regarded as inconsistency in Johnson's accounts: as news of the loan broke, Johnson told reporters he remembered no mention by Dortch that the kook had made sexual accusations against Bakker. Privately, as Burgund remembered, Johnson had acknowledged knowing that fact from the very beginning, though he also had told Burgund that Dortch said he didn't believe the allegations. For his part, Johnson described himself as an unwitting accomplice betrayed by his best friend Richard Dortch.

Soon PTL had a new trustee, a former CBN marketing executive named David Clark whom Bakker had considered hiring near the end of his tenure at PTL. Clark, like Falwell, declared that the Bakkers' future was not at PTL. Despite Clark's efforts to revive the ministry, donations and traffic into Heritage USA lagged, and in May 1988, Clark departed. Meanwhile, Bakker returned to the southern California desert and announced plans for a $2 billion religious retreat there, the heir to Heritage USA West. Nothing came of the plan. As the summer heat descended on the desert, the Bakkers moved back to Charlotte and into a house paid for by the Bring Bakkers Back Club.

The PTL scandal left its mark on the religious-broadcasting industry. TV ministries reported sharp declines in income, compounding the effects of a glutted market. In January 1988, the National Religious Broadcasters adopted tougher standards of financial accountability to take effect a year later. Those who failed to meet those standards would be denied membership in NRB and the seal of approval from NRB's new Ethics and Financial Integrity Commission. "You might say our board caught regulatory fever," executive director Ben Armstrong said. NRB recruited ECFA—the accountability group which PTL had held at bay for years—to administer the new NRB standards, which were similar to those already required of ECFA members. In mid-1989, however, it remained unclear how many broadcasters would submit to NRB's new standards.

In February 1988, a year after he began his final effort to unmask Jim Bakker's sexual misconduct, Jimmy Swaggart confessed to his own transgression. Swaggart, once the righteous accuser, begged for forgiveness, agreed to step down from the pulpit for three months, and declared, "I do not plan in any way to whitewash my sin." He offered few details to his public. Marvin Gorman, the New Orleans minister whose conduct Swaggart had attacked in 1986, had confronted Swaggart with evidence that the TV evangelist had visited a New Orleans prostitute. Swaggart denied having intercourse with the woman but admitted paying her to perform pornographic acts. National officials of the Assemblies of God demanded a more severe punishment than their brethren in the Louisiana district, ordering Swaggart to stay out of the pulpit for a full year. Swaggart chose to resign from the denomination instead, expressing regret and acknowledging that the Assemblies had no choice but to dismiss him. Swaggart contended that his absence for a year would bankrupt his Bible college and $142-million-a-year ministry. His decision to leave the Assemblies of God caused mass defections from his staff and college. Among those who departed were the father, mother, and brother of Jerry Ogg, Jr., my anonymous source Joe, who had himself taken a university teaching job in Tennessee the summer before.

More and more, the PTL story became a creature of the courts. PTL sued Bakker and Taggart for $52 million, alleging mismanagement, unjustified compensation, and personal use of sorely needed ministry dollars. After a trial in fall 1988, a bankruptcy-court judge ordered Jim and Tammy Bakker to pay $6.6 million and Taggart to pay $1 million. The judge condemned the defendants' expenditures as "outrageous, unbelievable, and shocking." He quoted Scripture in his ruling: "Be not deceived; God is not mocked: for whatsoever a man soweth, that shall he also reap." The Bakkers and Taggart appealed the judgment.

In pretrial depositions for the bankruptcy case, lawyers asked both Bakker and David Taggart about their physical relationship. Taggart was asked under oath whether he had had sexual relations with Bakker. His attorney invoked Taggart's Fifth Amendment right against self-incrimination. Asked if he had had a homosexual relationship with David Taggart, Bakker responded, "No, I'm not guilty of that."

A class-action lawsuit was filed on behalf of PTL's partners seeking damages from Bakker, Taggart, Messner, and several of PTL's banks and outside auditors, including Laventhol and Horwath. The case was expected to go to trial in late 1989. In a separate proceeding, a lawyer representing the hundred-thousand-plus lifetime partners sued to seek more of PTL's assets for his clients, whose lifetime of free lodging and recreation had vanished with PTL's financial crisis. Bakker sued Roy Grutman, accusing his onetime lawyer of tricking him into resigning.

In April 1988, the IRS revoked PTL's tax-exempt status dating back to 1980. Four months earlier, the IRS had sued the bankrupt PTL for nearly $56 million in back taxes, the nightmarish claim that Bakker and Dortch had stalled for years with administrative appeals. An IRS report put the Bakkers' excess 1981–87 compensation at more than $9 million.

In April 1988, with PTL unable to generate enough income to pay its debts, the bankruptcy court ordered Heritage USA put up for sale. In late August, Jim Bakker emerged as the leading candidate to buy the complex. "Bakker Nears a Return to PTL," read the headlines. But Bakker failed to come up with the $3 million down payment on his $172 million offer. Bakker remained optimistic. "I believe God called me to build Heritage USA, and God doesn't change his mind." With Bakker out of the picture, the bankruptcy court agreed on December 13, 1988, to award PTL's assets to Toronto real-estate developer Stephen Mernick for $65 million in cash. Mernick, thirty-four, is an Orthodox Jew and ordained rabbi with an aversion to publicity.

Mernick took partial control of Heritage USA in February 1989, with a deadline of September 30, 1989, for closing the purchase. With an estimated 50,000 hard-core supporters, Heritage Ministries continued to lease PTL's TV studio and the Upper Room, while the affiliated Heritage Church held services in the Barn. In May 1989 the ministries announced their intention to buy and move into a twenty-acre site in South Charlotte, leaving Heritage USA behind. Heritage USA continued to operate despite sparse traffic, the resort a pitiful shadow of itself in the go-go days of Jim and Tammy.

A day before the eighth anniversary of Jessica Hahn's trip to Florida, the federal grand jury in Charlotte indicted Bakker and Dortch for mail fraud, wire fraud, and conspiring to defraud the public through the sale of lifetime partnerships. The indictment alleged that the two men had failed to disclose the true number of partnerships sold to PTL partners and, by use of the mails and public airwaves, had sold tens of thousands more partnerships than PTL had lodging to accommodate. The grand jury also accused the men of concealing the Hahn payoff and the true financial condition of PTL from the ministry's board of directors. The case was expected to go to trial in late August 1989.

The grand jury indicted the Taggart brothers for tax evasion and conspiracy to impede the IRS in collecting taxes, alleging that they had diverted $1.1 million of PTL money to pay personal bills and expenses, failed to report the funds as income on their tax returns and thus evaded taxes of nearly half a million dollars. The Taggarts' trial began in July 1989.

On Bakker's forty-ninth birthday, January 2, 1989, Jim and Tammy Bakker returned to the air with an hour-long weekday TV show produced from the Charlotte home of Dexter Yager, a wealthy Amway distributor and longtime Bakker friend. The broadcast was carried on a handful of stations and cable systems—none of them in Charlotte. Soon the Bakkers were informed that they could no longer use a private home for a TV broadcast because they were violating zoning restrictions. In April 1989, they moved to Orlando, Florida. In May, they resumed their broadcast from a little-used shopping center. On June 1, 1989, the Bakkers learned that the IRS had filed a lien claiming the Bakkers owed $666,492 in back taxes for 1981 and $565,434 for 1982.

While Bakker insisted that he had done no wrong, Richard Dortch exhibited more pain and contrition from his new home in Clearwater, Florida, near the site of Bakker's encounter with Jessica Hahn. Dortch began seeing a psychotherapist, opened a ministry to serve pastors and others in crisis, and talked publicly about the failings of PTL's former leaders. He tried to explain what went wrong.

> At PTL, there was no time taken for prayer or for family because the show had to go on. We were so caught up in God's work that we forgot about God. It took the tragedy, the kick in the teeth, to bring us to our senses. . . .
>
> A television camera can change a preacher quicker than anything else. Those who sit on the sidelines can notice the changes. . . . It turns good men into potentates. Television must be used only as a tool for evangelism. It's so easy to get swept away by popularity. Everybody loves you, cars are waiting for you, and you go to the head of the line. That's the devastation of the camera. It has made us less than what God has wanted us to become.

The Bakkers were not the only players to cling to the limelight. After his recovery from a self-proclaimed suicide attempt, John Wesley Fletcher declared, in the January 1989 issue of *Penthouse* magazine, that he had been Bakker's sexual partner. Jessica Hahn turned her peculiar brand of fame into a lucrative, if hollow, career. She posed nude a second time for *Playboy* after plastic surgery on her nose and breasts, an effort to bury forever her "ugly duckling" identity. She toured the country making promotional appearances on local radio stations and appeared in a celebrated music video. Her former boss and lover, Gene Profeta, went to jail after pleading guilty to two of the eighteen counts against him. For evading taxes and tampering with a witness—Hahn—Profeta was ordered to serve six months. Some saw Hahn as a symbol of women's liberation, a victim who fought back. To others she seemed the essence of sexist stereotyping, a sexy secretary willing to display her body in a girlie magazine. Back home in Massapequa, her mother and stepfather severed communication with the twenty-nine-year-old. Like Bakker, Jessica had paid a high price for fame.

* * *

The world will never know for sure what happened in room 538 of the Sheraton Sand Key Resort in Clearwater Beach on December 6, 1980. Each of the three principal witnesses—Bakker, Hahn, and Fletcher—have similar proclivities either for willful deceit or stunning self-deception. Just as baffling is the puzzle of Jim Bakker himself; the enthusiastic man-child riding the miniature train at Heritage USA one moment, the tyrannical boss infuriated by burned-out light bulbs the next. The compassionate creator of a house for crippled children, the fund-raiser willing to mislead his audience. The doting husband on-camera, the sexual philanderer off-stage. What truly motivated this man who had so many identities, so little perspective on himself, and so much to hide?

I believe the answer can be found in a psychological profile with remarkable parallels to Bakker's conduct and life story: the narcissistic personality disorder, or what one writer has called pathological narcissism. A person of this personality type is self-centered and grandiose. He has a remarkable lack of interest in and empathy for others even though he is eager to win their love and admiration. Typically, his value system is corruptible and his relationships with others are exploitive, sometimes even parasitic, although the individual may not recognize it. "It is as if they feel they have the right to control and possess others and to exploit them without guilt."

When a narcissist secures a position of importance in the world, he tends to surround himself with admirers. From these people he extracts the adoration he savors. Once that has been accomplished, he exploits these "shadows" mercilessly. He protects himself from emotional conflicts and anxiety "by withdrawing into the splendid, grandiose isolation which gives the specific seal to the narcissistic organization."

It is not unusual for the narcissist to act in contradictory ways. He may display great charm, and still he can withdraw from social life as effectively as a severe schizoid personality, acting cold and aloof to protect himself from meaningful emotional interaction. His grandiosity may coexist with shyness and a conscious feeling of inferiority.

The narcissist may function well in society. Often he appears quite creative, and he may become prominent in the arts or an institution. But over time his work shows signs of superficiality, revealing an "emptiness behind the glitter." The narcissist has little tolerance for feelings of boredom and restlessness. He is unable to accept the mundane nature of ordinary life and searches constantly "for gratification of strivings for brilliance, wealth, power, and beauty."

Self-love may appear to motivate the narcissist; in fact, it's self-hatred that shapes his character. One psychiatrist described finding this pattern in the homes of narcissistic patients he treated: a parental figure, usually the mother, "who functions well on the surface in a superficially well-organized home, but with a degree of callousness, indifference, and nonverbalized, spiteful aggression." That promotes frustration, resentment, and aggression in the young child, who comes to see the world as devoid of love and himself as unworthy. As an adult, the narcissist fears above all depending on others, "because to depend means to hate, envy, and expose themselves to the danger of being exploited, mistreated, and frustrated."

The narcissist has some quality or skill that arouses envy or admiration in others and provides the building blocks for his idealized concept of himself. Perhaps he has some special talent. Or he might have been an only child, the only brilliant child, or the sibling who was expected to fulfill the family's aspirations. This idealized self-image compensates for the child's frustration and masks "a hopeless yearning and love for an ideal mother who would come to his rescue."

In adolescence and early adulthood, the narcissist often finds the gratification for which he thirsts. Eventually, due to age, illness, loss, or some other intrusion, the narcissist confronts reality.

> It is dramatic how intense the denial of this long-range reality can be in narcissistic personalities, who under the influence of the pathological, grandiose self are unconsciously (and sometimes consciously) convinced of their eternal youth, beauty, power, wealth, and the unending availability of supplies of confirmation, admiration, and security. For them, to accept the breakdown of the illusion of grandiosity means to accept the dangerous, lingering awareness of the depreciated self. . . .
>
> Perhaps the most frightening experience that narcissistic personalities need to ward off and eventually may have to face

is that of a surrounding world empty of love and human contact, a world of dehumanized objects within which animate as
well as inanimate objects have lost their previous magically
satisfying qualities."

It started as a marketing idea in the early days of Bakker's Charlotte
ministry: package the name PTL not only as the acronym for Praise
the Lord but also as shorthand for People That Love. The cuddly
slogan served the young organization in several ways. PTL was
reaching beyond old-time Pentecostals to charismatic Christians
unsatisfied with their home churches and to those who had been
completely divorced from religion. The catchword conveyed the
altruism of the traditional church, an image PTL was eager to
perpetuate as it sought viewers' dollars. The new name also captured the gentle, caring character of many of Bakker's rank-and-file
staff members and partners.

It was at PTL that Jim Bakker found his People That Love, the
collective substitute for a mother who was cold and self-involved
and a hard-working father who was tight with money and quick
with stern judgments. Bakker's audience—the awestruck visitors in
the studio and the loyal, generous audience across America—believed in Jim Bakker with the same devotion Bakker attributed to
Armilda Irwin, his idealized maternal grandmother. The PTL partners were always willing to forgive the failings of this man with the
face and stature of a boy.

Bakker's God was a complement to his loving partners. The
Divinity was generous with material blessings, tokens of the unfet-
tered love that Bakker seemed sure he had been denied as a boy.
And, in the years of Bakker's sexual infidelities and marital collapse,
Bakker's God was quick to supply all-cleansing forgiveness. Bakker
couldn't tolerate a church where God condemned or demanded
unrequited sacrifice. His God was his most loyal friend: "God loves
you, He really, really does," Bakker would say at the close of each
day's program.

As a boy, young Jim Bakker found pride in his gift for speech and
sales. He took the Bakker gift of gab and polished it in front of a
mirror, his reel-to-reel tape recorder capturing his delivery. He had
the Irwin knack for selling and practiced it on the neighbors who
bought the vegetables, fruit, and housewares he and Sonny Singer

hawked and on the ladies he fitted in the shoe store in downtown Muskegon. He had an intuitive sense for what worked. When his friend Marlene Way, the Elvis impersonator, bombed at the old-folks' home, he knew the song and dance that would win over the audience. With his variety-show fund-raisers at Muskegon High, Bakker found a way to marry his fondness for the stage with his gift of salesmanship. It would soon serve him well before the TV cameras in Portsmouth, Orange County, and Charlotte.

It was, perhaps, his older brother Bob's failure that determined the path young Jim Bakker took as he left Muskegon. Bob Bakker was Raleigh and Furn Bakker's firstborn and the child for whom they had the greatest aspirations. Bob Bakker's divorce and disregard for church orthodoxy gave Jim Bakker, the youngest child, then in his teenage years, an opportunity to take over the place of honor within the family—as, indeed, he would do despite his disdain for the Pentecostal church. "Bob was the one that was called . . . the tallest one, good looking, dynamic, people liked him." But with Bob's fall, Bakker said, "this whole thing . . . kind of slid on down and I have to do it."

It would have been an arduous road from Muskegon to Broadway, where some of Jim's high-school friends had expected Bakker to make his career. At Russell and Fern Olson's Minneapolis Evangelistic Auditorium, Bakker found a speedy path—the kind he preferred—onto the stage and into the company of celebrities. In the church world, the narcissist slid from view, masked by the selfless cause of Christ but influencing every turn. Bakker prayed all night and announced "I want to save the world for Jesus" with a grandiosity that invited snickers from his classmates in Bible school. A poor student, he took the opportunity that his passion for Tammy offered to drop out of Bible school without completing the most basic training for a minister. He chose the job of evangelist—a religious performer traveling to a new audience each week—over the job of pastor, with its mundane routine and intimate personal relationships. On the road, he measured success much as he had for his high-school variety shows: by the turnout of people and money.

Pat Robertson and the TV camera offered a reservoir of admiration far beyond what Bakker could have reached by appearing in a single church each week on the revival circuit. He and Tammy were a hit. Soon they were stars of sorts—in Tidewater, Virginia, southern California, Charlotte, and, with syndication, across the country. At PTL, Bakker's rapidly expanding ministry supplied money, power, and prestige—and put an even greater distance between Bakker and the individuals he was ostensibly winning to Christ.

Bakker believed in himself with intense certainty, a potent companion to his skills as an on-air performer. He deftly controlled the flow of information to his constituency, manipulating the truth to box others in his reality. He drew the audience into the "personal" lives of Jim and Tammy, replacing the aloofness of the preacher in the pulpit with the false intimacy of television. He used tears, humor, righteous anger, bruised self-pity, and gentle ministry to touch viewers in their living rooms. He was a man of uncanny seductive power. To women on his staff, he could seem a lost boy who needed nurturing and protection. To some men, he represented a resource of great promise, a master fund-raiser and gifted performer who, with the right help, had a ministry of unlimited potential.

The man at the top set the tone for his ministry. Bakker was not one to entertain grave doubts, to question his own motives and wisdom. His rush-rush schedule left no opportunity to look back, and his employees were swept downstream by the same white water. Their sense of what was right was a common casualty; few had the strength of character to take a public stand, as Bill Perkins had in 1978.

This was the full-gospel church, not a secular corporation, and that fact further strengthened Bakker's hand. Not only was Bakker the boss, he was also a pastor, doing God's work. His constituents accepted the imperatives of ecclesiastical hierarchy. They were ready, often eager, to sacrifice for their church and God. In Bakker's Pentecostal-charismatic world, reason routinely succumbed to the subjective and supernatural. When Bakker said that God had directed him to build Heritage USA, his followers believed.

If his God and partners supplied the affection Bakker had wanted so desperately as a boy, PTL and Heritage USA provided the setting in which Bakker could try to ease his childhood pain. He put his entire family—mother, father, brother and sister—on staff. With Kevin's House, Bakker erected a Victorian mansion as big as any on Webster Avenue. His ready access to PTL cash and credit

Coda

cards fostered a life-style that dimmed his exaggerated memories of threadbare coats and an orange house on Sanford Avenue. The staff members whose allegiance he secured with high salaries, alluring perks, and a seat in the throne room provided talents that Bakker used to enhance his own image: Doug Oldham gave PTL a well-known name in the gospel-music world, Roger Flessing brought creativity, wit, and polish to PTL's TV programs, John Wesley Fletcher displayed a gift for healing ministry. Others in Bakker's innermost circle did not shine as bright, but they had passed the stiff Bakker loyalty test, demonstrating a willingness to put Bakker's needs first. They were rewarded accordingly. Vi Azvedo, the omnipresent marriage counselor, acquired a position of power in the ministry. Jay Babcock, who offered a discreet source of sexual release, kept his job. David Taggart, willing to work slavelike hours and to protect Bakker's darkest secrets, took home enormous sums of money.

Still, the path to Bakker's door was littered with the corpses of the men and women he used and shoved aside. One day they were in, the next they were out. Some had gotten too close; Bakker got bored easily, with people as well as with cars and homes. Some were the idealists who set a rigid standard of morality and excellence alien to the corporate culture that Bakker promoted of deceitfulness, incompetence, and disregard for the law. Bakker confused disagreement at the office with disloyalty; there was no place in his universe for sustained dissent.

In the end, Bakker's partners and loyal staff began to see how they had been used. They had given their money, their sweat, and their trust. But the pathological grandiose self hungered for more; to borrow a phrase Bakker often used to justify his latest project, "If you stop growing, you start dying." He kept alive on the thrill and psychic gratification of constant change, another project, and a bigger building, on the reassurance of bigger bonuses, fancier cars, and more houses, on the clandestine "love" he received from his male sex partners, and on his righteous battles with the IRS, Jimmy Swaggart, ECFA, sundry lawyers, creditors, and the *Charlotte Observer*. Bakker had wasted millions of dollars, spent millions more on himself, run PTL to the brink of insolvency, and failed to build an institution capable of surviving his absence.

The February 1988 fall of Jimmy Swaggart was a stunning display of hubris; with his righteous condemnation of two fellow TV ministers guilty of moral indiscretion, Swaggart set the stage for his own unmasking. Bakker had done the same in March 1987 by trying to use Jerry Falwell, a man with a righteous public image, the president of the Moral Majority, as a cover for his sham resignation. Bakker's brief interlude with Jessica Hahn—the sin from which Falwell was supposed to proclaim Bakker's restoration—was merely a symptom of Bakker's wholesale failure as a moral leader. He had survived at PTL by creating a universe where right and wrong were relative; he wrote the rules, and if he needed to break one, he found reason to rewrite or ignore it. Employees could be fired for homosexuality while Bakker himself engaged in sex with men. Falwell brought to PTL a set of absolute standards—a crucible Bakker could not survive.

In the months that followed, some openly questioned Falwell's motives, suggesting he had forced Bakker aside to steal PTL's satellite network. Certainly the righteous, no-holds-barred, occasionally irresponsible style of the newcomers from Lynchburg fostered such conspiracy theories. But watching the Virginians turn away from Bakker in the pivotal month of April 1987 convinced me that the principal force at work was not greed but the devastating facts that the outsiders had discovered as they examined the ministry Bakker had asked them to protect.

Finally the truth had come out. This time God's people that love could not so easily forgive.

CHAPTER TWENTY-SIX

AFTERWORD

"Never in my life did I ever intend to defraud anyone."

Behind Jim Bakker's pose of righteousness, down deep beyond his thirst for adoration, there had always resided a demon bent on self-destruction. It seemed to guide Bakker's clumsy efforts to regain PTL through the Holy Wars of 1987, spawning more scandal and making his hoped-for resurrection even more improbable. In the third year after his fall, Bakker seemed again in the clutches of the demon within. What public esteem he might have mustered from mainstream America washed away during a six-week trial that convinced most of America that he was capable of the worst brand of fakery and the rest of America, those with compassion to spare, that he was a man on the brink of mental collapse. And what chance Bakker might have had for a gentle exodus from the world of grand juries and federal courtrooms vanished, replaced by a future that promised no exit at all.

The courtroom drama began quietly on July 5, 1989, with the little-noted trial of David and James Taggart, accused by the latest government count of using $1.2 million of PTL money to pay personal bills—and failing to pay $525,487 in taxes due on that unreported income.

Eleven days of testimony produced startling details of the brothers' lifestyle—conduct so egregious it was hard to imagine that Bakker, so close to the brothers, could not at least have suspected.

Merchants from exclusive Manhattan shops paraded in to recall a ring, pin, and bracelet of precious metals and stones bought for $96,900, $85,000, and $75,000, respectively; alligator-skin shoes purchased for $8,775; and a pair of antique ivory incense burners purchased for $25,000. Former PTL employees and PTL's tax consultants chronicled their efforts to get David Taggart's receipts for what the young aide had calmly described to them as legitimate ministry spending. In four years' time, the brothers' combined net worth increased tenfold, or by $1.5 million—a sum twice their taxable income.

To the end the brothers guarded their low profile, stepping forward only to testify. The whispers and stories about David Taggart's relationship with Bakker never reached the jurors, at least not in the courtroom. Nor would the jurors find out what Bakker had in fact known of the brothers' clandestine use of PTL money. Summoned by the Taggarts' attorney to prove the boss had authorized the brothers' spending, a nervous Bakker declined to answer questions, citing his Fifth Amendment right against self-incrimination. In ten minutes in the courtroom, Bakker made no visible gesture of greeting to his long-time friends.

The brothers' words did little to help their cause. James Taggart, thirty-five, testified that he had been storing, for eventual delivery to PTL, the furniture and precious artwork purchased with PTL money but delivered to the Taggarts' homes in Charlotte and in New York's Trump Tower. Prosecutors had expected David, thirty-two, to claim that his spending as well had been done on PTL's behalf. Instead, he claimed that Bakker—in his successful effort to recruit his trusted aide back to PTL in 1983—had agreed that PTL would pay David Taggart's travel and vacation costs and even his personal credit-card charges. "I wanted access to the same resources he had," David Taggart asserted. With his father admitting from the stand that he was not wealthy (in 1984 Henry Taggart had reported adjusted gross income of $5,035), David Taggart acknowledged misleading friends and colleagues about his parents' financial situation to deflect questions about the money he had gotten thanks to Bakker's pay offer.

The jury needed less than four hours to convict the brothers. The handful of former PTL partners inside the courtroom saw little reason to doubt the verdict. "I felt like I had been made a fool of," one Charlotte woman told me after hearing the details of the Taggarts' luxury purchases.

With a month left before Bakker's trial, prosecutors found themselves with three new cooperative inside witnesses—the Taggarts, who hoped to cut their prison terms with belated cooperation, and Richard Dortch, once scheduled for trial with Bakker. On August 8, two weeks after the Taggarts' conviction, Dortch shrewdly pleaded guilty to conspiracy and a handful of mail- and wire-fraud charges. Dortch agreed to cooperate with the government's effort to convict Bakker, the man he had protected so doggedly for so long. Dortch received a prison sentence of eight years and $200,000 in fines. "I participated in deceiving people . . . in doing something I know was wrong," he told U.S. District Judge Robert Potter before sentencing. "I lost the most cherished possession I had, that was my integrity." Privately Dortch told investigators he had never known what pay had been going to David and James Taggart or even to Bakker's secretary, Shirley Fulbright—he had learned it first, he confided, in the *Observer.*

Bakker's attorneys had tried their best to avoid Potter, a sixty-six-year-old Reagan appointee whose stiff prison sentences had earned him the nickname "Maximum Bob." But pretrial publicity, the lawyers' argument for moving the trial out of Potter's district, failed to convince the judge. Potter, poised to hold the trial out of town if he had trouble picking a jury, found the twelve people he needed within a day.

From August 28, the opening day of Bakker's trial, the televangelist's fate was front-page news across the country. To ensure their place inside Potter's small courtroom, some journalists even hired stand-ins to arrive before dawn to wait in line outside the courthouse, a handsome classical edifice set in a downtown of antiseptic skyscrapers. The press corps eventually swelled to include correspondents from CBS, ABC, NBC, Cable News Network, the *Washington Post,* the *New York Times,* the *Los Angeles Times,* the *Chicago Tribune,* and the *Atlanta Constitution.*

From opening day, the Bakker trial proved as unpredictable and theatrical as its celebrity defendant's tenure at PTL. Potter and George Davis of Hawaii, Bakker's eighty-two-year-old senior attorney, rubbed each other the wrong way from the start—establishing a pattern that, by trial's end, suggested that Davis's chief contribution to the defense, in the courtroom at least, had been his efforts to lay a foundation of judicial bias for any needed appeal. "Mr. Davis, be quiet," Potter admonished after the lawyer delivered his latest lengthy objection to the words a prosecutor had used to question a witness. "You don't have to make a speech. Now sit down."

David Taggart opened the government's case. With furtive glances at his former boss, an uneasy Taggart took the jury behind the scenes. During one Bakker visit to Tulsa, Oklahoma, Taggart recalled, the PTL president had complained that he lived shabbily compared to that city's leading evangelist, Oral Roberts. Bakker's power bill at Tega Cay had run $2,000 a month, Taggart said, because Jim and Tammy liked their outdoor pool heated to ninety degrees year-round.

Then followed a stream of mostly little-known PTL employees, whose testimony served to piece together the prosecutors' picture of fraud against the too-trusting lifetime partners. One recalled his 1985 memos warning that the Heritage Grand lifetime partnerships had been oversold. Former PTL vice president Steve Nelson alleged that Bakker had ordered him to keep two sets of lifetime partner tallies—one accurate count for Bakker, a second, lower tally for public display during telethons.

Suddenly, as defense attorney Harold Bender challenged Nelson's credibility on the trial's third day, the trim thirty-nine-year-old witness fell silent. His head slumped against his chest as if he had fallen asleep. "He just died!" someone in the audience muttered. With that, a nurse serving on the jury rushed to Nelson's side. Courtroom marshals, with help from prosecutor and former college football player Jerry Miller, struggled to hoist Nelson, frozen akimbo like a spent wind-up toy, out of the witness box.

The scene was terrifying: it seemed for several minutes as if Nelson had indeed died, his soul whisked away to the hereafter with merciless swiftness. As the witness lay on the floor, Bender, his eyes wet with tears, prayed with two Bakker supporters. And Bakker, apparently acting on his own initiative but with what he thought to be the judge's permission, drew near Nelson and began praying quietly. Some looking on said they saw Bakker touch the former staff member as he summoned the spirit.

With emotions running high and Nelson heading to the hospital, court was called off for the day. Later, while Bakker prepared for his daily exit out a side door, down a set of stairs past the omnipresent cameras to a waiting car, he looked distraught, like a frightened child; he had been sobbing in a private conference room. "Harold, don't leave me here," he cried out as Bender stepped out the courthouse door, momentarily leaving him behind.

That night, former PTL security chief Don Hardister watched the nightly news footage of Bakker's exit. Hardister knew how squeamish Bakker could be and how hard a time he had letting go of emotional experiences. Hardister had seen Bakker at his most broken, crying constantly, talking unintelligibly, and unable to walk unassisted, in the days of spring 1987 after Bakker began to suspect that Falwell would not return PTL. "I saw a very broken man," Hardister told me the next day, describing the Bakker he'd seen on the tube after Nelson's collapse. "I saw a man who was in desperate trouble and had no one to reach out to because all of the people like me, his friends, have turned their backs on him."

Nelson's collapse was blamed on dehydration, and the next morning he was back, ready to testify. But Bakker was not. With the jury out, George Davis surprised the courtroom with a request that Judge Potter recess for two weeks so Bakker could check into a psychiatric hospital. Davis summoned a psychiatrist who testified that Bakker had lapsed into an "acute depressive and confusional reaction," leaving him unable to adequately judge reality—or to aid in his own defense. Leaving the courthouse after Nelson's collapse, Bakker had perceived the crowd of photographers and reporters waiting for him as frightening insects or animals. Restless during the night, Bakker had taken Xanax, a tranquilizer. But the next morning, he was far from tranquil, "lying in a corner of his attorney's office, with his head under a couch, hiding, expressing thoughts that someone was going to hurt him."

The psychiatrist warned Potter that Bakker might not recover if committed to a government hospital. Potter said he had no choice under federal law: Bakker had to be sent to a federal prison hospital for evaluation.

Within minutes a platoon from the media ranks had gathered outside the restored Victorian home that housed Bender's office.

Five grim U.S. marshals pulled up, and soon a glum Bender and Davis arrived. A few minutes later the minicams stood at attention, reporters clutched their pens. The front door opened, and in the foyer inside I could make out Bakker—a Bakker I had never seen before.

This man who cared so about his appearance looked disheveled, his hair out of place, his eyes disoriented, his face puffy and twisted with anguish. Only his suit jacket, draped over his hands to cloak the standard-issue manacles around his wrists, seemed to suggest any of his preoccupation with appearance. "Please don't do this to me," he sobbed, over and over, struggling against the marshals trying to shuffle him onto the front porch, down four steps and along a short walk shaded by a crape myrtle flush with purple blossoms. "Please don't do this to me."

The fifteen reporters and photographers watched at curbside as Bakker pulled into a fetal position on the brown velour backseat of the LTD Crown Victoria, known as a "cage car" because of the wire barrier between the front and back seats. The scene—which would be reshown many times on local and national news programs—was pitiful and entirely convincing. Though several reporters had planned to bark out questions to the passing Bakker, the pack remained silent as this man unraveled before them.

Bakker had shed many theatrical tears in his career, using his childlike emotionalism to manipulate his caring audience. Indeed to many the wrenched face and the pleas for freedom seemed simply another act. But watching Bakker that day, recalling his autobiography's description of the nervous breakdown at CBN, and hearing anew from former aides about his periodic retreats to his Tega Cay bed with spells of depression, I concluded that the public had just glimpsed Bakker's fundamental inability to cope with the reality of the outside world. From his pain we now could infer just how thick and how high were the walls protecting Bakker's climate-controlled universe. The collapse of Nelson, a healthy-looking man younger than his one-time boss, had driven home to Bakker, a man always fearful of his own death, how fragile his sanctuary had become. That most frightening moment for the narcissist had arrived: "a surrounding world empty of love and human contact, a world of dehumanized objects within which animate . . . objects have lost their previous magically satisfying qualities" (Otto Kernberg, *Borderline Conditions and Pathological Narcissism,* pp. 310–11).

Later that day, Bakker was ushered to a federal prison hospital north of Durham, North Carolina. There psychiatrists would diagnose the episode as a panic attack, while back in Charlotte family members—always looking for some external bogey man—blamed the Xanax. The prison psychiatrists reported finding no mental disease but suggested that Bakker might suffer from a personality disorder with elements of dependency, passive aggressiveness, and narcissism. To them, one testified, Bakker seemed "somebody who was in a long-term habit of presenting themselves as very normal—very conventional, very much with the set of accepted values for society and someone who routinely would tend to deny any personal difficulties."

By the close of his first day back in court Bakker appeared animated and cheerful. The crack in the wall had been sealed, the sanctuary was safe for now.

While the Taggart prosecutors had used Manhattan merchants to make their case, the Justice Department called a procession of lifetime partners—many conspicuously elderly, disabled, or poor—to document each instance of Bakker's allegedly fraudulent money-raising. One partner had even kept a videotape of the Bakker pitch on which he'd relied when he plunked down his $1,000. A former PTL lawyer disclosed on the stand that PTL had mailed its original lifetime-partnership solicitation without taking his recommendation that the ministry wait until he had arranged a careful legal review.

The Bakker case unveiled the first family's lifestyle as prosecutors argued that the Bakkers personally profited from the tens of millions of dollars cascading in from lifetime partners. Bonuses had come out of lifetime-partnership accounts—contrary to PTL's claim that Bakker's pay originated in the Sunday church. Prosecutors produced a list of personal valuables that had earlier been drafted for the Bakkers' insurance company: it included a $45,000 diamond ring and two other rings each valued at $27,500—hardly the costume jewelry Tammy used to tell her fans she wore. James Taggart recalled his efforts in 1982 to give Bakker's Florida condo the "theatrical presence" Bakker had requested—plenty of mirrors and motorized drapes and a designer Christmas tree put together overnight that cost PTL $5,000. And he took the jury on a video-taped tour of the presidential suite in the Heritage Grand, stopping off for a glimpse of Tammy's sixty-foot-long closet.

Finance director Peter Bailey's written warnings of financial ca-tastrophe were damning to Bakker's cause. So was the govern-ment's eight-hour distillation of 130 broadcasts, videotape showing Bakker committing the very acts that prosecutors characterized as fraudulent. "I am sincere," he said in one 1984 clip, "I would not lie to you about anything."

Jessica Hahn would never be summoned to testify, but her specter hovered over the trial. Scott Furstman, the Los Angeles lawyer who helped Dortch execute the 1985 Hahn payoff, testified that he advised Dortch to fight Hahn's threatened lawsuit because her claim was legally frivolous. A solemn, contrite Dortch recalled from the stand Bakker's orders to resolve, once and for all, the problems that Hahn's threats were causing. Dortch said he had told Bakker how much PTL would have to spend. "His response was, 'I hate to give them anything. I hate to give them a dime, but do what you have to do to get it solved.' "

Dortch explained why Bakker's bonuses had always been so timely. Before board meetings David Taggart would tell Dortch how much money Bakker needed. Dortch would then pass the figure along to a cooperative board member. In notes he had made in the summer of 1987, which he drew from during his testimony, Dortch had written: "Jim told me once, 'As long as I pay the income tax, I can take what I want.' " Once, when Taggart tried to tell Bakker that he had spent all his bonus money, Bakker had answered back, "I must have it anyway."

Dortch invoked Bakker's enthusiastic private declaration that the lifetime partnerships were a money-raising gold mine. "He told me there's no limit to the amount of people we can offer these to because I can control crowds of people." Bakker believed he could use the airwaves to tell people when to come and when to stay away.

Bakker's lawyers struggled to mount a defense, and as none materialized the trial became for Bakker an exercise in self-inflicted humiliation, robbing him of what stature he might have recouped with his mass Christian audience. Only the radical fringe remained passionately at his side, a reminder that even the most outrageous cause can always find a few foot soldiers in modern day America. Harold Bender, a former assistant U.S. attorney, occasionally drew blood on cross-examination, but his co-counsel, Davis, a charming, chatty man outside the courtroom, seemed to ramble, incurring more of Judge Potter's wrath. (It would come as little surprise when Davis abruptly disappeared from the defense team at the trial's conclusion.)

The defense introduced its own videotapes of Bakker, but chose not to edit them—forcing the jury to endure pointless singing and chitchat. The tapes featured several of Bakker's favorite celebrity guests, as if the presence of singer Pearl Bailey, actor Gavin Mac-Leod of TV's "Love Boat" program, evangelist Robert Schuller, or even the so-often-run Billy Graham could somehow prove Bakker's innocence.

Judge Potter flashed his impatience with the stream of still-loyal PTL partners testifying to Bakker's good works and good intentions. After one woman claimed that Bakker had been "the most grossly underpaid man in America" Potter complained, "We have people coming in who know very little about what they're talking about."

On the twenty-first day, the drama climaxed with Bakker's appearance on the stand. He did well, at first. Relaxed, confident, and chatty as Davis lofted gentle questions, Bakker challenged the government's claim that PTL didn't have room to house the lifetime partners. In fact, he asserted, Heritage USA could accommodate as many as 211,000 donors—three times the capacity claimed by the prosecutors. To arrive at this stunning total, Bakker relied on about thirty buildings and a campground never completed—and assumed that the Towers, by then a favorite roosting spot for Heritage USA's birds, had also been completed. Bakker would never explain where PTL might have gotten the money to finish all that building without issuing even more lifetime partnerships. Bakker spoke in words reminiscent of his FCC testimony in 1979 and 1980: "You live by faith in God, not by fact. . . . You say, I'm going to build because I feel this is what God tells us to do."

On cross-examination, prosecutor Deborah Smith's accusatory questions did little to shake Bakker. By late afternoon it seemed Bakker would survive the cross-examination with a draw. But the government was lucky: Bakker had taken the stand on a Friday, and now prosecutors had the entire weekend to orchestrate their final challenge to the defendant. By Monday morning, Smith had embraced a more effective approach—less passionate, but still incredulous, shrewdly mapping out the conflict between Bakker's account of the facts and the facts themselves. Smith dismissed Bakker's tally of 211,000 spaces available for lifetime partners as a "very recent fabrication." As Bakker talked of managing by faith, she snapped, "How about truth? Did you tell [PTL's board] the truth about the financial condition of PTL before you told them you had faith?"

Smith, a thirty-six-year-old former reporter detailed from the Justice Department fraud section in Washington, drove the point home in her devastating closing argument. For years, she told the jury, Bakker had victimized his supporters with lies and the half-truths of which he was a "world-class master. . . . That's gone on too long. And it's your job to announce the truth to the world."

The defense's final pitch suffered at the hands of the meandering Davis, who complained at one point that the government had never introduced testimony about the pay given other ministers—information that the government then openly protested defense lawyers had themselves kept out of the record. With Davis's closing running long, the more effective Bender was forced to rush his argument (a pitch delivered so quietly that few reporters heard enough of it to report the next day). A few days later, when the jury finished its work, one juror dismissed the defense as a blend of sophistry, diversion, and theatrics.

Tammy Bakker had stayed away from the trial, apparently at the urging of her husband's lawyers, instead launching her tirades on Potter and the prosecutors from the airwaves, as if the battle for the hearts of the TV audience might make a difference in the courtroom. She now joined Bakker to sing songs of praise, read Scripture, and await the verdict in a courthouse conference room. A jarring buzz in Potter's court a few minutes before noon on October 5 announced that the jury had finished its work. They had deliberated for ten hours.

With the chamber packed with reporters, Bakker, by now reconciled to his fate, listened impassively as the jury verdict was read—guilty on the single count of conspiracy and all twenty-three counts of mail and wire fraud.

Minutes later, Potter stunned his audience with a blunt assessment of the PTL partners who testified for Bakker, the judge's words chiseling a sobering epitaph for a mass ministry that once seemed to hold such promise. "They really have what I would call the Jim Jones mentality. I mean, anything that he does is all right," Potter said, mentioning the minister who led the 1978 mass murder–suicide in Jonestown, Guyana. "I've seen these people up here, and they just think that he could walk on water."

Tammy emerged from the courthouse to sing "On Christ the Solid Rock I Stand," with backup vocals provided by a handful of supporters. "It's not over till it's over," she told the cameras, with a nervous smile that barely cloaked her pain. "I have a strong faith in God, and He will not let us down." A few hours later, Bakker, freed on bond to await sentencing, proclaimed his innocence once again.

The Bakkers retreated to their rented home in Orlando. Their struggling TV ministry, which had been taking in $100,000 a month, soon went dark, a victim, it was said, of dwindling cash flow.

On October 24, Bakker returned, accompanied by his daughter, Tammy Sue. Minutes after their entrance, a rainbow appeared in the sky outside the building. But Bakker's fantasy land lay behind, not ahead of him. Inside, Bakker told Potter he was sorry for those who had been hurt. "I have sinned, and I have made mistakes. But never in my life did I ever intend to defraud anyone." Prosecutor Jerry Miller, reading from a fund-raising appeal mailed to Bakker's supporters in the weeks before, cautioned Judge Potter that Bakker would be "right back at it as soon as he gets the chance"—unless he was sent away, far from the TV screen and his mailing list.

> A PTL employee who has asked that I not attribute the observation to, gave us the general theory of this case back long before trial. That is, that Mr. Bakker in the beginning was a person who loved people and used things, and that he evolved into a man, a ruthless man, who loved things and used people.

The halo over the building disappeared as Potter ignored a defense lawyer's suggestion that Bakker be put on probation, sent to Heritage USA, and given five years to complete his dream and fulfill his promise to partners. Instead, Potter sentenced the stoic Bakker to pay a $500,000 fine and spend forty-five years in prison, of which he will have to serve at least the first ten years. "He had no thought whatever about his victims, and those of us who do have a religion are ridiculed as being saps for money-grubbing preachers or priests."

Potter refused to delay Bakker's incarceration, sending Tammy Sue Bakker from the courtroom sobbing. Bakker spent the night in prison in Alabama, a way station for his new permanent home—a federal prison in Rochester, Minnesota, where he arrived during a driving snowstorm and was soon put to work cleaning toilets. The Taggart brothers, meanwhile, were dispatched to a comfortable prison in Alabama. David was sentenced to eighteen years and five months, James, seventeen years and nine months, and each was fined $500,000 and ordered to pay the taxes he had been accused of evading.

The weeks of courtroom drama had been a time of trial for Heritage USA as well. Stephen Mernick decided not to buy the complex for $65 million, explaining that a long-standing, unresolved Indian land claim in the area had prevented him from securing title insurance. Two days after his announcement, a hurricane expected to dissipate long before it neared Heritage USA blasted through Charlotte with ninety-mile-an-hour winds. The city was paralyzed, and Heritage USA battered. With Heritage drawing meager crowds, the bankruptcy trustee shut down the complex to all but the 450 families still living there. No buyer had been found by spring 1990.

The PTL drama was one that would never die, it seemed, and in early December prosecutor Jerry Miller obtained two new PTL indictments, each for perjury before the grand jury that had indicted Bakker, Dortch, and the Taggarts. Reverend Sam Johnson, the former Assemblies of God missionary and PTL missions director by whom Dortch felt betrayed, was accused of failing to tell the truth when he claimed not to remember where he had obtained $10,000 loaned to Dortch in 1984—money Dortch later gave Jessica Hahn. Johnson, still pastoring the remnants of Bakker's church and working with the remnants of the PTL television ministry, proclaimed his innocence and portrayed the indictment as the final vengeance of his one-time friend Dortch, who had testified before the grand jury that indicted Johnson.

After prosecutors presented their case in trial in April 1990,

Judge Potter directed a verdict of not guilty, agreeing with Johnson's attorney that the government had not proven perjury.

John Wesley Fletcher, the troubled one-time evangelist who had arranged Hahn's trip to Florida in 1980, was indicted based on contradictory testimony he'd given about his purpose in inviting Hahn to Florida—was his purpose all along to procure a woman for Bakker? In May 1990, Fletcher pleaded guilty to perjury and received three years' probation from Judge Potter. During the sentencing hearing, Potter was told that Fletcher was working as a roofer, had twice tried to commit suicide, and had taken an antidepressant drug before his first appearance before the grand jury.

Also expected to go to trial as early as summer 1990 was the class-action lawsuit brought on behalf of lifetime partners. At the center of that case is the conduct of PTL's two outside audit firms, particularly Laventhol and Horwath, whose annual audits PTL had used so effectively as badges of supposed financial integrity. Individual defendants in the case included Bakker, David Taggart, and board member Aimee Cortese, setting the stage for an awkward courtroom reunion.* Roe Messner, the loyal contractor who funneled PTL's money to Furstman for the Hahn payoff and who erected the buildings Bakker was supposed to be paying for with the lifetime partnership money, was also a defendant in the case. But in March 1990 Messner filed in bankruptcy court for Chapter 11 protection from his personal and corporate creditors, gaining at least temporary reprieve from the class-action case.

Dortch, who had been shrewd enough to plead and cooperate with the government, finally began serving his prison term in February in a so-called "Club Fed" prison at a Florida air force base—close to his wife and far from the harsh cold of Minnesota. In late April, just three days short of the third anniversary of his firing, Dortch won a reduction of his sentence from Potter. Instead of eight years, he now will serve no more than two and a half years. He'll likely be released from prison in early 1992, when he's sixty—about the same age Bakker will likely be upon his release.

*In early 1990, Rock Hill National Bank, which had helped PTL supporters finance purchases of lifetime partnerships, settled out of court in the lawsuit for $125,000.

Behind the prison gates in Rochester, Bakker kept a low profile, turning down regular requests for interviews as his lawyers awaited completion of a trial transcript—a necessary first step for filing his intended appeal. Tammy continued to minister each Sunday morning in Orlando to about 125 partners gathered in a former Tupperware distribution center.

After Bakker spent his fiftieth birthday in prison, his ministry in Florida dispatched a four-page letter written in Jim's hand. Bakker had bid Tammy and the kids a tearful good-bye a few days earlier, on Christmas day, he recalled in the letter: "I never felt so all alone in all my life. . . . The pain was almost more than I could bear." He was, he declared again, not guilty.

Bakker closed his letter with a request for prayers for those in prison in Rochester and around the world—and with words that seemed to say a prison's just a place for everyday folks:

> There are people here from all over the world, lawyers, medical doctors, druggist, corporation owners, sports figures, a mayor, a sheriff, the son-in-law of a former U.S. vice president, a U.S. presidential candidate, and yes drug dealers and members of organized crime. These are the people Jesus died for, many good people, some guilty, some not. Pray for revival inside here and out.
> "For all have sinned and come short of the Glory of God."

NOTES

The facts, quotations, and anecdotes that make up *Forgiven* are taken from an abundant collection of sources. These include hundreds of hours of interviews with Bakker's relatives, friends, and former employees between August 1987 and May 1989. I have also drawn from interviews and experiences that I had as I reported about PTL for the *Charlotte Observer* from 1984 to 1987.

I have been blessed with a bountiful documentary record. It includes materials amassed in my reporting for the *Observer* and by my colleagues, particularly Allen Cowan and John Wildman; transcripts of PTL broadcasts videotaped by the newspaper in 1984–87; PTL's publications, including books written by the Bakkers, fund-raising appeals, *Together* and *Action* magazines, and the *Heritage Herald* newspaper; the voluminous record of testimony and exhibits compiled by Federal Communications Commission investigators; the personal files of Roger Flessing from his first tour of duty at PTL; records of lawsuits, deaths, marriages, property ownership, and voter registration in Charlotte, NC, York, SC, Lancaster, SC, Muskegon, MI, Detroit, MI, Portsmouth, VA, Los Angeles, CA, and Santa Ana, CA; PTL documents made available by PTL officials after Bakker's departure in 1987; and depositions, exhibits, and testimony in the 1988 U.S. Bankruptcy Court trial of Jim Bakker and David Taggart.

Though these documents offer invaluable points of reference in the telling of the PTL story, they cannot resolve all the conflicting accounts in the story of Jim Bakker and his PTL ministry. I have attempted to rely principally on sources who have demonstrated an ability to recall events accurately, fairly, and insightfully. Where I believed that the source of my information was of special significance, I have identified it in the text or in a footnote.

I am thankful to those persons who have reviewed portions of my draft manuscript to identify any errors of fact. They include: George Bakker, Jon Buchan, Mark and Wanda Burgund, Dana and

Dave Cadwell, Jim Cobble, Al Cress, Roger Flessing, Bill Flint, John Gilman, Rolfe Neill, Jerry Ogg, Jr., Rich Oppel, Pat Robertson, John Stewart, Ed Stoeckel, and Alex Valderrama.

CHAPTER ONE

Among those interviewed by the author were Raleigh Bakker, Furnia Bakker, Norman Bakker, Dorothy Bakker, George Bakker, Marge Klages, Beverly Halgren, Charles "Lonnie" Irwin, Joan Saltsman (formerly Joan Bakker), Marlee Bakker, Bernard Ridings, Gary Reiben, Sonny Singer, Tony Kowalski, Ron Hughes, Daryle Hughes, Orville Johnson, Jr., Marlene Way, Steve Zarnas, Louis St. Louis (formerly Michael Zenone), Ana Zenone, Doris Summerfield (Jimmy's mother), Orville Johnson, Sr., Ruth Harms, Art Freeman, Denton "Hop" Moore, Bill Harrison, Sarah "Sally" Wickerink Hankins, Lou Meisch, Carl Burgess, Terry Gibson, Jim Borgeson, and Char Bonner. Thanks to Barbara Martin of the Muskegon County Museum.

2 "preservationists have rescued"
Details on the houses on Webster Avenue are taken from *Heritage Village Neighborhood,* a booklet produced by the Muskegon County Museum.

3 "doubted his own suitability"
When Joe Bakker posted signs on the hillside near his home bearing misspelled scriptural messages, one of his sons-in-law built a fire and paid one of Joe's grandsons to help torch the placards.

7 "wage earners"
Muskegon County: Harbor of Promise, Jonathan Eyler, Windsor Publications, 1986, p. 109.

"The one friend"
Move That Mountain, Jim Bakker with Robert Paul Lamb, Logos International, 1976, p. 8.

8 "At war's end"
Harbor of Promise, pp. 109–111.

9 "the woman he later married"
His first wife, Joan Bakker.

"spacious Dutch colonial home"
The house is located at 2332 Sanford Street. The Loescher House is located at 458 West Webster Avenue.

13 "Jim persuaded"
In a 1987 interview, Furnia Bakker told the author, "Well, Jim was the one that talked us into that house. . . . He loved big houses."

"wealthiest woman"
In *Jim and Tammy Bakker: The Real Story,* an unpublished 1986 manuscript written with Mel White, Bakker wrote, "I was a poor little kid from Muskegon. Martha was my Auntie Mame. . . . [She] would sweep into my life and make me feel good again."

14 "as a child"
Excerpt from a May 26, 1978, Jim Bakker interview with *Charlotte Observer* reporter Frye Gaillard.

15 "in its infancy"
The history of the Assemblies of God is recounted in *Anointed To Serve,* William W. Menzies, Gospel Publishing House, 1971. On p. 78, Menzies writes of the pre–World War I Pentecostal revivals from which the denomination was born in 1914.

> The Pentecostals . . . met the psychological needs of the people, providing in their music and worship for a high degree of participation and for emotional release. . . . To many who were frustrated by their circumstances in the present world the Pentecostal message gave a shining new hope, bursting with vitality and enthusiasm.

"he . . . spun records"
When he was sixteen years old, Bakker was told by a church deacon that he couldn't be a Christian and continue to change records at school dances. "Though my parents defended me, [the] deacon . . . demanded that I be kicked out of church for my sinfulness," Bakker wrote in *The Real Story.* Five days after the deacon chastised him, Bakker stopped working as a disc jockey, he wrote.

17 "a variety show"
Bakker's church buddies remember his arranging a small variety show at the Central Assembly of God too, spicing it up with his own imitation of the flamboyant Liberace.

22 "my brother, Bob"
This and the following quotes about Grandpa Bakker and the mantle are taken from the verbatim transcript of an October 11, 1985, staff meeting discovered in PTL files after Bakker's resignation. In the same meeting, Bakker suggested that his father also had ambitions to preach.

> Something that's not known and we don't tell it, but from what I can gather (and I've never really talked to my father about it), my father was called to preach. And he got up to preach and they made fun of him, and he never spoke again.

In a 1989 interview, Raleigh Bakker said he had no ambition to be a minister. At a church meeting during his early adult years, a sermon had flashed into Raleigh Bakker's mind as he sang choruses with fellow church members waiting for a church committee to end its private meeting. He was ready to deliver the sermon, but the committee emerged and Raleigh Bakker said nothing. He later mentioned the incident to his son, but, Raleigh Bakker said in 1989, he never suggested to Jim that he had been made fun of or been silenced.

23 "became the only thing"
Move That Mountain, pp. 14–15.

CHAPTER TWO

Among those interviewed by the author were Don Argue, John Phillipps, Arvid Kingsriter, Tom Byrtus, Bob Cilke, Sam Johnson, Peggy Elliott Webster, Barbara Flanagan, Wilbur Bell, and Gordon Churchill. I owe many thanks to head librarian Bob Jansen at the *Minneapolis Star-Tribune.*

25 "sleep through his classes"
In an October 1985 staff meeting, one of Bakker's deputies cited the hours Bakker spent praying in the Bible-college basement as evidence that God had led him from the very start.

26 "Without even thinking"
Move That Mountain, p. 18.

27 "hitch himself to a star"
During his second year at North Central, Bakker returned from a concert by organist E. Power Biggs and confided to roommate Bob Cilke that Biggs had offered him a job touring and introducing the organist at performances. Bakker decided against taking the job.

"spiritual mother"
In *The Real Story,* Tammy Bakker describes Fern Olson as the "spiritual mother" to both Bakkers. In the eighties, years after Fern's death from stomach cancer, Russell Olson moved to Heritage USA.

"simple, childlike trust in God"
Move That Mountain, p. 28.

28 "The Tea Room"
Bakker identifies the restaurant in his PTL books as the Fountain Room. Though named the Tea Room, it also went by the nickname the Fountain for the fountain located inside.

28 "long cigarette"
I Gotta Be Me, Tammy Bakker with Cliff Dudley, New Leaf Press, 1978, p. 47.

29 "I don't know why"
May 1978 interview with Gaillard.

30 "330 radio stations"
This description of the Oral Roberts crusade, as well as the 1953 dedication of the Minneapolis Evangelistic Auditorium and the 1959 Rock for Teens rally, are drawn from articles published in the *Minneapolis Star* and *Minneapolis Tribune.*

31 "He weighed 130"
I Gotta Be Me, p. 44. The Bakkers later identified the date of this first kiss as December 1, 1960.

"Tammy and I"
Move That Mountain, p. 23.

32 "I had no sooner"
I Gotta Be Me, p. 45.

"warning letter"
Had he known of the couple's plans, Raleigh Bakker said later, he never would have sent the letter. The letter and Raleigh Bakker's earlier confiscation of the gown left Jim feeling very hurt, Tammy wrote later.

33 " 'what's the key' "
Move That Mountain, pp. 27–28.

35 "unbelievable revival"
Move That Mountain, pp. 45–46.

36 "Come On Over"
In *The Real Story,* Bakker wrote, "I would shout the name of our first show on Channel 27 and kids would pour out of the makeshift bleachers and onto the steps of our little set."

CHAPTER THREE

Among those interviewed by the author were Hertha and Wiley Allen, Margie Carraway, Gordon Churchill, Barb Conti, John Gilman, Jerry Horstmann, Fred House, Bob and Laura Whyley, and Roger and Linda Wilson.

38 "Jim and Tammy Show"
After establishing themselves in Charlotte, the Bakkers gave the same name to their flagship broadcast at PTL.

39 "Our entire purpose"
Shout It from the Housetops, Pat Robertson with Jamie Buckingham, Logos International, 1972, pp. 188–89.

40 "Exaggeration . . . a pardonable sin"
In the world of traveling evangelists and, even more so, in the religious broadcasting industry, some refer to this practice jokingly as "evangelistically speaking" or "evang-elastically speaking."

"the holiness of God"
Shout It from the Housetops, pp. 215–16.

41 "faith healer Kathryn Kuhlman"
During Bakker's interview with Kuhlman, she had a word of knowledge that a woman was being healed. Later that day, as the tape was played on the air, a woman viewer telephoned to say she was the woman described by Kuhlman. Bakker was greatly impressed.

"experience, emotion, phenomena"
The Charismatics: A Doctrinal Perspective, John F. MacArthur, Jr., Lamplighter Books, p. 63.

43 "scraping together donations"
The Bakkers were capable of generosity, however. Tammy gave clothes to friends. Jim trimmed a hedge and hung pictures for his secretary, Hertha Allen. In 1971, the Bakkers gave Bob and Laura Whyley, friends, newlyweds, and new CBN arrivals, a bed, dining-room table, couch, and chairs that they no longer needed.

"a nervous breakdown"
Bakker's autobiography places this event in May 1969. In *The Real Story,* Bakker wrote that the birth of his daughter Tammy Sue in March 1970 ended his spell of dizziness, nausea, and depression.

"Problems loomed"
Move That Mountain, p. 78.

44 "She didn't want"
Charlotte Observer, July 9, 1978.

"fine or resign"
Bakker tells the story in *Move That Mountain,* p. 61.

45 "determined to expose"
In a 1987 interview, Horstmann attributed his cynicism to his own immaturity as a Christian. During Bakker's tenure at PTL, Horstmann apologized to Bakker for his conduct.

46 "A secretary who baby-sat"
The Bakkers could elicit steadfast loyalty and tireless dedication. Hertha Allen, twelve years older than Bakker, met Jim and Tammy when the couple spoke at her church. She befriended the couple when her daughter became a favored presence in the Bakkers' studio audience. Soon Allen, a gentle, nurturing woman whose husband fought fires for a living, was opening the Bakkers' mail at night and on weekends. She baby-sat and took care of the dogs. She delivered the dozen roses that Jim gave Tammy when she was hospitalized. Eventually, Jim convinced Robertson to put her on CBN's payroll.

It was a thrill to be a part of the excitement around the Bakkers, but Allen wasn't there for money or glory. She felt that she worked at CBN for the Lord, that to hear children come forward and say they had accepted Christ as their Saviour was payment in full.

"He threatened"
Later in his time at CBN, Bakker telephoned Horstmann to ask about a water heater that had been donated by a local businessman. As Horstmann remembered it, Bakker needed a new water heater at home and thought he was entitled to the appliance. Horstmann told him he would have to buy it if he wanted it. He never heard back from Bakker.

47 "things couldn't have been better"
Tammy showed less restraint than her husband in her autobiography, *I Gotta Be Me,* six years later. She blamed the Bakkers' troubles on the jealousy of other employees. "Pat was the kind of person I liked and yet disliked. One minute I would love him more than anything in the world, and the next minute I would dislike him for letting people manipulate him."

"the eighth day"
Move That Mountain, p. 106.

"God could not have comforted"
Move That Mountain, p. 108.

CHAPTER FOUR

Among those interviewed by the author were Jim Atkins, Sandy Barnard, Mike Cloer, Bill Flint, Larry "Phil" and Carolyn Hall, Tim Kelton, Reidy Lawing, Jim Moss, French O'Shields, Roger Flessing, Del Holford, Marsha Martin, Sam Orender, Syvelle Phillips, Paul Toberty, Alex Valderrama, and Stan Ditchfield.

49 "After being here"
Charlotte News, June 21, 1972.

50 "That praise story"
Move That Mountain, p. 93.

53 "began broadcasting"
At first, the new California ministry broadcast over Channel 46, a station licensed for Guasti in San Bernardino County. A few months later, Bakker and Crouch moved to another UHF station, Channel 40, which serves today as the flagship of Crouch's network of twenty full-power Christian TV stations.

"Robertson was fed up"
The Bakkers represented the bulk-erase order a different way in Tammy's autobiography, *I Gotta Be Me.* "Eight years of videotapes of the 'Jim and Tammy Show' that had brought thousands of boys and girls to Jesus [that could have been rerun for years] were erased. Satan really had a field day making certain that we would never return to CBN."

54 "they were sisters"
Tammy Bakker offers this description in *I Gotta Be Me,* p. 94.

"preferred to save money"
When Sam Orender called from Greenville, South Carolina, asking if Bakker wanted him to come to California, Bakker simply said, "If you feel like that's what the Lord would have you do." Orender came—and Crouch informed him the ministry couldn't afford to pay him.

"the pastor from Paul's"
I Gotta be Me, pp. 95–96.

56 "former PTL employee recalled"
Bakker offered a similar account in his confidential testimony to the Federal Communications Commission staff in 1979. Then, he said, he had waited "actually to the exact day" that Robertson asked before agreeing to allow tapes of his California show to be broadcast in Charlotte.

57 "conspiracy theory"
This scenario is developed in *Pat Robertson: The Authorized Biography,* John B. Donovan, Macmillan, 1988, pp. 108–9.

"bent the truth"
Bakker's autobiography, *Move That Mountain,* doesn't suggest that Bakker had any plans to establish a base in North Carolina. Instead, Bakker wrote that the Charlotte group had asked him to send tapes of his California broadcast, which they then alternated with "a local program . . . being produced through the efforts" of the Wheelers. According to the autobiography, Bakker agreed but told Charlotte that equipment troubles would delay the first shipment.

59 "Jim and I, who"
Ten Years of God's Miracles, booklet published by Trinity Broadcasting Network, p. 7.

63 "I was not actually"
Move That Mountain, pp. 151–52, 157. For Bakker, the transfer of power became neatly packaged testimony to his sound moral leadership. In fact, PTL would be hobbled by failure to pay bills on time throughout Bakker's tenure.

CHAPTER FIVE

Among those interviewed by the author were Phil and Ruth Egert, Henry Harrison, Robert Paul Lamb, and Bill Perkins.

65 "expensive-to-maintain buildings"
Move That Mountain, p.168.

66 "sister afternoon newspaper"
In a May 13, 1975, article, Bob Wisehart, then TV critic for the *Charlotte News,* described the admiration he found for Bakker, whom he described as equal parts evangelist, showman, and hard-headed businessman.

> Hero is not too strong a word to use to describe the way the people at the network feel about Bakker. Every time they talk about Bakker with strangers, it is nothing but praise.
> "I've seen him talk for almost twenty-four hours straight on telethons," said David Carver, an ex–disc jockey from Gainesville, Florida, who now handles promotions for the network. . . . "He never runs down."

67 "Newspapers, he explained"
Bakker was also worried they would make too much of his denominational affiliation. In a 1972 interview with a *Charlotte News* reporter, Bakker asked that he not be identified as a minister in the Assemblies of God for fear it might turn off members of his audience.

69 "There have been times"
Second Fiddle, Henry Harrison with Cliff Dudley, New Leaf Press, 1977, pp. 132–33.

70 "ready to publish"
Bakker had wanted Robertson's writer, Jamie Buckingham, to ghost his book too, but Buckingham was busy with *Daughter of Destiny,* his biography of Kathryn Kuhlman. Instead, the job fell to Lamb, a friend of Buckingham's.

71 "storybook-handsome"
Charlotte Observer, July 4, 1976.

72 "Osgood, Indiana"
PTL received these praise reports in 1982.

74 "I felt Jim"
I Gotta Be Me, p. 112.

"subsidized life-style"
When a business refused to allow a charge on a PTL American Express card because PTL had failed to pay its monthly bill, Bakker dispatched a terse memo to finance in March 1977. "I want the American Express paid the day the statement arrives (whether we have the money in the bank or not)." The finance office obliged.

77 "a Spanish version"
A dubbed translation of Bakker's show was considered less effective and less likely to take root in native soil.

78 "Jim Bakker is not"
Charlotte News, September 6, 1977.

"take a back seat"
From August 4, 1977, broadcast. A little more than a month earlier, in a June 28, 1977, broadcast, Bakker said, "Instead of me building and putting large sums of money here or there and building a kingdom and trying to, you know, maybe stash away for my rainy day, we believe in investing everything we have in the work of the Lord."

"And I am going"
August 4, 1977 broadcast. Bakker went on to say, "I believe the time is short. . . . I believe it is not time to build the retirement center and the other things."

79 "Talk negatively and"
From PTL transcript of Bakker's comments to his studio audience after his December 14, 1977, broadcast.

80 "a ministry in need"
On a visit to Charlotte before taking the PTL job, Perkins joined Bakker in a meeting with a Charlotte banker. Bakker wanted another $485,000 in short-term financing. PTL's past-due bills totaled $1.8 million. The banker refused the loan and warned that PTL was running on the edge.

82 "the role of victim"
In September 1977, the *Charlotte News* published a five-part series on PTL. The last few weeks of publicity have been "the hardest of my life," Bakker told the newspaper. "If I did not care for the souls of men and the people I believe it's helping, I would not continue. I would prefer a private life. I'm a very private, bashful person."

83 "I believe our partners"
July 20, 1977, broadcast.

"jewelry worth $8,500"
The value of the jewelry was subsumed in the $18,100 total for the category of household furnishings and other personal property, including jewelry.

85 "tempted to take him up"
Of course Robertson wouldn't have had Bakker. That wasn't Bakker's only deception. He claimed that he was "too busy to check up to see what ratings [CBN has] or what ratings we have." In fact, nine months earlier Bakker's staff had prepared a detailed comparison of the audiences of the two "Clubs," PTL and 700. The statistics sent to Bakker showed PTL with 230,000 households to CBN's 294,000. But PTL's audience had grown at a 105% clip over the previous year, CBN's at thirty percent.

86 "Scott complained"
For Scott, the issue was of practical concern. His station, KHOF, was under investigation. The Federal Communications Commission wanted to know if the station had spent donations on the same projects for which it had solicited money over the air—the very issue the FCC would soon pursue at PTL. Scott was refusing to cooperate with authorities. In his letter to Bakker, he alluded to the dispute.

> How do I tell you without furthering friction between us that there is no way that Faith Center in its current crisis with governmental reporting can let stand the implication that the funds you handled for us were not restricted but were gifts as you have indicated. Surely your accountant will tell you that restricted funds are restricted funds and not at all like undesignated funds.

Six years later, the FCC took away Scott's broadcast license.

87 "boosted Bakker's salary"
Five other executives—including three of Bakker's deputies on the board—also got higher pay.

CHAPTER SIX

Among those interviewed by the author were Allen Cowan, Frye Gaillard, Bob Manzano, and F. Brooks Sanders.

92 "Really this whole thing"
From a May 1978 interview with Gaillard.

92 "a very appealing thing"
From a transcript of private comments by Bakker to two representatives of a leasing company whom he was showing around the grounds of Heritage USA on July 7, 1978. Pat Robertson had announced in early 1976 that he planned to open a seminary and radio-TV school in Virginia Beach, and Oral Roberts already had such a school in Tulsa.

93 "People talk like"
From a May 1978 interview with Gaillard.

94 "really creating money"
Bakker was either out of touch or less than honest with his supporters. On June 2, 1978, Bakker told his studio audience that he wasn't interested in borrowing money. "I don't believe God wants us to borrow . . . I believe He wants us to pay cash so PTL will be a haven of rest and debt-free when the time comes of financial lack in this country." Two weeks later, PTL's board authorized a search for long-term financing, and Bakker signed a formal agreement with a loan broker seeking the $50-million loan. When Bakker resigned in 1987, PTL's Heritage USA property was heavily mortgaged, making it more difficult for PTL to survive the severe drop in donations prompted by the Bakker scandal.

"You may not like"
From Roger Flessing's handwritten notes of the meeting.

"personnel director was let go"
The PR man was later rehired.

96 "It's been a policy"
From a November 30, 1978, interview with Allen Cowan, then of the *Charlotte Observer.*

97 "The richer you get"
From a PTL transcript of comments made by Bakker after his June 2, 1978, broadcast.

"I believe the trumpet"
from a PTL transcript of comments made by Bakker after his June 14, 1978, broadcast.

100 "not simply cash flow"
Bakker's high-crisis appeals had raised $5.7 million in July, nearly three times more than PTL had ever received in that month. As soon as the money came in, Bakker spent it.

101 "he, not Manzano,"
Bakker later told FCC investigators that he had taken the trip when he learned of continuing problems with PTL's missions. Robert Manzano told the investigators a different story: Bakker, depressed and under tremendous pressure in Charlotte, wanted to get out of town for a vacation.

Bakker's secretary had collected a stack of travel brochures. Asked for his advice, Manzano suggested a trip to Bermuda. Instead, Bakker—who had never before left the North American continent—decided to go around the world. Bakker insisted Manzano stay behind and help Moss run PTL, Manzano told the FCC.

The pressure on Bakker included complaints from Owen Carr, then president of WCFC, Channel 38, a Christian TV station carrying Bakker's show in Chicago. In his letter of August 18, 1978, Carr shared the criticism he was beginning to receive. Viewers were complaining that Bakker's show was getting frivolous and lacked spirituality, that Bakker was getting arrogant and raising too much money, and that the " 'PTL Club' is cutting back on the 'ministry' to do things for which Jim has no calling."

> For the first time since we have had you on Channel 38, we are hearing people say they would rather watch "700 Club" than "PTL Club" . . . I know it hurts to receive a letter like this . . . [Viewers are calling with] questions about why "PTL Club" has lost its spiritual vitality.

102 "Manzano arrived"
Bakker told the FCC he was surprised that Manzano had come all the way to Singapore when he knew McAlister wasn't going to be there; he only wanted Manzano to bring the $50,000 check. In reply, Manzano said he could simply have wired the check instead of spending thousands on his airfare, if he had been invited only to deliver the check and not to salvage Bakker's reputation as well.

"I said 'Dr. Cho' "
Bakker testimony to FCC, pp. 1355–56.

103 "Bakker hired one man"
That man, Donald Barnhouse, Jr., later described how he was hired in a letter to Flessing.

> [Bakker] walked over to talk to the studio audience and told them that he felt God had given him the man to "head the new college," but that he wasn't announcing the name right then since the person properly needed to pray about it. But he smilingly looked around at me as he said this and caught my eye. The studio audience . . . was in no doubt about what was going on.

In a second letter to Bakker, Barnhouse pressed the PTL president to explain his firing.

> I would like to know the real reason for your change of heart toward me, from January 5th when you said that God had told you to ask me to join you, to June 19th or 20th when you decided to let me go, without ever having exchanged thirty seconds conversation with me personally in the time between. I was told by others that you had decided I was not spiritual. How could you have decided that? If you

have some fault to find, why did I never hear of it from you or my superiors?

109 "another side of the man"
Gaillard also described Bakker in other, unflattering terms:

> He is also preoccupied by the physical trappings—by satellite termi-
> nals and cross-shaped office buildings he designs himself. They are
> crucial ingredients in his total vision of PTL, and when that vision is
> criticized, belittled, or even vigorously questioned, he instantly as-
> sumes the stance of a martyr—his instinctive compassion for others
> replaced by his own defensiveness.

113 "firing Manzano"
Manzano announced his resignation at a press conference at his home October 24, 1978. Manzano lied and said he was not being forced out. He had, he said, cleared up any of Bakker's suspicions that he was to blame for PTL's troubled overseas missions. "I love the man. There is no man I love more."

For his part, Bakker released a statement saying he had accepted the resignation with "deep regret. . . . I count [Bob] a very valuable friend and co-worker and look forward to working with him on projects to further the Kingdom of God in the future."

" 'have been lied to' "
Perkins wasn't the only executive concerned about PTL's treatment of its creditors. In an August 29, 1978, memo to fellow executives, Alex Valderrama wrote:

> I am appalled and embarrassed at the manner in which we have
> conducted business in this year of 1978. Our creditors have a better
> chance of getting their money back in Las Vegas. It is not our credibil-
> ity that is at stake, it is our souls at Judgment Day.

114 "those hungry children"
On his trip, Bakker visited Calcutta, India, where heavy rains had caused serious flooding. "As tears streamed down my face, I cried, 'Oh Lord, please make it possible for us to do more,' " Bakker said later. When he had arrived at a stopover in Brussels, Belgium, Bakker later told his staff, "the culture shock . . . was so great all I could do in the airport was stand there and cry and cry."

Bakker was scheduled to stop over in Brussels before continuing his trip. At a hotel there, Bakker pitched a fit that Phil Egert hadn't booked the presidential suite. Egert arranged a switch. When Bakker arrived in the presidential suite—with its leather sofas, several interior levels, and a plaque establishing that the suite had been decorated personally by Gucci—Bakker told his staff he hadn't needed all of this. A day and a half later, the entourage left. Its tab for the stay was about $7,500.

Months later, after Bill Perkins told the story to an ABC reporter,

Bakker called Perkins to complain. Bakker supplied another version of events.

> Jim said he was so tired after leaving India that he didn't even pay attention to the hotel nor the room. . . . He said that the staff had made all the reservations for him and he paid no attention to the room.

Perkins didn't tell Bakker that Flessing, Bakker's traveling companion, had told him that Bakker had refused the room that had been reserved for him.

115 "$200,000 donated house"
Bakker said that he had asked the donors—Harry and Juda Ranier of Prestonburg, Kentucky—to give the money they were going to spend on the house to PTL's college instead, but they had refused. The couple wanted to give him the house, but he declined, he claimed. It wouldn't be right and he couldn't afford the taxes, he said; so the Raniers gave the house to PTL for Bakker's use. Bakker's claim was strange, the *Observer* pointed out, since Bakker's monthly tax-free housing allowance of eight hundred dollars could have easily paid the home's $187-a-month tax bill.

117 "Valderrama . . . announced"
Three months earlier, in his memo to fellow executives, Valderrama bluntly talked of his revulsion at working

> with so called 'peers' who are here only as status seekers and exploit-ers. I am tired of continually combating their deadly corporate games and observing their selfish and insincere manipulation. . . .
>   Some of my peers and I have, for the last three years, attempted and in some cases, successfully helped in the development of this organiza-tion; but it appears only futile, and I am beginning to see the decline and fall of the PTL Television Network.

Valderrama was more tactful in his December 4, 1978, resignation letter. To it, he attached his philosophical thoughts on furthering the Gospel. At one point, he touched on the chilling news of nine hundred deaths that had come from Guyana two weeks before.

> Artists and writers of any culture are the ones who first pick up signs of spiritual anguish. They are more sensitive than the rest of humanity to the world about us. These men suffer and express our common pain. They hold the mirror up to nature and to man. . . .
>   The artists portray man as a being who creates and clings to illusions in order to avoid facing the absurdity of reality. The writers have written of the need for illusions and the tragedy when the illusions collapse, as they must, under the pressure of reality. *Modern tragedy is not heroic, it is pathetic. Its central character is not a hero, but a victim.* . . . (The Rev. Jim Jones and his followers fell victim to their illusions)
>   . . . My desire is to reach out and put into motion the creative talents the Lord has given me. . . . I must try to reach my God given potentials to help sound a clear note to the world.

CHAPTER SEVEN

Among those interviewed by the author were Forbes Barton, Larry Bernstein, Jim Moss, and Ed Stoeckel.

120 "finding ways to raise money"
Some inside the ministry preferred PTL's early reliance on God; if He wants us to succeed, they thought, He will provide money. Marsha Martin, the first employee hired by Martha Wheeler, was one of those disturbed by the shift to gift offers for donors. She believed that gimmickry would raise money for any organization, even one that lacked God's anointing. Martin feared that PTL would find itself worrying about ways to raise money instead of taking care to listen to God. A few weeks after Bakker's June 1974 telethon, she quit.

121 "a truth together"
On this January 26, 1979, broadcast, Bakker reeled off statistics showing all that PTL had done: 443,640 calls into PTL's twenty-four-hour phone system, eleven thousand calls made by follow-up pastors, more than sixty thousand Bible correspondence-study courses mailed out, nearly 1.5 million partner gifts mailed, sixteen million letters mailed to partners, another 950,000 received back, more than 630 seminars taught to an average audience of one hundred, and more than eight thousand inmates sent salvation packets.

122 "proposal for a Cyprus transmitter"
PTL's $56,000 was among the $74,000 spent by Malki's ministry on travel and temporary radio broadcasts to the Middle East while it sought to find and secure the transmitter. Eventually, Malki chose to begin TV broadcasts on a TV station in Lebanon owned by CBN. He ended his effort to erect the radio transmitter.

"Like Bill Perkins"
In a letter to Bakker, PTL's vice presidents, and a new committee of elders, Perkins had belittled the explanations Bakker offered for PTL's failure to make good on its promises on foreign missions.

> The ministry has not grown "so fast that we can't keep up with it!" Nothing grows faster than management will let it! . . .
> I soon learned, after coming to PTL, that when people in high positions don't know or understand basic management concepts, they tend to spiritualize success as being "God's hand," and failure as being the devil or human error—"someone else's." . . .
> When God expects a miracle, He does it Himself. When He works through a man, He gives him the plan and allows ample time for preparation and planning and construction.

122 "master salesman"
Bakker had called him "the finest salesman in the world," Moss later told federal investigators.

"questioned his veracity"
Moss's moral rectitude was questioned as well. At one point, someone anonymously sent Moss's wife, now his ex-wife, a tape recording of her husband talking on his car phone with a beauty-contest winner who had appeared on Bakker's broadcast. It was one of those moments in which life at PTL became indistinguishable from a soap opera.

123 "I told him."
Jim Moss's 1979 testimony to the FCC staff, p. 931.

125 "Sunday-ghetto shows"
Among the network's biggest attractions were the weekly broadcasts of Oral Roberts, Jerry Falwell, Rex Humbard, and Robert Schuller. PTL produced Tammy's half-hour show on being a Christian woman, the "PTL Club," an hour of Bible teaching, and a music show hosted by a PTL staff member.

126 "heard only Bakker's version"
Observer stories were picked up by the wire services, but the news services typically shortened and sensationalized the stories. Sometimes they wrote errors into them, giving Bakker more cause for complaint.

"would not acquiesce"
Later, Bakker blamed a PTL lawyer for his own refusal to cooperate. The man "was very paranoid about everything. He thought there were Communists outside the gates at times. I think he had an emotional problem," Bakker told investigators.

127 "consumed Bakker's attention"
PTL went to court to resist the FCC in 1979. The effort failed. That summer, a US district-court judge dismissed the ministry's lawsuit. As he listened to PTL lawyers present their case, the judge scoffed and laughed at their arguments, according to the *Observer* account.

"$350,000 to underwrite"
Jim Bakker's testimony to the FCC staff, p. 1583. "We felt we needed to be honorable. I was not willing to live the rest of my life saying that you didn't give one dollar to Korea."

129 "This corporation has"
Charlotte Observer, July 22, 1979.

130 "Jim said he was referring"
From Bill Perkins's letter to his attorney, Stu Mitchell, undated, apparently written in summer 1979.

131 "I have never met"
Moss's FCC testimony, p. 877.

132 "Bakker's top priority"
As Moss predicted, Bakker denied this assertion in his testimony, saying
that "winning souls is the most important project to me"

"magazine captured the changes"
In his interview with *Christianity Today,* Bakker vented his frustration with
the religious press. "The Christian press picks up material that was in error
when it went into the paper here—half-truths mixed with lies—and then
they go with the same spirit as publishers who are atheists and whose
reporters are Jewish. All that is repeated in a Christian magazine as being
gospel truth."

The complaint was directed in part at the *Observer:* reporter Allen
Cowan was Jewish; the year before, publisher Rolfe Neill, a Presbyterian
who considered himself an agnostic, had written that he didn't know if
there was a God.

Two Charlotte Jewish leaders took offense and accused Bakker of foster-
ing anti-Semitic stereotypes.

Bakker then denied making the statement, saying that the comment was a
misquote taken out of context. But the interviewer had taped Bakker, and
the recording confirmed the quote's accuracy. The day after his denial,
Bakker wrote to the *Observer* to explain that he had been voicing concerns
about specific individuals, not a people. "I can't imagine that I said it, but if
there are recordings, it is obvious that it was said. I am not above making
mistakes, but there has never been any intention to privately or publicly
embarrass or offend the Jewish community. So I do apologize."

The controversy was over quickly, but it had illuminated Bakker's
willingness to deceive and his rage at those who found fault with him.
Usually, his distortions were subtle enough to escape such embarrassment.
This time, a tape recorder had trapped him.

133 "prosperity gospel"
In *The Big Three Mountain-Movers,* Jim Bakker with Robert Paul Lamb,
Logos International, 1977, pp. 48–50, Bakker presented the central lesson
of PTL's success.

> Decide on what you need. Is it a house? A solution to a problem? A
> healing? Money? Salvation of a loved one? Maybe you just want to
> lose weight.
>   The Bible tells us clearly we can have "whatsoever we say." . . .
> I've seen God work some unbelievable miracles in supplying the
> needs of His people when they step out in faith. . . .
>   Some people think you needed plenty of money in the bank before
> you can begin to operate in faith. I never have. PTL had no collateral
> when we began the Heritage Village project. All we had were some
> rented studios and faith in God.
>   Faith is not something you can reason out in your mind.

137 "average bank balance"
In his January 1979 letter to Bakker, PTL's vice presidents, and a new committee of elders, Perkins challenged similar statements by Bakker in a local TV interview.

> Jim [implied] . . . it would have been ridiculous for PTL to divert $300,000 from the committed missions projects to pay ministry bills, etc., since that amount only represented about one day's deposit. He failed to say, however, that at one point we needed twenty such "one day deposits" ($6 million) to pay *past due* bills. . . .
> I know Jim has said "some do while others criticize." However, when one does all he can to point out deficiencies that *must* be changed, and he is totally ignored, then they forfeit their right to stand above criticism. "Evil triumphs when good men are silent." Remember, the Old Testament prophets weren't popular either!

145 "to rejoin PTL's staff"
Bakker later confirmed for the FCC that Ed Stoeckel had been asked to resign and that he had told a PTL staff meeting that Herb Moore, not Stoeckel, had improved PTL's finances.

"severance-pay settlement"
In his sworn affidavit to the FCC, Moore wrote that he had been entitled to only two weeks' severance, or $1,700, when he was dismissed, and he didn't consider PTL's ten thousand dollars to be severance pay but a payment in exchange for attorney Midlen's appearance. When Moore got PTL's settlement check, the total was not ten thousand dollars, but slightly more than seven thousand dollars. Moore was told that PTL now called the settlement severance pay and had deducted taxes from the total.

Later that year, Moore sought to renounce the affidavit, which the FCC investigators had drawn up after a conversation with Moore and which Moore had then signed. Moore had been hospitalized with heart problems at the time, he said, and his "thought patterns" were not functioning properly. He had also been upset at the time that PTL had failed to correct the impression that he was the source of PTL's financial problems.

"not consider employing"
Herb Moore would reappear at Bakker's side in 1988 as Bakker struggled to start a new ministry in Charlotte.

148 "back to work"
Stoeckel and his staff considered a move into an office building in south Charlotte once occupied by Exxon. During a bus tour one day, Stoeckel and Roger Wilson made a pitch to board members to buy the office building instead of finishing the pyramid-shaped World Outreach Center. As the bus passed the Exxon building, Bakker stood up and declared, "But we're moving to the Total Living Center and we're going to complete the pyramid." With those words, Stoeckel's proposal was dead. Shortly after, Stoeckel left PTL.

CHAPTER EIGHT

Among those interviewed by the author were Jean Albuquerque, Greg Flessing, Kathy Flessing, Don Hardister, Gary Paxton, Karen Paxton, and Gary Smith.

151 "spending time in Nashville"
In *The Real Story,* Tammy Bakker recalled this era of her life:

> At last I was out from under the load of daily television and full-time child care. Life was fun for me again. My friends and I stayed up late at night in the recording studio. We worked hard, but we laughed and cried a lot. I enjoyed those intimate times together. I got so I hated going back home again.

153 "an uneducated trivialization"
In his August 1978 letter to Bakker complaining about changes in PTL's direction, Owen Carr, president of Chicago's WCFC, Channel 38, wrote that his station received a "floodtide of complaints" whenever Tammy hosted Bakker's show. "She may do very well hosting the Tammy Faye show, but the "PTL Club" needs the guiding hand of a mature man. Why not use Jim Moss, Roger, [or] Henry . . . when you can't host the program?"

155 "by themselves"
In a 1989 interview with the author, Gary Paxton said that a PTL employee was with him and Tammy whenever they worked in his studio.

156 "despite the claims"
In *Run to the Roar,* Tammy Bakker with Cliff Dudley, New Leaf Press, 1980, p. 99, Tammy stated she no longer needed drugs to fly. "I knew I could not write this book unless I was totally honest. I felt like taking the pills to fly [was] . . . nothing but a crutch. The only time I ever took them was when I flew."

157 "steadily converted many members"
By the late seventies, some staff members had objected to the charismatics' rising influence in the hospital. In court documents, three doctors who opposed what they regarded as the domination of a "cult group" complained that they had been forced off the staff. The doctors said that Gross performed "exorcisms"—a measure of the suspicion between the secular world and Christians who believe in divine healing.

"The Bible"
Los Angeles Times, December 17, 1977. Details of the routine of patients in the program are drawn from the same article.

160 "a noncommittal position"
In a draft of the board minutes for February 12, 1981, Bakker is quoted

as saying, "The media appreciated Jim's being a minister, not a politician, in the election [presidential]. That gave us a new dimension. All over there is a deep respect for PTL that we have not had."

162 "one of ten children"
Most of the biographical details of Fletcher's life here are drawn from the reporting of *Charlotte Observer* reporter John Wildman.

"the con artist"
From author's interview of Phil Egert, Bakker's former administrative assistant, who briefly worked for Fletcher.

164 "On Labor Day"
On his "victory day," as he called it, Bakker found a divine endorsement. "Three days ago, I received the occupancy permit for this building . . . and I've cried almost nonstop ever since," Bakker said. "It was like God Himself said, 'It's over, the battle has been won.'"

"flew to Acapulco"
PTL paid a travel agency $4,139 for expenses that included the Egerts' airfare. The IRS would later include the money in its tally of the millions of dollars that it believed the Bakkers took from PTL above what would have constituted reasonable compensation.

166 "cool, classy, and even"
The reporter was Louise Lione of the *Observer*.

"would have been shocked"
Taggart's misleading claims of family money were reminiscent of the impressions Bob Manzano had cultivated among his colleagues at PTL several years before.

167 "bizarre story about"
The ghostwriter later denied making any such statement. As Smith tells it, Bakker's response was to chew the ghostwriter out. In April 1986, the ghostwriter wrote to Bakker,

> Even though I don't hear from you anymore, I want you to know my love for you has not diminished one bit! I don't know what is going on there, but someone keeps telling the paper to call me and I'll give them the info they need to destroy you. Jim, I'll die before I would ever betray you. Someone there is out to get you . . . I still am trying to find out what I did that you have totally rejected me."

168 "He sent a copy"
A few days later, one of Bakker's secretaries called, telling Smith that Jim wanted to talk to him. Smith drove over to Heritage Village. Bakker was busy when he arrived, so Smith sat down to wait. One of Bakker's secretaries reassured him. "Hey, everything's OK."
As Smith tells it, he was afraid that Bakker would talk him out of

leaving. After a moment's thought, he got up and walked out of the office. He didn't tell anyone where he was going, and he didn't come back.

169 "we've straightened them out"
In the later, unpublished *Real Story,* Tammy acknowledged the make-believe in this article. "Most of the article was true. . . . But our marriage was not 'ideal' as the article implied."

CHAPTER NINE

Among those interviewed by the author were John Wesley Fletcher, Jessica Hahn, and Don Hardister.

175 "on his houseboat"
The staff member refused to comment on the matter in 1989.

176 "the Palmdale hospital"
In *The Real Story,* Tammy Bakker says that Fred Gross had arranged for her to get a job and take classes in nursing. The unpublished 1986 manuscript describes the Hawaii marital crisis without mentioning the Bakkers' April 1980 crisis and counseling. Jim Bakker wrote in the manuscript, "Tammy had a perfect right to be angry with me. I had failed my wife in so many different ways. At the heart of it all, however, was my failure to communicate."

178 "The author was Tammy"
Unlike Flessing, Roger and Linda Wilson remember Bakker identifying the author of the letter as Spurr. Spurr, who would return to run his company in Orlando, has declined comment on the matter.

181 "to enhance security"
As a national TV personality, Bakker had some cause to be concerned about his safety and that of his family. There were occasional threats against the Bakkers over the years, and after his resignation, police would learn that the kidnappers of a York County woman had considered kidnapping Tammy Sue Bakker until they had realized how well she was guarded. To some of his security guards, however, Bakker's morbid preoccupation with security seemed extreme.

"Security guards changed"
The work offended the guards and made it hard for Bakker's security chief, Don Hardister, to keep good employees. Bakker, frustrated that his pool wasn't cleaner, his driveway tidier, his yard more handsome, even surprised Hardister one day by placing the household security staff under the supervision of the head housekeeper.

184 "on Lake Wylie"
Chappell's letter was written nearly a year before the Bakkers' move to
Tega Cay.

187 "Fletcher to fill Tammy's place"
More likely than a permanent job as Bakker's co-host would have been
a more prominent position for Fletcher on the program during his appearances at PTL one week each month.

188 "Dortch decided to dismiss"
Dortch ordered an envelope containing the accusations of homosexuality
against Fletcher sealed and kept in Fletcher's file in the Assemblies of God
office in Carlinville, Illinois.

"What are you going"
In his 1989 *Penthouse* article, Fletcher claimed that he had told Dortch
specifically about Bakker's homosexuality and consumption of wine.
Dortch, he said, was uninterested. "This is not the time to be pointing the
finger at others, John."

189 "and began masturbating"
In *The Real Story,* Bakker lists the prohibitions the church imposed on him
as he grew up in Muskegon. In the middle of the list, after "having
'unclean thoughts' " and before "having un-Christian friends" was masturbation.

CHAPTER TEN

Among those interviewed by the author were Frank Marklin, Jeff Park,
and Porter Speakman.

192 "Bakker seemed tired"
The Bakkers had already enjoyed PTL's generosity the weekend before.
They had flown to Atlanta with David Taggart, stayed overnight, and
returned with $5,200 in personal purchases, according to an IRS audit.
The IRS later concluded that PTL had picked up the tab for the three at
a cost of more than six thousand dollars. A few weeks later, the Bakkers
would leave for a working vacation in Hawaii, one year after their disastrous marital crisis there.

"dined at Cafe Eugene"
PTL had served no food at the earlier staff party.

193 "won't believe this one"
Bakker contented himself with the Somerset, however. In late 1983, he
would give the boat to PTL during a church service. The boat was taken

to Heritage USA, ostensibly for use by the church youth but soon the houseboat returned to the dock at Bakker's house where it would remain.

194 "comply with federal tax"
Details on Franklin's tax advice are taken from interviews with Roger Flessing.

196 "the Upper Room"
Work began after the Bakkers led a delegation to Jerusalem to collect drawings and photographs of the original Upper Room. PTL estimated that the two-story, five-thousand-square-foot building would cost about $180,000. Dedicated on July 4, 1982, the Upper Room cost nearly twice that much.

"People need to learn"
Together, December 1982.

197 "$90,000 a year"
Gross was put on a consulting fee of one thousand dollars a week beginning in July 1981, one of several financial arrangements between the psychologist and PTL.

198 "People That Love center"
A few weeks earlier, President Reagan had appealed to Bakker and other church leaders to take the initiative to solve human problems. Bakker came back and asked his staff what they could do. The love center was the result.

201 "One of the things he said"
From the transcript of a July 20, 1983, meeting with officials from the Evangelical Council for Financial Accountability.

"taken aback"
As one of Bakker's employees remembered, when Tammy saw her reconstructed husband, his face still bruised from surgery, she told him, "You look like your brother Bob." Bakker answered, "Bob? He's dead." "I know," Tammy said.

202 "If it got permission"
FCC rules prohibited license holders from profiting from the sale of a station if they sold it under a cloud of misconduct.

"founded in 1966"
Historical details on the David Livingstone Missionary Foundation are taken from "Tulsa's Golden Missionary," a series of reports broadcast by KTUL-TV in Tulsa, Oklahoma, in 1985.

203 "not been PTL's first choice"
Ironically, the David Livingstone Missionary Foundation later sold station WJAN to Trinity Broadcasting Network, the TV ministry run by Paul Crouch.

203 "Full Gospel Business Men's"
This group, formed by Californian Demos Shakarian in 1951, describes itself as a worldwide evangelistic fellowship of Christian businessmen. It offered its members—including many Catholics and members of main-line Protestant churches—a regular forum for Pentecostal prayer and testimony outside the walls of Pentecostal and charismatic churches. In December 1978, Bakker recommended that Shakarian become a PTL board member, and Shakarian attended an April 1979 board meeting as an advisor. Minutes for the meeting end with Shakarian's appointment to the board. He soon changed his mind and stepped down from the board.

204 "The majority gave"
The four were Mark Fowler, chairman, appointed by President Reagan in 1981; James Quello, appointed by President Nixon in 1974 and reap-pointed by Reagan in 1981; Stephen Sharp, a 1982 Reagan appointee; and Mimi Dawson, a 1981 Reagan appointee.

205 "eight strident pages"
Fogarty had been appointed in 1976 by President Ford, Rivera in 1981 by Reagan.

205–06 "substantial and material questions"
Bernstein didn't have to meet the tougher standard for conviction on a criminal charge—guilt beyond a reasonable doubt.

206 "minutes made no mention"
In April 1982, Dortch had asked the board's previous recording secretary to change her minutes so that they no longer identified those who made motions in board meetings. He also asked her to stop mailing copies of the completed minutes to board members. Unhappy with Dortch, she resigned three weeks later.

"attorney was not needed"
Six years later, a federal grand jury would identify this as the first overt act in an alleged conspiracy by Bakker and Dortch to continue lavish and extravagant life-styles at PTL's expense.

CHAPTER ELEVEN

Among those interviewed by the author were Jay Babcock, Mark Bur-gund, Jim Cobble, Al Cress, Sam Johnson, Richard Robbins, Robert Spence, Juleen Turnage, Doug Wead, and Thomas Zimmerman.

212 "I'm so pleased"
State Journal-Register of Springfield, Illinois, July 14, 1980. The pastor Bakker was referring to was Bernard Ridings, who took over the Central Assembly of God in Muskegon in 1960, after Bakker had left for Bible college.

213 "Since that meeting"
April 9, 1986, letter from T. W. Wilson to Mrs. John C. Fosgate of Winter Park, Florida.

"three-page article"
TV Guide, March 5, 1983. Graham named Robert Schuller, Oral Roberts, Pat Robertson, and Jerry Falwell as among those he admired.

214 "A smattering of partners"
Because reporters Cowan and O'Neill could be recognized, my editors asked me to attend the day's show to note any comments made by Bakker. I sat in the back, discreetly scribbling notes while Bakker talked.

"actively discouraging pastors"
Eventually, Fletcher would prevail upon Phil Egert, then a member of his staff, to ask Richard Dortch for permission to preach again at PTL and to halt all efforts to hinder Fletcher's business on the revival circuit. Without explanation, Dortch told Egert that Fletcher couldn't return to preach. But Dortch sent a memo to PTL staff members saying that they were not to talk about any minister who had been at Heritage USA. Egert would later feel that Fletcher had taken advantage of his reputation to try to rebuild his tarnished ministry.

219 "a detailed look"
To generate these statistics, PTL randomly selected 3,241 respondents to an October 1985 PTL questionnaire sent to 450,000 partners.

222 "had heard rumors"
Account of Zimbalist's frustration from author's interviews with Doug Wead.

228 "fastest-growing denominations"
In 1987, the Assemblies of God reported that it had 2.1 million adherents, having doubled its size in the preceding ten years. That total made it the tenth-largest Protestant denomination and the home church to about one of every four Pentecostals in the country. Worldwide, where membership in the denomination was growing even faster, 16.3 million of an estimated 75 million Pentecostals belonged to the Assemblies of God.

CHAPTER TWELVE

Among those interviewed by the author were Don Barcus, Jim Barger, Dana Cadwell, Lloyd Caudle, Grace Cosenpino, Rick Rathbun, Walter Richardson, and Terry Zinger.

238 "steep fees"
The access to cable systems wasn't entirely free. In 1987, PTL paid about $2.4 million a year, some of it fees to cable systems and some of it in personnel, marketing, and related costs. The network offered enough revenue to offset the costs. In 1982, Bakker had reversed his earlier decision to charge nothing for airtime, and by 1986, PTL was drawing $4.3 million in gross receipts from the evangelists whose programming it carried and from limited commercials it broadcast.

"discovered Jim and Tammy"
America also got to know Pat Robertson. PTL's satellite network remained second to CBN's, which had access to at least twice as many households by cable. By fall 1988, CBN claimed access to 43 million households.

"a second path"
In 1985, for instance, cable subscribers in the city of Charlotte paying for expanded service could watch Jim and Tammy Bakker on three channels—the PTL network and independent broadcast stations in Charlotte and Washington, D.C., from which PTL purchased airtime.

239 "won its full claim"
The jury reached its decision in just sixty-five minutes. In a pretrial deposition given months before, Bakker had said that he knew only secondhand about the disputed contract. On the air, Bakker complained that the Ohio company "had represented to me personally," as well as to his staff, that the contract merely kept PTL's place in line without binding the ministry until PTL chose to make a payment.

> Money that is so difficult for me to raise, that I have to give a quarter of a million dollars of it to a company that misrepresented to my people. Now the law's on their side because we were foolish and we signed an agreement. We should not have done so. It's our fault, really when you get down to the bottom line . . . but we trusted. . . . I want to be honorable. I always want to pay all my bills. . . . You know, I trusted somebody, and I've learned I really can't trust people today. I've got to be more careful.

241 "lawyers attend all board"
Yorke had been the attorney asked to leave the board meeting nearly a year earlier.

242 "a January trip"
Just days after Bailey told Bakker that spending needed to be curtailed, the Bakkers and their entourage flew to southern California for a stay in a Palm Springs hotel. The trip cost PTL more than $11,000. Later, the IRS claimed that the payment wasn't a proper ministry expense.

Bakker himself described the trip a few months later as a vacation. "We tried to find rest. . . . We went to a hotel, people came up for autographs, there was pictures being taken and here I am in a bathing suit. . . . We were more exhausted at the end of the vacation than we were before."

"couldn't remember the reason"
Years later, Bakker denied ever telling Dortch or Taggart ahead of time that he needed or wanted a bonus. Yet Don Hardister remembered hearing Bakker talk with Taggart about bonuses and Bakker's personal needs. Not that Taggart needed reminding, Hardister said; Bakker's aide knew Bakker's finances as well as or better than Bakker himself.

243 "Tammy was taking"
The Edge of Disaster, Mike Richardson, St. Martin's Press, 1987, p. 113.

245 "misled him"
As REC began work, Jim Swaim informed Richard Dortch by memo of the payments PTL was required to make under the water-park contract. "These payments are not negotiable. . . . I just wanted to make you aware of the financial obligations PTL has in the next four months with REC Associates."

246 "If Mr. Bakker"
Undated two-page letter, apparently early 1986, Rick Rathbun to Terry Zinger. PTL had hired Rathbun to serve as project manager for the water park and the other efforts to develop a theme park at Heritage USA. Rathbun and PTL parted ways when PTL disputed his receiving a finder's fee and project-management fee from REC in addition to his consultant's fee from PTL.

249 "house in Palm Desert"
Details of household purchases in June 1984 from The Edge of Disaster, chapter 11.

"acquired a new Mercedes"
Bakker said later that he purchased the 1953 Rolls Royce and the new Mercedes with money he had borrowed from a bank. On June 11, 1984, David Taggart wired $90,000 of PTL money to California, apparently to supply cash to complete some of the Bakkers' purchases. On June 25, Bakker reimbursed PTL the full sum with a check drawn on his personal checking account.

249 "a new bonus check"
Twenty days after the Bakkers got the money, David Taggart drafted a
note for his files listing the sums and stating "this memo will supersede
the memo of July 10, 1984." After Bakker's resignation, investigators
could find no July 10 memo. They did locate a July 3 document showing
that the Bakkers were owed after-tax bonuses of $50,000 and $25,000,
half of what the Bakkers had actually received. The unexplained contradiction in the paperwork illustrates the potential for abuse in PTL's handling
of bonuses.

253 "only a broad description"
The plan, as Bailey understood it, was to raise the Towers money "on a
general basis . . . so that the money can be used where you feel it is
needed."

CHAPTER THIRTEEN

Among those interviewed by the author were Bobbie Garn and John
Wildman.

259 "the ministry's new jet"
In his public comments about the jet, which had been purchased used,
Dortch waxed enthusiastic about Bakker's greater availability for ministering and his hope to pay all the jet's expenses with charter business. Apparently, others were less confident. An agenda for the board-of-directors
meeting on September 11, 1984, had proposed sale of the jet. "It is in the
best interest of the Corporation, because of operating costs and limited
use, that the airplane be sold." The minutes for the meeting indicate that
the board agreed to make the plane available for "charter, lease, or sale."
The sale would not come for nearly two years.

264 "exceeded $2.1 million"
The total benefits calculation was made by the Internal Revenue Service.

265 "Tammy had taken"
However, the Bakkers had donated more than two thousand dollars to the
ministry that year.

266 "assign all your existing royalty rights"
Bakker chose another path in an effort to allay Chappell's concerns, selling
his publication rights to the outside publishing house for the $50,000. The
publishing house in turn paid the ghostwriter and publication costs.

269 "You know, even"
From a December 3, 1984, PTL broadcast.

CHAPTER FOURTEEN

Among those interviewed by the author were Jim Bakker, Richard Dortch, Jessica Hahn, Rolfe Neill, and Paul Roper.

284 "Carla Hammond"
Hammond's real name was Christine Fredricks. She would later be charged with and plead guilty to multiple counts of welfare fraud in Suffolk County, New York, according to New York officials.

287 "Profeta . . . obsessed"
She had used cocaine for several months in late 1984 and 1985 to cope with him, she claimed, stopping because she didn't like what the drug was doing to her. Hahn had also developed what a New York State investigator later characterized as an addiction to Fiorinal, a prescription barbiturate.

288 "a man's woman"
This biographical material is drawn in part from the interviews that my wife, then–*Observer* reporter Jody Jaffe, held with Hahn and Jessica and Eddie Moylan in spring 1987. Her profile of Hahn—the first press portrait of the Moylans—was published in the *Observer* on May 21, 1987.

294 "Cortese had kept quiet"
In a 1988 deposition, Bakker testified that he had "confessed my sins to [Aimee Cortese] and told her what happened and asked for her prayers and help." He also asked her to help counsel Hahn. On January 14, 1985, Bakker sent a thank-you note to Cortese for coming to his birthday-party gala twelve days earlier. "I appreciate so much your kind words. Your ability to understand and see the vision of what God is doing here means everything in the world to me. I can't tell you how much your support and encouragement has meant to me."

CHAPTER FIFTEEN

Among those interviewed by the author were Dave Cadwell, James Robison, and John Stewart.

300 "with Gene Profeta"
Roper's draft lawsuit listed Hahn's address as 4100 Jerusalem Avenue, the location of Profeta's Massapequa church.

300 "He stood looking"
St. Petersburg Times, July 2, 1988.

301 "said nothing more":
In early 1988, Dortch told *Christianity Today* magazine, "I made a deliberate decision not to report a friend to the denomination over an isolated
incident that took place four years [earlier]." In an interview published
in the magazine's March 18, 1988, issue Dortch also said: "The main thing
I've had to work through with Jim is that I feel I should have been told
about the Jessica Hahn matter before going to PTL."

302 "DeLorean participating"
After his arrest on the drug charges, John DeLorean found the Lord. He
worshipped at the Church on the Way, the charismatic church in Van
Nuys that Gross attended.

"weeks of reruns"
The day after his return to the air, February 12, 1985, Bakker circulated
a memo about Tammy to his staff, who still didn't know of the drama in
California.

> I am pleased to announce that Tammy Faye has been appointed a vice
> president of PTL.
>   She will be working closely with personnel and different areas of
> the Ministry, learning your problems and finding solutions to them.
> This will help us to be a more closely-knit team.

303 "spared no expense"
Each night, the staff of the hotel restaurant carried a tray of hors d'oeuvres,
perhaps boiled shrimp or small sandwiches, to the suite before the kitchen
closed. Occasionally, someone from the restaurant cooked fettucini Al-
fredo for the Bakkers in the suite's kitchen.

305 "One account"
Earlier, PTL had run its executive payroll account in-house, making special efforts to assure confidentiality.

306 "third supplied money"
The $25,000 check, which carried the signatures of Dortch and the
trusted secretary in charge of Bakker's personal finances, gave no indication of the purpose for the payment. PTL would also repay missionary Sam
Johnson for the borrowed ten thousand dollars that Dortch had used to
pay Hahn in November 1984. In a letter dated March 15, 1984, David
Taggart sent a check for $13,700, explaining that he had added $3,700
to cover taxes on the sum—even though it was, in fact, not income to
Johnson, simply repayment of a loan. Johnson answered with a letter
expressing his appreciation. "It has ALL been put to good use. Thank you
so much."

306 "Woodmansee gave his blessing"
Woodmansee received five hundred dollars for his work. In a March 1, 1985, letter, Furstman told the retired judge, "I look forward to working with you again in the future, although I am sure this type of situation is rather unique."

"check for $115,000"
Roper had done business at the Yorba Linda bank and could convert the check to cash without difficulty. As Roper told it later, Hahn took the initiative to offer Roper thirty-five percent of the entire settlement, the sum she would have had to pay a lawyer, not the much smaller sum he would have been willing to accept. So she received about $20,000 of the $115,000. Roper later explained that he considered $50,000 of the total—$2,500 for each of the twenty years of the trust—to be compensation for his expected duty as trustee.

307 "At the March board meeting"
On March 28, PTL's board was told that PTL no longer planned the West Coast expansion that had alarmed Peter Bailey in early January. The turnabout was sudden. Bakker had relocated a vice president to California, and as late as January 29, 1985, the executive was meeting with the savings and loan selling the swim-racquet club Bakker hoped to buy and resell as time-shares. A few days earlier, a PTL lawyer had warned that the lease for the club could limit PTL's flexibility in developing the property. He suggested that PTL exercise its option to cancel its contract to purchase. By early February, Dortch had ordered the vice president home without explanation.

"In mid-April"
In a Bakker fund-raising letter making the same appeal, the PTL president warned in a postscript, "Remember, I can only hold these for ten days. Don't wait even one day. I need to hear from you now!"

308 "fifty percent more"
On June 7, 1985, PTL staff member Hollis Rule reported to his boss that PTL had issued 44,375 fully paid lifetime partnerships in the Heritage Grand Hotel. "I am concerned about this," Rule wrote, "because this would require seventy-three percent occupancy to completely fulfill our obligations." Two months later, Bakker was notified by a memo from the hotel's management that PTL had exceeded the fifty-percent threshold, giving 1,145 room-nights free above the cutoff and costing the hotel $85,000 in revenue. With lifetime partners now being told that there was no room left for them in 1985, the memo read, "Our reservations department is beginning to receive many abusive phone calls from many irate lifetime partners, who are demanding a $1,000 refund."

308 "only $3.5 million"
PTL used what CPAs call the sum-of-the-years-digits method to derive the

amount the ministry would amortize each year. Using a seven-year cycle,
PTL reported twenty-five percent of the lifetime partnerships the first year
(or seven divided by twenty-eight, the sum of digits one through seven).
Under that method, PTL would have amortized the final 3.6% (or one
twenty-eighth) of the total in the seventh year.

"year-end deficit"
PTL's audited financial statements reflected the cost of Bakker's building
program; construction in progress tallied $14.4 million alone. PTL was
cash poor. It had $204,345 on May 31, 1985, less than half the total for
the same day a year before. It had written more than $700,000 in checks
against future bank deposits. PTL's current liabilities outnumbered its
current assets—the money and other valuables to which PTL had ready
access to pay its bills—by more than two to one, $33 million to $14.7
million.

311 "heaven and hell"
Water-park contractor REC suggested either a dark ride, akin to Disney's
Pirates of the Caribbean, a seventy-millimeter film, or a theater of the
senses that would combine a 3-D movie, 360-degree sound system, seat
shakers, and Scentavision.

313 "Wilkerson, an Assemblies of God"
David Wilkerson has subsequently resigned from the Assemblies of
God on friendly terms as he continues to pursue his ministry in New York
City.

"My reasons are deeply prophetic"
Wilkerson and Jimmy Swaggart were not the only evangelists raising
questions about the direction in which Bakker had taken PTL. Bakker's
zeal to build had alarmed evangelist James Robison, who had mended
fences with Bakker since speaking so bluntly about him during the late
1970s. On Feb. 21, 1984, two weeks after a visit to Heritage USA,
Robison wrote Bakker. He was diplomatic, warm, and perceptive. He
recognized a strident letter would get nowhere.

> To be quite frank, I have never observed a purer and more unselfish
> vision than yours. It is truly of God and for the people. There is
> nothing of personal value in it.

Robison cautioned Bakker not to be distracted from his ministry—a message Robison had also delivered to an uncomfortable meeting of the PTL
staff.

> Keep your eyes on Jesus and minister to His people. You are building
> His body, not physical structures, monuments and memorials. The
> buildings are merely places in which the body gathers for fellowship,
> instruction, edification and worship.
> . . . beware of the tendency and temptation to accomplish what God
> supernaturally commissions in the superficial energy of the flesh.
> . . . God will build your dreams as long as they are His visions and

you will let Him direct. Be careful, seek wise counsel only. (Read Isaiah 31:1–7, chapter 30:1–3)

. . . I also believe that the overall ministry will be strengthened as you find yourself surrounded by those willing to do the ministry of Jesus with no ego or selfish ambitions involved. . . . Remember, Jim, when God says, "No weapon formed against you shall prosper" [Bakker was using the inscription on a sculpture being offered to donors at the time] He is saying that only to those whose hearts are pure before Him, who walk in righteousness and heed His Word.

On March 11, ten days before Wilkerson's letter, Robison again wrote Bakker, inviting him to come to Texas for a few days.

Jim, the Lord has made me aware in the Spirit that you have been going through an extremely difficult period in your life. I know that just over a year ago God really spoke to you when I was there. Please do not forget those things which God said. God wants to lift the burdens from your shoulders but you have difficulty allowing Him to do so.

314 "Dortch two-faced"
In a July 1988 deposition, Peter Bailey was asked about Dortch.

To put it bluntly, I just never really trusted Mr. Dortch. . . . He just seemed to have his own agenda. I just felt he—he was very smooth, very gracious. He worked hard. But . . . [he always talked] to not just me but to people condescendingly, patronizing people. . . . I know a lot of people didn't trust Mr. Dortch.

316 "unseat the Southeast incumbent"
Some in the denomination say that Dortch was resented for his 1983 decision to run for executive presbyter from the Great Lakes region after he had already decided, or come close to deciding, to leave for PTL. Bakker announced Dortch's departure from Illinois the month after the vote in Anaheim. Candidates for executive presbyter are elected by region but aren't considered to represent their home region as would, for instance, a member of Congress. Dortch had taken steps to reestablish roots in the North Carolina church in time for the upcoming August election. Early in 1985, Dortch directed his staff at PTL to send a letter and leather-bound PTL Bible to each Assemblies of God minister in North Carolina.

317 "concocted excuses"
One day years before, as the Federal Communications Commission began its inquiry into his ministry, Bakker began to tell his audience, "If I'm wrong, I would be the first to admit it." But that day, as one of his employees remembered later, Bakker had a rare insight, a passing moment of self-knowledge. "No," Bakker said, "I would be the last one to admit it."

318 "another seven months"
As always, there was more to the story than Bakker told. Documents suggest that PTL, not Bakker, paid off Bakker's loan on the car; if so, his donation wasn't truly the car but the down payment he had paid and any principal he had retired on the loan in a year's time. Asked in a 1988 deposition what he had done with the Rolls, Bakker said that he had asked that it be given to a Shriners' burn hospital. In fact, Bakker had donated it first to his friend and regular TV guest, Dallas-based evangelist Mike Murdock, a fact he seemed to prefer to avoid admitting. In a February 1986 broadcast, with Murdock on the set, Bakker told his audience that PTL had donated the Rolls to another ministry, which Bakker didn't identify. Hauled to Dallas in April 1986, the Rolls was delivered to the burn hospital in early 1987 after Bakker had decided to donate it elsewhere. As Hardister remembered, Bakker left it to Taggart to tell Murdock that he was taking back the Rolls.

To replace the donated Rolls, Bakker had one of the Bakkers' PTL cars, a 1985 Cadillac, driven to Palm Desert. Nearly four months later—after an IRS audit report challenged the vast sums PTL was spending on Bakker—Bakker bought the Cadillac from PTL for its wholesale book value of $17,825.

"the Mississippi firm"
Eng-Land Design had completed about sixty percent of its work at a cost of $36,332. Two months after ordering work halted, Bakker unveiled a sketch of what he called Jerusalem City, "the newest addition to Heritage USA that will be built in the future." Eventually, Eng-Land Design— which had given PTL a price break because a principal in the Mississippi firm belonged to the Assemblies of God—sued PTL, complaining that the ministry had failed to pay for the services as it had agreed. A few months before Bakker's resignation, PTL settled out of court.

319 "finished by fall"
PTL gave no hint of the project's troubles in the *Heritage Herald.* "Heritage Island Is Nearing Its Finish," the headline read on the August 3, 1985, edition. A picture caption said that the water park would be opening "shortly."

CHAPTER SIXTEEN

Among those interviewed by the author were Art Borden, Neil Eskelin, Ernie Franzone, Doug, Laura Lee, and Dee Oldham, and Pete Teeley.

321 "provided the money"
Don Hardister had complained about the mileage put on his guards'
cars—without reimbursement—as they ferried the Bakker children to and
fro. Bakker gave the OK to buy a car, and Tammy Sue's bodyguards
would drive the Mazda off the grounds. To buy the Mazda, PTL drew a
check for $12,514. The remaining $4,500 was credited on the trade-in of
a PTL car, a red convertible Dodge 600.

Bakker had purchased the Dodge 600 in his own name and with his own
money at a time when he had felt the urge to drive around in a convertible.
He told Tammy Sue that the Dodge was for her, too, and soon she was
driving the car on the grounds. Three months after Bakker bought the
Dodge, he sold it to PTL for $9,967. His daughter continued to drive the
car.

322 "most of the work"
The Tega Cay water slide wasn't Bakker's first public show of paternal
dedication at PTL's expense. During the summer of 1984, Bakker had
talked to his partners about the tree house he had promised his son, Jamie
Charles, for years.

> I said I don't care what it takes we're going to build . . . a tree house,
> and we've got a tree house now. But oh, why live with regrets as an
> old man thinking someday, boy, I was going to build my kids a tree
> house and never did.

It sounded as if Bakker had spent a Saturday afternoon hammering two-by-
fours. In fact, PTL employees had spent nearly six thousand dollars to
erect a miniature two-level house, with twin heating–air conditioning
units, carpeting, wood paneling, and roll-out windows.

323 "You're fired"
The Edge of Disaster, p. 167.

325 "You read outrageous"
Daily Record, Dunn, N.C., September 12, 1985. The author was Hoover
Adams.

327 "elder Bakkers are not"
Restoration, fall 1979 issue. In its stern rebuttal to a critical article in
another Christian magazine, the Pentecostal magazine edited by Bakker's
friend Doug Wead reported that

> The elder Bakkers are not, nor ever have been, on PTL salary. Now
> in their 70's, they live in a fifteen by twenty foot bedroom with all
> their earthly possessions and share a hall bathroom with the many
> transient television guests passing through. Their role as "greeters"
> to the hundreds of PTL partners who descend on Charlotte, N.C. is
> described by PTL sources as "indispensable." Their sometimes ten-
> hour work days are given freely "as unto the Lord."

327 "discount off the combined price"
PTL contended the price break was available to all employees. The IRS found that PTL hadn't offered staff members a discount until three months later.

328 "donated $50,000 to Cortese's church"
In giving $50,000, PTL had donated more than seventy-five percent of the sum Cortese had begun raising in February 1985. In a letter sent to Dortch and other supporters in February, Cortese wrote that her church was buying its home in the Bronx for $65,000. "Let this letter be challenge. To give, to pray, to ask God to loosen the necessary funds."

329 "obsessed with the aesthetics"
Bakker was terribly conscious of personal appearances as well. He pressured one new executive to trade in his trusted Honda Accord for a Cadillac. He bought his bodyguard, Don Hardister, five pinstriped suits at a Beverly Hills clothier that opened by appointment only. He complained that reporters drove beat-up cars and didn't wash their hair; one journalist was so poorly dressed Bakker felt like taking him to a mission store for new clothes, he said.

Bakker liked to think he was ahead of the latest clothing fads. He was sure the oversized V-neck sweaters he wore would set a trend. He had a fetish about coats. Convinced he had had too few as a young boy, he would walk into a store and buy what seemed to be one of every kind of jacket in stock.

"burned-out bulbs"
After one trip to the grounds in April 1986, Bakker dispatched an angry memo to Jim Swaim:

> There have been light bulbs burned out at the Grand, light bulbs out of the chandeliers, and light bulbs burned out in the lobby. Now I'm finding light bulbs burned out on the merry-go-round. There is one spot along on the merry-go-round that has fifty light bulbs out of their sockets. Also, there are many burned out light bulbs and broken globes in the train tunnel. We need to take care of this right away so please make sure Maintenance knows we will approve the expenditure for light bulbs.

330 "PTL's internal systems suffered"
The staff members in charge of PTL's telephone system faced chronic frustration at their bosses' neglect of the integral, if unexciting utility. Workers at the telephone building had to pay for toilet paper out of their own pockets. They struggled to get money—even money authorized in their budget—to buy spare phones, cords, and supplies to repair phone cables. Accidentally severed cables were a routine at PTL, a symptom of chronic poor planning and constant construction.

On April 13, 1984, a staff member described his frustrations to Bakker by memo.

> ... There is a stack of "Requisitions for Purchase Orders" about 1½" high somewhere between Roger Flessing's signature and a check for materials. We have not received a cent in over a month. I understand the money is low; however, even miracles need material with which to be performed. As of the date it will be a MAJOR MIRACLE to have ANY phones working in the Grand Hotel by July.
> Why?
> No money; no materials; no place to put anything; no time; and very, very little cooperation.
> Can you do anything to help us?

Ron Ritch, PTL's telecommunications manager, had selected a new telephone system in 1984. It was designed to accommodate as many as 16,000 phones, tying together the hotels, PTL offices, and the Heritage Village campus. The first part cost more than $2 million. PTL made a $50,000 down payment, but then failed to make its first payment. The manufacturer sold the system. Later PTL bought another, smaller system and began paying for it. But it never finished. The system was never delivered or installed.

330 "Upper management is"
The memo was authored by the head of PTL's attractions department, David Griffith, who left PTL in mid-1985.

331 "the Hampton Court"
Open to partners at night, the restaurant served PTL insiders and their guests at lunch.

"winning my trust"
In June 1985, Dortch ordered a memo sent to his PR man, Neil Eskelin, with a reminder to use Charlie Shepard's wife as a feature writer for Heritage USA. I had probably mentioned to Dortch that my wife, Jody Jaffe, was a feature writer for the *Observer*. PTL made no effort to involve or hire Jody, however.

"a smile that could survive"
It seemed fitting that Eskelin had titled one of his books, *Yes, Yes Living In a No, No World*. Eskelin was already a familiar face around PTL. He had done work off and on for the ministry, spending one summer signing TV stations.

335 "Speakman had encountered"
In late October 1983, Bakker claimed to ECFA that Speakman was being asked to return to the job of budget director "so that we could bring about the policies that you have mentioned." As Speakman saw it, he was merely being moved back to the budget-director's job to make room for the returning David Taggart.

336 "Borden's March 25 letter"
Borden also told Bakker "because of the size of your ministry, the high
visibility of both the ministry and the Bakker family, the nature of your
message and the work of Satan, there is a certain vulnerability to attacks,
criticisms, unfavorable press accounts, and litigation. It is out of this concern for PTL and for ECFA members that the Standards Committee has
been urging the enlargement of your Board commensurate with your
growth for your responsible management and protection."

"Christian TV station"
Once PTL was notified of ECFA's concern over the back bill, PTL paid
the station for six months of back airtime.

337 "failed to mail"
The assistant Dortch was blaming was Al Cress. PTL later sent ECFA a
copy of the "missing" July 26 letter. Oddly enough, Cress had resigned
from PTL and walked out on July 23, 1985, three days before the date
on the typed letter. The letter also lacked the initials that Cress and his
secretary put on documents they typed.

340 "chose to ignore"
In two letters in early 1985, lawyers at Caudle and Spears, the firm then
handling PTL's tax case, warned that operating the hotels within the
church "could immediately jeopardize the tax-exempt status of the church
by having one of the largest and most elegant hotel complexes in the world
owned by a church" and "will undoubtedly continue to provide [the IRS]
with a reasonable basis to authorize further tax inquiries."

345 "moving up fast"
Private letter from Wead to Bakker, September 7, 1983.

"Sometimes helping somebody"
Private letter from Wead to Bakker, December 19, 1983.

347 "no-agenda kind of meeting"
Charlotte Observer, November 9, 1985.

CHAPTER SEVENTEEN

Among those interviewed by the author were Neil Eskelin, Eddie Karnes,
and Stan Cottrell.

351 "PTL had had the machine"
After Bakker's departure in 1987, one of Swaim's former deputies hired
out PTL's gunite machine to secure cash for the ministry. The machine was

reported stolen before anyone realized why it was gone, and the Falwell administration fired the employee for what once might have been considered admirable resourcefulness.

352 "make some sacrifices"
While Bakker laid off workers and canceled TV programs, money continued to hemorrhage from the third floor. On November 21, David Taggart allegedly used an $11,000 cash advance drawn on a PTL Visa card to pay the personal American Express account he shared with his brother. Eight days later, he allegedly did the same with a $9,500 credit-card cash advance. The two transfers were portrayed in an 1988 indictment as overt acts in an alleged conspiracy to evade taxes.

On November 25, $10,540 was paid from the executive checking account for furniture for Dortch's lakefront home. On November 30, finance director Peter Bailey wrote off $221,278.44 to travel and entertainment expenses after Taggart failed to provide supporting documentation for the spending. That same day, Bakker was given a five-thousand-dollar cash advance from a confidential parsonage checking account. At year's end, PTL also completed the $120,000 purchase of a sixth house in the Tega Cay compound, this one across the street from the house that overlooked Bakker's.

358 "it is beautiful"
The Mazda, which had cost $17,000 in June 1985, was sold to a PTL contractor for $11,250.

359 "For the first time"
Of course, PTL had only been in existence for eleven years, not forty-five.

"such a program"
The Bibles to China fund-raiser was a fiasco. PTL raised $600,000, far less than it had hoped. By October 1986, PTL had paid $221,000 to the South Carolina man who was supposed to orchestrate printing of the Bibles. No Bibles were ever distributed.

360 "programs would disappear"
With the overseas TV programs being phased out, Bakker moved to dispose of the Heritage Village property in Charlotte. PTL had taped the French, Italian, and Spanish TV shows in the studio there and used the facility for editing videotape. In spring 1986, PTL agreed to sell the Heritage Village site to a local church for $5 million.

363 "the worst scenario"
In a 1986 manuscript he wrote for PTL, Doug Wead described these events from PTL's point of view. Eskelin and Dortch had wracked their brains to figure the story out, Wead wrote. "For the life of them, they could not find any slip in any corner. There were no rumors that had not been examined. The finances had been checked as thoroughly as possible." As described in Wead's manuscript, the reaction to my disclosure

that day was a lifting of the sense of gloom that had hovered over the third floor.

CHAPTER EIGHTEEN

Among those interviewed by the author were Paul King and Sandra Sims.

366 "Enough Is Enough"
Lyrics to the song's chorus went

> I won't turn around
> I won't give ground
> In God I'm standing strong and tough
> I'm taking back what's rightfully mine
> My health, my joy, my peace of mind
> Watch out Satan, I'm calling your bluff
> Enough is enough.

"didn't, however, call attention"
Bakker also didn't mention a letter McAlister had sent to him in December 1983—evidence that McAlister had harbored strong feelings about Bakker's failure to live up to his word in 1978.

> It is important for me to tell you that I deeply regret the differences that have arisen between us, and to say that I have prayed for the Lord to bless and sustain you.
> Finally, I want to, with this letter, release you and PTL from any promises made to me in the past and assure you from my heart that I will not raise my hand against one of God's anointed—which you indeed are.
> This letter is written so that my heart can be released from any negative or unworthy feelings that I have had towards you, Jim.

367 "read a wire-service story"
Bakker also read aloud a 1983 letter that Bob Manzano had sent him. He identified the former aide only as the FCC's key witness, not by name. "I then testified with an anger towards you, trying to get even," Bakker read. He omitted the context of Manzano's letter.

Bakker had written to Manzano in 1981 saying that he had forgiven Manzano and asking for forgiveness, but without saying what either man needed forgiveness for. Manzano replied two years later with the letter from which Bakker read during the 1986 broadcast.

In his letter, Manzano recalled reading Bakker's testimony prior to his second appearance before the FCC staff in 1980.

> Jim, I wept through many pages. I then testified with an anger towards you, trying to get even.

> I . . . fell apart emotionally, spiritually and physically. . . . A root of bitterness towards you continued to grow . . .
>
> Recently, the Holy Spirit has dealt with me about you. I therefore ask your forgiveness for not being loving, forgiving, and kind towards you.

After Bakker produced the letter, Manzano told me that he had written the letter hoping to get into Bakker's good graces to help his new employer—who was, ironically, Reverend Cho from Korea. Angry or not, Manzano said, he had told the FCC the truth. But Bakker's excerpt suggested to viewers that Manzano had admitted lying.

If Bakker had any doubts how to interpret Manzano's "apology," they should have been cleared up in February, when a private detective working for PTL reported this conversation with Manzano.

> And when I read [Bakker's testimony] . . . I was shocked, literally shocked, that he had lied about me and basically tried to put the blame on me. . . . I got up in the witness stand and decided that's when I'm gonna tell everything.

367 "a vindication"
Though Bakker pronounced himself exonerated, lawyers for PTL cautioned in May 1986 that "if the Commission's original action was part of a 'deal' whereby PTL could get out of broadcasting, an attempt to reenter licensee ranks may engender official ill will." At the time, PTL considered the acquisition of a TV license in Rock Hill, South Carolina, the largest city in PTL's principal home, York County.

"mink coat Bakker had purchased"
The mink coat allegation was the weakest in the FCC staff report. Manzano had testified that a $2,500 PTL check had been used to buy a mink coat for Tammy Bakker. He said that he had learned that from Moss. I called Moss and then reported in my story that Moss remembered hearing both that PTL and that Bakker had paid for the coat. Later, Bakker produced a letter from the furrier stating that Bakker had paid for the mink with his own personal checks.

Unbeknownst to me, a similar mink coat allegation had surfaced inside PTL six years earlier. In his confidential April 1980 letter warning that PTL was jeopardizing its tax-exempt status, tax lawyer Paul Chappell told PTL that he had encountered "persistent reports" in interviews with staff members that the Bakkers had used four or five thousand dollars in petty cash in fall 1977 to buy a fur coat in Charlotte. Chappell also had been told that a diamond had been purchased for Tammy with PTL petty cash.

In his 1986 rebuttal, Bakker put his own spin on the Corvette story. He implied he hadn't picked out the car, as he in fact had. "It was not a Corvette bought for me, and it was not bought with missions money. It was a company car provided for me to drive. . . . I guess most churches provide a car for their [pastors]."

Bakker represented the issue in question to be whether PTL should provide a car for him at all. Bakker didn't say that he already had a luxury sedan courtesy of PTL or that the Corvette was kept at his home.

To blunt the suggestion that he had been two-faced when he bought his first houseboat in 1978, Bakker produced Herb Moore to speak on his behalf. It had been then–finance director Moore who had given fellow PTL executive Bill Perkins several conflicting accounts of the six-thousand-dollar ministry check Bakker used to make his houseboat down payment. Moore had been fired from his PTL job in summer 1979; Bakker, according to his FCC testimony, had deemed Moore unsuitable for rehiring.

But the TV audience knew nothing of that history, and Moore loyally confirmed that he had told Bakker he had accrued enough salary to cover the houseboat down payment.

370 "The time has"
Chicago Tribune, April 19, 1986.

371 "to file lawsuits"
PTL seized the opportunity to press for corrections when a wire service, newspaper, or broadcaster wrote errors into our FCC stories. Some papers had taken the overseas-missions story and blended it inaccurately with the accusations of personal misuse of donor money.

PTL warned a Baptist minister in Chadbourn, in southeastern North Carolina, that he could be sued for errors in his column in the local newspaper. Radio newsman Paul Harvey broadcast a correction that entirely embraced PTL's point of view. He then mused on Bakker's behalf about the negative publicity that afflicted evangelical ministers. PTL trumpeted the corrections as wholesale vindications and asked aloud why the *Observer* hadn't printed a retraction too. Bakker and Dortch didn't bother to explain that the corrected errors hadn't been ours.

"The problems I unearthed"
Buckingham Report, March 19, 1986. A similar report was carried in *Charisma* magazine, May 1986.

376 "had disappeared"
A newspaper in nearby Rock Hill, South Carolina, had profiled Brady three months earlier as part of its Christmas charity drive. She told the paper that she had left Colorado after her landlord threatened her with a gun. She had lived in PTL's campgrounds and in a PTL trailer until PTL began building a new entrance road through the trailer site. She hoped to find a job, she said; she had fallen in love with Rock Hill.

379 "an accountant working with ECFA"
The confidential report was written by W. H. Altman, a partner in Ernst and Whinney based in Los Angeles.

384 "PTL had wasted"
By April 23, Bakker declared on his TV show that he had read the advance
material from a book that "three investigative reporters are writing,"
apparently a reference to the research effort headed by Wead. "I do not
own the book. It is not my book. I am not paying for the book. But I'll
tell you one thing. These guys have done their homework."

386 "we love you"
Testimonials rolled in. Vice President George Bush and Barbara Bush
conveyed their "warmest best wishes" by letter. Jerry Falwell appeared by
videotape to wish the Bakkers a happy anniversary. "Jim and Tammy
don't look old enough to have been married twenty-five years," Falwell
said. Assemblies of God executive presbyter Marvin Gorman, also by
video, told the Bakkers "there is not a minister that you have not been
a challenge to, an inspiration to . . . you have made each one of us look
at what you have been able to do as you've yielded your life to God."

CHAPTER NINETEEN

Among those interviewed by the author were Jeannie Falknor and Rich
Oppel.

391 "salary was $45,000"
In April 1986, Bakker talked to a UPI reporter about his pay. "We have
a double standard. Johnny Carson can be paid $5 million a year, but if a
preacher asks more than $30,000 it's too much money. The Bible teaches
us we should prosper and be in health even as our soul prospers."

392 "certification of action"
Charles Cookman signed the document. He had been asked to do so the
evening after a board meeting, although he had missed the meeting due
to a conflict in his schedule.

"awkward and embarrassing circumstances"
Bakker took the theme up briefly on his April 30, 1986, broadcast. "Some
of our older pastors have retired and have nothing. They're broke. And
that's been the shame of [churches] who haven't even taken care of their
pastors."

393 "hardly a propitious time"
Bakker was capable of recognizing those realities. Later that spring, Bakker sent a message to Taggart telling him to work out the ten-year transfer
to the Goodmans. "I don't believe we should have to pay anything for
them, that the house is furnished as a gift to them as is over the next

ten-year period. . . . If there's anything they want done to it, that they're free to do it on their own, but PTL can no longer afford to upkeep all the houses." The same logic, of course, didn't apply to Bakker's home.

394 "it doesn't mean anything"
To hear Bakker on the air, PTL was in sound fiscal condition. Two days before Bailey's April 16 memo, Bakker posed a question on the air to his TV-affiliates director. "I didn't ask you this ahead of time. But don't you feel through this telethon time, by the end of this telethon, there is the closest possibility in our history of paying all of our TV stations current with the new budget controls and all that we've done, PTL is in the best shape it's ever been in?"

396 "to pay $120,000"
This settlement was also to remain secret. But the seller's lawyer disclosed the settlement in a memo inadvertently filed in the county clerk's office with other legal papers.

409 "cover Furstman's costs"
Furstman offered this explanation to Dortch for the $60,000 in billings in a confidential June 18, 1986, letter. But Furstman portrayed the checks differently in a subsequent letter to PTL's accounting firm, Laventhol and Horwath.
  The outside accountants had written to Furstman inquiring about the two executive-account checks for legal services rendered. In his November 1986 reply, Furstman described the ten thousand dollars as a bill "for legal services rendered . . . for general West Coast operations" and the $50,000 as a "retainer fee on account for continuing legal services rendered to [PTL] for general legal services to be rendered with regard to West Coast operational matters."

CHAPTER TWENTY

Among those interviewed by the author were Wanda Burgund, Joy Cole, J. B. Griffin, Steve Nelson, and Walter Richardson.

411 "another 180-degree turn"
To explain the sudden resurrection of the Towers partnerships in late May, Bakker again blamed partners who had failed to fulfill their promises. "So many of the pledges were false, I just didn't have the heart to go back to the TV audience and say I've got to pay this bill (to Messner). And God took it right out of my hands," Bakker said as his new lifetime offer propelled his late May telethon. "I've seen miracles, but I've never seen a miracle where God just took and pulled it out of our hands."

411 "Towers memberships remained"
In an aside on his April 15, 1986, broadcast, Bakker mused about the total number of lifetime partnerships, talk he had avoided since fall 1984. "I don't know how many lifetime members, between the Grand and the Towers. I'm sure there's almost a hundred thousand people in lifetime memberships. I'm not sure, I don't know the exact numbers. I don't even know. Do you know?" Off-screen, Dortch corrected Bakker. "Uh, it's near about seventy thousand, I think." Bakker had been closer to the truth. The lifetime count had reached $100 million at the end of March 1986.

413 "refused space"
Between June 1986 and March 1987, PTL refused hotel rooms to about 23,300 lifetime partners.

414 "he always seemed to care"
Though he preferred to keep his distance from them, Bakker wanted his audience, whether on TV or at Heritage USA, to be happy. "We're a great big ministry that wants to think like a little ministry," he told his viewers September 4. "We want to be caring and loving and personable."

Bakker's daily checklists were littered with orders to his staff to accommodate the customer. The lines are too long at the hotel counter. The restaurants weren't open after a late-night television taping. Main Street merchants were taking up choice public parking spaces. Employees were being rude to Canadians. And the breast of turkey served at dinner theater was too skimpy. As he tried to correct a mailing-room problem in 1985, Bakker ordered signs hung from the wall reading, "Labels Are People" and "Each Letter Represents a Person."

Bakker rarely treated his staff with the sensitivity he demanded they show the partners. When he ordered a swimming pool open after seeing six buses of visitors head into Heritage USA, he didn't stop to think his managers might not have anyone to staff the pool. In moments of great frustration, Bakker talked about dismissing those who didn't follow his orders. When he found out that singers performing around the hotel were still taking money from their impromptu audience, Bakker declared that the singers would be fired if it happened again. Later that day, he told his staff he was thinking about firing the managers who allowed the practice.

"drain on the ministry"
On December 19, 1985, Bill Mabrey of Brock Hotel Corporation told Richard Dortch that "with the increasing number of lifetime-partner usage, it is becoming extremely difficult to manage this hotel financially."

417 "Three years later"
In June 1989, Kevin Whittum and his adoptive parents David and Ione Whittum left Kevin's House and returned to Grand Rapids, Michigan.

417 "no mention of any problems"
On his July 1 broadcast, Bakker disclosed a small piece of the truth. "Our goal is to request the state to be able to have the largest amount of crippled children we can have for a home. We're told that we can only have eight in wheelchairs," Bakker said. A few minutes later, Bakker said in passing that Kevin's House is "a home, not an institution." He seemed to be talking about the feel of the structure, though, not the way it could be used. He continued: "Every room is decorated. Beautiful wallpaper. All different furniture."

420 "open the doors"
A glossy brochure sent with the "urgent" appeal claimed that the doors of Kevin's House couldn't be opened to the children until the house was paid for.

"PTL assigned more than $1 million"
Carrying these additional costs, Kevin's House ultimately appeared on PTL's records to be a money loser, pushing PTL $264,291 farther into the red.

421 "ill-considered corporate jet"
Bakker had soured completely on the corporate jet and was eager, as he said to his tape recorder one day in fall 1985, to "bring this airplane thing to a conclusion fast and immediately."

On January 3, 1986, PTL notified its chief pilot that PTL no longer needed his services. Two months earlier, the pilot had been assured that PTL would continue to pay him for a year, as it had agreed to do when he was hired.

Four days after his layoff, the pilot sued PTL, demanding $112,000. The total included $31,000 he claimed to have lost, in part because PTL failed to charter the plane as promised. The pilot was supposed to receive a share of any charter revenues.

Publicly, Dortch had used the prospect of charter business to justify the purchase of the plane. But the third floor had insisted on immediate access to the jet, an insurmountable impediment to charter operation. In their audit work, IRS agents found limited records explaining the purpose of the jet's travels. Ultimately they concluded that nearly two-thirds of the Sabreliner's trips had been for the personal benefit of Bakker or Dortch. Those personal trips for Bakker had cost PTL more than $100,000, the IRS reported, and Dortch's personal use had a price tag of nearly $86,000.

With the pilot's lawsuit attracting embarrassing attention from the local media, PTL quickly settled out of court.

CHAPTER TWENTY-ONE

Among those interviewed by the author were John Ankerberg, Ron Kopczick, Jerry Ogg, Jr., Wally Stalnaker, and Jimmy Swaggart.

424 "one of the great ministers"
The next month, PTL quietly arranged for a $75,000 short-term loan for Gorman at a bank in Rock Hill, South Carolina. PTL provided a certificate of deposit to serve as collateral for the loan. Shortly after Bakker's resignation, the loan came due and the bank asked that the loan be repaid. When no money was forthcoming, the PTL CD was forfeited.

425 "old-fashioned camp-meeting preacher"
Prime Time Preachers, Jeffrey K. Hadden and Charles Swann, Addison-Wesley, 1981, p. 39.

"generous contributor"
Swaggart's ministry supported missionary work in the denomination totalling $11 million in 1986.

"PTL ministry remained suspect"
In many respects, PTL and the Bakkers represented the antithesis of the denomination's standards.

The Assemblies' bylaws cautioned that biblical standards should prevail over all forms of worldliness. "Scripture warns against participation in activity which defiles the body, or corrupts the mind and spirit; the inordinate love of or preoccupation with pleasures, position, or possessions, which lead to their misuse; manifestation of extreme behavior, unbecoming speech, or inappropriate appearance; [and] any fascination or association which lessens one's affection for spiritual things." Among the causes listed for disciplining a minister are moral indiscretion, "assumption of dictatorial authority over an assembly," and a habit of running into debt.

426 "visit to Springfield"
PTL was eager to maintain good relations with the denomination. In December 1985, PTL hosted a four-day conference of top Assemblies of God officials, including the resident executives from Springfield, Missouri, and district superintendents from around the country.

When the church officials arrived, Bakker offered their wives a chance to buy an outfit for themselves, at PTL's expense, in the shops on Main Street. The offer appeared spontaneous, if ill-timed, given PTL's layoffs and Bakker's current pledge to cut costs. Some of the visitors found the offer embarrassing and viewed it as an attempt to buy their favor.

PTL's biweekly *Heritage Herald* had included a story about the upcoming conference in its latest forty-thousand-copy press run. When Dortch saw the article, he ordered the page pulled and reprinted—the sort of change of direction that chronically afflicted PTL.

The new article was shorter and listed a new purpose for the gathering. The first article had reported that the officials were gathering to become familiar with PTL. The second, sanitized story said that the officials had come "to share mutual ideas, familiarize church officials with ongoing administrative procedures, and spiritual encouragement through fellowship." The new version omitted details of the conference schedule, including an appearance on Bakker's show, Sunday-night welcoming banquet, and a Christmas special sung by the PTL Singers.

427 *"The Seduction"*
The Seduction of Christianity, Dave Hunt and Tom McMahon, Harvest House, 1985.

428 "Dick, what about the"
From Charles Cookman's testimony at the fall 1988 PTL-Bakker-Taggart trial in the U.S. Bankruptcy Court for the District of South Carolina.

429 " 'get-rich-quick' schemes"
The Evangelist, February 1987, p. 10.

431 "The three-day trip"
The travelers left their mark on PTL's credit cards. As the trip stretched to a week, they spent more than ten thousand dollars, mostly for food and lodging in Virginia and Tennessee. After his return home, as Bakker pitched a lifetime-lodging offer with praise for the "free benefits" PTL was offering, he said, "I just took a week off with my children. We paid for everything we did. Nobody gave us one thing free. There wasn't one event we went to, there wasn't one place we went into that was free. Except to go shopping, which you pay for yourself."

"massive renovation"
Back home at Tega Cay, Bakker's staff was beginning work on a $20,000 conversion of a family room into a rehearsal room/recording studio for Bakker's daughter. The renovation costs included five thousand dollars in hardwood floors and six thousand dollars in sound equipment.

432 "Charles Cookman proposed giving"
In a statement to the press when the story of the Gatlinburg house broke in mid-November, PTL said, "Mr. Bakker's home in Gatlinburg, Tennessee, is a personal matter and not owned by this ministry." No mention was made of the PTL money being spent on the property.

A day after the *Observer* published its story about Bakker's new house, Cookman wrote to Bakker,

> Sometimes our critics can be our greatest asset. Not because they are right or wrong . . . but because they make us think—examine.
> Let's examine the "Gatlinburg house:"
> 1. It provides seclusion without prohibitive distance.
> 2. It is surely not extravagant.

3. The Board of Directors of PTL, *unbeknown* to you, moved to provide security and remodeling.

4. No matter what you do, the press will find fault and be critical.

5. If it was *wrong,* then we should apologize and withdraw. But if buying the house was right, and I believe it was, then we should move straight ahead and you should enjoy the house to the fullest extent.

You are doing a ministry for the Lord that is "trend setting." Don't be surprised if people don't understand. We love you!"

433 "fight with the IRS"
The fight was costly. In July 1986, finance director Bailey drew down the Victory Warriors savings to pay Chapel's colleague, Michael Wigton, $111,273.

435 "PTL's best chance"
In their September 1986 letter, Chapel and Wigton told Bakker that "political help can be useful in some respects, but you cannot solve your problems politically." The letter offered no further explanation. Bakker's staff had discussed taking PTL's complaints about the IRS to sympathetic US senators, and Washington liaison Pete Teeley would accompany a lawyer from Baker and McKenzie to Senator Strom Thurmond's office registering PTL's procedural objections to the second IRS audit with a member of the senator's staff.

Wead said he had never discussed PTL's IRS audit with Bakker and believed that Bakker saw the meeting with Bush in November 1985 merely as a public-relations asset.

440 "visited the house"
Stalnaker's suspicions were deepened when he found that there had been additional construction at Dortch's house, but not until late 1985. That work, too, had been billed to a construction project at Heritage USA.

"failure to complete the Towers"
On November 1, Bakker celebrated completion of the top (twenty-first) story of the Towers, 230 feet off the ground. PTL had found a superlative for the occasion. The high rise, it declared, was the country's tallest masonry load-bearing building. The building was still months from completion.

441 "had gone to great lengths"
In his 1986 manuscript about PTL and the FCC, Doug Wead had written, "Bakker's executive assistant did not need a job. He was well off financially."

443 "had never approved"
David Taggart didn't discuss his salary with Dortch or Bakker or give them a copy of the agreement. Instead, he put it in his executive-payroll file. In fact, his salary never rose beyond $100,000, But large bonuses pushed his income well beyond $150,000 during the next two years.

The lawyer drew up a similar document for James Taggart, a consulting contract between PTL and the brother's interior-design firm, JHT Ltd. David Taggart asked Bailey and Fulbright to sign it for PTL.

The document guaranteed James Taggart ten thousand dollars a month, but it seemed to be little more than a piece of paper. James Taggart would eventually receive the ten thousand dollars a month from PTL, but not for another year.

In testimony after his resignation, Bakker said that he saw nothing wrong with David Taggart's contract.

446 "new $60,000 Mercedes"
A few days after the purchase, a PTL employee telephoned me to pass along the joke a co-worker had made after the Mercedeses appeared on the grounds. "There go our raises."

"ordered two more 560 SELs"
To get the Bakkers' sedans and the station wagon for Jamie Charles, PTL was obliged to pay the Alabama car dealer $150,000 in expenses and commissions that he had been seeking for his efforts to obtain financing for PTL. The dealer then bought the cars in his trust's name and loaned them to PTL for the Bakkers' use.

CHAPTER TWENTY-TWO

455"this was not true"
In July 1987, after Bakker's resignation, the Assemblies of God's legal counsel, Richard Hammar, wrote to ECFA to correct PTL's claims that PTL was an Assembly of God church and had submitted to the denomination's strict code of ethics. Both statements were false, Hammar wrote. PTL's church was affiliated with the denomination, but the rest of Bakker's ministry was not.

Also, Hammar wrote, the Assemblies of God had no code of ethics for an organization like PTL. It had adopted criteria for determining if an independent corporation was reputable enough for an Assemblies of God minister to work in it. But, Hammar wrote,

> PTL *never* submitted even to these limited criteria even though it employed several Assemblies of God ministers. It was a blatant untruth for PTL to represent that it "submitted to the stringent code of ethics" of the Assemblies of God.

457 "no member of its congregation"
A. T. Lawing, the only board member from Charlotte besides Bakker and Dortch, worshipped at a church in Charlotte.

457 "why I left"
By coincidence, just seven days earlier, a memo from Bakker had warned the staff that "sarcastic comments and foolishness" over headsets wouldn't be tolerated.

459 "make their own rules"
By April 1984, nothing more had been heard from Operation Antichrist. But the IRS—prompted by information that it had received from the Anaheim police—had begun investigating finances at Melodyland.

463 "worried about the consequences"
In a later deposition, Winters recalled PTL's request. "They said, 'Please continue. If you stop building on the Tower, we'll all get in trouble. We've got to keep the Tower going.' They meant just the effect. They—they didn't want to show on television that the Tower had stopped construction."

464 "on February 16"
By then, Winters had applied to Rock Hill National Bank for a one-year, $2-million line of credit to help finance PTL's debt to Messner. The financing was in place by early March.

"On Wednesday, February 4"
In the waning days of January, Reverend Tim Kelton had twice woken up from troubling dreams about Jim Bakker, the man who had taken his place thirteen years earlier on the fledgling "PTL Club" broadcast in Charlotte. He had had little contact with Bakker since the mid-1970s and had left Charlotte in 1981 to work as a missionary in New Guinea. Since 1983 he had lived in the Shenandoah Valley of Virginia.

The summer of 1986, Kelton had been admitted to a hospital with massive internal bleeding, the result of Wegener's granulomatosis, the same rare disease that had killed Bob Bakker. Kelton survived on a devastating therapy of chemotherapy and steroids.

Troubled by his dreams of doom for the Bakkers, Kelton telephoned a friend who worked at PTL. He learned that the Bakkers were in Palm Springs. He decided to go to California and find Bakker; he knew he would be put off if he called ahead. Kelton was convinced that God was dealing with him through a dream. There was a need, a problem in the Bakkers' lives, he feared, and he felt he should respond as a friend. He knew nothing of Tammy Bakker's drug dependency or the evening sessions at Betty Ford.

The afternoon of February 4, as I searched court records on Long Island, Kelton flew from Charlottesville to Los Angeles. Never before, he would say later, had he felt such urgency to spend one thousand dollars. The next day, Kelton pulled up at the Indian Wells, California, resort where David Taggart was staying; it was his best lead on the Bakkers. No one was in, the concierge told him, so he waited. Finally James Taggart appeared and took a message from Kelton. Later that night, David telephoned Kelton's hotel room in Palm Desert.

David explained that he had read Kelton's letter to Jim. He told Kelton that Jim appreciated his effort and compassion, but that he couldn't see him. Kelton told Taggart he had spent one thousand dollars and did not intend to leave without seeing the Bakkers. The next morning David Taggart telephoned again. He had talked to Jim a second time, and Jim had decided not to see anyone. Taggart chided Kelton for not calling before he took the costly flight. He told Kelton that Jim and Tammy needed rest and relaxation, that they were going through a time of tremendous stress, and had refused to see even ministers with national reputations. Eventually, as Kelton continued to press, Taggart said good-bye and hung up.

Kelton was determined. He tried everywhere to get the Bakkers' address. Finally he could think of nothing else to do besides driving his rented car around town. After a half hour he realized he was not likely to find a mailbox that read Jim and Tammy Bakker.

Desolate, he called his wife, Claudia. I've done everything I knew to do. I'm coming home, he told her.

Later, after the revelations of Tammy's drug problem, after Jim's resignation, after the Bakkers' fall from grace, Kelton felt in his soul that he had been given insight from God. Had he been able to reach the Bakkers that Thursday and Friday, he believed, he somehow could have changed the way Bakker faced the scandal that soon consumed him. He could not have changed what Bakker already had done, but his testimony, he believed, could have swayed the Bakkers' hearts and minds.

In March and April 1987, as the PTL scandal dominated the news shows on their television, Tim and Claudia Kelton sat breathless, awed at the sense that ever so briefly they had inhabited a realm beyond rational comprehension.

465 "named Jessica Hahn"
Hahn told the writer that Profeta's ministry had a mailing list of forty thousand names.

467 "she had considered"
In early 1987, Jessica Hahn signed a document declaring, "I renounce any and all claims as to funds, payments, or trust corpus involved in a certain transaction between me and James Bakker." Profeta signed as the witness. The document was dated January 15, 1987, three weeks before I had approached either Hahn or Profeta.

In 1989, Hahn told the author that she had decided to give up the money because she suspected it was "dirty." Hahn said the date on the document was correct and not backdated. She had given the paper to Profeta, who eventually gave it to Roper.

NOTES

However, Roper said that PTL had already stopped payments on the trust by that time, and no effort was made to execute Hahn's renunciation.

467 "PTL warned him not to talk"
Roper soon heard about my visit to Hahn and Profeta in New York, and he, like Profeta, counseled Hahn to say nothing to the press. On February 6, the day after my meeting with Hahn, Richard Dortch scribbled a note to his secretary to remind him to call Scott Furstman in mid-afternoon.

472 "with this new purchase"
On February 17, 1987, the Bakkers signed documents giving power of attorney to David Taggart and a Palm Springs lawyer so that the two could buy the home and two neighboring lots. The two representatives were directed to put the property in the name of the FSCO Trust—a name that included the middle initial of every member of the Bakker family. On February 20, the sale was recorded officially. The Bakkers bought only the house, not the neighboring lots.

474 "Perhaps $20,000"
Roper would tell me later that he was saying how much of the expense money had gone to Hahn.

CHAPTER TWENTY-THREE

482 "Before hanging up"
The next day, Joseph Flower—one of the top executives of the Assemblies of God—telephoned Orender. Orender refused to talk to him until he had talked to Bakker. Later, Cookman called Orender with the same appeal. Again, Orender—who hadn't grown up in the Assemblies of God—refused to help.

"pastor of an Assemblies"
Schmidgall would later take the position of board chairman for Heritage Ministries, PTL's successor.

487 "to curry sympathy"
On March 5, Bakker dispatched a memo to his staff to promote the sort of goodwill he would need to ride out the storm. He ordered each department to gather each morning for prayer and asked his employees to pray for him and his family. "The key to this Ministry is love. Everyone needs to reach out in love to everyone around you so that Heritage USA will be enveloped in love. God knows your hearts and all your needs and desires. He honors faithfulness . . . as we join together in one accord, we can expect God to move in a mighty way."

628

490 "We published the story"
As the show closed, Oral Roberts offered another unfortunate prophesy from the studio at Heritage USA. "I believe that Jim and Tammy are going to know the greatest years of their ministry just in the few weeks when they get back, than we've ever witnessed."

"forty-fifth birthday"
That day in California, David Taggart ordered $161 worth of flowers from a shop in Palm Springs. He paid with a ministry credit card. The purchase was the most recent in a succession of fresh-flower orders paid for by PTL during the Bakkers' California stay.

492 "the injunctions in Matthew 18"
The passage in Matthew is a few words away from a verse Bakker often cited to justify PTL and his brand of prosperity gospel. "Again, I tell you that if two of you on earth agree about anything you ask for, it will be done for you by my Father in heaven."

496 "whom Dortch had tried to recruit"
PTL was looking for someone to run its TV operations. In December 1986, PTL rolled out the red carpet for Marcus, showing him the attention lavished on VIPs at PTL. He and his wife were each given thirty dollars a day in spending money. Marcus, who had just left CBN, asked if he should get receipts for any money he used. Don't worry, Dortch told him, it's yours, we do this all the time. As it was, Marcus didn't have time to spend the cash. He was escorted everywhere. He was given meals, fine chocolates, a basket of expensive soaps and perfumes—reality, Bakker style.

Neil Eskelin cautioned Marcus gently. The place is great, Eskelin said with his customary good cheer. But he cautioned Marcus that he would be treated better as a potential hire than he would if he went to work at PTL. At dinner with Dortch, the Burgunds, and Sam Johnson and his wife, Joyce, Marcus sensed his hosts were tired and under tremendous pressure.

Dortch gave Marcus the grand tour of Heritage USA. Marcus asked if he could look inside Kevin's House. No, Dortch told him, the handi-capped children would be uncomfortable. Marcus left with the impression that a sizable number of kids lived inside. Dortch made no mention of the problems PTL was having just opening the home.

After a taping of Bakker's weekday show, Marcus was introduced to Jim and Tammy Bakker in the hallway outside their dressing room. Tammy told Marcus she hoped he would come to work at PTL—indeed, he would, during Falwell's tenure. We need creative people, she said. Dortch had already told Marcus he was eager to see more inventive treatment of Tammy's weekday show, "Tammy's House Party," and of the Sunday church service, which was Dortch's responsibility.

As usual, Bakker had little to say. He asked Marcus's daughter her name. She cast her eyes down, and Marcus explained the girl was shy. "So am I," Bakker replied.

As Marcus walked away with Dortch, Dortch assured him that the Bakkers had liked him. Dortch told him he had asked Bakker if he should hire the visitor. "You've hired everybody else at this place," Bakker replied. "You want to hire him, hire him too."

Marcus left with the impression money was flowing freely at PTL. Dortch had squired him about in his new Mercedes, and the number-two man had talked of a six-figure salary for Marcus. At CBN the most Marcus could make for the same work was sixty thousand dollars. But Marcus's wife had sensed something amiss. She told her husband she could not make the move to Heritage USA and PTL, that she could not live there in peace. Marcus told Dortch he would keep in touch.

499 "Eskelin asked when"
Early Friday morning, I telephoned Eskelin again. I had a few minor facts to check for the story, I explained to Linda Ivey, his friendly aide. I did need Dortch's age, but I also wanted PTL to know that the story was coming out in case the ministry chose, at the eleventh hour, to make a statement that truly responded to my February 24 questions.

502 "the story no longer"
We had never made what I had expected to be one of our toughest decisions: whether or not to name Hahn in the story. Naming her would give us the most credibility, omitting her name would follow a newspaper custom—the *Observer* and most newspapers don't identify the victim in reporting alleged rapes. For now, the draft stood without her name.

504 "broadcast about forgiveness"
Another topic that day was the injunction that those without sin should cast the first stone. Dortch complained of gossip. He quoted the Bible, "To quarrel with a neighbor is foolish. A man with good sense holds his tongue. A gossip goes around spreading rumors, while a trustworthy man tries to quiet them."

"jets of Swaggart and Oral Roberts"
Roberts usually spent winters in the California desert. A spokesman for his ministry declined to confirm that he was in the Palm Springs area at the time, however.

508 "Ben Armstrong"
After an NRB committee told Armstrong that it saw the board appointment as a conflict of interest, Armstrong resigned. He was replaced by DeWitt Braud of Lynchburg, a contractor and chairman of Falwell's ministry. The Reverend Charles Stanley would step down before the first meeting of Falwell's board. He was replaced by the Reverend Bailey Smith, another former president of the Southern Baptist Convention.

509 "A few minutes after two"
At the *Observer,* we could do little more than wait. Ethridge and Grutman talked again early in the week. Dortch wanted to exclude me from the interview. Ethridge refused. Instead, the two men agreed to hold the interview by telephone. The conference call was set for Thursday afternoon.

I was worried about losing the story to competition. A TV station from California called, pursuing rumors of a forthcoming story. So did an Assemblies of God radio station in Illinois.

I telephoned Weitzman and Furstman. Furstman didn't return the calls. Weitzman refused to answer any questions but cordially wished me luck. I checked with Cookman. He was now willing to confirm that he had resigned from PTL because of a conflict of interest. He was still uneasy with anything suggesting a betrayal of PTL. At the close of the call, I asked if he was getting help from Springfield, as others had told me. "Charles," he said in a half-pleading voice, "don't ask me those type of questions."

515 "twenty thousand extra papers"
The *Observer*'s weekday circulation averaged 232,000 at the time.

CHAPTER TWENTY-FOUR

Among those interviewed by the author were Jerry Falwell, Jerry Nims, and Bailey Smith.

517 "the syrupy, patronizing tone"
Dortch had a disingenuous air on television. His smile was a bit too tight, and his head moved with an occasional tic as if his collar were too small. His exaggerations strained belief, while Bakker's somehow seemed to convince the audience. Dortch's treatment of the Bakkers was saccharine. "All of us in the studio audience want to say, 'Jim and Tammy, we love you,'" was a familiar refrain.

525 "a move well-timed"
That same night, I talked to Gorman's attorney in Louisiana. He declined to say whether Bakker's attack had any bearing on the timing of Gorman's lawsuit.

529 "a curious denial"
In a later deposition, Bakker acknowledged having learned from David Taggart that Messner had supplied the money.

"Dortch's deceit"
In his letter, Franzone recalled his February 25 meeting with Dortch to

discuss the Hahn rumors and Dortch's denials. Franzone accused Dortch of two other deceptions—his July 1985 claim before the TV cameras that the board had voted to give Bakker the Mercedes roadster and a similar claim about a Christmas gift of a music box. Franzone also complained about the pressure Dortch and Grutman had put on the board to resign on March 18. "Reflecting upon these actions and the circumstances surrounding them . . . I realize I should not have agreed to such action in such haste."

530 "some changes in the hotel"
While Dortch suggested that design changes were to blame, a letter to partners that Bakker had drafted in the days before his resignation said, as Bakker often had said before, that unfaithful partners had necessitated the new fund-raising.

> I am very disappointed that some of those partners who have pledged to be a part of the Towers have not followed through on their commitment.
> I need several partners to help stand in the gap and make up the hedge for those who have fallen by the wayside and have been unfaithful in their commitment

532 "Johnson told him"
Johnson's annual salary, housing allowance, and retirement-fund contribution from PTL totaled $57,200. He had also received $19,508 in bonuses in 1986.

"it wouldn't be a good idea"
Johnson had learned his first lesson in compromise one Sunday morning in December 1985. Dortch had telephoned him at home and asked the new arrival to preach for him. Later that morning Johnson got a message from Bakker. We need a big offering—let the hundred-dollar Bibles go for fifty dollars, and let the records go three for fifteen dollars. For a half hour in church that morning, Johnson hawked Bibles, records, and Susie Moppet dolls in front of the congregation. Scores of people walked out in disgust.

539 "the man at whom"
This executive hasn't been identified publicly because he fears that the incident would hinder his ability to work with ministries. His accusations had considerable impact among Bakker's former staff. His identity is known to Bakker.

540 "status for 1981–83"
The audited financial statements I had obtained earlier in April revealed that the IRS was likely to extend its arguments for fiscal 1981, 1982, and 1983 to cover 1984 and 1985. The statements also showed that the South Carolina Tax Commission's claim—the other half of PTL's twin tax troubles—totaled $5.5 million and could escalate to $10 million.

541 "Watt would take over"
Three days later, Watt joined Humbard in resigning, leaving PTL's board without any charismatic-Christian members. Watt declined to detail all his reasons for resigning but wrote to Falwell that he could no longer serve "as a matter of conscience, personal integrity, and management philosophy."

In a brief April 30 interview, Watt characterized Dortch as a "man of tremendous integrity and capability and a dear friend. And I stand with my friend." Watt's son, Eric, had served as a church administrator at PTL under Dortch. At the time of Bakker's resignation, Eric Watt was attending Yale Divinity School with financial support from PTL.

"Dortch telephoned Messner"
Apparently, Dortch had already tried to enlist Messner's help in his effort to hide the trail leading from PTL to the Jessica Hahn trust. In a letter written by Messner associate Otis Winters to Messner on April 9, 1987, Winters wrote, "Reverend Dortch recently suggested you create an invoice now and back date it to March 1985 to support the charge [of $265,000] to the Amphitheater. I believe this would be a serious mistake because you have nothing to cover up."

" 'Roe,' he said,"
Dortch wasn't going to get any help from Messner. Later that day, the contractor shared that account of the telephone call with Falwell.

CHAPTER TWENTY-FIVE

547 "his large bonuses"
In 1988, a year after the Nightline appearance, a lawyer deposing Bakker asked the former PTL president about his decision to take the bonuses he had voted against.

> Bakker: How do you reject a decision by the board of directors?
>
> Lawyer: You don't cash the check. You didn't pass up any checks, did you?
>
> Bakker: I never cashed checks.
>
> Lawyer: Who cashed them for you?
>
> Bakker: They were put in the bank. Several times I tried to leave the checks in and I was told that I was in violation of Internal Revenue if I did not allow the checks to be put in my account, that I would be guilty of tax evasion.

Lawyer: Who told you that?

Bakker: From the accounting and attorneys.

Lawyer: Who?

Bakker: I don't remember. I don't recall the exact name.

Lawyer: . . . Did anybody ever tell you if you took it into income that you could turn right around and donate it back to PTL and take a tax deduction?

Bakker: I don't think so . . .

547 "six million people . . . visited Heritage"
PTL had used this statistic to establish that PTL was the third-largest family resort in America behind Walt Disney World in Florida and Disneyland in California.

The claim was another PTL exaggeration. While PTL said it had an estimated 4.1 million visitors in 1984, its security department counted just 977,079 vehicles entering the main gate of Heritage USA. To generate the higher count, PTL chose to assume that each arriving car contained at least three persons, according to a 1985 appraisal report. It considered few of the arriving cars to hold staff members.

The appraiser adopted a more conservative approach than PTL, assuming that just three out of ten cars entering the grounds contained tourists and other visitors.

548 "Falwell . . . abruptly resigned"
A month later, Falwell would announce that he was resigning as president of the Moral Majority and rededicating his life to preaching the Gospel. Falwell turned over leadership of the Moral Majority to Jerry Nims, the Atlanta businessman and "Old Time Gospel Hour" board member who had been instrumental in the ouster of Dortch.

550 "You might say"
Associated Press, September 12, 1987.

"pornographic acts"
Later, a prostitute claimed that Swaggart had indeed had sex with her.

551 "Be not deceived"
Galatians 6:7.

"Bakker failed"
Press reports identified Bakker's go-between to unidentified Greek investors as a Florida man who had served three prison terms on fraud charges.

551 "I believe God"
Charlotte Observer, September 10, 1988.

553 "Dortch exhibited more pain"
Shortly after Dortch's arrival in Florida in 1987, local press reports revealed that he had claimed a homestead tax exemption on two homes in
Florida while he lived in Charlotte. That violated Florida state law, which
allows such an exemption only on a property owner's primary residence—
which, in Dortch's case, was out of state in North Carolina. Later, Dortch
and his wife pleaded no contest to misdemeanor crimes, paid court costs
and back taxes, and were put on probation.

"At PTL, there"
Christianity Today, March 18, 1988.

554 "pathological narcissism"
My description of the narcissistic personality disorder draws heavily from
Otto Kernberg's words and analysis in *Borderline Conditions and Pathological
Narcissism,* Otto Kernberg, Jason Aronson, Inc., 1975, pp. 227–342.

"It is as if"
Pathological Narcissism, p. 228.

"by withdrawing into"
Pathological Narcissism, p. 282.

555 "emptiness behind the glitter"
Pathological Narcissism, p. 230.

"for gratification of"
Pathological Narcissism, p. 331.

"because to depend means"
Pathological Narcissism, p. 235.

"a hopeless yearning"
Pathological Narcissism, p. 257.

"It is dramatic how"
Pathological Narcissism, pp. 310–11.

INDEX